Business Ethics
The Pragmatic Path
Beyond Principles to Process

Rogene A. Buchholz

Legendre-Soule Professor of Business Ethics
Joseph A. Butt, S.J. College of Business Administration
Loyola University of New Orleans

Sandra B. Rosenthal

Professor of Philosophy
College of Arts and Sciences
Loyola University of New Orleans

Prentice Hall, Upper Saddle River, NJ 07458

Executive Editor: *Natalie Anderson*
Acquisitions Editor: *Lisamarie Brassini*
Editorial Assistant: *Dawn-Marie Reisner*
Editor-in-Chief: *James Boyd*
Marketing Manager: *Stephanie Johnson*
Production Editor: *Maureen Wilson*
Managing Editor: *Dee Josephson*
Manufacturing Buyer: *Diane Peirano*
Manufacturing Supervisor: *Arnold Vila*
Manufacturing Manager: *Vincent Scelta*
Composition: *Accu-color, Inc.*
Copyeditor: *Donna Mulder*

Copyright © 1998 by Prentice-Hall, Inc.
A Simon & Schuster Company
Upper Saddle River, NJ 07458

Library of Congress Cataloging-in-Publication Data

Buchholz, Rogene A.
   Business ethics : the pragmatic path beyond principles to process
 / Rogene A. Buchholz, Sandra B. Rosenthal.
   p. cm.
  Includes bibliographical references and index.
  ISBN 0–13–350786–6
  1. Business ethics. 2. Social responsibility of business.
 I. Rosenthal, Sandra B. II. Title.
HF5387. B829 1998
174'.4—dc21   97–13237
                                                CIP

Prentice-Hall International (UK) Limited, *London*
Prentice-Hall of Australia Pty. Limited, *Sydney*
Prentice-Hall Canada Inc., *Toronto*
Prentice-Hall Hispanoamericana, S.A., *Mexico*
Prentice-Hall of India Private Limited, *New Delhi*
Prentice-Hall of Japan, Inc., *Tokyo*
Simon & Schuster Asia Pte. Ltd., *Singapore*
Editora Prentice-Hall do Brasil, Ltda., *Rio de Janeiro*

Printed in the United States of America
10 9 8 7 6 5 4 3 2 1

For Our Mother, Rose Brener

Whose love, vitality, and practical wisdom
have shaped four generations
in a way that no text on ethics could ever explain

Contents

LONG CASES

Listing of Short Cases

PART ONE: A CONTEMPORARY CONCEPTUAL FRAMEWORK FOR BUSINESS ETHICS

PART TWO: THE CORPORATION IN SOCIETY

Preface

The subject of business ethics is not just a modern concern. There have been many articles and books written on the subject ever since management has emerged as a professional activity in corporations with business organizations growing in size and power so as to affect varied aspects of modern society. Several attempts have been made over the years to develop a moral philosophy for management and delineate a set of ethical principles to guide management decision making. These efforts reflect a continuing concern about ethical issues in business, a concern that has, however, accelerated in the past several years in both the corporate world and in schools of business and management.

What is new about today's concern is the development of business ethics as a field of study in its own right, not as a peripheral subject to be added onto existing courses as time and interest permit. Over the past several years, a large and growing body of literature has developed, journals in business ethics have been established to promote writing and research in the area, many business schools have added business ethics courses to their curriculum, and many centers and endowed chairs for the study of business ethics have emerged around the country.

Philosophers provided much of the initial leadership for the field and have written most of the textbooks used in teaching courses in business ethics. Their books are usually based on traditional ethical theories, such as utilitarianism or Kantian formalism, which may seem overly abstract and oftentimes far removed from the decision making involved in dealing with real-life ethical issues and dilemmas in the business world. Though differing greatly in their claims, these standard ethical positions contain certain common features found in a tradition of philosophy that sets the parameters for what kinds of questions can be asked, what alternative answers are possible, what kinds of dilemmas must be resolved, and ultimately, how one thinks about the moral dimensions of corporate life.

Management scholars bring different perspectives to the issues than do philosophers and have made valuable contributions to the field because of their immediate acquaintance with management problems and the functioning of a business organization. However, books written from a so-called managerial perspective often set forth practical issues and solutions in business ethics based on implicit but unexamined assumptions that are themselves grounded in traditional ethical theories. When the resulting alternatives prove to be unworkable, they often grope toward solutions which require philosophical foundations not available in the literature. Without a clear theoretical structure which gets beyond traditional ways of viewing ethical issues and possible solutions in business, these efforts are generally unsuccessful in providing a firm basis for making ethical decisions.

As a result of much discussion of issues and problems as we have heard them presented at conferences during the past several years, we have come to realize that there is need for a book that can provide a philosophical framework for rethinking the nature of the corporation and its mode of embeddedness in its social, cultural, and natural environments to bring out its pervasive relational and moral dimensions, and rethinking as well the nature of moral reasoning and the process by which it takes shape. This, in turn, provides a novel context for understanding and analyzing the kinds of ethical issues and problems that arise in business. The present text is intended to provide both a unique and unified approach to the study of business ethics and a way of bridging the gulf between liberal arts-oriented philosophical approaches and more practical managerial approaches.

This book will provide first a brief look at traditional positions utilized in business ethics and explore some basic assumptions which are operative in various views but which are taken for granted and never made explicit. Following this exposition, the basic ideas of pragmatic process philosophy will be introduced, showing the way these ideas differ from traditional approaches. While these chapters may be perceived as quite challenging, we believe it is important to treat philosophical concepts in some depth at the beginning of the book to lay a firm foundation that will enable students to come to grips with the pervasive moral dimensions of business and its activities.

The second part of the book will build on these philosophical foundations and deal with the nature of the corporation and its relationship to society. The way business functions in a market context and the problems that arise because of marketplace transactions will be discussed. These problems give rise to a concern with the social responsibilities of corporations and to the increasing importance of public policy as a means of shaping corporate behavior to respond to social concerns. The nature of the corporation itself and the manner in which a corporation can incorporate ethics into its organizational culture will be explored. Concepts discussed in the first part of the book will not be treated as philosophical abstractions but as fundamentally important tools for management students as they try to understand what business ethics is all about and how it applies to the function of business within society.

In the third section of the book, the focus will be on the diverse moral contexts in which business functions. Technology is the first of these contexts, as business is the primary institution in our society through which new technology is introduced. The way technology is used and structured and the purposes for which it is used raise many moral questions. Business and its relationship to the natural environment is a subject of increasing importance, and this chapter will show how the philosophical position developed in the first section of the book is an environmental ethic as well as a framework for business ethics. Problems in the natural environment give rise to questions regarding a changing cultural environment in which the traditional meaning and purpose of business organizations are being challenged. Finally, business increasingly functions in an international context, which raises many moral questions concerning its activities in foreign countries.

The fourth section will treat issues in the marketplace and workplace that students will most likely be dealing with on a day-to-day basis in their decisions and actions as employees of corporations. These issues include consumer issues and the rights that are of importance to consumers, issues related to a changing workplace, discrimination and equal opportunity in the workplace, and various rights and obligations of employees and employers including the topics of job ownership, plant closings, safety and health, insider trading, confidentiality and trade secrets, conflicts of interest, whistle-blowing, and privacy.

The last section of the book treats the subjects of moral leadership in business and the implications of ethics for the educational process. In some respects, these chapters provide a way of summarizing and reunifying important points made about ethics throughout the book, through focusing them on the subjects of leadership and education. These chapters provide a means of discussing important issues with respect to management organizations and the implications for the education of students of business and management.

While cases can be used in conjunction with any ethical position, the use of cases is especially important in dealing with the philosophical position outlined in this book, for the philosophical theory itself incorporates the absolutely essential role of concrete situations in moral decision making. Thus, short cases are provided at the end of every chapter that are of particular relevance to the issues discussed in that chapter. Longer cases are presented at the end of the book that deal with several important issues that can be used where an instructor thinks they are most relevant. All of these will give students a chance to combine reflective moral awareness and concrete decision making in coming to grips with ethical issues in business as they emerge in specific contexts. These cases will be presented to the students in as factual a manner as possible, and will give them the opportunity to grapple with real business situations from an ethical perspective.

This book is meant to be used as a primary text that can be supplemented, if desired, by readings chosen by the instructor in the various application areas such as advertising, conflicts of interest, employee rights, and similar issues. It offers a contemporary philosophical perspective that we have not found in other business ethics textbooks, one that we believe students and instructors will find attractive and relevant to their concerns. For courses focusing on the more purely philosophical dimensions of applied ethics, selected portions of this textbook can be utilized and supplemented by relevant primary texts chosen by the instructor.

If the primary focus of the course is on cases, this book can be used as an introductory text to deal with questions that are fundamental to the discussion of ethical issues raised in the case situations. It contains enough cases to get students started in this mode of analysis, but more cases can be used as supplements by the instructor if desired. The fundamental issues discussed in this text will be reflected in the various solutions that students develop to deal with the problems presented by the cases. This text can lay the groundwork for an intelligent discussion of these solutions.

Corporations that have an ethical module or introduce ethical concerns into their management training programs should find the book extremely useful. It raises fundamental questions that are important to management ethics in a relevant manner that managers will be able to understand. Thus, they will be led to see the importance of basic philosophical concepts, and the discussion of these concepts can again provide a solid foundation for the discussion of more specific issues related to the functional areas of management and the actual ethical situations managers face in their day-to-day activities.

Acknowledgments

There are several people and institutions that must be acknowledged for having helped in the writing of this book. William C. Frederick of the Katz Graduate School of Business at the University of Pittsburgh has been a constant source of inspiration and stimulation on matters pertaining to values and ethics and in the writing of this book. His continual work in this area has contributed considerably to our understanding of ethics and values within a business context, and his dedication to scholarship and discussion of ethical issues has provided an example that has guided our efforts.

The friends and acquaintances we have made over the past several years in the Society of Business Ethics have stimulated us to devote more time to developing a new theoretical approach to business ethics and to relating this approach to practical management concerns. Many people in this society have encouraged our efforts and have provided us with numerous opportunities to present our ideas at conferences, where we have received important feedback that has benefited us greatly.

Many thanks are also owed to Loyola University of New Orleans for giving us both leave for a year so we could spend the time necessary to work on this book. Several faculty at this institution have also been supportive of our efforts. Thanks are also due to the reviewers of the proposal and the first draft for their helpful comments: Craig Dunn, San Diego State University; Don Huffman, Cedar Crest College; Joseph Petrick, Wright State University; Georgia Holmes, Mankato State University; and Fred Diulus, University of North Florida. Finally, we would like to thank the people at Prentice Hall, particularly Lisamarie Brassini, who have been willing to take a risk with a new business ethics textbook, and have been supportive and helpful at every step of the process.

CHAPTER 1

The Nature of Business Ethics

Some would say that there is no such thing as business ethics, either jokingly or seriously advocating the position that business and ethics don't go together, that business ethics is an oxymoron. This kind of comment could be meant to imply that business is immoral by its very nature and needs to be accepted as such, but it also could be made to suggest that business is amoral, and that moral considerations are inappropriate in business. There may be many people who perceive that ethics only has application to their personal lives and not to their organizational lives in a business institution. The business of business is to make a profit, and people who work for a business organization must concern themselves with producing goods and services to earn a profit—with buying and selling, developing new products, increasing market share, and other such business concerns rather than with morality.

The reason this view is popular in some circles may be because it is easier to deal with dollars and cents than with explicit value judgments. People are more comfortable when discussing a business problem in terms of its bottom-line impact than in terms of its ethical impact. Most people in business are probably not very well trained in ethical analysis and are not familiar with ethical language and concepts. What they know about ethics may come from their religious background where they have some vague notions of justice and other ethical concepts but have difficulty in applying them in a business context, or from some acquaintance with philosophy that they may have picked up somewhere along the way in their educational experience.

That business organizations have ethical impacts and that they are treated as moral entities should be readily apparent to anyone who reads in the newspapers about business scandals and unethical practices that are exposed to the public and the appropriate authorities who may take action against the company. Those who are concerned with the social responsibilities of business treat business as a moral institution that has impacts on society that go beyond the production of goods and services to make a profit. Thus, the way many people treat a corporation in daily life would seem to disprove the belief that business is an amoral institution.

If the problem is truly one of ethical ignorance, then some exposure to ethical concepts and problems might help to provide business managers and students with some moral sensibilities that can help them in recognizing the ethical dimensions of their activities and provide a way of thinking about these problems. Such exposure should help them to see problems that they might otherwise ignore, often at their peril and at great cost to the organization. An exposure to concepts and problems in business ethics will not necessarily lead people to behave more morally, but it may help them to live more thoughtful and better-informed lives as employees in a business organization. The study of business ethics presupposes that people are moral beings who want to do the "right" thing; however, there is often a great deal of confusion as to what actions and practices are morally appropriate.

Definitions and Approaches

Business ethics is a subset of the study of ethics in general. Thus, a definition of what ethics in general means may be helpful in clarifying the concept of business ethics and distinguishing it from other kinds of ethical approaches. Ethics in general is concerned with actions and practices that are directed at improving the welfare of people. Ethicists explore the concepts and language that are used to direct such actions and practices to improve human welfare.

> Some are primarily concerned with the justification of this concern itself, others with the delineation or justification of principles that specify appropriate welfare-meeting conduct, and others with the relationship between these principles and the rules or character traits that guide people toward specific behavior to achieve human welfare. In essence ethics is concerned with clarifying what constitutes human welfare and the kind of conduct necessary to promote it.[1]

Ethics is the quest for an understanding of what constitutes a good life and a concern for creating the conditions for people to attain that good life. Thus, ethics deals with questions that relate to making a life worth living and helping people to achieve such a life. Ethics is largely a matter of perspective, putting every activity and goal in their place, knowing what is worth doing and not worth doing, knowing what is worth wanting and having, and what is not worth wanting and having. The objective of living a good life is to enhance one's life experience and enjoy the fullness of the good things life has to offer.[2]

Ethics is the study of what is good or right for human beings, and what goals people ought to pursue and what actions they ought to perform. Ethics in general is a systematic attempt, through the use of reason, to make sense of our individual and social moral experience in such a way as to determine what ought to govern human conduct and the values worth pursuing in life. Ethics concerns itself with human conduct, meaning human activity that is done knowingly and to a large extent willingly.[3]

The study of ethics is thus a philosophical inquiry into various theories of what is good for people and what is bad or evil, what constitutes right and wrong kinds of behavior with respect to human welfare and the good life, and what one ought to do and ought not to do to promote human welfare and attain a life that is worth living. Ethics also deals with theories of justice and injustice, the meaning of fairness and unfairness, and what rights and responsibilities are operative in certain situations. These ethical theories are philosophical systems that deal with the nature and justification of ethical principles, decisions, and problems.[4] This study of ethics is usually categorized into the following approaches.

DESCRIPTIVE APPROACHES

The descriptive approach consists of scientific studies or factual descriptions and explanations of moral behavior and beliefs in various societies or institutions. No attempt is made to pass judgment on the superiority or inferiority of these various ethical systems that are operative in different parts of the world or in different institutions. This approach is neutral because it does not advocate one set of values and beliefs over another, but merely states that a certain set of values and ethics seems to be dominant in a society or in an institution.

METAETHICS

Metaethics or conceptual ethics, as it is sometimes called, consists of an analysis of the central terms in ethics in an attempt to understand the foundations of ethical systems and the functions of ethics in a social system. This approach involves clarifying and evaluating presuppositions and investigating questions of meaning and justification with regard to ethical statements.

NORMATIVE ETHICS

Normative ethics is in general concerned with the formulation and defense of basic moral norms governing moral life. Normative ethics is concerned about presenting a particular set of principles and standards that would be best for people to follow in all areas of their lives. This approach to ethics seeks to uncover, develop, and justify the basic moral principles or the basic moral values of a moral system. Normative ethics is thus not morally neutral.

APPLIED ETHICS

Applied normative ethics is a species of general normative ethics. It focuses the tools, concepts, and concerns of normative ethics to help specify and clarify the obligations of agents who regularly encounter ethical issues in particular sectors or spheres of activity. It is concerned about applying the principles of general normative ethics to specific moral problems that appear in certain areas of human life, such as those problems peculiar to a particular profession or to a particular institution in society.

Business ethics is concerned with the application of moral standards to the conduct of individuals involved in organizations through which modern societies produce and distribute goods and services. In business ethics, an analysis of moral principles and norms is applied to the behavior of people in business institutions. It is a type of applied ethics that is concerned with clarifying the obligations and moral responsibilities of managers and other employees who make business decisions.

Business ethics is thus a normative endeavor that has to do with how managers and other employees ought to act in certain situations. As such it is distinguished from other normative endeavors that specify right and wrong conduct and deal with good and evil. Religion, for example, deals with permissible behavior as defined by some religious authority. The law specifies behavior that is considered to be legal and illegal as defined by some legislative or judicial body within a specific society. Etiquette also deals with proper and improper behavior, dress, and other areas as defined by the culture. There are thus several sources of normative guidance in a society, but ethics has to do with moral behavior and moral reasoning to arrive at a justifiable decision with respect to an action or practice.

At the common sense level, the terms *ethics* and *morality* are often used interchangeably, yet it may be useful to distinguish between them to reduce confusion in certain situations. Ethics is concerned with the justification of actions and practices in specific situations. Ethics generally deals with the reasoning process and is a philosophical reflection on the moral life and the principles and values embedded in that life. Morality, on the other hand, generally refers to traditions or beliefs that have evolved over several years or even centuries in societies concerning right and wrong conduct. Morality can be thought of as a social institution that has a history and a code of conduct that are implicit or explicit about how people ought to behave.[5] The two terms are very close in meaning, and this distinction does not always hold true in practice or in discussions about ethics and morals.

The terms *ethics* and *values* are also used interchangeably in many discussions. Ethics is usually considered to be the more general term referring to conceptions of human welfare and the development of principles to attain human welfare. Values can be thought of as specific desires for concrete objects or beliefs that are held to be important. We can value specific goods and services that are available on the market or we can value more abstract concepts such as freedom or equality. Whatever we value, however, stems from some general conceptions of a good life or a life that is worth living. We value freedom because we believe freedom is a fundamental human characteristic or need that makes for a better society. Human welfare is promoted if people are free to pursue their own interests and objectives. Ethics and values are thus closely related, making them interchangeable concepts in many discussions.

The Evolution of Business Ethics

Tracing the development of business ethics as a field in its own right will help to understand where ethics fits into the business school curriculum and what factors have been responsible for the evolution of ethical concerns. While the subject of business ethics received some attention prior to the 1960s, it was with the rise of the social responsibility debate that ethical concerns became of major importance to business organizations.[6] The years from 1960 to 1970 were years of sweeping social change that affected business organizations and the management of those organizations. Concerns about civil rights for minorities, equal rights for women, protection of the physical environment, safety and health in the workplace, and a broad array of consumer issues have had far-reaching and long-lasting impacts on business organizations. The long-term effect of this social change has been a dramatic change in the "rules of the game" by which business is expected to operate.

Given this kind of social revolution, it is not surprising that the social environment of business was given increasing attention during the 1960s and 1970s by business corporations and schools of business and management. The concept of social responsibility came into its own during this period of time as a response to the changing social values of society. Business executives began to talk about the social responsibilities of business and to develop specific social programs in response to problems of a social, rather than economic, nature. Schools of business and management implemented new courses in business and society or in the social responsibilities of business.

Although there are many definitions of social responsibility, in general it means that a private corporation has responsibilities to society that go beyond the production of goods and services at a profit—that a corporation has a broader constituency to serve than stockholders alone. Corporations relate to society through more avenues than marketplace transactions and serve a wider range of values than the traditional economic values that are prevalent in the marketplace. Corporations are more than economic institutions and have a responsibility to help society solve some of its most pressing social problems, many of which corporations helped to cause, by devoting some of their resources to the solution of these problems.

The concept of social responsibility received increasing attention during the 1960s because of the need for corporations to respond to the changing social environment of business. The concept of social responsibility is fundamentally an ethical concept involving changing notions of human welfare and emphasizing a concern with the social dimensions of business activity that have to do with improving the quality of life in society. The concept provided a way for business to be concerned with these social dimensions and pay some attention to its social impacts. The word *responsibility* implies an obligation to deal with social problems that business organizations are believed to have toward the society in which they function. It is thus a normative concept dealing with activities in which business ought to engage to be socially responsible.

The debate about social responsibility reflected many dimensions. Proponents of the concept argued that (1) business must accommodate itself to social change if it expects to survive; (2) business must take a long-run or enlightened view of self-interest and help solve social problems in order to create a better environment for itself; (3) business can gain a better public image by being socially responsible; (4) government regulation can be avoided if business can meet the changing social expectations of society before the issues become politicized; (5) business has enormous resources that would be useful in solving social problems; (6) social problems can be turned into profitable business opportunities; and (7) business has a moral obligation to help solve social problems that it has created or at least perpetuated.

The opponents of social responsibility developed many persuasive arguments against the concept. These arguments included (1) the social responsibility concept provides no mechanism for accountability as to the use of corporate resources; (2) managers are legally and ethically bound to earn the highest possible rate of return on the stockholders' investment in the company they manage; (3) social responsibility poses a threat to the pluralistic nature of our society; (4) business executives have little experience and incentive to solve social problems; and (5) social responsibility is fundamentally a subversive doctrine that would undermine the foundations of a free enterprise system if taken seriously.

After the smoke began to clear from this debate, it was obvious to many that there were several key issues in the debate that had not, and perhaps could not, be settled. One key issue concerned the operational definition of social responsibility. How shall a corporation's resources be allocated to help solve social problems? With what specific problems shall a given corporation be concerned? What priorities shall be established? Does social responsibility refer to company action taken to comply with government regulations or only to those voluntary actions that go beyond legal requirements? What goals or standards of performance shall be established? What measures shall be employed to determine if a corporation is socially responsible or socially irresponsible?

The traditional marketplace provided little or no information to the manager that would be useful in making decisions about solving social problems. But the concept of social responsibility in itself did not make up for this lack and provided no clearer guidelines for managerial behavior. Given this lack of precision, corporate executives who wanted to be socially responsible were left to follow their own values and interests or some rather vague generalizations about changing social values and public expectations. What this meant in practice, however, was often difficult to determine.

Another key problem with the concept of social responsibility was that the concept did not take into account the competitive environment in which corporations function. Many advocates of social responsibility treated the corporation as an isolated entity that had almost unlimited ability to engage in unilateral social action. Eventually, it was recognized that corporations are severely limited in their ability to respond to social problems. If a firm unilaterally engages in social action that increases its costs and prices, it will place itself at a competitive disadvantage relative to other firms in the industry that may not be concerned about being socially responsible.

The debate about social responsibility never took this institutional context of corporations seriously. Concerted action to solve social problems is not feasible in a competitive system unless all competitors pursue roughly the same policy on these problems. Since collusion among competitors is illegal, however, the only way such concerted action can occur is when some other institution, such as government, makes all competitors engage in the same activity and pursue the same policy. And this is, in fact, what happened. While the debate about social responsibility was going on and corporate executives were asking for a definition of their social responsibilities, government was rewriting the rules under which all corporations must operate in society by developing a vast amount of legislation and regulation pertaining to the physical environment, occupational safety and health, equal opportunity, and consumer concerns.

The last issue that remained unresolved in the debate about social responsibility concerns the moral underpinnings of the notion. The term *responsibility* is fundamentally a moral one that implies an obligation to someone or something. It is clear to most people that business has an economic responsibility to produce goods and services efficiently and perform other economic functions for society. These economic responsibilities constitute the reason for having something like a business organization. But why does business have social responsibilities? What are the moral foundations for a concern with its social impacts?

The proponents of social responsibility produced no clear and generally accepted moral principle that would impose upon business an obligation to work for social betterment.[7] Ascribing social responsibility to corporations does not necessarily imply that they are moral agents that are then responsible for their social impacts. But various moral strictures were used to try to impose this obligation on business and various arguments were made to try to link moral behavior to business performance. Little was accomplished, however, in developing solid and acceptable moral support for the notion of social responsibility. Thus, the debate about social responsibility was very moralistic in many of its aspects, a debate that often generated a good deal of heat but very little light in most instances.

The intractability of these issues, according to one scholar, "posed the dreadful possibilities that the debate over corporate social responsibility would continue indefinitely with little prospect of final resolution or that it would simply exhaust itself and collapse as a viable legitimate question."[8] But beginning in the 1970s, a theoretical and conceptual reorientation began to take place regarding the corporation's response to the social environment. This new approach was labeled corporate social responsiveness, and while initially it appeared that only semantics was involved, it gradually became clear that the shift from responsibility to responsiveness was much more substantive. This shift represented an attempt to escape the unresolved dilemmas that emerged from the social responsibility debate. This new concept of social responsiveness was defined by one author as follows.

> Corporate social responsiveness refers to the capacity of a corporation to respond to social pressures. The literal act of responding, or of achieving a generally responsive posture, to society is the focus of corporate social responsiveness. . . . One searches the organization for mechanisms, procedures, arrangements, and behavioral patterns that, taken collectively, would mark the organization as more or less capable of responding to social pressures. It then becomes evident that organizational design and managerial competence play important roles in how extensively and how well a company responds to social demands and needs.[9]

Thus, attention shifted from debate about a moral notion, social responsibility, to a more technical or at least morally neutral term, social responsiveness. Research in corporate responsiveness reflected this same shift and focused on internal corporate responsiveness to social problems, examining the ways in which corporations responded to such problems. Attempts were made to identify key variables within the organization that related to its responsiveness and to discover structural changes that would enable a corporation to respond to social pressures more effectively. The important questions asked in this research were not moral, related to whether or not a corporation should respond to a social problem out of a sense of social responsibility, but were more practical and action oriented, dealing with the ability of a corporation to respond and the changes that were necessary to enable it to respond more effectively.

One of the advantages of this approach is its managerial orientation. The concept ignores the philosophical debate about responsibility and obligation and focuses on the problems and prospects of making corporations more socially responsive. One of the reasons for research into response patterns is to discover those responses that have proven to be most effective in dealing with social problems. The approach also lends itself to more rigorous analytical research in examining specific techniques, such as environmental scanning and the social audit, to improve the response process. Such research can also discover how management can best institutionalize social policy throughout the organization. Questions to investigate concern what organizational structures are most appropriate, what role top management can play in enabling corporations to respond, what changes in the reward structure can improve the corporation's response to social problems, what role public affairs departments should play in the response process, and how social policy can be best formulated for the organization as a whole.

Given these advantages, however, the concept of social responsiveness was still plagued with the same key problems that faced the concept of social responsibility. The concept of social responsiveness does not clarify how corporate resources shall be allocated for the solution of social problems. Companies respond to different problems in different ways and to varying degrees. But there is no clear idea as to what pattern of responsiveness will produce the greatest amount of social betterment. The philosophy of responsiveness does not help the company to decide what problems to get involved in and what priorities to establish. In the final analysis, it provides no better guidance to management than does social responsibility on the best strategies or policies to be adopted to produce social betterment. The concept seems to suggest that management itself, by determining the degree of social responsiveness and the pressures it will respond to, decides the meaning of the concept and what social goods and services will be produced.[10]

The concept of social responsiveness does not take the institutional context of business into account any more seriously than did social responsibility. Research in social responsiveness did not deal very thoroughly with the impact that government regulation was making on the corporation and how the corporation was responding to this change in the political environment. Individual corporate institutions were again treated as isolated entities that could choose a response pattern regardless of the institutional context in which a corporation operated. There was not enough concern with business-government relations and the role government played in the social response process.

Finally, while the question of an underlying moral principle or theory is ignored in the research dealing with corporate social responsiveness in favor of more action-oriented concerns, this turns out to be a dubious advantage. Social pressures are assumed to exist and it is believed as an article of faith that business must respond to them in some fashion. This more or less places business in a passive role of simply responding to social change. The concept of social responsiveness provides no moral basis for business to get involved in social problems. It contains no explicit moral or ethical core and provides no moral direction for business to follow in making social responses.[11]

In the mid-1970s, academics and business managers began to realize that a fundamental change was taking place in the political environment of business—that government was engaged in shaping business behavior and making business respond to a wide array of social problems by passing an unprecedented amount of legislation and writing new regulations pertaining to these problems. The political system responded to the social revolution of the 1960s and 1970s by enacting over a hundred new laws regulating business activity. Many new regulatory agencies were created and new responsibilities were assigned to old agencies. These agencies issued thousands of new rules and procedural requirements that affected business decisions and operations.

This regulatory role of government continued to expand until the 1980 election of the Reagan administration. The new type of social regulation, as it came to be called, affected virtually every department or functional area within the corporation and every level of management. The growth of this new type of regulation was referred to as a second managerial revolution, involving a shift of decision-making power and control over the corporation from the managers of corporations to a vast cadre of government regulators who were influencing and, in many cases, controlling managerial decisions in the typical business corporation.[12] The types of decisions that were becoming increasingly subject to government influence and control were basic operational decisions such as what line of business to pursue, where products can be made, how they can be marketed, what products can be produced, and other such decisions.[13]

During the late 1970s, more and more attention was paid to the changing political environment of business. Books were written that provided a comprehensive overview of the impacts of government regulation on business.[14] Studies were completed that attempted to measure the costs of social regulation to the private sector.[15] This activity drew attention to the political environment of business and showed that this environment had become increasingly hostile, giving rise to legislation and regulation that interfered with the ability of business to perform its basic economic mission. Largely because of this activity, a national debate on regulation was initiated that culminated in the election of an administration in 1980 that promised to reduce the regulatory burden on business.

Thus began a serious concern with public policy as a new dimension of management. Many business leaders recognized the importance of public policy to business and advocated that business managers become more active in the political process and work more closely with government and other groups to help shape public policy. The motivation for this concern with public policy is clear. If the rules of the game for business are being rewritten through the public policy process and business is being forced to respond to social values through complying with laws and regulations, then business has a significant interest to learn more about the public policy process and become involved in helping to write the rules by which it is going to have to live. These rules should not be left solely up to public interest groups, Congressional representatives, or agency employees.

Business has since come to adopt a more sophisticated approach to public policy, an approach that has been called the proactive stance. This means that rather than fighting change, which has often proved to be a losing battle, or simply accommodating itself to change, business attempts to influence change by becoming involved in the public policy process. Business can attempt to influence public opinion with regard to social issues of concern, and it can attempt to influence the legislative and regulatory process with regard to specific laws and regulations.

The public policy approach has some distinct advantages over the corporate social responsibility and social responsiveness concepts discussed earlier. For the most part, there is no question about the nature and extent of management's social responsibilities. Once regulations are approved, these responsibilities are spelled out in detail. The government gets involved in specifying technology that can be employed, publishing labeling requirements, developing safety standards for products, specifying safety equipment, and hundreds of other such management responsibilities. Where questions arise about the legality or feasibility of regulations, the court system is available to settle disputes of this nature. Management is thus told in great detail what social problems to be concerned with and to what extent it has to respond.

Obviously, the public policy approach treats business in its institutional context and advocates that managers learn more about government and the public policy process so that they can appropriately influence the process. Government is recognized as the appropriate body to formalize and formulate public policy for the society as a whole. Some form of response by government to most social issues is believed to be inevitable, and no amount of corporate reform along the lines of corporate social responsibility or corporate social responsiveness is going to eliminate some form of government involvement. Government has a legitimate right to formulate public policy for corporations in response to changing public expectations.

> Society can choose to allocate its resources any way it wants and on the basis of any criteria it deems relevant. If society wants to enhance the quality of air and water, it can choose to allocate resources for the production of these goods and put constraints on business in the form of standards. . . . These nonmarket decisions are made by those who participate in the public policy process and represent their views of what is best for

themselves and society as a whole. . . . It is up to the body politic to determine which market outcomes are and are not appropriate. If market outcomes are not to be taken as normative, a form of regulation which requires public participation is the only alternative. The social responsibility of business is not operational and certainly not to be trusted. When business acts contrary to the normal pressures of the marketplace, only public policy can replace the dictates of the market.[16]

There is also, at least on the surface, no need for a moral underpinning for a business obligation to produce social betterment. Society makes decisions about the allocations of resources through the public policy process based on its notions about social betterment. The result is legislation and regulation that impinge on business behavior. Business, then, has a moral obligation to obey the law as a good citizen. Failure to do so subjects business and its executives to all sorts of penalties. The social responsibility of business is thus to follow the directives of society at large as expressed in and through the public policy process.

The public policy approach seems to offer a more democratic and public basis for judging business performance than can be had either by relying on a vaguely formulated notion of social responsibility or by leaving corporate responses in the hands of a managerial elite to decide the meaning of corporate social responsiveness. Initially, it seemed possible that, by using the public policy approach, scholars and students could escape the values and ethics that underlie these efforts and substitute a more objective and value-neutral basis by which to measure and judge business's social performance. If business adheres to the standards of performance expressed in the law and existing public policy, it can be judged to be socially responsive to the changing expectations of society.

When one digs beneath the surface of the public policy approach, one finds public policy questions plagued by the same kinds of ethical dilemmas that have plagued earlier attempts to address the social responsibilities of business. Those who confront social issues in the public policy context cannot ignore the normative dimensions of these issues because public policy issues are saturated with value-laden phenomena. Public policy is, in the final analysis, about values and value conflicts, and public policy solutions to these problems are built on a conception of ethics that concerns the promotion of human welfare.

As business becomes more politically involved in writing the rules of the game or preventing new ones from being written, the question of managerial guidelines and principles again becomes relevant. What criteria, other than self-interest, are relevant to guide the corporation in the development of its political strategies? Shall these strategies be judged solely on their short-term effectiveness, say, in helping to defeat a certain bill that business doesn't like? What candidates should a corporate political action committee support—only those who are judged to have the company's best interests in mind and share traditional business values? Again, the nagging question of defining social betterment, or in a public policy context, of defining the public interest, reappears.

Regarding the institutional context, there is the question of the appropriate role for government to play in shaping business behavior. Should government continue with a command and control system of regulation to accomplish social objectives, or should it adopt other incentive mechanisms more consistent with market behavior? On the other side of the coin, what is the appropriate role for business to play in the political process? If business is perceived as being too influential in the political process and constituting a threat to the pluralistic nature of American society, and if its behavior is perceived as being too self-serving and not cognizant of the broader public interest, adverse public reaction can be expected. How can business avoid this kind of reaction and yet look after its own legitimate interests in the public policy process?

And finally, the absence of a clear moral underpinning for public policy involvement still presents a problem. Does the proactive approach simply mean that business attempts to minimize the impact of social change on itself? Does not business have more of an obligation to society than is evident in self-serving attempts to manipulate the political environment for its own advantage? Does not business have a moral obligation that goes beyond obeying the law and complying with government regulations? If business does have social and political responsibilities as well as economic responsibilities, what is the moral basis of these responsibilities?

Ethics is thus an important component of the social-political context in which public policy is formulated. The ethical standards that society holds help to shape public opinion and impact the values and attitudes that are dominant at any given time in the society at large. Ethical standards interact in a very complex fashion with other components of the social-political environment and thus help to determine the public issues that are given attention by a society and the eventual outcome of the debate about issues that reach the public policy agenda.

From equal opportunity to the physical environment, public policy issues involve questions about fairness, equity, justice, and other such normative concepts. Resources are allocated through the public policy process, and costs and benefits are distributed on some ethical basis, even if unrecognized. It is important to address the ethical assumptions on which the resolutions to specific issues are based. Management has a responsibility to participate in the public policy process, and this participation must involve more than self-interest to be effective. Some concern must exist for the public interest, the good of the community, and the larger social context in which business functions. For regulations to work where needed, some commitment must exist, at least to obey the law, as even the best-run government cannot police every business organization. Managements must show some commitment to implement the law effectively in their organizations and must even go beyond what the law requires to solve problems not covered by public policy.

The Field of Business Ethics

All of these questions about social responsibility, social responsiveness, and public policy are difficult because they are fundamentally moral and ethical questions having to do with a definition of human welfare, the meaning and purpose of life, the nature of the human community, and similar questions that are basic to human existence. These questions cannot be answered by appeal to an economic calculus such as profit and loss, nor can they be answered satisfactorily through a political process based on power and influence. For business to be effective in responding to social and political issues, these moral and ethical dimensions of the issues must be explicitly recognized and discussed. Ethical questions are fundamental to an institution such as business because society allows institutions to be developed and to continue to operate based on society's conceptions of human welfare and the things that make a life worth living. These institutions have to change as society's notions of these ethical concepts change.

These moral concerns surfaced in the early 1980s, as the subject of business ethics received a great deal of increased attention in schools of business and management around the country as well as in corporations. Ethical issues were given explicit attention, not subsumed under the topic of social responsibility, social responsiveness, or public policy. Several studies of business ethics were completed, including the highly influential report entitled "Ethics in the Education of Business Managers," published by the Institute of Society, Ethics and the Life Sciences at the Hastings Center. New centers for the study of business ethics and values cropped up around the country. Corporate support for research and teaching about the subject of business ethics increased as did corporate efforts to include business ethics as an important component of a management training program.

Many more conferences on various aspects of business ethics were held at locations around the country. The number of textbooks and casebooks in the field of business ethics proliferated, most being written, incidentally, by philosophers rather than by the faculty in management schools.[17] Endowed chairs in business ethics were established at several schools, some on a rotating basis.[18] And finally, many more courses in business ethics were taught in schools of business and management. A survey conducted by the Center for Business Ethics at Bentley College in 1980 found that almost half of the 655 schools of business and management that responded to its survey offered a course in business ethics. Of the 338 schools that did not offer a course, 48 were planning to offer such a course, and another 144 said they would like to at some time in the future.[19]

These trends have continued into the 1990s as business ethics has become a field of study in its own right with an extensive body of literature, several journals devoted to the subject, and a number of national and international professional bodies consisting of scholars and practitioners in the field who are concerned with advancing teaching and research and the application of business ethics to the business world. More chairs have been established and more conferences held on the subject around the world. Most large corporations have written ethics codes and many have established some institutional means for addressing ethical concerns within their companies.

Although there are several reasons behind this interest in business ethics, in general it can be said that this increased interest reflects some fundamental changes in society regarding a consensus on ethical standards and the conduct of institutions including business organizations. The debate about business ethics reflects the confusion that has resulted from a breakup of the notions previously held about how a business ought to act in a market-oriented society. This broader view of the problem is held by Powers and Vogel, writing in the Hastings Center report:

> In our view, the new concern for corporate ethics and managerial ethics is the logical culmination of a series of social transformations through which the connecting tissues that make up the "organic" connection between management, institution, and society have eroded. What constitutes "ethical custom" is evaporating. The ability of the market mechanism to carry the normative freight between corporations and society is deteriorating as the society increasingly turns to other ways to try to connect its changing values to corporate practice.[20]

The authors list four factors they believe have contributed to this erosion of a consensus about appropriate corporate and managerial practice. These factors include: (1) the growth in the size of corporate institutions so that the market does not govern many current corporate activities and decisions—in a sense, corporations have outgrown the market mechanism; (2) a growth in the scope of legal constraints and requirements on business and of governmental involvement in corporate activities; (3) public concern about the externalities (such as pollution) that are not amenable to direct market control; and (4) "human dignity" and the "value of human life" as new priorities in the agenda of social values.[21]

Other reasons for the interest in business ethics include the general decline of confidence in business leadership as shown by polls of public attitudes. Scandals such as illegal campaign contributions in this country and foreign payments abroad contributed to this decline of confidence and raised questions in the public mind about the degree to which corporate leaders believe in and abide by the rules of the market mechanism. The growth of management as a "profession" may be another factor, which carries with it a corresponding interest in developing ethical standards for management that are uniformly accepted. Finally, questions about the legitimacy of the management function as raised in the debate about corporate governance may motivate business managers to find a new ethical justification for their role in society.

The emergence of this concern about business ethics is thus consistent with the emergence of public concern about business policies and practices. As long as there is a consensus as to the appropriateness of the market mechanism in allocating all or at least the great majority of society's resources, the ethical notions embedded in the market concept are also accepted as appropriate with respect to business and managerial conduct. There is no need to raise these basic ethical assumptions to a conscious level and debate them. Concern about ethics is limited to situations where the accepted standards are violated. But as that consensus begins to crumble and management is pressured to respond to concerns that are not reflected in marketplace transactions, ethical notions increasingly come to the surface and are the subject of intense and very conscious debate.

Business ethics involves an effort to confront the normative issues that were a part of the social responsibility debate but were not handled very effectively, and that tended to be ignored by advocates of social responsiveness and public policy. These normative issues are at the heart of concerns about the future of the corporation and the appropriate roles for business to play in society. Normative concerns can provide a foundation for continuing managerial efforts to respond to public pressures in an effective manner and learning to appropriately balance different interests in corporate activities. Managerial activities must be based on ethical principles that are acceptable in the society at large and consistent with notions of human welfare and fulfillment that are important in Western societies.

Objections to Business Ethics

Not everyone agrees that ethics should be of concern to business organizations or corporate managers. One such objection is based on the free market argument, as first enunciated by Adam Smith. If the free market is left alone, and everyone pursues his or her self-interest, the good of society will automatically be the result. Thus, ethical concerns are peripheral to the workings of a free market and no one need give self-conscious thought to ethical conduct of corporations and managers.

Such an outright appeal to blatant egoism, however, is not generally acceptable, as society does have ethical standards and a tradition of morality to which it expects its institutions to adhere in some sense. Markets are also not perfectly competitive, and competition itself is threatened when the system is completely unregulated. And profits, which are considered to be the lifeblood of a corporation in a free enterprise system, are not in all cases socially beneficial if they do not reflect the full social as well as economic costs of production.

A second objection to business ethics is the loyal agents argument. Managers of business organizations are merely agents of the owners, and as such they are legally bound to earn the highest rate of return they can on the owners' investment. Employees of the corporation are bound by the nature of their contract with the company to be loyal agents and carry out the directives of their superiors. Thus, everyone is absolved of ethical responsibilities.

This argument rests on an unproven moral standard, however, and there is no reason to assume that it is acceptable without qualification. The argument also assumes there are no limits to the duty managers have to serve their employer, when in fact the law of agency requires business or professional ethics to be considered and the loyal agent is under no duty to perform acts that are illegal or unethical. Finally, the argument assumes that an agreement between the manager and the firm automatically justifies whatever the manager does on behalf of the firm. But agreements to serve other people do not automatically justify doing wrong on their behalf.[22]

A third objection was raised by Albert Z. Carr in an article that appeared in *Harvard Business Review* several years ago and caused quite a bit of discussion. Carr argued that business operated according to a special set of ethical principles that was different from the ethics of society in general. Business, Carr argued, has the impersonal characteristics of a game—a game that demands both a special strategy and an understanding of its special ethics.[23]

Business executives, Carr states, are compelled to practice some form of deception. This deception could take the form of conscious misstatements, concealment of pertinent facts, or exaggeration—behaviors that Carr believes are all forms of bluffing. The need to bluff is a central fact of life for business executives, according to Carr; if they feel obligated to tell the truth in all situations, they will be ignoring many business opportunities and putting themselves at a great disadvantage in many business dealings.[24]

From this view of business comes the analogy of business as poker. The ethics of poker are different from the ethical ideals of civilized human relationships. Poker calls for distrust, cunning deception, and concealment of one's strengths and intentions. The game of poker ignores the claim of friendship and does not involve kindness and openheartedness. But no one thinks any worse of poker on that account. Such behavior is accepted as part of the game. Thus, if the analogy holds, neither should one think any worse of business because its standards of right and wrong differ from those of society at large.

Carr's article, when it first appeared, received a good deal of comment. Some agreed with his basic thrust. One executive, after citing several examples that supported Carr's view of business as being realistic, stated: "What is universal about these examples is that these managers, each functioning on a different corporate level, are concerned with one thing—getting the job done. Most companies give numerous awards for achievement and accomplishment, for sales, for growth, for longevity and loyalty, but there are no medals in the business world for honesty, compassion or truthfulness."[25]

Others disagreed with the thrust of the article, however, and argued that the comparison of business to poker was unfair and inaccurate, that business is too important an area of human endeavor to be regarded as a game. Other readers complained that the article condoned unethical business practices, that a business executive cannot separate the ethics of his or her business life from the ethics of his or her home life, and that the article is one-sided and extreme in its description of what goes on in business.[26]

Another general objection to the field of business ethics is that students' values are already formed by the time they are in college, and that business ethics courses are a waste of time. As stated by Lester Thurow, dean of MIT Sloan School of Management: "If they haven't been taught ethics by their families, their clergymen, their elementary and secondary schools, their liberal arts colleges or engineering schools or the business firms where most of them worked prior to getting a business degree, there is very little we can do."[27] Such a view, however, assumes a rigidity to human growth and development that is unrealistic. Humans change throughout their entire life span and come to adopt other values and interests as circumstances change. In fact, it could be argued that when people attend college, particularly as undergraduate students, they have their first and best opportunity to break away from parental and other childhood influences and adopt their own set of values that they deem appropriate.

Finally, it is argued that ethics can't be taught, any more than leadership or entrepreneurship can be taught in the classroom. These particular characteristics are ingrained in people, so it is believed, and one either has leadership qualities, for example, or one does not, and no course in the subject is going to make one into a leader. The point is, however, that people can be taught to recognize an ethical problem when it confronts them, and this in itself is half the battle. Many ethical problems are simply not recognized as such by managers. Students can also be taught how to think about such problems and how to engage in moral reasoning to arrive at a solution that is morally acceptable and defensible. It is hoped that this book will contribute to this endeavor.

Questions for Discussion

1. Do you agree with the definitions of ethics presented in the chapter? Why or why not? What is the difference between ethics and morality? Between ethics and values? How does ethics as a normative endeavor differ from the normative approaches of religion, law, and etiquette? Are these distinctions important?

2. Describe the different approaches to ethics mentioned in the chapter. How do they differ from each other? What are some of the major differences between a descriptive approach to ethics and a normative approach? What are the implications of these differences for the applied area of business ethics?

3. Define the basic meaning of the concept of social responsibility. What common elements are found in all the definitions offered in the text? What specific kinds of responsibilities are usually referred to by the term *corporate social responsibility?* Isn't a firm being socially responsible by producing goods and services at a profit? Is this not enough in today's world?

4. Examine the arguments against the social responsibility of business. Are there any that you personally agree with? Why or why not? Which do you regard as weak arguments? Which arguments are the strongest in your opinion? Can you think of any other ways to support the notion that business has social responsibilities?

5. How does corporate social responsiveness differ from corporate social responsibility? Why do you think this shift has taken place in academic thinking? What are the advantages of a responsiveness approach? What are its disadvantages? On the whole, do you believe the concept of corporate social responsiveness represents a theoretical advance in business-society relationships?

6. Are there severe limitations on a corporation's ability to be socially responsible or responsive? Do these limitations render the concepts of social responsibility and responsiveness inadequate to provide a conceptual underpinning for the social and political roles of business in society? Should they be abandoned in favor of some other conceptual framework?

7. What advantages does the concept of public policy have over the previous concepts in describing and understanding the social and political roles of business in society? Why have most social issues become public policy concerns? Is government the legitimate institution to formalize and formulate public policy for the society as a whole? Why or why not?

8. Why are ethical considerations basic to any discussion of the role of business in society? What does ethics mean and with what kinds of issues is ethics concerned? Do business executives need to learn something about ethics in order to meaningfully discuss the role of business in society? Or does a discussion of economics take care of all ethical questions?

9. What are the usual objections to business ethics? Is it really an oxymoron? Which objections are most important or damaging to the ethical endeavor with regard to business organizations? Are the answers to these objections mentioned in the text sufficient? How would you answer these objections?

10. Why should managers be concerned about ethical behavior? What does it mean to say that ethics is central to the management task? Do you agree with this statement? If your response is yes, what implications does your answer have for business organizations?

Endnotes

[1] Charles W. Powers and David Vogel, *Ethics in the Education of Business Managers* (Hastings-on-Hudson, NY: The Hastings Center, 1980), p. 1.

[2] Robert C. Solomon and Kristine R. Hanson, *Above the Bottom Line: An Introduction to Business Ethics* (New York: Harcourt Brace Jovanovich, 1983), p. 9.

[3] Richard T. DeGeorge, *Business Ethics,* 2nd ed. (New York: Macmillan, 1986), p. 15.

[4] Tom L. Beauchamp and Norman E. Bowie, *Ethical Theory and Business,* 2nd ed. (Englewood Cliffs, NJ: Prentice-Hall, 1983), pp. 1, 3.

[5] Ibid., pp. 1–2.

[6] See Richard T. DeGeorge, "The Status of Business Ethics: Past and Future," Business Ethics Research Workshop, Stanford University, August 14–17, 1985.

[7] William C. Frederick, "From CSR1 to CSR2: The Maturing of Business and Society Thought," Graduate School of Business, University of Pittsburgh, 1978, Working Paper No. 279, p. 5.

[8] Ibid.

[9] Ibid., p. 6.

[10] Ibid., pp. 12–13.

[11] Ibid., pp. 14–16.

[12] Murray L. Weidenbaum, *Business, Government, and the Public* (Englewood Cliffs, NJ: Prentice-Hall, 1977), p. 285.

[13] Murray L. Weidenbaum, *The Future of Business Regulation* (New York: AMACOM, 1979), p. 34.

[14] Ibid.

[15] See Murray L. Weidenbaum and Robert DeFina, *The Cost of Federal Regulation of Economic Activity* (Washington, DC: American Enterprise Institute, 1978); and Arthur Anderson, *Cost of Government Regulation* (New York: The Business Roundtable, 1979).

[16] Rogene A. Buchholz, "An Alternative to Social Responsibility," *MSU Business Topics* (Summer 1977), pp. 12, 16.

[17] Powers and Vogel, *Ethics in the Education of Business Managers,* pp. 31–34.

[18] In a novel settlement in 1983, U.S. District Judge Warren K. Urbom ordered a highway contracting company that had pleaded guilty to bid rigging to donate $1,475,000 to endow a chair in business ethics at the University of Nebraska. The idea apparently came from a former student who said he had never heard anyone mention bid rigging while he was in school.

[19] W. Michael Hoffman and Jennifer Mills Moore, "Results of a Business Ethics Curriculum Survey Conducted by the Center for Business Ethics," *Journal of Business Ethics,* Vol. 1, no. 2 (May 1982), pp. 81–83.

[20] Powers and Vogel, *Ethics in the Education of Business Managers,* p. 7. Reproduced by permission. Copyright © The Hastings Center.

[21] Ibid., pp. 7–8.

[22] Manuel G. Velasquez, *Business Ethics: Concepts and Cases* (Englewood Cliffs, NJ: Prentice-Hall, 1982), p. 19.

[23] Albert Z. Carr, "Is Business Bluffing Ethical?" *Harvard Business Review,* Vol. 46, no. 1 (January–February 1968), pp. 143–153.

[24] Ibid., p. 428.

[25] Timothy B. Blodgett, "Showdown on Business Bluffing," *Harvard Business Review,* Vol. 46, no. 3 (May–June 1968), p. 163.

[26] Ibid., pp. 163–166.

[27] Kirk Hanson, "What Good Are Ethics Courses?" *Across the Board* (September 1987), pp. 10–11.

Suggested Readings

Ackerman, Robert W. *The Social Challenge to Business.* Cambridge, MA: Harvard University Press, l975.

Ackerman, Robert W., and Raymond Bauer. *Corporate Social Responsiveness: The Modern Dilemma.* Reston, VA: Reston Publishing Co., 1976.

Aram, John D. *Managing Business and Public Policy: Concepts, Issues and Cases,* 2nd ed. Boston: Pitman, 1986.

Baron, David P. *Business & Its Environment.* Englewood Cliffs, NJ: Prentice Hall, 1992.

Bowen, Howard R. *Social Responsibilities of Businessmen.* New York: Harper & Row, 1953.

Carroll, Archie B. *Business & Society: Ethics and Stakeholder Management,* 2nd ed. Cincinnati: South-Western, 1993.

Carroll, Archie B., ed. *Managing Corporate Social Responsibility.* Boston: Little Brown, 1977.

Chamberlain, Neil W. *The Limits of Corporate Responsibility.* New York: Basic Books, 1973.

Chamberlain, Neil W. *Remaking American Values: Challenge to a Business Society.* New York: Basic Books, 1977.

Eells, Richard, and Clarence Walton. *Conceptual Foundations of Business.* Homewood, IL: Richard D. Irwin, 1961.

Frederick, William C., and James E. Post. *Business and Society: Corporate Strategy, Public Policy, Ethics,* 7th ed. New York: McGraw-Hill, 1992.

Friedman, Milton. *Capitalism and Freedom.* Chicago: University of Chicago Press, 1962.

Hay, Robert D., Edmund R. Gray, and Paul H. Smith. *Business & Society: Perspectives on Ethics and Social Responsibility.* Cincinnati: South-Western, 1989.

Luthans, Fred, Richard M. Hodgetts, and Kenneth R. Thompson. *Social Issues in Business,* 6th ed. New York: Macmillan, 1990.

McGuire, Joseph W. *Business and Society.* New York: McGraw-Hill, 1963.

Powers, Charles W., and David Vogel. *Ethics in the Education of Business Managers.* Hastings-on-Hudson, NY: The Hastings Center, 1980.

Preston, Lee E., and James E. Post. *Private Management and Public Policy.* Englewood Cliffs, NJ: Prentice-Hall, 1975.

Research and Policy Committee of the Committee for Economic Development. *Social Responsibilities of Business Corporations.* New York: Committee for Economic Development, 1971.

Sethi, Prakash, and Ceclia M. Falbe. *Business & Society: Dimensions of Conflict and Cooperation.* New York: Free Press, 1987.

Steiner, George A., and John F. Steiner. *Business, Government, and Society: A Managerial Perspective,* 6th ed. New York: McGraw-Hill, 1991.

Sturdivant, Frederick D., and James E. Stacey. *The Corporate Social Challenge: Cases and Commentaries,* 4th ed. Homewood, IL: Richard D. Irwin, 1990.

Sturdivant, Frederick D., and Heidi Vernon Wortzel. *Business and Society: A Managerial Approach,* 4th ed. Homewood, IL: Richard D. Irwin, 1990.

Tombari, Henry A. *Business and Society: Strategies for the Environment and Public Policy.* New York: Dryden, 1984.

Wood, Donna J. *Business and Society.* Glenview, IL: Scott, Foresman/Little Brown, 1990.

S H O R T   C A S E S

Manville Corporation

On August 26, 1982, Denver-based Manville Corporation, a diversified manufacturing, mining, and forest products company, filed for bankruptcy under Chapter 11 of the Federal Bankruptcy Act to protect itself from the overwhelming number of product liability lawsuits relating to the manufacture and use of asbestos. The company decided to seek protection after a study showed that Manville faced a potential total of 52,000 lawsuits at a projected cost of around $2 billion, which was nearly twice the company's net worth.[1] The chief executive officer of the company, John A. McKinney, said that its businesses were in good shape but that Manville was completely overwhelmed by the cost of the asbestos lawsuits filed against the company.[2]

Manville's unprecedented bankruptcy case stunned the financial community, outraged those who had filed asbestos suits against it, put stockholders in a panic, and raised a complex tangle of issues that had far-reaching implications for toxic tort litigation. By filing for bankruptcy, Manville won at least a temporary reprieve as all future claims were suspended. These future claimants then had to look to the bankruptcy court for relief, taking their place in line behind secured creditors. The bankruptcy court had the power to discharge or cancel any debts or potential claims against the company.

Manville was given many extensions to work out the differences with its creditors and litigants over its proposed reorganization plan. After several attempts, a plan began to take shape that eventually became the basis for a settlement. In the summer of 1985, Manville agreed to a flexible scheme to fund the claims against the company that would use some cash left over after normal operations, but that could also take as much as 80 percent of the company stock. Under the plan, Manville agreed to a trust fund to deal with asbestos-disease claims. The trust wouldn't be part of the company, but would be funded by it with a $1.65 billion bond to be paid in annual installments of $75 million over 22 years, $646 million in insurance, and 50 to 80 percent of the company's common stock, depending on the size of the claims that had been filed. Voting rights on the stock would be restricted for four years after Manville emerged from bankruptcy, but after that time the trust could use its stock to essentially take over the company. The trust would be controlled by five people appointed by the bankruptcy court. The company would also pay the trust $200 million in cash and allocate 20 percent of its annual profit indefinitely if the funds were needed. Overall, the company would contribute $2.5 to $3 billion, depending on the value of the stock and future earnings.[3]

The company initially balked at giving up control when the board said it had to have the final say in who would run the company after it emerged from bankruptcy. Representatives of current and future health claimants insisted that any director be acceptable to all the creditor groups, and the company eventually agreed to let creditors have the final say in board appointments, thereby removing the last major obstacle to gaining approval of the plan.[4] The board also agreed to look for an outsider to run the company after the present chief executive officer (CEO) and chair, John A. McKinney, retired in September 1986. At this news the president of the company, J. T. Hulce, who had been the heir apparent, resigned.[5] The board then named George C. Dillon, an outside director, as chair, and W. Thomas Stephens, the chief financial officer of the company, as the chief executive officer.[6] The company then paid McKinney and Hulce more than $1.8 million in a severance agreement.[7]

During the time this reorganization plan was being debated, an estimated 2,000 of the 16,500 personal-injury plaintiffs died. These victims had not received a penny for their claims because the bankruptcy filing froze the litigation. The money their relatives will eventually receive is little consolation. The company itself, after a four-year reorganization effort, is subject to be taken over by the trust, which could liquidate the company if the money isn't enough to pay claims. The only winners are the lawyers who will make about $1 billion in fees from settlements paid by the trust.[8]

Manville thought that bankruptcy would be a quick fix to the endless stream of lawsuits it was facing, and that it could emerge from Chapter 11 in a relatively short period of time after having set aside enough money to cover these claims. It now seems that the company drastically underestimated the complexity of using the bankruptcy code to deal with toxic torts litigation. The company had to deal with not only commercial creditors and shareholders, but also with about 20 representatives for the plaintiffs, another dozen or so lawyers representing co-defendants, and one representative for future claimants. Given this kind of a political context, Manville simply lost control of the situation and lost the store in the process.[9]

1. Was the use of bankruptcy laws an effective strategy for Manville to adopt? What was Manville's objective in using this strategy? Was this strategy appropriate? Was it ethical? Should bankruptcy be used to deal with toxic torts litigation?

2. Identify the parties at fault in this case. How should responsibility be assigned to these parties? Who is legally liable? Who is morally responsible? How should liability and responsibility be divided among the company, the insurance companies, the government, and other responsible parties?

3. Who should decide about the risks involved in using a hazardous substance? Employees? The company? The government? What kind of risk analysis is useful in making these decisions? Who should bear the risk and how should liability be distributed?

4. Apply concepts of justice to this situation. Was the final settlement a just agreement? Why or why not? Were anyone's rights violated or ignored in the settlement? Were important rights appropriately respected?

[1] "Company Besieged by Claims, Files Bankruptcy," *Monthly Labor Review* (November 1982), p. 48.

[2] William Marbach, et al., "An Asbestos Bankruptcy," *Newsweek,* September 6, 1982, p. 54.

[3] Jonathan Dahl, "Manville Offers $2.5 Billion Plan to Settle Claims," *The Wall Street Journal,* August 5, 1985, p. 3.

[4] Cynthia F. Mitchell, "Manville Is Said to Have Agreed to Let Creditors Decide Board Appointments," *The Wall Street Journal,* April 30, 1986, p. 7.

[5] Cynthia F. Mitchell, "Manville President Quits After Dispute with Asbestos Plaintiffs over Top Posts," *The Wall Street Journal,* April 30, 1986, p. 34.

[6] "Now Comes the Hard Part for Manville," *Business Week,* July 7, 1986, p. 76.

[7] Cynthia F. Mitchell, "Manville to Pay Large Severance to 2 Executives," *The Wall Street Journal,* June 24, 1986, p. 10.

[8] Cynthia F. Mitchell, "Negative Verdict: Manville's Bid to Evade Avalanche of Lawsuits Proves Disappointing," *The Wall Street Journal,* July 15, 1986, p. 1.

[9] Ibid.

Source: Rogene A. Buchholz, *Public Policy Issues for Management,* 2nd ed. (Englewood Cliffs, NJ: Prentice Hall, 1992), pp. 212–214.

Plasma International

The Sunday headline in the Tampa, Florida, newspaper read: "Blood Sales Result in Exorbitant Profits for Local Firm." The story went on to relate how the Plasma International Company, headquartered in Tampa, Florida, purchased blood in underdeveloped countries for as little as 15 cents a pint and resold the blood to hospitals in the United States and South America. A recent disaster in Nicaragua produced scores of injured persons and the need for fresh blood. Plasma International had 10,000 pints of blood flown to Nicaragua from West Africa and charged the hospitals $25 per pint, netting the firm nearly a quarter of a million dollars.

As a result of the newspaper story, a group of irate citizens, led by prominent civic leaders, demanded that the City of Tampa, and the State of Florida, revoke Plasma International's licenses to practice business. Others protested to their Congressmen to seek enactment of legislation designed to halt the sale of blood for profit. The spokesperson was reported as saying, "What kind of people are these—selling life and death? These men prey on the needs of dying people, buying blood from poor, ignorant Africans for 15 cents worth of beads and junk, and selling it to injured people for $25 a pint. Well, this company will soon find out that the people of our community won't stand for their kind around here."

"I just don't understand it. We run a business just like any other business; we pay taxes and we try to make an honest profit," said Sol Levin as he responded to reporters at the Tampa International Airport. He had just returned home from testifying before the House Sub-Committee on Medical Standards. The recent publicity surrounding his firm's activities during the recent earthquakes had once again fanned the flames of public opinion. An election year was an unfortunate time for the publicity to occur. The politicians and the media were having a field day.

Levin was a successful stockbroker when he founded Plasma International Company three years ago. Recognizing the world need for safe, uncontaminated and reasonably priced whole blood and blood plasma, Levin and several of his colleagues pooled their resources and went into business. Initially, most of the blood and plasma they sold were purchased through storefront operations in the southeast United States. Most of the donors were, unfortunately, men and women who used the money obtained from the sale of their blood to purchase wine. While sales increased dramatically on the basis of an innovative marketing approach, several cases of hepatitis were reported in recipients. The company wisely began a search for new sources.

Recognizing their own limitations in the medical-biological side of the business, they recruited a highly qualified team of medical consultants. The consulting team, after extensive testing, and a worldwide search, recommended that the blood profiles and donor characteristics of several rural West African tribes made them ideal prospective donors. After extensive negotiations with the State Department and the government of the nation of Burami, the company was able to sign an agreement with several of the tribal chieftains.

As Levin reviewed these facts, and the many costs involved in the sale of a commodity as fragile as blood, he concluded that the publicity was grossly unfair. His thoughts were interrupted by the reporter's question: "Mr. Levin, is it necessary to sell a vitally needed medical supply, like blood, at such high prices especially to poor people in such a critical situation?" "Our prices are determined on the basis of a lot of costs that we incur that the public isn't even aware of," Levin responded. However, when reporters pressed him for details of these "relevant" costs, Levin refused any further comment. He noted that such information was proprietary in nature and not for public consumption.

1. Is there such a thing as a "socially unacceptable" business activity?
2. Should Mr. Levin have revealed the costs that he considered relevant, when questioned by reporters? Would revealing these costs help his situation?
3. What rights should the public have concerning information about the activities of corporations, especially in areas that seem to involve public moral issues?
4. Should there be regulation of the collection, distribution, and sale of such products as blood? Who should do the regulating? What regulations should be instituted?

Source: Robert D. Hay, Edmund R. Gray, and Paul H. Smith, *Business and Society: Perspectives on Ethics & Social Responsibility,* 3rd ed. (Cincinnati: South-Western, 1989), pp. 124–125.

Computer Capers

Jim Langford had been a computer programmer for Pacific Corporation for the past ten years. He was the best programmer in the department and was known for his ability to solve complex programming problems. Systems on which he worked were usually implemented on time and had fewer problems than systems programmed by some of the other employees in the department.

Because of his skills and speed, the controller of the company and Jim's department head came to him one day with an unusual request. They wanted him to write a one-time program that would duplicate the format of a yearly summary page that was the end result of one of the systems Jim had programmed. This page contained yearly income and expenses for one of the other departments of the company, and was based on figures supplied to the computer over the course of the year. The only problem was that the controller wanted to use other figures than those that had come out of the regular year-end running of the system.

Because it was near tax time, Jim suspected the change in figures had something to do with taxes. The controller wanted the new figures to be printed on the computer so nothing would look suspicious. Jim was being considered for a project manager job he wanted very badly, and he knew the decision about this job would be made very shortly. Jim also knew that if he refused this request, his colleague, who was also in the running for the job, would not hesitate to do it and gain some points with management. Jim felt uneasy about the request because of his ethical standards, to say nothing of the legal implications should actual fraud be involved.

1. Should Jim be a loyal agent and do as his superiors requested? Would this absolve him of responsibility? How would the legal system in our country treat this situation?
2. What are the ethical issues in this situation? How should Jim weigh his own self-interest with regard to his decision? What would you do if you were in Jim's position?

Source: Rogene A. Buchholz, *Business Environment and Public Policy: Implications for Management,* 5th ed. (Englewood Cliffs, NJ: Prentice Hall, 1995), p. 493.

Swimming Pool Problems

The manager of the public swimming pools in the city of Happy Homes is faced with a major crisis. He accepted the responsibility for a large municipal pool system, which includes the hiring, training, and supervision of individual pool managers and lifeguards, several years ago to help pay for his college education. The manager is expected to take care of all budget matters, supply, repair, and scheduling for all the pools in the city, which are open from late spring to early fall. The pools are open seven days a week for competitive swimming, swimming lessons, and scuba diving classes. It was made clear by city officials that any problem that occurs is solely the responsibility of the general pool manager, with the very clear message that any problem that gets out of hand and causes either loss of revenue or excessive downtime will result in immediate termination.

Three weeks into the season, the general manager is notified that shipments of soda ash, which are needed to balance the water in pools using a gas chlorine purification system, will be curtailed due to problems of supply. The implications of this cutoff include the following: (1) Without soda ash it will be difficult to keep the acid level of the swimming pool water from reaching dangerous levels, and (2) the available substitutes, while keeping the water in balance for a short time, are troublesome in that they are much more expensive, upset the overall chemistry of the water, and decrease water clarity. The end result will be decreased water quality and reduced safety for swimmers. Furthermore, in a relatively short period of time, the water quality will become so degraded that the health department will close an affected pool until the condition is improved. Clearly, the situation threatens not only the swimming program but has the potential to get the manager fired due to disruptions in schedules and revenue.

Pointing out these serious implications to the supplier of soda ash, the manager is told that if he is able to come up with an extra couple of dollars for each bag needed, he might be able to get enough soda ash to see him through the summer. Given the quantity of soda ash on hand and the amount needed to complete the summer, the pool manager figures that the extra cost will be about $5,000 in total. He reasons that having the soda ash is better than being closed even though profits will be reduced overall. Thus, he agrees to pay the extra cost and a schedule for delivery is agreed upon with the supplier. The manager is then informed, however, that the extra charge should be paid in cash at the time of each delivery to "simplify bookkeeping."

This request severely bothers the manager and he calls the supervisor of recreation for the city to explain the situation. The manager is informed that if he can't take care of such a simple transaction, maybe someone else should be hired who can handle it without bothering city officials. After this conversation, the pool manager again called the chemical supply company and arranged to have the cash available with each delivery. Furthermore, he instructed each pool manager to set aside sufficient cash from funds taken in during public swimming to cover the costs of the "special delivery fee."

The pool system was thus able to stay open the entire summer with no major problems. The revenue generated that season was the best in several years. Problems that other municipalities had, caused by the lack of soda ash, such as pool closings, safety problems, lawsuits due to poor water quality, and injuries resulting from swimming in cloudy water, were avoided. For having such an outstanding record, the general manager was given a positive recommendation to the city officials and a substantial bonus, and told that he will be rehired for the next season at a substantial increase in salary.

1. Did the manager do the "right" thing? What were the ethical issues in this situation? Where did self-interest enter into this situation? Who benefited from the manager's decision? Who was hurt by this decision?

2. What other alternatives did the manager have in this situation? Could he have been more "creative" in his response to the soda ash supplier? Were there other things he could have done with regard to his superiors?

Source: Rogene A. Buchholz, *Business Environment and Public Policy: Implications for Management,* 5th ed. (Englewood Cliffs, NJ: Prentice Hall, 1995), pp. 493–494.

Traditional Approaches to Business Ethics

The usual approach to ethical theory in business ethics texts is to present either in cursory form or sometimes in greater detail the theory of utilitarianism based on the writings of Jeremy Bentham and John Stuart Mill as representative of a more general class of teleological ethics, and the Kantian ethical theory of duty as representative of the deontological approach to ethical decision making. These texts then go on to present certain notions of justice, usually going into the egalitarianism of John Rawls and the opposing libertarianism of Robert Nozick. They also generally include a discussion of rights and perhaps some variation of virtue theory based on Aristotle or more modern virtue theorists.

This chapter will present these various approaches, indicating the generally accepted strengths and weaknesses of each theory. It will also summarize, at appropriate times, common presuppositions concerning key concepts that need to be reconsidered to avoid the dilemmas and impasses to which these theories give rise. This kind of discussion and analysis will prepare the way for grasping the significance of the reoriented approach, which will be discussed in successive chapters in the first part of this book. It will be shown how this new approach undercuts some of the dilemmas that traditional theories pose for the field of business ethics.

Utilitarianism

Teleological theories of ethics, sometimes called consequentialist theories, hold that the moral worth of an action or practice is determined solely by the consequences of the action or practice. The rightness or wrongness of actions and practices is determined by the results that these actions or practices produce. What makes an action right or wrong is the good or evil that is produced by the act, not the act itself. Thus, teleological theories do not hold that an act has intrinsic value in and of itself, but all acts and practices must be evaluated in terms of the good and bad consequences they produce.

Several different kinds of teleological theories can be mentioned, but utilitarianism is the most popular theory that has application to business decisions.[1] Utilitarianism holds that whether an action is right or wrong depends on the good or bad consequences produced for everyone affected by the action. Thus, the way in which the action affects oneself is relevant, as is how the action affects all others. Utilitarian theory is thus universal or comprehensive and considers the consequences for all the parties affected by the act. Each individual is considered atomically in arriving at a sum total of good or bad consequences. Utilitarianism involves the consideration of alternatives, as an action or practice is judged to be correct if it leads to the greatest possible balance of good consequences or the least possible balance of bad consequences for everyone affected by the action or practice when compared with alternative actions or practices that are available. Utilitarianism thus promotes human welfare by minimizing harms and/or maximizing benefits as a whole.

Making a utilitarian decision, then, involves the following steps: (1) determining the alternative actions that are available in any specific decision situation, (2) estimating the costs and benefits that a given action would produce for each and every person affected by the action, and (3) choosing the alternative that produces the greatest sum of utility or the least amount of disutility.[2] If these steps are followed, the action chosen can then be defended as a morally correct action. Thus, utilitarianism advocates a specific method to arrive at a correct decision and grounds that method in a conception of the greatest good that can be produced for the greatest number of people who are affected by the decision considered as a whole.

Utilitarianism involves some conception of the "good" or ultimate utility in terms of which the effects of all the alternatives are to be evaluated. In this regard, there are hedonistic utilitarians who argue that the ultimate "good" or utility is pleasure and the ultimate "bad" or disutility is pain, and all actions or practices ought to be evaluated in terms of how much pleasure or pain they produce for all the people affected considered as a whole. Pluralistic utilitarians, on the other hand, argue that there is no single "good" that people pursue in an ultimate sense, but that friendship, knowledge, courage, beauty, and health are also "goods" worth pursuing, and that a utilitarian decision ought to take account of the effects of an action or practice on all these values.

Philosophers also make a distinction between act and rule utilitarianism. The former holds that in all situations one ought to perform the act that maximizes utility for all the persons affected by the action. What utility means is different in different situations, and these different situations are unique enough to justify separate analysis. Thus, in each and every situation, one needs to make a utilitarian analysis and apply the general rule of utilitarianism to determine the right action or practice. Rule utilitarianism, on the other hand, holds that utility can be applied to classes of actions rather than to each individual action. Thus, rules, which can be considered to be lower-level rules when compared with the general rule, or perhaps even called rules of thumb, can be developed that when followed, will tend to maximize utility in situations that are similar.

Thus, an act utilitarian, when faced with the temptation to break a promise, would have to evaluate the consequences of breaking a promise in each and every situation where the question arose. The concept of utility and the general rule would have to be applied to the breaking of a promise in a particular situation under a particular set of

circumstances. A rule utilitarian, on the other hand, would look at the general consequences of breaking promises in any situation, and might develop a rule of thumb that it
is immoral to break promises because, in general, keeping promises produces more good
than breaking them. The advantage of having these kinds of rules is that one does not have
to take time to think through the consequences of alternatives in each and every situation
but can use rules as guidelines to determine the right action. This is a particular advantage
when time pressures are involved, and one does not have the time to perform a thorough-
going utilitarian analysis. The disadvantage is that rules can become inflexible when
applied to situations that are truly unique and deserve new thinking.

Utilitarianism is obviously committed to the good and asserts that we ought always
to choose that action which produces the greatest possible balance of good for all persons
affected by the action. Concepts of duty and rights, which will be discussed later, are subordinated to or determined by that action which maximizes the good or promises the best
outcome for all affected parties considered as a whole. In making a utilitarian decision,
the well-being of each individual is totaled to yield the size of the benefits pie, but the conclusion then ignores the individual in favor of the sum total of benefits. Thus, a utilitarian
decision could bring about harm or disutility to a minority group and violate basic rights
they believe they possess in the interests of producing the greatest good for the greatest
number. Some philosophers hold that there are basic human rights that ought not to be violated in the interests of the general welfare.

A related criticism points out that utilitarianism only considers how much total
utility is produced by an action, and fails to take into account how that utility is distributed. Various distributional patterns can result from different actions, and yet utilitarianism is indifferent between different distributions as long as they produce the same
amount of total utility. A purely aggregative principle like utilitarianism neglects a distributive dimension, and many would hold that a sound morality cares not only about the
size of the benefits pie but also how it is divided among persons. Thus, philosophers argue
that justice, which is a basic concept of morality, cannot be derived from a utilitarian analysis, and they question the moral validity of utilitarian theory. Some ways of distributing
benefits and burdens are believed to be unjust, regardless of how great the store of benefits such distributions produce.[3] How the good of the individual may be linked with or
intertwined with the good of others remains a problem for utilitarian analysis.

Utilitarianism is also committed to the measurement and comparison of goods, and
assumes that all benefits and costs of an action can be measured on a common numerical
scale and then added or subtracted from each other. In our modern economic society, the
hedonistic calculus advocated by Jeremy Bentham has been replaced by the price mechanism. Utility is measured by the price people are willing to pay for something in the
market. Thus, benefits and costs of alternative courses of action can be measured by determining a market price that will express the positive benefits or negative impacts of a particular action on the people affected.

Criticisms are leveled at this process and questions raised about the possibility of
quantifying goodness or badness in this or any other manner. Philosophers argue that
attempts to quantify utility and measure benefits and costs of alternative actions involve
arbitrary and subjective assessments of value. It is difficult in many cases to determine
what is a benefit and what is a cost, let alone trying to place some dollar value on them that
is realistic and acceptable to all the parties concerned. When we get into the problem of
valuing the benefits of pleasure, health, knowledge, and happiness, or measuring the costs

of pain, suffering, sickness, death, and ignorance, we are faced with an apples and oranges problem, and it is impossible to find a common denominator that will do justice to valuing all these goods and evils appropriately and uniformly.[4] Nonetheless, the utilitarian method has value as a way of thinking, even if it cannot be strictly followed in a quantitative sense. Thinking about alternatives and arriving at some rough estimates of their consequences is still a useful method for a decision maker who is faced with making an ethical judgment.[5]

Ethical Formalism

The deontological approach to ethical decisions maintains that actions are not justified by their consequences, that factors other than good or bad outcomes determine the rightness or wrongness of actions and practices. Thus, actions or practices themselves have intrinsic value apart from their consequences. The value of actions lies in motives rather than consequences. It makes a difference to deontologists whether one's motive is based on duty or on self-interest. Doing one's duty is a matter of satisfying the legitimate claims or needs of others as determined by applicable moral principles. The sources of duty can be a divine command, reason, intuition, or a social contract arrived at by the members of a society.

For example, promises ought to be kept and debts paid because of one's duty to keep promises and pay debts, not because of the good or bad consequences of such actions. If a person borrows money from someone with a promise to pay the debt at a later date with interest, this payment should be made because of the moral obligation inherent in the agreement. Not to pay the debt would violate a principle of great moral significance. From a utilitarian perspective, however, the debt should be paid because of the consequences involved.

The theories of Immanuel Kant are most often cited in further explanation of deontological theory. According to Kant, the ultimate basis of morality is to be found in pure practical reason, not in intuition, conscience, or production of utility. By analyzing reason as applied to action (practical reason), the key to morality can be found. Since reason is assumed to be the same in each individual, what is rational and moral should be the same for each individual. Thus, morality has an objective basis that is independent of our own personal goals and preferences. The ultimate basis of morality must be founded on principles of reason that all rational agents possess in common. Individuals act morally when they willingly choose to act in the way reason demands.[6]

This demand to be moral comes to us in the form of a categorical imperative, something that everyone must do because it is a command of reason. These moral commands are categorical rather than hypothetical because they admit of no exceptions and are absolutely binding. They are imperative because they give instructions about how one must act in all circumstances. A categorical imperative tells us what must be done whether or not we wish to perform the action, and prescribes maxims that are binding regardless of the circumstances and consequences. If one wants to be a rational human being, one is duty bound to obey these categorical imperatives.

How does one tell a valid moral principle from one that is not morally valid? Kant's theory has been called ethical formalism because Kant holds that an action or principle is right if it has a certain form and is morally wrong if it does not have that form. Thus, the moral law at its most general level states the form an action must have to be moral; it does not state the content an action must have to be a right action. This approach involves certain criteria that we can use to judge whether or not an action or a lower-level moral principle is indeed moral. For an action or principle to be moral, (1) it must be possible for it to be made consistently universal, (2) it must respect rational beings as ends in themselves, and (3) it must stem from and respect the autonomy of rational beings.[7]

> **Universalizability.** An action is morally right for a person in a given situation if and only if the person's reason for carrying out the action is a reason that he or she would be willing to have every person act on, in any similar situation. If an action is moral for one person, it must be accepted as moral for everyone. Can dishonesty, for example, be justified as a valid moral principle on these grounds? Not according to Kant, because the principle cannot be applied universally. If dishonesty were the rule, nobody could believe a statement made by anyone, including a statement that one was being dishonest. One would have no way to sort out claims to truth. Thus, the principle cannot be applied consistently across all people, has no meaning in and of itself, and is self-defeating. Dishonesty only has meaning against a general presumption of honesty, which can be advocated as a valid moral principle because it can be applied consistently in all situations.[8]

> **Respect for rational beings.** An action is morally right if and only if in performing the action, the person does not use others merely as means for advancing his or her own interests, but respects people as ends in themselves. To treat people as means is to exploit them or otherwise use them without regard to their interests, needs, and concerns. People should be treated with dignity and have rights that should not be violated in pursuit of the general welfare or a so-called social good. People are not to be sacrificed on the altar of a utilitarian approach to morality that defines some general good as the ultimate end of human existence.[9]

> **Autonomy.** An action is morally right if and only if the action respects people's capacity to choose freely for themselves. People are to treat each other as free and equal in the pursuit of their interests. Deception, force, and coercion fail to respect a person's freedom to choose and are therefore immoral. The moral law is self-imposed and self-recognized; all persons determine its content for themselves in accordance with reason. All persons impose the law upon themselves and accept its demands for themselves. Those who possess moral dignity are the determiners of their own destinies and are self-governing beings. Autonomous persons are both free of external control and are also in control of their own affairs.[10]

Actions and principles must meet all three of these tests to be valid moral actions or principles. Actions and principles such as truth telling and keeping promises must be subjected to these criteria, and if they pass they then have the status of a categorical imperative. Thus, the right action to perform in a given situation is determined by these formal criteria rather than by an appeal to consequences. An action has moral worth when performed by an agent who possesses a good will, defined as a person whose sole motive for action is performance of a moral duty based on a valid moral principle.

As in utilitarianism, there are act and rule deontologists. According to act deontology, individuals in a decision-making situation must grasp immediately what ought to be done without relying on rules or guidelines. Each situation is unique and is not subsumable under general rules of moral behavior. This view emphasizes the particular and changing features of moral experience and relies on individual intuition, conscience, faith, or love as the basis for moral judgments. Kant's theory would seem to rule out this kind of deontology, as it provides a weak basis for moral action. What happens when people immediately grasp different "oughts" when confronted with the same or similar situations? There is no way to sort out these conflicting claims by appeal to rules, procedures, or consequences. Rule deontology, on the other hand, is consistent with Kant's theory, as it states that acts are right or wrong because of their conformity or nonconformity to one or more moral principles. Such rules facilitate decision making and are binding on individuals.

There are also monistic deontological theories that advocate a general rule, such as the golden rule, as the supreme moral principle from which all other moral rules and principles are derived, and pluralistic deontological theories, such as the ten commandments, which hold that there are a number of moral principles that have more or less equal validity. Ross, for example, lists a number of moral maxims such as faithfulness, promise-keeping, justice, beneficence, nonmalevolence, and gratitude, that are prima facie moral duties. They are always to be acted on unless they conflict on particular occasions with equal or stronger duties. Prima facie duties are thus not absolute and can be overriden under some conditions.[11]

Deontologists have been accused of making a covert appeal to consequences to demonstrate the rightness of actions. It is often argued that the consequences of an action cannot be separated from the action itself. Even Kant's theory is said to rely on a covert appeal to the utilitarian principle. If the consequences of the universal performance of a certain type of action can be shown to be undesirable overall, then the action is wrong. However, Kant never advocated that consequences be disregarded entirely, only that the judgment about the morality of a particular act should not rely on consequences.[12]

There is something of a problem of evaluating actions with regard to deontological theories. There can be legitimate disagreement as to exactly what action reason demands in a given situation. If one cannot turn to consequences, how is this disagreement to be resolved? Furthermore, what happens when moral rules conflict? Which one should be overriden in favor of the other? How should conflicting rights and principles be adjusted to each other? If one rule demands truth telling while another rule demands the protection of a person from serious harm, what is one to do when asked to disclose a piece of information that will bring serious harm to someone? Should one tell the truth and disclose the damaging information, or lie to protect a person from being harmed?[13]

Neither theory is free from problems, but deontology is again valuable as a way of thinking about ethical problems and arriving at valid moral actions and principles. Even if the categorical imperative can't be applied to all actions, thinking about one's duty and examining motives are important elements of ethical decision making. There are instances where doing one's duty is of overriding importance, even if adverse consequences for oneself and others result. Doing one's duty is an important motive that is emphasized at various times by every society and constitutes an important part of morality.

Rights

The notion of rights has received a great deal of attention in our society in the last several decades. Various movements have appeared to press for the rights of specific groups, such as the civil rights movement concerned about fundamental rights for blacks and other minorities; women's rights movements developed to press for equal treatment of women in our society; and more recently, right to life movements that attempt to protect the rights of unborn children and oppose abortion. Where do these rights come from and what gives rise to these kinds of movements that support certain kinds of rights?

People have used the notion of rights throughout history to overthrow systems of governance and establish new forms of social and economic power. In the Middle Ages, kings claimed a divine right to govern in order to throw off the shackles of the church, and they went on to claim ever more extensive powers over the subjects they came to dominate. Fledging democracies claimed a natural right to liberty in order to overthrow kings and establish a new system of government. Rights seem to emerge as a significant force in history when there are enough people who feel a basic injustice is being perpetuated, and are able to organize or be led to force a basic change of some kind in the society.

Our declaration of independence refers to certain basic rights that are believed to be self-evident. Such rights may be based on some kind of a natural law concept, proposing that there is an ideal standard of justice fixed by nature that is binding on all persons. This standard takes precedence over the particular laws and standards created by social convention. This concept provides absolute standards against which the laws and policies of particular states and institutions are to be measured.

This notion of natural rights may be seen to arise out of a need to check the sovereign power of kings, as was the case in the establishment of our country. Such rights can also be used to put a check on the sovereign power of the state, as do the rights contained in the Bill of Rights to the Constitution. These are considered to be fundamental rights regardless of merit, due to be respected because they are rooted in a knowledge of certain universal regularities in nature. The concept of nature refers to a proper ordering of the universe, and knowledge of this structure was believed to be accessible to all people by virtue of the reason they possessed.[14]

Today we speak more about human rights than natural rights and attempt to promote such human rights throughout the world (see box). Rights are no longer derived from the operations of natural reason, but rather from ideas of what it means to be human. It is assumed that human beings have an essential nature that determines the fundamental obligations and rights that are to be respected by other people and social institutions. The rights that are asserted as fundamental to the development of humanity are believed to stem from knowledge of these essential properties of human nature.

A person can only exercise a right to something if sufficient justification exists, that is, that a right has overriding status. Moral rights are important, normative, justifiable claims or entitlements. Basic human rights cannot be overriden by considerations of utility. Rights can be overriden only by another, more basic right of some kind. Property

---

BOX 2-1

United Nations Universal Declaration of Human Rights

The right to own property alone as well as in association with others.

The right to work, to free choice of employment, to just and favorable conditions of work, and to protection against unemployment.

The right to just and favorable remuneration ensuring for the worker and his family an existence worthy of human dignity.

The right to form and join trade unions.

The right to rest and leisure, including reasonable limitation of working hours and periodic holidays with pay.

rights, for example, can be overriden by a program of affirmative action to promote equal opportunity, on the basis that equality of opportunity is a more basic human right, not because it promotes social welfare. The right to liberty on the part of employers can be overriden in the interests of the rights of workers to a safe workplace. In this respect, certain rights can be considered as fundamental because (1) other rights are derived from them while they are not derived from any more basic rights, and (2) they are preconditions or necessary conditions of all other rights.[15]

There is a difference between moral and legal rights. One may have a legal right to do something immoral, or a moral right without any corresponding legal guarantee. Legal rights are derived from political constitutions, legislative enactments, case law, and executive orders of the highest state official. Moral rights exist independently of and form a basis for criticizing or justifying legal rights. Legal rights can be eliminated by lawful amendments or by a coup d'état, but moral rights cannot be eroded or banished by political votes, powers, or amendments.[16]

A right is an individual's entitlement to something. A person has a right when that person is entitled to act in a certain way or is entitled to have others act in a certain way toward him or her. These entitlements may derive from a legal system that permits or empowers the person to act in a specified way or that requires others to act in certain ways toward that person. Legal rights are limited to the particular jurisdiction within which the legal system is in force.[17]

Entitlements can also be derived from a system of moral standards independently of any particular legal system. They can be based on moral norms or principles that specify that all human beings are permitted or empowered to do something or are entitled to have something done for them. In this case, rights are not limited to a particular jurisdiction. The most important moral rights are those that impose prohibitions or requirements on others and that enable individuals to pursue their own interests.[18]

There are negative rights, which can be considered to be duties others have not to interfere in certain activities of the person. A negative right is a right to be free to hold and practice a belief, to pursue an action, or to enjoy a state of affairs without outside interference. Negative rights protect an individual from interference from the government and from other people. Government is to protect this basic right to be left alone and is not to encroach on this right itself. Libertarian theories of justice emphasize negative rights because human beings are viewed as ends in themselves, free to act according to their own purposes, and this right is to be respected by other people as well as by the institutions of society.

Positive rights, on the other hand, mean some other agents have a positive duty of providing the holder of right with whatever he or she needs to freely pursue his or her interests. Positive rights are rights to obtain goods and services, opportunities, or certain kinds of equal treatment. Egalitarian theories of justice emphasize more positive rights in that society should correct for the arbitrariness of nature by providing goods and services to its least advantaged members and assuring them equal opportunities. These are fundamental rights that require an obligation on the part of people and institutions to respect.

Moral rights of either kind, however, are tightly correlated with duties. Rights can be defined in terms of moral duties other people have toward that person. Rights are therefore often discussed as part of an ethics of duty. Even negative rights imply a duty on the part of other people to respect the right to be left alone. Negative rights imply a duty on the part of government to protect these rights. These correlative duties may not fall on any specific individual but on all members of a group or society.[19]

Moral rights provide individuals with autonomy and/or equality in the free pursuit of their interests. These rights identify activities or interests that people must be left free to pursue or not pursue as they themselves choose, and whose pursuit must not be subordinated to the interests of others except for special and exceptionally weighty reasons. Moral rights provide a basis for justifying one's actions and for invoking the protection or aid of others. They express the requirements of morality from the point of view of the individual instead of society as a whole, and promote individual welfare and protect individual choices against encroachment by society.[20]

Utilitarian standards promote society's aggregate utility and are indifferent to individual welfare except insofar as it affects this social aggregate. Moral rights, however, limit the validity of appeals to social benefits and to numbers. If a person has a right to do something, then it is wrong for anyone or any institution to interfere, even though a large number of people might gain much more utility from such interference. If utilitarian benefits or losses imposed on society become great enough, they may be sufficient, in some cases, to breach the walls of rights set to protect a person's freedom to pursue his or her interests.[21]

Justice

There are several kinds of justice that need to be mentioned at the outset of this discussion. Distributive justice is concerned with a fair distribution of society's benefits and burdens. This type of justice is concerned with the proper distribution of the goods and services society has available through its major institutions, including business organizations and governmental institutions. Distributive justice poses a special problem for business, which relies on inequalities as incentives to induce people to be more productive. How can these inequalities be morally justified?

Compensatory justice is concerned with finding a just way of compensating people for what they lost when they were wronged by others. The amount of compensation should be somehow proportional to the loss suffered by the person being compensated. This type of justice is of particular relevance to business organizations facing huge lawsuits involving products that are alleged to have caused harm to human health. What is a just compensation for the loss of a loved one or the loss of one's health, if indeed the product was the causal agent and the manufacturer was at fault? Theories of strict liability assign more of the responsibility to the manufacturer and make it easier for complaints about defective products to be brought against companies.

Retributive justice has to do with just imposition of punishments and penalties upon those who do wrong. The wrongdoer needs to be punished, especially if the wrong was done intentionally, so that justice is served and the wrongdoer's behavior is changed. Business is affected by this type of justice in the area of punitive damages, which some juries have been prone to award in damage cases. Punitive damages are awarded over and above compensatory damages and have no limit in most cases, although they should be consistent and proportional to the wrong committed.

Justice is often expressed in terms of fairness or what is deserved. A person has been treated justly when he or she has been given what is due or owed to him or her, what he or she deserves, or what he or she can legitimately claim. The so-called formal principle of justice states that like cases should be treated alike—equals ought to be treated equally and unequals unequally. This is called the formal principle of justice because it states no particular respects in which equals ought to be treated the same or unequals unequally. The principle merely states that whatever particulars are under consideration, if persons are equal in those respects, they should be treated alike. Individuals who are similar in all respects relevant to the kind of treatment in question should be given similar benefits and burdens, even if they are dissimilar in other irrelevant respects; and individuals who are dissimilar in a relevant respect ought to be treated dissimilarly, in proportion to their dissimilarity.[22]

This formal principle of justice can be considered to be a minimal moral rule. It does not tell us how to determine equality or proportion and, therefore, lacks substance as a specific guide to conduct. Material principles of justice, on the other hand, specify in detail what counts as a relevant property in terms of which people are to be compared, what it means to give people their due, and what are legitimate claims. These theories put material content into a theory of justice and identify relevant properties on the basis of which burdens and benefits should be distributed. Some of the most difficult questions about the nature of justice arise over the specification of the relevant respects in terms of which people are to be treated equally or unequally.[23]

> Each material principle of justice identifies a relevant property on the basis of which burdens and benefits should be distributed. The following is a sample list of major candidates for the position of valid principles of distributive justice: (1) to each person an equal share; (2) to each person according to individual need; (3) to each person according to the person's rights; (4) to each person according to individual effort; (5) to each person according to societal contribution; (6) to each person according to merit. There is no obvious barrier to acceptance of more than one of these principles, and some theories of justice accept all six as valid. Most societies use several in the belief that different rules are appropriate to different situations.[24]

Conflicts among these properties come up in the typical classroom situation, particularly when it comes time for grading. Most of us try to assign grades on the basis of merit, and accept this as the relevant principle for distributing grades. We try and develop tests, papers, and other exercises that will determine merit so that we can be just and fair in our allocation of grades. But students will attempt to make need a relevant property, arguing that they should be given a higher grade than they deserve on the basis of merit because they need it in order to graduate or receive an honors award. Other students will be offended by a merit-based approach because they feel they have worked harder and put more effort into the class than someone who received a higher grade. They believe they should be rewarded for their effort, and that this is a relevant property to be considered.

Theories of justice have been developed to provide general guidelines in determining what justice requires in a given situation. These theories systematically elaborate one or more of these material principles of justice and show how they are relevant properties on which to distribute burdens and benefits. Two such theories will be discussed here that have relevance to management decision making. These theories are egalitarian theories, which emphasize equal access to primary goods and services, and libertarian theories, which emphasize rights to liberty. The acceptability of either of these theories depends on the quality of the moral argument they contain as to whether one or more of the material properties they advocate ought to be given priority.[25]

EGALITARIAN THEORIES

Egalitarians base their view of justice on the proposition that all human beings are equal in some fundamental respect, and in virtue of this equality, each person has an equal claim to society's goods and services. The theory implies that goods and services should be allocated in equal portions regardless of people's individual differences. In its radical form, distributions of burdens and benefits are considered just to the extent that they are equal and deviations from absolute equality are considered to be unjust without respect for other properties in which members of the society may differ. The only relevant property in radical egalitarian theory is the simple possession of humanity, which is the sole property to be used in determining the justice of distributions.

Such a radical view overlooks the fact that there is no quality that human beings possess in precisely the same degree. Human beings are unequal in most respects, and some of these differences are relevant properties in determining what people deserve. Radical egalitarianism ignores some characteristics that should be taken into account, such as need, ability, and effort. The theory stated in this form also ignores the incentive effects of distributing benefits and burdens solely on the basis of the possession of humanity. Why should anyone produce more than another if they are going to get the same amount in return?

Most egalitarian theories of justice are qualified in some respects so that they are not this radical, even though they still hold to a central egalitarian thrust. One of the most influential egalitarian theories of recent years, for example, was developed by John Rawls, who was concerned about the lack of just distributions that could result from utilitarian theory. His objection to utilitarianism is that the social distributions produced by maximizing utility could entail violation of basic individual liberties and rights expressive of human equality and deserving protection as a matter of social justice. Utilitarianism is indifferent, he argued, to the distribution of satisfactions among individuals and would permit infringement of some people's rights and liberties if such infringement genuinely promised to produce a proportionately greater utility for others.[26]

Rawls's theory is based on a hypothetical social contract to which people would agree behind a so-called veil of ignorance, where no one knows his or her place in society. They know nothing about their status, their fortune in distribution of natural assets and abilities, their intelligence, or their race. Valid principles of justice are those to which people would agree if they could freely and impartially consider the social situation from a standpoint outside of any actual society behind such a veil of ignorance, and are principles that free and rational persons concerned with furthering their own interests would accept in an initial position of equality. This view of justice prevents people from promoting principles of justice that are biased toward their own combinations of fortuitous talents and characteristics. Thus, no one is advantaged or disadvantaged in the choice of principles because no one knows what his or her position in the society would be when the principles are formulated.[27]

The initial situation is thus symmetrical, and parties are forced to be fair and impartial and show no favoritism toward any special group. All people will want to secure a maximum amount of freedom so they can pursue whatever interests they have on entering society. All parties will want to protect themselves against the possibility of ending up in the worst position in society. Under these conditions, according to Rawls, people would unanimously agree on the two following fundamental principles of justice.

1. Each person is to have an equal right to the most extensive basic liberty compatible with a similar liberty for others.
2. Social and economic inequalities are to be arranged so that they are both (a) reasonably expected to be to everyone's advantage, and (b) attached to positions and offices open to all (difference principle).[28]

The first principle requires equality in the assignment of basic rights and duties. Each person is permitted the maximum amount of equal basic liberty compatible with a similar liberty for others. This principle defines and secures equal liberties of citizenship, such as political liberty, freedom of speech and assembly, liberty of conscience, freedom of thought, the right to hold personal property, and freedom from arbitrary arrest and seizure. The second principle says that inequalities in wealth and authority are just only if they result in compensating benefits for everyone, and in particular, for the least advantaged members of society. The hardship of some being offset by a greater good in the aggregate cannot be justified.

This division of advantages, it is argued, should draw forth the willing cooperation of everyone, including those less well situated. Everyone should benefit from social and economic inequalities. Inequalities of birth, historical circumstances, and natural endowment are undeserved. Persons in a cooperative society should correct them by making more equal the unequal situation of naturally disadvantaged members. Society must give more attention to those with fewer native assets and correct for arbitrariness of nature. In justice as fairness, humans agree to share one another's fate and avail themselves of the accidents of nature and social circumstance only when doing so is for the common benefit. Such accidents are not relevant moral properties for the distribution of burdens and benefits in society.[29]

In criticism of Rawls's theory, some have argued that it is not clear exactly what principles people would agree to behind a so-called veil of ignorance. People might agree to a riskier system of basic rules that permitted more dramatic wins as well as losses. The way people have responded to the lotteries sponsored by some states would suggest that this is a real possibility. The difference principle has been attacked by both sides in the debate as being at once too weak and too strong. Some claim it would still allow for unjust inequalities and others claim that it would deny justice to those who have worked harder or been more innovative and thus deserve greater benefits.[30] This theory has caused a good deal of controversy because of its implications for the distributions of goods and services in our society.

Another kind of egalitarian theory of justice has been proposed by William K. Frankena, who argues that if people who compete for the goods and positions that society has to offer have not had a chance to achieve all the virtue they are capable of achieving, then virtue is not a fair basis of distribution. If virtue is to be adopted as a relevant property for distribution, there must be a prior equal distribution of the conditions for achieving virtue. Thus, equality of opportunity, equality before the law, and equal access to the means of education are important considerations. Recognition of virtue as a basis of distribution is reasonable only against background conditions that acknowledge the principle of equality. The primary criterion of distributive justice is thus equality rather than merit in the form of some kind of virtue.[31]

The basic standard of distributive justice should be equality of treatment, according to Frankena. Justice requires that we give extra attention to people with certain kinds of handicaps, for example, because only with such extra attention do they have something approaching an equal chance to compete with others in enjoying a fulfilling life. Helping them in proportion to their needs is necessary for making an equal contribution to their lives. Treating people equally in this sense, however, does not mean making their lives equally good or maintaining everyone's life at the same level of goodness. In other words, equality of results is not a requirement of justice as equal treatment. However, justice, in this sense, does mean "making the same relative contribution to the goodness of their lives (this is equal help or helping according to need) or asking the same relative sacrifice (this is asking in accordance with ability)."[32]

LIBERTARIAN THEORIES

Libertarian theories of justice emphasize rights to social and economic liberty. These theories advocate distinctive processes, procedures, or mechanisms for ensuring that liberty rights are recognized in economic practice. Because the contributions people make to the economic system are freely chosen, they can be considered morally relevant bases on which to discriminate among individuals in distributing economic burdens and benefits. People are not deserving of equal economic returns because they do not make the same contribution to the production of economic goods and services. People are free to choose the kind of contribution they want to make; they have a fundamental right to own and dispense with their labor as they choose. This right must be respected even if its unrestricted exercise leads to greater inequalities of wealth in a given society.[33] Human agents are considered to be ends in themselves, free to act according to their own purposes. This basic liberty should not be interfered with in order to achieve a more equitable distribution of the benefits and burdens in society.

Robert Nozick has developed what has been called an entitlement theory of justice, proposing that there are certain basic rights to liberty people are entitled to that should not be interfered with by government or any other groups or institutions in society. Government action is permissible only to the extent it protects these fundamental rights or entitlements. This entitlement theory holds that whether or not a distribution is just depends upon how it came about. The set of holdings people end up with is not or should not be patterned according to some notions of equality. Whoever makes something, having bought or contracted for all other held resources used in the process, is entitled to it regardless of the inequality that may result. According to Nozick, there are three fundamental principles that society needs to concern itself with in order to ensure justice in the distribution of benefits and burdens.

1. **Principle of justice in acquisition:** the process by which things come to be held. This principle refers to the original acquisition.

2. **Principle of justice in transfer:** the process of acquiring things from another or of divestiture.

3. **Rectification of justice in holdings:** what, if anything, ought to be done to correct injustices.[34]

A person who acquires a holding in accordance with the principle of justice in acquisition is entitled to that holding. A person who acquires a holding in accordance with the principle of justice in transfer, from someone else entitled to the holding, is entitled to the holding. And finally, no one is entitled to a holding except by repeated applications of the first two principles. Any outcome is just as long as it results from consistent operation of these specified procedures. To maintain a pattern of equality, one must continually interfere to stop people from transferring resources as they wish or continually interfering to take from some persons resources that others for some reason choose to transfer to themselves. This is a violation of people's basic rights and entitlements.[35]

Libertarianism has been criticized as passing too quickly over the fact that the freedom of one person necessarily imposes constraints upon other persons. If constraints require justification, so does freedom. There are many different kinds of freedom. The freedom of one group to pursue its interests restricts the freedom of other agents to pursue their interests. Arguments for a specific freedom must show that the interests that can be satisfied by that kind of freedom are somehow better or more worth satisfying than the interests that other opposing kinds of freedom could satisfy.[36]

Libertarianism also enshrines a certain kind of value—freedom from the coercion of others, and sacrifices all other rights and values to it without persuasive reasons why this should be done. Other forms of freedom must also be secured, such as freedom from ignorance and freedom from hunger. These other forms of freedom may in some instances override freedom from coercion. Those with surplus money may have to be taxed to provide for those who are starving.[37]

The theory has also been criticized as generating unjust treatment of the disadvantaged. Under libertarianism, a person's share of goods depends wholly on what the person can produce or what other persons choose to give out of charity. But people have vastly unequal opportunities to make a contribution to the economy and be productive. People born into favorable circumstances have the chance to attend good educational institutions to develop their native abilities and talents. Thus, they can attain better positions and be rewarded for being more productive. People born into unfavorable circumstances may have just as much innate ability but never have the chance to develop those abilities. The conditions necessary to be productive may be unavailable through no fault of the person. If people through no fault of their own are unable to care for themselves, their survival should not depend on the outside chance that others will provide them with what they need. They should have these needs attended to as a basic right of humanity.[38]

Common Features of the Preceding Positions

In all of the preceding traditional approaches one can see that the traditional concern of moral reasoning has been to rationalize the moral life, to establish clear normative directives and clear standards of rational justification for guiding and evaluating the moral life. Traditionally, some moral judgments are taken as basic, while others are derivative, though controversy arises concerning the issue of which kinds of judgments are basic and which are derivative. For example, deontologists, such as Kant, hold that judgments about what is right are basic and judgments about what is good are derivative, while teleologists or consequentialists, such as Mill, generally hold that what is good is basic and what is right is derivative.

There is also disagreement about the way in which moral reasoning takes place and what kind of moral reasoning is actually involved in arriving at basic moral decisions. For example, Mill's utilitarian approach involves rational calculation of sensible consequences, and these consequences must focus on taking account of the good of the whole rather than the good of the individuals affected as individuals. Kant's position is based on the rational grasp of a first moral principle, and the practical work of reason then consists of enabling us to work out the dictates of reason, which tell us how to act operating solely on reverence for duty. Our moral reasoning is guided by duty, not by fulfillment of desire, and the major concern is the autonomy of the individual.

Sometimes the basic moral precepts by which one reasons to moral conclusions are concerned not with utilitarian consequences or what is good for the group as a whole, or Kantian rights and duties of individuals, but on what is just or fair. Here the issue of communitarianism versus libertarianism comes to the fore in the differing positions of Rawls and Nozick. Concern about rights is again an individualistic approach in focusing on the rights of the individual as set against utilitarian considerations that emphasize the good of the whole.

In these examples the function of moral reasoning is to rationalize and provide clear standards of rational justification for directives by which to live the moral life and evaluate the moral practices of other individuals and institutions. Furthermore, in all of these instances, it is presumed that if people use reason to approach moral problems and avoid the mistake of letting emotion, desires, or personal interests get in the way, they will arrive at the same position concerning moral principles and judgments. There is the common assumption that people are essentially rational beings who have the possibility of reasoning their way to universally acceptable moral standards.

In this manner, the tradition attempts, through different avenues, to provide rational legitimacy for moral claims. Morality is in some sense postulated in moral rules, and moral reasoning is by and large the application of the rule to the particular case. Moral reasoning thus works itself downward from first principles to specific cases which fall under the rule either directly or through intermediate steps of reasoning. It can also be seen that all of the preceding examples involve reasoning toward fixed ends in some sense. Furthermore, while Mill's position stresses the good of the whole, Kant's position stresses the moral autonomy of the individual, Rawls's position emphasizes the self-interest driven principles of abstract justice, and Nozick's theory points to the libertarian rights of individuals, they all begin with the assumption that individuals are atomic or discrete units isolatable from the social contexts in which they develop. The paradigm is that of discrete events obeying universal laws of moral behavior. And they all use moral reasoning to transcend individual desires, interests, or inclinations.

Virtue Theory

The problems that utilitarianism and ethical formalism pose with respect to moral reasoning bring us to another body of ethical theory sometimes called virtue theory. In the final analysis, it could be argued, ethics boils down to individual action. Ethics does not consist of a set of rules or prescriptions that determines how people ought to act, it consists of the actions and motives of ethical people who are concerned to do the right thing in all the situations they face. Ethical actions stem from virtuous people who are concerned about doing the good, not slavishly following a set of rules that hopefully is connected with the good in some fashion.

> An ethical rule never actually resolves an ethical dilemma. For the good, which is the central concern of ethics, is finally what a good man does. Being ethical is, after all, just that: a matter of being. The problem before the businessman who aspires to be ethical is

not that of doing, but of becoming and being. . . . An ethical decision will be made only by an ethical man who knows the situation, discerns what ought to be done, and does it. Those who persist in the belief that if only certain rules are obeyed, we shall have ethical conduct in business are much too abstract about ethics, far too disrespectful toward the particular and the concrete, naive in the failure to recognize the rationalizing talent with which each of us can escape an onerous rule, and doomed to continual frustration of their expectations.[39]

The former theories of teleological and deontological ethics dealt with principles and rules that prescribed what we ought to do, not what kind of persons we ought to be or strive to become. The task of ethics in these approaches is to provide guides to action that are consistent with general notions of what it means to be ethical or moral. In our everyday judgments about ethics and morals, however, we not only judge actions as being right or wrong, we also make character-centered judgments, which describe a person or character as being good or bad, praiseworthy or blameworthy, admirable or reprehensible. We give people credit or criticism not only for what they do but also for what they are and the kind of inward character they exemplify.

Thus, virtue ethics deals with the cultivation of virtuous traits of character as being among the primary functions of morality. Correct choices that are made out of a sense of duty do not necessarily signify that a person is virtuous. People who act only out of a sense of duty can sometimes despise and grudgingly fulfill their moral obligations. We would tend not to call such a person virtuous and possessed of a good and moral character. We might admire their actions and decisions without admiring the persons themselves.[40]

An ethics based on virtues depends on an assessment of selected traits of character, and should not be confused with principles or statements of what ought to be done. Virtue ethics deals with dispositions, habits, or traits that a person possesses or aspires to possess. Moral virtues can be defined as "a fixed disposition, habit, or trait to do what is morally commendable."[41] Thus, virtues deal with the kind of person one is, the qualities he or she possesses internally that are exemplified in daily activities. Virtue ethics is based on a way of being rather than a rule for doing.

Philosophers differ as to which virtues are central to the moral life. The Christian religion mentions the virtues of faith, hope, and love as central traits of a moral character. To these could be added the virtues of wisdom, courage, temperance, and justice that were advocated by classical philosophy. These were held to be cardinal virtues in that they cannot be derived from each other and all other moral virtues were believed to stem from them. Other virtues such as fairness, faithfulness, and gratefulness are also believed to be qualities that a moral person should possess and exemplify.

Aristotle held that moral virtues are universally praiseworthy features of human character that have been fixed by human habituation. The virtuous person is one who aims at moderation between extremes, who avoids the vice of excess (too much) and the vice of defect (too little). The proper balance between these extremes is best determined by persons of practical wisdom who have experience and great skill of judgment. A person possessed of practical wisdom knows which goals are worth attaining and knows how to achieve them, keeping emotions within proper bounds and thus exhibiting a proper balance among reason, feeling, and desire.[42]

An ethics of virtue is thus quite different from an ethics of principle. Virtue ethics focuses on character traits that a good person should possess, and holds that what we need to direct us toward ethical behavior are fundamental directives about the kinds of persons

---

BOX 2-2

Aristotle's Virtues

Courage: particularly courage in battle.

Temperance: which includes the enjoyment of pleasure as well as moderation; a man who abstained from sex, food, and drinking would not be considered virtuous by the Greeks, as he might be by some people today.

Liberality: what we would call charity.

Magnificence: spending lavishly and doing great deeds.

Pride: appreciation of one's own worth (humility was a vice).

Good temper: but it is important to get angry when appropriate.

Friendliness: a very important virtue for the Greeks, not just a personal pleasure or necessity.

Truthfulness.

Wittiness: people who can't tell or take a joke aren't virtuous. Aristotle would not equate "seriousness" with being moral, as some people do.

Shame: being sensitive to one's honor and feeling appropriately bad when it is besmirched. "Feeling guilty," on the other hand, did not even seem to be worth talking about.

Justice: the sense of fair treatment of others.

Source: Robert C. Solomon and Kristine R. Hanson, *Above the Bottom Line: An Introduction to Business Ethics* (New York: Harcourt Brace Jovanovich, 1983), p. 8.

---

we should strive to become. Those who believe virtue ethics should be primary in ethical theory believe that "morality does not consist in obedience to Kant's categorical imperative; rather, it is the expression of a virtuous character internal to the person—a character needing no external rules specifying right conduct."[43] The good is what the virtuous person does, not some abstractly defined notion of human welfare.

Moral ideals can be a part of virtue ethics because they are directed at the kind of person it is commendable to become, but they do not state specifically what that person ought to do in any given circumstance. One can pursue moral ideals and aspire to certain actions apart from belief in a morality of obligation. Saints and heroes are often used as role models and examples of what a moral person should be like and the virtues that are worth attaining. These people help us to learn to be virtuous and show us what a moral life looks like in the contemporary world. Their actions often go beyond what duty alone would seem to require, and stem from an inward commitment to live a virtuous and good life rather than a commitment to implement a set of principles. They are attractive individuals because they seem to have their act together and are moderate in all things. They provide a concrete example of ideals that we may deem important and show that in actuality these ideals can be lived out and become reality.[44]

There are several questions that can be raised about an ethics of virtue. One concerns the motivation to live a virtuous life and follow the example of those saints and heroes we admire. Does virtue ethics actually contain a subtle form of obligation, in that if we know what it means to live a virtuous life, is there not some kind of a demand or imperative that we should so live our own lives? The presumption behind virtue ethics is that we ought to be virtuous, and does not this presumption entail an obligation? If such an obligation is not a part of virtue ethics, then how do the moral ideals that we admire in heroes and saints become a reality for the vast majority of people, particularly when these ideals may conflict with living a prosperous and rewarding life in terms other than feeling good about being virtuous? Can virtue indeed be its own reward for people in a society like ours that is success oriented?[45]

Since virtue theory does not focus on actions, how can such a theory be used to determine the rightness or wrongness of actions? Suppose two people whom we regard as virtuous in all of their daily activities have two different opinions as to the appropriateness of abortions. This is not just an abstract example because there are instances every day where people we admire and regard as virtuous often hold different opinions as to what course of action to take with regard to specific situations. Which action, then, is the right one, and how are we to decide between two different actions on the basis of virtue theory alone?[46]

Likewise, the fact that a virtuous person chooses a certain action does not in itself make that action moral. Actions may be misguided and still be done with the best of intentions by virtuous people. The virtuous person may not know what should be done in certain circumstances because he or she is not aware of all the alternatives and does not have enough information. Judging the moral quality of an action by solely judging the moral quality of the person does not seem to be completely satisfactory. Even saints and heroes are fallible and may need rules to follow in morally ambiguous situations. They may need obligations to rely on when the will is weakened. Even virtuous people can act out of character and commit moral wrongs. The fact that they are usually virtuous does not make this wrong a right, but if we rely solely on virtue ethics, we have no way of knowing when an act is wrong and thus deciding when they may be acting out of character.

Virtue ethics is sometimes thought to exclude moral reasoning, since virtue ethics is concerned with the cultivation of virtuous traits of character as being among the primary functions of morality. A virtue is a state or disposition to act in a certain way, and moral virtue is promoted by regular practice, which provides the inculcation of dispositions or habits. In insisting on a state, rather than a pattern of behavior, Aristotle shows that he is concerned with virtues as something more than means to virtuous action. An ethics based on virtue depends on an evaluation of selected traits of character and is very different from one based on principles of statements of what ought to be done. Yet, moral reasoning plays an important role nonetheless. Indeed, since a human being is essentially a rational agent, the essential activity of a human being, according to Aristotle, is a life guided by practical reason.

Moral virtue, which is promoted by regular practice, involves following a mean course between extremes. But action is not virtuous because it follows a mean course—it is virtuous because it is in conformity with reason, and as a result it will, in fact, involve a mean. Virtue of character is thus inseparable from virtue of intellect. Practical wisdom discovers what is right in action and makes it possible for desire to conform to reason by discovering ends and then relating means to these ends of moral behavior.

For Aristotle, moral reasoning is a form of practical reasoning that involves a type of syllogism called the practical syllogism. The conclusions of such practical syllogisms are not propositions but dispositions. The conclusion is not a proposition stating what I ought to do, but an intention to do something. The ultimate end, living well, is not a matter of deliberation or choice, but rather is something given in the nature of the human qua human. Humans tend to realize a pregiven teleology, as there is a preordained end determining the continuity of character of dispositions. The good for humans is the fulfillment of their function.

More recent variations of virtue ethics have distanced themselves from the particulars of Aristotelian teleology, but they all depend on an assessment of selected traits of character as opposed to principles or statements of what ought to be done. All those who hold to the primacy of virtue ethics believe that morality is not obedience to abstract moral principles but rather morality is the expression of a virtuous character internal to the dispositions of an individual and needing no external rules specifying what ought to be done.

Correct choices that are made out of a sense of duty do not necessarily indicate that a person is virtuous. We might judge people's acts to be good, but not their character. In virtue ethics, moral ideals are directed toward the kind of person it is commendable to become, but they do not indicate what one ought to do in particular circumstances. What is judged moral are the character and the intentions from which an act flows, not specific actions and their empirical consequences or their conformity to "the moral law" grasped by reason.

Choosing Ethical Frameworks

Each of the foregoing ways of providing a moral evaluation of actions, persons, institutions, or situations is held by its proponents to be absolute and applicable to the full range of problems and issues that occurs in moral experience. But more and more today it is being recognized that no one of them captures all of the factors that must be taken into account in making moral decisions. What we are left with is a kind of ethical smorgasbord where one has various theories from which to choose and which will hopefully shed some light on the ethical problems under consideration, thus leading to a justifiable decision. Sometimes the rules of Kant's position emphasizing the autonomy of the individual are put to use, and sometimes utilitarian principles stressing the aggregate social welfare are considered.

Operative here is what has recently become known as moral pluralism, the view that no single moral principle or overarching theory of what is right or good can be appropriately applied in all ethically problematic situations. There is no one unifying, monistic principle from which lesser principles can be derived. Different moral theories are possible depending on which values or principles are included. Moral pluralism generally advocates two different approaches to moral reasoning: first, that each relevant principle be considered in every instance, or, second, that one principle be operative in one type of domain or sphere of interest, and another principle be operative in another type of domain or sphere of interest. The right act is the one that is subsumed under the proper balance of rules or principles.

But the conceptual framework on which Kant's deontological ethics is based is radically different from the conceptual foundations on which either act or rule utilitarianism is based. To be Kantians at one time and Benthamites at another is to shift conceptual frameworks at will and results in what has been called conceptual "musical chairs." Furthermore, in none of these supposedly absolute theories can there be guidance in deciding when to use a particular theory, for each theory is self-enclosed or absolute; no principle or rule can provide any guidance for the moral reasoning that underlies the choice among the various principles or rules. The basis for this choice, which now becomes the heart of moral reasoning, the very foundation for moral decision making, remains mysterious. Some authors of business ethics textbooks have noted this problem but consider it to be beyond the scope of ethical analysis.

> Our morality, therefore, contains three main kinds of moral considerations, each of which emphasizes certain morally important aspects of our behavior, but no one of which captures all the factors that must be taken into account in making moral judgments. Utilitarian standards consider only the aggregate social welfare but ignore the individual and how that welfare is distributed. Moral rights consider the individual but discount both aggregate well-being and distributive considerations. Standards of justice consider distributive issues but they ignore aggregate social welfare and the individual as such. These three kinds of moral considerations do not seem to be reducible to each other yet all three seem to be necessary parts of our morality. That is, there are some moral problems for which utilitarian considerations are decisive, while for other problems the decisive considerations are either the rights of individuals or the justice of the distributions involved. . . . We have at this time no comprehensive moral theory capable of determining precisely when utilitarian considerations become "sufficiently large" to outweigh narrow infringements on a conflicting right or standard of justice, or when considerations of justice become "important enough" to outweigh infringements on conflicting rights. Moral philosophers have been unable to agree on any absolute rules for making such judgments. There are, however, a number of rough criteria that can guide us in these matters. . . . But these criteria remain rough and intuitive. They lie at the edges of the light that ethics can shed on moral reasoning.[47]

Without some comprehensive moral theory, however, how are we to decide which theory to apply in a given situation? What guidelines are we to use in applying these different theories and approaches? What criteria determine which theory is best for a given problem, and what do we do if the application of different theories results in totally different courses of action? Moral pluralism does not provide a rule for the balancing of principles, but the right act is nonetheless the one that is subsumed under the proper balance of rules of principles. And on further reflection, it becomes evident that not only is there no mechanical way to decide the proper balance, but for neither moral pluralism nor moral monism is there a mechanical way to decide if a particular act falls under a rule in a given situation.

When one has to deal with a radically new kind of situation, where one cannot call on old decisions for precedence, this problem is even more pronounced. Furthermore, actions done with the best of intentions by virtuous people may nonetheless be misguided, and can only be so judged by something other than intentions. And the application of a moral rule to a specific case can be used by ill-intentioned individuals to justify all sorts of behavior that common sense judges to be immoral. Rules seem to judge intentions, yet bad intentions can misuse rules. It would seem that calling on good intentions or the application of some rule to a particular case can be used to justify all sorts of morally unacceptable behavior. Where does one go from here?

A position is emerging in business ethics that attempts to provide a theoretical basis for moral reasoning as inherently pluralistic. It does not involve a synthesis of existing theoretical alternatives, or a balancing act among them, but involves a radical reconstruction of one's understanding of what it is to think morally. The basic concepts of this position and its contrast with the traditional approaches discussed earlier will occupy the following chapters in the first part of the book.

Questions for Discussion

1. What are the two main types of ethical theories discussed in the first part of the chapter? Which theory do you identify with most strongly? Do you find yourself switching theories to justify different kinds of ethical decisions? If so, what does this suggest about ethical decisions?

2. How do these theories differ in terms of making ethical decisions? What do they focus on as the primary emphasis in deciding what is the right thing to do? What problems do they have that need to be taken into account?

3. Where do rights come from? How do certain rights find their way into public policy measures and others go unrecognized? Are there certain universal rights that should be respected by all institutions? If so, what are these rights? Does a business institution and a market-oriented economy respect them sufficiently?

4. What is the difference between justice and rights? How do concepts of justice affect business decisions? Which theory of justice is most compatible with a market orientation? Which theory is most compatible with public policy? Which do you agree with most strongly?

5. How does virtue theory differ from the foregoing approaches? What does virtue theory emphasize in terms of making ethical decisions? Can virtue theory be combined with any of the other theories? What are its major problems?

6. How can a manager use the ethical theories presented in the chapter as an aid in decision making? How can they be used to analyze and support a decision? What happens when conflicts between the different approaches result? How can these conflicts be resolved?

Endnotes

[1] For example, ethical egoism holds that whether an act is morally right or wrong depends solely on how good or bad the consequences of the action are for oneself. Ethical altruism, on the other hand, holds that whether an action is right or wrong depends solely on the good and bad consequences produced by the action for everyone except oneself.

[2] Manuel Velasquez, *Business Ethics: Concepts and Cases* (Englewood Cliffs, NJ: Prentice-Hall, 1982), p. 47.

[3] Tom L. Beauchamp, *Philosophical Ethics: An Introduction to Moral Philosophy* (New York: McGraw-Hill, 1982), p. 99.

[4] Ibid., pp. 97–98.

[5] Richard T. DeGeorge, *Business Ethics,* 2nd ed. (New York: Macmillan, 1986), p. 47.

[6] Ibid., p. 67.

[7] Ibid., p. 69.

[8] Ibid., pp. 69–70.

[9] Ibid., pp. 70–71.

[10] Ibid., pp. 71–72.

[11] William David Ross, *The Right and the Good* (Oxford, England: Clarendon Press, 1930).

[12] Beauchamp, *Philosophical Ethics,* pp. 138–139.

[13] DeGeorge, *Business Ethics,* pp. 74–76.

[14] Kenneth Minogue, "The History of the Idea of Human Rights," *The Human Rights Reader,* Walter Laqueur and Barry Rubin, eds. (Philadelphia: Temple University Press, 1979), pp. 14–15.

[15] Beauchamp, *Philosophical Ethics,* p. 194.

[16] Ibid., p. 189.

[17] Velasquez, *Business Ethics,* p. 59.

[18] Ibid., pp. 59–60.

[19] Ibid., p. 60.

[20] Ibid., p. 61.

[21] Ibid., p. 62.

[22] Beauchamp, *Philosophical Ethics,* p. 223.

[23] Ibid., pp. 225–229.

[24] Ibid., p. 229.

[25] Ibid., p. 230.

[26] Ibid., pp. 243–244.

[27] John Rawls, *A Theory of Justice* (Cambridge: Harvard University Press, 1971), pp. 136–142.

[28] Ibid., p. 60.

[29] Ibid., pp. 175–183.

[30] DeGeorge, *Business Ethics,* p. 78.

[31] William K. Frankena, *Ethics,* 2nd ed. (Englewood Cliffs, NJ: Prentice-Hall, 1973), p. 50.

[32] Ibid., p. 51.

[33] Beauchamp, *Philosophical Ethics,* pp. 231–232.

[34] Robert Nozick, *Anarchy, State, and Utopia* (New York: Basic Books, 1974), pp. 150–153.

[35] Ibid., p. 151.

[36] Velasquez, *Business Ethics,* p. 73.

[37] Ibid., p. 84.

[38] Ibid.

[39] Paul T. Heyne, *Private Keepers of the Public Interest* (New York: McGraw-Hill, 1968), pp. 111–113.

[40] Beauchamp, *Philosophical Ethics,* p. 149.

[41] Ibid., p. 150.

[42] Ibid., pp. 158–159.

[43] Ibid., p. 163.

[44] Ibid., pp. 170–173.

[45] Ibid., pp. 174–175.

[46] Ibid., pp. 177–179.

[47] Manuel G. Velasquez, *Business Ethics: Concepts and Cases,* 3rd ed. (Englewood Cliffs, NJ: Prentice Hall, 1992), pp. 104–106. Other books note the same problem. Tom Donaldson and Patricia Werhane, for example, after presenting the theories of consequentialism, deontology, and what they call human nature ethics—which seems to be a variation of virtue ethics—state: "Indeed, the three methods of moral reasoning are sufficiently broad that each is applicable to the full range of problems confronting human moral experience. The question of which method, if any, is superior to the others must be left for another time. The intention of this essay is not to substitute for a thorough study of traditional ethical theories—something for which there is no substitute—but to introduce the reader to basic modes of ethical reasoning that will help to analyze the ethical problems in business that arise in the remainder of the book." Thomas Donaldson and Patricia H. Werhane, *Ethical Issues in Business: A Philosophical Approach*, 4th ed. (Englewood Cliffs, NJ: Prentice Hall, 1993), p. 17. John R. Boatright notes that: "The differences between theories should not lead us to despair of resolving ethical issues or to conclude that one resolution is as good as another. Nor should we be discouraged by the fact that agreement on complex ethical issues is seldom

achieved. Unanimity in ethics is an unreasonable expectation. The best we can do is to analyze the issues as fully as possible, which means getting straight on the facts and achieving definitional clarity, then to develop the strongest and most complete arguments we can for what we consider to be the correct conclusions." John R. Boatright, *Ethics and the Conduct of Business* (Englewood Cliffs, NJ: Prentice Hall, 1993), p. 25.

Suggested Readings

Aristotle. *The Nicomachean Ethics.* Trans. by Sir David Ross. London: Oxford University Press, 1961.

Bayles, Michael D., ed. *Contemporary Utilitarianism.* Garden City, NY: Doubleday & Co., Inc., 1968.

Beauchamp, Tom L., and Norman E. Bowie. *Ethical Theory and Business,* 4th ed. Englewood Cliffs, NJ: Prentice Hall, 1993.

Bedau, Hugo A., ed. *Justice and Equality.* Englewood Cliffs, NJ: Prentice-Hall, 1971.

Bentham, Jeremy. *An Introduction to the Principles of Morals and Legislation.* London: Athlone Press, 1970.

Blackstone, William T., ed. *The Concept of Equality.* Minneapolis: Burgess Publishing Co., 1969.

Blanshard, Brand. *Reason and Goodness.* London: George Allen & Unwin, 1961.

Boatright, John R. *Ethics and the Conduct of Business.* Englewood Cliffs, NJ: Prentice Hall, 1993.

Bowie, Norman E. *Towards a New Theory of Distributive Justice.* Amherst: University of Massachusetts Press, 1971.

Cranston, Maurice. *What Are Human Rights?* New York: Taplinger Publishing Co., 1973.

DeGeorge, Richard T. *Business Ethics,* 4th ed. Englewood Cliffs, NJ: Prentice Hall, 1995.

Des Jardins, Joseph R., and John J. McCall. *Contemporary Issues in Business Ethics.* Belmont, CA: Wadsworth, 1985.

Donaldson, Thomas. *Corporations and Morality.* Englewood Cliffs, NJ: Prentice-Hall, 1982.

Donaldson, Thomas, and Patricia H. Werhane. *Ethical Issues in Business: A Philosophical Approach,* 4th ed. Englewood Cliffs, NJ: Prentice Hall, 1993.

Dworkin, Ronald. *Taking Rights Seriously.* Cambridge, MA: Harvard University Press, 1977.

Flathman, Richard E. *The Practice of Rights.* Cambridge, England: Cambridge University Press, 1977.

Foot, Philippa. *Virtues and Vices.* Oxford, England: Basil Blackwell, 1978.

Frankena, William K. *Ethics,* 2nd ed. Englewood Cliffs, NJ: Prentice-Hall, 1973.

Frankena, William K. *Thinking About Morality.* Ann Arbor: University of Michigan Press, 1980.

Geach, Peter. *The Virtues.* Cambridge, England: Cambridge University Press, 1977.

Gert, Bernard. *The Moral Rules: A New Rational Foundation for Morality.* New York: Harper & Row, 1970.

Grice, Geoffrey Russell. *The Grounds of Moral Judgment.* Cambridge, England: Cambridge University Press, 1967.

Hare, R. M. *Moral Thinking.* Oxford: Clarendon Press, 1981.

Hartland-Swann, John. *An Analysis of Morals.* London: George Allen & Unwin, 1960.

Hayek, Friedrich. *Individualism and Economic Order.* Chicago: University of Chicago Press, 1948.

Hoffman, W. Michael, and Jennifer Mills Moore. *Business Ethics: Readings and Cases in Corporate Morality.* New York: McGraw-Hill, 1984.

Kant, Immanuel. *Foundations of the Metaphysics of Morals: Text and Critical Essays.* Indianapolis: Bobbs-Merrill, 1969.

Kant, Immanuel. *Lectures on Ethics.* New York: Harper Torchbooks, 1963.

Lyons, David. *Rights.* Belmont, CA: Wadsworth, 1979.

Mayo, Bernard. *Ethics and the Moral Life.* London: Macmillan, 1958.

Melden, Abraham I. *Human Rights.* Belmont, CA: Wadsworth, 1970.

Mill, John Stuart. *Utilitarianism.* New York: The Liberal Arts Press, 1957.

Miller, David. *Social Justice.* Oxford, England: Clarendon Press, 1976.

Moore, George E. *Ethics.* New York: Oxford University Press, 1965.

Nozick, Robert. *Anarchy, State, and Utopia.* New York: Basic Books, 1974.

Paton, H. J. *The Categorical Imperative.* Chicago: University of Chicago Press, 1948.

Pojman, Louis P. *Ethics: Discovering Right and Wrong.* Belmont, CA: Wadsworth, 1990.

Rawls, John. *A Theory of Justice.* Cambridge, MA: Harvard University Press, 1971.

Rescher, Nicholas. *Distributive Justice.* Indianapolis: Bobbs-Merrill Company, Inc., 1966.

Ross, William D. *Foundations of Ethics.* Oxford, England: Clarendon Press, 1939.

Shaw, William H. *Business Ethics.* Belmont, CA: Wadsworth, 1991.

Shaw, William, and Vincent Barry. *Moral Issues in Business,* 6th ed. Belmont, CA: Wadsworth, 1995.

Sidgwick, H. *The Methods of Ethics.* Indianapolis: Hackett Publishing Company, 1981.

Smart, J.J.C. *An Outline of a System of Utilitarian Ethics.* Melbourne: Melbourne University Press, 1961.

Solomon, Robert C. *Ethics and Excellence: Cooperation and Integrity in Business.* New York: Oxford University Press, 1993.

Sterba, James. *The Demands of Justice.* Notre Dame, IN: University of Notre Dame Press, 1980.

Velasquez, Manuel G. *Business Ethics: Concepts and Cases,* 3rd ed. Englewood Cliffs, NJ: Prentice Hall, 1992.

Wallace, James D. *Virtues and Vices.* Ithaca, NY: Cornell University Press, 1978.

Warnock, Geoffrey J. *The Object of Morality.* London: Methuen & Co., Ltd., 1971.

S H O R T   C A S E S

The Ford Pinto Case

Ford Motor Company is the second largest producer of automobiles. With annual sales of over 6 million cars and trucks worldwide, it has revenues of over $30 billion per year. In 1960 Ford's market position was eroded by competition from domestic and foreign subcompacts, especially Volkswagens. Lee Iacocca, president of Ford, determined to regain Ford's share of the market by having a new subcompact, the Pinto, in production by 1970.

Although the normal preproduction testing and development of an automobile takes about 43 months, Iacocca managed to bring the Pinto to the production stage in a little over two years. Internal memos showed that Ford crashtested early models of the Pinto before production "at a top-secret site, more than forty times and . . . . every test made at over twenty-five mph without special structural alteration of the car . . . . resulted in a ruptured fuel tank."[1] Stray sparks could easily ignite any spilling gasoline and engulf the car in flames. Several years later, a spokesperson for Ford acknowledged "that early model Pintos did not pass rear-impact tests at twenty mph."[2]

Nonetheless, the company went on with production of the Pinto as designed, since it met all applicable federal safety standards then in effect and was comparable in safety to other cars then being produced. Moreover, a later Ford company study released by J. C. Echold, director of automotive safety for Ford, claimed that an improved design that would have rendered the Pinto and other similar cars less likely to burst into flames on collision would not be cost-effective for society. Entitled "Fatalities Associated with Crash-Induced Fuel Leakage and Fires," the Ford study (which was intended to counter the prospect of stiffer government regulations on gasoline tank design) claimed that the costs of the design improvement ($11 per vehicle) far outweighed its social benefits:

> The total benefit is shown to be just under $50 million, while the associated cost is $137 million. Thus the cost is almost three times the benefits, even using a number of highly favorable benefit assumptions. (See Table 2-1.)

TABLE 2-1	
BENEFITS:	
Savings	180 burn deaths, 180 serious burn injuries, 2100 burned vehicles
Unit cost	$200,000 per death, $67,000 per injury, $700 per vehicle
Total benefits	180 x ($200,000) plus
	180 x ($ 67,000) plus
	2100 x ($ 700) = $49.15 million
COSTS:	
Sales	11 million cars, 1.5 million light trucks
Unit cost	$11 per car, $11 per truck
Total costs	11,000,000 x ($11) plus
	1,500,000 x ($11) = $137 million

Source: From memorandum attached to statement of J. C. Echold.[3]

Ford's estimate of the number of deaths, injuries, and vehicles that would be lost as a result of fires from fuel leakage was based on statistical studies. The $200,000 value attributed to the loss of life was based on a study of the National Highway Traffic Safety Administration, which broke down the estimated social costs of a death as shown in Table 2-2.[4]

On May 28, 1972, Mrs. Lily Gray was driving a six-month-old Pinto on Interstate 15 near San Bernardino, California. In the car with her was Richard Grimshaw, a 13-year-old boy. Mrs. Gray was a unique person. She had adopted two girls, worked 40 hours a week, was den mother for all the teenagers in the neighborhood, sold refreshments at the Bobby Sox games, and had maintained a 22-year-long happy marriage.

Mrs. Gray was driving at about 55 mph when the Pinto stalled and was rear-ended by a 1963 Ford convertible. On impact, the Pinto gas tank ruptured and the car burst into flames. Inside the car, Mrs. Gray was burned to death and Richard Grimshaw was severely burned over 90 percent of his body. It was a hundred-to-one shot, but although badly disfigured, Richard survived the accident and subsequently underwent 70 painful surgical operations. At least 53 persons have died in accidents involving Pinto fires, and many more have been severely burned.[5]

TABLE 2-2	
COMPONENT	1971 COSTS
Future productivity losses	
Direct	$132,000
Indirect	41,300
Medical costs	
Hospital	700
Other	425
Property damage	1,500
Insurance administration	4,700
Legal and court	3,000
Employer losses	1,000
Victim's pain and suffering	10,000
Funeral	900
Assets (lost consumption)	5,000
Miscellaneous accident cost	200
TOTAL PER FATALITY:	**$200,725**

1. Using the Ford figures given in the memo, calculate the probability that a vehicle would be involved in a burn death (that is, the number of burn deaths divided by the total number of cars and trucks sold). In your opinion, is there a limit to the amount that Ford should have been willing to invest in order to reduce this figure to zero? If your answer is yes, then determine from your answer what price you place on life and compare your price to the government's. If your answer is no, then discuss whether your answer implies that no matter how much it would take to make such cars, automakers should make cars completely accident proof.

2. In your opinion, was the management of Ford morally responsible for Mrs. Gray's "burn death"? Explain. Was there something wrong with the utilitarian analysis Ford management used? Explain. Would it have made any difference from a moral point of view if Ford management had informed its buyers of the risks of fire? Explain.

3. Suppose that you were on Mr. J. C. Echold's staff and before the Pinto reached the production stage you were assigned the task of writing an analysis of the overall desirability of producing and marketing the Pinto as planned. One part of your report is to be subtitled "Ethical and Social Desirability." What would you write in this part?

[1] Mark Dowie, "Pinto Madness," *Mother Jones,* September/October 1977, p. 20. See also Joanne Gamdin, "Jury Slaps Massive 'Fine' on Ford in '72 Pinto Crash," *Business Insurance,* February 20, 1978, p. 76.

[2] "Ford Rebuts Pinto Criticism," *National Underwriter,* September 9, 1977.

[3] Ralph Drayton, "One Manufacturer's Approach to Automobile Safety Standards," *CTLA News,* VIII, no. 2., February 1968, p. 11.

[4] Dowie, "Pinto Madness," p. 28.

[5] "Ford Fights Pinto Case: Jury gives 128 million," *Auto News,* February 13, 1978, pp. 3, 44.

Source: Manuel G. Velasquez, *Business Ethics: Concepts and Cases* (Englewood Cliffs, NJ: Prentice-Hall, 1982), pp. 94–96.

Poverty in America

The official figures regarding poverty in the United States over the past several years are rather depressing. After several years of decline, poverty rose in 1990 to 13.5 percent of the U.S. population, or one out of every seven people, reflecting the effects of the recession. Blacks had a poverty rate of 32 percent, Hispanics 28 percent, and whites 11 percent.[1] This increase continued into 1991, with 14.2 percent of the population, or 35.7 million Americans, in poverty. This figure represented a 27-year high. Forty percent of these poor were children, while only 11 percent were elderly. Blacks again had the highest poverty rate at 32.7 percent, compared with whites at 10.7 percent.[2] Thus, the decade ended about where it began without much improvement in the poverty picture.

A report released in 1991 by the Joint Center for Political and Economic Studies stated that among industrial nations, the United States had the highest incidence of poverty among the nonelderly and the widest distribution of poverty across all age and family groups. The report also noted that poor people in the United States also experience the longest spells of poverty compared with other industrial countries, and that the United States is the only Western democracy that has failed to give a significant proportion of its poor a measure of income security.[3] Other researchers indicated at a conference in 1993 that Americans living in poverty are poorer than they were 20 years ago and that their numbers have increased.[4]

The poverty rate for children under 18 years old continued to be one of the most serious problems. According to a report issued by the Children's Defense Fund, the number of children in poverty grew by 1.1 million to more than 11 million between 1979 and 1989, with the poverty rate reaching 17.9 percent in 1989, up from 16 percent a decade earlier.[5] These figures reflected a continuing problem with child poverty that bode ill for the future of American society. The increases of poverty in this category were said to be the result of a drop in the real earnings of many working Americans over the past several years, the rise in the incidence of out-of-wedlock births and of female-headed households, and cutbacks in the major welfare programs aimed at the young.[6] In 1993, the National Research Council stated that more U.S. children than ever before were growing up in poor neighborhoods and facing futures of unemployment and more poverty.[7] While nearly one out of every three poor children live in urban areas, the fastest-growing poverty problem with regard to children is in the suburbs, where nearly a fourth of all poor children live.[8]

The problem of female-headed families and the child poverty that results is a social welfare challenge that is likely to plague society for many years to come. This so-called "feminization of poverty" is a deep, long-term poverty problem. Mothers without husbands and their children are the only poverty category whose total number is currently higher than when poverty first began to be officially measured in 1959.[9] The percentage of white children living with one parent almost tripled to 19.2 percent over the past three decades, and for the black population, it has more than doubled.

In the mid-1980s, a new aspect of poverty appeared in the plight of the homeless, those in our society who have no fixed address and wander the streets to find shelter in bus stations, cardboard boxes, or whatever else is available. Although the immediate cause of the problem is a shortage of housing that the poor could afford, there are diverse circumstances that helped to cause the problem. Some of the homeless are mentally ill, others are poor families who have no money to pay rent, and still others are single men without work or family. Estimates of the homeless population have ranged from 250,000 to more than 3 million.[10] A study by the National Alliance to End Homelessness stated that on a given night there are about 735,000 homeless in the country. Between 1.3 and 2 million people may be homeless for one or more nights during the year. Another study by the Urban Institute concluded that about 600,000 Americans live in shelters or on the streets on a given night.[11]

Federal support for housing was slashed 77 percent from $32.2 billion in 1981 to $7.5 billion in 1988. The Department of Housing and Urban Development authorized the construction of only 88,136 subsidized dwellings in 1987, compared with more than 224,000 in 1981. Some 2.5 million units of low-income housing disappeared between 1980 and 1988 through a combination of market forces and government indifference. Tenements that provided housing for the disadvantaged were torn down or renovated to make way for high-priced apartments or high-rise office buildings. During the past decade, half of the single-room occupancy hotels in the nation were lost. These were often the housing of last resort for the poor. An additional 200,000 units of low-income housing were expected to disappear over the next five years as loans expired from the tax-break programs of the seventies and eighties. The result would be hundreds of thousands more people in shelters.[12]

The market system offers large rewards, in some cases, to winners of the competitive race, but can also impose severe penalties on some of the losers. These losers often fall so far behind in terms of economic wealth that they end up in a seriously deprived condition. They have such small quantities and low qualities of resources at their disposal that they are not able to take care of themselves or their families. The market places a very low value on what they do have to offer, and often promotes wide disparities in income and wealth, allowing the "haves" to amass increasing wealth and the "have-nots" to fall further into relative poverty.

> Poverty cannot be ignored by a society that proclaims democratic values, insisting upon the worth of all its citizens and the equality of their political and social rights. Our commitment to freedom of speech, equality of suffrage, and equality before the law rests on a broader commitment to human values that is violated by the persistence of economic misery in an affluent society. I cannot imagine how a sane society could decide deliberately to guarantee every citizen a fair trial before a judge and jury and at the same time permit some citizens to be condemned to death by the marketplace.[13]

An unregulated market system can produce inhumane results, locking some people into a vicious cycle of poverty, and preventing them from ever really entering into the race for the rewards society has to offer. As Arthur Okun states: "Vast disparities in results—living standards, income, wealth—inevitably spawn serious inequalities in opportunity that represent arbitrary handicaps and head starts. . . . The children of the poor are handicapped in many ways—their nutrition, their education, their ability to get funds to start businesses and buy homes, and their treatment on many of the hiring lines for both private and public jobs."[14]

    1. Does the existence of poverty imply that our economic system is unjust? Does the concentration of poverty in certain groups make it more unjust than it would be otherwise?

2. What moral obligation, if any, do we have individually and as a society to reduce poverty? What steps should be taken to reduce poverty? What role can business play?

3. How can poverty be analyzed from a utilitarian perspective? What, if anything, would Kant's categorical imperative say about obligations to reduce poverty?

4. How would a libertarian like Nozick view poverty in the United States? How plausible do you find the libertarian's preference for private charity over public welfare? How would Rawls's difference principle apply to poverty? Does our system work to benefit the least advantaged in society?

[1] Timothy Noah, "Number of Poor Americans Is Up 6%, Real Income Is Off 1.7%, Agency Says," *The Wall Street Journal,* September 27, 1991, p. A2.

[2] Bruce Alpert, "Poverty Ratio Fill in '91, But La. Still Near Bottom," *Times-Picayune,* September 4, 1992, p. A-4. Poverty increased again in 1992 to 14.5 percent of the population or 36.9 million people. Income inequalities also continued to widen. See Paulette Thomas, "Poverty Spread in 1992 to Total of 36.9 Million," *The Wall Street Journal,* October 5, 1993, p. A2.

[3] Andrew Mollison, "Study: U.S. Has More Poor Than Other Democracies," *Times-Picayune,* September 22, 1991, p. A-14.

[4] Ann Mariano, "Poor Americans Getting Poorer, Researchers Say," *Times-Picayune,* June 26, 1993, p. A-16.

[5] Chrystal Caruthers, "Surge in Children Living in Poverty Is Cited in Study," *The Wall Street Journal,* July 8, 1992, p. C9.

[6] "… But U.S. Children Are Slipping Past the Safety Net," *Business Week,* October 12, 1987, p. 26.

[7] "Conditions Worsening for Poor Children, Panel Says," *Times-Picayune,* June 23, 1993, p. A-9.

[8] Kristin Huckshorn, "Myth: Most Poor Children Are Black, Urban," *Times-Picayune,* June 3, 1991, p. A-3.

[9] "Children Having Children: Teen Pregnancies Are Corroding America's Social Fabric," *Time,* December 9, 1985, pp. 79–90.

[10] Elizabeth Ehrlich, "Homelessness: The Policy Failure Haunting America," *Business Week,* April 25, 1988, pp. 132–138.

[11] Patti Davis, "For an Instant, She Met My Eyes," *Parade Magazine,* September 23, 1990, pp. 4–5.

[12] Jacob V. Lamar, "The Homeless: Brick by Brick," *Time,* October 24, 1988, pp. 34, 38.

[13] Arthur M. Okun, "Our Blend of Democracy and Capitalism: It Works But Is in Danger" (Washington, DC: The Brookings Institution, Reprint no. 351, 1979), p. 73.

[14] Ibid.

Source: Rogene A. Buchholz, *Business Environment and Public Policy: Implications for Management,* 5th ed. (Englewood Cliffs, NJ: Prentice Hall, 1995), pp. 274–278.

Employee Wages and Salaries

The Busy-Bee Sewing Machine Corporation is in the process of designing and implementing a new computer system to keep track of all its inventory and sales at more than 700 dealerships across the country. It is quite a complicated system that is taking a good deal of time and effort to put together. The company has a rather small programming staff that is working to design and implement the system with the help and advice of the computer manufacturer. This staff has had to put in a good deal of overtime work during the past several months, and is expecting to work even more overtime as actual implementation of the system draws closer.

The programmers who work for the company are considered exempt employees, meaning they do not get paid extra for overtime work. Such a provision is in their contract and was explained to them when they were considering employment with the company. Such overtime work is just expected of them from time to time as professional employees who are paid a salary rather than wages. To help with the work, the company has hired another programmer on a part-time basis who has had a good deal of experience and is something of a whiz when it comes to computer systems. He is a full-time student at a local college and thus is only available to work about 20 hours a week while school is in session.

During the summer, however, he can work as much as needed, and has recently been putting in as many as 80 hours a week. Since he is a part-time employee, however, he receives an hourly wage, which continues in effect no matter how many hours he works during a week or month. The other employees do not know how much per hour he is being paid, but they suspect that with the kind of overtime hours they have all been putting in lately, his total earnings for the week exceed what they are earning. This makes most of the full-time programming staff quite angry, and even though they like the part-time employee and believe he does excellent work, they do not think they are being treated fairly and are thinking of complaining to the manager.

1. Do the full-time programmers have a legitimate gripe in this situation? Are the terms of their contracts with the company being fulfilled? Why do they feel they are being treated unfairly? Are they getting anything as full-time employees that the part-time employee does not get? Should this be taken into consideration?

2. What light would some of the traditional ethical theories shed on this situation? Would a utilitarian analysis be helpful in analyzing this dilemma? What would Kant's categorical imperative suggest regarding the fairness of this situation? How would the egalitarian and libertarian positions differ?

Benefit-Cost Analysis

Business organizations for the most part do not like government regulations, as a good deal of time and effort are required to comply with them. Studies have shown that the compliance costs, the costs that business incurs to meet the regulations, can be significant. During the early 1980s, a serious effort was made by the administration in power to cut back on regulations and get government off the backs of business. While this effort experienced some success, government regulation again increased during the latter part of the decade. This increase continued into the 1990s, as the federal government implemented new laws passed by Congress with respect to the environment, disabled people, and family leave.

When the Republicans took control of Congress in the 1994 elections, an effort was made to pass legislation that would require a benefit-cost analysis to be performed for all new regulations. This procedure would require that all agencies justify the issuance of new regulations by showing that the benefits the regulation would provide for society would exceed the costs imposed on business and other parties. If the benefits did not exceed the costs, the regulation would have to be dropped or other less costly alternatives considered. Proponents of the process argued that benefit-cost analysis would introduce some scientific rationality into the regulatory process.

Critics of this process argued that such a procedure would stack the deck against the issuance of any new regulations, particularly in the environmental area. While the costs can be objectively quantified in most instances, the benefits are very subjective to quantify and can easily be manipulated for political purposes. Quite often, the benefits involve the saving of human lives, the prevention of serious illnesses, the protection of animals, or the saving of an ecosystem. How can realistic values be placed on these benefits so that comparison with the costs can be made fairly? What is the value of a human life? How much is a sea otter worth? This and other problems made critics label the process nothing more than a political means to stop regulations from being issued.

1. Does benefit-cost analysis seem like a reasonable way to proceed in the issuance of new regulations? Is something like this needed? What are the advantages and disadvantages of this approach?

2. Is this process based on utilitarian theory regarding the greatest good for the greatest number? If so, is it subject to the shortcomings that have been pointed out regarding utilitarianism? Which of the shortcomings is most important in your opinion?

A Process Approach to Ethical Theory

The remaining chapters of this part will lay out the key concepts involved in rethinking the basis of moral decision making in terms of an underlying process, rather than focusing on the application of principles or the development of a virtuous character. In this discussion, it should become clear the way this rethinking moves beyond traditional assumptions, tensions, and dilemmas, most of which are still to be found in the positions that form the core of theoretical approaches to business ethics discussed in the previous chapter. Since this process approach draws heavily from the collective corpus of the writings of the classical American pragmatists, a brief word about this movement will be helpful.

The development of classical American pragmatism occurred roughly from 1850 to 1950 when the doctrines of its five major contributors took shape, but it represents a spirit and vitality that is in an ongoing process of evaluation. The attempt to get at the significance of this philosophy has been long and complex. Because of initial confusion about the meaning and import of pragmatism, interest in it began to wane in philosophical circles. In recent years, however, interest in pragmatism has been growing rapidly from two interrelated directions. First, it is becoming recognized that pragmatism, though prior to what is considered mainstream philosophy today, anticipated its problems and dilemmas and offers a framework for moving beyond the impasses that these problems pose. Second, and ultimately intertwined with this first, more technical direction, it is becoming evident that pragmatism has a unique relevance for life—for social and cultural issues, for the values or goals that guide our activities. The implications of its unique focus have already begun to make their mark in such areas as environmental ethics, social and political thought, and feminist philosophy. In making use of pragmatism's insights for a new approach to business ethics, the remaining chapters of this part will roam freely through its collective corpus to clarify and make use of its common conceptual framework.[1]

The following explication of the various features of this process-oriented framework will highlight these features in their opposition to the traditional positions presented in the previous chapter. For, as indicated at the conclusion of that chapter, this position does not involve a synthesis of existing theoretical alternatives, but a radical reconstruction of the understanding of what it is to think morally. The best place to begin this exposition is with the understanding of the individual and the community that is contained in pragmatic thought.

The Individual and the Community

Sometimes terms we use quite frequently are so much taken for granted that we never stop to consider what they really mean. The terms *individuals,* or *selves,* or *persons* are examples of this phenomenon. However, the view of the self has serious implications for many issues relating to ethics. And the most important question concerning the self for these issues is whether the self is an isolatable, "atomic," discrete entity, or is by its very nature part of a social process.

The view of the atomic individual is firmly rooted in traditional thinking and is very much taken for granted. The view that singular or atomic individuals exist and have moral claims apart from any associations except those they choose to form for their own purpose was the philosophical basis for the French and American revolutions. This view is clearly embedded in John Locke's social contract theory, which is the position linked to the American revolution. Rawls's contemporary view of the social contract is itself rooted in the atomistic presuppositions of Locke and other social contract theorists of the tradition. These presuppositions are also the basis for understanding the nature of the corporation as a voluntary association of individuals.

While external ties may be established when antecedent individuals enter into contract with one another or come together through other means of collection in order to more readily secure their own individualistic goals, these bonds cannot root them in any ongoing endeavor that is more than the sum of their separate selves, separate wills, separate egoistic desires. This situation perhaps achieves its culmination in the economic theory of Adam Smith, to be more fully described in a later chapter. And even Henry David Thoreau, who unequivocally rejected capitalist values, revels in the isolatable individual, free from social interference.

This view of the atomic, singular self or person is also found in the utilitarian view that the community is a collection of atomic individuals, and moral decisions are justifiable by their consequences for this collective whole, consequences that may well be at the expense of particular individuals. It is likewise found in Kant's view of the autonomy of the person, which can stand over against the common good. Indeed, this accepted, unquestioned, presupposed view of the atomicity of the person or self is the common basis for positions as diverse as traditional individualistic or interest-group liberalism and traditional conservative laissez-faire economics, pitting the individual squarely against communitarian constraints such as government regulations. Once the individual is taken as an isolatable unit, then the individual and the community become pitted against each other in an ultimately irreconcilable tension.

The view of the self as inherently an aspect of an ongoing social process is a radically different way of understanding the self that denies the atomistic view. According to this view, in the adjustments and coordinations needed for cooperative action in a social context, human organisms take the perspective or the attitude of others in the development of their conduct. In this way there develops the common content that provides a community of meaning, such that communication can take place because there is a common basis of understanding. Without this shared meaning, people in a society have no way of understanding each other; in fact, it could be said that no society exists unless there is some common content.

Selfhood comes about through awareness of one's role in a social context. It involves the ability to be aware of oneself as an acting agent within the context of other acting agents. Not only can selves exist only in relationship to other selves, but no absolute line can be drawn between our own selves and the selves of others, since our own selves develop only insofar as others enter into our experience. The origins and foundation of the self are social or intersubjective; the self is not a given that constitutes the basic building block of society as in atomic individualism.

In incorporating the perspective or viewpoint of, taking the attitude of, or taking the role of the other, the developing person comes to take the perspective of others as a complex, interrelated whole. In this way one comes to incorporate the standards and authority of the group, the organization or system of attitudes and responses that Mead calls "the generalized other," but which could also be called the "common other" or "group other." Thus, there is a passive dimension to the self, the dimension structured by role taking, that aspect of the self Mead refers to as the "me." This generalized other is not merely a collection of others, but an organization or structural relation of others.

Mead uses the example of a baseball team as an instance of a generalized other or social group. The person who plays must be ready to take the attitude of everyone else involved in the game, and these different roles must have a definite relationship to each other. A participant must assume the attitudes of the other players as an organized unity, and this organization controls the response of the individual participant. Each one of the participants' own acts is set by "his being everyone else on the team," insofar as the organization of the various attitudes controls each participant's own response. "The team is the generalized other in so far as it enters, as an organized process or social activity, into the experience of any one of the individual members of it."[2] The common or generalized other consists of the organization of the roles of individual participants in the social process into some kind of structural relationship. In this sense, we are the roles we take in society and understand ourselves in terms of these roles.

Yet, an individual responds to the viewpoint of the other in a unique manner. There is a creative dimension to the self, which Mead refers to as the "I." The "me," then, represents the conformity of the person to the past and to the norms and practices of society, while the "I" represents its unique, creative dimension, which brings novel reactions to present situations. Any self incorporates, by its very nature, both the conformity of the group perspective or group attitudes and the creativity of its unique individual perspective. Thus, the tensions between tradition and change, conformity and individuality, conservative and liberating forces emerge as two dynamically interacting poles, which form the very nature of selfhood (Figure 3-1).

FIGURE 3-1 The Nature of Selfhood

I	ME
Creative Dimension of the Self; Novelty	Conformity to Norms and Practices of Society

Novel Perspective		Common Perspective
Conditions the	⟶	as Condition for
Common Perspective	⟵	Novel Perspective

FIGURE 3-2 Dynamics of Community

A person consists of a creative, ongoing interplay between the individual and social perspectives, and in this way freedom of the self lies in the proper relation between these two poles or dimensions. Freedom does not lie in opposition to the restrictions of norms and authority but in a self-direction, which requires the proper dynamic interaction of these two dimensions within the self. Thus, freedom does not lie in being unaffected by others and by one's past but in the way one uses one's incorporation of "the other" in novel decisions and actions. While a self or a person is not an isolatable individual apart from a social process, a self or person does have its own unique individuality, which is in an ongoing process of development.

It has been seen that any individual both reflects the group or common perspective and reacts to it in its own original manner. And this originality in turn enters into the group attitude or perspective and changes it in some fashion. Thus, a new perspective emerges because of its relation to institutions, traditions, and patterns of life, which conditioned its emergence, and gains its significance in light of the way it changes the common perspective. The dynamics or process of community is to be found in this continual interplay of adjustment of attitudes, aspirations, and factual perceptions between the common perspective as setting the context for the novel perspective and the novel perspective as it affects the common perspective[3] (Figure 3-2).

Thus, to ask if a new perspective is a product of an individual or a community, or to ask which is prior, the individual or the community perspective, is a false question. The creativity of the individual can be contrasted with the conformity represented by the common perspective, but not with community. True community occurs in the interactive process between the individual and the generalized other, and this takes place through ongoing communication in which each adjusts to or accommodates the other. It is this ongoing adjustment or accommodation between these two poles that is essential for community.

This adjustment is neither assimilation of one perspective by another, nor the fusion of perspectives into an indistinguishable unity, but can best be understood as an "accommodation" in which each creatively affects and is affected by the other through accepted means of adjudication. Thus, a community is constituted by, and develops in terms of, the ongoing communicative adjustment between the activity of the novel individual perspective and the common or group perspective, and each of these two interacting dimensions that makes a community gains its meaning, significance, and enrichment through this process of accommodation or adjustment (Figure 3-3).

A free society, like a free individual, requires both the influencing power of authority as embodied in institutions and traditions and the innovative power of creativity as contextually set or directed novelty. Thus, in Dewey's terms, "No amount of aggregated collective action of itself constitutes a community. . . . To learn to be human is to develop

FIGURE 3-3 Adjustment Process: Growth of Self and Society

Individual Perspective	Accepted	Common Perspective
Novelty	Organs of	Traditions
Creativity	Adjudication	Authority

through the give-and-take of communication an effective sense of being an individually distinctive member of a community; one who understands and appreciates its beliefs, desires, and methods, and who contributes to a further conversion of organic powers into human resources and values. But this transition is never finished."[4]

It can be seen that the very intelligence that transforms societies and institutions is itself influenced by these institutions. In this sense even individual intelligence is social intelligence. And social intelligence, as the historically grounded intelligence operative within a community and embodied in its institutions, though not merely an aggregate of individual intelligence but rather a qualitatively unique and unified whole, is nonetheless not something separable from individual intelligence. There is an intimate functional reciprocity between individual and social intelligence, a reciprocity based on the continual process of adjustment. Though the generalized other indeed represents social meanings and social norms, social development is possible only through the dynamic interrelation of the unique, creative individual and the generalized other. James expresses this interrelation in his observation that "the influence of a great man modifies a community in an entirely original and peculiar way, while the community in turn remodels him."[5]

It is often said that a community, to be a community, must be based on a common goal. The ultimate "goal" of this open-ended, dynamic process is enriching growth or development, not final completion. This in turn indicates that differences should not be melted down, for these differences provide the necessary materials by which a society can continue to grow. The development of the ability both to create and to respond constructively to the creation of novel perspectives, as well as to incorporate the perspective of the other, not as something totally alien, but as something sympathetically understood, amounts to growth of the self. Growth of self incorporates an ever more encompassing, sympathetic understanding of varied and diverse interests, thus leading to tolerance not as an infringement on one's self, but as an expansion of self. Thus, to enrich and expand the community is at once to enrich and expand the individuals involved in ongoing community interactions.

The understanding of a different way of making sense of things is not to be found from above by imposing one's own reflective perspective or abstract principles upon such diversity. Rather such understanding comes from beneath a conflict of principles by penetrating through such differences to a more fundamental level of human rapport. This kind of understanding can emerge because human beings are fundamentally the same and confront a common reality in an ongoing process of change. It is this deepened level of accommodation of perspectives that is necessary for a society to grow.

Such a deepening may change conflict into diversity, or it may lead to an emerging consensus that one of the conflicting positions is simply wrong for that time and place. In this way, over the course of time, incompatible perspectives, though not proved right or wrong in an absolute sense, are resolved by the weight of argument as reasons and evidence are brought to bear in the ongoing course of inquiry and things are worked out that are mutually acceptable. If such adjustments do not emerge, then community has broken down; what remains is sheer factionalism.

For example, in the winter of 1996, the Congress and the president of the United States were engaged in battle over the budget. The Republican-dominated Congress wanted to cut entitlement programs such as Medicare rather severely and grant a tax cut to certain groups of Americans. The president and most Democrats argued that the cuts in Medicare were too deep and that the tax cut was going to mainly benefit wealthy Americans. The differences between these positions were so great and so strongly ideologically held that a good part of the government had to shut down for the longest time in the nation's history when it came time for Congress to raise the debt ceiling. Some 800,000 so-called nonessential employees of the government were dismissed from their jobs for this period of time. Sheer factionalism reigned supreme through this period and community had broken down as neither side was willing to adjust its position to work toward a common agreement. Neither side was willing to get beneath abstract ideological principles to a deepened level of dealing with their conflicting positions.

A true community, by its very nature incorporating an ongoing process and a pluralism of perspectives requiring ongoing growth or integrative expansion, is far from immune to hazardous pitfalls and wrenching clashes, but these provide the material for such ongoing development. What needs to be cultivated in a society is the motivation, sensitivity, and imaginative vision needed to change irreconcilable factionalism into a growing pluralistic community. The deepening required for this growth does not negate the use of intelligent inquiry, but rather opens it up, frees it from the products of its past, from rigidities and abstractions, and focuses it on the dynamics of concrete human existence.

In some of the management literature today, there is growing interest in what is called "irrationality" in management decisions. This is based on the perception, becoming ever more widespread, that decisions are not based on the weighing of abstract, "objective," calculative alternatives, that the process of reasoning in concrete situations is not understandable as the application of abstractly grasped principles, nor can it be subjected to step-by-step analysis. What is operative instead in management decision making, it is held, is something akin to irrationality that cannot be examined or understood by traditional rational methods of examination.

What this view brings up, however, is the need for a new understanding of rationality. The process view advocated in this book does not destroy reason but brings it down to earth, so to speak. What has been destroyed is only the belief that the role of reason is to provide access to truth and value in the abstract and that its truth is for all time. Reason, brought down to earth, is concrete, imaginative, and deepened to operate with possibilities that have been liberated from the confines and rigidities of abstract rules and procedural steps in reaching a decision about something. This understanding of reason leads to a discussion of reasoning about value.

Value and Moral Reasoning

Within pragmatic process philosophy, all knowledge is understood as fallible, to be tested by ongoing consequences in experience. And knowledge emerges through intelligent reflection on experience within nature. Our experience within nature undergoes continual change, and while some aspects of experience are relatively stable, other aspects are unstable. Humans have a strong and deeply entrenched desire for some value to hold onto as a permanent basis of security in an uncertain world, and thus it is easy to focus on certain value aspects of experience and then falsely hold to them as absolute and unchanging, to be grasped with certitude.

With the rise of modern science, this means of attaining a feeling of security began to dissolve, though some still held rigorously to a view of absolute values. To hold onto absolute values in the face of science, a sharp distinction was made between the experimental method of science and the methods of pure reason or intuition by which values are grasped. Thus, one way to deal with this problem was to assert that there are absolute, unchanging values for all to know if they are knowing properly. Others, rejecting this claim, held that science showed the universe is valueless and put forth the view that values are whatever an individual thinks or feels is valuable. Value is merely subjective. Arbitrary relativism readily emerged from this view of value, as value is then a highly individualistic affair. Experimental method again was not needed because value was no more than a subjective feeling.

The process approach described in this chapter rejects all of the foregoing views. Value is not something subjective, merely housed within us in some sense, but neither is it something "there" in an independently ordered universe. Rather, objects in nature and contextual situations within which they emerge in human experience possess qualities such as being alluring or repugnant, fulfilling or stultifying, appealing or unappealing. These qualities are just as objective as qualities like color, sound, resistance, and so on. These former types of qualities, like all qualities, are "there" in nature; they are real emergents in the context of our interactions with our cultural and natural environments. Furthermore, they are not reducible in any way to other qualities. As qualities of interactions within nature, they are immediately experienced qualities that emerge in the context of organism-environment interaction. It is the immediately "felt" or immediately "had" qualities of experience that provide the basis, along with intelligent evaluation, for the values we hold and come to appropriate.

A scientist, for example, would reduce water to its components of hydrogen and oxygen in certain proportions. Water is reducible to and is nothing but a combination of these two elements as far as the scientist is concerned. The advocates of emergence, however, would hold that by reducing water to its components in this manner, one loses hold of the qualities of water that make it an important factor in human experience. These qualities include wetness, buoyancy, thirst quenching, and so on, all of which are dependent on the context of interaction between hydrogen and oxygen, but which are as real in their emergence as the elements themselves. To ask where the wetness is located, in the hydrogen or oxygen, is an incorrect question. It is in neither, but emerges in the context of their interaction. Similarly, to ask where is the experienced value—in me or in nature independently of me—is a false question. Value emerges in the context of the interactions of humans in nature and is there in that context.

Value is not something that the individual experiences in isolation from a community, nor are individual values something to be put in conflict with or in opposition to community values. Yet, community values are not merely the sum of individual values, nor are individual values merely a reflection of community values. Rather, values in their emergence within everyday experience are dimensions of social experience. The experience of value emerges as both shared and unique, as all experience is both shared and unique. It is the adjustment between these two aspects, the shared and the unique, which gives rise to the novel and creative aspects within moral community.

And, finally, value situations, like all situations, are open to experimental inquiry. This method involves the progressive movement from a problematic situation to a meaningfully resolved situation. It requires creatively organizing or reinterpreting the problematic situation, directing one's activity in light of that creative reorganization, and testing for its truth in terms of consequences: Does it work in bringing about the intended result? With respect to value, the intended result is, of course, the valuable result, one that can harmonize and integrate the diversity of conflicting values operative within the situation.

Normative claims have their normative function because they make claims concerning consequences of conduct as leading to the integration and harmonizing of values. Our values must constantly be reevaluated. "Yes, I hold this as a value, but ought I to do so? What are the consequences of holding such a value? Is it worthy?" Moral action is planned, rational action rooted in the awareness of its potentialities for enriching the experience of value for all involved. And when habitual modes of organizing behavior do not work in resolving problematic situations, situations with conflict, new evaluations take place and new moral claims emerge through the dynamics of experimental method. Experimental method, as applied in the moral context, is the attempt to increase the value ladenness of a situation through a creative growth of perspective, which can incorporate and harmonize conflicting or potentially conflicting values.

For example, a situation arises where there is a conflict between the corporation's need for maximum productivity from its employees and the need for some employees to have time to spend on family matters, whether taking care of children, parents, or whatever. An intelligent and creative solution to this situation of conflict is to institute flexible working hours where employees have to be working for some number of core hours, but have some flexibility to come in later than usual and leave later or come in earlier and leave earlier than usual to take care of family matters. Both the employees and the corporation are able to reach their respective goals in this solution. This solution will be constantly evaluated in terms of its workability. In resolving this conflict, intelligent inquiry restructured a problematic situation to harmonize and resolve conflicting demands. At the outset, the employer held as a value the need for all employees to be working during the same time period. As the reconstructed situation proved workable, this value was reevaluated and shown to be unworkable and, therefore, one that ought not to prevail.

Part of the development of the harmonious life is to make immediate experience as reflective of our ongoing, evaluated moral beliefs as possible. Only when one gets positive qualitative experiences from that which reason sees as justifiable in the foregoing experimental manner can one have a truly integrated self. Thus, taste, as Dewey notes, far from being that about which one cannot argue, is one of the most important things to argue about.[6] The cultivation of taste is the cultivation of the correct infusion of our value-related, qualitative experience with the moral beliefs that color this experience. If one finds value only in experiencing what reflective inquiry shows not to be worthy, then one is living a life of internal conflict.

People who consider good health valuable, for example, know that they need to keep their weight under control, and their eating habits reflect this value. They may be careful about their caloric and fat intake and practice moderation with regard to eating. They may actually come to find the taste of fatty foods unappealing. Others may go on crash diets to lose weight, but their craving for rich food is still so strong that, when they get off the diet, they immediately put on weight again, leading to another period of dieting, and so on, because their weight never stabilizes. In this case the value quality of their immediate experiences are not consistent with what intelligent reflection tells them is valuable, and they lead less than a harmonious existence.

As another example, people who come to value their health more highly than before and stop smoking because of the evidence that has accumulated about the potential harm smoking can cause may actually come to experience smoking as a disgusting habit and find it very distasteful. The change in what they believe is valuable has come to affect the qualitative character of their immediate experience such that they no longer even have a desire to smoke. Others, however, may still crave smoking even though they know it is not good for their health. Occasionally these people may give in to these cravings, thus creating internal conflict.

Our moral claims, then, can change the very quality of experience. And our moral claims are themselves always subject to evaluation and revision in terms of their ability to provide for the ongoing, enriched value ladenness of existence. There is nothing immune from potential revision. In this ongoing process not all value-related experience can be accepted, for some, if pursued, would lead to conflict and disintegration. Thus, while moral claims are about the production of value and not about anything else, the production of harmonious situations, which allow for the unimpeded experience of value, requires that we at times attempt to alter the quality of our value-related experience because of new "oughts" that have emerged as a result of experimental inquiry (Figure 3-4).

The preceding discussion has indicated that the social context itself affects the vital drives and desires operative within a situation. The experience of value and the emergence of moral norms do not occur apart from social interaction. Yet the creativity of the individual in its uniqueness brings unique tendencies and potentialities into the shaping processes of moral norms. The individual organism brings creative solutions to the resolution of conflicting and changing value claims and restructures the very moral behavior or moral practices and the institutionalized ways of behaving that helped shape its own developing potentialities.

Thus, Dewey claims that although moral deliberation involves "social intelligence," the reaction of the individual against an existing scheme becomes the means of the transformation and restructuring of habits and institutional practices.[7] Or, as he further notes, "Man is under just as much obligation to develop his most advanced standards and ideals as to use conscientiously those which he already possesses."[8] And, as new standards and ideals emerge, the rational order which underlies a moral community and which provides the adjudication process for conflicts is re-created as well. Though the slow evolution of such a re-creation may at times be difficult to discern, it may at times seem to manifest itself with startling energy and immediacy.

Here again, the resolution of conflicting moral perceptions, which provide the context for new ideals, cannot be resolved by appeal to abstract principles but through a deepening sensitivity to the demands of human valuings in their commonness and diversity. Such a deepening, as stressed earlier, does not negate the use of intelligent inquiry, but rather opens it up, frees it from the products of its past in terms of rigidities and abstractions, and focuses it on the experience of value as it emerges within concrete human existence. This allows us to grasp different contexts, to take the perspective of "the other," to participate in dialogue with "the other" in determining what is valuable.

What the foregoing indicates is that in place of the traditional understanding of moral reasoning as abstract and discursive it is now understood as concrete and imaginative. Moral reasoning as concrete is not working downward from rules to their application, but working upward from concrete moral experience and decision making toward guiding moral hypotheses. For pragmatism, rationality itself is imaginative, for imagination

FIGURE 3-4 Valuing Activity

Conflicting Values ⟶ Experience as Experimental ⟶ Reconstructed, Expanded Context; Harmonized Values

provides the capability of understanding what is actual in light of what is possible to create, of seeing conflicting fragments in light of a projected creative synthesis. Moral reasoning is not the inculcation of a past, either in terms of rules or dispositions. But it is inherently historical, for moral reasoning involves a creative reorientation of the present toward the future in light of the past. It involves dealing with a changing world, which manifests both stabilities and possibilities to be utilized. It does not ignore the lessons of the past, nor past theory-data relations, but reinterprets, reappropriates them in light of an imaginative grasp of what might be based on possibilities operative in the present. One grasps a situation historically not just in terms of the past but in terms of the future.

This past is, of course, not to be ignored. We make decisions and evaluations within the context of a prephilosophical traditional heritage that gives us a somewhat general consensus about working hypotheses from which to begin our decisions and actions. For example, in our society we tend to agree to a certain extent and in a rough, general fashion that lying, cruelty, stealing, killing, selfishness, and so on are to be avoided in favor of fairness, kindness, concern for others, and so on. But these can serve only as guides whose contours are shaped and reshaped by ongoing novel concrete situations and the conflicting values that must be concretely integrated. Guidelines such as these are working hypotheses that have emerged from past concrete situations and are held so strongly because they continue to work well in new situations.

It can be seen that the pragmatic process approach denies the understanding of moral reasoning as rule application. And it may seem that what results is a turn to virtue ethics as a concern with character development. However, the turn to an exclusive concern with being a virtuous person again oversimplifies, in its own way, the richness of moral decision making. In moral decision making we are, and should be, concerned with the kind of character we are developing. But the decision cannot be reduced to what kind of character one should develop. This can be a very important concern, but some moral decisions are less relevant than others regarding their role in forming good habits, but they are of intense moral concern nonetheless. Morever, the demands of concrete moral situations may lead to morally responsible decisions that go against character traits we have cultivated as important.

As habits develop from actions in previous situations and in turn enter into the new situations that arise, they modify both themselves as well as the new situation through the actions taken. The reconstruction of situations and the reconstruction of ourselves and the habits that constitute the ongoing process of self-development are inseparably interrelated. What is needed is not rigid adherence to what we consider good character traits, but the intelligence, sensitivity, and flexibility to deal with concrete situations in an ongoing context of moral growth. The exclusive focus on character is an abstraction from the contextual richness of moral decision making and the evaluation of consequences. As Dewey so well stresses,

> Consequences include effects upon character, upon confirming and weakening habits, as well as tangibly obvious results. To keep an eye open to these effects upon character may signify the most reasonable of precautions or one of the most nauseating of practices. It may mean concentration of attention upon personal rectitude in neglect of objective consequences. . . . But it may mean that the survey of objective consequences is duly extended in time.[9]

Understanding moral action as adherence to preestablished rules encourages rigidity and lack of moral sensitivity. Understanding moral action as the development of a good character or a good will encourages the self-engrossed concern with meaning well or of having good intentions. Each of these provides a comfortable substitute for the difficult task of bringing about good consequences in concrete situations. Morality is more than following rules and more than manifesting a set of inculcated virtues. At no time can one say, "The consequences turned out to be terrible, but at least I know I did the morally right thing." Such a statement is, from the pragmatic process perspective, a contradiction. The most important habits we can develop are habits of intelligence and sensitivity, for neither following rules nor meaning well can suffice. Morality is not postulated in abstract rules to be followed or virtues to be inculcated but discovered in concrete moral experience. Bringing about good consequences in concrete situations through moral decision making helps develop, as by-products, both good character traits as habits of acting and good rules as working hypotheses needing ongoing testing and revision.

Moreover, as seen earlier, the individual and the community, in this view, are not isolatable atomic entities, but rather they are inextricably interwoven. Given this inherent interrelatedness, neither individuals nor whole systems are the bearers of value. Rather, value emerges in the interactions of individuals, and wholes gain their value through the interactions of individuals, while the value of individuals cannot be understood in isolation from the interrelationships that constitute their ongoing development. When we slide over the complexities of a problem, we can easily be convinced that absolute moral principles are at stake. And the complexities of a problem are always context dependent and must be dealt with in the context of a concrete situation.

Our concrete decision making is influenced by all sorts of conflicting guidelines, and decision making cannot be simplified to accord with any single one of them. It is not that moral theories presented in the previous chapter do not get hold of something operative in our concrete moral decisions, but that in lifting out one aspect, they ignore others, reducing moral action to some fixed scheme. Utilitarian theories, deontological theories, virtue theories, individualisms, and communitarianisms all get at something important, but they each leave out the important considerations highlighted by the other theories. And the relative weight given to any of these, as well as to a host of other considerations in coming to a decision as to what ought to be done, will depend on the novel and concretely rich features of the situation in which the need for the decision arises. There is no formula, but there is the need for ongoing concrete, creative intelligence in action and sensitivity to the conflicting demands emergent within concrete situations.

Furthermore, added together the various theories are contradictory because they are attempting to substitute for a concrete, rich moral sense operative in decision making some one consideration, which is found operating there in various degrees at various times and in various situations, turning it into a moral absolute to determine what is the moral course to follow in all times and all situations. Any rule, any principle, any scheme is an attempt to make precise and abstract some consideration that seems to be operative in concrete moral experience, but this experience is ultimately too rich and creative to be adequately captured in that manner.

In this view, moral reasoning involves an enrichment of the capacity to perceive the complex moral aspects of situations rather than a way of simplifying how to deal with what one does perceive. It involves sensitivity to the rich, complex value ladenness of a situation, and to its interwoven and conflicting dimensions, the ability to utilize creative intelligence geared to the concrete situation, and an ongoing evaluation of the resolution. Moral reasoning involves being responsive to the possibilities that experience presents to us and taking responsibility for the decisions we make. And, decisions that change a situation will give rise to new problems requiring new integrative solutions (Figure 3-5). One cannot just "put the problem to bed" and forget about it for all intents and purposes. The goal of moral reasoning is not to make the most unequivocal decision, but to provide the richest existence for those involved. Moral maturity, in fact, thus increases rather than decreases moral problems to be mediated, for it brings to awareness the pervasiveness of the moral dimension involved in concrete decision making.

It has been seen that our moral claims are about something that requires experimental integration, the emergence of concrete value experiences of humans in their specific situational concrete interaction with their world. We create and utilize norms or ideals in the moral situation as working hypotheses by which to organize and integrate the diversity of concrete valuings. This pluralistic process, of course, rules out absolutism in ethics. But what must be stressed is that it equally rules out subjectivism and relativism, for it is rooted in the conditions and demands of human living and the desire for meaningful, enriching lives. While the experience of value arises from specific, concrete contexts shaped by a particular tradition, this is not mere inculcation, for the deepening process in getting beneath rules or principles offers the openness for breaking through inculcated tradition and evaluating one's own stance. In this way we are operating in open rather than closed perspectives.

This openness of perspectives is frequently denied. In the area of moral value, such a denial leads, on the one hand, to the false assumption that the individual is operating in the value situation from a personal perspective closed to others and to objective evaluation. It leads, on the other hand, to the false assumption that one should be acting from an absence of any perspective and thus achieving a common and ultimate agreement with all others. The assumption of a closed perspective results in moral relativism, while the assumption of the absence of perspective leads to moral absolutism. In the latter case, one is not claiming to be acting from a perspective or viewpoint as such, but rather claims to have a grasp of absolute truth. Moral relativism results in the extreme of irresponsible tolerance, while moral absolutism results in the extreme of dogmatic imposition of one's own principles or framework on others.

The present view attempts to combine the commonness of humans qua human with the uniqueness of each human qua human in a way that allows for a value situation of intelligently grounded diversity accompanied by an ongoing process of evaluation and continual testing. This understanding of value leads neither to a relativism of arbitrary choice nor to an absolutism of no true choice in shaping values; it involves neither

FIGURE 3-5 The Process of Moral Reasoning

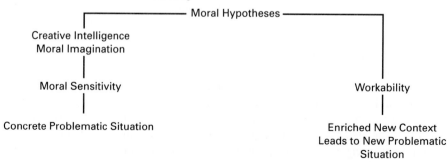

Moral Hypotheses

Creative Intelligence
Moral Imagination

Moral Sensitivity

Concrete Problematic Situation

Workability

Enriched New Context
Leads to New Problematic
Situation

nihilistic despair nor utopian wholesale optimism. Rather, it is a meliorism that holds, in Dewey's words, that "the specific conditions which exist at one moment, be they comparatively bad or comparatively good, in any event may be bettered. . . . it arouses confidence and reasonable hopefulness as (wholesale) optimism does not."[10] Though moral diversity, just as diversity in general, can flourish within a community, when such diversity becomes irreconcilable conflict, intelligence must offer growing, reconstructed contexts that can provide a workable solution.

Here something should be said about *growth* and about *workability,* for both of these terms have been subject to great distortion. First, growth cannot be understood only in terms of one's own interests alone. The growth of the self or person is a process by which one achieves fuller, richer, more inclusive, and more complex interactions with one's environment. Thus, workable solutions cannot be understood just in terms of the artificiality of oneself in isolation, but rather they must be workable for all those whose interests are there to be adjudicated. Because the very sense of self is a sense of "being with," the process of recognizing the interests of others does not require that one become a sacrificed self, but rather that one becomes a larger self.[11]

As seen earlier, growth incorporates an encompassing sympathetic understanding of varied and diverse interests. Dewey, then, can hold that growth itself is the only moral "end," that the moral meaning of democracy lies in its contribution to the growth of every member of society,[12] and that growth involves the rational resolution of conflict, conflict between duty and desire, between what is already accomplished and what is possible.[13] Thus, also, Peirce can "bless God for the law of growth with all the fighting it imposes."[14]

Critics of this position have wrongly interpreted growth as mere accumulation. This leads to charges that increases in morally detrimental activity or unfounded beliefs could be considered instances of growth. It has been seen, however, that a pragmatic process understanding of growth involves reintegration of problematic situations in ways that lead to expansion of self, of community, and of the relation between the two. In this way growth has an inherently moral and esthetic quality.

Although Dewey refers to growth as an "end," he does not intend this in a technical sense of "end," and indeed, growth can best be understood not as an end to be attained but as a dynamic embedded in the ongoing process of life, just as experimental method is not an end to be achieved but a dynamic embedded in the ongoing course of experience. Experimental method, as applied in the moral context, is in fact the melioristic attempt to increase the value fullness of a situation through a creative growth of perspective, which can incorporate and harmonize conflicting or potentially conflicting values. It should be stressed here that the expansion of a moral perspective, although not independent of intelligent inquiry, is not merely a change in an intellectual perspective but rather is a change that affects and is affected by the individual in its total concreteness, its desires, drives, and so on.

This leads directly to the issue of workability. First, workability cannot be taken in the sense of workable for oneself only, for the entire discussion has stressed that oneself is inextricably tied to the community of which it is a part. Second, workability cannot be taken in terms of the short-range expedient, for actions and their consequences extend into an indefinite future and determine the possibilities available in that future. Finally, workability in the moral situation cannot be taken in terms of some abstract aspect of life such as economic workability. Because moral situations are concrete, workability in the moral situation must concern the ongoing development of the concrete richness of human experience in its entirety. The full significance of the consequences of choice among values is found in Dewey's assertion that: "The thing actually at stake in any serious deliberation is not a difference of quantity, but what kind of person one is to become, what sort of self is in the making, what kind of a world is making."[15]

It should be noted here that what is being made is not only self but world. Our moral choices affect not only our developing selves, but the concrete contexts in which the decision arises in all their richness and interrelationships. What the entire foregoing discussion has attempted to show is that thinking morally is not merely applying rules of community interest, self-interest, universalizability, and so on to some specific act; nor is it acting according to some ultimate value, or to some set of ultimate values within which all others can be seen as subsets. Indeed, the application of a moral rule to a specific case can be used by ill-intentioned individuals to justify all sorts of behavior that common sense judges to be immoral. Nor are virtuous persons those who act merely from good intentions or through the inculcation of tradition. Neither good will nor inculcated habit is enough. For actions done with the best of intentions by virtuous people may nonetheless be misguided, and can only be so judged by something other than intentions. And inculcated traditions themselves require ongoing evaluation and reshaping.

What is needed for moral reasoning is the development of the reorganizing and ordering capabilities of creative intelligence, the imaginative grasp of authentic possibilities, the vitality of motivation, and a deepened sensitivity to the sense of concrete human existence in its richness, diversity, and complexity. The importance of this latter cannot be overemphasized. As Dewey holds, a problem cannot be stated until it is felt. It is this "felt" dimension that regulates the way one selects, weighs, and conceptually orders what one observes.

This deepening sensitivity or attunement, as stressed earlier, does not negate the use of intelligent inquiry, but rather opens it up, frees it from the products of its past in terms of rigidities and abstractions, and focuses it on the dynamics of concrete human existence and the direct sense of value as it emerges from the very core of human existence. The vital, growing sense of moral rightness comes not from the indoctrination of abstract principles but from attunement to the way in which moral beliefs and practices must be rooted naturally in the very conditions of human existence. It is this attunement that gives vitality to diverse and changing principles as working hypotheses embodied in concrete moral activity. And it provides the ongoing direction for well-intentioned individuals to continually evaluate and at times reconstruct their own habits and traditions. Humans cannot assign priority to any one basic value, nor can their values be arranged in any rigid hierarchy, but they must live with the consequences of their actions within concrete situations in a process of change.

Other Topics

FEMINIST PHILOSOPHY

Before leaving this chapter, something should be said about the relation of this position to feminist philosophy in business ethics, or what is sometimes called the ethics of care. This philosophy focuses on traits of character that are valued in close relationships, traits such as sympathy, compassion, fidelity, friendship, and so forth. Along with this focus, it rejects such abstractions as Kant's universal moral rules and utilitarian calculations, for these abstractions separate moral decision makers from the particularity of their individual lives and separate as well moral problems from the social and historical contexts in which they are embedded. Such abstractions involve rationally grasped rules and/or rational calculations and ignore the role of sensitivity to concrete situations and to the attitudes and interrelations of those involved. This leads to a so-called "moral impartiality" that, instead of fostering respect for all individuals, in fact negates respect for concrete individuals by impersonally viewing them as anonymous and interchangeable.

This concern for the individual in feminist philosophy is not a focus on the individualism of atomic agents, but rather on relationships and the caring, compassion, and concern these relationships should involve. This philosophy points out that this feminine "voice" or perspective is by and large radically different from the male voice of abstract rights and justice which has dominated the development of moral theory.[16] Feminist thought rejects the notion of rights involving contracts among free, autonomous, and equal individuals in favor of social cooperation and an understanding of relationships as usually unchosen, occurring among unequals, and involving intimacy and caring. The model used is often that of the parent-child relationship and communal decision making. The focus on relations leads feminist philosophy to the importance of the need to be attuned to other perspectives and to enter sympathetically into them.

It can be seen from the preceding overview that feminist philosophy focuses on the same features of moral experience that form part of the central structure of pragmatic process ethics. Pragmatic process ethics offers a philosophical foundation for a relational view of the self, for the communal nature of relations, for the indispensability of taking the perspective of the other, for self-growth and community growth as involving the enrichment of the esthetic-moral dimensions of concrete human existence, for the deepening of reason beneath formalized abstract rules and procedures, and for the central importance of attunement or sensitivity to concrete individuals and the unique concrete situations in which they are enmeshed and within which moral problems emerge. Pragmatic process philosophy, in having united the various insights of feminist philosophy or a philosophy of caring within a unified theoretical structure before feminist philosophy came into being, would seem a rich field for those interested in a philosophy of caring to explore.

RIGHTS

Something should also be said about pragmatic process philosophy and its relationship to the issue of rights, as rights and the conflict between them will be an important topic in later chapters, particularly those dealing with issues in the marketplace and workplace. As was briefly indicated earlier, traditional rights theories are usually based on an understanding of humans that is highly individualistic in nature; yet these theories negate respect for concrete individuals by impersonally viewing them as anonymous and interchangeable. Rights theories focus on abstract, individualistic humans coming together by entering into contracts that bind them through external ties, contracts that require they give up certain absolute rights. Thus, society is always in some sense an impingement on one's absolute rights.

From the pragmatic perspective, it can perhaps be said that what is more natural is not absolute individual rights but contractual rights. However, this view of rights does not mean merely that individuals are born into societies that have already been formed, at least in theory, through a social contract of original participants. Nor does it mean that rights are merely the result of government legislation or contractual agreements. Finally, it does not mean that abstract principles can be substituted for caring attunement to concrete situations and the individuals involved. Rather, what this view of rights is intended to point out is that the "natural" state of being human is to be relationally tied to others and that apart from the dynamics of community there can be no individual rights, since individuals emerge within and develop in the context of community adjustments. Thus, in the very having of rights one has community obligations.

There can be no absolute individual rights, for the need for adjustment between freedom and constraint, it will be remembered, is built into the internal structure of the self in the form of the I-me dynamics. The self consists of a creative, ongoing, interpretive interplay between the individual and social perspective, and thus freedom of the self, in a general sense, lies in the proper relation between these two poles. Freedom, as stressed earlier, does not lie in opposition to the restrictions of norms and authority, but in a self-direction that requires the proper dynamic interaction of these two poles within the self. It does not lie in being unaffected by the other, but in the way one uses one's incorporation of "the other" in novel decisions and actions. Individual rights are at once social rights, though responsible social rights are not possible without individual freedom. In developing moral perceptions that bestow rights on individuals or groups or the common other, the process of communicative adjustment is at the same time bestowing obligations on everyone, those whose rights were increased as well as those who must respond to the granting by adjusting their own actions.

Ongoing community adjustments, then, must be understood not as pitting the individual with absolute rights against the common other that limits these rights, but rather as community attempts to find the proper balance between the dimensions of novelty and conformity, neither of which can function without the other. A free society, like free individuals, requires this balance. In this way, the good of the whole is not the good of the common or group other over against the individual. The good of the whole is the proper relation between the individual and the common other, for the whole is community and community encompasses both. If rights are understood as an absolute individual possession upon which society infringes, thus pitting one individual against another or pitting the individual against the group, then rights will lead to self-interested factionalism and adversarial relationships rather than to communal cooperation.

Questions for Discussion

1. How is the process of moral reasoning outlined in this chapter different from the moral reasoning involved in utilitarianism and in Kant's ethical formalism? How does the way the concrete situation is treated differ from the way a concrete situation is treated when principles are involved?

2. What are the key elements of a pragmatic process approach to ethical theory? What role do moral sensitivity and moral imagination play in this process theory? How are moral principles treated in this theory? What does workability mean? How are morally problematic situations resolved?

3. What does it mean to say that the self is inherently social? How are the passive and the creative self related to each other? How does this view of the self differ from the notion of atomic individualism found in other ethical theories?

4. Describe the process of community dynamics outlined in the chapter. How are differences between the individual perspective that is represented by novelty and creativity and the common perspective represented by traditions and authority resolved? How does the resolution of these differences lead to growth of the self and community?

5. What is the difference between the valuing experiences of people and what they know "ought" to be? What happens when these two are not in harmony? How can a conflict between these two be brought into alignment?

6. How does an ethics of process differ from an ethics of principle and an ethics of virtue? In what ways are they similar? What are the important characteristics of each approach? What are the strengths and weaknesses of each approach? Which seems most applicable to business situations that involve ethical problems? Defend your answer.

BOX 3-1

Summary of Important Elements of Process Thought

THE SELF IS INHERENTLY SOCIAL

Passive feature of the self.

Incorporation of the generalized other-conformity.

Creative feature of the self.

Unique individual-change-novelty.

Freedom does not lie in opposition to restrictions of norms and authority, but in a self-direction that requires the proper dynamic interaction of these two poles within the self.

COMMUNITY DYNAMICS

The common perspective, as representative of the generalized other, is the condition for the novel perspective.

The novel perspective reshapes the common perspective.

True community occurs in the interplay between the individual and the generalized other in which each adjusts to and accommodates the other through the accepted means of adjudication.

Growth of the self incorporates an ever more encompassing sympathetic understanding of varied and diverse interests.

Differences provide the necessary materials by which individuals and a society can continue to grow.

MORAL REASONING AND VALUES

Value is not something subjective housed solely within us in some sense. Rather, value-laden qualities emerge in the context of organism-environment interaction and are immediately experienced and irreducible to anything else. These, along with intelligent evaluation, form the values we hold. Like all experience, value experience is both shared and unique. The adjustment between these two aspects gives rise to the novel and creative aspects within moral community. Part of the harmonious life is to make immediate valuing experiences reflective of what reason tells us is valuable.

Our moral claims, our claims concerning what is valuable, our evaluations are about something that requires integration, our concrete value-laden experience as it emerges in specific situational concrete interactions with our world. Morality is not postulated in moral rules but discovered in concrete moral experience. The growing sense of moral rightness comes not from indoctrination of abstract principles but from sensitivity to concrete situations.

Moral action is planned rational action rooted in the awareness of the potentialities for the enrichment of the value ladenness of experience for all involved. We create and utilize norms or ideals as working hypotheses by which to organize and integrate the diversity of concrete values into a reconstructed context that resolves the conflict. In this process the values we hold must be reevaluated, giving rise at times to new values, new normative claims.

The ongoing resolution of conflicting values requires growth. Growth is inherently moral for it involves enrichment of value within concrete contexts for all those whose interests are to be adjudicated. It is not mere accumulation of something but ongoing expansion and integration of selves and the contexts in which they function.

MORAL REASONING REQUIRES

- Reorganizing and ordering capabilities of creative intelligence.
- Imaginative grasp of authentic possibilities.
- Vitality of motivation to think morally.
- Deepened sensitivity to the sense of concrete human existence in its richness, diversity, and complexity.

Endnotes

[1] Sandra B. Rosenthal has argued elsewhere in *Speculative Pragmatism* (Amherst, MA: University of Massachusetts Press, 1986) that the positions of these five major classical American pragmatists, including Charles Peirce, William James, John Dewey, C. I. Lewis, and G. H Mead, form a systematic and unified movement. Paperback edition (Peru, IL: Open Court Publishing Co., 1990).

[2] Ibid., p. 154.

[3] A person may be a member of more than one community, for there are diverse levels and types of communities. Any community consists of many subgroups, and though individuals may feel alienated from a particular society, they cannot really be alienated from society in general, for this very alienation will only throw them into some other society. Ibid., pp. 353–354.

[4] John Dewey, The Public and Its Problems, *The Later Works,* Vol. 2, Jo Ann Boydston, ed. (Carbondale and Edwardsville, IL: Southern Illinois University Press, 1984), pp. 330, 332.

[5] William James, "Great Men and Their Environment," *The Will to Believe and Other Essays: Works of William James,* Frederick Burkhardt, ed. (Cambridge, MA: Harvard University Press, 1979), p. 170.

[6] John Dewey, The Quest for Certainty, *The Middle Works,* Vol. 4, Jo Ann Boydston, ed. (Carbondale and Edwardsville, IL: Southern Illinois University Press, 1984), p. 209.

[7] John Dewey, Ethics, *The Middle Works,* Vol. 5, Jo Ann Boydston, ed. (Carbondale and Edwardsville, IL: Southern Illinois University Press, 1978), p. 173.

[8] John Dewey, Reconstruction in Philosophy, *The Middle Works,* Vol. 12, Jo Ann Boydston, ed. (Carbondale and Edwardsville, IL: Southern Illinois University Press, 1982), p. 180.

[9] John Dewey, Human Nature and Conduct, *The Middle Works,* Vol. 14, Jo Ann Boydston, ed. (Carbondale and Edwardsville, IL: University of Southern Illinois Press, 1983), pp. 216–217.

[10] Dewey, Reconstruction in Philosophy, pp. 181–182.

[11] George Herbert Mead, *Mind, Self, and Society,* Charles Morris, ed. (Chicago: University of Chicago Press, 1934), p. 386.

[12] Dewey, Reconstruction in Philosophy, pp. 181, 186.

[13] Dewey, Ethics, p. 327.

[14] Charles Hartshorne and Paul Weiss, eds. *Collected Papers of Charles Sanders Peirce* (Cambridge: Belknap Press of Harvard University, 1931–35), Vol. 6, Sec. 479.

[15] Dewey, Human Nature and Conduct, pp. 216–217.

[16] Carol Gilligan, *In a Different Voice* (Cambridge: Harvard University Press, 1982).

Suggested Readings

Dewey, John. Authority and Social Change. *The Later Works,* Vol. 11, Jo Ann Boydston, ed. Carbondale and Edwardsville, IL: University of Southern Illinois Press, 1987.

Dewey, John. Ethics. *The Middle Works,* Vol. 5, Jo Ann Boydston, ed. Carbondale and Edwardsville, IL: University of Southern Illinois Press, 1978.

Dewey, John. Human Nature and Conduct. *The Middle Works,* Vol. 14, Jo Ann Boydston, ed. Carbondale and Edwardsville, IL: University of Southern Illinois Press, 1983.

Dewey, John. The Public and Its Problems. *The Later Works,* Vol. 2, Jo Ann Boydston, ed. Carbondale and Edwardsville, IL: Southern Illinois Press, 1984.

Dewey, John. The Quest for Certainty. *The Later Works,* Vol. 4, Jo Ann Boydston, ed. Carbondale and Edwardsville, IL: Southern Illinois University Press, 1984.

Dewey, John. The Theory of Inquiry. *The Later Works,* Vol. 12, Jo Ann Boydston, ed. Carbondale and Edwardsville, IL: University of Southern Illinois Press, 1986.

Gouinlock, James. *John Dewey's Philosophy of Value.* New York: Humanities Press, 1972.

James, William. Essays in Radical Empiricism. *The Works of William James,* Frederick Burkhardt, ed. Cambridge, MA: Harvard University Press, 1976.

James, William. Talks to Teachers on Psychology. *The Works of William James,* Frederick Burkhardt, ed. Cambridge, MA: Harvard University Press, 1983.

James, William. The Will to Believe and Other Essays. *The Works of William James,* Frederick Burkhardt, ed. Cambridge, MA: Harvard University Press, 1979.

Lewis, Charles Irving. *The Ground and Nature of the Right.* New York: Columbia University Press, 1955.

Lewis, Charles Irving. *Our Social Inheritance.* Bloomington, IN: Indiana University Press, 1957.

Mead, George Herbert. *Mind, Self, and Society.* Chicago: University of Chicago Press, 1934.

Mead, George Herbert. *Selected Writings,* J. A. Beck, ed. New York: Bobbs-Merrill, 1964.

Peirce, Charles. *Collected Papers,* Vol. V, Charles Hartshorne and Paul Weiss, eds. Cambridge, MA: Belknap Press of Harvard University, 1960.

Rosenthal, Sandra B. *Speculative Pragmatism.* Amherst, MA: University of Massachusetts Press, 1986. Paperback edition. LaSalle, IL: Open Court Publishing Co., 1990.

SHORT CASES

Air Bags

Reducing automobile accidents in the United States is a major public policy problem, as approximately 50,000 people die each year from such accidents and over 5 million are injured. Despite improved highways and driver training programs, accidents continue at a high level. The National Highway Traffic Safety Administration (NHTSA) was created in 1966 to develop and enforce safety standards for motor vehicles. One of the first acts of the new agency was to emphasize use of the air bag in automobiles to reduce the chance of serious injury in an accident. The agency published a notice in 1969 entitled "Inflatable Occupant Restraint System" that required air bags to be installed in all vehicles manufactured in the country. The automobile industry opposed this standard and raised questions about safety research, engineering design, financial burdens, and possible legal violations, and was able to postpone implementation for nearly a decade.

Air bags are passive restraints that deploy automatically in an accident without any action by the occupants of the automobile. The bag inflates upon impact in a fraction of a second and acts as a cushion to prevent the occupants from striking the interior of the car or hitting the windshield and shattering the glass. Seat belts would perform much the same function, but the problem with such devices is that they require positive action from the occupants to "buckle up." Research has indicated that the percentage of people who use seat belts was very low. Use of the air bag would not require any such action and was thereby considered to be a superior technology.[1]

Initial research conducted for NHTSA showed that air bags would be effective in preventing injuries and fatalities to adults in frontal crashes. Evaluations done by General Motors and Ford also showed air bags would be effective, especially when used in combination with seat belts.[2] Proponents of air bags stress the desirability of reducing fatalities by whatever means and that this is reason enough for requiring their installation. Automobile companies and their supporters argue that there are many unresolved problems that make the use of this technology questionable. Opponents of the air bag generally raise the following objections: (1) It is a complex and untested contraption, (2) they can go off when they shouldn't causing a startled driver to lose control, (3) they work only in head-on crashes, (4) they need to be used in conjunction with a seat belt to be effective, (5) they can injure a child standing on the seat or otherwise out of the normal passenger position, and (6) they are costly.[3]

The controversy over the installation of air bags continued when a passive restraint rule was adopted by the Carter administration in 1977 that would have required some 1982 models to be equipped with air bags or belts that automatically fold across front seat occupants.[4] The Reagan administration first delayed the effective date a year and then rescinded the rule entirely. A federal appeals court overturned this decision in response to lawsuits filed by State Farm Mutual Automobile Insurance Co. and the National Association of Independent Insurers. The appeals judge called the decision "arbitrary and illogical" and said that NHTSA had failed to consider any alternatives to recession of the requirement.[5]

The government estimated that air bags would boost car prices $300 to $1,100, and GM estimated that it would have to invest $285 million to comply with the passive restraint requirement. Ford Motor Co. estimated an investment of $183 million.[6] The Center for Auto Safety, a Nader watchdog group, estimated a cost of $1 billion annually, but stated that society pays $2.4 billion annually in medical, rehabilitation, and loss-of-work-time expenses linked to auto-related injuries.[7]

The head of the Transportation Department, Elizabeth Dole, issued a ruling in the summer of 1984 to deal with the controversy. Beginning with 1987 models, new cars would have to be built with either air bags or automatic seat belts. Automakers would have to equip 10 percent of their 1987 models with passive restraints for the driver and front-seat passengers. This percentage would rise to 25 percent in 1988, 40 percent in 1989, and all of the 1990 models. Alternatively, new cars could be built with new kinds of safer, "friendly interiors" if such interiors would provide as much passenger protection as air bags or automatic belts. None of these measures would be required, however, if states representing two-thirds of the population were to enact laws requiring people to fasten their seat belts. States had until April 1989 to pass such mandatory seatbelt laws.[8]

In mid-1986, 26 states and the District of Columbia, which accounted for 68 percent of the nation's population, had passed seat belt laws. Legislation was pending in 26 other states. However, efforts to repeal the laws were underway in ten states, including some in which the law hadn't yet taken effect. Compliance with the laws also seemed to be waning.[9] In September 1986, an appeals court in Washington said that none of the laws being enacted by the states to require motorists to buckle their seat belts appeared to meet the standards set by the agency. Thus, in the court's opinion, it appeared unlikely that the passive restraint rule will be rescinded when the deadline for mandatory seat belt laws was reached.[10]

Because the states failed to reach the required level of coverage with seat belt laws, the phase-in procedure for passive restraints began. After September 1, 1986, an increasing number of automobiles had to be equipped with passive restraints on both the driver and passenger sides of the vehicle. These restraints could include air bags, passive seat belts, or other protective measures such as padded dashboards and shock-absorbent steering columns. In May 1988, Chrysler Corporation announced that it had started putting driver-side air bags in six of its car lines and, by 1990, would meet the federal standard in all of its passenger vehicles. Ford also stated that it was planning to install air bags on more than half of its cars before the 1990 deadline arrived.[11]

1. Does the community have a legitimate interest in promoting safety with regard to automobile usage? Why does there need to be laws with respect to automobile safety? Should not people's freedom to do as they please be respected?

2. Why don't people value safety more highly making laws unnecessary? How can safety be promoted throughout the society? Do people need to be protected from their own folly? Do individual decisions have an impact on the community?

[1] Judith Reppy, "The Automobile Air Bag," in Dorothy Nelkin, ed., *Controversy: Politics of Technical Decisions* (Beverly Hills, CA: Sage Publications, 1977), pp. 145–146.

[2] Richard M. Hodgetts, "Air Bags and Auto Safety," *The Business Enterprise: Social Challenge, Social Response* (Philadelphia: W. B. Saunders, 1977), pp. 130–131.

[3] Albert R. Karr, "Auto Air Bags: U.S. Resumes Debate on Use," *The Wall Street Journal,* November 29, 1983, p. 31.

[4] See Susan J. Tolchin, "Air Bags and Regulatory Delay," *Issues in Science and Technology,* Vol. 1, no. 1 (Fall 1984), pp. 66–83, for an excellent summary of the air bag controversy.

[5] Albert R. Karr, "U.S. Move to Scrap Air Bags in New Cars Is Overturned by a Federal Appeals Court," *The Wall Street Journal,* June 2, 1982, p. 2.

[6] "Cars Must Have Air Bags by 1984, U.S. Court Rules," *The Wall Street Journal,* August 5, 1982, p. 4.

[7] Stephen Wermiel, "High Court's Decision on Air Bags Makes It Tougher for Agencies to Rescind Rules," *The Wall Street Journal,* June 27, 1983, p. 7.

[8] Christopher Conte and Donald Woutat, "Rule on Air Bags Won't End Safety Battle as U.S. Agency Plan Allows Alternatives," *The Wall Street Journal,* July 12, 1984, p. 3. In November 1985, Ford announced that it would offer driver-side air bags in Tempo and Topaz models, the first company to offer such gear on nonluxury vehicles since the mid-1970s. Christopher Conte, "Ford Plans to Offer Airbags as Option on 2 Compact Cars, *The Wall Street Journal,* November 4, 1985, p. 12.

[9] Jan Wong, "Despite Recent Laws, Many Motorists Are Still Casual About Wearing Seat Belts," *The Wall Street Journal,* March 7, 1986, p. 19.

[10] Albert R. Karr, "Rule on Air Bags, Automatic Safety Belts Unlikely to Be Rescinded, Court Says," *The Wall Street Journal,* September 19, 1986, p. 10.

[11] Joseph B. White, "U.S. Auto Makers Decide Safety Sells," *The Wall Street Journal,* August 24, 1988, p. 17.

Source: Rogene A. Buchholz, *Public Policy Issues for Management,* 2nd ed. (Englewood Cliffs, NJ: Prentice Hall, 1992), pp. 46–48.

Plant Closings

By the early 1980s, General Motors, the giant of the American auto industry, had begun to feel the effects of aging auto plants and the need to compete with low-cost, high-quality auto imports. In the spring of 1985, General Motors (GM) announced the construction of an all-new manufacturing plant to be built in Spring Hill, Tennessee, and that an all-new automobile called the Saturn would be built in that new and highly automated manufacturing facility. The Saturn was an automobile that was designed to compete with foreign imports. This announcement pointed to a movement that would logically result in the closing of aging production plants owned by General Motors.

One such aging facility was the Norwood plant just outside the city of Cincinnati. The news of the plant closure (Norwood) was reported in a trade journal in June 1986. The journal reported that General Motors was planning to close six of the company's 25 North American assembly plants by 1990. The Norwood plant was built in 1923 and was producing the GM Chevrolet Camero and Pontiac Firebird. The trade journal, the weekly *Metal Working News,* reported that GM intended to close two of its auto assembly plants in the United States over the next two years. The trade journal stated that in addition to the Norwood plant, GM was studying whether or not to close older plants in Detroit; Lakewood, Georgia; North Tarrytown, New York; Ste. Therese, Quebec; and Fairfax, Kansas.[1]

A week after the announcement in the trade journal, Roger Smith, chairman of General Motors, reported that General Motors "has no firm plans to close any of its assembly facilities." He went on to say that, "there is no doubt there is going to be significant overcapacity in the market, and that we hope that the overcapacity is somebody else."[2] On November 6, 1986, Roger Smith spoke at a major GM press conference. He began by stating that GM had begun to see the economic benefits of its North American automotive reorganization. Due to a $10 billion plant construction and modernization program as well as other management actions, GM was a more competitive company. He followed this upbeat statement with the announcement of GM's "Strategy of the Eighties." The plan was to "replace obsolete facilities with new or modernized plants."[3]

The Norwood manufacturing plant, as well as the Hamilton-Fairfield, Ohio, plant (also in the Cincinnati area), which makes body parts for assembly at other plants including Norwood, would be closed because of the lack of competitive labor agreements and the age of the two plants. The two Cincinnati area plants were among 11 that would be closed by General Motors by the end of the decade. No definite date for the plant closings was announced.[4] The announcement of the plant closings came after a story reported in the *Detroit Free Press* on Sunday, November 2, 1986, that the automaker would make an announcement of plant closings because the automaker was reeling from a $338 million loss in the third quarter and a declining share of the market.[5] It was estimated by General Motors that the plant closings would cost greater Cincinnati more than $229 million in annual wages and $111.5 million in annual payments to subcontractors. The Norwood plant employed 4,300 workers and the Fairfield-Hamilton plant employed about 2,400 workers.[6]

Although GM had indicated that the auto plants would probably be closed before the end of the decade, there was no definite closing date given for the Norwood plant. It was thought that the plant would remain open until mid-1986. However, on Tuesday, March 3, 1987, General Motors announced that the Norwood plant would close permanently on August 26, 1987. The closing date was almost a year earlier than expected. General Motors indicated that continued production of the Camero and Pontiac Firebird would take place at its plant in Van Nuys, California.[7]

The announcement was devastating to the Norwood community. The plant closing would have a direct impact on the 4,300 workers who would lose their jobs. However, the indirect economic impact on the community would be even greater. Already immersed in an economic downturn, the city would lose $2.7 million in earnings and property tax revenues. The city's school system would also lose $2.3 million in tax revenues. "It was estimated that the loss of income from GM jobs would remove over $100 million annually from the greater Cincinnati economy."[8]

General Motors could not estimate the number of jobs that would be offered to the Norwood workers at other plants. GM had made the announcement in March in order to give the workers at least six months' notice. Ohio Governor Celeste was disappointed at the announced closing, but was encouraged by what the company had offered the community in the way of assistance. Senator Howard Metzenbaum (D–Ohio) charged that the company continues to move operations abroad and that it was bad business for American companies to move American jobs abroad and expect loyalty from Americans.[9]

The GM plant accounted for almost $3 million of tax revenue collected in the city of Norwood, which represented about 25 percent of the proposed 1987 budget of $11.5 million. General Motors said that it would continue its corporate contribution to the local United Appeal campaigns for the next two years. The present year's contribution had been $182,000. In addition, it promised to spend at least $9 million to clean up the Norwood plant site; engage a private consultant to find a new use for the old site; and provide up to $100,000 to help the 4,300 workers relocate to new jobs within General Motors, provide retraining assistance, and pay supplemental unemployment benefits that had been negotiated between the company and the union.[10]

GM tried to compensate for the sudden job losses by enacting worker retraining, job placement, and transfer programs. Also, based on the GM-UAW contract, GM was required to give additional unemployment benefits, guaranteed income flow benefits, relocation allowances, and continued health benefits. These benefits were valued at over $100 million. GM also hired economic development consultants to evaluate the future utility of the plant's facilities and surrounding land and a company to market the Norwood property. GM also saved Norwood about $2 million in tax revenues by not seeking a property tax reassessment on the site.[11]

City officials considered GM's actions a mere public relations ploy. They explained to the citizens that the $100 million that GM would pay in closing costs were required by contract. The gesture was not one of generosity but a legal requirement. Negotiations between city officials and representatives from GM took place between March and July 1987. The city of Norwood filed a lawsuit against GM for $318 million. GM was charged with breach of contract and fiduciary duty by closing the plant. On September 2, 1988, the suit was dismissed by the Hamilton County Court in Ohio as "totally without merit or basis in fact."[12]

1. What factors led General Motors to consider plant closings? Were there any other strategies the company could have adopted to deal with these factors in its environment? Were plant closings the only viable alternative as far as the company was concerned?

2. From the standpoint of the workers, what other alternatives were available? What has been done in other situations where plant closings were proposed? Have these efforts been successful?

3. What are the pros and cons of plant closing legislation? What forms have some of the proposals and legislation taken? Should such legislation be encouraged or discouraged? Why?

4. What are the impacts of a plant closing on a local community? What steps can the community take to deal with a plant closing? Does the company owe anything to the community? What steps, if any, should a company take to mitigate its impact on the community?

[1] "Report Says GM May Leave Norwood," *Cincinnati Enquirer,*" June 17, 1986, p. D6.

[2] "GM Chairman Plans No Closings," *Cincinnati Enquirer,* June 26, 1986, p. B8.

[3] "General Motors and the City of Norwood, Ohio," *Up Against the Corporate Wall,* 5th ed., S. Prakash Sethi and Paul Steidlmeier (Englewood Cliffs, NJ: Prentice Hall, 1991), p. 67.

[4] Mike Boyer, "Age Doomed GM Plants," *Cincinnati Enquirer,* November 7, 1986, p. A1.

[5] Mike Boyer and Mark Braykovich, "The Pricing of Closing," *Cincinnati Enquirer,* November 4, 1986, p. A1.

[6] "Plant Closing Soon," *Cincinnati Enquirer,* November 3, 1986, p. A3.

[7] Mike Boyer, "The Other Shoe Drops," *Cincinnati Enquirer,* March 4, 1987, p. A4.

[8] "General Motors and the City of Norwood," pp. 68–69.

[9] Boyer, "The Other Shoe Drops," p. A4.

[10] "D-Day for Norwood: GM Close Means City Faces Crisis," *Cincinnati Enquirer,* March 4, 1987, p. A1.

[11] "General Motors and the City of Norwood," p. 75.

[12] Ibid., pp. 76–78.

Source: Adapted from Rogene A. Buchholz, et al., *Management Responses to Public Issues,* 3rd ed. (Englewood Cliffs, NJ: Prentice Hall, 1994), pp. 181–191.

Ideology

In 1975, George Cabot Lodge conducted research into the nature of American ideology. He described five key ideas that he believed comprised traditional American ideology based on Lockean notions of private property and individualism. This ideology was being challenged, according to Lodge, by five other key ideas that went under the general heading of communitarianism. These ideas included the rights of membership in a community as being more important than property rights and increasing government intervention in the economy.

Lodge surveyed almost 2,000 readers of the *Harvard Business Review* in several countries. Not surprisingly, most of the respondents preferred the traditional ideology and believed it was the dominant ideology in American society at that time. Nonetheless, they sensed its replacement by the communitarian principles of the challenging ideology, as a majority of the respondents believed the new ideology would be dominant in American society by 1985, just ten short years away. By 1985, however, a conservative revolution had taken place in American society and an administration was in federal office that espoused the traditional ideology and attempted to reduce the size of government. The traditional ideology seemed to be alive and well, and many believed a knockout blow had been delivered to its challenger.

1. How can this discrepancy be explained? Why did so many *Harvard Business Review* readers, most of whom were executives, believe that, by 1985, the challenging ideology would be dominant? What evidence existed in 1975 that made this a real possibility? What changes took place in American society in the ten-year interval that prevented this change in ideologies from happening?

2. Does the market appeal more to the individualistic tendencies of its participants? Can community interests be taken care of through market transactions? What kind of balance should be struck between individual rights to property and regulation of property for community interests?

Source: Rogene A. Buchholz, *Business Environment and Public Policy: Implications for Management,* 5th ed. (Englewood Cliffs, NJ: Prentice Hall, 1995), p. 126.

Charitable Contributions

XYZ Corporation was a charter member of the 5 percent club, that is, those companies that gave the maximum amount allowed by law to charitable causes. Now that the law had been changed to allow 10 percent of before-tax profits to be deducted, XYZ Corporation had to decide whether to take the lead in establishing a 10 percent club, or at least to increase its contributions to something above the 5 percent level.

XYZ had also given the majority of its contribution money to educational institutions, believing this policy was justified because the company at least could be said to benefit from having a better educated pool of potential employees from which to draw its work force. Now that the federal administration had cut back on traditional welfare programs and had asked the private sector to respond to community welfare needs, XYZ wondered whether or not it should give more to community agencies that provided services for the disadvantaged in towns and cities where its plants were located.

There was considerable disagreement within the company itself as to the need for a contributions program, let alone its distribution. Many employees believed that a private corporation had no responsibilities to society other than to produce goods and services, provide jobs and income to employees, and earn profits for stockholders in the process. Other employees believed giving to education was acceptable but did not want to provide welfare services for people who were unemployed and living in poverty. They believed welfare was a proper function of the government but not private corporations.

1. What are the arguments for and against a contributions program? Should XYZ continue its program and perhaps even increase its giving? Why or why not? What does the company hope to gain from having a contributions program? Does the corporation owe anything of this nature to the community?

2. How should the funds from a contributions program be distributed? Should top management have the only say in where the funds are spent? Should employees be involved in the decision? Stockholders? How would you go about resolving the distribution question facing XYZ Corporation? Should it respond to the administration's request?

Source: Rogene A. Buchholz, *Business Environment and Public Policy: Implications for Management,* 5th ed. (Englewood Cliffs, NJ: Prentice Hall, 1995), pp. 300–301.

CHAPTER **4**

Scientific Method and Human Experience

The application of ethical theory to business problems and the development of normative statements about what business ought to be doing with respect to these problems are problematical because of the scientific approach that is taken toward most business problems. Much research conducted in schools of business and management is based on one or more of the social sciences, such as economics, political science, anthropology, psychology, and sociology, all of which claim some form of positivist orientation. The way business problems are researched is to develop a theory regarding the problem, gather supposed value-free data, and then analyze the data using appropriate statistical techniques to prove or disprove the theory.

The result of this scientific orientation is a trained incapacity, or at the very least, a strong reluctance, to engage in normative analysis. Schools of business and management that are dominated by a scientific culture often do not find normative analysis that is characteristic of applied ethics very useful in dealing with business problems. The research base, the research methods, and the research literature are shaped by the combined forces of positivist social science, which deals with human behavior in a reductionistic manner, and the expectations of schools of business and management.[1]

While on the surface this reluctance to deal with normative analysis may not seem very important in a business or management school context, a closer examination shows that it is of critical importance. Instructors who argue that normative concerns are best left to "ivory tower" philosophers who are trained to debate at this level may be doing their students as well as themselves a great disservice. This issue has to do with the degree to which normative concerns are considered relevant to business issues and the acceptance of ethical theories and statements as legitimate objects of study in a business or management school setting.

Scholars who are interested in business ethics have dealt with this issue by talking about two kinds of business ethics, the normative and the empirical, where the former is considered to be a prescriptive approach, and the latter is explanatory, descriptive, and/or predictive in its approach. Normative business ethics is the domain of philosophers and theologians, while the latter is considered to be the domain of management consultants and business school professors. Scholars who represent these different domains are said to be guided by different theories, assumptions, and norms, which often result in misunderstanding or lack of appreciation for each other's endeavors.[2]

The normative approach is rooted in philosophy and the liberal arts, and focuses its attention on questions of what ought to be, how an individual or business ought to behave in order to be ethical. The empirical approach is rooted in management and the social sciences and is generally concerned with questions of what is, assuming that the organizational world is basically objective and is "out there" awaiting impartial exploration and discovery. Empiricists answer questions of what is by attempting to describe, explain, and/or predict phenomena in the natural world utilizing the agreed-upon methodologies of their social scientific training.[3]

The social scientist may devalue the philosopher's moral judgments because they cannot be understood in empirical terms and cannot be verified by empirical test or be used to predict or explain behavior. The social scientist's statements about morality, on the other hand, are seen to be of little value to the philosopher because they do not address the essential questions of right and wrong. Normative ethical theories develop standards by which the propriety of certain practices in the business world can be evaluated. In contrast, the empirical approach focuses on identifying definable and measurable factors within individual psyches and social contexts that influence individual and organizational ethical behavior.[4] The differences between the normative approach and empirical approach to business ethics are nicely summarized in the following table (Table 4.1).

Various attempts have been made to overcome this split in the field. Weaver and Trevino have outlined three conceptions of the relationship between normative and empirical business ethics. The parallel relationship rejects any efforts to link normative and empirical inquiry for both conceptual and practical reasons. The problems with this approach are that if empirical inquiry ignores normative issues, it may lose sight of why and for whom it pursues some questions rather than others, and self-contained normative inquiry may become too abstract to be of any practical value. The symbiotic relationship supports a practical relationship in which the two domains may rely on each other for guidance in setting agendas or in applying the results of their conceptually and methodologically distinct inquiries. Information from each type of business ethics inquiry is potentially relevant to the pursuit and application of the other form of inquiry. A full-fledged theoretical integration countenances a deeper merging of distinct forms of inquiry, involving alterations or combinations of theory, assumptions, and methodology, a task the authors believe few people in the field are equipped to even attempt, let alone resolve.[5]

Victor and Stephens call for a unification of the two domains, arguing that ignoring the descriptive aspects of moral behavior in a business context is to risk unreal philosophy, and ignoring the normative aspects is to risk amoral social science.[6] Patricia Werhane suggests that there is no purely empirical or purely normative methodology, that social science cannot be purely objective and that ethicists cannot be purely nonempirical.[7] Finally, Donaldson and Dunfee develop what they call an integrative social contracts theory that incorporates empirical findings as part of a contractarian process of making normative

	Normative Approach	Empirical Approach
TABLE 4.1 Normative and Empirical Approaches to Studying Business Ethics		
Categories		
1) Academic home	Philosophy, theology liberal arts	Management Social Sciences
2) Language	Evaluative	Descriptive
Definition of ethical behavior/ action	Act on what is right just, fair	Ethical choices, decisions (right or wrong)
3) Underlying assumptions human moral agency	Autonomy, responsibility	More deterministic Reciprocal causation
4) Theory purpose, scope, and application	Perscription and proscription Abstract Analysis and critique	Explanation/prediction Concrete and measurable Influence actual behaviors
5) Theory grounds, evaluation	Reflection on business practice Rational critique of moral judgments	Empirical study of business practice Ability to explain, predict, solve business problems

Source: Linda Klebe Trevino and Gary E. Weaver, "Business ETHICS/BUSINESS Ethics: One Field or Two?" *Business Ethics Quarterly,* Vol. 4, no. 2 (April 1994), p. 115.

judgments. They seek to put the "ought" and the "is" in symbiotic harmony that requires the cooperation of both empirical and normative research in rendering ultimate value judgments.[8]

The Fact-Value Distinction

None of these approaches has been very successful in addressing the issue of normative versus empirical business ethics because this split between the two approaches to business ethics is another manifestation of a problem that has existed between philosophy and science for several centuries. This problem is most often expressed as the difference between facts and values, but other ways of stating the problem have also appeared, such as the difference between objective versus subjective approaches, the "is" versus the "ought," and descriptive versus prescriptive statements. This distinction was briefly touched upon in the previous chapter, and involves questions related to the seriousness with which normative or ought statements should be taken. Are ethical oughts in any way scientific or empirical propositions that say something significant about the world in which we live, or are they merely matters of opinion? Do ought claims relate in any significant way to factual claims that are the subject matter of scientific endeavors?

In terms of the framework of traditional empiricism, within which this question is usually raised, the difference between descriptive and prescriptive claims boils down to the issue of whether or not morality is in any way objective. Descriptive claims deal with matters of "fact" and attempt to make clear to people the way things are or the nature of reality. Such statements, it is held, are the purview of science in its attempt to objectively analyze real-world problems and establish relationships between variables to understand the way the world works. Prescriptive statements, on the other hand, deal with questions of value and attempt to prescribe the way things should be in order to obtain the "good" life, or be consistent with notions of human welfare and fulfillment or enrichment of human experience. They are believed to be inherently subjective, representing opinions about what ought to be done. Given this assumption, if values cannot be reduced to facts, if there is a fact-value distinction, then objective morality becomes impossible.

The implications of the fact-value distinction for traditional empiricism in ethics can best begin with Bentham's utilitarian position discussed in the previous chapter. The fact-value distinction is completely ignored by Bentham in his utilitarian position, for he slides back and forth between the factual claim that individuals are motivated by pleasure and the normative claim that individuals ought to be motivated by pleasure. The unexpressed assumption that runs through his position is that the supposed truth of hedonism as a psychological theory about the way individuals behave is an automatic justification for the moral claim about the way individuals ought to behave.

John Stuart Mill, a utilitarian writing after Bentham, tried to explicitly prove that the "ought" claim could be derived from the "is" claim, but he was ultimately shown to have failed in this endeavor. The claim that the production of pleasure is good is a normative claim having no more or no less justification in factual evidence than many other normative claims, and must be judged like all other normative claims. For example, even if psychological hedonism was a "proven" scientific fact, a moral philosopher could well claim that though we are motivated by pleasure we ought not to be, for the human being has the ability to transcend such inclinations and be motivated by a higher moral calling.

Furthermore, G. E. Moore, known for his presentation of the "naturalistic fallacy," attacked the very attempt by empiricists to define moral goodness in terms of anything sensible. He argued that a normative concept, such as the morally good, cannot be equated with pleasure or any other sensible or "natural" quality, for the two are never identical in meaning. Value predicates are never identical in meaning with factual predicates. No list of what is the case could ever determine what ought to be the case or what is good. Therefore, no factual term entails a value term, and no factual judgment entails a value judgment. There is a complete separation between facts and values, and an empiricism, which holds that value judgments are a species of factual judgments, is mistaken.[9]

The separation of fact and value that Moore advocates can lead one to hold a view that ethics is noncognitive in nature, that neither ethics nor moral philosophy has the status of genuine knowledge. Ethics consists solely of opinions that express our likes and dislikes, our preferences or predilections, our wishes and aversions. This is the position taken by A. J. Ayer, largely as a result of Moore's writings. He holds that if statements of value cannot be reduced to statements of fact, then value claims are meaningless, for any meaningful claim must be reducible to sensible facts. Our guides to action, our praises and condemnations are merely emotive. Statements of what ought to be are unverifiable because they do not express genuine propositions about the world.[10]

However, those who hold to a source of knowledge other than sense experience can maintain this general type of distinction without falling into relativism, for this other source of knowledge provides awareness of the "ought." Thus, Moore held that moral goodness is a nonsensible quality grasped by a nonsensible intuition. Kant's position, as seen in the previous chapter, makes moral duty or obligation, expressed in prescriptive or ought claims, totally independent of our desires and totally devoid of any reference to facts, especially the facts of human nature and its inclinations. The categorical imperative, as was previously seen, is a prescriptive statement that is regarded as a moral law by which all reason must be bound because it is self-evidently and universally true for all human beings in all circumstances. The source of morality is reason, not empirical observation.[11]

At one extreme, then, are those who claim moral philosophy is not a body of genuine knowledge, that judgments of value or prescriptive claims about what ought or ought not to be done are neither true nor false. They express nothing but our personal preferences, our likes and dislikes—in other words, our subjective feelings about the objects or actions in question. Thus, moral judgments are mere opinion, concerning which there is no point in arguing and certainly no way of investigating a proposition to determine its validity. Descriptive statements are the only kind of statements that can be examined by a scientific method to determine their so-called truth value.

At the opposite extreme are those who believe that there are absolute and universal standards of right and wrong and of what ought to be done or ought not to be done in specific circumstances. They believe there is a universal morality that applies to all people at all times and places and feel secure in a dogmatic assertion that the existence of objective moral standards and values is incontrovertible. People who enunciate this view claim an authority to make moral judgments and expect them to be accepted by others on the basis of this claimed authority. Again, there is nothing to argue about or examine as far as prescriptive claims are concerned, as adherents to this view claim to be speaking absolute truth that need not be validated by external criteria such as factual descriptions.

The question as to whether or not moral values and prescriptive claims about what ought to be have any "objective validity" often is also stated in terms of relativism versus absolutism. The relative is that which varies from time to time and changes with alterations in the circumstances, while the absolute is that which does not vary from time to time and does not change with alterations in the circumstances. According to cultural relativism, moral beliefs and principles that prescribe acceptable forms of human behavior are closely connected in a culture to other cultural characteristics, such as language and political institutions. Anthropological studies show that moral beliefs—the particular actions and motives that are deemed worthy of approval or disapproval—differ greatly from culture to culture. Thus, moral standards are held to be simply historical products sanctioned by customs that have developed over a long period of time in response to conditions in which the society functions. Moral beliefs and principles are relative to groups and individuals who make up a culture, and consequently there are no universal norms that apply to all people and all cultures.[12] Nor can there be debate when conflict of cultures arises, for each is "playing by a different set of rules." One cannot judge checkers by the rules of chess.

Subjective relativism, which is sometimes called normative relativism in the business ethics literature, concerns differences among individuals rather than cultures. This view holds that when individuals differ on what is right or wrong, this difference is merely one of opinion or feeling. In other words, moral statements are simply statements of opinion or feeling; they have no objective basis where their truth value can be determined. People can never really disagree about the morality of an action, nor can they be mistaken in their moral judgments. Statements of opinion or feeling are relative; one cannot in any real way show an opinion about a moral action to be false or invalidate a particular feeling about morality.[13]

The fact-value distinction in a broad sense thus leads to the view that facts are not action guiding in the sense of indicating that something ought to be done. They are descriptions and causal explanations of human or natural phenomena. Value judgments, on the other hand, do have an action-guiding function and commend or condemn particular courses of action, whether this commendation or condemnation is held to merely express subjective feeling or state an absolute standard.

Most of us probably fall somewhere in between these extreme positions of absolutism and relativism, but in a business school or business organization that adheres to a positivistic orientation toward reality—where empirical data are collected and analyzed to solve problems—the first view is likely to be more strongly held. This poses a special problem for moral philosophers who want to make normative statements about what business ought to be doing or what it ought not to be doing. How can the validity of these statements be established, and how can they be seen as anything other than mere opinion or dogmatic assertion, which can then be easily dismissed?

If this question is not dealt with, and an instructor plunges right in to deal with cases and issues without examining the ethical assumptions people are making, arguments about what is right and wrong are very likely to be a my-opinion versus your-opinion type of argument. This may be satisfactory for some people but certainly very frustrating to those who are trying to learn something of a more objective nature that can be applied to real-world situations. It would seem that for business ethics to establish itself as a legitimate subject for study in a business school and not be just a passing fad, it must establish that prescriptive claims about the way things ought to be done have some validity about them that can be examined and discussed the same way one can examine and discuss descriptive claims.

Process Ethics and the Scientific Method

The process approach to ethics outlined in the previous chapter provides a way of dealing with science and scientific method that undercuts the fact-value distinction and the traditional dichotomies between subjective and objective and absolute and relative. When properly understood, the process approach provides an important perspective from which to understand what is involved in "thinking scientifically." The philosophy of pragmatism with which the process approach is intertwined arose in part as a reaction against the modern-world view Cartesian understanding of the nature of science and of the scientific object. This modern-world view understanding resulted from the general belief that the method of gaining knowledge, which was the backbone of the emergence of modern science, was linked with the content of the first "lasting" modern scientific view—the Newtonian mechanistic universe.

Such a linkage, based largely on the presuppositions of a spectator theory of knowledge, led to the view that scientific knowledge provided the literal description of objective fact, and excluded our lived qualitative experience as providing access to the natural universe. This world view resulted in a quantitatively characterized nature, and the atomicity of discrete individual units that must be brought together through mechanistic laws or related to each other through a mechanistic process. This in turn led to the alienation of humans from nature and a radical dehumanizing of nature. Nature as objectified justified nature as an object of value-free human manipulation.

The human being was saved from being reduced to a mechanistic object by being truncated into a dualism of mind and matter, Cartesian dualism, the dualism of Descartes, in which the body was a part of this mechanistic nature, but mind was "outside" of nature and beyond the realm of scientific study. Such a view was not amenable for the emerging sciences of the human, and the human being became understood as part of this mechanistic nature rather than set apart from nature. As a result, humans, like atoms, were understood in terms of isolated, discrete entities who interact through mechanistic relationships. Humans and their behavior were "reduced" to the mechanistic atomism of nature as characterized by Newtonian physics. The social and behavioral sciences, as they began to develop, thus became reductionistic in nature.

A deep-seated philosophical tendency completely rejected by the process approach to business ethics is the acceptance of the framework of Cartesian dualism. Humans are within nature, not outside of nature, and inexplicably linked to it. Such an assertion, however, when interpreted in the light of the preceding framework, can be glibly read as a type of reductionism. If humans are a part of nature, then they are reducible to nature. In brief, the phenomenon of humans and their behavior must be reducible to a level that is no longer human. This alternative, however, is definitively rejected. The process approach is naturalism in that humans are within nature. But nature is not the mechanistic universe of the Newtonian world view. And it is precisely the pragmatic refocus on science in terms of method rather than content that provides the key to its radical correction of this view.

What, precisely, is the content of science? There are many sciences, each with its own subject matter, its own content. The content of the science of botany is different than the content of the science of geology, for example, and the contents of both of these are different than the content of physics. The language of physics is quantitative, but botanists and geologists use the language of our everyday experience. What unifies them all as science is not a reduction of everything to quantitative, calculative language and mechanistic laws but the method by which they gain an understanding of the data with which they deal. Scientific method is practiced by the scientist; it is something that the scientist does, not something that the scientist finds.

The very first stage of scientific inquiry requires human creativity. Scientists are not mere passive spectators gathering brute data, but rather they bring creative theories that enter into the very character and organization of the data grasped. Second, there is directed or goal-oriented activity dictated by the theory. The theory requires that certain activities be carried out and certain changes brought about in the data to see if anticipated results occur. Finally, the test for truth is in terms of consequences. Does the theory work in guiding us through future experiences in a way anticipated by its claims? Truth is not something passively attained, either by the contemplation of absolutes, or by the passive accumulation of data, but by activity shot through with the theory that guides it. And the theory itself is constituted by possible ways of acting toward the data and the anticipated consequences of such theory-laden activity.

This role of purposive activity in thought and the resultant appeal to relevance and selective emphasis, which must ultimately be justified by workability, are key features of the scientific method. Furthermore, in any science, when a theory does not work well, when it cannot integrate its data in meaningful ways that lead to anticipated consequences, when some data just do not seem to fit, then new creative theories are developed that provide a broadened context, which can encompass the problem areas in a newly integrated whole. And so the process continues, and in this way scientific method is self-corrective.

It was seen in the previous chapter that this experimental method is embedded in the very nature of experience, for all experience involves an interpretive perspective that directs our activity, which is tested by its workability, by the consequences it brings about, and is revised when it does not work properly.

By focusing on the method of science rather than its contents, the proper understanding of human experience is not one that reduces it to quasi-scientific mechanistic laws or attempts in any way to substitute for the full richness of human experience a quantitative, calculative focus. In this way, a proper understanding of the lessons of the scientific method reveals that the nature into which the human organism is placed contains the qualitative fullness revealed in lived experience, and that the grasp of nature within the world is not a mere passive assimilation of data but rather is perspectival and creative. The human being is within nature. Neither human activity in general nor human knowledge can be separated from the fact that this being is a natural organism dependent upon a natural environment. But the human organism and the nature within which it is located are both rich with the qualities, values, and meanings of our everyday experience.

Thus, as was indicated in the previous chapter, workability from an ethical perspective cannot be limited to economic workability, but rather workability must apply to the richness of concrete human existence in its entirety. Furthermore, when problematic contexts emerge, when our creative approaches are not working properly, it has been seen that what is needed, as in the technical sciences, is the creative development of an expanded context that can resolve the conflicts. Thus, the resolution of conflicts involves expanded or growing contexts. Problem solving in concrete human existence involves the resolution of conflict in a way that enriches it with values and meanings.

From the backdrop of the nonpassive or nonspectator understanding of human experience, humans and their environment—organic and inorganic—take on an inherently relational aspect. To speak of organism and environment in isolation from each other is never true to the situation, for no organism can exist in isolation from an environment, and an environment is what it is in relation to an organism. The properties attributed to the environment belong to it in the context of that interaction. What we have is interaction as an indivisible whole, and it is only within such an interactional context that experience and its qualities function.

Such a relational view of humans and their environment at once has pluralistic dimensions, for environments are contextually located, and significant solutions to problematic situations emerge within such contextually situated environments. Diverse perspectives grasp the richness of reality in different ways but must be judged in terms of workability. And here it should perhaps be stressed again that workability requires growth, resolution of conflicts in terms of enlargement of context that can adjust or adjudicate the conflicting perspectival claims. Growth cannot be reduced to material growth, nor to mere accumulation, but rather is best understood as an increase in the moral-esthetic richness of experience.

The Fact-Value Distinction Revisited

Not only does the complete separation of fact and value constitute a serious problem for moral philosophy in a world that is scientifically and empirically oriented in the traditional sense, but in fact the problem as traditionally posed comes about because, in the traditional sense, to be scientifically and empirically oriented meant to "just collect the brute facts" that are empirically "there" and value free. Facts provide value-free descriptions and causal explanations of human or natural phenomena. But, as seen earlier, pragmatism rejects the view that nature is merely a value-free universe. Nature is rich with contextually emergent qualities, including value as an emergent in the interactive context of organisms within nature. Value need not be, nor can it be, reduced to some experienced quality other than itself, for it is among the qualities that pervade our experience within nature.

As seen in the previous chapter, this distinction between valuing and the valuable, between what is satisfying and what is satisfactory, is not an attempt to derive an "ought" from an "is," a value from a fact. There is no fact-value distinction. The occurrence of the immediate experience characterized by value is a qualitative dimension of a situation within nature on an equal footing with the experiencing of other qualitative aspects of nature. Values are as real as all other qualities within nature. Furthermore, any experienced fact within the world can have a value dimension, for the value dimension emerges as an aspect of the context within which the fact functions as value relevant. Indeed, the experience of value is itself a discriminable fact within our world. And valuing gives rise to the valuable through the operation of scientific or experimental method. Moreover, the valuable, what ought to be, is about the enrichment of value, about creative ways of organizing valuing experiences, which will direct activity toward what works in enhancing valuing experiences of all those involved. The entire fact-value problem as it has emerged from the past tradition of moral philosophy is misguided from the start.[14]

The resolution of conflicting moral perceptions, which provides the context for new ideals, cannot be accomplished by appeal to abstract principles or to a moral absolutism, but neither are such resolutions to be evaded because such conflicts are merely expressions of different feelings or because dialogue is closed off by the self-enclosed relativism of each position. While the experience of value arises from specific, concrete contexts shaped by particular traditions, this is neither a relativism nor a subjectivism, for the openness of perspectives, developed in the previous chapter, indicates the way for breaking through to grasp different contexts, to take the perspective of "the other," to participate in dialogue with "the other," and to critically evaluate the very context that gave rise to one's own beliefs. Our moral rules are about ways of organizing and enriching the experience of value as a contextual emergent within concrete situations, and if one is not attuned to the experience of value, then there is nothing for one's moral rules to be about. One cannot debate conflicting moral directives without attunement to the experience of value anymore than one can debate conflicting aesthetic principles of utilizing color in creating works of art if one has never experienced color.

Furthermore, our factual beliefs are not about something brutely given and value free. This view that they are stems directly from the mechanistic view of nature discussed previously. Experience need only be broken down to smaller and smaller units until the real essence is known. In this way, so-called organic systems, having their own emergent qualities, such as persons and societies, are actually mechanistic systems obeying universal laws, all of which are separate from the knower and can be grasped in their brute thereness. Such a view gives rise to the widespread understanding of economic systems as separate from the rest of society and as knowable without entanglement with our knowledge of the larger context in which an economy functions. A disinterested observer can collect the facts of this deterministic, mechanistic system. These facts are brutely there and value free. Thus, economics can be a science in which one collects the facts and determines the mechanistic laws governing them, and avoids the "fuzzy," unscientific realm of values.

However, what we hold as valuable enters into our very perception of the facts. Our judgments about what the facts are, what is acceptable as fact, what evidence we will believe, and what methodology is appropriate to answer questions about a particular part of reality are all influenced by what we hold as valuable. This also enters into an interpretation of the facts, in describing what the facts mean. Various interest groups can arrive at different conclusions from looking at the same set of "facts."

Facts do not just come to us ready-made, announcing their brute givenness. Eventually, human beings have to decide what they accept as a fact and what they believe to be the nature of reality. They have to decide what constitutes adequate evidence and what are valid methodologies so that they will be persuaded that a descriptive claim deserves to be accepted as true and thus labeled as fact. Reality is not merely a given that we can passively absorb but is partly defined by us as we progress in knowledge and understanding. This progression is influenced by values as we make judgments about the facts in building a store of knowledge. Indeed, a proper understanding of scientific methodology in its most general sense as actually practiced by scientists itself rules out such an understanding of fact as brutely given and passively received. The scientist, as seen previously, creatively interprets data, and this creativity is guided by the theory he or she accepts. This creative interpretation, which guides what is seen as fact, is directive of action in the laboratory and must be tested in terms of consequences. Thus, the scientist's observation itself cannot be reduced to brute fact.

Perhaps the relationship between fact and value can be illustrated by some examples. One of the most frustrating areas of controversy affecting business these days is the attempts of medical science to establish the truth of claims about human health. Does smoking cause cancer? Are certain substances used in the workplace dangerous to workers' health? Is dioxin really one of the most toxic substances known? The examples are endless, as debates about health matters and causes of certain illnesses continue. The outcomes of these debates are crucial to business because of the liability involved.

One would think that science could answer these questions conclusively to the satisfaction of all parties, particularly in a society where science is so dominant. But in most of these situations, the facts are never conclusively established, and the debate continues. Business comes up with its studies that show no linkage between a substance and human health, and government comes up with other studies that show such a linkage. Who is right, and which studies should be accepted as the basis of policy?

Several years ago there was a controversy about the safety of ethylene dibromide (EDB), a substance that was widely useful in fumigating grain milling machinery, as a bulk fumigant in grain storage bins, and as a soil fumigant by the citrus industry.[15] Studies began to be conducted that showed EDB appeared to induce cancer in laboratory animals, and on the basis of these studies and its own analysis of EDB's risk to human health, the Environmental Protection Agency (EPA) eventually banned all uses of EDB and ordered grain products to be removed from grocery shelves that contained what were considered to be harmful residues of the substance. Many reputable scientists, however, disputed the implications of these studies and argued that the results of animal studies could not be extrapolated to humans and that there were no credible studies connecting cancer in humans to trace elements of EDB in food products.[16]

The smoking controversy has been going on for some years now and is a terribly complex situation, involving all sorts of people and institutions, and all kinds of conflicting claims and values. We have moved more and more toward a smoke-free society in the past several years, but there are many unanswered questions involved in the controversy. The discovery that secondhand smoke could have harmful health effects on innocent parties changed the nature of the issue and has led to all sorts of restrictions on where smokers can practice their habit. The Tobacco Institute, however, keeps claiming that no one has proven conclusively that smoking causes cancer because many people who smoke do not get cancer, and not everyone who has cancer has smoked. Thus, it is obvious, so they claim, that there is not a one-to-one correlation between smoking and cancer and, thus, smoking does not necessarily cause cancer.

While technically they may be right, the question is whether or not anyone really cares if it has been proven conclusively that smoking causes cancer. The Tobacco Institute seems to live in a cause-and-effect world, an abstraction from the world in which most of us live and experience. We live in an uncertain, probabilistic world where increasingly it is known that most complex issues of this nature cannot be proven conclusively by science or any other method. However, common-sense experience strongly suggests that smoking is related to cancer in some fashion, and what is most relevant to people's concerns is knowing what the probability is that they will get cancer if they smoke or inhale secondhand smoke.

Could it be that such controversies are not solely about the facts but are also questions of value? The values we hold about smoking as a human activity enter into our judgments about the validity of scientific evidence and influence what we accept as the facts about this question. These values reflect our interests, financial and nonfinancial, that we have in the question of smoking. Do we own stock in a tobacco company? Do we work for such a company? Do we gain a great amount of satisfaction from smoking? Has one of our relatives died of cancer? All such interests are reflected in our values as they relate to a specific activity such as smoking and its relation to certain possible effects.

In the EDB case, the EPA had the authority to make the decision about continued use of the substance, basing its decision on its judgment about the validity of certain studies and their implication for the risk humans faced from continued exposure to the substance. Its decisions about what the "facts" were in this situation reflected its mission to protect human health and the conservative values inherent in its decision-making process. If business organizations had been making the decision, they undoubtedly would have questioned the validity of animal studies and interpreted the risks involved in a much different fashion, reflecting the values of business as a profit-making institution.

Most of the facts about our complex world with its manifold complex organically integrated systems of interrelations are disputable and changing. They are no more brutely objective and absolute than the values we hold. Descriptions of ethical reasoning processes stating that to make an ethical decision involves gathering value-free facts about the situation do not recognize this complexity. It is precisely the facts that are often in dispute, and how this dispute is resolved reflects the values of the disputants. The way most of these situations work is that evidence begins to mount against a substance such as asbestos or dioxin, such that it becomes apparent to most people that the substance is harmful. But no one study is definitive in this regard, and we are never certain in a factual sense that the substance is harmful enough to warrant drastic measures. Arguments for and against the taking of drastic measures embody conflicting interpretations of the relevance and significance of the data stemming from conflicting value-laden contexts. This contextual dependence of facts upon the frameworks within which they emerge as relevant is continuous with the understanding of the scientific method as described previously.

Conversely, evidence as to what the facts are influences what we hold as valuable. For years we did not pay much conscious attention to our environment and used it as a gigantic waste dump for disposing of our waste material. We did not value our environment very highly and polluted it so badly that our quality of life was affected. Then we began to learn how important our environment was to us; we began to learn about ecosystems and how our pollution was disrupting such systems on which human life depended. In a matter of a few short years, our values relative to the environment changed dramatically because of additional evidence of what was happening to the environment, and the nation began to devote a great deal of attention to cleaning up pollution. When we began to learn more about our environment and the nature of ecosystems, we changed our values and came to believe the environment was worth spending money on in order to preserve human life and promote a higher quality of life in the world. Our value-laden choices result in bringing about new interpretations of reality, and these interpretations give rise to new values and new possible choices among them.

All of this is meant to suggest that what we believe about the world and what we value are intertwined in manifold ways. So-called "facts" about the world cannot be reduced to values any more than values can be reduced to facts. But neither can they be so neatly separated as some philosophers, and especially those who claim to study business and social issues in a "scientific" way, would have us believe. They are not separate, so that facts are objective and absolute, and values are subjective and relative. Both facts and values emerge as wedded dimensions of complex contexts, which cannot be dissected into atomic bits or reduced to mechanistic laws to show relationships. We need to be more aware of where the factual dimensions of a problem are relevant to advance our knowledge and enlighten our discussion, and where the evidence about something is well enough known that we can focus our efforts on the values that lead to diverse views and recommended courses of action, thus making an intelligent decision on the basis of what is believed to promote human welfare and human fulfillment and lead to an enrichment of the human experience.

The problem for most of us is not that we are unethical but that we are ethically ignorant. We do not know how to argue value questions intelligently, and we do not know how to recognize the complex value dimensions that pervade all situations. So we hide our ignorance behind more empirical studies and so-called value-free–oriented activities, which actually further confuse the issue. If a decision is necessary, we eventually make it, but probably on grounds that are more political in nature rather than on a conscious view of the "good" in relation to the particular area under consideration. We avoid enacting, or even stating, what we think "ought to be" because it is hard to justify such statements and have them accepted as more than just mere opinion. We are victims of our narrow scientific and empirical outlook, which lets us avoid moral responsibility by hiding under the security blanket of statistics and supposed objective, value-free facts about the world.

Moral disagreements can be resolved only by engaging in open and honest dialogue about what kind of world we want to live in and what we believe constitutes human fulfillment. Hiding behind either a bogus scientific or moral authority does nothing to promote this dialogue. No one knows any absolute truth, but we can search for better versions of the truth if we engage in human discourse with our fellow human beings. We should not let scientific and technical people resolve questions of value under the guise of dealing with "factual" information. Nor should a moral authority be imposed on the situation by applying principles that are supposedly developed in the realm of pure thought separated from experience. The development of normative principles is guided by experience just as empirical studies are guided by values.

We must deal with value and ethical questions explicitly and debate them on both philosophical and empirical grounds. The process approach to moral reasoning being presented in this book will hopefully take the dialogue and debate about normative versus empirical business ethics beyond the dead ends too often offered by traditional alternatives. This process approach does not accept the traditional alternatives offered, nor does it bounce between them, but presents a different philosophical way of looking at humans and the moral situations in which they are enmeshed in a way that undercuts or renders irrelevant many of the traditional dichotomies.

Perhaps this framework takes away the sense of clarity and security offered by some of the old ways of thinking. Perhaps one feels that instead of providing a way of dealing with moral issues that gives us some "safety" and allows us to put problems to bed, what has been offered is something that makes what once seemed safe, the value-free facts and mathematical statistics, appear more fuzzy, less secure, or more threatening. Must we be accountable and responsible everywhere we turn? Is there no point at which we can just stick to facts and absolve ourselves of moral responsibility? Is there no way in which we can at least fall back on some moral rule and absolve ourselves of responsibility when we must make a moral decision? The answer is, of course, "no." Recognizing this is the beginning of understanding business from a moral perspective.

Questions for Discussion

1. What is the difference between normative and empirical business ethics? Why is this a problem for the relevance of ethics to business problems? What are the different approaches that have been taken to try to resolve this distinction?

2. Describe the fact-value distinction. What is the difference between an "is" and an "ought"? What is the difference between the subjective and the objective, the relative and the absolute? Are these all different ways of saying the same thing?

3. How does a process approach to business ethics based on pragmatic philosophy undercut some of these distinctions? What is the difference between scientific content and scientific method? What are the implications of this difference for the fact-value distinction?

4. How are facts and values related? How do facts come about? What role do values play in the determination of facts? How do the examples presented in the chapter illustrate this process? What implications does this view have for business organizations and the decision-making process in these organizations?

Endnotes

[1] William C. Frederick, "Are SIM and Business Ethics Different Fields?" Paper presented at a Joint Session of the Society for Business Ethics and the Social Issues in Management Division of the Academy of Management, Dallas, Texas, August 14, 1994, p. 2.

[2] Linda Klebe Trevino and Gary E. Weaver, "Business ETHICS/BUSINESS Ethics: One Field or Two?" *Business Ethics Quarterly,* Vol. 4, no. 2 (April 1994), pp. 113–114.

[3] Ibid., pp. 116–117.

[4] Ibid., pp. 120–121.

[5] Gary E. Weaver and Linda Klebe Trevino, "Normative and Empirical Business Ethics: Separation, Marriage of Convenience, or Marriage of Necessity?" *Business Ethics Quarterly,* Vol. 4, no. 2 (April 1994), pp. 129–141.

[6] Bart Victor and Carroll Underwood Stephens, "Business Ethics: A Synthesis of Normative Philosophy and Empirical Social Science," *Business Ethics Quarterly,* Vol. 4, no. 2 (April 1994), pp. 145–155.

[7] Patricia H. Werhane, "The Normative/Descriptive Distinction in Methodologies of Business Ethics," *Business Ethics Quarterly,* Vol. 4, no. 2 (April 1994), pp. 175–179.

[8] Thomas Donaldson and Thomas W. Dunfee, "Toward a Unified Conception of Business Ethics: Integrative Social Contracts Theory," *Academy of Management Review,* Vol. 19, no. 2 (April 1994), p. 254.

[9] Tom L. Beauchamp, *Philosophical Ethics: An Introduction to Moral Philosophy* (New York: McGraw-Hill, 1982), pp. 345–352.

[10] Mortimer J. Adler, *Ten Philosophical Mistakes* (New York: Macmillan, 1985), pp. 119–120.

[11] Gilbert Harman, *The Nature of Morality: An Introduction to Ethics* (New York: Oxford University Press, 1977), pp. 66–67.

[12] Beauchamp, *Philosophical Ethics,* pp. 34–35.

[13] Richard T. DeGeorge, *Business Ethics,* 2nd ed. (New York: Macmillan, 1986), pp. 34–38.

[14] At least one other author questions the validity of this dichotomy between fact and value or normative and empirical business ethics. The suggestion is made that all of the authors who debate this dichotomy accept as fact that this distinction is valid as a descriptive category. In other words, this distinction is posited as a real one that then needs to be discussed. They overlook the possibility that they have posed a false dichotomy. What such distinctions may represent is merely a sociocultural reality and an institutional history. See William C. Frederick, "The Virtual Reality of Fact vs. Value: A Symposium Commentary," *Business Ethics Quarterly,* Vol. 4, no. 2 (April 1994), pp. 171–173.

[15] See Rogene A. Buchholz, et al., "The EDB Controversy," *Management Responses to Public Issues: Concepts and Cases in Strategy Formulation,* 3rd ed. (Englewood Cliffs, NJ: Prentice Hall, 1994), pp. 100–121.

[16] See Robert Bernstein, "Traces of Pesticide Found in Food Products," *The San Antonio Light,* January 4, 1984, p. 1. See also American Council on Science and Health, *Ethylene Dibromide* (New York: ACSH, May 1984), p. 12.

Suggested Readings

Ayer, Alfred J. *Language, Truth and Logic,* 2nd ed. New York: Dover Publications, 1936.

Brandt, Richard B. *Ethical Theory.* Englewood Cliffs, NJ: Prentice-Hall, 1959.

Ewing, Alfred C. *The Definition of the Good.* New York: Macmillan, 1947.

Foot, Philippa, ed. *Theories of Ethics.* Oxford, England: Oxford University Press, 1967.

Hare, Richard M. *The Language of Morals.* Oxford England: Oxford University Press, 1952.

Harnock, Roger N. *Twentieth-Century Ethics.* New York: Columbia University Press, 1974.

Harrison, Jonathan. *Our Knowledge of Right and Wrong.* New York: Humanities Press, 1971.

Hartland-Swann, John. *An Analysis of Morals.* London: George Allen & Unwin, 1960.

Hudson, W. D., ed. *The Is/Ought Question: A Collection of Papers on the Central Problem in Moral Philosophy.* New York: St. Martin's Press, 1970.

Hume, David. *A Treatise of Human Nature.* Oxford, England: Oxford University Press, 1978.

Ladd, John, ed. *Ethical Relativism.* Belmont, CA: Wadsworth Publishing Company, 1973.

Monro, David H. *Empiricism and Ethics.* Cambridge, England: Cambridge University Press, 1967.

Moore, George Edward. *Principia Ethica.* Cambridge, England: Cambridge University Press, 1903.

Nagel, Thomas. *Moral Questions.* Cambridge, England: Cambridge University Press, 1979.

Ross, William David. *The Right and the Good.* Oxford, England: Oxford University Press, 1930.

Stevenson, Charles L. *Facts and Values: Studies in Ethical Analysis.* New Haven: Yale University Press, 1963.

Warnock, Geoffrey J. *Contemporary Moral Philosophy.* New York: St. Martin's Press, 1967.

Westermarck, Edward. *Ethical Relativity.* Paterson, NJ: Littlefield, Adams & Co., 1960.

S H O R T   C A S E S

Ethylene Dibromide

A major scandal over ethylene dibromide (EDB) erupted in late 1983. The chemical was widely used as a soil fumigant for crops and as a fumigant for citrus and other fruits and vegetables after harvest as well as an antiknock agent in gasoline. It was also used to protect stored wheat, corn, and other grains against destruction by insects and contamination by molds and fungi, and as a fumigant to keep milling machinery free of insects. EDB proved useful to keep grain supplies free from insect fragments, insect excrement, and mold toxins and thus made a major contribution to the safe storage of grain products over extended periods.

Ethylene dibromide (EDB) had been produced in the United States since the 1920s. It was used primarily as a lead scavenger in leaded antiknock gasoline additives. During the 1950s and 1960s, federal pesticide registrations for uses of EDB as a fumigant were granted under the Federal Insecticide, Fungicide and Rodenticide Act (FIFRA). EDB has been registered as a pesticide since 1948, and thus became subject to EPA regulations after the agency was formed and given responsibility for pesticide control.

Eventually the chemical was tested to be an animal carcinogen, linked to cancer and reproductive disorders. Many scientists, however, were confident that the minute levels of EDB found in grain-based products posed no imminent health hazard. Roughly 350 million pounds of EDB were produced annually in the United States of which about 245 million pounds were used domestically. About 230 million pounds (about 93 percent) of this amount was used as an additive in leaded gasoline. The remaining 7 percent, which was about 15 million pounds annually, was used for various agricultural activities.

On September 30, 1983, the EPA ordered immediate suspension of the use of EDB for soil fumigation. Soil fumigation accounted for over 92 percent of the more than 20 million pounds of EDB used annually as an agricultural pesticide. Appeals to this suspension could be made, but use of the product ceased during the appeals process. The

September 30 decision also proposed immediate cancellation of EDB fumigation of stored grain, grain milling machinery, felled logs, and proposed cancellation of quarantine use on citrus and other tropical fruits to control the fruit fly effective September 1984. Minor uses of EDB were retained with added safety precautions and the requirement that applicators be trained and certified. Appeals were made to have administrative hearings for each use the EPA proposed to cancel.

Shortly after the EPA announced its decision to ban EDB, the state of Florida began testing food products for EDB residues. Dr. Stephen King, the state's health officer, decided that if EDB could be detected at a level of one part per billion, the food should not be sold. As a result of this discovery, on February 3, 1984, the EPA administrator, William D. Ruckelshaus, announced the immediate emergency suspension of EDB for use as a fumigant for treating stored grain and milling machinery and recommended residue levels for grain and grain-related products already in the "pipeline" to protect the public from EDB contamination.[1]

Ruckelshaus said that the emergency suspension of EDB use as a grain fumigant will result in the "clearing of EDB from the food pipeline in this country. I firmly believe that the guidelines we are recommending today are fully protective of public health. I expect the residue levels on all grain products will begin to decline almost immediately as a result of the actions we are announcing today. In fact, in the very near future, that rate of decline should become quite pronounced."[2]

The EPA recognized its responsibility to take action at the federal level to deal with EDB residues in a way that would protect public health. The balance between the risks and benefits of EDB usage changed in recent years due to increased concern about potential health effects and the development of alternatives for most major uses of EDB. Based on a detailed evaluation of health effects and economic benefits, the EPA concluded that for all the major uses of EDB as a pesticide, the risks of continued usage outweighed the benefits and thus registrations of EDB for use as a pesticide should be canceled.[3]

1. How could the public be affected by the severe contradictions among the opinions on the health effects of EDB of a large number of respectable scientists and organizations in charge of protecting public health? What might be the consequences of these differences in terms of public trust in scientists and federal agencies?

2. Given the fact that the public has a right to know the truth about the safety of products that it is consuming, particularly if a cancer issue is involved, how much information and what type of information should be disclosed to the public? Are there indisputable facts in a highly complicated controversy such as the EDB situation? Where do values enter into the discussion? To whom should the public listen?

3. Since evidence about EDB was not conclusive and the issue was not clear-cut, could government agencies be blamed for being conservative and being on the safe side? Is it acceptable to say that safety comes first when there is a reasonable doubt about the safety of a product?

4. How should trade associations, the industry in general, and individual companies conduct themselves in this kind of situation? Should there be any self-imposed constraints on promoting and marketing such a substance? What precautions, if any, should be taken? How should responsibilities to stockholders and consumers be weighed?

[1] Office of Public Affairs, United States Environmental Protection Agency, "EDB Facts," Washington, D.C., February 3, 1984, pp. 2–3.

[2] Ibid., p. 3.

[3] Testimony of Edwin L. Johnson before the Senate Committee on Agriculture, Nutrition, and Forestry, Orlando, Florida, January 23, 1984.

Source: Rogene A. Buchholz, *Business Environment and Public Policy: Implications for Management,* 5th ed. (Englewood Cliffs, NJ: Prentice Hall, 1995), pp. 45–46.

Chlorofluorocarbons

Chlorofluorocarbons (CFCs) were invented in the 1930s and became widely used in a variety of products because they were chemically stable, low in toxicity, and nonflammable. They became the leading heat transfer agent in refrigeration equipment and air-conditioning systems for buildings and vehicles. They were used in the manufacture of various kinds of foam, including building insulation. And they were used as solvents and cleaning agents in semiconductor manufacturing and other businesses. CFCs were once widely used as propellants in aerosol containers, although they were banned for this use in the United States several years ago, while in Europe and Japan they continued to be used for this purpose.

Du Pont became the world's largest manufacturer of CFCs, receiving $600 million in 1987 in revenues from this business. Du Pont was the only firm that produced CFCs in all three major markets that included the United States, Europe, and Japan. In 1985, Du Pont produced 882 million pounds of CFCs in these three markets, with 706 million pounds being produced in the United States alone. U.S. sales of CFCs peaked in 1973, when concern began to develop about depletion of the ozone layer. Aerosol uses accounted for about half of CFC consumption in the United States, and when this use was banned in 1978 because it was a nonessential use of the product, consumption of CFCs fell by 50 percent. Sales began climbing slowly back toward mid-1970 levels as more uses were found and demand in nonaerosol sectors grew.

As concern about CFCs and their role in depleting the ozone layer mounted, Du Pont led producers and users in opposing CFC regulation, citing scientific uncertainty as the primary reason for this opposition. In the absence of regulation, CFC use was expected to grow at about the level of GNP in the industrialized world, and somewhat faster in developing countries. All of these forecasts changed with the signing of the Montreal Protocol in 1987, where virtually all of the world's industrial nations agreed to cap production. The countries that signed the protocol could decide for themselves how to allocate production among CFC compounds and among producers, subject to an overall ceiling for each country that was expressed in terms of ozone depletion potential.

While opposing regulation because of scientific uncertainty, Du Pont also made a public promise to change its position if the scientific case against CFCs should solidify. Subsequent findings led Du Pont to change its position. The company stated that "it would be prudent to limit worldwide emissions of CFCs while science continues to work to provide better guidance to policymakers."[1] But only international action would be effective, the company argued, because unilateral action by the United States would provide an excuse for other nations to delay regulating their own producers. Thus, Du Pont supported ratification of the Montreal Protocol.

The issuance of the NASA Executive Summary Report on ozone depletion caused the company to reassess its position again. This report described a fundamental change in the scientific understanding of the CFC-ozone connection. It presented hard evidence of reductions in stratospheric ozone concentrations over temperate populated regions as well as Antarctica, firmly established the link between CFCs and ozone depletion, and suggested that implementation of the Montreal Protocol would result in little net depletion of ozone and that continuing ozone decreases were expected even if the protocol were implemented.

Soon after this report was released, Du Pont decided to stop production of CFCs altogether. Because of difficulties in developing substitutes and obtaining regulatory approval to produce them, this exit would be phased in over a ten-year period. But by 1999, when the protocol would require a cutback to 50 percent of 1986 levels, Du Pont planned to stop manufacturing regulated CFC compounds entirely. The company received widespread accolades for this announcement, while competitors either kept silent, or commented that they were still reviewing the evidence and were not at all sure that such drastic action was warranted.

1. Did Du Pont do the right thing with regard to this controversy? Did it act responsibly to shareholders? Why did Du Pont decide to do more than the protocol actually required? What was their decision based on?

2. How should companies deal with controversies of this nature? Are international solutions necessary for these kinds of global environmental problems? What role can companies play in bringing about such international agreements?

[1] Forest Reinhardt, "Du Pont Freon® Products Division," in Rogene A. Buchholz, Alfred A. Marcus, and James E. Post, *Managing Environmental Issues: A Casebook* (Englewood Cliffs, NJ: Prentice Hall, 1992), p. 281.

Source: Rogene A. Buchholz, *Business Environment and Public Policy: Implications for Management,* 5th ed. (Englewood Cliffs, NJ: Prentice Hall, 1995), pp. 646–647.

Bioengineered Foods

A whole new area of concern for consumers arose in the early 1990s as bioengineered foods began to appear on the market. Products such as sweeter tomatoes, longer-lasting peppers, leaner pork, and healthier cooking oils, all bioengineered with these characteristics, posed problems for consumers and regulators. Critics were concerned about the possible adverse effects these products would have on the environment and on human health. The biotech industry asked for clarification as to the manner in which food additive regulations would be applied to bioengineered products. The government issued guidelines for these products in May 1992 by stating its concerns extended only to food from plants and did not affect biotechnology research involving meat, poultry, fish, or dairy products.[1]

With regard to plants, the FDA intended to invoke its power to regulate food additives only if a totally new substance was added to the food or if the composition of the food had been altered enough to raise safety concerns. In other words, if a new substance is introduced, such as a sweetening agent that did not exist before, or if an existing substance were significantly increased, then marketers must obtain Food and Drug Administration approval. Otherwise, marketers would be spared from having to obtain approval for each and every genetically engineered product.[2] There was a good deal of concern in some circles that these guidelines were not stringent enough to protect consumers and the environment.

1. Do these guidelines seem sufficient enough to protect consumers from unknown hazards with regard to bioengineered foods? Should they be more stringent? What additional safeguards should be provided? Is the regulatory process capable of responding to these concerns? Can the market alone adequately protect consumers from any adverse health effects?

2. Many people are opposed to the introduction of bioengineered foods in the marketplace, citing safety and health concerns. How should the marketing of these foods be accomplished? Should they be marketed to a small segment of the public before being introduced more widely, and should these people be monitored for any adverse health effects? Should these products be clearly labeled so consumers can avoid them if desired?

[1] Bruce Ingersoll, "New Policy Eases Market Path for Bioengineered Foods," *The Wall Street Journal,* May 26, 1992, p. B1.

[2] Diane Duston, "Food Tests Not Required for Gene-Altered Crops," *Times-Picayune,* May 27, 1992, p. A-4.

Source: Rogene A. Buchholz, *Business Environment and Public Policy: Implications for Management,* 5th ed. (Englewood Cliffs, NJ: Prentice Hall, 1995), pp. 398–399.

Carbon Dioxide Emissions

Global warming is said to occur because trace gases, such as carbon dioxide, form a shield around the earth to trap the infrared rays of the sun and prevent them from escaping into space. They thus act like a greenhouse in trapping heat, leading to increases in the earth's temperature. Scientists agree that there has been an increase in the trace gases emitted into the atmosphere over the past several decades, and further increases are expected. There is also general agreement that the earth has warmed over the past several years, but the critical question is whether or not there is a connection between increases in trace gases and warming of the earth. Such warming could be the result of natural causes, as the earth has warmed and cooled throughout history.

If the earth warms significantly, many low-lying coastal areas would be flooded because of rising sea levels from melting of the polar ice caps. Temperate zones would also move further north, resulting in massive dislocations of people, plants, and animals.

Your company is a utility in the Midwest that emits carbon dioxide into the atmosphere. There is concern in the company about carbon dioxide emissions, but because of the uncertainty surrounding global warming, the company is afraid to spend money to reduce these emissions. There is also no guarantee that other companies would do the same. Thus, the company could be spending a good deal of money that would have no real effect on global warming.

1. How should companies deal with this kind of issue? Are they able to respond on their own, or is there a need for some kind of regulations that would make all companies meet the same standards? Can companies do anything to help reduce the uncertainty? Where do values enter into their understanding of the situation and the determination of their responsibilities?

2. How should companies weigh their responsibilities to shareholders and the society at large in these kinds of situations? Should they initiate actions to deal with the problem or wait until governments act to formulate regulations? What can they contribute to the discussion about the "facts" regarding global warming?

CHAPTER 5

The Market System and Business Organizations

Now that the basic foundations for a process approach to business ethics have been established, this section will focus on a discussion of business and its relation to society. The nature of this relationship needs to be dealt with before turning to specific ethical problems facing business organizations. These problems arise out of the relationships business has with its major constituencies, be they employees, customers, or other groups of people or individuals who interact with the corporation, and are largely a function of the systems that have evolved over time, which prescribe the roles business is to play in society. These systems, including the market system and public policy, constitute the way in which our society is organized to provide itself with certain kinds of goods and services that people need to survive and grow in terms of human enrichment.

The market is believed to be, according to classical economic theory, the principle means by which modern Western societies organize themselves to provide goods and services people need to live and enhance their economic welfare. The market system is usually considered to be an economic system where economic wealth is created and where economic growth is promoted based upon private ownership of the means of production. The role of the corporation in this kind of system is to produce goods and services people need and want to materially enhance their lives, pay dividends to shareholders who in theory are the owners of the corporation, provide employment for people who choose to work for corporations, pay taxes to the government, and perform other economic functions that are considered to be appropriate for such an entity in the market system. In this manner, the corporation creates wealth and distributes it throughout society so people can buy the goods and services the corporation produces.

Every society has to make decisions about what to produce as far as goods and services are concerned, and in what quantities the goods and services shall be produced.

Decisions also have to be made about how the goods and services that are produced shall be distributed in the society. In a market-oriented society, these decisions are made by individuals acting in their own self-interest, so it is held, and the market aggregates these individual decisions into a collective demand schedule that faces corporations. These productive mechanisms then have to meet the preferences of individual consumers who express their values by the decisions they make about the purchase of products and services that are available in the marketplace.

Thus, business organizations do not function in a vacuum but instead are part of a larger system where business activity is connected to the society as a whole and is made to serve its economic purposes. Business activity is guided by a so-called invisible hand to do what society wants done as far as production of goods and services is concerned. A corporation cannot just do as it pleases; it must be sensitive to consumer tastes and preferences so that it produces something people are willing to buy, and it must try to better the competition to make a product that can be sold at a price people are willing to pay. In this way the business can make a profit and continue in operation.

In a socialistic society, these decisions are made by a planning agency, or perhaps one should say a government bureaucracy, based on some scientific or quasi-scientific assessment of the needs of people as weighed against other needs of the society for military goods and services. The demand schedule that faces productive organizations is put together through a bureaucratic mechanism rather than a free market, and factories are given quotas to meet as far as production of goods and services is concerned. While consumers still have a choice to make relative to the purchase of the available goods and services, these choices do not affect the kinds of goods and services that are available nor the quantities that are produced. The distribution principle is from each according to one's ability and to each according to one's needs, and prices set by the bureaucracy are supposedly consistent with this principle.

These systems haven't worked out very well in practice, and recent years have seen a wholesale abandonment of socialistic systems across Eastern Europe and the former Soviet Union in favor of some kind of market system. The socialist system in these countries degenerated into a kind of state-run economy where the bureaucracy that made economic and political decisions made sure its needs were adequately taken care of while the rest of the population suffered in relative poverty. Members of the bureaucracy had special stores in which to shop that not surprisingly were well stocked, and they were able to have second homes in some of the better vacation spots in the country in which they lived. The self-interest principle apparently was alive and well in socialistic countries, and played itself out in ways that were not very productive for the society as a whole.

In a free market society, at least in theory, self-interest is harnessed to serve the social good, as the energies people expend in the pursuit of their own interests are coordinated by the market mechanism to create economic wealth for the society as a whole. Thus, the market system, as far as a moral justification is concerned, is given a utilitarian justification in that the greatest good for the greatest number of people is produced through the pursuit of self-interest. The fact that socialist systems have been abandoned in recent years gives ample testimony to the superiority of market systems in producing a greater economic product for the citizens of a society to enjoy than socialistic systems. It seems rather clear that socialistic systems were held together more by force than by the consent of the people. Once that force was removed or at least was less of a threat, revolution seemed to be inevitable.

Elements of the Market System

The market system could be discussed as a whole, as is done in most literature, by describing its operation in allocating scarce resources for the production of goods and services. But it seems that our purposes would be better served by taking a more analytical approach and breaking a concept like the market down into various conceptual elements that make up the whole, so that a more detailed picture can be obtained of the way in which decisions are made through a market mechanism. This procedure allows for some interesting comparisons to be made between the working of the market system and the public policy process, which will be described in a later chapter. Exhibit 5-1 lists the key elements of the market system that will be discussed from the standpoint of traditional market theory.

THE EXCHANGE PROCESS

At the heart of a market system is an exchange process where goods and services are traded between the parties to a particular transaction. In a strictly barter type of situation where money is not used, goods and services are exchanged directly for other goods and services. Where money is present, it serves as an intermediate store of value in that goods and services are exchanged for money and then the same money can be used to purchase other goods and services immediately or some time in the future. Money has little or no value in and of itself, but it is valued for what it represents and what it can purchase. The use of money greatly facilitates exchange over a barter type of economy and greatly increases the number of exchange transactions that are possible.

Thus, in the market system, all kinds of exchanges between people and institutions are continually taking place. People exchange their labor for wages and salaries, and in turn exchange this money for goods in a retail establishment or for services they cannot or do not wish to provide for themselves. Investors exchange money for new stock or bond issues in a corporation, which exchanges this money for purchases of raw materials or new plant and equipment. Farmers exchange their produce for money, which may be used to buy new farm machinery or seed for the next planting.

Decisions as to whether or not to exchange one thing for another are made by individuals and institutions acting in their own self-interest as defined by them and based on the particular value they attach to the entities being exchanged. That is, people decide

EXHIBIT 5-1 Key Elements of the Market System

Exchange Process
Private Goods and Services
Economic Value System
Self-Interest
The Invisible Hand
Economic Roles (Producers–Consumers–Investors–Employees)
Consumer Sovereignty
Profits as Reward
Business as the Major Institution
Operating Principles: Efficiency, Productivity, Growth

whether or not the item they want is of sufficient value to warrant the sacrifice of something they already have that is of value to them. Exchanges will not normally take place unless there is an increase of value to both parties of the exchange. The exchange process is usually a positive sum game as both parties believe themselves to be better off as a result of the exchange.

Based on these individual decisions in the market, then, resources are allocated according to the preferences of individuals for one kind of merchandise over another, one job over another, the stock of one corporation over another, and so forth across the entire range of choices the market offers. Thus, the values assigned to particular goods and services and the decisions that result with respect to the allocation of resources for the production and distribution of these goods and services are made through an exchange process.

PRIVATE GOODS AND SERVICES

The nature of the goods and services that are exchanged is a second element of the market system. These goods and services are private in the sense they can be purchased and used by individual persons or institutions. They become the private property of the persons who obtain them and are of such a nature that they do not have to be shared with anyone else. The goods and services exchanged in the market are thus divisible into individual units and can be totally consumed and enjoyed by the people or institutions that obtain the property rights to these goods and services.

Thus, one can buy a house, a car, or a piece of furniture, and these items become one's property to enjoy and use entirely in one's own self-interest. People can also contract for or purchase services and have a legal right to expect that the services will be provided. The legal system supports this concept of property rights and enables people to enforce these rights if necessary to protect their property from unwanted encroachment by others. This social arrangement provides a degree of security for people regarding their own property and forces them, in turn, to respect the property rights of others. Thus, property rights can be assigned to the goods and services traded in the market because of their divisibility into individual units that can be privately owned and consumed.

COMMON ECONOMIC VALUE SYSTEM

The value of all these entities that are exchanged in the market system is able to be expressed in common units that stem from an underlying economic value system. The worth of an individual's labor, the worth of a particular product or service, and the worth of a share of stock can all be expressed in economic terms. This is not to suggest that the fundamental value of everything is economic in nature. One person might value a particular piece of residential property because of the view it commands of the surrounding countryside, thus making the aesthetic value of the property of primary concern. Another person might desire a particular art object because of its religious value in reminding that person of certain events that are important in the history of the religion to which he or she belongs. But, in order for exchange to take place where money is involved, these other values eventually have to be translated into economic values.

This economic value system thus serves as a common denominator in that the worth of everything can be expressed in a common unit of exchange, such as dollars and cents in our society. The terms on which an object can be acquired in the marketplace reflect the collectivization of subjective evaluations of the worth of that object to many different people. This fact facilitates the exchange process and makes it possible for individuals to assess trade-offs much more easily than if such a common denominator were not available. People can make an informal benefit-cost analysis when making a decision in the marketplace by comparing the benefits a good or service will provide with the costs involved in acquiring the product or service. People enter a store, for example, with money they have earned or will earn and assess the price of the goods available by comparing the benefits these goods will provide to the real costs (the effort involved in earning the money) of obtaining them. Since both sides of this benefit-cost equation are expressed in the same units, this assessment can be made rather easily.

This common value system allows a society to allocate its resources according to the collective preferences of its members. All the diverse values that people hold in relation to private goods and services are aggregated through the market system into a collective demand schedule. If a particular product is not valued very highly by great numbers of people, aggregate demand for that product will not be very high and its price will have to be low in order for it to be sold, if it can be sold at all. Thus, not many resources will be used for its production and it may eventually disappear from the market altogether.

Depending on general economic conditions, if a particular job is valued very highly by society and the people who can perform the job are scarce relative to demand, the wage or salary paid to perform the job will have to be high to attract people to perform the job. Resources are thus allocated according to the values of society as expressed through the exchange process. Resources will go where the price, wage and salary, and return on investment are highest, all other things being equal, and are thus allocated to their most productive use where they can be combined to produce the greatest wealth for society in comparison with other alternatives.

SELF-INTEREST

People are free in a market economy, according to traditional theory, to use their property, choose their occupation, and strive for economic gain in any way they choose, subject, of course, to limitations that may be necessary to protect the right of all people to do the same thing. Society may also place limitations on the use of property and choice of occupation because of moral standards or because of other reasons that are believed to be important enough to override market forces. The selling of drugs, for example, is illegal, even though there is a huge market for them in most countries. The same is true for other uses of property for purposes that are not seen as contributing to the welfare or real wealth of society. A strict libertarian approach to the use of property, however, would oppose these latter types of restrictions.

The pursuit of self-interest is assumed to be a universal principle of human behavior, with a powerful advantage, as far as motivation is concerned, over other forms of human behavior. The pursuit of one's own interest is believed to elicit far more energy and creativity from human beings than would the pursuit of someone else's interests, especially under coercive conditions. Not only is it difficult to determine what the interests of other people are, in most cases; it is also difficult to find a way to sustain a high level of motivation if much of the effort one expends goes for the benefit of other people.

The definition of self-interest in a market economy is not provided by government for all its citizens but by each individual participating in the exchange process. If the self-interest of an individual were defined by someone else, the concept would have no meaning. Thus, self-interest is an individual concept. Yet, within a market system, the definition of self-interest is not completely arbitrary, depending on the whims of each individual. The existence of a common underlying economic value system makes the definition of self-interest take on a certain economic rationality.

If one is engaged in some aspect of the productive process, economic rationality dictates that self-interest consists of maximizing one's return on his or her investment. Entrepreneurs are expected to maximize profits, investors to maximize their returns in the stock market, and sellers of labor are expected to obtain the most advantageous terms for themselves. On the consumption end of the process, consumers are expected to maximize satisfaction to themselves through their purchases of goods and services in the marketplace. If one were to seek the lowest return on investment or the least satisfaction from goods and services, this would not be viewed as rational behavior under normal circumstances, and one might be a candidate for a mental health clinic if such an irrational pursuit of self-interest persisted.

THE INVISIBLE HAND

Resources are allocated in a market system by an invisible hand, which is something of a mythological concept, but one that is a crucial element of a market system. There is no supreme authority in government such as a planning commission that makes decisions for the society as a whole about what goods and services get produced and in what quantities, and allocates resources accordingly. These decisions are made by the individuals who participate in the marketplace and express their preferences as based on their self-interest. These preferences are aggregated by the market and, if strong enough relative to particular goods and services, elicit a response from the productive mechanism of society to supply the goods and services desired.

The invisible hand consists of the forces of supply and demand that result from the aggregation of individual decisions by producers and consumers in the marketplace. Resources are allocated to their most productive use as defined by these individuals collectively. According to Adam Smith, society as a whole benefits more from this kind of a resource allocation process than if someone were to consciously try to determine the best interests of society. Pursuit of one's own selfish ends, without outside interference, is believed to result in the greatest good for the greatest number of people. Thus, the market system is given a utilitarian justification as far as ethics is concerned.

> As every individual, therefore, endeavors as much as he can both to employ his capital in the support of domestic industry, and so to direct that industry that its produce may be of the greatest value; every individual necessarily labours to render the annual revenue of the society as great as he can. He generally, indeed, neither intends to promote the public interest, nor knows how much he is promoting it. By preferring the support of domestic to that of foreign industry, he intends only his own security; and by directing that industry in such a manner as its produce may be of the greatest value, he intends only his own gain, and he is in this, as in many other cases, led by an invisible hand to promote an end which was no part of his intention. Nor is it always the worse for the society that it was no part of it. By pursuing his own interest he frequently promotes that of the society more effectually than when he really intends to promote it.[1]

ECONOMIC ROLES

The marketplace requires certain roles to be performed in order for it to function. All of these roles have an economic character to them. People can be producers who take raw materials and give them utility by producing something that will sell on the market, consumers who buy these goods and services for their use, investors who provide capital for the producers, or employees who work for producers and receive wages or salaries in exchange for their contributions to the production process. All of these roles are vital to the functioning of a market system. They are called economic roles because people are thought to be pursuing their economic self-interest in performing them. There are other important roles to be performed in society, of course, but economic roles are by and large dominant in a society organized around free market principles, where people spend most of their time pursuing economic interests.

CONSUMER SOVEREIGNTY

The most important economic role in a market system, however, is supposedly performed by the consumer. At least in theory, consumers, through their choices in the marketplace, guide the productive apparatus of society and collectively decide what goods and services get produced and in what quantities. When there is enough demand for a product, resources will be allocated for its production. If there is not enough demand, the product will not be produced and resources will go elsewhere.

Consumer sovereignty is not to be confused with consumer choice. In any society, consumers always have a choice to purchase or not purchase the products that confront them in the marketplace. Consumer choice exists in a totally planned economy. But consumer sovereignty implies that the range of products with which consumers are confronted is also a function of their decisions, and not the decisions of a central planning authority. Thus, consumers are ultimately sovereign over the entire system.

There are those who would argue that consumer sovereignty in today's marketplace is a fiction, that consumers are manipulated by advertising, packaging, promotional devices, and other sales techniques to buy a particular product. Sometimes this manipulation is said to be so subtle that the consumer is unaware of the factors influencing his or her decision. Thus, the demand function itself, so it is maintained, has come under control of corporations and consumer sovereignty is a myth. Producers are sovereign over the system, and consumers are made to respond to the producers' decisions about what to produce.[2]

While there may be some truth to these views, they do not constitute the whole truth. It is hard to believe that consumers are totally manipulated by these techniques. They still have to make choices among competing products, and the producers selling these products are all trying to manipulate the consumers. In the final analysis, the individual consumer is still responsible for his or her decision, and undoubtedly many factors besides the particular sales techniques employed by a company influence the purchase decision. In the absence of a central authority making production decisions for the entire society, it is safe to assume that some degree of consumer sovereignty exists. As long as there are competing products or acceptable substitutes, some products may not sell well enough to justify continued production. Thus, they disappear from the marketplace, not because producers desire to remove them, but because consumers have decided not to buy them in sufficient quantities.

PROFITS AS REWARD

The reason products disappear when they do not sell is because there is no profit to be made. Profits are the lifeblood of a business organization, and without profits, a business organization normally cannot survive. Profits are a reward to the business organization or entrepreneur for the risks that have been taken in producing a good or service for the market. If the management of a business organization guesses incorrectly and produces something people do not want and cannot be persuaded to buy, the market is a stern taskmaster, as no rewards will be received for this effort. Thus, the product will be removed from the market.

Profits are also a reward for combining resources efficiently to be able to meet or beat the competition in producing a product for which there is a demand. Some entrepreneurs may be able to pay lower wages or employ a more efficient technology or have some other competitive advantage. Thus, a lower price can be charged and high-cost producers are driven from the market. This effort is rewarded with increased profits as society benefits from having its resources used more efficiently.

BUSINESS AS THE MAJOR INSTITUTION

The major institutional actor in the market system is the business organization that is driven by the profit motive to produce goods and services to meet consumer demand. This is not to suggest that business is the only institution that is producing something useful for society. Hospitals provide medical services and governments produce a wide range of goods and services for citizens. But these other institutions are not driven by the profit motive as business is and cannot offer the full range of goods and services that business can when functioning in a market economy. The business organization is the primary productive institution in a market economy, and most of the decisions about the allocation of society's resources for the production of private goods and services are made by the business institution.

OPERATING PRINCIPLES

The primary operating principles that are used to measure performance in a market system are concepts such as efficiency, productivity, and growth. These are basic concepts to the operation of a market system and are given a specific economic meaning in order to judge performance. There are quantitative measures for these concepts, and while they may be imprecise in many respects, these measures at least provide some idea as to how well the market system is functioning. If economic growth is declining or negative, for example, the economy is judged to be functioning poorly, and policy measures are taken to try and correct this deficiency. These principles are thus crucial to the operation of a market system, and good performance along these dimensions of efficiency, productivity, and growth helps a great deal to make market outcomes acceptable to society.

Ethics and the Market

The question of the way in which ethical concerns relate to the market system is an interesting one that bears on the way we view business organizations and their ethical responsibilities. The so-called traditional view on this question assumes that there is and can be no divergence between the operation of a successful business organization in a market context and ethical behavior on the part of that organization. Such a divergence cannot exist because ethics is subsumed or totally contained in terms of marketplace performance. What is considered to be ethical is exactly the same as what is considered to be good business in a competitive process. The ethical notion that forms the basis of this view is the principle of economizing. A business organization is formed to provide goods and services that people in a society are willing to buy at prices they can afford. In order to do this successfully, business must economize in the use of resources—combine resources efficiently—so that it can earn profits to continue in business and perhaps even expand into new markets.

The ethical performance of business is thus tied up with marketplace performance. If a business organization is successful and earns a satisfactory level of profits, this means that the business has economized in the use of resources, assuming that competition exists in the markets it is serving. The business has produced something people want to buy, and has done so in such a way that it has met the competition. Successful performance in the marketplace is ethical behavior, and there is no divergence between being ethical and being successful in the marketplace. Successful business performance and acceptable ethical behavior are believed to be one and the same thing.

The traditional view was stated some years ago by a management theorist by the name of Oliver Sheldon, who strongly advocated the development of a professional creed for management in the closing chapter of his book on management.[3] Sheldon believed that the managerial function was a constant factor in any industrial organization no matter what external forces exist or the nature of the economic system in which the organization operates. The function of management remains much the same under any set of external conditions and is that element charged with guiding the organization through periods of change. Management is the one stable element in the process of evolution. There is no structure or system where management does not fulfill approximately the same functions as under the present system in this country.

Because management was such an important factor in modern societies all over the world, Sheldon thought it was important to develop a managerial creed, to devise a philosophy of management or a code of principles that is "scientifically determined and generally accepted," which will act as a guide for the daily practice of the profession.[4] Without such a creed, says Sheldon, there can be "no guarantee of efficiency, no hope of concerted effort, and no assurance of stability."[5] Such a creed, in other words, can help to establish the legitimacy of the managerial function and ensure its continuity.

Sheldon's creed links the managerial function to the well-being of the community of which it is a part, and encourages management to take the initiative in raising the general ethical standards and conception of social justice that exists in the community. The goods and services produced by a company "must be furnished at the lowest prices compatible with an adequate standard of quality, and distributed in such a way as directly or indirectly to promote the highest ends of the community."[6] Such a statement calls for management to be responsible and ethical in relation to broader community interests. Management is encouraged to look beyond the bottom line and the interests of stockholders to be concerned about what could be called the public interest. The creed recognizes that management serves at the discretion of society and derives its legitimacy from being a useful social function, a theme found in modern social responsibility literature.

But what are the interests of the community, at least as Sheldon sees them? A close reading of the creed shows that it is based on the ethic of economizing, that the primary concern of management, according to Sheldon, is to promote the efficient use of resources, both personal or human resources and capital or material resources. The primary focus of the creed is on economic utilization of the factors of production, which can be determined by scientific principles. Thus, the community is presumably interested in an efficient use of resources in order to increase its standard of living. Management thus derives its legitimacy from applying scientific principles in running corporate organizations to accomplish this objective.

> Industry exists to provide the commodities and services which are necessary for the good life of the community, in whatever volume they are requested . . . . It is for Management, while maintaining industry upon an economic basis, to achieve the object for which it exists by the development of efficiency—both personal or human efficiency, in the workers, in the managerial staff, and in the relations between the two, and impersonal efficiency, in the methods and material conditions of the factory.[7]

There is no mention in the creed about what is now called the social responsibilities of management. While Sheldon recognizes the importance of certain aspects of the external environment, such as government, public attitudes, foreign trade, and so on, social issues are not mentioned. Perhaps it is not fair to criticize Sheldon for this omission, as his creed only reflects the times in which he wrote. Problems such as pollution, equal opportunity, occupational safety and health, and other social issues were not generally recognized as serious problems that needed attention in those years. However, a more modern statement of the same view by Milton Friedman, who engages in the debate about social responsibility, argues that the social responsibility of business is to increase its profits.[8] In other words, the social and ethical responsibilities of business are exhausted in terms of marketplace performance. As long as business performs its economizing function well, it has fulfilled its social and ethical responsibilities and nothing more need be said.

Another characteristic of this view exists in the method Sheldon advocates to make the creed specific and develop a set of standards to guide managerial practice. These standards, according to Sheldon, can be determined by the analytical and synthetical methods of science. The aim of those who are practicing the management profession should be to develop a "science of industrial management," which is distinct from the technique of any particular industry.[9] Yet if management is truly a science, and the practice of management can be circumscribed by a set of scientific principles, what need is there for a philosophy of management or a professional creed for management? In this view, management becomes nothing more than the application of scientific principles to concrete situations. It involves no consideration of responsibilities to the larger community outside of marketplace behavior or any conscious ethical reflection that is a part of a true professional activity.

Thus, the traditional view of ethics and business subsumes ethics under marketplace performance and does not necessitate any conscious ethical considerations of business's responsibilities to society other than successful economic performance. Ethics is totally captured by the notion of economizing, which can be promoted by the development of scientific principles related to an efficient combination of resources. One advantage of this view is that it does at least place ethics at the core of managerial behavior and makes ethics central to the performance of the management function. The disadvantage of this approach is that it removes any need for conscious ethical reflection on the part of management, but leaves it for the management scientists and economists to develop guidelines and principles that promote efficiency.

Problems with the Market

There are many problems with this approach to ethical behavior in relation to markets. For one thing, markets are not perfectly competitive and do not function as economic theory would have us believe. There are many problems with competition in the real world that have to be dealt with in order to keep the system going. Market systems also enshrine property rights at the expense of human rights to safety and health and equal opportunity, for example, problems that are dealt with by legislation and regulation. Finally, there is difficulty with the way externalities such as pollution and other environmental problems are treated in a market system.

COMPETITION

The ideal form of competition is pure competition, where the industry is not concentrated, where there are insignificant barriers to entry, and no product differentiations exist. In this kind of competitive system, the firm has no other choice but to meet the competition, since buyers and sellers are so small that they have no influence over the market, thus ensuring that the forces of supply and demand alone determine market outcomes. In this kind of context, competition will cause resources to be allocated in the most efficient manner, thus minimizing the cost of products and benefiting the consumer.

In practice, completely unregulated markets tend toward concentration, as competition in any industry is never perfectly balanced. If the object is to win out over competitors, as is true in a market system, the natural expectation is that eventually one or a few firms will come to dominate their industries because they were better competitors or were lucky enough to be in the right place at the right time with the right products. Thus, most industries in today's economy are oligopolistic, containing a few large firms that recognize the impact of their actions on rivals and therefore on the market as a whole. In an oligopolistic system, firms deal with each other more or less directly and take into account the effect of their actions on each other. What they do depends very much on how their rivals are expected to react. Oligopolistic firms adjust prices in response to changing market conditions or to changes introduced by rivals in the industry.

Modern large corporations are not simply passive responders to the impersonal forces of supply and demand over which they have no control. These large firms do have some degree of economic power and some influence in the marketplace. Economic power can be understood as the ability to control markets by the reduction of competition through concentration. Thus, markets may fail if the dominant firms in an industry are allowed to engage in collusive actions to maintain prices or interfere with the workings of supply and demand and the price mechanism in some other fashion. For these reasons, the society saw fit to establish antitrust laws to deal with this problem of concentration.

The purpose of these antitrust laws is to limit the economic power of large corporations that can control markets by reducing competition through concentration. The role of government is to maintain something called a "workable competition" on the theory that resources are allocated more efficiently and prices are lower in a competitive system than one dominated by large corporations. Workable competition refers to a system where there is reasonably free entry into most markets, no more than moderate concentration, and an ample number of buyers and sellers in most markets. The government accomplishes this goal by enforcing policies that deal with the size of corporations and the structure of the industries in which they function.

The competitive process is thus not a natural mechanistic process that maintains itself indefinitely. It is not some mechanistic process that automatically holds the economic power of atomic corporations in check through forces that are beyond the control of any economic actor. Rather, competition is something that the community strives to maintain because it is a community-held value, one that the community views as essential for the enhancement of its welfare. The realization of this value is an achievement of society, not a naturally given fact embedded in a certain kind of economic system.

Furthermore, competitive behavior tends to sink to the lowest common denominator in an unregulated market system. If the object is again to win in terms of market share or profits or some other economic indicator, there is always likely to be one or more competitors that will engage in predatory or anticompetitive practices to destroy the competition in an effort to emerge as the sole victor. If these unethical practices do allow the perpetrator to succeed, these practices will have to be engaged in by all competitors if they are to stay in business and compete successfully.

For example, suppose a competitor begins to mislead the public in its advertising as to the health benefits its product provides and gains a larger market share as a result of this strategy because the public believes its claims and has no way of sorting out the truth regarding its advertising. Then all competitors will have to engage in the same kind of misleading advertising to stay competitive, and will have to tout the health benefits of their products and most likely exaggerate these claims to counter the effects of the advertising being done by their competitors. The conduct of the companies involved will then sink to the lowest common denominator, as ethical behavior is not necessarily rewarded in an unregulated market system.

Thus, the government passes regulations related to truth in advertising and food labeling to deal with this situation. The antitrust laws also deal with corporate conduct in addition to structure and promote fair competition by making certain forms of anticompetitive practices such as price fixing and price discrimination illegal. These practices, if allowed to continue, could eventually destroy the system and destroy trust in the fairness of competition.

The business community itself has a common interest in keeping the competitive game going. No matter how strongly various members of this community may object to specific legislative and regulatory requirements and decisions by the courts, they all hold the common value of maintaining a competitive system and doing what is necessary to keep the game going. They have no interest in letting the game degenerate into a free-for-all where anything goes and the system eventually is destroyed. Determining what is necessary to keep the game going is an ongoing, experimental enterprise involving the entire society.

PROPERTY RIGHTS

The market system is also based on the assumption that property rights override all other rights, and that people's right to use their property in their best interests takes precedence over other human rights related to safe workplaces, equal opportunity, safe products, and other such human concerns. The owners of capital or their representatives should be able to hire whom they please, produce products that have whatever level of safety they deem appropriate, and provide for the safety and health of their work force in whatever ways they please. If these concerns are consistent with earning profits, then they are likely to be given consideration. If they are not, human rights are subservient to property rights, and any interference by some external force to see that human rights are respected interferes with an efficient allocation of resources.

The market is based on a libertarian view of justice in that people should be free to use their property to advance their own interests, and concerns for social justice are of no importance. Thus, if the market system produces vast inequalities in income and wealth, these are considered appropriate if they are the result of an efficient use of property. This view of the market is consistent with the utilitarian justification given by Adam Smith, for a utilitarian view of ethics is indifferent concerning the way in which the good is distributed, as was seen in an earlier chapter. The total good produced is what is important, not how it is distributed.

This emphasis on property rights causes problems when other groups in society begin to assert their rights, such as rights to be treated equally in the workplace with respect to hiring and promotion decisions, rights of consumers to safe products, rights of workers to hazard-free workplaces, and rights of employees to know when managers are considering closing of plants, to name only a few. Thus, over the past several years, these human rights, as they are called, have taken precedence over property rights, and there have been continual clashes over these rights that are difficult to resolve. There are also continual debates in our society over the scope and extent of entitlement programs that redistribute wealth in our society.

EXTERNALITIES

Finally, when it comes to externalities such as environmental problems, the market does not respond very well if left to its own devices. The term *externality* is often used to refer to this condition and generally means that a third party who is not involved in the exchange is unintentionally harmed. The consenting parties to the transaction are able to damage the third party without compensating it; thus, the exchange does not adequately reflect the true costs to society. If a river is polluted and the fish are unsafe to eat and the water unsafe to swim in because of transactions between producers and consumers who have an interest in the lowest prices possible and want to dump environmental costs onto someone else, third parties who may not have been involved in any transactions with the producers have to pay the costs in that they may not be able to fish in the river anymore and swimming may be prohibited because it is unsafe.

There is no way the value of the environment or any of its components can be determined through a market process, since there is nothing to be exchanged. People cannot take a piece of dirty air, for example, and exchange it for a piece of clean air on the market, at least given the current state of technology. Some might want to argue that certain environmental goods could be provided through marketplace transactions. Suppose, for example, the market offered a consumer a choice of two automobiles in a dealer's showroom that are identical in all respects, even as to gas mileage. The only difference is that one car has pollution-control equipment to reduce emissions of pollutants from the exhaust while the other car has no such equipment. The car with the pollution-control equipment sells for $500 more than the other.

If a person values clean air, it could be argued that he or she would choose the more expensive car to reduce air pollution. However, such a decision would be totally irrational from a strictly economic point of view. The impact that one car out of all the millions on the road will have on air pollution is infinitesimal—it cannot even be measured. Thus, there is no relationship in this kind of a decision between costs and benefits—one would, in effect, be getting nothing for one's money unless one could assume that many other people would make the same decision. Such actions, however, assume a common value for clean air that doesn't exist. Thus, the market never offers consumers this kind of choice. Automobile manufacturers know that pollution-control equipment won't sell in an unregulated market.

Moreover, there is another side to the coin. If enough people in a given area did buy the more expensive car so that the air was significantly cleaner, there would be a powerful incentive for others to be free riders. Again, the impact of any one car would not alter the character of the air over a region. One would be tempted to buy the polluting car for a cheaper price and be a free rider by enjoying the same amount of clean air as everyone else and not paying a cent for its provision. Thus, there is kind of a double-whammy effect on the ability of a market mechanism to respond to environmental concerns that renders it ineffective as far as externalities are concerned.

Some call this inability of market systems to respond to environmental pollution and degradation as market failure, but to use this term is not entirely accurate. Market systems were not designed to factor in environmental costs and it is not fair to blame the system for not doing something for which it was not designed. Property rights are not appropriately assigned as regards the environment, and nature often lacks a discrete owner to look after its interests. The rights of nature can be violated by market exchanges, and as a common property resource, nature can be overused and degraded as it is subject to the tragedy of the commons.

Environmental degradation and pollution are external to normal market processes and are not taken into account in the price mechanism unless these costs are determined by some other process and imposed on the market system. The market system by itself cannot determine the value of the environment and determine the price of clean air or the value of preserving a particular piece of wilderness area in its natural state. These decisions have to be made through some other process and imposed on the market system in order for these values to be internalized and reflect themselves in market decisions. The ecological functions of environmental entities have no value as far as the market is concerned. It is only their economic utility or instrumental value that is of importance in a market economy.

Market systems evolved to serve human needs and wants; they are not constructed to protect the environment. The environment is treated as a source of raw materials to be used in the production process and as a bottomless sink in which to dispose of waste materials. The environment has no value in and of itself, but it is only worth something as it can be used to serve some human purpose such as enhancing living standards through the creation of more and more economic wealth. Market systems are limited in their scope and cannot be used to determine the value of the environment or any of its components.

A tree in the Amazon rainforest, for example, has no value as far as its ecological function is concerned. It only has value in Western market societies as it is cut down to be used for lumber, or left standing because it may be economically beneficial as far as providing nuts and fruits is concerned. Or perhaps, economic decision makers can be convinced that the tree has value because it is a rare species that may eventually have some kind of medicinal value in providing a cure for disease. But its ecological value in terms of providing the world with a carbon sink and contributing to the diversity of plant life in that part of the world has no economic value. From a strictly economic point of view, the tree has no value in its natural state and must be cut down and made into something useful or left standing as long as it is seen as productive in some other sense.

The same is true of wetlands, which cover vast areas of some parts of the world, both along coastal areas and inland. These wetlands perform valuable ecological functions that we are only now beginning to understand, yet from an economic point of view they only have value because they contain resources that can be exploited or because they can be filled in to provide land area for residential or commercial development. Most people probably consider wetland areas as wasteland and fail to appreciate the valuable ecological functions they perform in terms of providing a habitat for fish and other forms of wildlife and acting as water reservoirs to prevent flooding, just to mention a few.

The Market as a Social Process

Our traditional understanding of the market system and how it works, as described on the previous pages, is based on the assumption of the atomic individual acting in its own interests, and an assumption that the market acts in a mechanical fashion to provide for people's needs and wants. The market is based on an individualistic conception of human beings, as people are expected to act as individual or atomic units in expressing their preferences in the marketplace, preferences which are then aggregated into demand schedules facing corporations. The marketplace is seen as nothing more than some mechanical process that performs this coordination function through the forces of supply and demand so that business organizations know what to produce and in what quantities. Competition is seen as some sort of mechanical regulator that puts constraints on individual egos and prevents business organizations from attaining a monopoly position in which competition could not perform its proper function.

The market system, however, is a social system and not only an economic system, as many people spend the greater part of their lives working for corporations or some other economic entity and spend another major portion of their lives in stores shopping for goods and services. The market provides the context in which much of our social life takes place, and provides the means for many of our social interactions. These social relations are based upon economics as we spend a great deal of time producing and consuming economic wealth and playing the roles of producers and consumers, or employees and investors in corporate entities. Other roles such as parents and citizens are not given an economic value, and are not seen to be as important as our economic activities when viewed in a market context. But such a view is a distortion of their true importance in society as a whole.

When market societies came into existence, they replaced the traditional social systems that had been in place and had served to prescribe roles and functions of people. Economic activity had always been subordinated to the social system and was merely a part of a larger social reality that provided for social interactions and gave people a sense of identity and belonging. But market systems and the market principle took over, so to speak, and became social systems in and of themselves, and other aspects of social life became subordinated to market duties and roles. The market itself became the principal manner in which society organized itself, and the roles of producer and consumer along with other economic roles became the primary roles in society.[10]

Other parts of the social world such as family, church, and the like have had to adapt themselves to economic life, which is the primary driving force in our society. Most of the important decisions we have to make are economic in nature. The primary wealth of our society is economic. And the dominant roles we play are economic in nature. All of which is to say that the economy and the way in which we provide ourselves with goods and services have become the dominant concern for the majority of the population in a market-oriented society. The market organizes our activities and provides us with a motivation to do what the market requires.

The emergence of laissez-faire capitalism thus turned human and social relations around and altered the relationship of humans with nature. Whereas in earlier times economic relations were embedded in and secondary to their broader social context, market systems actually embedded social relations into the economic system. The evolution of market-oriented societies occurred through the transformation of nature, humans, and capital, the so-called factors of production, into fictitious economic commodities that can be bought and sold on the market. While such a fictionalizing as economic elements of things that are fundamentally social ushered in a period of production of goods and services never before experienced, it also set loose forces that caused social, political, and environmental dislocation of an unparalleled nature.[11]

The economy, however, cannot be so neatly separated from nor absorb the rest of society. The economic system is fully woven into the fabric of society as but one dimension, inseparable from others, of the sociocultural matrix in which we act out our day-to-day behavior. Indeed, from the process perspective developed in previous chapters, the very idea of the economic system as discussed above, far from being a reality engulfing the social, is a product of the fallacy of giving to a discriminatable dimension of the richness of concrete existence, an existence that is inherently social and value laden in all sorts of noneconomic ways, a supposedly independent status. This mistake results from making a discriminatable aspect within concrete social existence the causal mechanism of social existence. The problem with the foregoing market approach is that "the market," the "economic system," ultimately cannot even stand on its own conceptually, much less in reality, for to isolate it in this way for purposes of analysis severs it from the very context that makes it intelligible as a discriminable force in society. To fully explore the implications of this view, it will be necessary to first discuss changing views regarding the relationship of business to society, and then turn to a discussion of public policy and its role in society.

Questions for Discussion

1. What are the key elements of a market system? How is a market system differentiated from a socialistic system of economic organization? What problems exist in using a common economic value system to evaluate the worth of goods and services traded in the market? Can the "true" worth of goods and services be determined in this manner? What advantages are inherent in this process?

2. Define the concept of self-interest. Do you believe self-interest is a universal principle of human behavior? How does one determine what is in his or her self-interest? Are there any

other kinds of "interests" that motivate people? Can self-interest be differentiated from these other kinds of interests?

3. Does consumer sovereignty exist in our modern economic system? What evidence can you find that would help support your answer? What research would be relevant to answer this question? If consumers are not sovereign, who determines what goods and services are to be produced in society? What moral issues are raised by this question?

4. How can judgments be made as to whether or not the market system is working properly? What measures are relevant to answering this question? What other information would be useful in this regard? What assumptions are made in choosing criteria to make these judgments? What are the moral implications involved in these determinations?

5. What is the traditional view regarding the relation of ethics and markets? Is this view realistic in today's economy? What other approaches would you recommend? Where do moral issues come into play in the workings of a market economy? Are these issues being discussed in today's world?

6. What does it mean to say the market is a social process? How does this view differ from the traditional economic view of the market? Can the economy be separated from the rest of society? What kind of a philosophical system would allow for a more holistic view of the economy and its function in society? What moral implications are involved in this issue?

Endnotes

[1] Adam Smith, *The Wealth of Nations* (New York: Modern Library, 1937), p. 423.

[2] See, for example, John Kenneth Galbraith, *The New Industrial State* (Boston: Houghton Mifflin, 1967).

[3] Oliver Sheldon, *The Philosophy of Management* (London: Sir Isaac Pitman & Sons, Ltd., 1923), pp. 280–291.

[4] Ibid., p. 284.

[5] Ibid.

[6] Ibid., p. 285.

[7] Ibid., pp. 285, 286. Quoted by permission of Pitman Publishing, London.

[8] See Milton Friedman, "The Social Responsibility of Business Is to Increase Its Profits," *New York Times Magazine,* September 13, 1970, pp. 122–126.

[9] Sheldon, *The Philosophy of Management,* p. 290.

[10] See Karl Polanyi, *The Great Transformation* (Boston: Beacon Press, 1944).

[11] Robert H. Hogner, "We Are All Social: On the Place of Social Issues in Management," in *Contemporary Issues in Business and Society in the United States and Abroad,* Karen Paul, ed. (Lewiston, NY: Edwin Mellen Press, 1991), p. 8.

Suggested Readings

Ayres, Clarence E. *The Theory of Economic Progress.* Chapel Hill: University of North Carolina Press, 1944.

Block, Walter, et al., eds. *Morality of the Market.* Vancouver, British Columbia, Canada: The Fraser Institute, 1985.

Etzioni, Amitai. *The Moral Dimension.* New York: The Free Press, 1988.

Gauthier, David P., ed. *Morality and Rational Self-Interest.* Englewood Cliffs, NJ: Prentice-Hall, 1970.

Goudzwaard, Bob. *Capitalism and Progress.* Grand Rapids, MI: William B. Eerdmans Publishing Co., 1979.

Kornai, Thomas S. *The Road to a Free Economy.* New York: W. W. Norton, 1990.

Mirowski, Phillip. *Against Mechanism.* Totowa, NJ: Rowman and Littlefield, 1988.

Polanyi, Karl. *The Great Transformation.* Boston: Beacon Press, 1944.

Reddy, William H. *The Rise of Market Culture.* Cambridge: Cambridge University Press, 1987.

Steidlmeier, Paul. *People and Profits: The Ethics of Capitalism.* Englewood Cliffs, NJ: Prentice Hall, 1992.

Zohar, Danah. *The Quantum Self.* New York: Quill/William Morrow, 1990.

SHORT CASES

Standard Oil Company

The early history of the Standard Oil Company provides a very good example of corporate growth using the methods of combination, consolidation, and vertical integration, which so many U.S. companies followed in subsequent years. Standard Oil was one of the very first companies to dominate an industry by using these methods, and pioneered in creating new legal and administrative forms. It invented the trust device, which made it possible for a single business to hold stock in a number of companies in many different locations. This legal consolidation permitted administrative centralization, which rationalized the production facilities under the trust's control.[1]

The petroleum industry that emerged after the Civil War was characterized by numerous small firms competing vigorously in an "anything goes" atmosphere. The result was a wildly fluctuating market where there were perennial imbalances between supply and demand. These imbalances caused both producers and refiners to seek ways of stabilizing their positions. Voluntary efforts at cooperation such as informal agreements fell apart under the pressures of competition. It took a John D. Rockefeller to successfully analyze and manipulate this situation in order to gain control of the whole industry and mitigate competitive pressures.[2]

With the collapse of the National Refiners Association in 1872, which was created to control price and production in the oil industry, Rockefeller and his associates decided to bring a large part of the oil industry directly under their control. The trusteeship device allowed Rockefeller and his associates to set up separate companies in several states with a central legal entity to direct the entire combination. The Standard Oil Trust Agreement of 1882 established such a trust to be the sole and central holding agency for all the securities of 41 participating investors in 40 named companies. This agreement vested the original nine trustees (a third of whom were to be elected annually) with centralized administrative control over the operating companies, including the buying, transportation, storing, refining, and marketing of petroleum.[3]

Standard Oil thus grew into a multimillion-dollar integrated industrial enterprise dominating its industry for many years. Standard Oil was the first enterprise to take this route and become a modern industrial business corporation by creating a structure that allowed administrative centralization over a vast empire.[4] Eventually the federal government found Standard Oil guilty of violating both sections one and two of the Sherman Antitrust Act of 1890, which had been passed by a Congress concerned about use of the trust device to create huge industrial empires. It was believed that competition was disappearing as a regulator of business behavior as more and more combinations were taking place in several industries, and that the country needed a law that gave the government power to break up those combinations that were especially onerous in order to protect the public and preserve a competitive system. Standard Oil was found guilty of creating a conspiracy to restrain trade and of attempting to monopolize an entire industry. The trust was ordered to be dissolved into several separate companies.[5]

1. Does competition always work out best in terms of using resources efficiently and effectively? Was Standard Oil doing society a favor by trying to rationalize the industry and reducing waste and inefficiencies? Or was the Standard Oil Trust nothing more than a conspiracy against society?

2. What are the ethical issues in this kind of incident? Should companies be punished for being successful and controlling an industry? Does government need antitrust laws to preserve the competitive system? Is unregulated competition self-destructive?

[1] Alfred D. Chandler, Jr., and Richard S. Tedlow, *The Coming of Managerial Capitalism: A Casebook on the History of American Economic Institutions* (Homewood, IL: Irwin, 1985), p. 344.

[2] Ibid., p. 346.

[3] Ibid., pp. 358–359.

[4] Ibid., p. 369.

[5] Irwin M. Stelzer and Howard P. Kitt, *Selected Antitrust Cases: Landmark Decisions,* 7th ed. (Homewood, IL: Irwin, 1986), p. 9.

Source: Rogene A. Buchholz, *Business Environment and Public Policy: Implications for Management,* 5th ed. (Englewood Cliffs, NJ: Prentice Hall, 1995), pp. 69–70.

The Forgotten Dumps

The Pinelands National Reserve covers parts of seven counties in southern New Jersey. The reserve is a million-acre wilderness of prime forests, cedar swamps, tidal creeks, and cranberry bogs.[1] Beneath the reserve lies the pristine waters of the Cohansey Aquifer, said to be the largest on the East Coast. The aquifer contains about 17 trillion gallons of water, which is the equivalent of a 2,000-square-mile lake with a uniform depth of 37 feet.[2] This aquifer supplies drinking water for much of South Jersey, as well as supporting the region's fragile wetlands ecology, its blueberry and cranberry industries, and its coastal estuaries.[3]

Because it was remote and sparsely populated, the Pinelands was also popular as a dumping ground for toxic wastes. In 1984, the region contained at least seven industrial lagoons and 43 known landfills, 17 of which have been closed since 1980 by order of the Pinelands Commission or the State Department of Environmental Protection. From 1976 to 1979, 60,000 gallons of hazardous chemicals were spilled in the Pinelands—either deliberately or accidentally—in 41 separate incidents. Eventually, these wastes began to cause serious groundwater contamination problems and threatened the pristine quality of the water.[4]

Tests conducted through 1984 concluded that groundwater at more than a dozen sites in the Pinelands contained contaminants, but that pollutants had not spread beyond the immediate areas of those dumps. If the dumps were not cleaned up soon, the pollutants were expected to spread to other areas, particularly if large amounts of water were pumped from the aquifer to supply other cities. The groundwater movements caused by this pumping could disperse the contaminants now concentrated near the dump sites.[5]

Two abandoned chemical dumping sites surfaced during 1979 in the center of the Pinelands within the headwaters of the Wading River used to irrigate the many cranberry bogs in the Pinelands. Piles of rusted drums were strewn about each of the sites, and puddles of colored liquids were visible. The dumps were closed in the early 1960s, but odors of chemicals lingered in many sections of the dumps that were potent enough to give a visitor a slight headache.[6] The nearest home was more than a mile away, so there was little fear of a public health danger. The most severe threat was initially believed to be to cranberry production, which was the biggest industry in the area. Cranberries are not known to be particularly sensitive to water quality, and the impact on the cranberry bogs was not immediately known.

Samples of the chemicals found at the site were sent to the State Department of Environmental Protection for analysis. Scattered throughout one of the sites were patches of an asphaltlike substance that was found to contain carcinogens such as benzene, dimethylphenol, and other similar substances. More than 30 other chemicals were also found in various areas of the site. Groundwater tests indicated that if pollution had entered the ground, it had not yet spread to adjacent areas. At the other site, there were standing trenches of drum-laden water that were oddly colored and thickly coated with sticky tar along the bottom. One of the wells at this site was found to contain concentrations of several different agents, some of which were known toxins, and many of which were suspected of being carcinogenic. Thus, groundwater below the site was believed to be highly contaminated, but the contaminant plume was not detected in off-site wells. However, the Cohansey Aquifer is only 30 to 40 feet below the surface in that area and runs very deep.[7]

The chemicals were believed to have originated with the 3M Company and Rohm and Haas as well as the Hercules Company. None of these companies owned or operated the sites, but it was believed that waste material from the 3M plant in Bristol Township and a Rohm and Haas plant in Bristol, Pennsylvania, were dumped at the sites.[8] These firms indicated that Mr. Rudy Kraus of Industrial Trucking in Bucks County was hauler and operator of the sites. Mr. Kraus hauled wastes from their plants over a ten-year period beginning in 1950 and ending in the 1960s. Identification of the companies involved in dumping at the sites was important to the Department of Environmental Protection's investigation because these companies would be in the best position to know what was buried there and have the expertise to help neutralize whatever dangers exist.[9] Thus, the first step in cleaning up these dumps was to notify the potentially responsible parties requesting information on the types and quantities of wastes sent to the Woodland sites.

The 3M Corporation received a letter dated July 19, 1983, from Mr. John F. Dickinson with the Office of Regulatory Services in the Department of Environmental Protection of the state of New Jersey. The letter was addressed to Mr. Lewis W. Lehr, chairman of the board and chief executive officer of 3M Corporation. The letter indicated that the company had utilized the services of Rudolph Kraus to haul waste material from its plant in Bristol Township in Pennsylvania to the Routes 72 and 532 Woodland Township dumpsites. The letter stated that testing of the sites had disclosed that the soil and groundwater had been substantially contaminated by hazardous chemical compounds leaching from the disposed material.[10]

The letter mentioned that the sites sit directly on top of the Cohansey Aquifer and at the headwaters of the Wading River, which was stated to be the source of irrigation waters for the numerous cranberry farms in the area. In order to undertake remedial action at the sites, Mr. Dickinson asked 3M to supply the state of New Jersey with information about its disposal operations, including the types and quantities of waste placed with Mr. Kraus for disposal. The company replied to this letter and stated that a review had been made of files and records regarding operations at the 3M plant in Bristol, but that no records had been found pertaining to the disposal sites in Woodland Township. Nonetheless, the company did put together some information based on the recollections of former 3M employees. The types and quantities of waste were estimated based upon the product mix manufactured during the time Mr. Kraus would have hauled wastes from the Bristol plant.[11]

The letter mentioned that the company understood that the organic liquid waste was burned to facilitate recovery of the drums. These drums were sold to junkyards for scrap. The letter mentioned that the company would cooperate with the state of New Jersey regarding this matter. A copy of the letter went to Mr. Brian Davis, senior attorney with the Office of General Counsel for 3M Corporation. It mentioned a meeting that would be held with Mr. Dickinson on September 20 of that year.

The New Jersey Department of Environmental Protection (NJDEP) did call a meeting in Trenton for all the potentially responsible parties (PRPs), which at that time included three major dischargers, two minor dischargers, one transporter/operator, and two landowners. The NJDEP stated its concern about the potential environmental effects of waste material discharged at the sites, and called for the PRPs to conduct an investigation and begin remedial action to clean up the sites. If the PRPs did not do so, the NJDEP would carry out this action itself and seek treble damages from the PRPs under the provisions of the Spill Compensation and Control Act. The PRPs agreed to cooperate with the state and requested time to meet and prepare a response to the state's request.

1. What threats do toxic waste dumps pose for the environment and human health? Why were these threats not apparent when the dumps were first created? What happened to change perceptions regarding the disposal of toxic waste material?

2. Why didn't companies keep records of what waste material they disposed of and in what quantities? What ethical responsibilities did they have to dispose of their waste material safely? Were there any market incentives for them to pay attention to waste disposal?

[1] Marc Duvoisin, "The Tainting of the Pinelands' Most Precious Resource," *The Philadelphia Inquirer,* January 16, 1984, p. 4-B.

[2] Brett Skakun, "Chemical Dumps Found in Pines," *Atlantic City News,* April 29, 1979, p. 1.

[3] Duvoisin, "Tainting of the Pinelands," January 16, 1984, p. 4-B.

[4] Ibid.

[5] Ibid.

[6] Skakun, "Chemical Dumps," April 29, 1979, p. 1.

[7] Ralph Siegel, "Two Dumps in Woodland Pushed for Superfund Aid," *Burlington County Times,* November 19, 1982, p. 1.

[8] Siegel, "Two Dumps," November 19, 1982, p. 1.

[9] Tony Muldoon, "Pine Barrens Breeze Could Be Lethal," *Camden Courier-Post,* April 27, 1979, p. 3.

[10] Letter from John F. Dickinson, Office of Regulatory Services, Department of Environmental Protection, State of New Jersey, July 19, 1983.

[11] Letter from Russell H. Susag, Director, Environmental Regulatory Affairs, 3M Corporation, St. Paul, Minnesota, September 1, 1983.

Source: Rogene A. Buchholz, et al., *Managing Environmental Issues: A Casebook* (Englewood Cliffs, NJ: Prentice Hall, 1992), pp. 130–140.

Advertising at Better Foods

The Better Foods Corporation had been producing a cereal that tasted good and was nutritious for children as well as adults. When first introduced, the product captured a significant share of the market and had held this market share for several years. The company did not tout the health benefits of its cereal because of regulations that prevented companies from making such claims. Thus, its advertisements stressed the taste features of the product as well as other characteristics such as crispiness that might appeal to consumers.

When the government relaxed restrictions on making health claims, the company's competitors began to tout the benefits their cereals had on cholesterol levels as well as other areas of health that were of concern to consumers. The companies knew many of these claims were misleading to consumers because they implied that eating regular amounts of the cereal would have such health benefits. Actually, consumers would have to consume prodigious amounts of cereals to receive any such benefits. But consumers were not made aware of this fact and were beginning to be influenced by all the hype about health benefits of these cereals.

Better Foods Corporation experienced its first drop in market share in several years because of this new type of advertising. As an employee in charge of the advertising program, you have been asked to come up with a new advertising campaign that will stress the nutritious aspects of the company's product. This assignment puts you in something of a bind, as you find some of the outrageous claims being made by your competitors offensive from a moral standpoint. Yet, if you don't do the same, the sales of your company's product may continue to decline and your job itself may be in jeopardy.

1. What is the purpose of advertising in a free market society? Are there minimum standards of honesty that should be adhered to, or are advertisers free to do whatever the market will bear? How can consumers tell the outrageous health claims from honest ones so they can make a reasonable decision?

2. What advertising strategy should Better Foods adopt? Should it follow the lead of its competitors? Could it point out the misleading advertising its competitors are doing? Should it advertise more honestly and take the moral high ground even if it leads to a further decrease in sales?

Moving Superior Products

Your company, Superior Products, Inc., is facing increasing competition from overseas companies that can produce their products with cheaper labor and less stringent environmental standards. These factors give these companies a competitive advantage that is becoming increasingly difficult to overcome. The company has mounted a vigorous advertising campaign stressing the superiority of its product line and the advantages of buying from U.S. companies, but it is beginning to lose market share because the price differential is too great to overcome by these means.

Consumers are getting more and more price conscious and are willing to accept a little less quality for a cheaper product. Something has to be done, or the company will become less and less competitive and may have to close its doors. Management is considering moving most of its manufacturing facilities to another country where labor costs are lower and environmental standards are less stringent. This move would obviously have a severe impact on employees who have worked for the company for many years and on the communities where plants are located.

You are asked to draw up a plan for building plants in other countries and have already visited several potential sites where the company could build plants and find a readily available labor pool. You are in a moral quandary and find that you hate your job more and more because of the implications of what you are doing and what the company is contemplating. Yet you also have to face facts and realize that if the company doesn't do something, it may have to close its doors anyhow and its stockholders will take a bath because of foreign competition.

1. What other alternatives might the company have besides moving to another country? Are any of these alternatives feasible? What are companies to do in the emerging global economy where competition is worldwide and consumer loyalty is difficult to maintain?

2. What are the ethical issues in these kinds of situations? What does the company owe to its long-time employees who have stuck with it through good times and bad? What does it owe to the community? Can the company just pick up and leave with no moral responsibility to other stakeholders?

CHAPTER **6**

Business
and Society

While not everyone adhered to the traditional view of business and the marketplace and accepted the notion that business was solely an economic institution with only economic responsibilities, it does seem that this view of business and its relationship to society was the prevailing view in our society for several decades. And as long as the system worked well enough for most people, there were not likely to be any serious questions raised about the ethical behavior of business outside of the marketplace context. Questions about the ethical behavior of business were largely limited to issues such as fraud and deception, conflicts of interest, and other ethical problems that were seen to interfere with the proper workings of the market.

It was with concern over the social responsibilities of business that serious questions began to be raised about the traditional view of business and its relationship to society and the view of ethics and business embedded in a marketplace orientation. The problems that social responsibility advocates addressed, such as pollution and unsafe workplaces, were in large part created by the drive for efficiency in the marketplace. Thus, it began to be argued that there was a divergence between the performance of business in the marketplace and its performance as far as the social aspects of its behavior were concerned, and a gap began to develop between the social expectations of society and the social performance of business.

Many people began to believe that cleaning up pollution, providing safer workplaces, producing products that were safe to use, promoting equal opportunity, and attempting to eliminate poverty in our society had something to do with promoting human welfare and creating the "good life" in our society. Yet business was causing some of these problems and perpetuating others in its quest for an efficient allocation of resources. For example, by economizing in the use of resources and disposing of its waste material as cheaply as possible by dumping untreated wastes into the water, business was causing some serious pollution problems regarding the quality of the water. By always hiring the best qualified person for a job opening and not having some kind of an affirmative action program, business was helping to perpetuate the effects of discrimination against minorities and women.

It was at these points of intersection between the economic performance of business and changing social values of society that questions of social responsibility and ethics began to arise. Business increasingly came to be viewed as a social as well as an economic institution that had social impacts that needed to be considered by management. Social responsibility advocates strongly argued that management needed to take the social impacts of business into account when developing policies and strategies, and much effort was devoted to convincing management to take its social responsibilities seriously. A great deal of research was done to help management redesign corporate organizations and develop policies and practices that would enable corporations to respond to the social expectations of society more effectively and measure their social performance.

The deficiencies of the traditional view of the marketplace began to be exposed. It became clear to many that there were many points of divergence between good business performance and what society expected of its business organizations in terms of social and ethical behavior. An ethical creed based on the traditional view, such as the one proposed by Sheldon, did not include these social aspects of corporate activities and did not encourage management to pay attention to the social impacts of corporate operations. Thus, it provided no means or rationale for management to internalize the social costs of production and left this task to government regulation, a social control mechanism that is generally unacceptable to management as well as inefficient in many of its aspects.

While Sheldon wanted to see management in a broader social and ethical context, he ended up being a victim of his own scientific outlook, which was atomistic, mechanistic, and reductionistic. This outlook is not sufficient in and of itself to provide an ethical or moral philosophy for management. Such a philosophy no longer can be built solely on the notion of economizing, but must include the broader purposes of the community and its welfare, an ethical vision that Sheldon so eloquently stated but then failed to develop.

The problem facing modern management theorists who accept the fact that a divergence often exists between ethical behavior and marketplace behavior is how to connect ethics and social responsibility with management in such a way that they are not peripheral to business operations. One way to do this is simply to argue that good ethics is good business, that being ethical will lead to success in the marketplace. Socially responsible behavior will be rewarded by increased profits, improved performance on the stock market, and other relevant measures of business success.

The difference between this view and the traditional view of ethics and the marketplace is that ethics is not subsumed under marketplace performance and the notion of economizing. Ethics has some kind of separate grounding and is not totally subsumed by marketplace behavior. Ethical considerations are not exhausted by economizing in the use of resources and deserve conscious reflection and attention. But by choosing to be socially responsible in all aspects of business operations and following separate ethical principles relevant to these responsibilities, management will be economically successful, so it is often argued.

The social responsibility advocates tried to make this connection in convincing management to take the notion of social responsibility seriously. They made various arguments based on the notion of long-run self-interest, that by being socially responsible business was taking account of its long-range health and survival. Business could not remain a healthy and viable organization in a society that was deteriorating. Thus, it made sense for business to devote some of its resources to helping solve some of the most serious social problems of society, whether it be education, discrimination, or poverty, because business could function better in a society where most of its members shared in a high standard of living and enjoyed an improved quality of life.

Other arguments had to do with gaining a better public image, that by being socially responsible business organizations could improve their image in society and in this way gain more customers and provide more of an incentive for investors to put their money in the company. There are several examples of companies that have tried to present themselves as concerned about public health and the environment through their advertising program. Finally, other arguments had to do with the avoidance of government regulation, that by being socially responsible and effectively responding to changing social expectations, business might be able to eliminate the necessity of onerous government regulations that would affect its profits and other aspects of performance.

These arguments were never very convincing because they were never based on a solid moral philosophy about the nature of the corporation and its management but were more in the nature of moralizing about certain aspects of business behavior. Moreover, the transparent falsity of these claims, and indeed of the general claim that good ethics is good business, was evident to many critics of this view. Being socially responsible costs money. Pollution-control equipment is expensive to buy and operate. Ventilation equipment to take toxic fumes out of the workplace is expensive. Proper disposal of toxic wastes in landfills can be very costly and time-consuming. These efforts cut into profits, and in a competitive system, companies that go very far in this direction will simply price themselves out of the market. This is a fact of life for companies operating in a free enterprise system that the social responsibility advocates never took seriously.

The argument that good ethics leads to good business is subject to serious question. There is no guarantee that being "good" will lead to successful economic performance in the marketplace. Studies that have been done to try to demonstrate a relationship between socially responsible behavior and stock market performance or increased profitability are at best inconclusive and at worst irrelevant. Thus, being "good" has no necessary connection with being successful in economic terms, either on a philosophical or empirical level. This linkage all depends on the context in which socially responsible activities take place, and whether virtue will actually be rewarded by the marketplace. It could be argued that virtue is its own reward, and that if one expects to be economically rewarded for virtuous activity, the concept of ethics loses its meaning. Thus, the "good ethics is good business argument" may be only a more subtle variation of the traditional view of ethics and the marketplace.

If there is no close linkage between ethics and business performance, however, this could mean that ethics may remain peripheral to management concerns. Management has to be concerned about the economic performance of the organization. It cannot set aside these requirements to pursue some ethical or social objectives that conflict with economic performance and expect to remain in business for very long. When there is a choice to be made between an ethical "ought" and a technical "must," a choice business sometimes must make to remain a viable organization within the system, it seems clear which path most managements would follow. Technical business matters are the ultimate values—a technical business necessity is a must that always takes precedence over an ethical ought that would be nice to implement but is simply not practical under most business conditions.[1]

It could be argued that ethical ideals will not provide answers to the problems of finance, personnel, production, and general management decision making. The businessperson's role is defined largely, though not exclusively, in terms of private gain and profit, and to suggest that this can be set aside for adherence to a set of ethical principles that may conflict with that role is startlingly naive and romantic. The businessperson is locked into an ongoing system of values and ethics that largely determines the actions that can be taken. There is little question that at any given time individuals who are active within an institution are subject in large measure to its prevailing characteristics.

This divergence between good ethics and good business poses a serious problem for business ethics. For ethics to be taken seriously by business schools and by the management of business organizations, it must be related in some fashion to business performance. There must be a way to relate ethics to the core management functions or else it will be nothing more than the liberal arts frosting on the business school curriculum, something to be taught as long as the time and money exist, but one of the first courses to go if times change and resources become scarce. The problem is one of making ethics central to the task of management and linking ethics to business performance.

The Relationship of Business to Society

This question of the relationship between good business and good ethics is all tied up with the particular view one holds about the relationship of business to the larger society in which it functions. Those who adhere to the traditional economic view of the corporation hold that business relates to society through the marketplace and that marketplace transactions constitute the whole of its existence and reason for being. Those who argue for a broader view of the corporation believe that corporations are not only an economic institution but a social institution with social impacts that need to be taken into account. They usually talk about business and society and the social responsibilities that corporations have to the society at large that it needs to fulfill in addition to its economic responsibilities.

Proponents of social responsibility have developed various theoretical approaches to describe this broader relationship of business to society that includes its social impacts. Two of these theories that seem to be most popular are stakeholder theory and social contract theory. Both of these theories attempt to provide a grounding for a broader view of the corporation and society that goes beyond its economic responsibilities to society and a narrow focus on the stockholder as the only entity to whom the corporation is ultimately responsible in the sense of maximization of shareholder wealth.

STAKEHOLDER THEORY

Freeman is usually given credit for doing the seminal work on the stakeholder concept[2], even though Abrams urged business leaders to pay attention to their corporate constituents[3], a theme that was continued by the Committee for Economic Development 20 years later.[4] Since Freeman's work, however, the stakeholder concept has been widely employed to describe and analyze the corporation's relationship to society.[5] At least one conference has been held that dealt exclusively with the concept and was reported in a major journal.[6]

While each scholar may define the concept somewhat differently, each version generally stands for the same principle, namely, that corporations should heed the needs, interests, and influence of those affected by their policies and operations.[7] A typical definition is that of Carroll, which holds that a stakeholder may be thought of as "any individual or group who can affect or is affected by the actions, decisions, policies, practices, or goals of the organization.'"[8] A stakeholder, then, is an individual or group that has some kind of stake in what business does and may also affect the organization in some fashion.

The typical stakeholders are considered to be consumers, suppliers, government, competitors, communities, employees, and, of course, stockholders. However, the stakeholder map of any given corporation with respect to a given issue can become quite complicated.[9] Stakeholder management involves responding to the interests and concerns of these various groups and individuals in arriving at a management decision, so that they are all satisfied at least to some extent, or at least that the most important stakeholders with regard to any given issue are satisfied.

SOCIAL CONTRACT THEORY

The emerging social responsibilities of business have also been expressed in terms of a changing contract between business and society that reflected changing expectations regarding the social performance of business.[10] The old contract between business and society was based on the view that economic growth was the source of all progress, social as well as economic. The engine providing this economic growth was considered to be the drive for profits by competitive private enterprise. The basic mission of business was thus to produce goods and services at a profit, and in doing this business was making its maximum contribution to society and being socially responsible.[11]

The new contract between business and society was based on the view that the single-minded pursuit of economic growth produced detrimental side effects that imposed social costs on society. The pursuit of economic growth, some believed, did not necessarily lead automatically to social progress, but instead led to a deteriorating physical environment, an unsafe workplace, discrimination against certain groups in society, and other social problems. This contract between business and society involved the reduction of these social costs of business through impressing upon business the idea that it has an obligation to work for social as well as economic betterment. This idea was expressed by the Committee for Economic Development as follows:

> Today it is clear that the terms of the contract between society and business are, in fact, changing in substantial and important ways. Business is being asked to assume broader responsibilities to society than ever before and to serve a wider range of human values. Business enterprises, in effect, are being asked to contribute more to the quality of American life than just supplying quantities of goods and services.[12]

The changing terms of the contract are found in the laws and regulations that society has established as the legal framework within which a business must operate and through shared understandings that prevail as to each group's expectations of the other.[13] The social contract is a set of two-way understandings that characterizes the relationship between business and society, and the changes in this contract that have taken place over the past several decades are a direct outgrowth of the increased importance of the social environment of business. The "rules of the game" have been changed, particularly through the laws and regulations that have been passed relating to social issues such as pollution and discrimination.

More recent formulations of the social contract notion have emphasized a broad range of responsibilities related to consumers and employees[14] and the responsibilities of multinational corporations to home and host countries.[15] Social contract theory has even more recently been used, as described in an earlier chapter, to bridge the gap between two streams of business ethics research that have been developed in the last several years, the empirical and the normative.[16] Thus, social contract theory has a long and rich history in business and society thought and constitutes an entrenched way of thinking about the relationship of business to society.

Problems with These Approaches

There are two basic assumptions embedded in these approaches to business and its relationship to society that make them problematical in describing and analyzing this relationship. The first assumption is that the individual is the basic building block of a society or a community, and that the society is no more than the sum of the individuals of which it is comprised.[17] In this philosophical view, institutions as well as individuals are isolatable units that have well-defined boundaries, can be considered as separate from their surroundings, and are not an integral part of the environment in which they function. To relate individuals or institutions to society involves the invention of concepts and language involving interfaces or other such schemes to bring discrete entities together.

The second assumption is that the universe is basically mechanistic, a holdover from Newtonian mechanics, and that thinking about the resolution of problems is done primarily in mechanistic fashion. Thus, one can model the decision-making process as a stakeholder map attempts to do and show descriptively what relationships are important to a corporation, or one can describe the changing contract between business and society in terms of laws and regulations that have evolved over the past several decades. But these mechanistic approaches do not begin to capture the true nature of the business-society relationship nor adequately describe the decision-making process that takes place to adjudicate conflicts.

Thus, stakeholder theory assumes that stakeholders are isolatable, individual entities that are clearly identifiable by management, and that their interests can be balanced in some mechanical fashion in the decision-making process. Complications arise when the same person may be a member of several stakeholder groups, as when, for example, an employee may be a stockholder as well as a consumer, but such complications are not given due credence in applying the theory. Each stakeholder has identifiable interests that must be taken into account by the manager in arriving at a responsible and effective decision.

The notion of a social contract is plagued by the same assumptions that underlie stakeholder theory. Social contract theory assumes that there are two distinct parties to the contract, namely business and society, that are separable entities with conflicting interests. These conflicting interests have to be worked out in some fashion through a negotiation process so a mutual agreement can be reached that is satisfactory to both parties and allows harmony to be reestablished and problems addressed that both agree are important.

This whole way of talking about business and society or business and its environment, which is the usual way social responsibility advocates think about the relationship, is permeated by the problems of atomic individualism and mechanistic thinking. To talk about business and society implies that there are two separable, isolatable entities, business and society, that are roughly co-equal in their relationship to each other. Society is composed of individual business units that function in a competitive environment. These units also have social responsibilities to that society because of their social impacts. Taken as a whole, business and society have to negotiate with each other in some fashion to decide which social issues deserve attention and how many resources should be allocated for their resolution. This process is analogous to the way business relates to society through the marketplace in determining what goods and services to produce and in what quantities.

A Critique

The process approach to business ethics holds that the relationship between business and society is analogous to the relationship between the self and community as described in an earlier chapter. The relationship between business and society is inherently relational, for no business organization can exist in isolation from society or from its environment, and society is what it is in relation to its constituting institutions. Business is a social object, not an isolatable institution, and is an acting agent in society within the context of other acting agents. But no absolute line can be drawn between business and society, for the origins and foundations of business are social in nature. There is no such thing as an isolatable, atomic something called business.

This view means that the appropriate way to think about the relationship of business to society is to talk about business in society or the corporation in its environment. This way of thinking reflects the relational nature of business to the society of which it is a part, and implies that business organizations in relation to each other constitute a major part of American society and provide much of the meaning and values that inform our society. But they are inseparable parts of that society, not isolatable units that have certain kinds of responsibilities to a society that is considered to be something separate and external.

Thus, the second implication of this philosophy is that the whole notion of the social responsibilities of business was inadequate from the very beginning of the field, and all the subsequent language about social responsiveness, social performance, and the ethical obligations of business perpetuate this fundamental problem. For these concepts and ways of thinking about the corporation and society are again built on the notion of the corporation and society as isolatable units that are somehow separable from each other and that are coordinated in a mechanistic fashion.

> The notion of responsibility is very much a part of the atomistic individualism that I am attacking as inadequate, and the classical arguments for "the social responsibilities of business" all too often fall into the trap of beginning with the assumption of the corporation as an autonomous, independent entity, which then needs to consider its obligations to the surrounding community. But corporations, like individuals, are part and parcel of the communities that created them, and the responsibilities that they bear are not products of argument or implicit contracts but intrinsic to their very existence as social entities.[18]

Corporations have to take the perspective of the society as a whole and incorporate the standards and authority of society, even as they remain a unique center of activity that has a creative dimension to add to the total social experience. The corporation thus incorporates both the conformity of society's perspective and creativity of its unique individual perspective. A society is partially constituted by the dynamics of adjustment between the corporation and the generalized other as reflected in social expectations, which involves an accommodation in which each creatively affects and is affected by the other through accepted organs of adjudication.

And what are these accepted organs of adjudication? In the case of material goods and services, the accepted organ of adjudication is the market system, which coordinates the wishes and desires of millions of individuals in society into collective demands for certain kinds of goods and services that can be produced in sufficient quantities to earn a profit for corporations. This market system is not, however, a mechanistic process where individuals merely express their individual desires as consumers to autonomous corporations that are limited in their power over consumers by competition. The market is a social process, as discussed in the previous chapter, that expresses the collective wishes of society for a better life to which material goods and services produced by corporations can contribute. It is an interactive process where corporations and consumers mutually influence each other to reach a satisfactory resolution of what goods and services should be produced.

What about social problems such as equal opportunity, safety and health in the work-place, pollution control, consumer protection, and other problems of this nature that have been the subject matter of the field of business and society since its inception? What is the appropriate organ of adjudication for these issues? Is it the corporation itself that should adjudicate these issues out of a sense of social responsibility, responding to pressures from stakeholder groups, or to some abstract notions about a changing social contract?

For one thing, when the managers of these corporations assume the right to make decisions about social investment, they are involved in the realm of public decision making without being subject to any of the guidelines or limitations imposed by the market. Nor are they subject to any democratic political process as a check on their decision making.[19] Managers of corporations have no legitimacy for making these kinds of decisions as they would in effect be imposing taxes on the public by using money that appropriately belonged to stockholders, consumers, and employees for a public purpose. They would be spending this money on a social interest and exercising political power without any definite criteria for them to follow. Such actions leave the public with nothing more than a hollow claim that the corporation's actions are in the public interest, a claim that has no clear meaning and cannot be challenged by the public whose interests are at stake. It is dangerous to assume that corporate managers acting as isolatable units know what is best for society.

Furthermore, as mentioned previously, the marketplace in which business functions places severe restrictions on the ability of corporations to respond to social issues in an effective fashion, because to do so would put them at a competitive disadvantage. Where there is some consistency between profits and alleviation of social problems, as in the case of waste minimization, for example, where some companies have saved money through reduction of their waste stream by finding new uses for waste and reducing pollution in the process, these limitations may not be a problem. But most social problems are not of this nature and require expenditures on the part of corporations that are not going to be recovered through savings in operating expenses. Where there is no money to be made or where there are adverse financial impacts to be avoided, corporations cannot voluntarily deviate a great deal from their appointed task of producing goods and services at a profit in the interests of solving social problems.[20]

> every business . . . is, in effect, "trapped" in the business system that it has helped to create. It is incapable, as an individual unit, of transcending that system . . . the dream of

the socially responsible corporation that, replicated over and over again can transform our society is illusory. . . . Because their aggregate power is not unified, not truly collective, not organized, they [corporations] have no way, even if they wished, of redirecting that power to meet the most pressing needs of society. . . . Such redirection could only occur through the intermediate agency of government rewriting the rules under which all corporations operate.[21]

Practically all of the issues that have been of concern to business and society scholars have become matters of public policy in one way or another. This development in itself suggests that the public policy process is the appropriate adjudicatory organ with respect to social issues, and pragmatic process theory lends further support to this view of society. The public policy process represents the wishes of society for public goods and services such as clean air and water, national defense, safer products, goods and services that are indivisible and public by their very nature and thus are held in common by society. The marketplace cannot provide them and expectations for them cannot normally be expressed through marketplace transactions.[22] The public policy process, then, is the appropriate way for society to decide about the allocation of resources for the solution of social problems rather than by relying on corporations to be socially responsible, accurately discern stakeholder interests, or respond to some notions of a new social contract.

Thus, a further implication of process theory for the business and society field is that public policy must receive more theoretical attention if the field is to move forward. Much, if not most, of the theoretical work in the field that has been done to more adequately describe and analyze the interactions between business and the broader environment in which it functions has focused on corporate social responsiveness and corporate social performance, and on the development of stakeholder theory and social contract theories that undergird these approaches. These concepts and approaches are founded on theoretical underpinnings, which are different from those needed for illuminating and providing a foundation for the public policy context in which corporations function.

Public policy involves a different orientation for the field or a different perspective from which to view social issues and how they get resolved. The title of business and society logically leads to a focus on management's trying to discern the responsibilities of the corporation to society by responding to external stakeholder concerns, getting serious about its social responsibilities or ethical obligations to an external society, or responding to the requirements of a new social contract between separable entities. The phrase, "business *in* society," however, leads to the public policy perspective, which is more consistent with thinking about the corporation as an integral part of society, as it involves taking the perspective of society as a whole and discerning how society articulates its expectations regarding corporate behavior. Society is the entity in which corporations are embedded and it is society that in large part decides what corporations are to do with respect to social issues through the public policy process as a means of adjudication.

As stated so well by Preston and Post, public policy is, along with the market mechanism, the source of guidelines and criteria for managerial behavior.[23] The public policy process is the means by which society as a whole articulates its goals and objectives, and directs and stimulates individuals and organizations to contribute to and cooperate with them. Appropriate guidelines for managerial behavior are to be found in the larger society, not in the personal vision of managers or in the special interests of groups. Thus, a business organization should analyze and evaluate pressures and stimuli coming from public policy in the same way it analyzes and evaluates market experience and opportunity.

Through the constant adjustment process that goes on between the corporation and its environment by means of the market process on the one hand, and the public policy process on the other, values emerge, values with respect to goods and services for sale on the market, and values with respect to public goods and services provided through the public policy process. These values emerge in the interactions between different business organizations and consumers in a marketplace context or between business and citizens in a public policy context. As such these values are both shared and unique.

While the corporation finds itself continually adjusting to community interests as expressed through the public policy process, such adjustment is not a passive process and corporations need not be merely passive respondents to public policy, merely meeting the requirements that society imposes on corporate behavior in the form of new public policies. There must be a dynamic, creative interaction between these two dimensions, the same as takes place between the corporation and the market system. A corporation must continually take on the responsibility of providing creative input into its environment, which leads to ongoing revision and improvement of public policy. Value conflicts are inevitable, but the resolution of these conflicts leads to growth of the corporation and the society of which it is a part. For growth to take place, there must be openness to change and a willingness to reconstruct problematic situations.

When habitual modes of organizing the behavior of corporations in society do not work in resolving problematic situations involving conflicting valuings, new norms and ways of organizing behavior emerge that reconstruct the situation in an attempt at successful resolution of problems. When this adjustment happens, and when corporations are made to respond to social problems through new laws and regulations, this is not indicative of a new social contract between independent entities or new pressures from external stakeholder groups or a new set of responsibilities called social responsibilities that business must now accept. These changes are simply implicit in the nature of corporations as social entities that are subject to change along with the society of which they are an inextricable part. In other words, corporations do not stand apart from society; they are embedded in society and an ingredient in its changes of values and valuation.

The corporation and the public policy process are related to each other in a complex manner, and the actions taken by the corporation can have important effects on the public policy process, while the actions of the corporation are themselves shaped to some extent by events that take place in the public policy process.[24] The concept of public policy is thus not just another theoretical pillar of the field along with those mentioned previously; it is a different perspective based on different assumptions about the corporation and its role in society and the nature and functioning of the market system.

Current theoretical work in describing the relationship of business to society has reached an impasse because of its assumption about the atomic individual and mechanistic problem solving. These assumptions are shared with standard economic theory in which the individual is considered to be an isolated entity that expresses his or her preferences for goods and services in the marketplace, which then coordinates these preferences into a demand schedule facing producers in order that they know what to produce and in what quantities to meet consumer demand. Competition is viewed as a mechanistic regulator of supply and demand to ensure that any one producer does not come to dominate the system and attain a monopolistic position.

This economic view of the firm and its responsibilities to society remains largely intact, as neither stakeholder theory nor social contract theory has provided an alternative view of the firm that is powerful enough to replace standard economic theory. Responses to social issues are made within the established economic framework and the traditional view of the firm, in which the bottom line of the corporation is purely economic in nature. Such responses are shaped to correspond with the dominant economic value system that ultimately determines corporate behavior.

Pragmatic process philosophy, based on different assumptions, opens up the possibility of developing an alternative theory of the firm in society that overcomes the traditional dichotomies associated with attempts to relate them, dichotomies that have limited our ability to deal with problems effectively and unify our thinking. Such a unification will begin to come into focus in the following chapter, which will discuss public policy and the corporation, and argue that ultimately public policy is not just compatible with the market system, but that both are polar dimensions of an inextricably interwoven and dynamic whole.

Questions for Discussion

1. Where did questions about the social responsibilities of business begin to arise and how did this notion challenge the traditional view of business and its relationship to society? How did the notion of social responsibility raise questions about the view of ethics and business embedded in a marketplace orientation?

2. Does being ethical necessarily lead to being successful in business? What arguments did the advocates of social responsibility develop to promote this view? Were these arguments very conclusive? If not, what might motivate managers to be ethically and socially responsible?

3. What is atomic individualism and how does stakeholder and social contract theory reflect this notion? How does the notion of atomic individualism relate to mechanistic thinking? Do you agree that the traditional way of thinking about business and society is plagued by these assumptions?

4. How does the process approach based on pragmatic philosophy alter this perception of business and society? Does the notion of business in society better capture the inherently relational aspect of business and society? What implications does this philosophy have for thinking about business and society?

Endnotes

[1] See Benjamin and Sylvia Selekman, *Power and Morality in a Business Society* (New York: McGraw-Hill, 1956).

[2] R. Edward Freeman, *Strategic Management: A Stakeholder Approach* (Boston: Pitman, 1984).

[3] F. Abrams, "Management's Responsibilities in a Complex World," *Harvard Business Review,* Vol. 24, no. 3 (1951), pp. 29–34.

[4] Committee for Economic Development, *Social Responsibilities of Business Corporations* (New York: CED, 1971).

[5] See Abbass Alkhafaji, *A Stakeholder Approach to Corporate Governance: Managing in a Dynamic Environment* (New York: Quorum Books, 1989); Jerry W. Anderson, *Corporate Social Responsibility* (New York: Quorum Books, 1989); James J. Brummer, *Corporate Responsibility and Legitimacy: An Interdisciplinary Analysis* (New York: Greenwood Press, 1991); Kenneth E.

Goodpaster, "Business Ethics and Stakeholder Analysis," *Business Ethics Quarterly,* Vol. 1, no. 1 (January 1991), pp. 53–73; Charles W. L. Hill and Thomas M. Jones, "Stakeholder Agency Theory," *Journal of Management Studies,* Vol. 29 (March 1992), pp. 131–154.

[6] Max Clarkson, et al., "The Toronto Conference: Reflections on Stakeholder Theory," *Business & Society,* Vol. 33, no. 1 (April 1994), pp. 83–131.

[7] William C. Frederick, "Social Issues in Management: Coming of Age or Prematurely Gray?" Paper presented to the Doctoral Consortium of the Social Issues in Management Division of the Academy of Management, Las Vegas, Nevada, August 1992, p. 5.

[8] Archie B. Carroll, *Business & Society: Ethics and Stakeholder Management,* 2nd ed. (Cincinnati: Southwestern, 1993), p. 60.

[9] Ibid., pp. 69–73.

[10] Melvin Anshen, *Managing the Socially Responsible Corporation* (New York: Macmillan, 1974).

[11] See Milton Friedman, "The Social Responsibility of Business Is to Increase Its Profits," *New York Times Magazine,* September 13, 1970, pp. 122–126.

[12] CED, *Social Responsibilities of Business Corporations,* p. 12.

[13] Carroll, *Business & Society,* p. 19.

[14] Thomas Donaldson, *Corporations & Morality* (Englewood Cliffs, NJ: Prentice Hall, 1982).

[15] Thomas Donaldson, *The Ethics of International Business* (New York: Oxford University Press, 1989).

[16] Thomas Donaldson and Thomas W. Dunfee, "Toward a Unified Conception of Business Ethics: Integrative Social Contracts Theory," *Academy of Management Review,* Vol. 19, no. 2 (April 1994), pp. 252–284.

[17] One other author in the field of business ethics has recognized this problem of atomic individualism. "It is this emphasis on the primacy of institutional arrangements that has become essential in combating what many philosophers have taken to calling 'atomic individualism,' the appealing and long-standing idea that we are each first of all individuals who then enter into various agreements with one another, whether wholly voluntary or under considerable duress." See Robert Solomon, *Ethics and Excellence: Cooperation and Integrity in Business* (New York: Oxford University Press, 1993), p. 77.

[18] Ibid., p. 149.

[19] Friedman, "Social Responsibility," pp. 122–126.

[20] Rogene A. Buchholz, *Business Environment and Public Policy,* 4th ed. (Englewood Cliffs, NJ: Prentice Hall, 1992), p. 29.

[21] Neil W. Chamberlain, *The Limits of Corporate Responsibility* (New York: Basic Books, 1973), pp. 4, 6. Copyright © 1973 by Basic Books, Inc., Publisher. Reprinted by permission of the publisher.

[22] Buchholz, *Business Environment and Public Policy,* p. 80.

[23] Lee E. Preston and James E. Post, *Private Management and Public Policy* (Englewood Cliffs, NJ: Prentice-Hall, 1975).

[24] Preston and Post recognized this interactive effect in their interpenetrating systems model of the relationship between the market system and public policy. "It is this ability of one system to change the structure of the other, and not simply to alter the volume or character of inputs and outputs, that distinguishes the interpenetrating systems model from simpler collateral or suprasystems conceptions . . . we require a model that permits society to influence and constrain—but not necessarily dominate or control—an area of activity formerly reserved to the firm exclusively. Similarly, attempts by individual organizations to affect the course of public policy . . . may be described as an expansion of managerial activity into the decision system of society at large. In neither example does one system necessarily come to control the other completely, even with respect to the specific matter involved and certainly not in all matters. Nor can the relationship between the

systems be described in the simple terms of input-output exchange. On the contrary, the concept of interpenetration seems to be, if less precise, the more accurate general form of the relationship between micro-organizational management and its social environment." Ibid., p. 26.

Suggested Readings

Alkhafaji, Abbass. *A Stakeholder Approach to Corporate Governance: Managing in a Dynamic Environment.* New York: Quorum Books, 1989.

Anderson, Jerry W., Jr. *Corporate Social Responsibility.* New York: Quorum Books, 1989.

Anshen, Melvin. *Managing the Socially Responsible Corporation.* New York: Macmillan, 1974.

Baron, David P. *Business & Its Environment.* Englewood Cliffs, NJ: Prentice Hall, 1992.

Brummer, James J. *Corporate Responsibility and Legitimacy: An Interdisciplinary Analysis.* New York: Greenwood Press, 1991.

Buchholz, Rogene A. *Business Environment and Public Policy,* 4th ed. Englewood Cliffs, NJ: Prentice Hall, 1992.

Carroll, Archie B. *Business & Society: Ethics and Stakeholder Management,* 2nd ed. Cincinnati: Southwestern, 1993.

Chamberlain, Neil W. *The Limits of Corporate Responsibility.* New York: Basic Books, 1973.

Committee for Economic Development. *Social Responsibilities of Business Corporations.* New York: Committee for Economic Development, 1971.

Donaldson, Thomas. *Corporations & Morality.* Englewood Cliffs, NJ: Prentice Hall, 1982.

Donaldson, Thomas. *The Ethics of International Business.* New York: Oxford University Press, 1989.

Freeman, R. Edward. *Strategic Management: A Stakeholder Approach.* Boston: Pitman, 1984.

Preston, Lee E., and James E. Post. *Private Management and Public Policy.* Englewood Cliffs, NJ: Prentice-Hall, 1975.

Solomon, Robert C. *Ethics and Excellence: Cooperation and Integrity in Business.* New York: Oxford University Press, 1993.

Wood, Donna J. *Business and Society.* Glenview, IL: Scott Foresman/Little Brown, 1990.

S H O R T   C A S E S

Control Data Corporation

Control Data Corporation (CDC) was a high-tech company manufacturing computers and computer peripherals, and providing computer services. The major markets for CDC's computers were federal and state governments, educational institutions, and industrial companies. CDC was also a major supplier for space, defense, nuclear, and weather systems. Its computer service business included planning, accounting, and administrative systems for large and small businesses. The peripheral products division supplied products to other computer manufacturing concerns.

CDC was also a company with a social conscience. William C. Norris, the founder and longtime chair of the company, advocated a philosophical synthesis of capitalism and social consciousness. Consequently, he spent a good deal of his time and company assets on ventures far removed from the computer business such as training the jobless, helping to revitalize disadvantaged communities, and supporting small businesses. Norris tried to ingrain in all his employees the idea that addressing society's needs can be a profitable business opportunity.[1]

Growing out of this philosophy, the specific programs that the company had implemented to address these needs included the building of manufacturing plants in economically depressed inner-city areas that served the interests of each community by revitalizing urban areas and providing a path for disadvantaged persons to enter the mainstream of society, and developing a computer-based educational program called PLATO to address the need for better, more readily available, and lower-cost education throughout the world.[2]

The company tried to find problems where a profit could eventually be made and where there was a congruence between traditional business objectives and the interests of society. It believed that the foregoing social ills should not be viewed as problems but as opportunities for business. It should be noted that Control Data did not have a formal contributions program as do most major corporations. Consequently, it did not see its involvement in social problems as a philanthropic effort but as a normal business opportunity that had risks but also had profit-making opportunities. Thus, the company did not try to project the image of a do-gooder, but wanted to be seen as a company that expanded its horizons to reach out and embrace other opportunities that most business organizations ignored.

However, Control Data Corporation experienced financial difficulties in the 1980s because of an industrywide slump in the computer, office, and equipment supplies markets. Its 1985 annual statement showed a charge of $130.2 million on the peripheral products group after a loss of $269.6 million on $3.69 billion in revenues. The company was also under a class-action suit from shareholders for misrepresenting the financial health of the company. Many analysts blamed Norris for the company's financial difficulties for sidetracking it on ventures that distracted management, diluted resources, and left the company's core businesses vulnerable.[3]

In 1986, Norris was replaced as CEO by Robert M. Price, who immediately began restructuring the company. Price slashed employment by 25 percent from 1985 levels, eliminating nearly half of top-management jobs in the process. He sold off 82 percent of Commercial Credit Corporation, the company's financial services subsidiary. He also cut back on many of the social projects that Norris had started. The aim of this restructuring was to focus on the company's computer manufacturing, disk drive, and service business, which brought in 95 percent of revenues.[4]

Price changed the priorities of the company, and in the process began to change the culture of the company from one of seeing the company as a tool to meet society's unmet needs to a more traditional business-driven culture. The effort seemed to pay off financially, as CDC earned more than $75 million in 1987 after losing $832 million during the previous two years. Its disk drive business became profitable again and its 89 percent owned subsidiary, ETA Systems, delivered the first of its new supercomputers. After technically defaulting on some bank loans in 1985, in 1987 the company had $300 million in cash and marketable securities.[5]

1. Should companies profit from meeting social needs? Is there something morally repugnant in the idea that business should earn a profit from people's misfortunes? Does such a question make any difference as long as the quality of life for disadvantaged people is improved?

2. Would Milton Friedman approve of Control Data's actions? Would he view Control Data as a profit-seeking corporation or as more of a do-gooder? Did Control Data go too far in its social mission? Was its efforts to respond to social problems responsible for its financial difficulties?

[1] William C. Norris, "A New Role for Corporations," speech to the Social Needs and Business Opportunities Conference, Minneapolis, Minnesota, September 21, 1982.

[2] Control Data, "Addressing Society's Major Unmet Needs As Profitable Business Opportunities," Minneapolis, Minn., January 1982, pp. 1-48.

[3] Richard Gibson, "Control Data Betting Smaller Is Better," *The Wall Street Journal,* December 3, 1985, p. 6.

[4] "How Bob Price Is Reprogramming Control Data," *Business Week,* February 16, 1987, p. 102.

[5] Ibid.

Source: Rogene A. Buchholz, *Business Environment and Public Policy: Implications for Management,* 5th ed. (Englewood Cliffs, NJ: Prentice Hall, 1995), pp. 21–22.

Wedtech Corporation

In 1965, John Mariotta, a high school dropout, invested $3,000 to start a small manufacturing company in a desolate area of the South Bronx. The company struggled along for five years, when Mariotta entered into a partnership with Fred Neuberger, a mechanical engineer. The firm was named Welbilt Electronics, and was eligible for loans directed to minority contractors from the Small Business Administration (SBA). The SBA had a set-aside program, which allowed minority firms to obtain federal contracts without competitive bidding. By the early 1980s, Welbilt began winning million-dollar contracts for Navy pontoon bridges and Army smoke-grenade launchers. Eventually, about 95 percent of its business came from these set-aside contracts.[1]

The company changed its name to Wedtech in 1983 and moved to new facilities in the shadow of Yankee Stadium. The company hired more than 1,000 black and Hispanic workers from the local neighborhood, an area that had lost 40 percent of its manufacturing base during the previous decade. The company's profits increased to more than $72 million by 1984 from $8 million in 1981, and went public with a $30 million stock offering that made millionaires of Mariotta, Neuberger, and other executives. The company became a symbol of minority achievement, as President Reagan lauded the company's success, and called John Mariotta a hero for the 1980s. The company was hailed as a success story and an example of what minorities could achieve.[2]

Then federal and local prosecutors entered the picture, and a different story began to unfold. The prosecutors alleged that Wedtech prospered as a result of promiscuous bribery of city, state, and federal officials and engaged in a conspiracy to win government contracts by fraudulently depicting itself as a minority-owned business. The company was depicted as a racketeering enterprise dependent on bribes to public officials to win minority contracts. Payoffs were so routine, the prosecutors alleged, that the company maintained a secret bank account for depositing kickbacks from contractors and greasing public officials.[3]

When Wedtech wanted a multimillion-dollar contract for engines, for example, it hired attorney E. Robert Wallach as a consultant, and he was allegedly given some $500,000 worth of the company's stock over several years in addition to a retainer for his services. Wallach was an old friend and lawyer of then Presidential Counsellor Edwin Meese, who was kept informed of Wedtech's efforts to win the engine contract. Meese later became attorney general for the Reagan administration. The company also retained Lyn Nofziger who had formerly worked for the White House and left to set up his own consulting firm. Nofziger had written a letter on behalf of the company to Meese's chief deputy, who then set up a White House briefing on Wedtech that was attended by top officials and the Army and representatives of the SBA. Soon after this meeting, Wedtech was awarded the first of its many military contracts.[4]

When the stock sale took place, Mariotta was no longer the majority shareholder, which meant Wedtech no longer qualified as a minority-owned company. The local SBA office thus began proceedings to remove the company from the set-aside program. The company then quickly transferred 1.8 million shares of company stock to Mariotta's nominal control and retained the law firm of Richard Biaggi, the son and former partner of South Bronx Congressman Mario Biaggi. The law firm received more than $1 million in fees and stock for representing the company. Soon after these actions, the SBA approved Wedtech's stock transfer and allowed it to remain eligible for minority set-asides.[5] Eventually, Mario Biaggi and his son along with five others were indicted by a federal grand jury on charges of extortion, racketeering, and conspiracy. Prosecutors claimed that Biaggi received $3.6 million in Wedtech stock after he threatened to undermine SBA support for the company. A former SBA regional administrator was also indicted.[6]

Soon thereafter, Mariotta was replaced as Wedtech's chairman by Neuberger after they disagreed about management policies. The stock that Mariotta controlled was then returned to the company and it lost its status as a minority contractor. By October 1986, the stock had dropped from $11.44 a share in March to $6.50 a share. By the end of the year, the company had laid off 1,000 people and filed for bankruptcy. Debts were listed at $212 million. Four former executives, including Neuberger, pleaded guilty to a range of charges that included bribery and mail fraud. Mariotta himself was not indicted.[7]

The company tried to recover. New management took over and obtained a $500,000 loan from Chemical Bank and $38 million in government contracts that were not under investigation. However, the Cadillacs and limousines used by Wedtech's former officers were gone and a $305,000 condominium purchased in 1985 for entertainment purposes was put on the market. The scandal was a blot on the minority set-aside program and stimulated several proposals for reform. The incident also cast aspersions on the minority work force that some considered undeserved. In any event, the unfolding story was another example of how difficult it is to implement programs to aid disadvantaged people and avoid corruption and favoritism.[8]

1. What is a minority business organization? Is promotion of more minority business organizations an effective strategy in combating poverty in disadvantaged areas of the country? What special problems do minority businesses face in getting started?

2. What is a set-aside program? Is this kind of program a valid effort to promote the development of minority business enterprises? Should business organizations help establish minority enterprises as part of their social responsibility?

3. Describe the beginnings of Wedtech Corporation. Where did the company go wrong? What did management do to win government contracts under the set-aside program? Who benefited from the growth of the company? Who got hurt when the scandal began to unravel?

4. Is a program of this nature tailor-made for fraud and abuse? Can it be reformed to make it more effective? What should be done in this regard? Should the program be dismantled? What other things can be done to promote minority business enterprises?

[1] Bruce van Voorst, "A Tale of Urban Greed," *Time,* April 20, 1987, p. 30.

[2] Ibid.

[3] Ibid.

[4] Ibid.

[5] Ibid., pp. 30, 32.

[6] Walter Shapiro, "$4 Billion Worth of Temptation," *Time,* June 15, 1987, p. 20.

[7] van Voorst, "A Tale of Urban Greed," pp. 30, 32.

[8] Ibid., p. 32. Also see Paula Dwyer, "Wedtech: Where Fingers Are Pointing Now," *Business Week,* October 5, 1987, pp. 34–35.

Source: Rogene A. Buchholz, *Business Environment and Public Policy: Implications for Management,* 5th ed. (Englewood Cliffs, NJ: Prentice Hall, 1995), pp. 269–270.

Activist Shareholders

The annual meeting of the company was again a very disruptive affair. A coalition of church and public interest groups had garnered enough votes from the other stockholders to bring up issues such as the company's investments in South Africa, its compliance with hazardous waste disposal regulations, and other such social issues. Most of the CEO's time at the meeting was spent dealing with these issues and answering the coalition's questions. Financial issues that were of interest to the traditional shareholders did not get enough attention, and some stockholders were complaining.

The CEO knew something had to be done. He also knew that General Motors had tried to hold two annual meetings one year, only one of which dissident shareholders were allowed to attend. This idea did not work out, however, and was scrapped. The CEO also thought of including representatives of some of these groups, so-called special-interest directors, on the board of directors so they could bring up their concerns at this forum and hopefully not continue to disrupt the annual meeting. Another possibility was to have one public interest director represent all the social concerns of activist shareholders.

Since the CEO was a member of the Business Roundtable, he was well aware that the Roundtable had rejected political models of the board that included special-interest directors as unworkable. Something had to be done, however, and the CEO wanted to make a reasonable proposal at the next board of directors meeting.

1. What options are available to the company in this situation? Is the annual meeting the best forum where activist shareholders can voice their concerns about social issues? Do they not have this right if they own stock and get enough votes to raise the issues at the meeting?

2. Are political models of the board inherently unworkable? Why or why not? How would conflicts be resolved where radically different interests may be involved? Is this a good way for questions about the social responsibility of companies to be raised?

Source: Rogene A. Buchholz, *Business Environment and Public Policy: Implications for Management,* 5th ed. (Englewood Cliffs, NJ: Prentice Hall, 1995), p. 262.

Poverty Area Plants

Paperboard Company did not have a contributions program and was being pressured by other companies in the city to help make a better community by contributing to some aspect of community welfare. The company was being accused of being a free rider and benefiting from other companies' concern about city problems. Company management wanted to be a responsible company, but it doubted the wisdom of establishing a contributions program. The company wanted to do something different.

Paperboard had heard of Control Data's program to build plants in disadvantaged areas to employ local people and thus help the area to establish a sound economic base. The management of the company wondered if this strategy would work well for Paperboard and if it could make a better contribution to the community in this manner. Its manufacturing process lent itself to small plants that could make specialized products. The company also did not need many highly skilled employees to operate a typical plant.

The company was also aware that the federal government was considering a bill to create enterprise zones in disadvantaged areas to encourage companies to locate there. Due to budgetary considerations, however, political experts were saying that the bill had little chance of passage during the current congressional session. Paperboard was thus wondering whether to wait and see if this bill could be salvaged, or whether to go ahead on its own and plan to build plants in disadvantaged areas of the community.

1. What factors should the company consider in building plants in disadvantaged areas? What problems are likely to be encountered? Will small plants of this nature really make much of an impact on disadvantaged areas of communities?

2. Should the company lobby for passage of federal legislation to establish enterprise zones? Or should it begin to work at the state level for passage of similar legislation? Which would be the most socially responsible course of action?

Source: Rogene A. Buchholz, *Business Environment and Public Policy: Implications for Management,* 5th ed. (Englewood Cliffs, NJ: Prentice Hall, 1995), p. 301.

Public Policy and the Corporation

The business institution has been reshaped and the managerial role affected by many public policy measures designed to accomplish both economic and noneconomic goals and objectives of the larger society. Over the last two decades, public policy has become an ever more important determinant of corporate behavior, as market outcomes have been increasingly altered through the public policy process. These changes are making it increasingly clear that business functions in two major social processes through which decisions are made about the allocation of corporate resources and conflicts are adjudicated. These are the market system and the public policy process. Both processes are necessary to encompass the broad range of decisions that a society needs to make about the corporation and its role in society. The market mechanism and public policy are both sources of guidelines and criteria for corporate and managerial behavior.

There are many concepts related to public policy that can be discussed in order to better understand the nature of public policy. Regarding the concept of public policy itself, public policy can be defined as a specific course of action taken by society or by a legitimate representative of society, addressing a specific problem of public concern that reflects the interests of society or particular segments of society. This definition emphasizes a course of action rather than discrete actions taken with respect to particular problems; it does not restrict such action to government, and does not claim that each and every public policy represents the interests of society as a whole. Enough interests have to be represented, however, so that the policy is supported and can be implemented effectively. The general goals of public policy are determined through a political process in which citizens participate, constrained only by rights of the kind protected by the U.S. Constitution.[1]

The public policy agenda is that collection of topics and issues with respect to which public policy may be formulated.[2] There are many problems and concerns that various people in society would like to see acted upon, but only those that are important enough to receive serious attention from policymakers comprise the public policy agenda. Such an agenda does not exist in concrete form but is found in the collective judgment of society, actions and concerns of interest groups, legislation introduced into Congress, cases being considered by the Supreme Court, and similar activities. The manner in which problems in our society get on the public policy agenda is complex and involves many different kinds of political participation.

The specific course of action that is eventually taken with respect to a problem is decided through the public policy process. The term *public policy process* refers to the various processes by which public policy is formulated. There is no single process by which public policy is made in our country.[3] It is made by means of a complex, subtle, and not always formal process. Many agents who do not show up on any formal organization chart of government nevertheless influence the outcome of the public policy process.[4] The public policy process thus refers to all the various methods by which public policy is made in our society. Formulation of public policy is not limited to formal acts of government but can be achieved by interest groups that bring issues to public attention and attempt to influence public opinion as well as business and government.

Many of the policies in our country have been formed through a process involving public opinion, interest groups, institutions, demonstrations, the media, and a host of other actors. When public policy is formalized by government, there still is no single process involved. Public policy can be made through legislation passed by Congress, regulations issued by government agencies, executive orders issued by the president, or decisions handed down by the Supreme Court. The process of making public policy begins in the society as problems and issues are defined. These issues may find their way into formal institutions for some policy decisions, and then they are subsequently returned to society again for implementation.[5]

Elements of the Public Policy Process

The public policy process can be broken down into various elements (Exhibit 7-1) to facilitate discussion and comprehension of the concept. Such a procedure will enable a comparison with the market system to be made element by element, rather than trying to compare the two complex concepts as a whole. This procedure should introduce more precision into the discussion and provide a better understanding of how the public policy process responds to the values of society as expressed through political activities. It should be noted that this description of the public policy process is based on the traditional view of public policy as a means of providing the society with public goods and services.

POLITICAL PROCESS

Instead of an exchange process, values are assigned to particular entities in the public policy process and decisions are made about the allocation of resources through a political process. The political process is a complex amalgam of power and influence that involves many people pursuing different interests who try to persuade and influence other people in order to achieve their objectives. It is often difficult to determine who has the most power and influence in the political process, as it is a very complex mixture that is impossible to describe in scientific terms.

EXHIBIT 7-1 Conceptual Elements of the Public Policy Process

Political Process
Public Goods and Services
Diverse Value Systems
The Public Interest
The Visible Hand
Political Roles (Politicians–Citizens–Public Interest Groups)
Citizen Sovereignty
Power as Reward
Government as the Major Institution
Operating Principles: Justice, Equity, Fairness

Politics has often been called the art of the possible, which generally means that a balancing of interests is necessary to resolve conflicts between interests in order to arrive at a common course of action. People usually have to be willing to give up something of what they want in order to reach agreement among all the members of a group. The usual outcome of the political process reflects the principle that no one gets everything they want and yet everyone has to get something in order to be satisfied that the objective is worth pursuing. Thus, compromise and negotiation are necessary skills to participate effectively in the political process.

The function of a political process is to organize individual effort to achieve some kind of social goal or objective that individuals or private groups find it difficult, if not impossible, to achieve by themselves. People participate in the exchange process because they believe they can better achieve their individual objectives by making some kind of trade, but the parties to the exchange do not have to share objectives or agree on a common course of action. Let us say some people in a community want to build a road, which no one person in the community can or would want to build alone. To get the road built, enough people in the community have to agree they want a road and would contribute the necessary resources to getting it built. Even after this decision is made, these people are going to have different ideas as to what kind of road should be built, where it should be located, and other related matters. These differences have to be resolved through the political process in order for the road to be constructed.

The task of the political system is to adjudicate such conflicts by (1) establishing rules of the game for participants in the system, (2) arranging compromises and balancing interests of the various participants, (3) enacting compromises in the form of public policy measures, and (4) enforcing these public policies.[6] The outcome of the political process is not usually under the control of a single individual or group, as is the outcome of an exchange process. The outcome of the political process depends on how much power and influence one has, how skillful one is at compromising and negotiating, and the variety and strength of other interests involved. Decisions can be made by vote where the majority rules, by building a consensus, or by exercising raw power and coercing other members of a group to agree with your course of action.

The outcome of the exchange process is fairly certain as people usually know that their decisions are directly connected to the outcome. If people choose to part with a sum of money, they only do so because they know they will receive a product or service they want in return. Producers sell their products for a specific sum of money, not for some promise to pay an unspecified amount. The value of goods and services, as well as money, changes over time. But at the discrete moment of exchange, people usually have a pretty good idea of what they are getting, unless misrepresentation or outright fraud is involved.

Outcomes in the political process are highly uncertain, in most instances, and contain many surprises. In the political process, especially if it involves a representative democracy, people are not always certain what they are getting. They may vote for a candidate they believe will support the issues they favor and who seems to share similar values. But elected public officials are a very poor store of value in this sense. They may not carry out their campaign promises, and even if they do, their vote might count for nothing in the final outcome if few others voted the same way on the issues.

People pursue their interests through the political process based on the values they hold relative to the objectives being sought through the public policy process. But these values cannot be expressed directly or precisely, particularly in a representative democracy. Individual preferences are rarely matched because of the need for compromise, and the outcome is highly uncertain because of the complex interactions that take place among all the parties to a transaction. Yet resources for the attainment of public policy objectives are allocated through the political process that combines values expressed by individual participants into common objectives and courses of action.

PUBLIC GOODS AND SERVICES

The reason public policy decisions have to be made through a political process is the nature of the goods and services that are provided through the public policy process. These goods and services can appropriately be referred to as public goods and services (see box) as distinguished from the private goods and services described in the market system. Just as in the market system, these public goods and services are provided to meet the demands of people for these goods and services as expressed through the political system. The public policy process deals with things that are held in common.

Public goods and services are indivisible in the sense that the quantity produced cannot be divided into individual units to be purchased by people according to their individual preferences. For all practical purposes, one cannot, for example, buy a piece of clean air to carry around and breathe wherever one goes. Nor can one buy a share of national defense over which one would have control. This indivisibility gives these goods their public character because if people are to have public goods and services at all, they must enjoy roughly the same amount.[7] No one owns these goods and services individually—they are collectively owned in a sense, or held in common, and private property rights do not apply. Thus, there is nothing to be exchanged and the values people have in regard to these goods and services and decisions about them cannot be made through the exchange process.

Because of these characteristics of human behavior and the nature of public goods and services, the market system will not work to provide them for a society that wants them. When goods are indivisible among large numbers of people, the individual consumer's actions as expressed in the market will not lead to the provision of these goods.[8] Society must register its desire for public goods and services through the political process because the bilateral exchanges facilitated by the market are insufficiently inclusive.[9] Only through the political process can compromises be reached that will resolve the value conflicts that are inevitable in relation to public goods and services.

BOX 7-1

The concept of public goods and services needs further explanation. The literature about this subject usually refers to national defense as the best example of a public good—something tangible provided by government for all its citizens that cannot be provided by the citizens for themselves.

Pollution is generally considered to be an example of an externality, defined as either a beneficial or detrimental (pollution is detrimental) effect on a third party (homeowner who lives close to a polluting factory) who is not involved in the transaction between the principals (customer and producer) who caused the pollution because of their activities in the marketplace. Yet the results of pollution control (clean air and water) can also be called a public good as they are entities with beneficial physical characteristics for human health that are widely shared in different amounts by people in society.

Something like equal opportunity might be called a social value in that it is a particular goal of our society that is important for many of its members because of their individual values or ethical sensibilities. Yet if these values are widely shared or are an important part of a society's heritage, policies designed to promote equal opportunity also produce a public good in that it is good for society to implement its basic values and provide equal opportunity for its citizens.

Thus, the concept of public goods and services as used here is an all-inclusive concept that refers to all these various outcomes of the public policy process. This broader use also includes the maintenance of competition as a public good because Americans believe that resources are allocated more efficiently in a competitive economy than one dominated by one or a few firms in an industry.

DIVERSE VALUE SYSTEMS

Value conflicts are more pronounced in the public policy process because of the existence of diverse value systems. There is no underlying value system into which other values can be translated, no common denominator by which to assess trade-offs and make decisions about resource allocation to attain some common economic objective such as improving one's material standard of living or increasing the nation's gross national product.

What is the overall objective, for example, of clean air and water, equal opportunity, occupational safety and health, and similar public goods and services? One could say that all these goods and services are meant to improve the quality of life for all members of society. But if this is the objective, what kind of common value measure underlies all these goods and services so that benefits can be assessed in relation to costs, and trade-offs analyzed in view of this common objective of improving the quality of life?

The costs of pollution-control equipment, for example, can be determined in economic terms. The benefits this equipment provides should be positive in improving health by reducing the amount of harmful pollutants people have to breathe and improving the aesthetic dimension by making the air look and smell better. Safety may also be enhanced through an improvement of visibility for aircraft. The difficulty lies in translating all these diverse benefits into economic terms so that a direct comparison with costs can be made.

What is the price tag for the lives saved by avoiding future diseases that may be caused by pollution? What is the economic value of having three more years added on to one's life span because of living in a cleaner environment? What is the value of reducing the probability that children will be born with abnormalities because of toxic substances in the environment? What is the value of preserving one's hearing because money has been spent to reduce the noise emitted by machinery in the workplace? What is the appropriate value of being able to see across the Grand Canyon and enjoy whatever benefits this view provides?[10]

The difficulty of expressing all these intangibles in economic terms so that people's preferences are matched should be apparent. In spite of these difficulties, insurance agents, legal experts, scientists, and agency administrators routinely assign values to human life ranging from a few dollars to many millions of dollars, depending on the methods used to calculate these values. One of the most precise ways of calculating the value of a human life is to break down the body into its chemical elements. Some experts have determined that the value of a human life on this basis is about $8.37, which has increased $1.09 in six years because of inflation.[11] Obviously, such a method is not acceptable for public policy purposes.

There are at least five ways of determining the value of a human life: (1) calculating the present value of estimated future earnings that are forgone due to premature death, (2) calculating the present value of the losses others experience because of a person's death, (3) examining the value placed on an individual life by presently established social policies and practices, (4) using the "willingness to pay" method where people are asked how much they would be willing to pay to reduce the probability of their death by a certain amount, and (5) looking at the compensation people accept as wage premiums for dangerous jobs or hazardous occupations.[12]

The diversity of economic valuation that results from these techniques is not surprising. People are going to value their lives vastly differently from each other. Some people may believe they are worth any economic expenditure no matter how great. Others may feel their lives are relatively worthless. People's valuation of their lives will also change with age and other circumstances. Such diversity renders the use of analytical techniques such as those described previously highly questionable in most situations, even though they appear to introduce more precision into the determination of value with regard to human life.

When people are making individual choices about private goods and services, diverse value systems present no problems. They are forced to translate these diverse values into economic terms and make choices accordingly. Making choices about public goods and services is another matter. There seems to be no way to force a translation of the diversity into a common value system that is acceptable, realistic, and appropriate. Should more money be spent on reducing the emissions from coke ovens than on improving highway safety? How much money should be spent on cleaning up existing dump sites for hazardous wastes? For these kinds of public policy questions, the political process seems to be a reasonable way to respond to the diversity of people's values to make a decision about a course of action when there is no common value system to use for more calculative decisions.

THE PUBLIC INTEREST

According to the traditional view, the universal motivating principle in the public policy process is the public interest rather than self-interest. This principle is invoked by those who make decisions about public policy. Elected public officials often claim to be acting in the interests of the nation as a whole or of their state or congressional district. Public interest groups also claim to be devoted to the general or national welfare. These claims make a certain degree of sense. When politicians have to make a decision about the provision of some public good or service, they cannot claim to be acting in the self-interest of everyone in their constituency. When goods and services are indivisible across large numbers of people, it is impossible for individual preferences to be matched. Nor can public policymakers claim to be acting in their own self-interest; such a claim is not politically acceptable. A more general principle such as the public interest has to be invoked to justify the action.

The definition of the public interest, however, is problematical. The term can have at least four meanings.[13] The public interest can refer to the aggregation, weighing, and balancing of a number of special interests. In this view the public interest results through the free and open competition of interested parties who have to compromise their differences to arrive at a common course of action. The public interest is the sum total of all the private interests in the community that are balanced for the common good. This definition allows for a diversity of interests.

The public interest can also refer to a common or universal interest that all or at least most of the members of a society share. A decision is in the public interest if it serves the ends of the whole public rather than those of some sector of the public, if it incorporates all of the interests and concepts of value that are generally accepted in our society. Such a definition assumes a great deal of commonality as to basic wants and needs of the people who comprise a society.

There is also an idealist perspective as to the meaning of the public interest. Such a definition judges alternative courses of action in relation to some absolute standard of value, which in many cases exists independently of the preferences of individual citizens. The public interest is not only more than the sum of private interests; it is something distinct and apart from basic needs and wants of human beings. Such a definition has a transcendent character and refers to such abstractions as "intelligent goodwill" or "elevated aspirations" or "the ultimate reality" that human beings should strive to attain. The difficulty with this definition is finding someone with a godlike character who can define these abstractions in an acceptable manner.

Another definition of the public interest focuses on the process by which decisions are made rather than the specification of some ideal outcome. This definition involves the acceptance of some process, such as majority rule, to resolve differences among people. If the rules of the game have been strictly followed, which in a democratic setting means that interested parties have had ample opportunity to express their views, then the outcome of the process has to be in the public interest by definition.

These definitions all have their problems, making an acceptable definition as difficult to arrive at as a specific public policy itself. Most public policies undoubtedly reflect all of the features highlighted in these definitions in some manner. Before leaving this subject, one additional caveat must be mentioned. Those in a position of power and influence in society to shape public policy can never really escape their own self-interest and legitimately claim to be acting solely in the public interest or general good of society, however it is defined. Politicians want to get reelected and will vote for those goods and services they believe have an appeal to the majority of their constituency. Public interest groups want to extend their power and influence in society, and might more appropriately be called special interest groups. Thus, the definition of the public interest can never be entirely divorced from the self-interest of those who are making the decisions.[14]

THE VISIBLE HAND

Whatever definition of the public interest is invoked, resources are allocated in the public policy process by a visible hand. That visible hand is the group of decision makers in the public policy process who have been most active and influential in arriving at a common course of action. They are the ones who consciously allocate resources for the production of public goods and services they believe the public wants, that is, those goods and services they believe serve the public interest. If they make the wrong decisions and do not adequately serve the public interest, however it may be defined, they can be held accountable and removed from their position of power and influence.

Something of a supply and demand process occurs here in that if enough citizens demand something, at least in a democratic society, the system will eventually respond. But the decisions about resource allocation are visible in that certain people in the public policy process—elected public officials, government bureaucrats, public interest groups—can be held accountable for these decisions if they are not in the public interest and thus not acceptable throughout the entire society. The market system does not fix responsibility so precisely, as decisions about resource allocation are made by thousands of people participating in the marketplace. The concept of the invisible hand is thus appropriate for a market system but not for the public policy process.

POLITICAL ROLES

People play different roles in the public policy process than they do in the market system. These roles, of course, have a political character. Elected public officials are directly involved in the public policy process, but they are few in number relative to the total population. The same can be said of other government people such as those who serve on congressional staffs or regulatory agencies and have a real influence on public policy outcomes. These are the key decision makers in the public policy process and have the most visible impact on the outcome of the public policy process.

The average person simply plays the role of citizen by voting for a representative of his or her choice, contributing money to a campaign, writing elected public officials on particular issues, and similar measures. At the extreme, this role could involve driving one's tractor to Washington, D.C., and clogging the city streets in protest of certain governmental actions. Joining large social movements such as the civil rights movement is another way for the average person to exercise political influence. Widespread support for issues has an effect on the voting of elected public officials. Finally, people can join public interest groups or support them with contributions and fulfill a political role in this fashion. Most citizens, however, are probably content simply to elect others to engage in the business of governing in the public interest and go about their daily tasks with a minimum of political participation.

CITIZEN SOVEREIGNTY

Citizens are supposedly sovereign over the public policy process as consumers are supposedly sovereign over the market system. The vote is the ultimate power that citizens have in a democratic system. A public official can be voted out of office if he or she does not perform as the majority of citizens in his or her constituency would like. The citizens can then vote someone else into office whom they believe will make decisions about allocation of resources for production of public goods and services that are more consistent with the citizens' preferences as a whole. In the interim period between votes, citizens can express their preferences and try to influence the outcome of the public policy process either individually, through contact with public officials, or collectively, through interest groups.

There are two problems with this notion of citizen sovereignty that need to be mentioned. One concerns the idea of manipulation that was mentioned in connection with consumer sovereignty. Candidates for elected public office are advertised and packaged as are products, and in recent years, television advertising has been used more and more in political campaigns. Are citizens thus being manipulated by these promotional techniques and voting for an image created on television rather than for an individual whom they have little or no chance to know? Has citizen sovereignty been rendered obsolete by the packaging of candidates to appeal to the prejudices of people with little consideration given to the merits of issues important to the election?

Another problem with citizen sovereignty is the bad reputation that the average citizen has with regard to participation in the political process. Voter turnouts are often very low in many elections. Most of those who do vote probably know little about the candidates and the issues that are at stake in the election. Most people are not interested in public issues much of the time, particularly those that do not affect them directly. Taking such an interest means spending time on political concerns that might be more profitably devoted to the family or to leisure activities. Most citizens do not derive primary satisfactions from political participation, and unlike the marketplace, they do not have to participate to fulfill their basic needs and wants. The cost of participation in public affairs seems greater than the return. People who do not participate thus sacrifice their sovereignty and power to the minority in the society who do have a strong interest in political life and choose to actively participate in the formulation of public policy for the society as a whole.[15]

POWER AS REWARD

The reward for a public official or candidate for office is the attainment of power and influence in the public policy process. If an incumbent has done a good job in office—assessed citizen preferences correctly and been able to supply the public goods and services the citizens of his or her constituency want, that is, if the official delivers—he or she will most likely be reelected and retain the power that has been accumulated. If there is enough dissatisfaction with the incumbent, and a newcomer comes along who appears to be more responsive to citizen preferences and makes promises that people believe, that new person may be elected to office and granted the power that goes with the office.

The elected public official seeking power can be compared with the entrepreneur seeking profits. While power is not a quantifiable concept as is profit, it is no less a powerful motivator for those who want to be in positions of influence in supplying goods and services to the public. Power accrues to people who make correct decisions, who are skillful at compromise and negotiation, and who can persuade people that they can be trusted with power and will use it in the public interest so that the society as a whole benefits. Power is the lifeblood of politicians. Without it they will wither and die and eventually fade away into oblivion.

GOVERNMENT AS THE MAJOR INSTITUTION

The major institutional force operative in the public policy process is government, primarily the federal government and to a lesser extent state and local governments. Other institutions are, of course, also active in the public policy process. Business, for example, has always been and will continue to be an institutional force in the public policy process. Public interest groups are another institutional force that can be quite influential. As stated previously, not all public policies need to involve formal government action to be effective.

Government is the principal institution involved in formulating public policy that shapes the behavior of business organizations. Many policies do not become public policies until they are adopted, implemented, and enforced by some governmental institution. Government lends legitimacy to policies by making them legal obligations that command the loyalty of citizens. Government policies extend to all people in a society while the policies of other groups or organizations such as business reach only a segment of society. Government also monopolizes the legitimate use of force in seeing to it that public policies are followed by those who are affected. Only government can legitimately imprison violators of its policies.[16]

OPERATING PRINCIPLES

The operating principles of the public policy process are concepts like justice, equity, and fairness. These concepts are often invoked to justify the decisions made in the public policy process about resource allocation. While efficiency is certainly a consideration in many public policy measures, or at least should be, it will in many cases be sacrificed in the interests of justice, equity, and fairness. Government moves forward by a complex process of compromise and negotiation and divides authority and applies checks and balances to limit power that would never make sense for private business organizations.

There are no quantitative measures for these concepts of justice, equity, and fairness, but nonetheless, society has some idea as to how well the public policy process is performing along these lines. If certain courses of action are seen as grossly unfair to enough people in society, pressures will mount to change the policies. These principles are important to the operation of the public policy process and make the outcomes acceptable to society. If justice has been served by a policy, for example, an outcome will be accepted even though it may entail great sacrifice on the part of the citizens affected.

Public Policy and the Market System

Public policy is a social process and is not to be understood atomistically or as some mechanical process through which the individual preferences of citizens are aggregated into an overall public policy. People are not to be considered as atomic units who express their preferences for public goods and services in some mechanical fashion through the political process. In participating in the public policy process and expressing their values, people are revealing who they are and what kind of future they want to live in and enjoy through an interactive social process.

Mark Sagoff argues that people have different values and different objectives with respect to their roles as consumers and citizens. As consumers, people are out to satisfy self-interested preferences in markets, whereas in the public policy process they are concerned about the larger good of the community. According to Sagoff, the interests, goals, or preferences we entertain as citizens differ logically from those we seek to satisfy as individual consumers.[17] The public policy process allows people to express what they believe, what they are, and what they stand for, not simply what they wish to buy as individuals. The public policy process reflects values people choose collectively, and these may conflict with the wants and interests they pursue individually.[18] People may love their cars and hate buses, and yet vote for candidates who promise to tax gasoline to pay for public transportation.[19]

> Goals such as a cleaner environment are goals we determine for ourselves as a community, goals we could not conceive, much less achieve, as individuals trading in markets. People in communities are not an aggregate of individuals or set of preferences to be satisfied. People in communities know purposes and aspirations together they could not know alone.[20]

Public policy goals such as clean air and water, according to Sagoff, are not to be construed as simply personal wants and preferences; they are not interests to be priced by markets. They are rather views or beliefs that may find their way as public values into legislation and regulation. These goals stem from our character as a people, and a person who makes a value judgment or a policy recommendation claims to know what is right and not just what is preferred. People who participate in the public policy process regard themselves as thinking beings capable of discussing issues on their merits rather than as bundles of preferences capable primarily of revealing their wants.[21] Consumer preferences reveal a person's interests with regard to his or her own consumption opportunities, while value judgments made through public policy are concerned about the distribution of resources in society generally.[22] Ideas or convictions that can be supported by reasons in the political process are different from wants and interests satisfied in markets.[23]

Such a distinction between the market and the public policy process may not be entirely accurate, however, as many of the same points can be made about the market. In the process view, as discussed earlier, the market system is not a mechanistic process where individuals merely express their individual desires as consumers to autonomous corporations that are limited in their power over consumers by competition. The individual desires of consumers are not individualistic, but are part of the shared desires of an interactive community where corporations both shape and respond to these desires as expressed through the market.

The market is a social process that expresses the wishes of society for a better life to which material goods and services produced by corporations can contribute. It is an interactive process where corporations and consumers mutually influence each other to reach a satisfactory resolution of what goods and services should be produced. In expressing their needs and wants for certain kinds of goods and services, people are also revealing who they are rather than just their preferences, and determining what kind of future they want for themselves and their children through an interactive social process. Thus, the market system and public policy alike are social processes, each acting as an accepted organ of adjudication in society.

In the case of material goods and services, the accepted organ of adjudication is the market system that coordinates the wishes and desires of millions of individuals in society into collective demands for certain kinds of goods and services that can be produced in sufficient quantities to earn a profit for corporations. Regarding public goods and services such as equal opportunity, safety and health in the workplace, pollution control, consumer protection, and other problems of this nature, the public policy process is the accepted organ of adjudication.

Furthermore, for these social processes to work, there must be shared values. People have to share in a consumption-oriented outlook on life for the market system to work and have to share in a private property and individual ownership arrangement as the best way to organize their relationship to the goods and services provided by the market. People also have to agree that certain kinds of goods and services will meet their needs and desires for attaining a better life for themselves. Conversely, people have to agree on certain public goods and services as being in their common interest for the public policy process to work, and must have a shared set of values that certain things like clean air and competition are worth maintaining or attaining in order to live the kind of life they believe is worth living.

Through the constant adjustment that goes on between the corporation and society through the market process on the one hand and the public policy process on the other, specific values emerge, values with respect to goods and services for sale on the market, and values with respect to public goods and services provided through the public policy process. These values are both shared and unique, and emerge in the ongoing course of experience. Neither individual corporations nor society as a whole are bearers of value, but rather values emerge in the interactions between these two poles. While the corporation finds itself continually adjusting to community interests as expressed through the public policy process, such adjustment is not a purely passive one, and corporate response enters into the ongoing development of public policy. The more this dynamic, creative interaction is recognized as such, the more will corporations take responsibility for providing thoughtful, informed, and creative input into these ongoing dynamics in ways that enhance public policy.

When the usual ways of organizing the behavior of corporations in society do not work in resolving problematic situations involving conflicting valuings, new norms and ways of organizing behavior emerge that reconstruct the situation in an attempt at successful resolution of problems. When this adjustment happens, corporations are made to respond to social problems through new laws and regulations that change corporate behavior. These changes are simply implicit in the nature of corporations as social entities that are subject to change along with the society of which they are a part. In other words, corporations do not stand apart from society; they are embedded in society and subject to its changing values.

If corporations are to play a responsible role in a mutually enriching growth process, corporate leaders must be open to ongoing change and have a willingness and ability to reconstruct problematic situations, envision creative possibilities for doing so, and take the perspective of the other in providing a fair and open evaluation of consequences rooted in a sensitivity to the conflicting demands of the situation. The more corporate leaders are able to anticipate potential problems down the road by utilizing the foregoing capabilities, the more they will be able to direct the ongoing interaction between the market system and public policy in ways beneficial to both the corporation and the public at large.

Furthermore, the market and the public policy process in which corporations function are related to each other in a complex manner. The public policy process affects the market and values expressed in the market affect public policy. The way issues are dealt with through the public policy process, for example, increases public understanding of what is valuable to purchase and/or consume, what ought to be bought in the marketplace. These changes in turn provide changes in the public's experience of directly had value, thus making it profitable to produce different kinds of goods and services for sale in the marketplace. For as seen in Chapter 3, our awareness of what is valuable and ought to be promoted can enter into the directly felt value qualities of experience. On the other hand, what transpires in the market also feeds back into public policy, as companies experience ease or difficulty in responding to these expectations. The market provides information about costs and their consequences that are important to take into consideration.

As public policy measures related to landfills and other disposal methods make it more costly to dispose of waste using traditional methods, recycling becomes economically feasible and recycled products begin to have a distinct market, as more and more people change their individual value-driven choices in the marketplace. If a market for recycled products such as paper doesn't develop fast enough to deal with waste disposal problems, however, new incentives may have to be provided through additional public policy measures to make the market work effectively in addressing this problem.

As another example, the new labeling guidelines in effect showing fat content in foods more accurately will increase public consciousness about healthy eating habits, and this in turn should increase demand for nonfat foods. Thus, the marketplace itself becomes infused with a community perspective of what is valuable, and the changing desires this promotes. People come to dislike tasting the richness of foods with high-fat content, knowing that fatty foods have adverse health effects. Marketplace experience, however, will also feed back into public policy. If the new guidelines prove to be overly expensive, confusing, or simply unworkable in their present form, they will have to be changed to be more effective.

Over the last several decades, public policy has become an ever more important determinant of corporate behavior, as market outcomes have been increasingly altered through the public policy process. What happens in the public policy process has become more and more important to corporations as more and more laws and regulations affecting corporate behavior have been passed. Most corporate social behavior is the result of responding to government regulations of one sort or another or responding to a different legal environment where the corporation faces liability exposure because of laws related to its social behavior. These changes are making it increasingly clear that business must function in both the market system and public policy process. Both processes are necessary to encompass the broad range of decisions that a society needs to make about the corporation and its role in society.

Just as the relation between business and society is inherently relational, such that neither exists in isolation from the other, so to speak of the functioning of the market system and public goods and services in isolation from each other is to engage in a process of abstraction for purposes of discriminating aspects of an inseparably interwoven whole. Thus, as stressed previously, the market system is not a mechanistic process in which individuals merely express their individual desires as consumers to autonomous corporations that are limited in their power over consumers by competition. The market itself embodies demands created by a social process that expresses the collective wishes of the society for a better life to which material goods and services produced by corporations can contribute. And, as the market system adjusts to meet these demands, the direct and indirect results of the market adjustment affect the future course of public policy. Just as with self and community, one may speak of the two interactive poles in the process of adjustment, but each pole gains its meaning and significance, indeed its very being, in terms of the other. This ongoing adjustment reflects the dynamics of experimental method, as ideas for ongoing resolution of problematic contexts are tested by experience.

Thus, while both the market system and the public process can be seen as somewhat distinct, and for purposes of analysis and discussion keeping them distinct has some beneficial advantages, they are inseparably intertwined both in theory and practice. Indeed, while people may act differently and play different roles in the market and public policy process, they are essentially acting as human beings working within the dynamics of their creative selves and passive selves, bringing a unique dimension to their choices in the market and public policy processes, and yet conforming to the generalized other through the common purposes expressed through the market and public policy. The market cannot respond to individual preferences any more than can the public policy process. There must be some sense of community already present that is more than the sum of the parts and is prior to the individual.

The Role of Public Policy in a Market Society

Public policy plays the role of establishing a framework for the market system to function effectively. Perhaps this role can be best understood by describing a theory of social change called the mythic/epic cycle of social change and applying this to a market-oriented society. This theory or model grows out of the post-Enlightenment critical study of the history of religions.[24] As the name suggests, this theory consists of two major cycles. The mythic cycle addresses itself to the problem of maintaining a shared sense of meaning and continuity in a society. The epic cycle deals with radical change from essentially one society to another.

According to this theory, societies maintain a shared sense of meaning and a particular vision of reality through myth. Myth is that collection of shared stories that mediates ultimate reality to a given society, and is, therefore, directed toward personal development and social transformation. Societies usually do everything they can to keep myths alive to preserve themselves and maintain an ongoing continuity of traditional processes for as long as possible. Societies undergo radical change, however, through the process of an epic struggle of a cultural hero. The epic cycle focuses on emerging discontinuities in history, human relationships, and rupturing events. Together these cycles provide a model for a society in equilibrium and a society undergoing radical change.[25]

Applied to a capitalistic system (Figure 7-1), the primal mythical reality is Adam Smith's notion of the invisible hand, a mythical view of reality regarding how a society provides itself with material goods and services. The invisible hand is a secularized version of God, who promises abundance to his or her people. If the invisible hand is left alone to do its work (laissez-faire) and competition prevails, everyone's cup will run over with wealth and riches. People can pursue their own self-interest and society as a whole will benefit. Stories of free enterprise and entrepreneurship are all part of this primal reality.

This primal reality is eventually differentiated into a more scientific concept that provides a structural view of the way the system works. This view was provided by the mechanistic concept of supply and demand, which held that these forces are in effect the

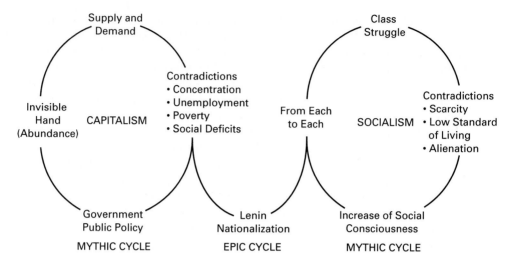

Source: Rogene A. Buchholz, *Business Environment and Public Policy: Implications for Management and Strategy Formulation,* 2nd ed., © 1986, p. 85. Reprinted by permission of Prentice-Hall, Englewood Cliffs, NJ.

FIGURE 7-1 Mythic/Epic Cycles Applied to Capitalism and Socialism

invisible hand and allocate resources to the appropriate places and provide full employment for all the members of society willing and able to work. Economic theories were thus developed to describe the workings of a market system in scientific terms so we could understand it better and prescribe policy changes when necessary.

Eventually, however, contradictions appear that challenge the primal view of reality. The competitive free enterprise system left to its own devices tends toward oligopoly or even monopoly. Thus, imperfections of competition appear. Unemployment also appears, particularly during recessions or depressions, which cannot be blamed on the people themselves. Many are not able to share in the abundance a capitalistic society produces and live out the Horatio Alger story. Instead they remain hopelessly rooted in poverty. Social deficits appear in the form of pollution or toxic wastes not disposed of properly.

These contradictions require some sort of adjudication if the primal vision of reality on which society rests is to be maintained. In American society, the government becomes the primary mediator to deal with these contradictions through public policy measures to enable the system to continue functioning. The mythic cycle is profoundly conservative, and as long as adequate adjudicating terms can be found, the society will remain stable. Change will have occurred, of course, but it will not be perceived as such because the change has been incorporated into the original mythic structure.

If these contradictions cannot be successfully mediated or reconciled, however, the epic cycle starts and the old order begins to break apart. The people who are affected by the contradictions express their alienation and oppression in what has been called a lament—a legal petition to the powers governing the universe to intervene. Eventually, a hero appears who delivers the people from their alienation and despair and becomes the leader of the new social order with new organs of adjudication and self-directive goals. That order then proceeds to maintain itself through the mythic cycle.[26]

Something like this must have happened in Czarist Russia during the Bolshevik revolution. The contradictions of the capitalistic system could not be reconciled in that country. Eventually a hero appeared (Lenin) who promised to deliver the oppressed people from their despair by abolishing the institutions of a capitalistic society (private property) and founding a new order based on a vision of reality appropriated from Marxist theory. This change involved an overthrow of old myths and the establishment of new ones to support the new order that emerged.

The primal vision of reality in this order was the myth "to each according to his need, from each according to his ability." The differentiating principle to describe how the system works was the notion of a class struggle. Contradictions that appeared include scarcity and a lower standard of living when compared with many nations of the world. Perhaps the most basic contradiction of all was the alienation of workers from the bureaucracy that ran the society and the formation of labor unions to promote workers' rights in a society that was supposed to be a worker's paradise. These contradictions were successfully mediated in the Soviet Union for many years by increasing the social cohesiveness of the people through propaganda and purges or other coercive means.

Eventually, however, new leadership appeared that attempted to change Soviet society through policies related to *perestroika* (internal reform) and *glasnost* (openness) that were meant to reform the existing society and make it more productive and democratic. But the contradictions that existed were too great to be dealt with by these measures, and once change was started by Gorbachev, it took on a life of its own, leading to a breakup of the Soviet Union and a breakaway of Eastern European countries from Soviet influence. In effect, what Gorbachev did was to lead the country into the beginning of a new epic cycle that was continued by Yeltsin after Gorbachev passed from the scene. But a new order has not yet been established, and the epic cycle continues as a struggle for power goes on in Russia and the other former Soviet republics.

Perhaps what is happening in modern Russia provides a good example of what happens when there is not a public policy framework in place to control market behavior. What has developed is something of an unregulated market economy where some people are getting rich and the vast majority of the population is suffering. Vast inequalities of wealth are resulting, inequalities that the population is not likely to tolerate for very long. Also, crime has been allowed to control emerging markets and take its share of the profits generated. Such a result seems inevitable when there is no system of laws and regulations in place to provide a framework in which markets can flourish. What happens is that the market becomes a free-for-all where anything goes and the devil takes the hindmost.

Ordinarily, then, societies operate in the mythic mode. Only when the underlying vision of reality on which the social order rests breaks down because of unreconciled contradictions does true epic appear. The epic cycle always deals with radical social change. Usually the outcome of an epic cycle is the establishment of a new social order. Should this not happen, people can face generations of oppression and anarchy. One destroys old myths and gods only at the risk that no new ones may appear to give life meaning and order.

Clearly the time frame for this model is unpredictable. The process of mythic stability can go on for generations, even thousands of years, without serious disruption. Even when the alienation stage is reached, the epic cycle may not take place for generations, or the hero figure essential to triggering rapid and radical social change may appear overnight and the revolution be accomplished in a matter of hours. The model gives no basis for estimating the time parameters for any stage or movement.[27] The former republics of the Soviet Union and the countries of Eastern Europe may take several years, if not decades, to settle on a new economic and social order that can survive into the next century.

Thus, public policy plays the role of mediator in our society, providing an ongoing organ of adjudication resolving conflicts that appear from time to time between the way the system is supposed to function and the way it is actually performing. If these contradictions can be resolved to the satisfaction of enough members in the society, radical change will be prevented and society will remain essentially stable as far as its basic institutions and mode of operation are concerned. The self-understanding of that society will be preserved and most people will still believe in the same myths and ideologies.

This is not to say that all myths are equally good, however, as they can have radically different outcomes. Myths must constantly withstand the test of their workability in reconstructing problematic situations of conflict and contradictory demands in ways that work in promoting enrichment of concrete human experience. But even the most workable is a mythic or imaginatively created structure for organizing human experience. The "truth value" of a myth lies in its workability in enriching human existence, not in supposed conformity to some ultimate law of the universe.

Questions for Discussion

1. Is the public policy process the appropriate adjudicatory organ with respect to social issues? Does the notion of public policy involve a different orientation or perspective from which to view social and ethical issues? Are both the public policy process and the market system the source of guidelines and criteria for managerial behavior?

2. Do you understand the difference between the conceptual elements of the market system and the public policy process? Be critical of the author's distinctions. Eliminate those you believe are either false or unimportant, and add others you believe are more relevant to an understanding of the differences between the market system and the public policy process.

3. Is the distinction between private goods and services and public goods and services valid? List all the public goods and services you can think of and describe how they are different from private goods and services. Describe the concept of the free rider. Can you think of instances where you have been a free rider? Does being a free rider have any moral implications?

4. What is the value of human life? What is the price of an arm, a leg, hearing, sight, and so on? How much is another three years added on to your life worth? How much would you pay to avoid cancer? What problems exist with regard to making such determinations? In light of such problems, is benefit-cost analysis a reasonable way to decide which regulations should be implemented through the public policy process?

5. What definition of the "public interest" do you agree with most strongly? What implications does your choice have for public policy? What does it mean to say that business should act in the "public interest" on any given issue? Are citizens sovereign over a democratic system? Why or why not? Does an individual's vote really count? Is there any logic to this kind of collective action?

6. Define the concepts of justice, equity, and fairness. How would you determine how well these concepts are being implemented in our society? Pick a recent public policy decision and discuss it with reference to these concepts. Are ethical issues of this sort behind public policy decisions? How can process theory contribute to the resolution of these issues?

Endnotes

[1] Mark Sagoff, *The Economy of the Earth* (Cambridge: Cambridge University Press, 1988), p. 70.

[2] Lee E. Preston and James E. Post, *Private Management and Public Policy: The Principle of Public Responsibility* (Englewood Cliffs, NJ: Prentice-Hall, 1975), p. 11.

[3] James E. Anderson, David W. Brady, and Charles Bullock, III, *Public Policy and Politics in America* (North Scituate, MA: Duxbury Press, 1978), p. 6.

[4] B. Guy Peters, *American Public Policy: Promise and Performance,* 2nd ed. (Chatham, NJ: Chatham House, 1986), p. vii.

[5] Ibid.

[6] Thomas R. Dye, *Understanding Public Policy,* 3rd ed. (Englewood Cliffs, NJ: Prentice-Hall, 1978), p. 23.

[7] John Rawls, *A Theory of Justice* (Cambridge, MA: Harvard University Press, 1971), p. 266.

[8] Gerald Sirkin, *The Visible Hand: The Fundamentals of Economic Planning* (New York: McGraw-Hill, 1968), p. 45.

[9] James Buchanan, *The Demand and Supply of Public Goods* (Chicago: Rand McNally, 1968), p. 8.

[10] See Michael J. Mandel, "How Much Is a Sea Otter Worth?" *Business Week,* August 21, 1989, pp. 59, 62.

[11] William R. Greer, "Pondering the Value of a Human Life," *The New York Times,* August 16, 1984, p. 16.

[12] Alasdair MacIntyre, "Utilitarianism and Cost-Benefit Analysis: An Essay on the Relevance of Moral Philosophy to Bureaucratic Theory," Donald Scherer and Thomas Attig, eds., *Ethics and the Environment* (Englewood Cliffs, NJ: Prentice-Hall, 1983), pp. 145–146.

[13] See Douglas G. Hartle, *Public Policy Decision Making and Regulation* (Montreal: The Institute for Research on Public Policy, 1979), pp. 213–218.

[14] There is a school of thought called public choice theory that looks at government decision makers as rational, self-interested people who are just like the rest of us, and view issues from their own perspective and act in light of the personal incentives. While voters, politicians, and bureaucrats may desire to reflect the "public interest" and often advocate it in support of their decisions, this desire is only one incentive among many with which they are faced and is likely to be outweighed by more powerful incentives related to self-interest of one sort or another. See Steven Kelman, "Public Choice and Public Spirit," *The Public Interest,* No. 87 (Spring 1987), pp. 80–94, for an interesting critique of the public choice school of thought.

[15] Aaron Wildavsky, *Speaking Truth to Power: The Art and Craft of Policy Analysis* (Boston: Little, Brown, 1979), pp. 253–254.

[16] Dye, *Understanding Public Policy,* p. 20.

[17] Sagoff, *The Economy of the Earth,* p. 8.

[18] Ibid., p. 17.

[19] Ibid., p. 53.

[20] Ibid., p. 121.

[21] Ibid., p. 44.

[22] Ibid., p. 56.

[23] Ibid., p. 92.

[24] See Owen Barfield, *Poetic Diction: A Study in Meaning* (New York: McGraw-Hill, 1964); Joseph Campbell, *The Hero with a Thousand Faces,* 2nd ed. (Princeton, NJ: Princeton University Press, 1971); Edward F. Edinger, *Ego and Archetype* (Baltimore, MD: Penguin Books, 1974);

Mircea Eliade, *Patterns in Comparative Religion* (New York: Sheed & Ward, 1958); and Claude Levi-Strauss, *Structural Anthropology,* trans. by Claire Jacobson and Brooke Grundfest Schoepf (New York: Basic Books, 1963).

[25] Ken Kochbeck, "The Mythic/Epic Cycle and the Creation of Social Meaning," unpublished paper (St. Louis, MO: Washington University, 1979), p. 3.

[26] Ibid., p. 4.

[27] Ibid., p. 7.

Suggested Readings

Anderson, James E., et al. *Public Policy and Politics in America,* 2nd ed. Belmont, CA: Wadsworth, 1984.

Buchanan, James. *The Demand and Supply of Public Goods.* Chicago: Rand McNally, 1968.

Dye, Thomas R. *Understanding Public Policy,* 7th ed. Englewood Cliffs, NJ: Prentice Hall, 1991.

Eskridge, William N., Jr., and Philip J. Frickey. *Legislation: Statutes & The Creation of Public Policy.* St. Paul, MN: West Publishing Co., 1992.

Galbraith, John Kenneth. *Economics and the Public Purpose.* Boston: Houghton Mifflin, 1967.

Galbraith, John Kenneth. *The New Industrial State.* Boston: Houghton Mifflin, 1967.

Hartle, Douglas G. *Public Policy Decision Making and Regulation.* Montreal: The Institute for Research on Public Policy, 1979.

Jones, Charles O. *An Introduction to the Study of Public Policy,* 3rd ed. Belmont, CA: Wadsworth, 1984.

Lineberry, Robert L. *American Public Policy.* New York: Harper & Row, 1978.

Luthans, Fred, and Richard M. Hodgetts. *Social Issues in Business: Strategy & Public Policy Perspectives.* New York: Macmillan, 1989.

Mills, Claudia. *Values & Public Policy.* New York: Harcourt Brace, 1991.

Nagel, Stuart S., and Lisa A. Bievenue. *Social Science, Law & Public Policy.* New York: University Press of America, 1992.

Olson, Mancur. *The Logic of Collective Action.* Cambridge, MA: Harvard University Press, 1977.

Perry, Huey L. *Democracy and Public Policy.* New York: Wyndham Hall, 1985.

Peters, B. Guy. *American Public Policy: Promise and Performance,* 2nd ed. Chatham, NJ: Chatham House, 1986.

Portney, Kent E. *Approaching Public Policy Analysis.* Englewood Cliffs, NJ: Prentice-Hall, 1986.

Preston, Lee E., and James E. Post. *Private Management and Public Policy.* Englewood Cliffs, NJ: Prentice-Hall, 1975.

Rawls, John. *A Theory of Justice.* Cambridge, MA: Harvard University Press, 1971.

Sirkin, Gerald. *The Visible Hand: The Fundamentals of Economic Planning.* New York: McGraw-Hill, 1968.

Smith, Adam. *The Wealth of Nations.* New York: Modern Library, 1937.

Wright, Gerald C., Jr. *Congress & Policy Change.* New York: Agathon, 1986.

S H O R T   C A S E S

Chrysler Corporation

In 1979, Chrysler Corporation, a once proud automotive giant, faced bankruptcy. Its share of the domestic car market had shrunk from 25.7 percent in 1946 to 9 percent in 1978. It had reacted too slowly to the decline in the market for standardized cars, and in 1979 had an unsold inventory valued at $700 million, which was mostly large cars. The company's stock plunged to new lows on the stock exchange. The company's losses reached $1 billion in 1979, the largest loss of any corporation in history for a single year. The firm's total indebtedness in 1979 stood at more than $5 billion spread among some 250 different banks and other financial institutions.

The company thus went hat in hand to Washington for help as its creditors refused to extend any more credit to the company. Chrysler couched its request for government aid in the form of a complaint about government regulation. Chrysler argued that government was responsible for Chrysler's situation and hence should aid the company. The solution to Chrysler's problem was believed to be a federal loan guarantee so creditors could safely extend the money Chrysler needed to continue operations.

Some 360,000 jobs were at stake, taxes would be lost to the government, people would be forced on the unemployment rolls, and other adverse effects would result. The failure of Chrysler would have affected a great number of groups and individuals. Chrysler served approximately 191,000 shareholders, 109,000 employees, 4,700 dealers, and 18,000 suppliers. Chrysler had facilities located in 57 communities that produced about 917,000 cars and 308,000 trucks in 1979. In order to keep these facilities operating, Chrysler had borrowed over $5 billion by 1979 and had sold almost 67 million shares of stock to 211,587 groups and individuals. Chairman Lee Iacocca estimated that if Chrysler were to fail, approximately 2 million Americans would feel a severe impact.[1]

Opponents of the guarantee blamed Chrysler's problems on bad management that had made a series of poor decisions and, therefore, should not be helped out in a state of emergency. Subsidizing a failing company, they argued, would undermine the very purpose of a competitive economy, which is to ensure that the resources of society are used efficiently. The management of Chrysler was inefficient, it was charged, and to save the company from bankruptcy would be rewarding poor management. If government played the role of guaranteeing the survival of inefficient companies, the incentives for big business to be efficient would be removed.

A Chrysler bankruptcy would have been the largest ever in the United States up to that time. It would have meant a rise in the national unemployment rate of between 0.5 percent and 1.09 percent.[2] A straightforward corporate fire sale would have threatened 113,000 production workers. More than half of these worked in Detroit, where 25,000 of the company's 38,000 minority workers were employed. The Michigan unemployment rate would have been jolted by another 4 percent while Detroit's rate would have risen by about 10 percent. There were predictions that the unemployment rate in Syracuse, New York, would double after a bankruptcy. Perhaps the largest impact would be on smaller communities that were dependent on a Chrysler factory.[3]

The cost to taxpayers in the form of unemployment compensation would have been large. A Chrysler shutdown would have cost about $1.5 billion a year in unemployment benefits. Bankruptcy would also have eroded federal income taxes by $500 million. In addition, the Federal Pension Benefit Guarantee Corporation, which was not designed to handle major failures, would have been swamped by the $800 billion of unfunded liabilities washing around in Chrysler's enormous pension funds.[4] The question of whether or not to bail out Chrysler with a loan guarantee was thus not a simple one that had an easy answer. There were many good arguments on each side of the issue.

Nonetheless, in December 1979, Congress passed the Chrysler Corporation Loan Guarantee Act of 1979. This act authorized up to $1.5 billion in loan guarantees. As a condition to this financing, Congress required Chrysler to obtain at least $1.43 billion in nonfederally guaranteed financing and to submit financing and operating plans to the Chrysler Corporation Loan Guarantee Board. The board consisted of the secretary of the Treasury, the chairman of the Federal Reserve Board, the comptroller general of the United States, plus two ex-officio nonvoting members, the secretary of labor and the secretary of transportation. This board had a good deal of say over Chrysler's operations during the time the loan guarantee was in effect.[5]

1. Was Chrysler correct in blaming government regulations for its problems? Or was this merely a politically expedient move to win support for the loan guarantee?

2. Should the loan guarantee have been granted? What were the main arguments for and against the action? In terms of costs and benefits to society, was the action justified?

3. Should business organizations turn to Washington for help when all else fails? What effect, if any, does such action on the part of American business have on free enterprise ideology and business credibility?

4. Given that the Chrysler loan turned out to be a success, does this mean the government ought to be in the business of bailing out failing companies on a continuing basis? Does this success provide any basis for the idea that government ought to develop an industrial policy for the nation that would include aid to failing businesses?

[1] Testimony by Lee A. Iacocca, Chairman of Chrysler, to U.S. House of Representatives, October 18, 1979.

[2] Seama Mority, *Going for Broke: The Chrysler Story* (New York: Doubleday, 1981), p. 279.

[3] Ibid., p. 280.

[4] "Should We Bail Out Chrysler," *Commonweal,* November 9, 1979, p. 613.

[5] Chrysler Corporation, *Annual Report,* 1982, p. 30.

Source: Rogene A. Buchholz, *Business Environment and Public Policy: Implications for Management,* 5th ed. (Englewood Cliffs, NJ: Prentice Hall, 1995), pp. 130–132.

Braniff Airlines

When the Airline Deregulation Act was passed in 1978 to give air carriers more freedom to fly routes of their own choosing, it ushered in a whole new era of competition to the airline industry. Some of the air carriers were able to adjust to this new environment and have survived and prospered. Others have had serious problems and have struggled along for years on the brink of bankruptcy. One airline that didn't make the adjustment was Braniff International, a Dallas-based carrier under the direction of Harding Lawrence, who had made the airline one of the giants in American aviation. The airline had grown from revenues of $100 million per year to revenues of $1 billion under Lawrence's leadership.[1]

While Braniff opposed deregulation, as did most of the other airlines, Lawrence had a plan in mind should deregulation become a reality. The strategic plan was to construct a sufficiently large route system, and thus a large revenue base, while the routes were there for the asking. This expansion would not only allow Braniff to survive in a deregulated world but would also give it a competitive advantage when regulation was reimposed on the airline industry. Lawrence was absolutely convinced that after several years of chaos, mergers, and ruinous competition in the industry Congress would admit its mistake and reregulate the industry. When that happened, Braniff would have grandfather rights to the routes it had acquired during the deregulatory period, and would thus be able to compete with the largest airline companies.

It was this critical assumption on which Braniff's strategy was based. Braniff had to expand, argued Lawrence, to continue Braniff's record of high profits. The size of the airline and its operations increased over 30 percent in just a few short months. Braniff began flying more and more overseas routes and schedule changes alone began costing the carrier a great deal of money. The rapid expansion began to cause problems, as many planes had load factors that did not reach the break-even level. This was particularly true of the new routes that the airline was flying overseas. It became more and more difficult for Braniff to raise the cash needed to buy aircraft to service the new routes it was acquiring and its fuel bills went tens of millions of dollars over budget.

Routes were cut back to stem the losses, pay cuts were proposed, airplanes were sold, but nothing could seem to stop the downward trend of the airline. Lawrence himself was eventually persuaded to leave the company and new management took over, but they too were unsuccessful. Finally on May 12, 1982, what was then the nation's eighth largest carrier suddenly halted all flight operations, and at 12:01 A.M. on the same night, filed for protection under Chapter 11 of the U.S. Bankruptcy Code. The company was to reappear under new ownership as a reorganized and much smaller airline. But the old Braniff had disappeared. It had simply expanded too rapidly based on a critical assumption that was false. The political environment was such that deregulation continued to be the order of the day, as the deregulatory trend was accelerated with the election in 1980 of the Reagan administration. Lawrence was wrong in his assumption about reregulation and thus the strategy based on this assumption was bound to fail, as the company did not prepare itself to survive in a competitive environment.

1. How important was public policy to Braniff? Should the company have implemented a more formal forecasting system rather than relying on the projections of one person? Should the CEO have this much power in the organization?

2. Did the government owe anything to Braniff in this situation? Should Braniff have asked for a loan guarantee or some other kind of help to bail it out of trouble? Did Braniff have any kind of moral claim on government because of its action?

[1] Information for this case came from John J. Nance, *Splash of Colors: The Self-destruction of Braniff International* (New York: William Morrow and Company, Inc., 1984).

Source: Rogene A. Buchholz, *Business Environment and Public Policy: Implications for Management,* 5th ed. (Englewood Cliffs, NJ: Prentice Hall, 1995), pp. 527–528.

Government Bailouts

The talk in the executive dining room was all about the sorry state of the company. Unless some miracle happened, most executives believed the company would go under. All of the creditors had refused to extend any more credit, and the company was faced with an imminent cash flow problem. It may not be able to meet the payroll at the end of the month and thus would be forced to take drastic action. It seemed incredible to Bill that a company the size of Invincible, Inc., should be faced with bankruptcy, but such was the reality.

As a last resort, top management was considering asking the federal government for a bailout in the form of a loan guarantee. Management believed it could make a good case for a bailout, as had Lockheed and Chrysler, because of the implications of a bankruptcy for employment and defense contracts.

This request bothered Bill because he knew how antigovernment management was on most other matters, grousing about government regulations, welfare programs, pork barrel waste, and crooked politicians. The dominant ideology in the company was strictly free enterprise with minimal government interference in business affairs. Yet here the company was about to get in bed with the "devil," so to speak, in asking for a helping hand. This inconsistency didn't seem to bother most of the other executives, but it did bother Bill, and he wondered if he should raise the question or keep his mouth shut.

1. Do most executives really believe in free enterprise and readily accept the implications of a competitive system? Why would they turn to government for help when they get in trouble?

2. Should we as citizens be concerned about government bailouts of failing companies? Was Bill's concern based upon his role as an employee of the company or on his role as a citizen? What should he do as a loyal agent of the company?

Source: Rogene A. Buchholz, *Business Environment and Public Policy: Implications for Management,* 5th ed. (Englewood Cliffs, NJ: Prentice Hall, 1995), p. 158.

Regulation and Competitive Advantages

Get-Well Drug Company made a decision several years ago that now has the potential of giving it a significant competitive advantage over other companies in the industry. For reasons that are now obscure, management decided some time ago to package all its over-the-counter drugs in plastic bottles when glass bottles seemed to be the standard in the industry. Even though the cost of plastic bottles was a bit higher, management decided to break ranks with the rest of the industry. Speculation has it that this may have been an effort to differentiate the company's products from those of its competitors.

Now that decision was about to pay off. There had been numerous instances over the past several years of people dropping the glass bottles on the bathroom floor, and then not sweeping up all the glass fragments. Later they would step on these fragments and cut their feet, sometimes quite severely. Because of these accidents, a bill was now before a House committee to require the use of plastic bottles for all over-the-counter drugs.

If this bill passed, Get-Well would have a significant advantage for a period of time while the other companies in the industry retooled for plastic bottles. It could advertise itself as a forward-looking company and perhaps even gain a permanent increase in market share for some of its products. Thus, top management has been talking with the company's Washington representative about lobbying for the bill's passage. Such lobbying would obviously have to be done very discreetly so as not to alienate its competitors and appear hypocritical about its stated opposition to government regulation in general.

1. Are there other instances where government regulation can give some companies significant competitive advantages? Is it proper for management of these companies to try and use the public policy process in these situations to gain an advantage? What possible adverse consequences might result from such activities?

2. What alternatives besides lobbying are available to the management of Get-Well to try to get the bill passed? Are some of these alternatives more acceptable than the bill under consideration? Would some of them be more effective than the current proposal? Which is the more important consideration?

Source: Rogene A. Buchholz, *Business Environment and Public Policy: Implications for Management,* 5th ed. (Englewood Cliffs, NJ: Prentice Hall, 1995), p. 194.

The Nature
of the
Corporation

The corporation is a dominant institution in American society in that the values promoted and created by the corporation are some of the most important values in society. The corporation creates economic value and promotes this particular kind of value through its activities. It is economic value that is most often used to measure success in American society and determine whether the society is in good shape or needs some serious attention. The corporation also distributes economic value, and the way it distributes this value determines the welfare of vast numbers of people. In this manner, the corporation is a dominant institution in American society in that the economic value it creates gives shape to the society and largely defines what the society is all about.

Characteristics of the Corporation

The corporation is a device that was formed to create economic wealth. This is simply another way of saying that the corporation creates a certain kind of value that the society believes is of central importance in contributing to its welfare. The corporation brings together people with different skills and talents, capital resources of many different kinds, and raw materials from many different places, and puts these all together to produce goods and services that are useful for the society. The corporation is a kind of social organization where people are organized to achieve a common purpose. They may not have a common purpose in mind when taking a job with a company, but nonetheless, their skills and talents are eventually directed to the common purpose of producing goods and services and creating economic wealth for the society.

The corporation is often described, particularly in classical economic theory, as a voluntary organization where people join together to accomplish purposes that they could not accomplish separately. They band together because of economic self-interest.

Employees are believed to be pursuing their self-interest in working to earn wages or salaries to support themselves and their families. Investors put money into the corporation because of the desire to earn an economic return on their investment. Customers buy the goods and services a corporation produces because they are pursuing their self-interest in attempting to enhance their welfare and gain personal satisfaction through their consumption activities.

The corporate form of organization was first used for a public purpose in that corporations were formed for purposes of building roads or canals in the early years of this country. But in the landmark Dartmouth College decision, corporations were held to be a voluntary organization that could be used by people to pursue their economic self-interest without an overriding public purpose. Thus, corporations were formed for private purposes and were freed from control by the government. People were encouraged to form corporations wherever they thought an opportunity existed that could be exploited for self-interested purposes.

The corporate form of organization enabled risk to be spread across a number of people and made individuals who invested in the company accountable only for the amount of money they had put into the organization rather than for the whole entity. They could thus minimize their risk and yet join with others in a cooperative enterprise that needed larger sums of capital and resources than they had individually. Thus, they could share in a larger endeavor that could exploit opportunities that were too large and risky for any one individual to take on alone. The legal fiction called the corporation enabled this kind of an arrangement to work for the advantage of society.

Such a view, however, is again based on the perspective of the individual as an atomic unit who bands together with other such individuals for certain common purposes. They have no other connection except this need to be part of the same organization for self-interested reasons. From a process perspective, however, the corporation is a community, an entity where individuals are in part what they are because of their membership in a corporate organization, and the organization is what it is because of the people who choose to become part of the organization. The organization needs a certain dimension of conformity to operate, but at the same time needs creative input from the unique individuals who work within it in order for it to grow and remain competitive. And like all communities, the corporation has a moral dimension.

Nor are these selves and their skills and abilities coordinated in some mechanical fashion to accomplish corporate objectives. Such a mechanistic view of the corporation is not consistent with the notion that people who work in the corporation do not sacrifice their essential humanness and become some kind of atomic unit that is treated in a machinelike manner. Managers who treat their employees in an economic sense as just another factor of production are not treating them as moral beings who are an essential part of the community. Moreover, treating people in a mechanical manner does not lead to an efficient or effective organization.

> What makes a corporation efficient or inefficient is not a series of well-oiled mechanical operations but the working interrelationships, the coordination and rivalries, team spirit and morale of the many people who work there and are in turn shaped and defined by the corporation. So, too, what drives a corporation is not some mysterious abstraction called "the profit motive." . . . It is the collective will and ambitions of its employees, few of whom work for a profit in any obvious sense. Employees of a corporation do

what they must to fit in, to perform their jobs, and to earn both the respect of others and self-respect. . . . To understand how corporations work (and don't work) is to understand the social psychology and sociology of communities, not the logic of a flowchart or the organizational workings of a cumbersome machine.[1]

The corporation is the primary organization in our society through which new technology is introduced. When science makes possible the development of new technologies, these technologies will most likely be developed and employed by a corporation in order to introduce a new product to the market that hopefully will be profitable. Thus, technology is made to serve the aims of the corporation, and the decision as to whether or not a new technology is introduced into society is primarily economic in nature. There may be some questions asked about the potential effect of the technology on the environment and whether or not it is safe to use, but the primary concern of the corporation will be whether or not the technology can be made profitable and serve the private interests of the people who benefit from corporate activities.

The corporation then is based primarily on a certain kind of value, or perhaps it is more appropriate to say that the corporation is an organization that creates economic value or adds economic value to something that is believed to have no such value in and of itself. This value is primarily economic in nature in that resources that have no economic value in themselves are combined in such a way that goods and services are produced that are of value to the society. These goods and services are then traded on the marketplace in order for the corporation to earn a profit that is a reward for having created something that is of value. Another way to describe this process is to say that the resources in the production process have no economic value in and of themselves or have no utility for anyone. Iron ore in the ground has no economic value in its natural state, for example; it is only as it is dug out of the ground and utilized for the production of iron and steel that it has economic value or utility in the society at large. Similarly, land in its natural state has no economic value in and of itself, but as land is cleared and plowed and used for growing crops, it comes to have economic value.

Purposes of a Corporation

One major purpose of a corporation, then, is to produce goods and services that contribute to the material well-being of society. But this is not the only purpose of a corporation. The business organization also exists to provide meaningful life experiences for its employees, to pay dividends to shareholders who have invested in its future, to develop new products and technologies through research and development that can improve society, to do those activities that enhance the environment and cease doing those activities that degrade the environment, to be a good citizen in obeying the laws of the country in which it operates, and where possible to help society solve some of its most pressing social problems. Thus, the corporation is truly a multipurpose organization and many of its purposes are noneconomic in nature.

If a company has done things right in the sense of producing things people want to buy and find useful, has done so efficiently so that people can afford to buy the things that are produced, and has hired and maintained an efficient and well-motivated work force, the company is rewarded with profits. In the best sense of the word, then, profits are the reward for having efficiently produced something useful, representing the corporation's share of the wealth that has been created. Profits are the lifeblood of the corporation and without profits corporations obviously would not survive. These profits are used to support the operations of the corporation and are paid out as dividends to the shareholders who have risked their money by investing in the stock of the corporation.

However, these purposes of a corporation are often lost sight of in the quest for profits, as managers are encouraged to maximize profits or earn the highest rate of return they can for the shareholders rather than produce goods and services that maximize utility to customers. In some sense, the cart is put before the horse, as the purpose of the corporation over time has become the generation of profits, and the production of goods and services has in large part become an incidental exercise in the unending quest for profits. Perhaps this is inevitable given the nature of the system, but in any event, the purpose of the corporation has gone through a transformation in our society to the point where economic value resides in the money a corporation can earn rather than in the goods and services it produces and the contribution it makes toward enhancing the welfare and quality of life in society.

Schools in business and management where future managers of these organizations are trained focus on the making of profits and the maximization of shareholder wealth rather than on the production of quality goods and services that increase the material well-being of society. From a moral point of view, there is no justification for shareholders holding such an important position in the scheme of things and having first priority as regards corporate activity. Shareholders can spread their risk by diversifying their investment portfolio, while employees cannot do the same by having a number of jobs in different organizations. They are usually totally dependent on the fortunes of a single organization. Consumers also put their lives at risk if there is some question about the safety of the product the company is producing. Thus, the idea that shareholders are the group that takes the greatest risk and thus deserves special treatment is a fiction.

This focus on profits, however, is found everywhere. Corporate strategy is formulated with an eye on increasing profits by increasing market share or eliminating the competition with more effective strategies. Rarely is there any emphasis on the production process and the efficient utilization of resources to create something that has utility for the customers. Only recently has there been a concern for quality that has gained the attention of managers and schools of business. However, one would have thought that quality should have been a major concern from day one and not something that suddenly has been discovered and is treated as a major revelation.

That this transformation should happen is probably a function of the nature of the economic value system in which corporations operate. While the real purpose of a corporation is to enhance the material well-being of society and provide meaningful opportunities for a major part of the work force, these purposes get lost and take a lesser priority as the economic purpose of the corporation begins to dominate. Because the only way to measure the success of a corporation is economic in nature, this measurement system becomes the focus of corporate activity, and the corporation comes to be viewed solely as an economic institution that creates economic wealth as measured by profits. Thus, the making of profits becomes the purpose of a corporation and the other values that are involved in the production of goods and services become of lesser importance.

Money has thus come to play a dominant role in society. It has changed from being a medium of exchange to becoming the embodiment of wealth. The wealth of the society is not tied up in the quality of life to which the corporation contributes, either positively or negatively, but in the money that is generated in the process of producing goods and services. But money in and of itself has no utility; it is what money can buy or the status that it confers that is important. The idea that money should become the all-dominant purpose is in some sense absurd; it has become a reified entity that somehow conveys a sense of real wealth, when in actuality it is only a piece of paper or a coin or a number in a bank account that has no real value in and of itself.

The modern corporation is a much different type of entity than it was in the early years of this country. The fact that it has become large is not necessarily the most important thing that has happened to this form of organization. What is perhaps most significant is the changing perceptions of what the corporation is all about and how it is viewed in the society as a whole. And in this regard, it seems that the corporation is not viewed as an organization that performs a service in society as the institution through which goods and services are produced that enhance the society's material well-being, or that since a large portion of the population spends a significant part of their lives working for the corporation, provides meaning and purpose for their existence. What has happened is a transformation of the corporation into a money-making machine where wealth is tied up with the money that a corporation can make, not in the goods and services it produces or the quality of life it provides for its employees. This is a form of corporate mercantilism where the most important aspect of corporate behavior is its ability to make money and the making of a product or the provision of a needed service is incidental to its main purpose of creating monetary wealth.

Corporate Moral Agency

The question of moral agency has to do with moral responsibility and moral accountability related to the corporate organization. Is the corporation a moral agent in some sense so that it can be held morally accountable for its actions? Or is the corporation no more than the people who are a part of the organization and, thus, moral responsibility and accountability only make sense when applied to these individuals? Can the corporation be considered as something distinct from its individual members and thus be held morally responsible as an organizational entity? Or in holding a corporation morally accountable, are we simply holding individuals in the corporation accountable?

Corporations are considered as persons under the law and have some of the same rights as persons. They can sue and be sued; they own property, conduct business, conclude contracts, and enter into agreements; they have freedom of the press and are protected from unreasonable searches and seizures the same as individuals. Corporations are considered citizens of the state in which they are chartered. They can be fined and taken to court by governments for violation of laws or regulations. Since the law treats corporations the same as individuals in many respects, does this mean that corporations are also a moral agent with moral responsibility?

Usually a moral act is considered to be an act that is done knowingly and intentionally and involving choice. The action is not forced but is done freely and deliberately. It would be folly to hold someone morally responsible for an act that was coerced or where little or no choice was involved. We also excuse people from moral responsibility if they are not in control of their mental faculties or have a temporary condition that renders them incapable of making a conscious choice.[2]

Moral responsibility generally involves a goal orientation, such that the action in question was brought about by a moral agent who acted knowingly and freely. If there are no excusing conditions, the act can be morally evaluated. Excusing conditions include (1) conditions that preclude the possibility of action such as an action being impossible for a person to perform, (2) conditions that preclude or diminish knowledge that is required to perform the action as when a reasonable person could not be expected to know the consequences of an action, and (3) conditions where freedom to perform or not perform an act is precluded or diminished, such as the existence of external coercion or internal compulsion.[3]

Given this definition, it may seem obvious to some people that the corporation cannot be held morally accountable for its actions. The corporation as such does not make choices—the people in the corporation make choices. People act intentionally and deliberately, but the corporation cannot act intentionally, at least not in the way we usually use and understand that concept. The corporation is not a moral person; it has no conscience and no feelings of moral compulsion or obligation. The corporation cannot act on its own volition; it can only act through the people who comprise its work force. What sense does it make, then, to say that the corporation is morally responsible for its actions?

While the corporation may not be a moral person, it may, however, be a moral agent in the sense that the corporation was created for specific functions in society and thus is responsible to society for the fulfillment of those functions. Corporations do act through some kind of a decision-making procedure and these decisions have impacts on people. When a decision is made to close a plant, that decision affects stockholders, employees, the community in which the plant is located, and other people. This decision has moral consequences and involves moral duties that should be taken into account by the corporation.

The corporation could thus be seen as an agent created by society for special purposes and accountable to society for its decisions. It has been created to fulfill certain roles in society and is allowed to function as long as these roles are adequately fulfilled. The primary role of a corporation is, of course, economic, but its social and political roles are of increasing importance. If the corporation does not fulfill its economic responsibilities, the marketplace may force it to declare bankruptcy. If its social role is not fulfilled adequately, the government may regulate the corporation in the public interest. The corporation has a responsibility connected with its agency and the roles it is expected to play in society.

Because the corporation has these characteristics of agency, it may be appropriate to ascribe moral responsibility to the corporation as an entity, rather than simply talk about the responsibility of the individuals who work for the corporation. The corporation can be held morally responsible and accountable for its actions even though it is not a moral person. There are certain practical advantages to this ascription of responsibility that stem from the complexity of a corporate organization and the difficulty of identifying the appropriate individuals and affixing responsibility for the decisions made by the corporation.

Because the corporation may be a moral agent, however, does not mean that it possesses other properties that are associated with human agents, such as intentions, feelings, pleasures, and human rights and responsibilities. The corporation as such has no right to vote in a democratic society, nor is it required to obtain a driver's license. There is a difference between corporate moral agency and personal or human moral agency. This difference is important to keep in mind because the moral agency of a corporation is of a special kind and deserves special consideration.[4]

THE PHILOSOPHICAL DEBATE

The question of corporate moral agency and responsibility has been debated extensively in the philosophical literature. People like John R. Danley, for example, argue that collective entities are not the kinds of things that are capable of intending. When we speak of corporations as being responsible, we are speaking elliptically of certain individuals in the corporation who are responsible. Only individuals within the corporation can be held responsible and punished for their actions.[5]

Danley compares the corporation to a machine and argues that if a complicated machine got out of hand and ravaged a community, there would be something perverse about directing moral outrage and indignation to the machine. Such moral fervor should be addressed to the operators and designers of the machine. They, and not the machine, are morally responsible.[6] In the Bhopal tragedy, for example, it would make no sense to direct our moral outrage to the technology in which MIC was stored and controlled. Such outrage is appropriately directed toward the operators of the plant, the designers of the facility, and the management of the company.

Michael Keeley agrees that it is difficult to talk intelligently about the corporation as a single collective entity. It does not make sense to talk about corporate intentions and responsibilities in contrast to the intentions and responsibilities of individual persons in the corporation. While a corporation can act in the sense of producing an effect, this does not mean that it acts in the sense of intending an effect. When we talk about intentions, it does not seem possible to speak of organizational intentions without resorting to the intentions of participating individuals. What we commonly call organizational goals are those potential consequences of organizational behavior, which are goals for at least some participating individuals.[7]

John Ladd asserts that corporations should not be expected to display the same moral attributes we expect of persons. Formal organizations or their representatives acting in their official capacities cannot and must not be expected to be honest, courageous, considerate, sympathetic, or have any kind of moral integrity. Because of its structure, a corporation is bound to pursue its goals single-mindedly, and cannot, by definition, take morality seriously. Decisions are made for the organization with a view to its objectives, and not on the basis of the personal interests or convictions of the individuals who make decisions. The decisions made by management must take as their ethical premises the objectives that have been set for the organization. They cannot take their ethical premises from the principles of morality. It is improper to expect organizational conduct to conform to ordinary principles of morality. Corporate decisions are subject to the standard of rational efficiency whereas the actions of individuals as such are subject to ordinary standards of morality. There exists a double standard, then, one for an individual when he or she is working for the company and another when the individual is at home among friends and neighbors.[8]

Kenneth Goodpaster and John Matthews in an article entitled "Can a Corporation Have a Conscience?" attempt to attack this notion of the double standard.[9] They argue that a corporation can and should have a conscience—that organizational agents such as corporations should be no more and no less morally responsible than ordinary persons. In supporting these assertions, they define and apply two key concepts of corporate behavior. One of these is rationality. Taking a moral point of view includes features usually attributable to rational decision making such as lack of impulsiveness, care in mapping out alternatives and consequences, clarity about goals and purposes, and attention to details. The other key concept is respect defined as awareness and concern for the effect of one's decisions and policies on others. Respect goes beyond seeing others merely as instrumental to accomplishing one's purposes and involves respect for the lives of others in taking their needs and interests seriously.

The principle of moral projection is then advocated as a means of projecting rationality and respect to organizations. It is not sufficient to draw a sharp line between an individual's private ideas and efforts and a corporation's institutional efforts. The latter can and should be built upon the former. The principle of moral projection helps to conceptualize the kinds of moral demands we might make of corporations and other organizations and offers the prospect of harmonizing those demands with the demands we make of ourselves. In this way the double standard between individual and corporate moral responsibility can be overcome.[10]

Peter French argues that corporations can be full-fledged moral persons and have whatever privileges, rights, and duties as are, in the normal course of affairs, accorded to moral persons. Moral responsibilities are created through promises, contracts, compacts, hirings, assignments, and appointments. French relies on a corporation's internal decision-making structure (CID) as the basis for corporate morality, claiming that the CID structure is the requisite device that licenses the predication of corporate intentionality. Corporations have policies, rules, and decision-making procedures, all of which when considered together qualify them for the status of a moral agent. A functional CID structure incorporates the acts of biological persons who can then be praised or blamed for decisions, and their decision-making capacity entails that they are intentional beings and have essentially the same responsibilities and rights as ordinary persons. When a corporate act is consistent with the implementation of established corporate policy, then it is proper to describe it as having been done for corporate reasons, and as having been caused by a corporate desire coupled with a corporate belief—in other words, as corporately intentional.[11]

Finally, Tom Donaldson argues that in order for a corporation to be raised above the level of a mere machine, the corporation must have reasons for what it does, not merely causes, and some of these reasons must be moral ones in order for the corporation to be considered a moral agent. A second condition for moral agency, according to Donaldson, is that corporations must be able to control the structure of policies and rules; in other words, they must have the freedom to develop policies and rules of operation free from internal compulsion or external coercion.[12]

IMPLICATIONS OF THE DEBATE

What are the implications of this debate for the question of corporate moral agency and responsibility? The argument by Peter French mentions corporate policies as a possible focus of moral responsibility. Policies can be defined as courses of action taken with respect to a particular problem or issue. These policies reflect the best thinking of the corporation and in a sense represent the collective wisdom of the organization. In modern complex organizations these policies are not the responsibility of one person but are the result of inputs from many different people. These policies are more than the sum of these individual inputs, however, and represent a true community product that has moral dimensions and impacts and can be evaluated from a moral point of view.

It seems reasonable to assume that corporations do have moral reasons for what they do, either implicit or explicit, and that they have certain degrees of freedom in the development of policies and rules of operation. It can be assumed that corporations act rationally according to a rational decision-making structure. These decisions affect people and hence can be morally evaluated. Thus, corporations can be held morally accountable for the moral dimensions of policies and the actions that result from these policies.

Corporate policies toward AIDS victims, for example, have moral implications. Do these policies respect the rights of individuals to privacy, the right to a job, and the right to equal opportunity? These are moral questions. Other policies regarding the disposal of toxic wastes have moral implications. Are these wastes being disposed of properly so as to protect drinking water and human health and thus promote human welfare and fulfillment? Policies with respect to customer complaints entail moral considerations. Do these policies respect persons as ends with valid concerns that the company has an obligation to treat in a responsible fashion?

These are all legitimate moral questions that apply to the policies of the organization. The organization accomplishes much of its work through the implementation of these kinds of policies. It does not seem realistic, let alone ethical, to assign moral responsibility for the effects of these policies solely to individuals in the organization. The organization is a community and many people at all levels of the organization are involved in policy making with regard to various issues and problems. The question of assigning or affixing responsibility solely to individuals in this kind of a context is difficult under the best of conditions.

Because of the size and complexity of modern corporate organizations, it is sometimes difficult to identify the individuals within the corporation to whom responsibility should be assigned. These difficulties are compounded when one recognizes that many of these decisions were probably made in a committee structure where no single individual can be held responsible for what is essentially a group decision. The modern corporation is a complex bureaucracy where it is often difficult to parcel out sole responsibility for policies and decisions to certain individuals that can be justified on principles of justice and fairness.

Who is responsible for the Bhopal disaster, for example, when so many people were involved? How much responsibility should be assigned to the workers who panicked and ran away when they realized that the tank containing MIC might explode? How much blame should be assigned to the designers of the facility who made a decision to store the chemical in large tanks rather than in smaller ones where the risks might have been lessened? How shall responsibility be allocated between the management of the Indian facility and top management of the company located in the United States? What responsibilities should be assigned to the board of directors of the parent company?

There are more than practical reasons, however, as to why all of the actions of a corporation cannot be reducible to individual actions. There are philosophical reasons as well having to do with the nature of a corporation as a community. The arguments against treating the corporation as a moral agent seem to be largely based on atomic individualism where the corporation is nothing more than the sum of the individuals who work within its boundaries. They are also based on a mechanistic view of the corporation where it is treated as nothing more than a machine rather than a community of people who have both common and individual purposes.

There is something called corporate action, even though the actors are individuals who make individual contributions to the corporate action. But one individual action in itself is not sufficient to produce a corporate action. In a corporate action, each individual action is mixed with others and transformed into an action or policy of the organization. Because of this process of transformation, the actions and practices of the corporation are quite different from the primary inputs of any of the individual contributors. In principle, at least, it is possible for an immoral corporate action to be the result of a mixture of moral primary actions, thus making the moral evaluation of corporate actions and policies different from the moral evaluation of individuals within the corporation who played a role in the action.[13]

Policies are truly acts of the corporation and the corporation as such can be held responsible for their effects. This does mean that the corporation is a moral agent, but it is a moral agent only in acting as an agent of society to accomplish specific purposes. The corporation can be held responsible for its policies that result in actions that have moral impacts. The corporation as such has obligations, it enters into contracts, it makes agreements and commitments. Thus, it belongs in some sense to a moral community and can be ascribed moral responsibility for its actions. While it may not have a conscience, it does have purpose and intentionality of a sort, and the people who make decisions within the corporate structure and formulate and implement policies for the organization are acting on behalf of the corporation and not strictly for themselves. While individuals make corporate policy decisions, these decisions are not personal but are choices made for and in the name of the organization.[14]

This argument about the moral status of a corporation has serious implications when it comes to controlling corporate behavior. If the corporation is viewed as essentially an amoral entity and in no sense a moral agent in its own right, if it is viewed in some mechanistic sense as nothing more than a means of coordinating the actions of atomic individuals, then guidance as far as moral purposes are concerned must be external. The law and the political process are then seen as the appropriate sources for this guidance. If corporations are similar to large machines that have capacity to harm society, then they must be externally controlled. If they are only profit-generating machines, for example, then they must be regulated to perform their activities in a morally acceptable manner.

If the corporation is viewed in some sense as a moral agent, however, and its policies and actions have moral impacts, then a different view of implementation results. Moral pressure can then be brought to bear within the organization so that each of those individuals involved in policy and decision making as agents of the corporation might consider the actions and policies of the corporation and their own participation in decision making within the corporation from a moral point of view and consider their moral responsibilities. They could, as Goodpaster and Matthews suggest, project rationality and respect into corporate actions and policies.

Individual responsibility is thus still important even if the corporation is considered to be a moral agent, but it must be considered in the context of the corporation as a community. If the corporation is considered to be a moral agent, an inquiry can be made into the nature of a corporation's rights and responsibilities. But a focus on moral agency should not allow us to ignore individual responsibility. While moral responsibility may be ascribed to corporations, this responsibility must be assumed by the individuals within the corporation in order for it to mean anything and for change to take place if it is necessary. Moral responsibility can be refused, in which case no action will be taken to correct whatever moral deficiencies are alleged to exist.

All too often such responsibility can be avoided in a large complex organization. Those who are at or near the end of the line as far as implementation of policies is concerned believe that they have little or no choice in the matter. They have received their orders and the choices open to them are limited. They did not initiate the action or practice; they are just following corporate policy or the orders of their superiors. Those at the top echelons of the company, who are responsible for major policies of the company, can claim that they do not see the specific results of the policies they initiated and are far removed from their concrete implementation. They may claim that they did not intend to cause the specific harms that people at the receiving end of the policy may have suffered. Thus, at both ends of the chain of command, people can escape moral responsibility for corporate policies and actions.

The law treats corporations and individuals in a way that perhaps has application to the question of moral agency. Some laws, such as those in the antitrust area, hold both the corporation and individuals guilty of violations and subject them to separate penalties. Both the corporation and the individuals who are determined to be responsible for the illegal action are fined some amount of money. In some cases the fine is the same; in other cases the corporation as such is subject to a greater fine than the individuals involved. Jail sentences, of course, can only be assigned to individuals and not the corporation, but even here, it has been rumored that corporations pick individuals whose job it is to serve the sentences on behalf of the corporation when individual responsibility cannot be determined.

There is, of course, a difference between legal and moral culpability. Some laws may be judged immoral, and some immoral acts may be judged perfectly legal. Nonetheless, just as the individual and the organization are held legally responsible, so both the individual and the corporation are important to consider from a moral point of view. Atomic individualism leads to views that stress either the individual, slighting the role of the whole, or the group as a whole, slighting the role of the individual. If the corporation is seen as nothing more than the individuals who make up its membership, then corporate responsibility can be avoided. On the other hand, if the corporation is seen as a whole that abrogates the freedom of individuals, then individual responsibility can be escaped. But the corporation understood as a community, as an irreducible relational whole, is more than the sum of its parts and embodies its own moral quality. Moreover, to function as a community, its ongoing dynamics must incorporate the poles of individual creative input and conforming constraint in an ongoing adjustment that does not abrogate but rather demands individual freedom and responsibility.

To develop a moral corporation, all persons within the company must hold themselves to be morally responsible for the job they were hired to do, and they must hold others morally responsible for doing their jobs. In this way, a culture of moral responsibility can be created where moral conduct is institutionalized throughout the organization. Where this takes place, there is more likely to be a consistency between moral actions on the part of individuals and moral actions that are the result of collective action on the part of the organization. Such a firm would have a moral integrity that is more than the sum of the integrity of the individuals who comprise the organization. The organization itself could be said to be moral in that it has accepted its responsibility and recognizes the moral dimensions of its policies and actions.

Creating an Ethical Business Organization

Many of the cases in this book illustrate how easy it is for management to cut corners and take unethical actions when under pressures to make profits and keep the company afloat. Financial pressures are often sufficient to explain why some companies play fast and loose with accepted ethical practices and try to deceive the public or the government. But there are other pressures as well that often cause management to abuse its power and engage in unethical practices that most often lead to disastrous results for managers and the companies they manage. In dealing with this problem, it may be useful to consider how an ethical organization can be created and prevented from engaging in unethical practices, to say nothing of breaking laws and regulations that expose it to criminal and civil penalties. What factors are important in creating and maintaining an ethical organization?

TOP-MANAGEMENT COMMITMENT

Ethical behavior starts at the top of the organization, in some sense, as strong ethical leadership from top management leads to an organizational climate in which ethical conduct is encouraged and promoted. Without commitment from the top, lower-level employees who are concerned about ethical standards often find themselves in conflicting situations between their own standards and those of the organization. Such commitment is lacking in many of the cases presented in this book, as top management gave in to financial and other pressures to keep the company going and save its own position. Top management serves as a role model by making it clear throughout the organization that unethical behavior will not be tolerated. This message has to be consistent in everything top management does, as ambiguous messages of the "do as I say and not as I do" variety leave employees confused as to what kind of behavior is expected of them. Ethical behavior has to be encouraged and rewarded consistently, even when hard times fall upon the company, for the commitment of top management to mean anything.

ETHICAL CODES

Written codes of ethics can be useful in specifying more precisely what kind of ethical behavior is expected of employees in their specific responsibilities. The code can clarify what the organization means by ethical conduct, and can be effective in encouraging ethical behavior throughout the organization. The best codes of ethics state what the company values and what it stands for as far as ethical conduct is concerned, rather than being rule-oriented codes that are just another part of a management control system. When standards of conduct based upon the values of the organization are integrated into a strong corporate culture, then behavior will become more ethically consistent throughout the entire organization.

There is often a tendency for corporations to prepare ethical codes for individuals to use in making judgments in particular cases, and then consider the issue "handled" successfully. However, these codes, like moral rules in general, cannot be taken as something that can be routinely applied in concrete cases. Rather, the thoughtful, tentative application of these codes in concrete cases may lead to decisions that alter the codes in various ways depending on the circumstances. The codes must be constantly evaluated in terms of concrete cases, and those applying them must have input into their ongoing evaluation.

Codes of ethics typically cover areas like conflicts of interest; protection of the company's proprietary information; the giving and receiving of gifts, gratuities and entertainment; discrimination and sexual harassment; kickbacks; employee use of company assets; bribery; insider trading; environmental protection; and other such areas where ethical issues are likely to arise. Corporate interest in codes of ethics has increased over the last several decades. Part of the reason is that in the 1970s, public confidence in business fell dramatically as shown by several poll-taking organizations. This trend was further exacerbated with numerous "ethics" scandals in the 1980s, including defense contracting irregularities, insider trading, the generic drug scandals, and other such problems involving whole industries or individual companies.

The response of many companies to this "crisis" of confidence has been to clarify policies and expectations through the development of standards of employee and business conduct. Many companies developed such codes for the first time. The types of codes that have been produced, the reasons for their development, and the uses to which they have been put vary considerably. Some are simple, one-page statements of company values or management philosophy. Others are multipage, even multivolume, attempts to prohibit or require specific conduct of employees over a broad array of situations.

Codes of ethics are living documents in the sense that they express the values of an organization and what it stands for as reflected in the kind of conduct it expects from its employees. Since organizations are dynamic entities, codes of ethics must also be dynamic to reflect changes in the organization and in external conditions. Codes of ethics are not to be viewed as static rules that the company is trying to impose on its employees, sort of another management control device. While some rulelike standards cannot be avoided in a written code, they are best viewed as statements about the values of the company rather than as a means to regulate employee behavior.[15]

There are many possible purposes for a code of ethics, and any one code will undoubtedly serve several purposes at the same time. The purposes of a code are important because they will affect the form as well as the content of the code, and will have implications for the way in which the code is promulgated. Some common purposes include (1) inspiring company employees and exhorting them to high standards of conduct, (2) regulating employee behavior by spelling out prohibited conduct and affirmative duties to the company, (3) providing guidelines for decision making in areas of employee discretion by articulating the standards governing the conduct of the company's business, and (4) defining the values of the company and capturing its ethos or spirit in the hope of uniting diverse elements of the organization into one coherent ethical culture.[16]

Ethical codes also have the advantage of (1) serving as sounder guides to acceptable and unacceptable behavior than other forms of communication, (2) providing guidance to employees in ethically ambiguous situations, (3) controlling the power of other employers and supervisors to solicit unethical and illegal behavior from employees and subordinates, and (4) communicating the importance of the ethical policy as the collective standard of the organization.

Some companies also claim that a code may lead to improvements in productivity, help with loss prevention, and provide a degree of legal protection for the company. Such objectives, however, are at best indirect in nature, and in most cases it may be extremely difficult to substantiate such claims. In any event, while it is hoped that the development and implementation of a code of ethics will have a positive bottom-line impact, such claims must be made carefully because of the complex nature of the relationships involved. It is best to be cautious in establishing objectives, as the objectives that are claimed are obviously key factors in determining the course of the ongoing development of the code of ethics.

If done appropriately, a company should be able to design an effective and useful code of employee business conduct, one in which it can take pride and which will help to make it a better company. If properly designed and implemented, the code can help to instill the highest standards of business conduct in employees and be a workable management tool to create a culture where the highest standards of conduct are a part of every worker and manager throughout the company. The creation of such a culture can help restore confidence and trust in business organizations and enable them to be good corporate citizens in whatever country they operate.

ETHICS EDUCATION AND TRAINING

Education and training in ethics are needed to sensitize managers and employees to ethical issues, have them learn how to make ethically defensible decisions, and discuss methods to implement and explain ethical policies to their colleagues and subordinates throughout the organization. If a code of ethics exists, it can serve as one of the major training tools in such a program, as employees learn about the code and are trained in applying its provisions to their situations. Many corporations have such education and training programs, as some surveys have found that 45 percent of the largest 1,000 corporations in the United States have such ethics programs or workshops.[17]

CORPORATE CULTURE

The term *corporate culture* generally refers to the constellation of beliefs, mores, customs, value systems, behavioral norms, and ways of doing business that are more or less unique to each corporation. These factors contribute to setting a pattern for corporate activities and actions and characterize life in the organization. The purpose of top-management commitment, ethical codes, and ethical training and education is to create a culture where ethical concern permeates the whole organization, where ethics has become institutionalized and made a regular and normal part of business activities. This process of institutionalizing ethics begins with top management and if done right will ultimately result in ethics being integrated into decision making at all levels of the organization.

DECISION MAKING

Many people avoid thinking in ethical terms because they are unsure what ethics is and why it matters. Managers and employees need a practical concept of ethics to apply to the problems they face in the workplace. Simply adding ethical considerations into an organization without providing a systematic method for integrating those considerations into decision making can cause a great deal of resistance throughout the organization. Since business ethics is primarily concerned with clarifying the moral obligations and ethical responsibilities of managers who make business decisions, it is important to discuss the nature of decision making in relation to ethical concerns. The problem is one of identifying the ethical dimensions of a decision. Are ethical dimensions present in every decision made by a manager, or only in certain decisions? What are the important ethical dimensions to consider in analyzing managerial decisions?

Perhaps the relation between decision making and ethics can be clarified by specifying certain levels of ethical decision making in a corporate context and illustrating ethical issues at these levels with specific examples. Kenneth Goodpaster has identified three levels of ethical issues with respect to corporate organizations that vary in scope or coverage. These levels are the individual level, organizational level, and system level.[18] At the individual level, the manager is making personal, day-to-day decisions that mostly involve the application of corporate policy to specific concrete situations. Judgments have to be made when the policy isn't clear or when exceptional circumstances arise. It is at these points that ethical issues arise and the personal judgment of managers on a day-to-day basis has important ethical dimensions.

The organizational level involves decisions about corporate policy where decisions are not merely personal, but are decisions made for and in the name of the corporation that will guide the behavior of all or at least significant numbers of employees within the organization. Thus, these decisions are broader in scope than those made at the individual level and involve more people and resources. It is at this level, Goodpaster argues, that questions of corporate social responsibility are relevant.[19]

At the system level, broad questions are raised about the ethical foundations of capitalism, and whether or not the system as presently constituted is fair, equitable, and just, and provides for and promotes human welfare better than some alternative system. Thus, questions are raised about the legitimacy of the fundamental components of capitalism such as private property and competition. Should property rights be overriden in the interest of the general welfare? What is the proper role of government in a capitalistic society? Questions at this level are obviously the most comprehensive in scope and are the most difficult to resolve. They are public policy questions, by and large, where the corporate manager is only one actor in a very complex and political decision-making process.

The specific nature of the decisions involved at each of these levels can be seen if a concrete example is used. Personnel decisions about hiring, firing, and promotions are fraught with ethical dimensions and provide a useful vehicle to illustrate ethical dilemmas at each of these levels. Let us assume that the basic corporate policy or decision rule in regard to personnel decisions is one of hiring, promoting, or retaining the best-qualified people. The criteria related to who is best qualified is most likely determined by testing procedures, interviews, performance evaluations, and other methods, all related to helping a decision maker judge the merit of the individual or individuals involved.

Ethical consideration enters into these decisions at the individual level in borderline or exceptional cases, which corporate policy does not cover. There may be situations where two candidates are equally qualified for only one position, or where an individual is in a gray area when it comes to meeting the criteria. These become difficult personal decisions as far as a manager is concerned. Corporate policy in most of these decisions is not a great deal of help, even where numerical scores are involved. Policy may state that a person has to receive a certain minimum score in order to be employed. But given the subjective and uncertain nature of the whole testing process, it hardly seems fair to apply this policy mechanically and exclude people who score one point below the minimum without considering other factors. Then there are exceptional cases where a person may be clearly less qualified for a job or promotion, but where something like need may be so great as to make a manager deviate from corporate policy in the interests of justice or rights.

At the organizational level, the ethical dimensions of decision making come into play when corporate policy is determined. Managers must make certain that the criteria and procedures that are established to determine who is best qualified do not discriminate against certain individuals or groups on the basis of irrelevant factors such as race, sex, religion, creed, or national origin. Such systemic discrimination is not only considered to be an injustice in our society, it is also illegal at this point. If the company has had discriminatory personnel policies in the past, then it is faced with a decision about establishing an affirmative action program where the decision rule of hiring the best-qualified person may be set aside in some cases in order to give preferential treatment to some groups who have suffered injustices in the past. There are complex and difficult questions of justice and rights involved in these kinds of policy decisions.

At the level of the system the ethical question concerns merit itself, which is one of the ethical pillars of a free enterprise system. Is merit the appropriate principle to use in distributing the benefits of society, such that those who merit rewards in the sense of better qualifications and job performance merit the better and higher-paying jobs society has to offer? Egalitarians question the justice of this arrangement arguing that merit, which is not earned and for which no individual can take credit, cannot be ethically justified as a valid distribution principle. They would advocate that benefits be distributed equally across all members of society. Others would argue that need is the appropriate and fair way to distribute benefits. These kinds of questions are settled through the public policy process and the eventual outcome is reflected in laws related to employment practices such as the Civil Rights Act and through the establishment and continuation of welfare or entitlement programs that transfer benefits and burdens between groups in society.

Exhibit 8-1 shows these various levels of decision making and the ethical issues that are relevant to each level. There are obviously conflicts among these various levels of decision making. Corporate policy may require that a corporate manager go against his or her personal ethical standards, causing a very agonizing dilemma for individual managers. And corporate policy may not always reflect the ethical standards of the society at large, requiring new laws to be passed to force a change in corporate policy and behavior.

This example can serve to illustrate where questions of justice and rights are relevant at different levels of decision making in organizations. The decisions that are made at all these levels distribute benefits and burdens in different ways and affect individuals and groups differently. Their welfare is enhanced or is affected adversely, thus making questions of justice and rights important. Since these concepts are central to making ethical decisions, some discussion of these concepts and the different meanings they have been given should be part of any ethical training program for managers.

EXHIBIT 8-1 Personnel Decisions

"Decision rule: Hire the best-qualified person."	
Individual Level:	Borderline and extraordinary situations.
Policy Level:	Are criteria discriminatory? Is some kind of affirmative action program just and equitable?
Social Level:	Is making decisions on the basis of merit just and equitable?

STRATEGIC MANAGEMENT

Ethical considerations must also be integrated into the strategic management process where the corporation defines its mission and makes long-term plans for its continued success or survival. This process has become more important to corporations as competition has become globalized, and ethical values must have a positive effect on the strategic management process for the corporation to avoid making some serious and costly mistakes. If management considers the ethical implications of what it is doing—not to mention the long-term effects of the possibility of eventually getting caught doing something unethical and illegal—it might make different decisions, not based on expediency or short-term profits alone.

Strategy with regard to ethical concerns needs to be developed at various levels and integrated into more traditional business concerns. These levels of strategy development include (1) the enterprise level that encompasses the development and articulation of the role of the organization in society; (2) the corporate level where product market decisions about entering, withdrawing, or remaining in an industry are considered; (3) the business level where the focus of strategy is how to compete within an industry; and (4) the functional level where operational decisions are of concern.[20] Strategy at all of these levels must be considered in developing an ethical organization.

Enterprise-level strategy deals with the basic question of what the corporation stands for, and involves an understanding of the role of the firm as a whole entity in society and its relationships to other social institutions. Enterprise-level strategy deals with such questions as the perception of the organization by major stakeholders, the principles or values the organization represents, the obligations the organization has to society at large, and the implications its allocation of resources has for the company's role in society. The point of enterprise-level strategy is that the firm needs to specifically and intentionally address these questions in its strategy formulation process. Enterprise-level strategy helps the firm in crisis situations when there is no time for deliberation and the company has to rely on its basic values and culture to respond effectively.[21]

At the corporate level, strategy has to do with mergers, acquisitions, diversification, divestment, and other corporatewide decisions. With regard to ethical issues, for example, the tobacco companies are faced with questions related to their main product line because of changing values in society and the emphasis on the rights of nonsmokers. In view of these environmental changes, should tobacco companies diversify into related lines of business where their advertising and marketing skills would be useful? Should they find new uses for tobacco that will eventually replace cigarette production? This is an example of a strategic decision at the corporate level involving ethical concerns that affect the basic product line of the company.

At the business level, the concern is with the industry and competitor environment and how ethical issues are likely to affect this environment. Certain kinds of regulations, for example, may give competitive advantages to some companies and penalize others in the same industry. Chrysler Corporation, for example, claimed that cutbacks in fuel mileage requirements that were instituted by the Reagan administration were unfair because they benefited Ford and General Motors at the expense of Chrysler, which already had planned its product line to meet the more stringent requirements. When these requirements were relaxed, Chrysler's competitive advantage was taken away and given to its competitors. Thus, regulation can affect companies in the same industry very differently.

New issues that are just appearing on the agenda may affect companies in various ways and, thus, are something that should be considered when developing strategies.

At the functional level, operational decisions are affected by government regulations in response to ethical issues of concern to society. The new regulations with regard to disabled people are going to affect operations of many companies, both large and small. New policies and procedures will have to be put into place and facilities changed to comply with these regulations. The same is true of the communication standards promulgated by OSHA with respect to handling of toxic substances. New labeling requirements had to be implemented at the functional level, data sheets had to be prepared, and workers trained in the interpretation of all this new information about toxic substances. These regulations involved substantial changes in policies and procedures at the functional level and entailed the development of new strategies to comply with the regulations.

Corporate strategy begins with a mission statement that announces the purpose of the organization and states the reason for the organization's existence. This mission defines the business the corporation is in and what it intends to accomplish as far as society and its stakeholders are concerned. These mission statements often involve a statement of the core values of the organization and the principles that guide its actions.

Companies can define their mission in terms of seeking to do social good as well as seeking profits, and try to find as many situations as possible where it can do both at the same time. More and more opportunities of this sort are appearing in the environmental area, where waste reduction plans can actually save the company some money. The corporation can also seek to produce life-sustaining and -enhancing goods and services, something the cigarette companies might consider as they continue to face pressures from society. Other companies may define their mission in terms of maximizing the interests of all their stakeholders rather than simply the stockholders.[22] Companies need to define their mission more broadly in keeping with the multiple purposes of the organization as described at the beginning of this chapter.

All of these factors are important in developing an ethical organization dedicated to the maintenance of high ethical standards. Yet the best designed ethical system does not guarantee that things still can't go wrong.[23] But more and more companies seem to be developing comprehensive ethics programs that cover all or many of the foregoing factors.[24] Several consulting organizations have been developed to help corporations in some of these efforts and, along with individual consulting on the part of academics, form something of an ethics industry that is promoting the development of an ethical organization.

Further interest in corporate ethics programs was provided by the new sentencing guidelines that took effect in November 1991, which involve severe and mandatory fines for corporations found guilty of fraud and antitrust offenses, instead of the modest penalties for white-collar crime that have been standard practice in past years. Companies could find themselves facing multimillion-dollar fines depending on the severity of the transgression.[25] Companies with meaningful ethics policies, however, will receive much more lenient treatment as long as they cooperate with prosecutors and their policies meet the guidelines' standards. If they have a comprehensive ethics program in place, including a code of conduct, an ombudsman, a hotline, and mandatory training seminars for executives, they could have their fines reduced substantially.[26]

Thus, there are penalties if corporations do not follow the law, penalties which can be mitigated to a certain extent by well-intentioned ethics programs. Anyone who does not obey these laws could be said to be acting irresponsibly from an economic point of view.

However, the law can most appropriately be seen as prescribing a minimum morality at best, and acting legally is not the same as acting morally. As this chapter has been concerned to emphasize, the moral behavior of a corporate community and the imposition of moral norms from without are two very different things. Corporate morality should emerge from within the organization rather than requiring imposition from without, and it involves a commitment to ethical behavior that reflects the corporate community in its entirety.

Questions for Discussion

1. What does it mean to say that the corporation is a voluntary organization? Why do people join corporate organizations? What advantages do corporations provide for investors? In what sense can the corporation be considered a community? How does this view differ from the traditional view of a corporation? What implications does the community view have for the treatment of employees?

2. What are the major purposes of a corporation? What values have come to dominate corporate purpose? Do you agree with the authors that the modern view of corporate purpose is skewed? What changes, in your opinion, are necessary? Are these changes of an intellectual nature or would they result in changes in corporate behavior?

3. What issues are involved in the question of moral agency? Why are these issues important? What are the different philosophical views on the question of moral agency? Which view do you agree with most closely? What implications does this have for the questions of moral responsibility and control of corporate behavior?

4. What problems arise with the attempt to hold individuals responsible for corporate actions and practices? Are both individual and corporate responsibility important? How does the law treat this situation? What does it take for the firm to have a moral integrity? Is such integrity important? Why?

5. What elements are important in creating an ethical business organization? Are there some elements that you think are more important than others? Where would you start in creating or changing an organization to be more ethical in its operations?

6. What are corporate codes of ethics? What areas do they typically cover? What purposes do such codes serve? What kinds of codes seem to work best in a corporate organization? What advantages do they provide for the corporation and its employees?

7. What are the different levels of decision making in a typical organization? What ethical issues arise at each of these levels? Show how this process works by taking a particular decision and analyzing it at the various levels described in the book.

8. What are the sentencing guidelines that now affect corporate behavior? How do they provide a positive incentive to create an ethical organization? What is the proper function of these guidelines? Should morality be imposed from the outside or is it best for the organization to commit itself internally to ethical behavior?

Endnotes

[1] Robert C. Solomon, *Ethics and Excellence: Cooperation and Integrity in Business* (New York: Oxford, 1992), p. 150.

[2] Richard T. DeGeorge, *Business Ethics,* 2nd ed. (New York: Macmillan, 1986), p. 83.

[3] Ibid., pp. 83–87.

[4] Ibid., p. 30.

[5] John R. Danley, "Corporate Moral Agency: The Case for Anthropological Bigotry," *Business Ethics: Readings and Cases in Corporate Morality,* W. Michael Hoffman and Jennifer Mills Moore, eds. (New York: McGraw-Hill, 1984), p. 173.

[6] Ibid., p. 178.

[7] Michael Keeley, "Organizations as Non-Persons," *Ethical Issues in Business: A Philosophical Approach,* 2nd ed., Thomas Donaldson and Patricia H. Werhane, eds. (Englewood Cliffs, NJ: Prentice-Hall, 1983), pp. 120–125.

[8] John Ladd, "Morality and the Ideal of Rationality in Formal Organizations," *Ethical Issues in Business: A Philosophical Approach,* 2nd ed., Thomas Donaldson and Patricia H. Werhane, eds. (Englewood Cliffs, NJ: Prentice-Hall, 1983), pp. 125–136.

[9] Kenneth E. Goodpaster and John B. Matthews, Sr., "Can a Corporation Have a Conscience?" *Business Ethics: Readings and Cases in Corporate Morality,* W. Michael Hoffman and Jennifer Mills Moore, eds. (New York: McGraw-Hill, 1984), pp. 150–162.

[10] Ibid.

[11] Peter A. French, "Corporate Moral Agency," *Business Ethics: Readings and Cases in Corporate Morality,* W. Michael Hoffman and Jennifer Mills Moore, eds. (New York: McGraw-Hill, 1984), pp. 163–171.

[12] Thomas Donaldson, *Corporations & Morality* (Englewood Cliffs, NJ: Prentice-Hall, 1982), p. 30.

[13] Patricia H. Werhane, *Persons, Rights, & Corporations* (Englewood Cliffs, NJ: Prentice-Hall, 1985), p. 56.

[14] Kenneth E. Goodpaster, "The Concept of Corporate Responsibility," *Just Business: New Introductory Essays in Business Ethics,* Tom Regan, ed. (New York: Random House, 1984), p. 295.

[15] Ethics Resource Center, *Creating a Workable Company Code of Ethics* (Washington, DC: Ethics Resource Center, 1990).

[16] Ibid.

[17] Bruce Hager, "What's Behind Business' Sudden Fervor for Ethics," *Business Week,* September 23, 1991, p. 65.

[18] Kenneth E. Goodpaster, "The Concept of Corporate Responsibility," *Journal of Business Ethics,* Vol. 2, no. 1 (February 1983), pp. 2–3. See also Kirk Hanson, "Ethics and Business: A Progress Report," *Stanford GSB* (Spring 1983), pp. 10–14.

[19] Ibid.

[20] Liam Fahey and V. K. Narayanan, *Macroenvironmental Analysis for Strategic Management* (St. Paul: West, 1986), p. 189.

[21] Archie B. Carroll, *Business and Society: Ethics & Stakeholder Management* (Cincinnati: South-Western, 1989), p. 453.

[22] See Charles E. Exley, Jr., "Stressing Corporate Values," *Management Digest Quarterly,* Vol. 3, no. 1 (Spring 1989), p. 10.

[23] See John A. Bryne, "The Best-Laid Ethics Programs," *Business Week,* March 9, 1992, pp. 67–69, for the story of what went wrong at Dow Corning relative to the safety of breast implants despite the existence of a sophisticated ethics program.

[24] See Ethics Resource Center and the Behavior Research Center, *Ethics Policies and Programs in American Business* (Washington, DC: Ethics Resource Center, 1990).

[25] Jeffrey M. Kaplan and William K. Perry, "The High Cost of Corporate Crime," *Management Accounting* (December 1991), pp. 43-46.

[26] Hager, "What's Behind Business' Sudden Fervor for Ethics," p. 65.

Suggested Readings

Alkhafaji, Abbass F. *A Stakeholder Approach to Corporate Governance: Managing in a Dynamic Environment.* Westport, CT: Quorum Books, 1989.

Bowie, Norman. *Business Ethics.* Englewood Cliffs, NJ: Prentice-Hall, 1982.

Brown, Courtney C. *Putting the Corporate Board to Work.* New York: Macmillan, 1976.

Burnham, James. *The Managerial Revolution.* Bloomington: Indiana University Press, 1941.

DeGeorge, Richard T. *Business Ethics,* 2nd ed. New York: Macmillan, 1986.

Donaldson, Thomas. *Corporations & Morality.* Englewood Cliffs, NJ: Prentice-Hall, 1982.

French, Peter A., Jeffrey Nesteruk, and David T. Risser. *Corporations in the Moral Community.* New York: Harcourt Brace Jovanovich, 1992.

Heyne, Paul T. *Private Keepers of the Public Interest.* New York: McGraw-Hill, 1968.

Hosmer, LaRue Tone. *The Ethics of Management,* 2nd ed. Homewood, IL: Richard D. Irwin, 1991.

Lorsch, Jay W. *Pawns or Potentates: The Reality of America's Corporate Boards.* Cambridge, MA: Harvard Business School Press, 1990.

Matthews, John B., Kenneth E. Goodpaster, and Laura L. Nash. *Policies and Persons: A Casebook in Business Ethics,* 2nd ed. New York: McGraw-Hill, 1991.

Michael, Rion. *The Responsible Manager.* New York: Harper & Row, 1990.

Regan, Tom, ed. *Just Business: New Introductory Essays in Business Ethics.* New York: Random House, 1984.

Useem, Michael. *Executive Defense: Shareholder Power and Corporate Reorganization.* Cambridge, MA: Harvard University Press, 1993.

Vogel, David. *Lobbying the Corporation: Citizen Challenges to Business Authority.* New York: Basic Books, 1978.

Werhane, Patricia H. *Persons, Rights, & Corporations.* Englewood Cliffs, NJ: Prentice-Hall, 1985.

SHORT CASES

RJR Nabisco

The largest leveraged buyout in history was proposed in the fall of 1988 when the CEO of RJR Nabisco, F. Ross Johnson, and seven other managers made a $75 a share proposal to take the company private in a leveraged buyout. With the stock selling at about $56 a share at the time, the stockholders stood to make a good deal of money. Johnson had good reason to believe that the board of directors would approve of the buyout, not only because of the benefit to shareholders but because of favors he had done for them over the years.[1]

However, the directors of the company were in a state of shock that turned to outrage when they learned about the kind of money that Johnson and the other executives would make for themselves. Some accused Johnson of raiding the company from the inside, as the total amount the executives might make was in the neighborhood of $2.6 billion in five years, depending on the amount of money the company made over that period.[2]

The directors then proceeded to retaliate by taking control of the buyout process and opening the bidding for RJR Nabisco to all comers. They believed they could get a better deal for the shareholders by putting the company up for auction rather than approving the buyout proposed by Johnson and the other managers. By taking matters into their own hands, the directors set a precedent on how boards should respond to such bids and think about the long-term interests of shareholders and other stakeholders such as employees and communities.[3]

After several bids were received, the board eventually awarded the company to Kohlberg Kravis Roberts, the leveraged buyout specialists, for about $25 billion in cash and securities or about $109 a share. This bid was even less than the $112 a share proposed by Johnson and the management group as their last offer. Members of the losing side thought that the board had discriminated against them. The board defended its action by suggesting that Kohlberg Kravis Roberts was going to have to sell fewer businesses and thus keep the company largely intact and that there was more protection for employees under the Kohlberg Kravis Roberts offer.[4]

1. What do such takeover proposals suggest about the way management sees itself with respect to the modern corporation? What are the ethical issues with respect to takeovers of this nature? Why was the board of directors offended?

2. Are takeovers good for the economy as a whole? What impact do such takeovers have on employees of the company? Have they made for more efficient companies that are better able to compete internationally? How would you judge antitakeover legislation that some states have adopted from an ethical point of view?

[1] Frederick Ungeheuer, "Will His Deal Go Up in Smoke?" *Time,* November 28, 1988, p. 76.

[2] Ibid.

[3] John Helyar and Bryan Burrough, "Nobody's Tool: RJR Nabisco Board Asserts Independence in Buy-Out Decisions," *The Wall Street Journal,* November 9, 1988, p. A-1. See also Laurie P. Cohen, "Directors' Decision on RJR Offers Deemed Likely to Survive in Court," *The Wall Street Journal,* December 2, 1988, p. A-4.

[4] John Greenwald, "$25,000,000,000," *Time,* December 12, 1988, pp. 56–57.

Source: Rogene A. Buchholz, *Business Environment and Public Policy: Implications for Management,* 5th ed. (Englewood Cliffs, NJ: Prentice Hall, 1995), pp. 231–232.

Breast Implants

On February 10, 1992, Dow Corning admitted that it had knowledge for 20 years that silicone breast implants might leak and replaced its chairman with a proven crisis manager.[1] On March 19, 1992, the company announced that it would completely abandon the breast implant business.[2] Such announcements were too late in coming to stave off the legal frenzy that ensued, as the company faced many lawsuits as more and more women with implants came forward. However, these implant recipients were not the only threat to Dow Corning, as the company also had to deal with shareholder class-action suits and civil and criminal investigations by the government.[3]

The breast implant division of Dow Corning made up less than 1 percent of the company's $1.84 billion in 1991 revenues, and had not been profitable since 1986, but now it faced hundreds of millions of dollars in costs from the lawsuits alone. Many analysts wondered if the company would seek protection by filing for bankruptcy following the lead of Manville and A. H. Robins corporations. By filing for bankruptcy, the company would put a halt to the private litigation and resolve all of the claims simultaneously.[4]

Lawyers were also investigating the liability of Dow Corning's joint owners, Dow Chemical and Corning, in the event Dow Corning would declare bankruptcy. Dow Chemical and Corning each maintained that they could not be held liable for Dow Corning's actions and could not be sued because they are separate companies. The parent companies argued that they were protected by a "corporate veil" that limited their liability. However, such legal distinctions were expected to be difficult to maintain in the face of mounting public pressure and politicians demanding satisfaction.[5]

The public first caught wind of the controversy surrounding silicone breast implants in a trial that ended in December 1991, with a $7.3 million verdict awarded to Mariann Hopkins from California who sued Dow Corning when her implants ruptured. She argued that the silicone leakage damaged her immune system. The jury found Dow Corning guilty of fraud and malice because it did not reveal what it knew about the health hazards associated with the product. Hopkins's lawyer said that the verdict sent a message to the company that it could not sacrifice the health and safety of women to enhance its bottom line.[6]

The jury was presented with internal memos, which revealed that company employees had concerns since 1970 about the safety of the implants. In a particularly damaging memo, a company scientist had stated that to his knowledge, the company had no valid, long-term data to substantiate the safety of gel for long-term usage. In another memo, a marketing executive said that he had told a group of plastic surgeons "with crossed fingers" that the company did have a safety study in progress. The company contended that it had never hidden any scientific data from the government, and that such memos were an airing of differences of opinion regarding the safety of the implants and did not represent a consensus of scientists.[7]

For several years, an engineer at Dow Corning by the name of Thomas D. Talcott had asserted that the company was practicing experimental surgery on humans. Talcott sounded the alarm in 1976 when he came to believe that the company's silicone breast implants could cause health problems by rupturing and leaking into a woman's body. People ignored his warnings, however, and in 1976 he quit his job of 24 years in frustration. Documents supporting Talcott's opinions were discovered in June 1991, suggesting that the company had been aware of implant problems for years and tried to hide them. In response to Talcott's allegations, the company stated that he left as a disgruntled employee, and that his motives were subject to question because he was earning $400 an hour to testify on behalf of those suing the company.[8]

The problems that emerged at Dow Corning were exceptionally interesting in light of the fact that the company had been considered a leader in corporate ethics programs. It was among the first companies to establish such a program, which many believed to the among the most elaborate in the country. In the early 1970s, John S. Ludington, the chairman of the company, set out to design a corporate culture that demanded high ethical standards. He created a Business Conduct Committee in 1976 composed of company executives who reported to a board committee, and began a series of audits to monitor employee compliance. The company also had training programs that touched on ethics, and included an ethics section in the company's opinion surveys.[9]

But however well designed and well intentioned, the program failed to pick up signs of internal dissent over the safety of breast implants. The audit program, in particular, apparently did not uncover the memos and concerns that later surfaced. Perhaps such programs are simply too broad to deal with specific situations. It was alleged that ethics programs of this nature were not designed to deal directly with complex problems, but instead were there to help cultivate an overall environment of proper conduct. In any event, the company had no plans to touch the ethics program, and although it failed to tip off the right people in the company as to potentially unethical behavior, it was expected to aid and guide the company through the difficult times ahead.[10]

1. Why don't companies pay more attention to concerns employees raise about the safety of their products? What motivates company executives to deny any allegations about the safety of their product, even in the face of mounting evidence to the contrary? Is there any way to make companies more responsive to safety concerns?

2. What went wrong with the ethics program at Dow Corning? Was it designed to respond to problems of this nature? What was missing, if anything, from its approach to creating an ethical culture? How can such problems be prevented from happening again?

[1] "Tat for Tit," *The Economist,* February 15, 1992, p. 33.

[2] Joseph Weber, "I Guess the Price of Salt Water Is Going Up," *Business Week,* April 6, 1992, p. 28.

[3] Michele Galen, "Debacle at Dow Corning: How Bad Will It Get?" *Business Week,* March 2, 1992, pp. 36–38.

[4] Ibid.

[5] "Tat for Tit," p. 33.

[6] Jean Seligmann, "Another Blow to Implants," *Newsweek,* January 6, 1992, p. 45.

[7] Ibid. See also Tim Smart, "Breast Implants: What Did the Industry Know, and When?" *Business Week,* June 10, 1991, pp. 94–98.

[8] Tim Smart, "This Man Sounded the Silicone Alarm—In 1976," *Business Week,* January 27, 1992, p. 34.

[9] John A. Bryne, "The Best-Laid Ethics Programs . . . ," *Business Week,* March 9, 1992, pp. 67–69.

[10] Ibid.

Defense Contracting

For the past several months, the newspapers had been full of stories about defense contractors overcharging the government for everything from ordinary wrenches and screwdrivers to coffee makers. These stories were great for the politicians who wanted to cut the defense budget and slap more stringent regulations on defense contractors. More serious was the admission by General Electric of falsifying employee time cards to overcharge the government on the production of missile components and the allegations against General Dynamics for charging the government for all sorts of items that were noncontract related such as dog care and fancy executive suites. These problems resulted in substantial fines against the companies involved and loss of contracts as well as management changes.

Carl Hendricks is CEO of Defense Unlimited, a major defense contractor in its own right even if not in the same league with the aforementioned companies. Mr. Hendricks wonders what motivates company employees to do this sort of thing when the country's security is at stake. Being a patriotic citizen and wanting to keep his company out of trouble, he does not want these sorts of things taking place at Defense Unlimited. The company cannot afford to lose the government's business and it has benefited greatly from the recent defense buildup.

Yet Mr. Hendricks wonders what he can do as CEO to make sure that these sorts of things aren't happening somewhere in his company. One thing he is considering doing is instituting a code of ethics regarding the company's posture toward the government and what kind of ethical standards are expected of employees when dealing with government contracts. Another possibility is some system of controls so that he or the controller of the company would have some indication at an early stage that something was remiss. Mr. Hendricks wonders whether or not either of these ideas would really work and whether or not something else would work better.

1. What are the advantages and disadvantages of codes of ethics? What conditions are necessary for them to work effectively in controlling employee behavior? Are those conditions present in this situation?

2. Are there other alternatives that Mr. Hendricks has available? What limitations are there on his power as CEO of the company? Should he be held responsible for the conduct of subordinates?

Source: Rogene A. Buchholz, *Business Environment and Public Policy: Implications for Management,* 5th ed. (Englewood Cliffs, NJ: Prentice Hall, 1995), p. 159.

Board Committees

Mr. Specific is a member of the board of directors for General Manufacturing Corporation, a large multinational company making diverse consumer products. He had been on the board for about two years and was well aware that management manipulated the board and was in almost total control of the company. While this bothered Mr. Specific, he did not have an issue of sufficient interest that could be used to mobilize the other board members to challenge the power of management.

But now perhaps such an issue was in the making. Mr. Specific had been reading about the fact that executive pay continued to rise right through the recent recession when other employees were taking pay cuts or getting laid off. Now that the economy had recovered, top management was still voting itself larger increases overall than the rest of the employees were getting, including lower levels of management. Most often, these pay increases bore no relationship to company performance.

Public sentiment was building against this practice and some politicians were making noises about passing legislation to cap executive pay increases or at least tie them more closely to company performance. Politicians who were making these noises claimed to have the stockholders' interests in mind, and were making a moral issue out of the situation.

Top management of GMC had notified board members that compensation would top the agenda items at next month's meeting. They were again proposing a generous increase in bonuses and stock options for themselves, even though the company had a mediocre year. Mr. Specific was considering proposing a compensation committee at the board level to take the power of proposing their own increases away from management. There seemed to be something of a trend toward establishing board committees in areas like compensation and nomination of board members.

Mr. Specific knew he would have a fight on his hands, but if he could mobilize the rest of the outside board members and gain some stockholder support, perhaps he could win over the opposition of management. He wondered where to start and whether or not the battle would be worth the effort.

1. Have board committees been effective in carrying out their assigned responsibilities and acting as a counterweight to total management control? Has the compensation committee in particular been effective in dealing with unjustified pay increases? What problems are involved?

2. What moral and ethical issues are involved in this situation? What is fair compensation for top management? How much credit should it take when things go right and how much blame should it be given when things go wrong?

Source: Rogene A. Buchholz, *Business Environment and Public Policy: Implications for Management,* 5th ed. (Englewood Cliffs, NJ: Prentice Hall, 1995), p. 263.

CHAPTER

Business in Its Technological Environment

Technology, to which the scientific enterprise gives rise, if it is not to be a dominating tool to ravage nature and fragment humans, must be placed in its proper context of the fullness and richness of humans and nature. Technology, at its best, can provide a full, free, flexible way of life, and extend the ability of humans to enrich their lives. But it can also alienate people and destroy the environment if not used properly. The problem with technology is not technology itself, but rather springs from the ideas, or perhaps better said, the absence of ideas, which too often operate in conjunction with technological factors and guide the way it is put to use in society. Technology can provide the means, but human vision as creative, as grasping possibilities for the betterment of the human experience in its holistic nature, is required to guide technology. Technology is not over nature, nor can it be set over against humanistic concerns, for it is a part of the natural process by which human beings, who are within and part of nature, alter their environment in order that it better enhance the qualitative fullness of their lives.

The Management of Technology

One problem with the application of technology in our society arises because the corporation is the primary institution through which new technologies are introduced. And the corporation, being primarily interested in profit or other organizational objectives, often asks very limited questions about the impacts of that technology on the environment and whether or not it is safe to use as intended. Where regulations exist, as in the case of new drugs to be introduced in the market, companies have to submit to extensive testing procedures to prove that the drug is both safe and effective. But in many cases, corporations are prone to ask minimal questions about safety, and unless required to do so because of government regulations, do not engage in extensive examination of environmental

193

impacts. While this traditional pattern is changing in many organizations, concern about the environment and safety and whether or not the technology will actually work as intended is still not of the highest priority in some organizations.

This problem is well illustrated in many cases where the concerns of engineers in corporations over the use of a particular technology or a particular decision related to the technology clash with managerial concerns. One of the most persistent and interesting problems in ethics relative to business organizations is the differences that arise from time to time between engineers or technical people over the safety or workability of a product or device and managers who often overlook such concerns in the interests of organizational objectives. There are several cases where engineers or technicians have raised questions about the technical problems inherent in some product or technology, and these concerns have been squelched or overriden by managers in the interests of profits, schedules, or some other organizational or administrative concern.

In a case involving production of a new plane for the Air Force called the A7D that appears in many business ethics books, the brake designed by the senior engineer of a subcontractor was not large enough to safely stop the aircraft upon landing. While initially the problem was believed to be with the materials used in the brake assembly, eventually it was determined that the fault was in the design itself as the brake repeatedly failed in lab tests no matter what materials were used.[1]

Yet management refused to deal with this technical reality and created a fictional reality of its own by having technicians falsify test data that were sent to the Air Force and the prime contractor. Management did not want to incur the expense and delay that a redesign effort would take and apparently believed that the brake would work in the actual aircraft despite the test results. When the brake did not work in an actual test situation, however, and almost resulted in a major accident with possible loss of life, it had to be redesigned anyway. The technical people involved in the incident eventually disclosed to investigators what had actually happened with regard to the original brake and were the ones who suffered while management either stayed in place or were even promoted.

In the Dalkon Shield case involving A. H. Robins, a technician had shown in a simple experiment that the tail used to extract the IUD could wick, meaning that infectious agents could enter a woman's body by this route causing pelvic inflammatory disease. But this evidence was ignored by management because the company had a product that was making a great deal of money and management didn't want to hear about potential health problems. Yet these problems couldn't be wished away and eventually came back to haunt the company in the form of lawsuits that eventually led to bankruptcy and takeover by another company.[2]

The most devastating case of all in this regard is the *Challenger* disaster. Engineers had raised a question long before the disaster occurred about an O-ring problem with the solid booster rocket joints. The design of the field joints did not work as intended and the seals were not able to seat effectively to prevent leakage. Blow-by had been noticed on several of the previous launches when the booster rockets were recovered, and a seal task force had been formed to study the problem. The O-rings had even been reassigned from a Criticality 1-R rating, where there was redundancy with a secondary seal, to a Criticality 1 rating where there was no backup because it was believed that the secondary seal would be ineffective should the primary seal fail in flight. This information, however, was not passed on to the highest levels of NASA management, and the criticality rating was continually signed off on by a lower level of NASA management so launchings could proceed on schedule while the problem was being studied.[3]

On the night before the launch of the *Challenger,* temperatures were much lower than had been experienced on any previous launch. Initially, the prime contractor, Morton Thiokol International (MTI), recommended against the launch because the temperature was outside of its experience base and there was concern that the primary seals would lose all resiliency and lead to an explosion on the launch pad. Under pressure from NASA, MTI reversed its decision leaving the engineers out of the decision-making process and making what was called a management decision to support the launch and please a customer. The most revealing event in this flawed decision-making process occurred when Robert Lund, the head of engineering for MTI, was asked by the rest of the managers to take off his engineering hat and put on his management hat and, in this kind of role, he supported the launch decision.

All of these examples have some common elements.[4] The differences between a decision based on technical concerns and a decision based on management concerns led to vastly different courses of action. In each of these examples, management decisions led to disastrous consequences. Supposedly an engineering decision is based on certain technical realities that the engineers and technicians believe are true relative to a brake, to an IUD, and to an O-ring seal that could cause problems. Engineers and technicians are concerned that a technology will work properly, that it is safe, and that there will be no unexpected problems. Their reality is a technical one and their values are based on concerns that are technical in nature.

Managers, however, live in a different world, and in addition to these concerns must base decisions on financial realities, budget considerations, schedules, customer desires, and similar kinds of organizational concerns. These concerns are no less real, but they are of a different nature than technical realities. The numbers related to finances, budgets, and schedules put pressures on managers that are of a different nature than the concerns of engineers and technical people. These numbers mean different things than the numbers engineers and technical people deal with, and lead to different kinds of decisions, as the examples illustrate.

In modern corporate organizations, however, managers control the decision-making process and are ultimately responsible for staying within budget, meeting schedules, satisfying customers, and other organizational objectives. And if the pressures on managers are great enough, they are inclined to either create technical fantasies by falsifying test data as in the A7D case, or ignore technical concerns and either shoot or exclude the messenger, as they did in the other cases. This difference between the concerns of engineers or technicians and managers constitutes a central ethical problem of the modern corporate organization regarding the management and use of technology (Figure 9-1).

While technical realities do not always take priority in decision making, they do take priority in the real world. When the brake is finally field-tested on an actual aircraft, it fails and the reality of this failure can no longer be ignored or falsified. The tail on the IUD does wick, causing many cases of pelvic inflammatory disease, and the company faces so many lawsuits that it seeks bankruptcy for protection. The O-rings finally do fail to seal properly, and while the *Challenger* does not blow up on the launch pad as expected, it later explodes in mid-air, killing seven people and putting the shuttle program on hold for several months.

Technical Concerns	Managerial Concerns
Work properly	Finances
Safety	Budgets
Minimize unexpected problems	Schedules
	Customers

Managers Control the Decision-Making Process

Create technical fantasies
Ignore technical concerns
Shoot or exclude the messenger

The issue is one of giving technical concerns greater
priority in decision making where appropriate

FIGURE 9-1 Framing the Issue

Previous Attempts to Define the Problem

How can this problem be addressed, and what kind of problem is it in the final analysis? It could be seen as a structural problem that is inherent in the capitalistic system where the corporate organization has to serve certain sets of values, and these values are antithetical to the demands of modern technology. It could also be seen as an organizational or policy problem that requires changes in the organization to give engineers more authority or to facilitate whistle-blowing on the part of engineers or technicians. There are several ways to view the problem that lead to different solutions, some of which will be mentioned in the following section. Following this analysis, a different way of viewing the problem based on the perspective of the pragmatic process approach will be introduced.

A STRUCTURAL APPROACH TO THE PROBLEM

One scholar who dealt with this problem on a structural level was Thorstein Veblen, who is best known for his book about conspicuous consumption and the theory of the leisure class. But perhaps his most insightful work has to do with the structure of the corporate organization, where he developed a model that involved a distinction between what he called the machine process and the business enterprise, two aspects of what is still a single, continuous activity. Veblen's analysis of the capitalistic system and its structural deficiency is, in many ways, more penetrating than standard Marxist analysis based on the abolition of private property.

The machine process as described by Veblen is a high-level abstraction that consists of an interlocking, detailed arrangement that requires disciplined habits of thought, regularity, coordination, uniformity, standardization, and interchangeability. People cannot do as they please with the machine process and expect it to function effectively. The process requires a certain kind of organization and certain kinds of attitudes. It requires the learning of certain skills and habits of mind. Such characteristics are necessary because the machine process, according to Veblen, is based on an impersonal and mechanical cause-and-effect relationship.[5]

Within the machine process, the elements of materials, machines, buildings, tools, skills, and techniques are organized in such a way as to efficiently produce material goods. The operatives of the industrial system are the engineers, technicians, mechanics, and scientists—people who have been trained in the use of tools and who have a scientific attitude and who have adopted technological procedures as part of their behavior. The guiding elements of this process are efficiency and productivity—to combine all these elements in such a way as to produce the most output with the least amount of input. The goal is to combine these elements and operatives as effectively as possible.

This machine process, however, is managed and controlled by another entity, what Veblen called the business enterprise. The business enterprise is able to control the machine process through control of the capital goods that are used in the production process. Control over these goods gives the business enterprise control over everything else in the machine process. The notion of private property is an important element of this kind of control, as the owners of capital are given the final right to determine how this capital shall be used and combined in the production of goods. These decisions as to how capital shall be employed are made on the basis of the pecuniary return to these owners.

The guiding principles of the business enterprise are thus pecuniary in nature and the questions of what to produce and how much to produce under certain conditions are made on the basis of what is judged to be the most profitable. The owners of capital are concerned about industrial efficiency only to the extent that it proves to be profitable. They are not technicians concerned about productivity and efficiency, but pecuniary specialists concerned about profitability. The decisions about employment of capital are made by people who have little or no direct knowledge of the machine process and who make their decisions on grounds other than industrial efficiency and productivity. The business enterprise, then, is guided by pecuniary principles, which serve as guidelines for business behavior, and these principles predominate in control of the machine process.[6]

The business enterprise is an institutional arrangement that includes operatives like accountants, lawyers, marketing and sales personnel, and financial people. It uses money as a standard of value and manages capital funds with a view to maximizing return on invested capital. This arrangement is surrounded by a system of legal property rights that supports the claim of owners to these rights of control and to the return on capital employed. The machine process is thus managed in terms of its ability to produce earnings and not in terms of its output of goods. The factors of production are combined in such a way as to earn the highest net gain for the owners and not on the basis of getting the most output with the resources that are available. The machine process is capitalized on its business capacity and not on its industrial capacity.[7]

Veblen saw problems developing between the machine process and the business enterprise that grow out of the fact that control over industrial affairs—over the planning and execution of projects that call for a comprehensive technical balancing and articulation of large industrial processes where lack of technical insight and sobriety would have particularly grave and far-reaching consequences—continued to be exercised by absentee laypeople who made decisions and took actions on other than technical grounds. Veblen believed that the technician would become of increasing importance in the machine process as it became more complex, and yet the technician is by no means master of the machine process. The businessperson is essentially an outsider as far as knowledge and contact with the machine process is concerned, but he or she is an outsider with a deciding vote on what goes on inside.[8]

Veblen predicted that the business enterprise would eventually be undercut by the machine process on which it depended.[9] The business enterprise would eventually pass the level of tolerance by continually working at cross-purposes with the requirements of the machine process in the allocation of energy resources, materials, and labor.[10] The vested interests of the business enterprise would constitute more and more of an extraneous interference and obstruction to the industrial system in the interests of making a profit and so badly misallocate resources so as to enter a stage of increasingly diminishing returns and reduction of the national dividend beyond limits of tolerance.[11]

The business enterprise is thus dependent on the machine process for its existence. The technical requirements of this process must be met for effective management. These requirements will eventually force changes in the business structure and constitute the secular trend that Veblen called the cultural incidence of the machine process. Eventually, Veblen predicted, a revolution in industrial society will take place when the engineers draw together, work out a plan of action, and decide to disallow absentee ownership out of hand.[12]

Veblen provided us with a useful distinction inherent in the corporate form of organization that aids in understanding the ethical dilemma illustrated by the examples at the beginning of this chapter. What Veblen called the machine process we might call the technical system and what he called the business enterprise could be called the management system. The point, which Veblen so ably described, is that these two systems have different operatives, different requirements, and the decisions made in each realm are based on different values. Since the management system is in control of the technical system, however, it is the values of this system that prevail when push comes to shove in particular instances, and the requirements of the technical system are ignored in the interests of reaching management goals and objectives. Management values override engineering or technical considerations.

The revolution Veblen predicted, however, has not come about, and given current realities, it is unlikely to happen. Such a revolution involves radically restructuring corporate organizations to make them serve different values—a new kind of system that is geared to different measures of success where technical realities take precedence over financial and other kinds of managerial realities. What such a system would look like is hard to imagine, and Veblen did not help us much in this regard, as he did not spell out in detail the implications of his revolution and what form a new industrial order would take. How would engineers disallow absentee ownership, for example, and what kind of governance structure would replace the current one involving management and boards of directors to represent the interests of the owners?

ORGANIZATIONAL AND POLICY CHANGES

A variation of Veblen's thinking is found in John Kenneth Galbraith's theory about the modern corporate organization and its structure and the role of technical employees in the governance process. He invented a new term, *technostructure,* to describe decision making within the corporation. The technostructure refers to all persons who contribute specialized information to group decision making in the organization. This technostructure consists of management, technical specialists, scientists, and other knowledgeable people who may be involved, depending on the type of decision.[13]

Galbraith's point is that the complexity of modern technology makes it impossible for top management to possess enough knowledge to make a decision that will work in the corporation's best interests. Management has to rely more and more on technical specialists within the organization and include them in the decision-making process. This need for information from numerous individuals derives from the technological requirements of modern industry. Decision making and control have moved from the top of the organization down into lower levels, involving more and more employees. Power has thus shifted to some degree to those who possess knowledge rather than just status or position.

Galbraith's analysis is much less revolutionary than Veblen's and basically makes the case for involving more engineering and technical people in the decision-making processes of the modern corporate organization. There has been movement in this direction, as companies have had to involve more engineering and technical people in decision making because of the complexity of modern technology. Managers need to rely on the judgment of these people in making decisions that work in the best interests of the organization. Yet as the *Challenger* case so clearly illustrates, engineering people can be shut out of the decision-making process when a management decision has to be made involving a particular incident.

Perhaps another solution is to give engineers more authority in corporate organizations. The reporting structure can be changed so that engineers report to other engineering personnel who will be more likely to understand their concerns and respond to them in an appropriate manner. In the A7D case, for example, low-level technical people reported to management people who were able to pressure them into falsifying test data. But even if the reporting structure is changed so that engineering has more authority at top levels of the organization, when a critical decision has to be made, the top engineer may be asked to put on his or her management hat and make a management decision.

The problem may be related to the lack of understanding that many managers have relative to how technology works and the role of technology in society. Managers may lack an appreciation for technology and may not be aware of the requirements that are necessary to meet for technology to work appropriately. Managers are used to working with numbers that are relatively imprecise and can be manipulated; they do not have the same meaning as do technical numbers. Profits can be manipulated by different accounting procedures, budgets can be changed without causing accidents, schedules can be rearranged to respond to changing conditions.

But a brake cannot be made to work by falsifying test data, a wicking tail on an IUD cannot be made safe by simply ignoring it in the interests of profits, and an O-ring cannot be made to seal properly because a schedule has to be met in order to satisfy a customer. Managers may not have an appropriate appreciation for technology and not realize the implications of what they are doing because they don't understand what the numbers mean when they refer to something physical rather than financial or pecuniary. They may tend to think of technology in organizational terms and not in the terms appropriate to technology itself. They indeed are laypersons when it comes to an understanding of technology.

Is the solution to have more engineering people become managers, and thus have more clout in the decision-making process? Some companies consider themselves to be engineering companies where many, if not most, managers have an engineering background. Where this kind of management prevails throughout the organization, one would expect technical values to carry more weight. But managers, even with an engineering background, have to make management decisions and worry about finances and budgets and other management considerations. They become part of what Veblen called the business enterprise and are subject to its values and requirements.

Should whistle-blowing be encouraged, making it easier for engineering and technical people to bring their considerations to the attention of top management? An enabling and empowering environment could be created where dissent is not equated with disloyalty. In order to implement this idea, many companies have instituted policies that encourage whistle-blowing and have established hotlines for employees to report activities that may involve criminal conduct or corporate policy violations. But again, this seems to be only a partial solution to the problem, as whistle-blowers can be silenced if necessary, and management objectives can take precedence over the objections of whistleblowers that may be based on technical considerations. Hotlines have their own problems and many people are skeptical about their usefulness, as such policies may be destructive of community and trust that are essential to a successful organization.[14]

In the final analysis, this problem of engineering versus managerial values is not a structural problem of capitalism that can be solved by developing some new kind of system in which private property or absentee ownership is abolished. Socialistic systems have fared even worse than capitalistic systems in managing technology efficiently and effectively, and have been almost totally unresponsive to concerns about environmental problems that have surfaced in recent years. Nor is it simply an organizational or policy problem that can be addressed by giving engineers and technical people more authority in corporate organizations or better and less threatening opportunities to blow the whistle.

Redefining the Problem

Those who control the machine process as organized by the industrial system are individuals who must discipline themselves to its requirements and learn the necessary skills to keep the process functioning. But as Veblen pointed out, the business enterprise is managed with a view to making the largest possible net gain and not with a view to the enhanced quality of human life. Rate and volume of output are regulated to correspond with this goal of the business enterprise. But these pecuniary terms, as Veblen well noted, are a very inadequate measure of serviceability to the community.[15] The conditioning force of any business move is its profit-yielding capacity. Business transactions are carried out with an eye to pecuniary gain and their bearing on the community's welfare is incidental to the transaction of business. Industry is not managed by the technological experts for the material advantage of the community, but by businesspeople for the material advantage of themselves and the absentee owners.[16] The population lives in the naive faith that such a practice benefits the community at large, according to Veblen, and thus continues to support and safeguard the pecuniary interests of these businesspeople.

Managers who do not have an engineering and technical background must develop a better understanding of technology. But this alone is not enough, as even those engineers who become managers must continue to remain attuned to the physical requirements of technology and never forget that physical realities take precedence in the real world. While profits are necessary for an organization to survive and grow and schedules must be met for customers to be pleased, the organization will not continue to be profitable and the customer will certainly not be pleased if the technology doesn't work and kills or injures people. The whole organizational apparatus based on pecuniary principles cannot function on its own; it has no independent existence. Its existence depends on an appropriate and safe technology that works and serves community interests.

The problems surrounding the misuse of technology lie in a lack of understanding of technology's inherently social and moral dimensions. And this lack of understanding in turn is related to the abstraction of technology from the concrete situations in which it operates and from its role in enhancing the fullness and richness of human life. Technology is not meant to serve the private interests of managers for power aggrandizement nor the interests of shareholders for an ever increasing return on investment. Technology is employed for the ultimate benefit of the community. It is a part of the natural process by which human beings, who are within and part of nature, alter their environment in order that it better enrich the qualitative fullness of their existence. Humankind has been able to reach unprecedented levels of affluence because of the effective use of technology, which has resulted in rapid material growth and the enhancement of human life. The machine or technical process has value when it operates effectively to advance the life process of human beings. The machine process is valued because it has proven to be of benefit to humankind.

Technology cannot be understood as an instrument for bringing about goals that are external to the contexts in which it operates. The relational contexts in which technology functions are imbued with values that demand consideration. Thus, technology as it actually operates in concrete situations has a contextually dependent moral quality. Technology creates a moral situation, and this situation should provide the context for decision making. Technology can be used irresponsibly if the inquiry and testing technology involves have been directed toward ends that do not take the nature of technology into account and are themselves immune from the results of experimental testing.

What these comments suggest is that technology itself is experimental, particularly in the kinds of examples described at the beginning of this chapter.[17] While the engineers and technicians raised questions about the safety and workability of these technologies, there was no certainty that they were right and that their concerns should thus override managerial considerations. But they did, at least, introduce an element of "reasonable doubt" into the decision-making process that the managers should have taken into consideration. There was a "reasonable doubt" that the technology would work properly, and what the managers were actually doing in each of these and similar incidents was conducting a real-world experiment that would hopefully falsify the concerns of the engineers and technicians.

Part of the moral problem is that the people who were most directly affected by this experiment were not informed as to the nature of the experiment in which they were participating. People have a right to know the nature of the risks they face when involved in such experiments and a right to refuse to participate if these risks are judged to be unacceptable. The final decision as to whether or not to go ahead with the experiment should involve those who put their lives at risk, and not merely rest in the hands of either managers or engineers who are not directly participating in the experiment.

The test pilot of the A7D had a right to know that there was some question as to whether or not the brake was designed properly and that he or she might not be able to stop the aircraft when landing. Women who were thinking of using the Dalkon Shield had a right to know that there was a potential problem with wicking that might cause serious illness.[18] And the people who boarded the *Challenger* had a right to know that there previously had been problems with blow-by relative to the O-rings and that the launch they were being asked to make was taking place at a temperature outside the experience base of previous launches such that the engineers had serious doubts about the rings seating properly.

It is highly doubtful that the test pilot would have flown the plane had he or she known about the brake problems, as there are enough risks with flying a new aircraft under the best of conditions. Women would most likely not have used the Dalkon Shield if they had known about the potential for serious illness. And the crew of the *Challenger* might not have boarded the space vehicle had they known about the conditions of the experiment in which they were participating. The people most directly involved in the experiments may have made different decisions than the managers, decisions that would have prevented disasters or near disasters from taking place.

The managers involved in these situations, because of their own interests and those of the organization, did not disclose the nature of the experiments they were conducting. They chose instead to falsify test data to cover up the problem, or ignore the problems the engineers and technicians had discovered. There is something morally perverse when the managers who made these decisions are rewarded and the engineers and technicians who raised legitimate questions about the safety and workability of the technology are punished. There should be severe sanctions for managers who willingly and knowingly place people in experimental situations without disclosing the full nature of the experiment to those who will be most directly affected.

While more right-to-know laws may be helpful and constitute at least a potential solution to the problem, they alone are certainly not the answer. What is ultimately needed is for managers themselves to recognize and respond to the moral dimensions of the situation. Technology is never neutral, it has positive and negative effects. Managers must be concerned about these effects and the consequences of their decisions with respect to technology. They must ask themselves if they would accept being part of the experiment to which they are subjecting others. They must envision themselves or their loved ones in the concrete situation engendered by the technology, rather than viewing the situation in terms of dehumanized and decontextualized abstractions.

And therein lies the nub of the problem. What seems to be missing in the examples mentioned at the beginning of this chapter is a moral sensibility. Technology demands moral sensibility, as technology creates and operates within moral situations. The managerial role involves nuts-and-bolts considerations that are primarily economic in nature. But economic considerations are an abstraction from a concrete situation involving technology, and concrete situations always have something that goes beyond mere economics—they have moral dimensions. Moral sensibility does not involve an abstraction from a concrete situation but involves a mode of integrating the conflicting dimensions of a concrete situation by reconstructing a pathway that is directed by a moral vision. Moral sensibility doesn't ignore technological factors, doesn't falsify technological data, and doesn't reduce the conflicting demands of a concrete situation to abstract probabilities, in which human lives and deadlines and profits become nothing more than equal weights in a probability matrix.

Concrete situations in their richness and complexity require the concrete human being functioning in his or her total concreteness. The engineers cannot run the organization solely on technical factors, as Veblen implied, nor can managers run it solely on economic factors. Furthermore, neither an engineer nor a manager is merely playing a role in the organization. When the head of engineering in the *Challenger* example was asked to take off his engineering hat and put on a managerial hat and think like a manager, he was in essence being asked to be just a manager, and he responded accordingly. Underneath the managerial or engineering role, however, is a concrete human being who, to function as such, must be attuned to the concrete situation and the conflicting values emergent within that situation.

Managers are thus being asked to be human beings with a sensibility to the moral nature of technology and the conflicting values within the concrete situation. They are not expected to be moral heroes who put their jobs and careers on the line when raising questions about the workability and safety of a particular technology. Rather, they must share their knowledge and responsibility with the rest of the organization and with the public at large. The board of directors, for example, needs to know the nature of and the risks involved in the experiment that is being conducted, as does the entire management team involved in a project. Everyone involved with a technology needs to ask the question as to whether or not the results of experimental testing conducted thus far warrant a real-life experiment. They need to ask themselves if they are willing, should that experiment fail, to take responsibility for the decision and show the public that it was rationally and morally justified based on the available evidence.

Such a moral sensibility seems to have been learned by Manville Corporation with respect to its fiberglass product. After having denied the long-term consequences of asbestos hazards and suffered through a painful reorganization as a result of bankruptcy proceedings, the company instituted a product stewardship program when the safety of its fiberglass product came into question. This program involved studying, analyzing, assessing, and above all, communicating to the customer what they knew about the hazards of fiberglass. The company learned that a consistent, conscientious commitment to the truth about a product enabled them to overcome fear, relativity, and cynicism. Customers came to depend on their you'll-know-when-we-know policy, and supported the company's actions with respect to the product.[19]

Moral sensibility requires the development of the concrete individual beneath the particular roles he or she appropriates, including, as stressed earlier in the book, the reorganizing and ordering capabilities of intelligence, the imaginative grasp of authentic possibilities, the vitality of motivation, and sensitivity to the "felt" dimensions of human existence[20], all of which are needed for the dilemmas emergent within the conflicting demands of concrete situations. Thus, the utilization of the total concrete human being, in all its dimensions, is necessary for ongoing constructive solutions to technological problems.

Managers thus need to incorporate some of these moral qualities and give appropriate concern to technology when real questions of safety and workability are raised by engineers and technicians, questions that deserve serious consideration. They must not get caught up in the world of profits, budgets, and schedules and ignore these technological questions. They cannot be "just managers" in distortive abstraction from their concrete functioning as human beings embedded in moral contexts. The organization in which they work must develop a culture where community interests come first, community interests in a safe and workable technology that will enrich the lives of people exposed to the results of technology.

Technology and the Worker

The previous discussion illustrated the way in which the conflict between managers and engineers over the employment and operation of particular technologies results from the reduction of concrete human beings to that of a single, myopic role in the organization. The ensuing discussion will turn to the way in which the humanness and richness of the workers in the corporation are undermined by the introduction of technology and the factors involved in this problem.

Technology can, of course, be liberating and contribute to the well-being of workers in a business setting.[21] It can eliminate some of the hardest, most physically demanding kinds of work and can be used to perform repetitive and boring tasks that would otherwise require human labor. In this sense, it can be used to benefit workers by freeing them from performing work that may eventually cause serious health problems and by allowing them to do work that is more interesting and intellectually demanding. But technology can also be alienating and cut workers off from essential parts of themselves. Technology can result in the loss of the concrete human being.

When technology was simpler and under the control of the users themselves, craftspeople working with tools understood technology as an extension of themselves. These craftspeople were closer to the technology they used and they saw the end product of their efforts. This gave them a sense of accomplishment; they felt at one with their tools and the products they made. These tools and products were extensions of themselves and their ideas and efforts, and the technology employed allowed these craftspeople to be creative and enrich their human experience. The craftspeople working with tools they understand can come to view them as extensions of their bodies. They can not only identify them as their own, they can identify with them.

When craftspeople made shoes, for example, the tools they worked with were virtually an extension of themselves. Craftspeople understood the tools and what they could do, and these tools were in a sense an extension of their hands to bring about the vision that guided their activity. Craftspeople experienced their handiwork unfolding as a unity of purpose. The vision in their minds as to what the shoe should look like extended itself through their hands into the tool itself, and hence, the tools were an extension of their vision as well as of their physical activity.

The expression "made by hand" can be said to capture this feature, for of course things "made by hand" are usually made with tools of one kind or another. The tools that allowed craftspeople to labor were an extension of their ideas, efforts, creativity, and sensitivity to the feel of the tool as it worked its way into the leather. There was a total concrete human being involved in the work, which allowed for creativity and demanded a certain amount of sensitivity to the sensational dimension of the experience.

As technology became more and more complex, it required more specialization, for workers could not master an entire technological process. As the tools used became more specialized, the humans who used the tools became more narrowly specialized. The rise of industrialization brought with it the counterpart of the large organization to manage this complexity in the interests of the owners. Craftspeople lost control of technology as they could no longer afford it nor manage it in their interests. Thus, technology came to be owned by capitalists, people who owned the capital that produced things to be sold on the market, and who were entitled to the profits these products earned.

As this process continued, and technology became more and more specialized and organizations more complex, it was inevitable that workers became alienated from the end product they produced as many workers never saw the end product and thus could no longer see it as an extension of themselves. Work, along with the end product, no longer became an extension of the self, but was externalized under the control of others. Many lost a sense of achievement and a sense of meaning as they became merely one specialized component that was part of a complex whole. They lost a sense of the whole as they became compartmentalized and separated from the end product. They also became separated from the consequences of their actions at least as far as performance of the end product was concerned. Workers lost a sense of creativity as well when they were asked to repeat a task over and over again in a boring mechanical fashion.[22]

These aspects of alienation found their most complete expression in the invention of the assembly line where workers repeated the same task over and over during the course of the workday. They were part of a larger machine and were expected to become proficient at performing their jobs in a mechanical fashion. The assembly line was invented, of course, to increase productivity and produce more end product that could be sold on the market. It was successful in accomplishing this task as products were produced more cheaply and thus were made available to more and more people. Such productivity also made more and more profits for the owners of capital.

The vision that guided the way the technology was structured was the view of humans as atomic units acting in a mechanistic fashion. In brief, the vision was that of the understanding of modern science embodied in reductionism as developed in earlier chapters. Workers were understood as cogs in a much larger machine and were expected to perform their tasks over and over again in machinelike fashion. They were expendable and interchangeable with other workers who could be quickly trained to perform the same tasks. They were not seen in their totality as human beings, as creative individuals, but rather were viewed in individual units to be fitted into some aspect of the mechanistic process of production. They were indeed merely factors of production.

The culmination of this view of the worker found expression in a school of thought called scientific management, the goal of which was to break down each task into its simplest components, which could then be learned quickly and performed efficiently. Work was treated as something completely external to the worker that could be broken down in mechanistic, scientific fashion. While this view was meant to apply only to the workplace, books such as *Cheaper by the Dozen* also extended the same principles into raising a family, where efficiency became an important goal in raising children, who were seen as comparable to a product.

Eventually, these aspects of alienation reached some kind of limit, in that a reaction emerged to treating the worker in such a dehumanized fashion. Many studies appeared that showed the cost to workers from such alienation in increased absenteeism, turnover, alcoholism, and other such problems, all resulting in lost productivity. Thus developed a human relations school that became concerned about the mental and physical health of workers, human resource management, and the development of a humanistic approach to the workplace.

From these concerns came many techniques and programs to deal with the alienation technology was causing. Some companies went to great lengths to combat some of the more obvious features of alienating workplaces. They flew workers from time to time to places where their products were used so that workers could see the results of their many individual efforts. If the company manufactured large electric turbines, for example, people who had worked on the various components of these turbines would be flown to a hydroelectric project where these turbines were installed so they could see the end product in action.

Other companies adopted job enrichment or job enlargement programs to give workers more and different tasks to perform on a given product and to encourage workers to change the job they were doing from time to time to relieve boredom. Other companies did away with the assembly line completely and formed teams to work on the product through all stages of the production process. Concepts such as quality control circles were implemented to give workers more control over the jobs they were doing in that teams could make their own work assignments rather than have supervisors determine who was going to do what tasks. Modern developments called total quality management treat workers as resources who have suggestions to make regarding improvement of the production process to improve quality.

These efforts to deal with alienation and humanize the workplace have met with varying degrees of success. One factor they all suffer from to some extent is the fragmentation that still exists in the workplace between labor and management. Many workers, particularly in unionized workplaces, see these efforts to humanize the workplace as merely more of the same, that is, as merely more efforts by management to squeeze more productivity out of the employees. To the extent that workers have this perception, they resist such efforts and, hence, these programs are not as effective as they might otherwise become. What is lacking in these situations is trust. Managers must again be concerned with the well-being of workers in their concrete situations rather than viewing them as abstractions in productivity and profit calculations. And it is important that workers come to recognize these efforts as expressive of genuine concern for their well-being as concrete individuals. In short, the fragmentation of workers and managers must be replaced by community interactions based on trust and a sense of mutual caring. If managers can accomplish this goal, profits and productivity will most likely follow.

It is the way technology is used, rather than technology itself, which is in large measure responsible for the alienation it can cause. And this usage depends, in large measure, on the concrete context in which it is embedded. Perhaps a good illustration of this comes from different uses of the computer. Writers, for example, can well experience the computer as an extension of themselves. Just as the hand that writes is an extension of the thoughts, feelings, and imagination of the writer, so the computer is an extension of these elements. Writers often "think with their hands or fingers," and in this case, the computer is not external to the writer. Instead, the insights of the author are translated into words more rapidly, the consequences are more in view of the writer, creativity is heightened, and the end product is more rapidly envisioned. Indeed, it is often in the very typing that the vision takes place. Furthermore, the use of spell-checkers relieves the writer of the laborious task of proofreading, allowing time for more creative dimensions of the activity.

The computer in business, where it is used merely for data entry, for example, can alienate people who sit in front of it hour after hour entering meaningless data in a mechanical fashion. Not only does this dull the mind and stifle creativity, it involves a health hazard in producing repetitive motion injuries for those who are susceptible to such problems. The computer can also be used as a substitute for first-hand communication, as it allows people to send messages back and forth to each other in record time. But such a process is not real communication in the same sense as people talking to each other over the phone or experiencing face-to-face communication. As an added dimension of communication, computer messages can be liberating. As a substitute for more personal forms of communication, overabsorption in computer "chats" can be stifling.

Thus, it isn't technology itself that is the problem, as this illustration shows that the same technology can be used to extend the self or alienate people. It all depends on the context in which it is used, the vision or purpose that guides its employment, and the way it is structured. The worker or anyone who uses technology is a concrete human being who has needs for achievement, creativity, and a sense of meaningfulness. He or she is not an atomic unit that is a mere cog in a mechanistic process dedicated to the pursuit of more and more product or profits. Technology can be used to liberate people or it can enslave and alienate people. It all depends on the moral vision that guides the employment of that technology.

Questions for Discussion

1. What is technology? How is technology primarily introduced in our society? What problems does this pose for its application? How can these problems be overcome? Would this lead to a change in the system of capitalism or merely a change of attitude or values?

2. What is the difference between the concerns of engineers or technicians and management personnel? Does it make sense to define the problem as one of technical concerns and realities versus managerial or administrative concerns and realities? Are these different parts of the same organization?

3. What are the essential components of Veblen's analysis of the capitalistic system? What is the difference between the machine process and the business enterprise? Which process controls the other? What problems does this pose for the use of technology? What did Veblen predict would eventually happen? Why has his prediction not come about?

4. What are other ways of dealing with the problem that arises between engineers and managers? Have these been successful? Which do you think has the most chance of success? How is the problem redefined by the authors? What does it mean to say that technology has inherent social and moral dimensions? Why is it important for managers to be aware of these dimensions?

5. Can technology be as alienating as the authors indicate? Are there other aspects of alienation that have not been mentioned? Is this alienation inherent in the nature of technology itself, or is it a problem of the vision and purposes for which technology is used? Is what the authors suggest "practical" in a business context?

6. How can managers develop a moral sensibility with respect to technology? How can they stay in touch with the concrete situation in which technology is being employed and not abstract themselves out of the situation? What does moral sensibility involve with respect to the problems mentioned in this chapter?

Endnotes

[1] "The A7D Affair," William H. Shaw and Vincent Barry, eds., *Moral Issues in Business,* 5th ed. (Belmont, CA: Wadsworth, 1991), pp. 31–35; William M. Hoffman and Jennifer Mills Moore, *Business Ethics: Readings and Cases in Corporate Morality,* 2nd ed. (New York: McGraw-Hill, 1990), pp. 116–125.

[2] "A. H. Robins: Product Safety," Rogene A. Buchholz et al., *Management Response to Public Issues,* 2nd ed. (Englewood Cliffs, NJ: Prentice Hall, 1989), pp. 296–321.

[3] Mark Maier, *A Major Malfunction: The Story Behind the Challenger Disaster* (Binghamton, NY: SUNY, 1992), pp. 2–44.

[4] The latest example of this kind concerns a former research scientist at Philip Morris who claims that his research was suppressed and that he was forced to leave the company after management became concerned that the work he was doing on the addictive potential of nicotine could pose a legal liability for the company. Thus, scientists can also be faced with the same problem mentioned in these examples. See Eben Shapiro, "Scientist Says Philip Morris Suppressed His Research on Nicotine Addiction," *The Wall Street Journal,* April 29, 1994, p. B4.

[5] "The machine process is a severe and insistent disciplinarian in point of intelligence. It requires close and unremitting thought, but it is thought which runs in standard terms of quantitative precision." See Thorstein Veblen, *The Theory of the Business Enterprise* (New York: Augustus M. Kelley, 1965), pp. 308–310.

[6] Thorstein Veblen, *The Instinct of Workmanship* (New York: Augustus M. Kelley, 1964), p. 217.

[7] Thorstein Veblen, *The Engineers and the Price System* (New York: Augustus M. Kelley, 1965), p. 107.

[8] Thorstein Veblen, *Absentee Ownership and Business Enterprise in Recent Times* (New York: Augustus M. Kelley, 1964), p. 259.

[9] "The growth of business enterprise rests on the machine technology as its material foundation. The machine industry is indispensable to it; it cannot get along without the machine process. But the discipline of the machine process cuts away the spiritual, institutional foundations of business enterprise; the machine process is incompatible with its continued growth; it cannot, in the long run, get along with the machine process." Veblen, *The Theory of Business Enterprise,* p. 375.

[10] Veblen, *The Engineers and the Price System,* p. 119.

[11] Veblen, *Absentee Ownership,* pp. 442, 445.

[12] "So soon—but only so soon—as the engineers draw together, take common counsel, work out a plan of action, and decide to disallow absentee ownership out of hand, that move will have been made. . . . The obvious and simple means of doing it is a conscientious withdrawal of efficiency; that is to say the general strike, to include so much of the country's staff of technicians as will suffice to incapacitate the industrial system at large by their withdrawal, for such time as may be required to enforce their argument." Veblen, *The Engineers and the Price System,* pp. 166–167.

[13] John Kenneth Galbraith, *The New Industrial State* (Boston: Houghton Mifflin, 1967), pp. 13–17.

[14] March Mason, "The Curse of Whistle-Blowing," *The Wall Street Journal,* March 14, 1994, p. A14.

[15] Veblen, *The Theory of Business Enterprise,* p. 44.

[16] "The producers, manufacturers, captains of industry, whose interests are safeguarded by current legislation, and by the guardians of law and order are the businessmen who have a pecuniary interest in industrial affairs; and it is their pecuniary interests that are so safeguarded in the naive faith that the material interests of the community at large coincide with the opportunities for gain so secured to the businessmen." Veblen, *The Instinct of Workmanship,* pp. 351–352.

[17] All technology is in some sense experimental, as even under the best of conditions, no one can be certain what effects a technology is likely to have on people and society. After all the testing has been done, even if it is done accurately, and all the problems that are discovered in testing dealt with rather than ignored, when technology is introduced into the real world it can have unforeseen consequences that may adversely affect people and society.

[18] What is ironic about the Dalkon Shield situation is that the product was introduced at a time when adverse side effects of birth control pills were beginning to manifest themselves. Thus, the time was ripe for a new birth control device that was safe and effective to capture a large market share, and executives at Robins were well aware of this market potential. The use of the pill itself was something of a mass experiment, however, and thus women who switched from the pill to the Dalkon Shield went from one experimental situation to another.

[19] Bill Sells, "What Asbestos Taught Me About Managing Risk," *Harvard Business Review,* Vol. 72, no. 2 (March–April 1944), pp. 76–90.

[20] As Dewey has so aptly summarized this need: "A problem must be felt before it can be stated. If the unique quality of the situation is had [experienced] immediately, then there is something that regulates the selection and the weighing of observed facts and their conceptual ordering." See John Dewey, "Logic: The Theory of Inquiry," in *The Later Works,* Vol. 12, Joanne A. Boydston, ed. (Carbondale and Edwardsville, IL: University of Southern Illinois Press, 1986), p. 76.

[21] For an in-depth study of the liberating humanistic dimensions of technology, see Larry A. Hickman, *John Dewey's Pragmatic Technology* (Bloomington and Indianapolis: Indiana University Press, 1990).

[22] For an interesting discussion of alienation in modern society, see John Lachs, *Intermediate Man* (Indianapolis and Cambridge: Hackett Publishing Company, 1981).

Suggested Readings

Buchholz, Rogene, et al. *Management Response to Public Issues,* 2nd ed. Englewood Cliffs, NJ: Prentice Hall, 1989.

Dewey, John. "The Theory of Inquiry," in J. A. Boydston (ed.). *The Later Works,* Vol. 12. Carbondale and Edwardsville, IL: University of Southern Illinois Press, 1986.

Galbraith, John Kenneth. *The New Industrial State.* Boston: Houghton Mifflin, 1967.

Hickman, Larry A. *John Dewey's Pragmatic Technology.* Bloomington and Indianapolis: Indiana University Press, 1990.

Hoffman, William M., and Jennifer Mills Moore. *Business Ethics: Readings and Cases in Corporate Morality,* 2nd ed. New York: McGraw-Hill, 1990.

Lachs, John. *Intermediate Man.* Indianapolis and Cambridge: Hackett Publishing Company, 1981.

Maier, Mark. *A Major Malfunction: The Story Behind the Challenger Disaster.* Binghamton, NY: SUNY, 1992.

Shaw, William H., and Vincent Barry, eds. *Moral Issues in Business,* 5th ed. Belmont, CA: Wadsworth, 1991.

Veblen, Thorstein. *Absentee Ownership and Business Enterprise in Recent Times.* New York: Augustus M. Kelley, 1964.

Veblen, Thorstein. *The Engineers and the Price System.* New York: Augustus M. Kelley. 1965.

Veblen, Thorstein. *The Instinct of Workmanship.* New York: Augustus M. Kelley, 1964.

Veblen, Thorstein. *The Theory of the Business Enterprise.* New York: Augustus M. Kelley, 1965.

SHORT CASES

Firestone Radials

Radial tires were big sellers in Europe before they were introduced into the United States. By the early 1970s, Michelin had been making only radials for 30 years, and Dunlop, another manufacturer of radial tires, had been aware of the design of radial tires for 60 years. These companies began moving into the U.S. market in the 1970s to find new opportunities. The U.S. tire market was dominated by Goodyear, which had achieved a large share of the bias belted tire market. Firestone, once a very strong competitor in the tire market, wanted to make a comeback and gain a larger market share.

In 1970, Ford Motor Company's decision to use more radial tires as original equipment on the cars it was producing looked like the chance Firestone needed. Ford wanted to use more radial tires and it wanted to find a domestic producer for these tires.[1] Firestone was quick to spot this unfilled need in the U.S. tire market. Firestone began U.S. production of radial tires for passenger cars in 1971. Since the switch from bias to radial tire production involved both new equipment and new skills, the switch required a large financial commitment by Firestone. By 1978, the company produced about 51 million Firestone brand steel belted radial passenger tires of all kinds, with about 23 million of these sold as Steel Belted Radial 500 tires.[2]

Preproduction testing of 23 million miles and the 660 million miles driven by customers by mid-1978 on Firestone Radial 500's did not keep the tire from falling into consumer and government disfavor. During the summer of 1977, federal officials stated that Firestone Steel Belted Radial 500 tires were unsafe. The tires were suspected of being prone to blowouts, tread separations, and other deformities and had been the target of thousands of consumer complaints. Records indicated that there had been hundreds of accidents associated with this tire and at least 34 deaths.[3] By the end of 1978, the National Highway Traffic Safety Administration (NHTSA), a government agency, had studied 6,000 consumer reports about 14,000 individual tire failures.[4]

Based on this information, NHTSA ordered a recall of the Radial 500 on November 29, 1978, "not because of any specific defect in the tires but rather, because it is claimed that the tire had a significant failure rate."[5] NHTSA's attempts to identify a specific defect were all unsuccessful but data gathered by the agency indicated an unusually large number of tire failures. "In public statements, Firestone denied any difficulties with the Radial 500's, and attributed the vast bulk of the tire failures to owner neglect or abuse."[6] Firestone maintained that the steel belted radials were safe and reliable and tried to keep the issue from becoming the subject of widespread public discussion.

But there was ample evidence that, for whatever reason, Firestone radials were failing to perform satisfactorily. Along with these road failures, the tire was the subject of investigation by consumer groups, courts, government agencies, and Congress. However, the company continued to state that "our steel belted radial tires have been repeatedly disparaged by an enormous amount of adverse and erroneous publicity."[7] In light of the 250 lawsuits against the company, a congressional investigation, a dealer revolt, consumer group prodding, and customer complaints, Firestone was well aware of a growing problem.

As overwhelming evidence mounted against the Radial 500, the pressure became too intense, and the company agreed to recall an estimated 10 million tires, the largest recall in the industry's history. The recall covered all Steel Belted Radial 500s manufactured during a 12-month period in 1975–76, plus tires made for individual department stores and gasoline companies.[8] Harry Millis, the respected tire analyst for the law firm of Prescott, Ball, and Turben in Cleveland, said the recall was going to be extremely expensive. He was not sure the cost could remain under $175 million, and guessed it would be between $180 and $210 million. Firestone officials set up a $200 million reserve fund to cover the expenses incurred from the recall.[9]

1. Why did Firestone's management not admit there were possible problems with the Radial 500 at an early stage of the controversy? Were there any legal implications that may have been a factor in this decision? What are the moral implications in trying to cover up a problem of this sort?

2. What kind of strategy did Firestone adopt with respect to this incident? Did this strategy make any sense in this situation? Would it make any sense under any circumstances? Is it a good idea to blame the customer for a problem with a product?

3. How did Firestone go about trying to correct its image problem? Is this a good way to deal with questionable performance? How would you go about trying to restore Firestone's good reputation after a debacle such as the Radial 500?

4. What role did the government play in this situation? Was it a constructive role? Were any interest groups active in this case? What role did they play? What interests did they have at stake in this incident?

[1] David Hess, "Killer Times," *Ohio Magazine,* October 1978, p. 54.

[2] John Floberg, Vice President Secretary and General Council of the Firestone Tire and Rubber Company, Statement Before the Sub-committee on Oversight and Investigations of the Interstate and Foreign Commerce Committee of the U.S. House of Representatives, May 23, 1978, p. 2.

[3] Arthur M. Louis, "Lessons From the Firestone Fracas," *Fortune,* August 28, 1978, p. 45.

[4] Ibid.

[5] Floberg, p. 2.

[6] Hess, "Killer Times," p. 46.

[7] Floberg, p. 2.

[8] "A Radical Radial Recall," *Newsweek,* October 30, 1978, p. 68.

[9] "The Case for Firestone," *Forbes,* November 13, 1978, p. 106.

Source: Rogene A. Buchholz, *Business Environment and Public Policy: Implications for Management,* 5th ed. (Englewood Cliffs, NJ: Prentice Hall, 1995), pp. 561–562.

Bhopal

During the evening of Sunday, December 2, 1984, an incident happened in Bhopal, India, that has been called the worst industrial accident in history. The first sign that something was wrong came shortly before midnight, when a worker at the Union Carbide pesticide plant on the outskirts of Bhopal (pop. 672,000) noticed that pressure was building up in a tank that contained 45 tons of methyl isocyanate (MIC), a deadly chemical used to make pesticides. Pressure in the tank continued to build until sometime after midnight, when the highly volatile and highly toxic MIC began to escape from the tank into the surrounding atmosphere. The escaping gas overwhelmed inadequate and reportedly out-of-commission safety backup systems and spread in a foglike cloud over a large and highly populated area close to the plant.[1]

Early reports indicated that 2,500 people had died and at least another 1,000 were expected to die within a two-week period. Some 150,000 people were said to have been treated at hospitals and clinics in Bhopal and surrounding communities. Most of the deaths were caused by the lungs filling up with fluid, causing the equivalent of death by drowning. Other people suffered heart attacks. Some of the survivors were permanently blinded; others suffered serious lesions in their nasal and bronchial passages. Doctors also noticed concussion, paralysis, and signs of epilepsy. Six days after the accident, it was reported that patients were still arriving at Hamidia Hospital in Bhopal at the rate of one a minute, many of them doubling over with racking coughs, gasping for breath, or convulsed with violent spasms.[2] While there was some dispute over the exact number of victims who were killed and injured by the cloud, it is clear that the disaster was of significant proportions.[3]

Methyl isocyanate (MIC) is a colorless chemical compound that was used by Union Carbide as an ingredient in producing relatively toxic pesticides known as Sevin and Temik. Isocyanates in general are reactive and resemble aldehydes and ketones in their propensity to undergo additional reactions with a variety of compounds containing active hydrogen atoms. This reactivity makes them useful as chemical intermediates, but also makes them tricky to handle.[4] MIC in particular will react with many compounds including water. At room temperature, the MIC-water reaction starts slowly, but the reaction produces heat, and if the reaction continues long enough, the MIC will start to boil violently and build up pressure.[5]

Because of its hazardous properties, great precautions were taken in handling and storing the chemical. At the Bhopal facility, MIC was stored in three double-walled stainless steel tanks, buried mostly underground to limit leakage and shield them from outside air temperatures. These tanks were refrigerated to keep the highly volatile gas in liquid form, and also equipped with thermostats, valves, and other devices to warn when the temperature of the chemical exceeded the boiling point. The Bhopal plant had two safety devices that were supposed to operate automatically in case a tank ruptured and the gas started escaping. The first was a scrubber that would neutralize the highly reactive gas by treating it with caustic soda. If the scrubber failed to do its job sufficiently, another mechanism was supposed to ignite the gas and burn it off in the air harmlessly before it could do much damage.[6]

Union Carbide was first incorporated in India some 50 years ago when it began manufacturing batteries. The Indian subsidiary was allowed to stay on after India won independence from Britain and is one of the few firms in India in which the parent company was permitted to hold a majority interest. Union Carbide owned 50.9 percent of the Bhopal facility. The Indian government long favored Union Carbide because of its interests in developing sophisticated industry and in promoting the "green revolution" in agriculture. Pesticides are an important ingredient in this revolution, which is vital to India because of its huge population, much of which is very poor by U.S. standards.[7]

The Bhopal plant was built in 1969 with approval from the local authorities and the blessing of the national government. When the plant was first built, it was located just outside the city limits in an open area, but by the time an expansion program got underway six years later, the area between the town and the plant had begun to be settled by squatters. Many of them were attracted by the roads and water lines that accompanied the plant. In 1975, the administrator of the municipal corporation asked that the plant be removed because of potential dangers to the people living nearby. Instead, the administrator was removed from office and the plant remained.[8]

The deadly cloud had hardly dissipated before lawyers became involved. Five American attorneys, including Melvin M. Belli, filed a class action against Union Carbide on behalf of the victims seeking $15 billion in damages. The suit sought to represent all those who were injured or who lost relatives as a result of the disaster and claims that the corporation was negligent in designing the Bhopal plant and that it failed to warn the area's residents about the dangers presented by the stored chemical. The suit charged that Union Carbide acted "willfully and wantonly" with utter disregard for the safety of Bhopal residents. This charge was partly based on the allegation that the Bhopal plant lacked a computerized early-warning system that had been installed in the company's plant in Institute, West Virginia, which was supposedly identical to the Bhopal facility.[9]

The Indian government got into the legal picture and further complicated matters. Union Carbide had been trying to work out a settlement with the government, and according to some sources, had offered the government an immediate $60 million and a further $180 million over the next 30 years as compensation for the victims of the disaster.[10] Whatever the amount was, it was rejected by the Indian government when it filed suit on April 8 in New York on its own behalf. The suit charged that Union Carbide was liable for any and all damages arising from the poison gas leak, but because of the enormity of the disaster, the government wasn't able to allege with particularity the amount of compensatory damages being sought. The suit also sought punitive damages "in an amount sufficient to deter Union Carbide and any other multinational corporation from the willful, malicious and wanton disregard of the rights and safety of the citizens of those countries in which they do business."[11]

The suit claimed that Union Carbide was negligent in designing and maintaining the Bhopal plant and that the company made false representations to the government about the plant's safety. The company is alleged to have encouraged the storing of MIC in "dangerously large quantities," failed to equip the storage tanks with alarm devices and temperature indicators, and didn't provide "even basic information" about appropriate medical treatment for exposure to the chemical.[12]

Thus, the legal problems for Union Carbide mounted and it faced a great deal of uncertainty regarding the eventual outcome of the situation. The greatest uncertainty, of course, involved the amount of eventual compensation awarded to the victims of the tragedy. With a reported $200 million in insurance coverage, Union Carbide could probably weather a settlement in the range of $250 to $300 million, but anything near $500 million would hurt the company's performance. If the final settlement were to be paid out over a period of time, this would substantially reduce the immediate burden for the company.[13]

John Tollefson, dean of the School of Business at the University of Kansas, stated that three things are crucial to successful management of such a crisis situation as the tragedy at Bhopal: (1) Executives must give long-range considerations priority over short-term costs and benefits; (2) action must be taken immediately; and (3) truthful information must be provided to the public from the beginning. The worst thing that could happen in a situation like Bhopal, added John D. Aram, professor of management at Case Western Reserve University, "is that [executives] get into a bunker mentality where assumptions get frozen and alternatives get closed down instead of opened up."[14]

While Union Carbide was conducting its own investigation of the incident, an inquiry was conducted by the government of India that identified a number of design flaws, operating errors, and management mistakes that helped cause the accident. Plant safety procedures were said to be inadequate to deal with a large-scale leak of the deadly chemical, despite the fact that the dangers such a leak would pose were well known. Nor had any precautions been taken to protect people living near the plant. No procedures were developed for alerting or evacuating the population who would be affected by an accident.

In addition, some important safety systems were not working at the time of the accident. Refrigeration units designed to keep MIC cool so that it could not vaporize had been shut down before the accident. Other equipment, including devices designed to vent and burn off excess gases, was so inadequate that it would have been ineffective even if it had been operating at the time of the accident. Finally, plant workers failed to grasp the gravity of the situation as it developed, allowing the leak to go unattended for about an hour. Brief and frantic efforts to check the leak failed. As the situation deteriorated, the workers panicked and fled the plant.[15]

Finally, the company issued its own report about what caused the disaster. The company report stated that it believed that the accident resulted from a large amount of water entering a storage tank and triggering a chemical chain reaction. The report stated that the water was put in the tank either "inadvertently or deliberately," but the chairman of the company couldn't say that it was an act of sabotage. One possible source of the water was a utility station where a pipe marked "water" was located next to one marked "nitrogen," which was used to pressurize the tank. Quite possibly, someone connected the wrong pipe to the tank allowing as much as 240 gallons of water to mix with the MIC in the tank. The report covered an investigation of nearly three months by a team of company scientists and engineers who conducted about 500 experiments to determine the technical aspects of the accident.[16]

The report also showed that the Bhopal plant was ill run, violated a number of standard operating procedures, and failed to maintain safety devices. Conditions were so poor at the time of the disaster that the plant "shouldn't have been operating," according to Warren M. Anderson, the chairman of Union Carbide. The report confirmed that the scrubber unit intended to neutralize the escaping gas wasn't operating prior to the accident, and that another safety device, a flare tower, also wasn't operating because it had been shut down for maintenance.[17]

1. Is there anything a company can do about citizens who choose to live near its facilities? Should companies be required to provide a buffer zone between their plants and the nearest residents? Should companies actively participate in the preparation of an evacuation plan for communities in the event a disaster like the one at Bhopal occurs? What moral and legal implications do these questions involve?

2. Are there some products that are simply too toxic and hazardous to handle and thus shouldn't be produced? Can the EPA administrator ban such substances from being produced in this country? If so, on what grounds? What about foreign nations? Did the safety systems at the Bhopal plant appear to be adequate? Can safety systems be designed and operated to prevent such accidents from happening?

3. How much is a life worth? What is adequate compensation for an ongoing illness that was the result of the Bhopal accident? How do courts usually deal with these issues? Is the present value of future earnings an adequate way to figure compensation for the family of a deceased wage earner?

4. Was Union Carbide, the parent company, responsible and liable for the actions of its Bhopal subsidiary? What criteria would you use to answer this question? What are the implications of your answer for multinationals in general? Under what circumstances should they continue to be shielded from the actions of their foreign subsidiaries?

5. How can technology be better managed so that safety systems aren't shut down or not working, as apparently was the case at the Bhopal facility? What kind of controls can management institute so that it can be assured on a day-to-day basis that all safety systems are up and operating properly? Is such a goal realistic? Is safety a management problem or a technical problem for the engineers?

6. Is more regulation the answer to controlling the use of chemicals and other hazardous substances? Do communities have the right to know what is being produced in their backyard so they can take appropriate action to protect themselves in the event of an accident? Should such a national right-to-know law be passed or can corporations be relied on to do the "right" thing in this regard?

[1] "India's Night of Death," *Time,* December 17, 1984, p. 22.

[2] Ibid., pp. 22–23.

[3] "Carbide Lawyer Says Number of Bhopal Victims Overstated," *Dallas Times Herald,* April 18, 1985, p. 28-A.

[4] Ward Worthy, "Methyl Isocyanate: The Chemistry of a Hazard," *Chemical and Engineering News,* Vol. 63, no. 6 (February 11, 1985), p. 27.

[5] Ibid., pp. 27–28.

[6] "India's Night of Death," p. 25.

[7] Ibid., p. 26.

[8] Ibid.

[9] "Union Carbide Fights for Its Life," *Business Week,* December 24, 1984, pp. 53–56.

[10] "India's Bhopal Suit Could Change All the Rules," *Business Week,* April 22, 1985, p. 38.

[11] Roger Friedman and Matt Miller, "Union Carbide Is Sued by India in U.S. Court," *The Wall Street Journal,* April 9, 1985, p. 14.

[12] Ibid.

[13] Matt Miller, "India Lifts Ban on Carbide Plan for Asset Sales," *The Wall Street Journal,* December 1, 1986, p. 2.

[14] Ron Winslow, "Union Carbide Mobilizes Resources to Control Damage from Gas Leak," *The Wall Street Journal,* December 10, 1984, p. 29.

[15] "Frightening Findings at Bhopal," *Time,* February 18, 1985, p. 78.

[16] Barry Meier, "Union Carbide Says Facility Should Have Been Shut Before Accident," *The Wall Street Journal,* March 21, 1985, p. 3. Union Carbide raised the possibility of sabotage again later in an apparent effort to lower expectations about the size of a final settlement. See Barry Meier, "Carbide's Bhopal Sabotage Claim Seen by Some as Effort to Shape Settlement," *The Wall Street Journal,* August 15, 1986, p. 5.

[17] Ibid.

Source: Rogene A. Buchholz, et al. *Management Responses to Public Issues,* 3rd ed. (Englewood Cliffs, NJ: Prentice Hall, 1994). pp. 301–322.

Video Display Terminals

Progressive Company was one of the first companies in its industry to fully computerize its information requirements by implementing a fully integrated, on-line system throughout the company. Orders are entered into the system as they are received from customers, shipments are logged on the system as soon as they leave the warehouses, and inventory is monitored on a daily basis. Every manager has access to the central database to find out the status of some item of interest.

Such an extensive computer system means there are many video display terminals (VDTs) scattered throughout the company. Most of these VDTs are used by women who key in the order entry data and other vital information. Recently the safety director of the company has brought to the attention of top management the controversy surrounding the possible health effects of radiation from VDTs, particularly the effects on pregnant women and their unborn fetuses. No definitive answers have been reached in this controversy, and it seems to be another one of those situations where scientific evidence is inconclusive.

Top management of the company doesn't want to ignore the situation, but it doesn't know quite what to do either. The company could establish a policy that limits the hours pregnant women can sit in front of a VDT, but if there isn't a real serious problem, Progressive doesn't want to alarm women needlessly and gain a reputation for being a "softie" in the industry. Most of the other companies in the industry have taken a hard line on this issue. On the other hand, if there is a problem, the company wants to live up to its name in every way and head off pressures for more government regulation.

1. Can issues like this ever be settled to everyone's satisfaction? Is there any possibility of arriving at a definitive answer to these kinds of controversies? How can one company contribute to the resolution of the issue? What are the moral issues?

2. Is this an area that lends itself to self-regulation? Would self-regulation work in the sense of meeting public expectations and eliminating the need for government regulation? What can Progressive do to convince the rest of the industry to take a more proactive approach to this issue?

Food Additives

The Eat-Right Company has introduced a new line of products that contains no fat in an attempt to appeal to health-conscious consumers. The company believes there is a market for such foods that it would like to exploit. These products have begun to appear on grocery shelves in certain parts of the country. The company has decided to conduct test marketing of the product on a limited basis before selling the product in stores around the country. In this way it hopes to discover any problems with the new line before its reputation is tarnished in all the markets where it eventually hopes to sell the nonfat products.

Eat-Right has been closely monitoring consumer reaction to the new line of products through surveys and other means. One problem that it has discovered is that many consumers are complaining about the taste of the nonfat foods, particularly cookies and pastries where the absence of fat leaves the products with a bland taste compared to those that contain fat. The company is getting the definite impression through its test marketing that consumers will trade off better taste for more fat with respect to these types of foods, and that its fat-free variety of cookies and pastries is not going to be competitive.

The company has put its chemists to work at developing some sort of additive that will put a decent taste back into this type of product. Recently its laboratory has come up with a new additive that seems to fill the bill in making cookies and pastries taste as good as those that contain fat. The management of the company is excited about this development and wants to pressure the chemists in the laboratory to begin making this additive available to the production lines as soon as possible.

The chemists, however, are adopting a cautious approach to the introduction of this new additive. They are well aware of the problems that other additives such as cyclamates and certain types of dye have had in the past regarding possible links to cancer. Thus, they are taking a great deal of time to test the new additive as thoroughly as possible. They want to be sure that the substance is safe and that the company will not experience any problems with the additive somewhere down the road. They know the law regarding food additives and want to be sure they can defend their practices should any problems develop in the future.

1. How safe is this type of situation? How much testing needs to be done before the additive can be used? What kind of balance should be struck between the need to be safe and the need to get the additive into production so the company can begin to make a profit on its products?

2. What are the moral issues in this incident? What kind of moral reasoning would be relevant to resolving questions about safety? How does the process approach lend itself to resolving these kinds of situations?

CHAPTER 10

Business in Its Natural Environment

There are some fundamental changes going on in American society and throughout the world that are impacting institutions and lifestyles as never before. These changes have to do with our relationship to the environment, and are being made in order to cope with some serious problems having to do with the depletion of the ozone layer, global warming, deforestation, species decimation, coastal erosion, wetlands protection, acid rain, water pollution, solid and hazardous waste disposal, toxic air emissions, and several other environmental problems of similar magnitude. Most if not all of these problems have become serious enough to require massive expenditures in the billions of dollars and changes in industrial processes that are unprecedented. Companies are phasing out highly useful products such as chlorofluorocarbons (CFCs), for example, and are spending billions to reduce their environmental impact. Technology has impacted the environment and given us the ability to alter the natural environment beyond what anyone would have imagined.

Events of the past few years have accelerated an already growing concern for the environment. Substantial attention has been given to the discovery of the ozone hole over the Antarctic and the link between depletion of the ozone layer and CFCs, which are believed to be the major culprit in destroying this layer. Subsequently, an international agreement was signed to eliminate the production of these substances over a specified period of time and accelerate the search for substitutes. The hot and dry summer of 1988 was confirmation enough for some scientists and policymakers to conclude, as did James Hansen, a NASA climatologist, that the greenhouse effect was for real, and was changing our climate in ways that are only beginning to be understood. Discovery that 1990 was an even hotter year gave further evidence that the earth was indeed warming.

The tenth anniversary of Earth Day celebrated in the spring of 1990 brought with it a new awareness of environmental problems and a new sense of urgency that enabled people to be mobilized for environmental causes all over the world. Public opinion polls in the United States reveal a steady and widespread growth in public concern for environmental quality, which even continued throughout the 1980s when a conservative administration tried its best to cut back on environmental expenditures. Data from a variety of polls indicate that the American public is increasingly aware of and concerned about the gravity of environmental problems and wants the federal government to become more actively involved in their solution. Many people believe tougher laws and regulations are needed and feel more money should be spent on environmental protection. They also say they are more willing than ever before to pay for environmental cleanup and believe economic growth must be sacrificed in order to protect the environment.[1]

Growing recognition exists among corporate leaders that environmental issues are here to stay, and that environmental protection must be considered a normal part of doing business. It is becoming increasingly clear that positive corporate environmental performance cannot be adequately addressed through either the enunciation of environmental policies by top management or the efforts of environmental staff specialists, but must be institutionalized by being incorporated into the fundamental responsibilities of line management. This task will require increased environmental awareness and sophistication on the part of managers throughout the organization and the development of new skills and strategies to respond to environmental problems.

While environmental concerns have been on the public agenda for over two decades, during which a good deal of environmental legislation has been passed and implemented, what is different about today's world is that the environment has rapidly become a survival issue rather than a quality of life issue as it was in the sixties and seventies. More and more business executives are identifying the environment as the issue that will most affect their companies as we move into the twenty-first century. And more and more scientists are suggesting that if we don't come to grips with environmental problems in this decade, irreversible processes will have been set in motion that will inevitably lead to serious environmental degradation all over the globe and widespread human suffering.

The End of Nature

The *End of Nature* is the title of a book by Bill McKibben that captures these concerns and provides a new way of viewing the present situation. The basic thesis of this book is that nature as we have known it in the past in its pure form no longer exists. Human beings have conquered nature as the entire natural world now bears the stamp of humanity, as we have left our imprint on nature everywhere and have altered it beyond recognition in some cases. We have made nature a creation of our own, and have lost the otherness that once belonged to the natural world. The natural world is so affected by human technology that it is more and more becoming one of our own creations and thus is no longer the autonomous nature in which we sought refuge from human civilization.[2]

> In our times . . . human cunning has mastered the deep mysteries of the earth at a level far beyond the capacities of earlier peoples. We can break the mountains apart; we can drain the rivers and flood the valleys. We can turn the most luxuriant forests into throwaway paper products. We can tear apart the great grass cover of the western plains and pour toxic chemicals into the soil and pesticides onto the fields until the soil is dead and blows away in the wind. We can pollute the air with acids, the rivers with sewage, and the seas with oil—all this in a kind of intoxication with our power for devastation at an

order of magnitude beyond all reckoning. . . . Our managerial skills are measured by the competence manifested in accelerating this process.[3]

What this view suggests is that the world has crossed a threshold with respect to the environment that can never be recrossed. We cannot return to a simpler age, something like the "small is beautiful" idea where human would tread much more lightly on the environment and be less disruptive of nature. We have no choice in these matters because our science and technology have taken us too far to turn back to a past age that may never have existed. Such notions of a return to a pristine past where nature was less affected by human activities are romantic and unrealistic. Human activities alter natural processes far more greatly than anyone can imagine, and nature has been subjugated and reconfigured according to human needs and desires.

Many are legitimately concerned that nature will be crowded out by such human interference, and oppose the idea that humans should exercise their dominion over nature for the sake of material progress. They have a sense of loss because nature's independence is being destroyed. For much of history, human beings have not experienced nature as kind and gentle, but as harsh and dangerous and, therefore, humans have felt compelled to subordinate nature in order to protect themselves. But humility toward nature is what is now being advocated, that human beings should neither control nor dictate to nature, but must learn to live in harmony with nature and take a responsibility for nature that has thus far largely been avoided.

The earth has finite resources and a fragile environment, all of which give us a responsibility to manage the human use of planet earth. We must develop new technologies and strategies that are environmentally sensitive and we must be more responsible in our use of resources. Not to take these kinds of steps and change our way of thinking will most assuredly lead to environmental degradation on a scale that far surpasses anything we have experienced in our lifetime. Nature no longer can take care of itself, and one of the most fundamental assumptions we have made about nature, namely, that it can take care of itself without any conscious thought given to the impacts human activities have on the environment, must be discarded. We simply cannot proceed, as we have in the past, to exploit nature and not worry about the environmental consequences of our activities. The leaders of business and industry, as well as of government and educational institutions, are beginning to think in terms of managing nature, which most often means taking responsibility for nature to ensure the survival of the world.

Managing nature involves making value judgments regarding the kind of planet we want. While science at least attempts to tell us what kind of planet we can have or are likely to have if certain trends continue, what we choose to have is a value judgment. Value judgments include the answer to such questions as: How much species diversity should be maintained? How much of nature and what natural resources do we wish to leave for our children? Should the size or growth rate of the human population be curtailed to protect the global environment? How much climate change is acceptable? How much poverty is acceptable throughout the world? Science can tell us something about the broad patterns of global transformation taking place, but value questions about the pace and direction of those patterns have to be answered through political and economic systems.

Through a gradual awakening, people are beginning to develop a new perception of humanity's relationship to the earth's natural systems. People are crossing perceptual thresholds without necessarily even being aware of it, and developing new ways of thinking. Such changes are necessary to respond to environmental problems effectively and in time to save the world from irreversible destruction. There is a growing sense of the world's interdependence and connectedness, and an understanding that progress is an illusion if it destroys the conditions for life to thrive on earth. The leaders of industrial and Third World countries alike recognize their common interest in and responsibility for participating in sustainable development. Looming threats to the world's climate and undermining of other global commons may soon make the transition to stronger international solutions inevitable.

New Directions in Environmental Ethics

As environmental problems impinge themselves on the public mind, intellectual disciplines such as philosophy are struggling to develop new environmental paradigms that overcome the traditional approach to the environment that has pervaded industrial societies. Sometimes called the greening of philosophy, new thinking in philosophy is attempting to provide alternatives to the dualism between humans and nature that has undergirded traditional approaches to the environment, approaches in which the environment is seen as something separate from humans to be dominated and manipulated for human purposes. This traditional paradigm was consistent with institutional practices in which environmental impacts were largely ignored with a "nature can take care of itself" attitude. Now that institutional behavior is changing, there is a need for new philosophical paradigms to provide a rationale for these changes and to indicate a path for future changes. Some believe that this task is vital to human survival on a planet that is being systematically destroyed by traditional ways of thinking and acting.

The upshot is that the dominant ethical systems of our times,

> those clustered as the Western ethic and other kindred human chauvinistic systems, are far less defensible, and less satisfactory, than has been commonly assumed, and lack an adequate and nonarbitrary basis. Furthermore, alternative theories are far less incoherent than is commonly claimed, especially by philosophers. Yet although there are viable alternatives to the Dominion thesis, the natural world is rapidly being preempted in favor of human chauvinism—and of what it ideologically underwrites, the modern economic-industrial superstructure—by the elimination or overexploitation of those things that are not considered of sufficient instrumental value for human beings. Witness the impoverishment of the nonhuman world, the assaults being made on tropical rainforests, surviving temperate wildernesses, wild animals, the oceans, to list only a few of the victims of man's assault on the natural world. Observe also the associated measures to bring primitive or recalcitrant peoples into the Western consumer society and the spread of human-chauvinistic value systems. The time is fast approaching when questions raised by an environmental ethic will cease to involve live options. As things stand at present, however, the ethical issues generated by the preemptions—especially given the weakness and inadequacy of the ideological and value-theoretical basis on which the damaging chauvinistic transformation of the world is premised and the viability of alternative environmental ethics—are not merely of theoretical interest but are among the most important and urgent questions of our times, and perhaps the most important questions that human beings, whose individual or group self-interest is the source of most environmental problems, have ever asked themselves.[4]

Treating nature as instrumental places the natural world in a utilitarian position in relationship to human beings. The material world has value only to the extent it can serve humans. Such an approach promotes an unhealthy separation between humans and the rest of nature. Humans must also ask how they can serve nature and recognize a mutual interdependence between human life and life in the natural world. Human life, in fact, is part of the natural world, and the dualism and individualism that are characteristic of Western thought is no longer functional. Such thinking leads to policies and practices that undermine the conditions for supporting human life and activities by destroying the natural world on which we all depend.

The development of a field of environmental ethics, which allows for a consideration of the moral responsibilities of business in relation to the environment, however, poses a problem. When it comes to environmental ethics, one is confronted with another field of ethics that has a separate group of scholars and a separate body of literature from the field of business ethics. As concern for the environment gains importance, this problem can only increase. Ideally, an ethical position must be able to encompass all areas of human endeavor under one general conceptual framework. The chasm between business and environmental ethics occurs, however, because of the inadequacy of traditional theories utilized in business ethics to provide an adequate conceptual framework for throwing moral light on our relation to the environment.

As discussed in Chapter 2, the theoretical foundations of business ethics come largely from the utilitarian theories of Bentham and Mill, deontological theories derived largely from Kant's categorical imperative, theories of justice derived from Rawls and Nozick, and to some extent from the virtue theories of Aristotle and more contemporary scholars such as MacIntyre. In the environmental literature, one finds little application of these theories to the natural environment.

One presupposition underlying Kant, Bentham, Mill, and social contract theories alike is that of atomic individualism. This external individualism cannot be overcome, for while peripheral ties may be established when antecedent individuals enter into contract with one another or come together through other means of collection in order to more readily secure their own individualistic goals, these bonds cannot root them in any ongoing endeavor that is more than the sum of their separate selves, separate wills, separate egoistic desires, much less bond them to anything beyond contractually established social structures. Furthermore, these positions lead to problems with the understanding of communities of any sort, for a community can be no more than the collective sum of the parts, with the individual in some sense pitted against or set over against the collective whole in an external relationship.

Such positions are not congenial to the needs of environmental ethics. Neither are the virtue ethics approaches of Aristotle and MacIntyre conducive for work in environmental ethics, for the self is now rooted in cultural traditions of self-enclosed societies, and there is no philosophical structure for moving beyond this impasse. Moreover, for all of the preceding positions, the source of ethical action lies either in the application of abstract rules to cases or in the inculcation of tradition, neither of which incorporates the type of attunement to experience in nature that is required for an environmental consciousness.

Philosophers in environmental ethics have thus devoted their efforts to developing new notions about environmental ethics and extending moral consideration to nature through new philosophical systems. Thus far, the greening of philosophy seems to be taking two paths, one path that deals with moral extensionism and eligibility, and the other path with biocentrism or deep ecology. Both these approaches are attempting to bring nature into the moral realm and make all or parts of nature an active moral agent that deserves moral consideration in our actions and practices.

MORAL EXTENSIONISM AND ELIGIBILITY

The concept of rights has come into standard usage in terms of extending moral consideration to entities and has changed a host of institutional practices that have impacts on human beings. The civil rights movement extended the notion of rights to blacks and other minorities, and had as a goal the extension and implementation of basic rights afforded to Americans of any race or color. Equal rights dealt with the same problems with regard to women, and were used to press for equal treatment for women in all aspects of society. The right to a safe and hazard-free workplace found its way into legislation and regulation regarding safety and health in the workplace. Something called a consumer bill of rights dealt with product safety and other aspects of the marketplace that needed attention. The concept of human rights has thus been extended into many aspects of life in our society and has been used as the basis of much legislation and regulation that have changed the nature of institutional behavior to respect those rights.

The question is whether this notion of rights can also be extended to the natural world or at least some of its components and whether this extension can help to deal with environmental problems in an effective manner. Where does the ethical cutoff fall with regard to moral eligibility? What aspects of nature should be brought into the moral realm and thereby given moral consideration? The philosophical approach to extending rights to nature has taken place around the issue of moral extensionism and eligibility.

Many philosophers extend ethics only so far as animals on the grounds that animals are sentient beings in that they are able to suffer and feel pain. But more radical thinkers widened the circle to include all life such as plants. Still others see no reason to draw a moral boundary at the edge of life and argued for ethical considerations for rocks, soil, water, air, and biophysical processes that constitute ecosystems. Some are even led to the conclusion that the universe has rights superior to those of its most precocious life form.[5]

Peter Singer argues that the view holding that the effects of our actions on non-human animals have no intrinsic moral significance is arbitrary and morally indefensible. He makes an analogy between the way we now treat animals with the way we used to treat black slaves. The white slaveowners limited their moral concern to the white race and did not regard the suffering of a black slave as having the same moral significance as the suffering of a white person. Thus, the black could be treated inhumanly with no moral compulsion. This way of thinking and treating blacks is now called racism, but we could just as well substitute the word *specieism* in regard to the manner in which animals are treated. The logic of racism and the logic of specieism are the same.[6]

Just as our concern about equal treatment of blacks through legislation and regulation moved us to a different level of moral consciousness, so will treating animals as beings that have interests and can suffer and therefore deserve moral consideration move us to a different level of moral consciousness. This level may involve stopping certain practices, such as using animals for testing purposes and subjecting them to slow and agonizing deaths. It may also involve stopping the practice of raising animals in crowded conditions solely for the purpose of human consumption. The decision to avoid specieism of this kind will be difficult, but no more difficult, states Singer, than it would have been for a white Southerner to go against the traditions of his society and free his slaves.[7]

The creatures in Singer's moral community have to possess nervous systems of sufficient sophistication to feel pain; that is, they have to be sentient beings. Ethics ends at the boundary of sentience. A tree or a mountain or a rock being kicked does not feel anything and, therefore, does not possess any interests or rights. Since they cannot be harmed by human action, they have no place in ethical discourse. There is nothing we can do that matters to them and thus they are not deserving of moral consideration.[8]

Other philosophers, such as Joel Fineberg, also limited their moral concerns to animals. Fineberg excluded plants from the rights community on the grounds that they had insufficient "cognitive equipment" to be aware of their wants, needs, and interests. He also denied rights to incurable "human vegetables," and using the same logic disqualified certain species from moral consideration. Protection of rare and endangered species became protection of humans to enjoy and benefit from them. Even less deserving of rights were mere things.[9] While many philosophers now find these requirements too limiting, Singer and Fineberg at least deserve credit for helping to liberate moral philosophy from its fixation on human beings.

Scholars such as Christopher Stone pushed the boundaries of moral eligibility further to include other aspects of the natural world. Stone saw no logical or legal reason to draw any ethical boundaries whatsoever. Why should the moral community end with humans or even animals? While this idea may sound absurd to many people, so did the extension of certain rights to women and blacks at one point in our history. The extension of rights in this manner would help environmentalists to better protect the environment and also reflects the view that nature needs to be preserved for its own sake and not just for the interests of human beings.[10]

The question of moral extensionism and eligibility also comes into play when we talk about the obligations we have to future generations. There is probably a general agreement that it would be wrong to use all of the earth's resources and to contaminate the environment that we pass on to our children. But at what point do we draw the line? How many resources do we leave to future generations and in what condition shall we leave the environment? Do future generations in any sense have any rights to the resources we are presently using and do they have a right to a clean environment? Since they are not yet alive, they cannot lay claim to a livable environment and do not seem, at least on the surface, to have any interests in our present activities.

But as Joel Fineberg argues, whatever future human beings turn out to be like, they will have interests that we can affect, for good or ill, in the present. The interests that these future generations will have do need to be protected from irresponsible invasions of those interests by present generations. Present generations have some responsibility to save something for the future, so their offspring can enjoy some of the amenities that we presently enjoy. Rather than focus solely on the rights and interests of present individuals, Fineberg argues that we have obligations to consider the good of the continuing human community.[11]

Richard DeGeorge, on the other hand, believes that future persons, either individually or as a class, do not presently have the right to existing resources. Future generations or individuals have rights only to what is available when they come into existence—when their future rights become actual and present. It is only when a being actually exists that it has needs and wants and interests. It then has a right only to the kind of treatment or to the goods available to it at the time of its conception. It cannot have a reasonable claim to what is not available. However, to argue that future generations do not have present rights does not mean that present generations do not have some obligations to try and provide certain kinds of environments and leave open as many possibilities as feasible for future generations. But the needs of the present and already existing people take precedence over consideration of the needs of future generations.[12]

TOWARD A BIOCENTRIC ETHIC

Kenneth Goodpaster argues that the extension of rights beyond certain limits is not necessarily the best way to deal with moral growth and social change with respect to the environment. The last thing we need, he states, is a liberation movement with respect to trees, animals, rivers, and other objects in nature. The mere enlargement of the class of morally considerable beings is an inadequate substitute for a genuine environmental ethic. The extension of rights to other objects or to future generations does not deal with deeper philosophical questions about human interests and environmental concerns. Moral considerations should be extended to systems as well as individuals. Societies need to be understood in an ecological context and it is this larger whole that is the bearer of value. An environmental ethic, while paying its respects to individualism and humanism, must break free of them and deal with the way the universe is operating.[13]

John Rodman, a political theorist at California's Claremont Graduate School, protested the whole notion of extending human-type rights to nonhumans because this action categorizes them as "inferior human beings" and "legal incompetents" that need human guardianship. This was the same kind of mistake that some white liberals made in the 1960s with regard to blacks. Instead we should respect animals and everything else in nature "for having their own existence, their own character and potentialities, their own forms of excellence, their own integrity, their own grandeur." Instead of giving nature rights or legal standing within the present political and economic order, Rodman urged environmentalists to become more radical and change the order. All forms of domestication must end along with the entire institutional framework associated with owning land and using it in one's own interests.[14]

Another philosopher from the University of Wisconsin, J. Baird Callicott, an admirer of Aldo Leopold's land ethic—a position to be discussed shortly—declared that the animal liberation movement was not even allied with environmental ethics, as it emphasized the rights of individual organisms. The land ethic, on the other hand, was holistic and had as its highest objective the good of the community as a whole. The animal rights advocates simply added individual animals to the category of rights holders, whereas "ethical holism" calculated right and wrong in reference not to individuals but to the whole biotic community. The whole, in other words, carried more ethical weight than any of its component parts. Oceans and lakes, mountains, forests, and wetlands are assigned a greater value than individual animals that might happen to reside there.[15]

Thus, biocentric ethics or deep ecology leads the more radical philosophers to devalue individual life relative to the integrity, diversity, and continuation of the ecosystem as a whole. This approach offended many proponents of animal rights, and presumably those who advocated rights for plants and other aspects of the natural community, to say nothing of those whose moral community ended with human society. According to Roderick Nash, this perspective on environmental ethics has created entirely new definitions of what liberty and justice mean on planet earth and an evolution of ethics to be ever more inclusive. This approach recognizes that there can be no individual welfare or liberty apart from the ecological matrix in which individual life must exist. "A biocentric ethical philosophy could be interpreted as extending the esteem in which individual lives were traditionally held to the biophysical matrix that created and sustained those lives."[16]

This new approach to the environment holds that some natural objects and ecosystems have intrinsic value and are morally considerable in their own right apart from human interests. Nature is not simply a function of human interests, but has value in and of itself apart from human interests. The naturalistic ethic respects each life form and sees it as part of a larger whole. All life is a sacred thing and we must not be careless about species that are irreplaceable. Particular individuals come and go, but nature continues indefinitely, and humans must come to understand their place in nature. Each life form is constrained to flourish in a larger community, and moral concern for the whole biological community is the only kind of an environmental ethic that makes sense and preserves the integrity of the entire ecosystem.[17]

Nature itself is a source of values, it is argued, including the value we have as humans, since we are a part of nature. The concept of value includes far more than a simplistic human-interest satisfaction. Value is a multifaceted idea with structures that are rooted in natural sources.[18] Value is not just a human product. When humans recognize values outside themselves, this does not result in dehumanizing of the self or a reversion to beastly levels of existence. On the contrary, it is argued, human consciousness is increased when we praise and respect the values found in the natural world, and this recognition results in a further spiritualizing of humans.[19] Thus, this school of thought holds that there are natural values that are intrinsic to the natural object itself apart from humans and their particular valuing activities. Values are found in nature as well as in humans. Humans do not simply bestow value on nature, as nature also conveys value to humans.[20]

Such a position was advocated several years ago by the land ethic of Aldo Leopold, a wildlife management expert in the state of Wisconsin. Such a land ethic changes the role of human from conqueror of nature to a plain member and citizen of nature. We abuse land, said Leopold, because we regard it as a commodity belonging to us. When we see land as a community to which we belong, we may begin to use it with love and respect. His most widely quoted precept with regard to land usage is that "a land-use decision is right when it tends to preserve the integrity, stability, and beauty of the biotic community. It is wrong when it tends otherwise."[21]

This approach calls us to a new kind of relationship with the earth, as it does not involve simply measuring water pollution, for example, and taking steps to reverse this pollution; it is a matter of coming to know water through being aware of it in a new way, as a fellow citizen of our earth community. This approach involves (1) the notion that other members of the earth community deserve respect or moral consideration of their own simply because they are there and not just because they are useful to humans, and (2) the notion that a consciously developed relationship with these fellow natural beings is essential to understanding what the ethics of respect demands.[22]

The world of nature is not to be defined in terms of commodities that are capable of producing wealth for humans who manage them in their own interests. All things in the biosphere are believed to have an equal right to live and reach their own individual forms of self-realization. Instead of a hierarchial ordering of entities in descending order from God through humans to animals, plants, and rocks, where the lower creatures are under the higher ones and are ruled by them, nature is seen as a web of interactive and interdependent life that is ruled by its own natural processes. These processes must be understood if we are to work in harmony with nature and preserve the conditions for our own continued existence. Protecting the rainforest is not just a matter of someone from the outside trying to preserve the rainforest as something apart from human existence—it is a matter of seeing oneself as part of the rainforest and acting to protect oneself from extinction.[23]

As stated by Thomas Berry, "any diminishment of the natural world diminishes our imagination, our emotions, our sensitivities, and our intellectual perception, as well as our spirituality."[24] Human beings are integral with the entire earth and even with the universe as the larger community we belong to by the very nature of our existence. But most of us do not live within this perspective and are not in intimate communion with the natural world. We have become autistic and do not hear the voices of nature. We have been blindly pursuing more and more economic growth and all the while replacing nature with our own view of reality, and in the process we have destroyed much that is good and beautiful.

> The mountains and valleys, the rivers and the sea, the birds and other animals, this multitude of beings that compose the natural world no longer share in our lives and we have ceased to share in their lives except as natural resources to be plundered for their economic value. . . . We might wonder how it was that we let this fascinating world be taken from us to be replaced with the grime of our cities disintegrating the very stones of our buildings, as well as increasing the physical and emotional stress under which we live. It was, of course, the illusion of a better life, foisted on us largely through hypnotic advertising and the promise of economic enrichment.[25]

Biocentrism or deep ecology thus accords nature ethical status that is at least equal to that of human beings. From the perspective of the ecosystem, the difference is between thinking that people have a right to a healthy ecosystem or thinking that the ecosystem itself possesses intrinsic or inherent value.[26] Deep ecologists argue for a biocentric perspective and a holistic environmental ethic regarding nature. Human beings are to step back into the natural community as a member and not the master. The philosophy of conservation for Holmes Ralston, for example, was comparable to arguing for better care for slaves on plantations. The whole system was unethical, not just how people operated within the system. In Ralston's view, nothing mattered except the liberation of nature from the system of human dominance and exploitation. This process involved a reconstruction of the entire human relationship with the natural world.[27]

The heart of deep ecology is the idea that identity of the individual is indistinguishable from the identity of the whole. The sense of self-realization in deep ecology goes beyond the modern Western sense of the self as an isolated ego striving for hedonistic gratification. Self in a new sense is experienced as integrated with the whole of nature. Human self-interest and interest of the ecosystem are one and the same. There is a fundamental interconnectedness of all things and all events that must be taken into consideration in our thinking and practices.[28]

On close examination, both these approaches prove useful in understanding the relationship between humans and nature. But these approaches treat the environment differently and make different assumptions about the locus of moral consideration. Moral extensionism and eligibility use the vehicle of rights to extend moral concern to more and more aspects of nature, but these rights are bestowed by human beings, they are not intrinsic to nature itself. The question is whether rights can meaningfully be extended to the natural world or at least to some of its components and whether this extension can help to deal with environmental problems in an effective manner. It seems clear that the attempt to extend rights in this manner represents an effort to build a wider moral community that includes all or part of the natural world, and in this sense, the dualism between humans and nature is overcome. But these rights are not possible through social contract theories utilized in business ethics because nonhumans, of course, cannot enter into covenants of this nature.

Biocentrism or deep ecology assumes nature already has intrinsic value that needs to be recognized by liberating nature from the system in which it is currently trapped. By recognizing the intrinsic value of nature, the last remnants of anthropocentrism, still operative in moral extensionism and eligibility, is excised. However, while moral extensionism and eligibility stress the individual to the exclusion of the whole, biocentrism or deep ecology subordinates the individual to the good of the whole. What can be seen here, though dressed now in new environmental garb, are the same traditional conflicting philosophical alternatives discussed earlier.

Bridging the Chasm: Pragmatic Process as a Unified Ethical Perspective

From the backdrop of the process understanding of human experience, humans and their environment—organic and inorganic—take on an inherently relational aspect. To speak of organism and environment in isolation from each other is never true to the situation, for no organism can exist in isolation from an environment, and an environment is what it is in relation to an organism. The properties attributed to the environment belong to it in the context of that interaction. What we have is interaction as an indivisible whole, and it is only within such an interactional context that experience and its qualities function.

Such a relational view of organism and environment at once has pluralistic dimensions, for environments are contextually located, and significant solutions to problematic situations emerge within such contextually situated environments. However, as was discussed earlier, pluralism is not relativism[29], for with the rejection of the spectator theory of knowledge, or knowledge as a passive finding, comes the rejection of the correspondence theory of truth, and instead, a view of reality as richer than or overflowing our conceptual awareness is stressed. Diverse perspectives grasp the richness of reality in different ways but must be judged in terms of workability. And workability requires growth, resolution of conflicts in terms of enlargement of context, which can adjust or adjudicate the conflicting perspectival claims. Growth, as already stressed, cannot be reduced to material growth, but rather is best understood as an increase in the moral-esthetic richness of experience.

Moreover, it was seen that value for the pragmatist is not something subjective, housed either as a content of mind or in any other sense within the organism, but neither is it something "there" in an independently ordered universe. Objects in nature and contextual situations, as they emerge in human experience, possess qualities such as being alluring or repugnant, fulfilling or stultifying, appealing or unappealing. These qualities are real emergents in the context of our interaction with our cultural and natural environments and are "there" in that context.[30] These immediately experienced qualities provide the basis, along with intelligent evaluation, for the values we hold and come to appropriate. What we hold as valuable, what ought to be, develops through the ongoing process of experimental inquiry. Conversely, new evaluations can give a different quality to immediate experience. A harmonious life requires the harmonizing of the evaluated claims of intelligent inquiry and the prized qualities of experience.

As this view relates to the environmental concerns of the present chapter, it may be objected that an individual can achieve a harmonious life in a totally artificial environment, with no concern for nature whatsoever. This, however, is to miss the point that humans are concrete organisms enmeshed in a natural environment with which they are continuous. Human development is ecologically connected with its biological as well as its cultural world.[31] Growth involves precisely the deepening and expansion of perspective to include ever widening horizons of the cultural and natural worlds to which we are inseparably bound. This receives its most intense form in Dewey's naturalistic understanding of experiencing the world religiously as a way of relating one's self with the universe as the totality of conditions with which the self is connected.[32] This unity can be neither apprehended in knowledge nor realized in reflection, for it involves such a totality not as a literal content of the intellect, but as an imaginative extension of the self, not an intellectual grasp but a deepened attunement to the universe. This is the reason poets get at nature so well.[33]

Such an experience brings about not a change in the intellect alone, but a change in moral consciousness. It allows one to "rise above" the divisiveness we impose through arbitrary and illusory in-group and out-group distinctions by "delving beneath" to the sense of the possibilities of a deep-seated harmonizing of the self with the totality of the conditions to which it relates. And this ultimately involves the entire universe, for the emphasis on continuity reveals that at no time can we separate our developing selves from any part of the universe and claim that it is irrelevant. Indeed, while environmentalists may seek to describe "objective" relationships among interacting individuals—human, nonhuman, organic, and inorganic that make up the biosphere—yet the properties attributed to the individuals are not possessed by them independently of the interactions in which they exhibit themselves. Nature cannot be dehumanized, nor can humans be denaturalized. Humans exist within and are part of nature, and any part of nature provides a conceivable relational context for the emergence of value. The understanding of "human interests," of what is valuable for human enrichment, has to be expanded not just in terms of long range versus short range and conceivable versus actual, but in terms of a greatly extended notion of human interest or human welfare. Furthermore, to increase the experience of value is not to increase something subjective or within us, but to increase the value ladenness of relational contexts within nature. Dewey's understanding of experiencing the world religiously provides the ultimate context within which such an ethics must be located. While every situation or context is in some sense unique, no situation or context is outside the reaches of moral concern. Pragmatic process ethics, properly understood, *is* an environmental ethics.

Such an ethics cannot be called an anthropocentrism. True, only humans can evaluate; and, without evaluation as a judgment concerning what best serves the diversity of valuings, the valuable could not emerge. Furthermore, humans can speak of nonhuman types of experience only analogically in reference to their own. But, though the concept of the valuable emerges only through judgments involving human intelligence, value emerges—either positively or negatively—at any level of environmental interaction involving sentient organisms. While the value level emergent in organism-environment contexts increases with the increased capacity of the organism to experience in conscious and self-conscious ways, as long as there are sentient organisms experiencing, value is an emergent contextual property of situations. As James stresses, as moral agents we are forbidden "to be forward in pronouncing on the meaningfulness of forms of existence other than our own." We are commanded to "tolerate, respect, and indulge those whom we see harmlessly interested and happy in their own ways, however unintelligible these may be to us. Hands off: neither the whole of truth nor the whole of good is revealed to any single observer."[34] Though some may question the claim that a distinction in levels of value emergence can be made, when push comes to shove, when all the abstract arguments are made, is it not the case that claims of the valuable must be seen in light of their promotion of or irrepressible harm to human welfare, actual or potential? Does anyone really think that the preservation of the spotted owl and the preservation of the AIDS virus have equal moral claim? Thus, we find the characteristic of "harmless" in the foregoing statement by James.

This evaluation of the relative merits of the AIDS virus and the spotted owl in terms of their promotion of or harm to human welfare cannot be pushed into a position of anthropocentrism. The attempt to do so comes from a failure to adequately cut beneath the either/or of anthropocentrism/biocentrism. In fact, both-and is closer to the position intended, but even this is inadequate, for it fails to capture the radical conceptual shift which, in making the conjunction, changes the original extremes of the positions brought together. There is no "all or none" involved. It is not the case that all value is such only in relation to humans. Yet, neither is it the case that all value has equal claim irrespective of its relation to the welfare of humans. Value is an emergent contextual property of situations as long as and whenever there are sentient organisms experiencing, yet the value level emergent in organism-environment contexts increases with the increased capacity of the organism to experience in conscious and self-conscious ways. The biological egalitarianism of biocentrism can perhaps be thought consistently, but it cannot be maintained in practice. Surely one is not willing to move from the theoretical egalitarianism of humans and the AIDS virus to an implementation of such theory in practice.

Yet, this does mean that humans can ignore the value contexts of sentient organisms within nature. To do so is not to evaluate in terms of conflicting claims, but to exploit through egocentric disregard for the valuings of other organisms. We must make judgments that provide protection for the welfare of humans, yet such judgments must consider the value-laden contexts involving other sentient organisms to the largest degree consistent with this goal. And, while this position does not allow for the emergence of value in nonsentient contexts, such contexts are ultimately included in moral deliberation. For, is it really possible to envision any aspect of nature, any relational context in nature, or any thing in nature that cannot provide a conceivable experiential context for sentient organisms?

The problem is not that environments are ultimately valuable in their actual or potential relational contexts of emergent value, but that valuings and the valuable environments that allow for them are taken far too narrowly. At no point can one draw the line between human welfare and the welfare of the environment of which it is a part and with which it is intertwined in an ongoing interactive process. Here many would object that to value nonsentient nature in terms of its potentiality for yielding valuing experiences is to say that it has merely instrumental value, and if nature is merely an instrument, then no real environmental ethic is possible. Yet, within the foregoing framework, the entire debate concerning instrumental versus intrinsic value is problematic from the start. Everything that can conceivably enter into experience has the potential for being an intrinsic relational aspect of the context within which value emerges, and any value, as well as any aspect of the context within which it emerges, involves consequences and is therefore instrumental in bringing about something further. Thus, Dewey holds that no means-end distinction can be made, but rather there is an ongoing continuity in which the character of the means enters into the quality of the end, which in turn becomes a means to something further.[35]

Moreover, evaluations grow, gain novel direction and novel contexts in the resolution of conflicting and novel interests, and it is with choice and creative resolution in these problematic contexts that morality is concerned. If everything has intrinsic value, then decision becomes somewhat arbitrary. If, for example, every tree has its own intrinsic value and the right to exist, irrespective of its potential for valuing experiences, how can we choose which trees to cut down? Yet, common sense tells us we cannot "save" them all. Arguments must be made, and the literature itself shows that arguments are ultimately made in terms of the potential for valuing experiences and, ultimately, when hard choices must be made, for the valuing experiences of humans.[36]

It may be further questioned as to whether or not the ideal of "fully attained growth" in the union of self and universe merges into an ecocentrism in which value is given to the system rather than to the individual. Here again, these alternatives do not hold within the present framework. Sometimes the system is more important, sometimes the individual, and this is dependent on the contexts in which meaningful moral situations emerge and the conflicting claims at stake. Furthermore, no absolute break can be made between the individual and the system, for each is inextricably linked with the other and gains its significance in terms of the other. The whole notion of an isolated individual is an abstraction, for diversity and continuity have been seen to be inextricably interrelated. Neither individuals nor whole systems are the bearers of value, but rather value emerges in the interactions of individuals, and wholes gain their value through the interactions of individuals, while the value of individuals cannot be understood in isolation from the relationships that constitute their ongoing development. When we slide over the complexities of a problem, we can easily be convinced that categorical moral issues are at stake. And the complexities of a problem are always context dependent or relational.

While this view cannot tell us what position to take on specific issues, it gives a directive for understanding what is at issue, for making intelligent choices, and for engaging in reasoned debate on the issues. What is needed for an environmental ethics are those same factors that were earlier seen to be needed for process ethics in general: the development of the reorganizing and ordering capabilities of creative intelligence, the imaginative grasp of authentic possibilities, the vitality of motivation, and a deepened attunement to the sense of concrete human existence in its richness, diversity, and multiple types of interrelatedness with the multiple environments in which it is embedded. The resulting deep-seated harmonizing can bring about the change in moral consciousness needed for the implementation of an environmental ethic.

Managers cannot make morally responsible decisions with respect to the environment based on an instrumental view, that nature is there to be simply exploited for human purposes. Nor do they find much guidance in holding abstractly that nature has rights or that the ecosystem supersedes the needs of individual societies or humanly structured functions. We cannot save all trees, nor can we be concerned equally with saving all species. What is needed is a recognition that the corporation has its being through its relation to a wider environment and this environment extends to the natural world.

Responsible corporate decision making, as contextually located and evaluated in terms of consequences, must include environmental considerations when these are relevant. What specific course of action should be followed in specific instances must, of course, emerge from the concrete situation and the unique conflicting demands it involves. But, as in all moral decision making, the more deeply one is attuned to one's embeddedness in and interconnectedness with ever widening contexts, the more a potential exists for decision making that enriches human existence.

Questions for Discussion

1. What does the end of nature mean with respect to understanding and responding to environmental problems? Does this view help us to understand our responsibility for nature? Or can nature take care of itself without human concern? What does managing nature involve?
2. With what issues are moral extensionism and eligibility concerned? On what basis are rights extended to animals? Should rights also be extended to the plant community? What about rocks and other inanimate objects?
3. Do future generations have any rights with respect to the resources we are using and the pollution we are producing? What do philosophers think about this issue? What is a common-sense view with respect to this issue?
4. What is a biocentric ethic? How does this approach to environmental ethics differ from extending rights to nature? How does intrinsic value differ from instrumental value? What is the approach of deep ecology to environmental ethics?
5. What are the important components of a relational view between the organism and its environment? How does this view deal with the problem of intrinsic versus instrumental value? How do values come about and where do they reside?
6. What does it mean to say that nature cannot be dehumanized nor can humans be denaturalized? How can humans make value judgments that take nature into account? How can we make morally justifiable distinctions among different parts of nature? Can we make justifiable decisions to use parts of nature for our own purposes?

Endnotes

[1] David Kirkpatrick, "Environmentalism: The New Crusade," *Fortune,* February 12, 1990, pp. 44–55.

[2] Bill McKibben, *The End of Nature* (New York: Random House, 1989).

[3] Thomas Berry, *The Dream of the Earth* (San Francisco: Sierra Club Books, 1988), p. 7.

[4] R. and V. Routley, "Against the Inevitability of Human Chauvinism," *Ethics and Problems of the 21st Century,* K. E. Goodpaster and K. M. Sayre, eds. (Notre Dame, IN: University of Notre Dame Press, 1979), p. 57.

[5] Roderick Frazier Nash, *The Rights of Nature: A History of Environmental Ethics* (Madison, WI: University of Wisconsin Press, 1989), p. 125.

[6] Peter Singer, "The Place of Nonhumans in Environmental Issues," *Moral Issues in Business,* 4th ed., William Shaw and Vincent Barry, eds. (Belmont, CA: Wadsworth, 1989), p. 471.

[7] Ibid., p. 474.

[8] Nash, *The Rights of Nature,* pp. 140–141.

[9] Ibid., p. 126.

[10] Christopher D. Stone, "Should Trees Have Standing?—Toward Legal Rights for Natural Objects," *Moral Issues in Business,* 4th ed., William Shaw and Vincent Barry, eds. (Belmont, CA: Wadsworth, 1989), pp. 475–479.

[11] "The Environment," *Moral Issues in Business,* 4th ed., William Shaw and Vincent Barry, eds. (Belmont, CA: Wadsworth, 1989), pp. 452–453.

[12] Richard T. DeGeorge, "The Environment, Rights, and Future Generations," *Ethics and Problems of the 21st Century,* K. E. Goodpaster and K. M. Sayre, eds.(Notre Dame, IN: University of Notre Dame Press, 1979), pp. 93–105.

[13] K. E. Goodpaster, "From Egoism to Environmentalism," *Ethics and Problems of the 21st Century,* K. E. Goodpaster and K. M. Sayre, eds. (Notre Dame, IN: University of Notre Dame Press, 1979), pp. 21–33.

[14] Nash, *The Rights of Nature,* p. 152.

[15] Ibid., p. 153.

[16] Ibid., p. 160.

[17] Holmes Ralston, III, "Just Environmental Business," *Just Business: New Introductory Essays in Business Ethics,* Tom Regan, ed.(New York: Random House, 1984), pp. 325–343.

[18] Holmes Ralston, III, *Philosophy Gone Wild: Essays in Environmental Ethics* (Buffalo, NY: Prometheus Books, 1987), p. 121.

[19] Ibid., p. 141.

[20] Ibid., pp. 103–104.

[21] Nash, *The Rights of Nature,* p. 71.

[22] Sara Ebenreck, "An Earth Care Ethics," *The Catholic World: Caring for the Endangered Earth,* Vol. 233, no. 1396 (July/August 1990), p. 156.

[23] Ibid., p. 157.

[24] Thomas Berry, "Spirituality and Ecology," *The Catholic World: Caring for the Endangered Earth,* Vol. 233, no. 1396 (July/August 1990), p. 159.

[25] Ibid., p. 161.

[26] Nash, *The Rights of Nature,* p. 10.

[27] Ibid., p. 150.

[28] Ibid., p. 151.

[29] For various arguments in the debate on moral pluralism, see Christopher Stone, "Moral Pluralism and the Course of Environmental Ethics," *Environmental Ethics,* Vol. 10, Summer 1988, pp. 139–154; Don Marietta, Jr., "Pluralism in Environmental Ethics," *Topi,* Vol. 12, March 1993, pp. 69–80; Baird Callicott, "The Case Against Moral Pluralism," *Environmental Ethics,* Vol. 12, Summer 1990, pp. 99–124; Anthony Weston, "On Callicott's Case Against Moral Pluralism," *Environmental Ethics,* Vol. 13, Fall 1991, pp. 283–286. It should be noted here that pragmatism is not suggesting a metaphysical pluralism or a pluralism of "absolute" principles, but rather a metaphysics and epistemology that demand pluralism. This is not a relativism of any type but rather an ontologically grounded perspectivalism or contextualism.

[30] The claim by Anthony Weston that pragmatism is a form of subjectivism is misplaced. "Beyond Intrinsic Value: Pragmatism in Environmental Ethics," *Environmental Ethics,* Vol. 7, Winter 1985, p. 321.

[31] Bob Pepperman Taylor's objections to Dewey as an environmentalist stem from an ongoing illicit abstraction both of the social, cultural, and biological dimensions of the human in Dewey's philosophy from concrete human existence, and of aesthetic sensibility from the very fiber of human life. See "John Dewey and Environmental Thought: A Response to Chaloupka," *Environmental Ethics,* Vol. 12, Summer 1990.

[32] It should perhaps be pointed out here that this is quite different from theistic beliefs, which often foster environmental indifference.

[33] And thus, James holds that the broadest forms of moral commitment are held by those who appreciate the religious dimension of existence.

[34] "On a Certain Blindness in Human Beings," in *Talks to Teachers* (New York: W. W. Norton, 1958). In "American Pragmatism Reconsidered: William James' Ecological Ethic," *Environmental Ethics,* Vol. 14, Summer 1992, Robert Fuller argues for a possible panpsychism in James such that even inorganic matter has sentience and thus engages in valuing in at least some rudimentary fashion. We are disinclined to accept this interpretation of James or this kind of justification for concern with inorganic nature.

[35] See the debate between Anthony Weston, "Beyond Intrinsic Value," and Eric Katz, "Searching for Intrinsic Value: Pragmatism and Despair in Environmental Ethics," in *Environmental Pragmatism,* Andrew Light and Eric Katz, eds. (New York: Routledge, 1996), pp. 285–318.

[36] Thus, for example, old-growth forest is valuable in that it has the potential for yielding valuing experiences for individuals. But here problematic situations emerge, for the old-growth forest, as cut down for lumber, has the potential for yielding valuing experiences for humans as they desire more housing. The old-growth forest, as a forest, has the potential for providing valuing experiences for individuals as they experience the joys of the outdoors. Furthermore, in these and various other value dimensions of the old-growth forest, its potential for the production of valuing experiences extends not just to actual valuings, or even to the valuings of actual individuals, but to its potential for the production of valuing experiences into an indefinite future. These potentialities for future valuing are not something that can be excluded from the present problematic context, for these potentialities to be affected are not in the future; they are there within the present context to be affected by our present decisions.

Suggested Readings

Attfield, Robin. *The Ethics of Environmental Concern.* New York: Cambridge University Press, 1983.

Brennan, Andrew. *Thinking About Nature: An Investigation of Nature, Value, and Ecology.* Athens: University of Georgia Press, 1988.

Cahn, Robert. *Footprints on the Planet: A Search for an Environmental Ethic.* New York: Universe Books, 1978.

Callicott, J. Baird. *In Defense of the Land Ethic: Essays in Environmental Philosophy,* Albany, NY: SUNY Press, 1988.

Chamberlain, Neil W. *The Limits of Corporate Responsibility.* New York: Basic Books, 1973.

Clark, Stephen R. L. *The Moral Status of Animals.* New York: Oxford University Press, 1984.

Daly, Herman E., ed. *Economics, Ecology, and Ethics.* San Francisco: W. H. Freeman, 1980.

DeGeorge, Richard T. *Business Ethics,* 2nd ed. New York: Macmillan, 1986.

Devall, Bill, and George Sessions. *Deep Ecology: Living As If Nature Mattered.* Salt Lake City: Gibbs M. Smith, 1985.

Goodpaster, K. E., and K. M. Sayre, eds. *Ethics and Problems of the 21st Century.* Notre Dame, IN: University of Notre Dame Press, 1979.

Hardin, Garret. *Exploring New Ethics for Survival,* 2nd ed. New York: Viking Press, 1978.

Hargrove, Eugene C. *Foundations of Environmental Ethics.* Englewood Cliffs, NJ: Prentice-Hall, 1989.

Leopold, Aldo. *A Sand County Almanac.* New York: Oxford University Press, 1949.

McCloskey, H. J. *Ecological Ethics and Politics.* Totowa, NJ: Bowman & Littlefield, 1983.

Midgley, Mary. *Animals and Why They Matter.* Athens: University of Georgia Press, 1984.

Nash, Roderick Frazier. *The Rights of Nature: A History of Environmental Ethics.* Madison, WI: University of Wisconsin Press, 1989.

Partridge, Ernest, ed. *Responsibilities for Future Generations: Environmental Ethics.* Buffalo, NY: Prometheus Books, 1981.

Passmore, John. *Man's Responsibility for Nature: Ecological Problems and Western Traditions.* New York: Scribner, 1980.

Ralston, Holmes, III. *Environmental Ethics: Duties to and Values in the Natural World.* Philadelphia: Temple University Press, 1988.

Ralston, Holmes, III. *Philosophy Gone Wild: Essays in Environmental Ethics.* Buffalo, NY: Prometheus Books, 1987.

Regan, Tom. *The Case for Animal Rights.* Berkeley: University of California Press, 1983.

Regan, Tom, ed. *Just Business: New Introductory Essays in Business Ethics.* New York: Random House, 1984.

Selekman, Benjamin, and Sylvia. *Power and Morality in a Business Society.* New York: McGraw-Hill, 1956.

Shaw, William, and Vincent Barry, eds. *Moral Issues in Business,* 4th ed. Belmont, CA: Wadsworth, 1989.

Singer, Peter. *Animal Liberation.* New York: New York Review Books, 1975.

Solomon, Robert C., and Kristine R. Hanson. *Above the Bottom Line: An Introduction to Business Ethics.* New York: Harcourt Brace Jovanovich, 1983.

Taylor, Paul W. *Respect for Nature: A Theory of Environmental Ethics.* Lawrenceville, NJ: Princeton University Press, 1986.

Tobias, Michael, ed. *Deep Ecology.* San Diego, CA: Avant Books, 1985.

S H O R T   C A S E S

The Exxon *Valdez*

The Exxon supertanker *Valdez* entered the port of Valdez on March 22, 1989, riding high in the water because its huge cargo chambers were empty. Tugs guided it into the dock at Berth 5 at the Alyeska oil terminal. Alyeska was the name given to a consortium of oil companies that had been formed to operate the terminal. The tanker, only two years old and built in the San Diego shipyards, cost $125 million. It was one of the best-equipped vessels that hauled oil from the port of Valdez, having collision-avoidance radar, satellite navigational aids, and depth finders.[1]

The commander of the *Valdez* was Captain Joseph Hazelwood of Huntington, New York, a 20-year veteran of Exxon and commander of the supertanker for 20 months. Hazelwood was 42 years old and had one characteristic typical of many sailors, a drinking problem. In 1985, he had been convicted of drunken driving in Long Island, New York, and was again found guilty of driving while intoxicated in September 1988 in New Hampshire. In the span of five years, his automobile driver's license was revoked three times. He informed the company about his drinking problem in 1985, and Exxon immediately sent him to an alcohol rehabilitation program. The company claimed that it was not aware that his drinking problem persisted after he left the treatment program; however, at the time of the incident, Hazelwood apparently was still not permitted to drive a car, but retained his license to command a supertanker.[2]

On Thursday, March 23, the ship was eased out into the harbor by the port pilot, which is a customary practice in most shipping facilities. The pilot apparently noticed alcohol on Hazelwood's breath, but noticed no impairment of the captain's judgment or faculties. Thus, he turned over command of the ship to Hazelwood and descended over the side of the tanker to a waiting pilot boat. The tanker increased its speed to 12 knots and entered the more open water of Prince William Sound. It was the 8,549th tanker to safely negotiate the Valdez narrows since the first tanker left Valdez fully loaded in August 1977. No serious accidents had happened during that time.[3]

There were icebergs, however, in the outgoing lane, and the ship radioed the Coast Guard for permission to steer a course down the empty incoming lane to avoid the icebergs. This permission was granted and the *Valdez* altered course. At some point after the pilot left the ship, Hazelwood left the command post and went below to his cabin, in violation of company policy, which requires the captain to stay in command of the ship until it is in open water. Third Officer Gregory Cousins was left in charge of the ship, even though he lacked Coast Guard certification to pilot a tanker in Alaskan coastal waters. The ship was in trouble almost immediately, as it had set out on a course that would take it due south on a potential collision course with Busby Island, five miles away.[4]

The Coast Guard station on Potato Point had been tracking the ship, but had not noticed a potential problem, apparently because the ship disappeared from the screen for a while. Apparently the Coast Guard had replaced its radar unit two years ago with a less powerful unit that was unable to maintain contact with the ship and warn it of potential danger. During this time, the ship rode over submerged rocks off Busby Island, and minutes later plowed into Bligh Reef and began dumping its cargo. The reef had torn 11 holes in the ship's bottom, some as large as 6 by 20 feet. Eight cargo holds that were big enough to swallow 15-story buildings were ruptured. While a command had been given to change the course of the ship to avoid disaster, it came too late to have effect. At 12 knots, it takes about half a mile for any rudder change to alter the course of the 987-foot ship substantially.[5]

The Coast Guard station in Valdez was notified of a vessel run aground about 12:28 A.M. on Friday. About 1 A.M. a Coast Guard pilot boat headed for the accident site following a tugboat that had already been dispatched. At 3:23 A.M. they arrived on the site and saw that the ship was losing oil at a rate that was later reported to be 1.5 million gallons an hour. At 5:40 A.M. it was reported that the *Valdez* had lost 210,000 barrels of oil or more than 8.8 million gallons. There are 42 gallons in a barrel of oil, which is the standard industry measure. Spotters aboard an Alyeska plane reported at 7:27 A.M. that the oil slick was 1,000 feet wide and five miles long and was spreading. Earlier a passing boat had reported encountering an oil slick about half a mile south of Bligh Reef. Later it was estimated that the *Valdez* had released about 240,000 barrels of oil equivalent to 10.1 million gallons into the sound.[6]

After Hazelwood's blood was tested fully nine hours after the ship ran aground, he still had a blood-alcohol level of .06, which is higher than the .04 the Coast Guard considers acceptable for captains. It was estimated that his blood-alcohol level at the time of the accident was about .19, assuming that he had not had anything more to drink after the accident and that his body metabolized at the normal rate. This level of .19 is almost double the amount at which most states consider a motorist to be legally drunk. After it learned of these test results, Exxon fired Hazelwood and the state filed criminal charges against him for operating a ship while under the influence of alcohol, reckless endangerment, and criminally negligent discharge of oil. The maximum penalty for the combined charges was 27 months in jail and a $10,000 fine. The state also issued a warrant for his arrest.[7]

After one day, the slick was eight miles long and four miles wide, and was clearly the worst spill in U.S. history. By the end of the week the slick covered almost 900 square miles to the southwest of Valdez, threatening the marine and bird life in the sound and spreading to the Chugach National Forest. On Thursday afternoon, the slick began taking its greatest toll of wildlife when oil began washing up on the beaches on Knight and Green islands. Scientists found many blackened animals huddled or dead on the beaches. Scores of cormorants and other birds were barely distinguishable from the oil-covered sand and gravel.[8]

The oil slick continued to spread, covering more than 1,000 square miles and hitting hundreds of miles of inaccessible beaches and drifting into the Gulf of Alaska where it threatened the port of Seward and the delicate shoreline of Kenai Fjords National Park. The area covered by the spill was said to be larger than the state of Rhode Island. Eventually the slick spread 100 miles out into the Gulf of Alaska, forcing federal officials to open a second front in their battle to contain its advancement. Scientists estimated that about half the oil lost by the *Valdez* had left Prince William Sound and had entered the gulf creeping south at about 15 to 20 miles a day.[9]

One of the first effects of the accident was to postpone indefinitely the fishing season for shrimp and sablefish, to which fishermen reacted bitterly. There was also some question as to whether the season for herring roe would also have to be canceled because of the spill. Herring roe, which are really eggs, are considered to be a delicacy in Japan and bring high prices that give fishermen an economic boost to carry them through to the summer salmon season.[10] The herring lay their eggs on floating kelp beds that fishermen feared would be smothered by the oil slick. Millions of salmon fingerlings from the hatcheries were scheduled to be released into the sound's inlets to begin a two-year migration cycle. These fingerlings feed on plankton that may be poisoned by the oil, thus beginning a contamination that would continue up the food chain. Clams and mussels were expected to survive, but hydrocarbons will probably accumulate in their body tissues, which would endanger any species that feeds on them.[11]

Before long, waterfowl by the tens of thousands would finish their northward migrations and settle in summer nesting colonies in the sound. More than 200 different species of birds were reported to be in the sound, and some 111 of them are water related. The Copper River delta, which is at the east end of the sound, is home to an estimated 20 million migratory birds, including one-fifth of the world's trumpeter swans. It was later estimated that thousands of sea birds such as cormorants and loons died either because oil destroyed their buoyancy or because they were simply poisoned.[12]

Emergency teams that were sent out to clean up the oil found ducks coated with crude and sea lions with their flippers drenched with oil clinging to a buoy that was located near the damaged tanker. Environmentalists feared that a significant part of the sound's sea otter population of 12,000 would be totally wiped out by the spill. Sea otters die of hypothermia when their fur becomes coated with oil. They may also sink under the surface of the water and drown. Thus, many different kinds of animals were placed under threat by the spreading oil slick.[13]

The long-term effect of the spill could be to change the balance of power between the oil industry and the environmentalists. The latter lost no time in getting their message across regarding oil and gas exploration on the North Slope. While they were unable to prevent development of the North Slope fields, the *Valdez* disaster gave them new ammunition in the fight against opening up the Arctic National Wildlife Refuge (ANWR) that lies between Prudhoe Bay and the Canadian border. As the name implies, the area teems with wildlife of all kinds, and the environmentalists want to keep the oil industry out of this preserve.[14]

Industry has lost the trust of the Alaskan people as they felt betrayed by believing the claims of the oil companies that they could protect the environment. People will be less likely to believe that the oil industry can develop the Arctic in a responsible manner. State lawmakers want assurances that current operations will not further harm the environment but are less likely to trust the oil companies to do this on their own without state regulation.[15] Federal officials began talking about stricter enforcement of existing laws as well as new requirements that tankers be equipped with double hulls for added protection. Other suggestions had to do with tougher personnel rules that would ban drunken drivers from commanding tankers, and proposals for updating the training standards for crews of tankers. Perhaps one of the most controversial proposals had to do with testing employees for drug and alcohol abuse.[16]

1. Why was Alyeska not better prepared to deal with an oil spill of this nature? What happened over the years to create an attitude of complacency? How can companies guard against this attitude and keep themselves alert to potential accidents?

2. Did Exxon accept responsibility for the spill? In what ways? Was the bad coverage it received from the media deserved? How could it have responded differently? How much should the spill be blamed on Hazelwood alone?

3. Is it possible for there to be a balanced approach to industrial development and preservation of the environment? Can industry and the environment live with each other in harmony? How can such a balance be achieved?

4. Who are the stakeholders in this incident? What rights do they have? What did Exxon owe each of them? How shall the rights of these stakeholders be balanced against each other? Do the animals whose lives were threatened have any rights?

[1] "Disaster at Valdez: Promises Unkept," *Los Angeles Times,* April 2, 1989, p. I-20.

[2] "The Big Spill," *Time,* April 10, 1989, p. 39.

[3] "Disaster at Valdez," p. I-20.

[4] Ibid.

[5] Ibid., p. I-22.

[6] Ibid., p. I-21.

[7] "The Big Spill," p. 40.

[8] Mark Stein, "FBI Starts Probe of Valdez Spill as Toll Mounts," *Los Angeles Times,* April 1, 1989, p. I-1.

[9] Larry B. Stammer and Mark A. Stein, "New Front Opened in Oil Spill Battle," *Los Angeles Times,* April 8, 1989, p. I-23.

[10] Mark A. Stein, "Arrest of Missing Tanker Captain Sought by Alaska," *Los Angeles Times,* April 2, 1989, p. I-1.

[11] Ken Wells and Marilyn Chase, "Paradise Lost: Heartbreaking Scenes of Beauty Disfigured Follow Alaska Oil Spill," *The Wall Street Journal,* March 31, 1989, p. A-1.

[12] Ibid.

[13] "Smothering the Waters," *Newsweek,* April 10, 1989, p. 57.

[14] "Tug of War Over Oil Drilling," *U.S. News & World Report,* April 10, 1989, p. 48.

[15] Michael D. Lemonick, "The Two Alaskas," *Time,* April 17, 1989, p. 63.

[16] Ibid., p. 66.

Source: Rogene A. Buchholz, *Public Policy Issues for Management,* 2nd ed. (Englewood Cliffs, NJ: Prentice Hall, 1992), pp. 292–294.

Oakdale: A Success Story

During the 1940s and 1950s, several companies, one of which was 3M, disposed of their wastes using the accepted practice of the day of hiring a contractor to dispose of waste material generated by their manufacturing plants. The contractor in this case disposed of the material in a 60-acre disposal site in an undeveloped, lowland area about 10 miles from St. Paul, Minnesota. The site consisted of an area for burning material, a drum recycling operation, and several waste disposal areas for both organic and inorganic residues.

As the amount and volume of waste increased and open burning was outlawed, the contractor dug trenches to dispose of the waste, and used other low areas in the site to try and keep up with the waste disposal activity. However, by 1960, most of the available disposal areas on the site were filled and the contractor ceased operations at this location. After the site was closed, it became covered with foliage and the property changed hands, which helped to obscure past usage. The state pollution-control agency, however, learned about this site from some of the area residents in 1978, and conducted a preliminary investigation. The agency subsequently notified the potentially responsible parties in early 1980, including present and past landowners, transporters, and waste generators.

Later in that year, the potentially responsible parties, including 3M, were called to a meeting at the state pollution-control agency to discuss a course of action. When no specific proposals were forthcoming, 3M pointed out the need for an immediate investigation of the site to determine the scope of the problem. The company offered to fund the investigation, and with the approval of the state pollution-control agency, hired Barr Engineering, a Minneapolis-based independent consulting firm, to conduct the investigation.

The results of the investigation showed that there were three separate disposal areas. These three sites were named the Abresch, Brockman, and Eberle sites after the owners of the sites at the time of disposal activity. Based on the data collected during these investigations, Barr Engineering recommended a remedial action plan that consisted of four major programs. The major objective of the remedial action plan was to remove the major sources of contaminants and prevent any future movement of contaminants into the deeper aquifers.

In July 1983, a detailed remedial action plan consisting of the four recommended programs of Barr Engineering was approved by 3M, the state pollution-control agency, and the EPA. The key ingredient in the development and acceptance of the remedial action plan was the inclusion of provisions in the agreement that allowed the government agencies involved some degree of flexibility in modifying portions of the program as work progressed and more knowledge of the site and waste encountered was acquired. The basic philosophy of 3M in the agreement was to cooperate with the regulatory agencies and local government units and resolve issues on the basis of actual data and the operating history of the system. The company tried to keep politics to a minimum.

The entire cleanup effort was completed in 1985, which meant that only five years elapsed from the first notification to completion of the effort. It is useful to reflect on this experience with the Oakdale project to determine if there are any lessons to be learned and generalizations that can be developed that might apply to other situations. The success of this cleanup effort certainly indicates that under certain conditions, a waste dump can be cleaned up effectively and rather quickly compared with other cleanup efforts.

1. What was the accepted practice in the 1940s and 1950s regarding disposal of hazardous waste material? What problems has this practice caused? Is there any way these problems could have been avoided given the state of our knowledge at the time? Was it possible at that time to take more precautions?

2. What were the key management factors that made this cleanup a success story? Can the lessons learned from this situation be transferred to other waste sites? Are there some unique factors about Oakdale that make any generalizations suspect?

Source: Rogene A. Buchholz, et al., *Managing Environmental Issues: A Casebook* (Englewood Cliffs, NJ: Prentice Hall, 1992), pp. 170–175.

Noise Pollution

The Wells Metals Corporation had planned to build a new foundry in a relatively rural area in Michigan. However, through tax breaks and other incentives, it was persuaded by the civic leadership of a large city in Ohio to locate its plant within three blocks of a residential district. Although the installation was quite attractive from the outside and incorporated the latest technology for controlling air pollution, the round-the-clock operation of the plant emitted sufficient noise, particularly at night, to disturb a number of residents. Some people had already begun to move out and it looked as if property values would plunge. It came to the attention of the company that a group of residents was organizing to bring a suit against the firm to have the noise completely abated, or the plant shut down. This neighborhood coalition was exploring eliciting the help of the Environmental Protection Agency and initiating a class-action suit of its own.

1. Comment on the quality of managerial decision making as exemplified in this situation. Include the decisions made by both private- and public-sector managers.

2. What action should Wells take regarding these developments? Are there specific things it can do to the plant to reduce the amount of noise? What should it do with regard to the neighborhood coalition?

Source: Rogene A. Buchholz, *Business Environment and Public Policy: Implications for Management,* 5th ed. (Englewood Cliffs, NJ: Prentice Hall, 1995), pp. 460–461.

Animal Rights

The management of Bigger & Better Feedlot Company is being pressured on all sides to change its methods of operation and/or get out of business entirely. Animal rights groups have been picketing the company because of the way it crowds animals together in its feedlots, in some cases not providing enough room for cattle to lie down if they desire. Bigger & Better is no different from other feedlot companies in this regard, and tries to utilize space efficiently. Animal rights activists, whose ultimate goal is to get people to stop eating meat entirely, have been receiving a good deal of favorable press coverage making the company look bad in the local newspapers.

At the same time, Bigger & Better has also drawn the fire of environmental groups who complain about the methane gas emitted by the feedlot, which is one of the trace gases believed to contribute to global warming. These developments have begun to affect the company, as it has seen its sales drop over the past several months because people are being persuaded to eat less meat to respect the rights of animals and protect the environment. The management of the company has to develop a strategy to deal with these issues, and has called a meeting of its top executives to deal with the situation.

1. What should the company do in response to these pressures? Should it mount an advertising campaign to promote the eating of meat? Should it use advertising to try and promote its image as a company concerned about animal rights and the environment? Would such an approach be believable?

2. With respect to the long-term prospects of the company and the industry, what should management be thinking about? Are major changes in store for the industry? Should Bigger & Better take the lead in developing more humane and environmentally safe ways to raise cattle and other animals? Or should it wait until it is forced to make changes by the pressure of public opinion or government regulation?

Source: Rogene A. Buchholz, *Business Environment and Public Policy: Implications for Management,* 5th ed. (Englewood Cliffs, NJ: Prentice Hall, 1995), p. 461.

Business in Its Cultural Environment

The natural environment in which business functions also has broad impacts on the cultural environment and the values and activities that comprise that environment. One of the most profound conceptual changes that the natural environment poses for business in its cultural context relates to the meaning and purpose of corporate activity. This change is the most recent of several conceptual shifts that have occurred over the years in the moral milieu of business activities.

While there has been a concern about pollution of the environment for several years, talk about limits to growth, or more recently, sustainable growth has also raised concerns about resource limitations and limits relative to the ability of the planet to provide everyone with an improved material standard of living. Such concerns lead to charges that the industrialized Western world is living beyond its means and taking more than its share of resources to produce a lifestyle that is not sustainable. The Western world is said to overconsume the world's resources and should share its wealth with emerging nations.

These concerns have profound implications for corporate activity that is based on the promotion of consumption and an ever increasing material standard of living. The corporation is the primary instrument of economic growth in industrialized societies, and one of its primary reasons for existing is producing goods and services to enhance people's material well-being. If this activity is to be curbed in the interests of conserving resources and reducing pollution, what will become of the corporation and the continued growth on which its legitimacy is predicated? Thus, the challenge of the natural environment is an important one and whether or not overconsumption is a reality and changing patterns of consumption are called for are questions that need examination.

The Protestant Ethic

The best place to begin such a discussion is to examine the moral system that informed the development of market systems and provided a legitimacy for their existence. The primary ethical emphasis behind the development of market systems has been called the Protestant ethic because this ethic had religious origins in the newly emerging industrial societies that developed after the Reformation period. The Protestant ethic helped to legitimize the capitalist system by providing a moral justification for the pursuit of wealth and the distribution of income that were a result of economic activity within this system. The Protestant ethic not only had behavioral implications regarding the economic conduct of people who were a part of the system, it also had moral implications in that belief in the Protestant ethic provided a moral legitimacy for the system and infused its adherents with moral purpose.

The Protestant ethic had religious origins, coming from the Protestants of Calvinistic or Calvinistically allied churches in post-Reformation Europe. For our knowledge of the Protestant ethic, we are indebted to Max Weber, who first discussed the concept comprehensively.[1] Weber sought to establish a relationship between these Calvinistic beliefs and a capitalistic mentality of which the bourgeoisie from Calvinistic churches was the leading exponent. These religious beliefs, which Weber called the Protestant ethic, produced a certain type of personality with a high motivation to achieve success in worldly terms by accumulating wealth and working diligently to overcome every obstacle.

The self-discipline and moral sense of duty and calling, which were at the heart of this ethic, were vital to the kind of rational economic behavior that capitalism demanded (calculation, punctuality, productivity). The Protestant ethic thus contributed to the spirit of capitalism—what might now be called cultural values and attitudes—a spirit that was supportive of individual human enterprise and the accumulation of wealth necessary for the development of capitalism. Within this climate, people were motivated to behave in a manner that proved conducive to rapid economic growth of the capitalistic variety and shared values that were consistent with this kind of development.[2]

Weber sought to provide an explanatory model, based upon religious elements, for the growth of capitalistic activity in the sixteenth and seventeenth centuries. In doing this, he was not claiming that religion was the most important factor in the rise of capitalism. Other secular elements could and had to be explained by appeal to other factors. Weber was simply isolating those elements in the development of capitalism that he felt could not be explained by other factors but only by an appeal to religious beliefs and attitudes.[3]

Weber's thesis was based upon certain sociological phenomena that he observed in post-Reformation Europe, especially in England and the Low Countries, which became the center of capitalistic development. He observed that the trading classes of the bourgeoisie were found chiefly in the ranks of Protestantism. He argued that the proportion of leading industrialists, traders, financiers, and technical experts was greater among Protestants than Catholics. Business leaders and owners of capital as well as the higher grades of skilled labor and the technically and commercially trained personnel of modern enterprise were overwhelmingly Protestant. These classes in the sixteenth and seventeenth centuries, said Weber, were mainly found not merely among the Protestants in general, but among the Protestants of Calvinistic or Calvinistically allied churches—the Huguenots of France, the Dutch traders, and the Puritans of England.[4]

The Weber thesis was an attempt to explain these differences through looking into the intrinsic character of these Calvinistic beliefs and establishing a relationship between these beliefs and the capitalistic mentality of which the Calvinistic bourgeoisie was the leading exponent. The religious element was of primary importance in his explanation and provided a basis for examination of the values that influenced the behavior of those people who understood the potentials of a newly emerging economic order and were able to benefit from this new order.

> it is a fact that the Protestants (especially certain branches of the movement to be fully discussed later) both as ruling classes and as ruled, both as majority and as minority, have shown a special tendency to develop economic rationalism which cannot be observed to the same extent among Catholics either in one situation or the other. Thus the principal explanation of this difference must be sought in the permanent intrinsic character of their religious beliefs, and not only in their temporary external historical-political situations.[5]

Thus, what Weber has done in this thesis is to develop an idealization of the kind of ethical imperatives that are a part of the Calvinistic belief system and show how they are logically related to rational economic behavior, which is conducive to the development of capitalism. Weber assumes a multiple-factor model of causality that includes ideals and values of religious belief systems as well as material conditions. His investigations showed how the religious ideals and values of Calvinism entered in a very real way into the development of capitalism and markets and offered an alternative to the Marxist view of historical causality, which placed an emphasis on material conditions alone through its materialistic interpretation of history.[6] Weber did not deny the importance of material conditions, but showed how religious ideals and values play their part in shaping history.

THE ROLE OF THE PROTESTANT ETHIC

While the Protestant ethic did indeed have a religious source, it was also developed in a specific historical context and played a very important function in the development of modern industrial societies. Moral support and guidelines for human and organizational behavior in an emerging industrial society were provided by Calvinistic Protestantism in the form of the Protestant ethic. This ethic contained two major elements: (1) an insistence on the importance of a person's calling, which meant that one's primary responsibility was to do his or her best at whatever station God had assigned the person in life, rather than to withdraw from the world and devote oneself entirely to God, as the Catholic Church had taught as a counsel of perfection, and (2) the rationalization of all of life as introduced by Calvin's notion of predestination, whereby work became a means of dispersing religious doubt by demonstrating to oneself and others that one was one of the elect.[7]

Thus, one was to work hard, be productive, and accumulate wealth. But that wealth was not to be pursued for its own sake or enjoyed in lavish consumption because the world existed to serve the glorification of God and for that purpose alone. The more possessions one had, the greater was the obligation to be an obedient steward and hold these possessions undiminished for the glory of God by increasing them through relentless effort. A worldly asceticism was at the heart of this ethic, which gave a religious sanction to acquisition and rational use of wealth to create more wealth.

> The upshot of it all was that for the first time in history the two capital-producing prescriptions, maximization of production and minimization of consumption, became com-

ponents of the same ethical matrix. As different from medieval or communist culture these norms were not reserved for or restricted to specific individuals or groups. Everyone hypothetically belonged to that universe from which the deity had drawn the salvation sample, without disclosing its size or composition. The sampling universe had no known restriction of biological or social background, aptitude, or occupational specialization. Nobody could opt out from the sampling process, indeed, everyone had to act as if indeed he had been selected. For the mortal sin was to mock the deity by contradicting through his behavior God's primeval sampling decision. Everybody not only could, but had to presume potential sainthood and correspondingly optimize his performance both as producer and consumer. The more his performance excelled relative to his reference group's, the higher the probability that indeed he had been selected. The new ethic then pressured equally towards effective production and efficient consumption which, while sustaining maximum productivity, also maximized savings and potential investment capital.[8]

Within this theology, work was understood to be something good in itself, not a curse as the early Hebrews believed and not something fit only for slaves as the Greeks thought. Work was considered to be a divine calling ordained by God, and each person's duty was to accept his or her involvement in worldly affairs as his or her calling. Relative to this calling, people were to devote themselves to a particular vocation by which their usefulness to their neighbors was distinguished. Hard work was exalted as a virtue, laziness or leisure was a sin to be avoided. Thus, work itself, which in the period before the Reformation was by and large considered to be a morally neutral activity, was given a clear moral sanction.

Furthermore, the pursuit of material wealth was also given a moral basis in that wealth, which was believed to be the fruits of hard work, was a sign of election—as sure a way as was available to disposing of the fear of damnation. Thus, one was not to rest on his or her laurels or enjoy the fruits of his or her own labor. Whatever wealth was earned must be reinvested to accumulate more wealth in order to please God and as a further manifestation of one's own election. This represented a new approach to acquisitiveness and the pursuit of profit over earlier periods. What had been formally regarded at best as something of a personal inclination and choice had now also become something of a moral duty.

The Protestant ethic thus proved to be consistent with the need for the accumulation of capital that is necessary during the early stages of industrial development. Money was saved and reinvested to build up a capital base. Consumption was curtailed in the interests of creating capital wealth. People dedicated themselves to hard work at disagreeable tasks and justified the rationalization of life that capitalism required. All of this was long before the development of formal economic theory and industrial institutions on a large scale, and required a major change from the way people behaved in medieval agrarian society.

> Until recently, the Protestant work ethic stood as one of the most important underpinnings of American culture. According to the myth of capitalist enterprise, thrift and industry held the key to material success and spiritual fulfillment. America's reputation as a land of opportunity rested on its claim that the destruction of hereditary obstacles to advancement had created conditions in which social mobility depended on individual initiative alone. The self-made man, archetypal embodiment of the American dream, owed his advancement to habits of industry, sobriety, moderation, self-discipline, and avoidance of debt. He lived for the future, shunning self-indulgence in favor of patient,

painstaking accumulation; and as long as the collective prospect looked on the whole so bright, he found in the deferral of gratification not only his principal gratification, but an abundant source of profits. In an expanding economy, the value of investments could be expected to multiply with time, as the spokesman for self-help, for all their celebration of work as its own reward, seldom neglected to point out.[9]

Thus, the Protestant ethic was an ingenious social and moral invention that emphasized both the human and capital sources of productivity and growth and in this sense was the first supply side theory. It emphasized the human side of production through hard work and the aspect of the calling. But it also advocated that people should not only work hard, but that the money they earn in the process, particularly the owners of capital, should also put their money to work and not spend it on lavish consumption. Inequality was thus morally justified if the money earned on capital was reinvested in further capital accumulation, which would benefit society as a whole by increasing production and creating more economic wealth.

The Protestant ethic served to pattern behavior and, for its adherents, make sense of what was happening to European culture. The definitions and understandings of work it provided were meaningful and relevant, especially to the rising middle-income business classes. As industrial civilization emerged and cultures were reorganized to adjust to this reality, as corporate institutions developed to provide guidelines for behavior, and as economic doctrines developed to explain people's actions in a capitalist society, the Protestant ethic became routinized and continued to serve as a means of supporting the status quo and legitimizing industrial civilization and capitalism. It provided a moral foundation for productive activity and legitimized the pursuit of profit and accumulation of wealth on the part of those who worked hard and invested their money wisely.

THE WORK ETHIC IN CONTEMPORARY SOCIETY

This notion of the Protestant ethic later became secularized in American society and was stripped of its religious trappings, but the basic assumptions about work and its importance remained pretty much the same. Secularization refers to the process of deemphasizing the religious elements of any particular entity and increasingly referring to worldly or temporal elements as distinguished from the spiritual or eternal realm. Thus, a secular view of life or of any particular matter is based on the premise that religion or religious considerations should be ignored or purposely excluded. The Protestant ethic thus became known as the work ethic and is now almost exclusively discussed in secular terms with very little reference made to its religious origins except in certain scholarly and religious circles.

One topic of interest and concern that appeared frequently in both popular and professional literature during the 1970s was the weakening or disappearance of the Protestant ethic or work ethic from the American scene. There was a good deal of evidence to suggest that the traditional values regarding work and the acquisition of wealth as expressed by the Protestant ethic were changing in some fashion. Many articles indicated that young adults, in particular, had little interest in the grinding routine of the assembly line or in automated clerical tasks. They were turning away, it was suggested, from their parents' dedication to work for the sake of success and were more concerned about finding meaningful work—something that was satisfying and personally rewarding in terms other than money. Young people were seeking to change existing industrial arrangements to allow these intangible goals to be pursued.[10]

This change in values was already noted as early as 1957 by Clyde Kluckhohn, who did an extensive survey of the then available professional literature to determine if there had been any discernible shifts in American values during the past generation. As a result of this survey, he discovered that one value change that could be supported by empirical data was a decline of the Protestant work ethic as the core of the dominant middle-class value system.[11] Kluckhohn cited numerous studies to support this conclusion and made the following statement:

> The most generally agreed upon, the best documented, and the most pervasive value shift is what Whyte has called "the decline of the Protestant Ethic." This is a central theme in Whyte's book. It is a clear-cut finding of the Schneider-Dornbusch study of inspirational religious literature. It is noted by essentially all the serious publications on recent value changes and on the values of the younger generation.[12]

Related to this fundamental shift are a number of others mentioned by Kluckhohn that have the Protestant ethic as their central point of reference. These shifts are interconnected and mutually reinforcing and are a result of the weakening of the Protestant ethic, but may also, in turn, contribute to this weakening. There has been a rise in value upon "being" or "being and becoming" as opposed to "doing," according to many studies cited by Kluckhohn. Another such shift is the trend toward "present time" in contrast to "future time" value orientation supported by other studies.[13]

Finally, there is a trend toward an increase of aesthetic and recreational values as good in themselves, a development of "values which the Puritan Ethic never placed upon recreation (except as a means to the end of more effective work), pleasure, leisure, and aesthetic and expressive activities. Americans enjoy themselves more and with less guilt than ever before. Moreover, there has been a remarkable diversification and broadening of the base of leisure-time activities within the population."[14]

The next comprehensive discussion of the weakening of the Protestant ethic in contemporary American society was written in 1976 by Daniel Bell, who argued that the Protestant ethic has been replaced by hedonism in contemporary society—the idea of pleasure as a way of life. During the 1950s, according to Bell, American culture had become primarily hedonistic, concerned with fun, play, display, and pleasure. The culture was no longer concerned with how to work and achieve, but with how to spend and enjoy.[15]

> In the early development of capitalism, the unrestrained economic impulse was held in check by Puritan restraint and the Protestant Ethic. One worked because of one's obligation to one's calling, or to fulfill the covenant of the community. But the Protestant Ethic was undermined not by modernism but by capitalism itself. The greatest single engine in the destruction of the Protestant Ethic was the invention of the installment plan, or instant credit. Previously one had to save in order to buy. But with credit cards one could indulge in instant gratification. The system was transformed by mass production and mass consumption, by the creation of new wants and new means of gratifying those wants.[16]

Thus, the cultural, if not moral, justification of capitalism had become hedonism. This cultural transformation was brought about by (1) demographic change that resulted in the growth of urban centers and a shift in political weight, (2) the emergence of a consumption society with its emphasis on spending and material possessions rather than thrift and frugality, and (3) a technological revolution which, through the automobile, motion picture, and radio, broke down rural isolation and fused the country into a common culture and a national society.[17]

Bell argued that this abandonment of the Protestant ethic left capitalism with no moral or transcendental ethic, and produced an extraordinary contradiction within the social structure of American society. The business corporation requires people who work hard, are dedicated to a career, and accept delayed gratification, all traditional Protestant ethic virtues. Yet in its products and advertisements, the corporation promotes pleasure, instant joy, relaxing, and letting go, all hedonistic virtues. In Bell's words, "one is to be straight by day and a swinger by night."[18] Capitalism thus continued to demand a Protestant ethic in the area of production but needed to stimulate a demand for pleasure and play in the area of consumption.[19]

Perhaps the crowning blow to the work ethic has been provided by Daniel Yankelovich in a more recent publication.[20] Yankelovich states that traditionally, Americans have been a thrifty and productive people adhering to the major tenants of the Protestant ethic, and in the process helping to create an abundant and expanding economy. But in the past two decades, Americans have loosened their attachment to this ethic of self-denial and deferred gratification and are committed in one way or another to the search for self-fulfillment. Yankelovich presents evidence from polls and life histories to describe this search and support his assertion that about 80 percent of contemporary adults are involved in this search to varying degrees.[21] The old ethic of self-denial that is giving way to a search for self-fulfillment is described by Yankelovich in terms of the giving-getting compact.

> The old giving/getting compact might be paraphrased this way: I give hard work, loyalty and steadfastness. I swallow my frustrations and suppress my impulse to do what I would enjoy, and do what is expected of me instead. I do not put myself first; I put the needs of others ahead of my own. I give a lot, but what I get in return is worth it. I receive an ever-growing standard of living, and a family life with a devoted spouse and decent kids. Our children will take care of us in our old age if we really need it, which thank goodness we will not. I have a nice home, a good job, the respect of my friends and neighbors; a sense of accomplishment at having made something of my life. Last but not least, as an American I am proud to be a citizen of the finest country in the world.[22]

This compact provided support for the goals of America in the post-World War II period. Most Americans pursued material well-being, and self-denial and sacrifice to attain a rising standard of living made good sense. But doubts about these rules have set in as more and more people question whether or not these rules are worth the bother.[23]

The search for self-fulfillment does not reject materialistic values, but it broadens them to embrace a wider spectrum of human experience. This search accepts social pluralism as the norm and includes a new freedom to choose one's lifestyle. The search for self-fulfillment involves a search for intangibles such as creativity, autonomy, pleasure, participation, community, adventure, vitality, and stimulation. It involves satisfaction of both the body and the spirit—the addition of the joy of living to the efficiency of a technological society.[24]

Finally, Christopher Lasch argues that a new ethic of self-preservation has taken hold in American society. The work ethic has been gradually transformed into an ethic of personal survival. The Puritans believed that a godly man worked diligently at his calling not so much in order to accumulate personal wealth as to add to the wealth of the community.[25] But the pursuit of self-interest, which was formerly identified with the rational pursuit of gain and the accumulation of wealth, has become a search for pleasure and psychic survival. The cult of consumption with its emphasis on immediate gratification has created the narcissistic man of modern society.[26] Such a culture lives for the present and does not save for the future because it believes there may not be a future to worry about.

Behavioral Changes in American Society

The weakening of the traditional work ethic with its inherent restriction on consumption is consistent with a behavioral change in American society. Prior to World War II, people by and large were savings oriented and lived by the ethic of deferred gratification. They would not buy houses with large mortgages and run up huge credit card balances, but would save their money until they could buy things outright. Gratification of their desires was deferred until they could afford to satisfy them, and then, and only then, was it proper to buy things to enjoy. In other words, people lived within their immediate means and did not borrow for purposes of increased consumption.

During the 1950s, however, this ethic changed into one of instant gratification, as a consumption society was created where people were encouraged to satisfy their desires now rather than wait until they had the money in hand. Buying on credit was encouraged and long-term mortgages became the order of the day with regard to housing. Why defer gratification when one could buy and enjoy things immediately and pay for them in the future? Companies helped to create this kind of society by making credit easy to obtain through the use of credit cards and by using more sophisticated forms of advertising to increase consumption of their products. In fact, there were even some theories that advocated that companies not only controlled the supply of products but controlled the demand function as well through manipulation of consumer desires.[27]

These were the days when the throwaway society was created and obsolence was built into products so that people could buy newer products faster. Packaging was improved so that products looked more attractive and could be purchased more easily. This meant that the amount of stuff to be disposed of increased dramatically as products that had outlived their usefulness had to be discarded along with all the packaging materials that were used to encase new products. The United States became a society where consumption was emphasized and money was made available so people could buy on credit and pay their debts some time in the future.

This change in ethic was also a change in the culture. Television fed this change with sitcoms that portrayed the typical American family as one that lived in a nice house in the suburbs with two cars and all the latest kitchen appliances and electronic gear in the rest of the house. Advertising on television also became more sophisticated to stimulate demand for products. Companies fed the consumption binge with a proliferation of products that appealed to every taste that could be imagined. Perhaps the development of the atomic bomb had an impact on generations growing up after World War II because the future has never been as certain since that time, and we all have had to live with the knowledge that humans have the ability to destroy the planet. Thus, one might as well live as well as one possibly can now rather than defer gratification for some future time that may not be there.

There were thus many factors behind the change in behavior of the American people, but there is no doubt that we became a nation where instant gratification became a cultural trait in contrast to earlier times when saving was emphasized. The implications of this change were profound for lifestyles and habits of people, as society became more wealthy and prosperous. Many people lived more interesting lives and had more diversity available to them as never before. They traveled more miles, wore more and different clothes, drove more expensive and sophisticated cars, and in general, enjoyed rising standards of living that involved consumption of the latest products.

Environmental Impacts of Instant Gratification

There were adverse implications to this change as well, particularly as far as resource usage and environmental impacts were concerned. In the 1960s, concern about the natural environment began to emerge, and a great deal of legislation related to the environment was passed. Most of this legislation focused on pollution control, as before the advent of this legislation, air, water, and land were treated as free goods available to anyone for dumping wastes. This caused no problem when the population was sparse, factories small, and products few in number compared to today. The natural environment's dilutive capacity was rarely exceeded and was perceived as infinite in its ability to absorb waste. Changes in society, however, began to cause serious pollution problems.

Current environmental concerns, while still dealing with pollution control, also emphasize resource limitations, as serious questions are being raised about the wisdom of a continued emphasis on economic growth. During the close of the 1970s, there was intense debate about the limits to economic growth in the world in general and in the advanced industrial nations in particular.[28]

These efforts came to naught, however, during the 1980s when talk about limits to growth came to an end except perhaps in some isolated corners of academia. Instead the emphasis was on opportunity and the unlimited potential of technology and the human spirit. The limits to growth movement was something of an elitist concern, and did a great deal of harm to the environmental movement of earlier years in getting it labeled as anti-growth and obstructionist to those on the lower rungs of the economic ladder.

There was a need for a new concept to capture many of the concerns about resource usage raised in the limits of growth movement, and these concerns were eventually encapsulated in the idea of sustainable growth, which became a much discussed concept during the latter part of the decade. Sustainable growth has a much better chance of being accepted and implemented in public and corporate policy. This concept is concerned with finding paths of social, economic, and political progress that meet the needs of the present without compromising the ability of future generations to meet their own needs. This concept reflects a change of values in regard to managing our resources in such a way that equity matters, equity among peoples around the world and equity between parents and their children and grandchildren.[29] It thus has an appeal to people at all levels of development, and in particular has appeal to people and nations at early stages of economic development. They obviously don't want to see resources depleted before they have had their share, and must be concerned about growth that is sustainable for many years to come.

Efforts to manage the sustainable development of the earth must have three specific objectives according to one author: (1) to disseminate the knowledge and the means necessary to control human population growth, (2) to facilitate sufficiently vigorous economic growth and equitable distribution of its benefits to meet the basic needs of the human population in this and subsequent generations, and (3) to structure the growth in ways that keep its enormous potential for environmental transformation within safe limits yet to be determined.[30] The greatest responsibility and greatest immediate potential for the design of sustainable-development strategies may be in the high-income and high-density regions of the industrialized world.[31]

Implications for Society and the Corporation

These environmental concerns about pollution and resource usage run headlong into cultural values related to increased consumption and immediate gratification. The question now being asked increasingly is whether or not advanced industrial societies like the United States are sustainable from an environmental point of view, and whether or not they are just in relation to the rest of the world from a moral point of view. Questions are being raised about the feasibility and morality of our society hooked on an ever increasing standard of living, using up more and more of the world's resources, and causing more and more pollution of the environment.

Do the United States and other advanced industrial societies need to cut back on consumption and share some of their largess with developing nations? Do developed societies need to save something for future generations if they take the concept of sustainability seriously? These are moral questions thus related to intragenerational and intergenerational equity. Is there a need for some new kind of ethic that would essentially function like the work ethic did in terms of providing moral limits on consumption? These are critical questions that need to be raised as more and more nations around the world develop some form of market economies and economic growth is promoted. Does the earth have sufficient carrying capacity to sustain economic growth for the entire population?

Alan Durning has written a book appropriately entitled *How Much Is Enough?* in which he argues for the creation of what he calls the culture of permanence—a society that lives within its means by drawing on the interest provided by the earth's resources rather than its principal, a society that seeks fulfillment in a web of friendship, family, and meaningful work.[32] Yet he recognizes the difficulty of transforming consumption-oriented societies into sustainable ones and the problem that the material cravings of developing societies pose for resource usage. These forces cause what he calls a conundrum that is described as follows.

> We may be, therefore, in a conundrum—a problem admitting of no satisfactory solution. Limiting the consumer life-style to those who have already attained it is not politically possible, morally defensible, or ecologically sufficient. And extending the lifestyle to all would simply hasten the ruin of the biosphere. The global environment cannot support 1.1 billion of us living like American consumers, much less 5.5 billion people, or a future population of at least 8 billion. On the other hand, reducing the consumption levels of the consumer society, and tempering material aspirations elsewhere, though morally acceptable, is a quixotic proposal. It bucks the trend of centuries. Yet it may be the only option.[33]

For the past 40 years, the overriding goal of people in Western industrial societies has been buying more goods, acquiring more things, and increasing their stock of material wealth. Companies have profited from this consumer culture by catering to the consumers, making goods more convenient to buy, bombarding them with advertising, in general, promoting a consumer society by creating a certain materialistic conception of the good life. Because of this trend, the world's people have consumed as many goods and services since 1950 as all previous generations put together. Since 1940, according to Durning, the United States alone has used up as large a share of the earth's mineral resources as did everyone before them combined.[34]

Aside from the question as to whether or not all this consumption has really made people happier and more fulfilled, the environmental impacts have been severe as more and more resources have become depleted and it becomes more and more difficult to dispose of waste material. Consumer society is built on two critical assumptions: (1) the world contains an inexhaustible supply of raw materials, and (2) there are bottomless sinks in which to continue to dispose of waste material. Both of these assumptions are now in question, causing many to take a serious look at the sustainability of consumer culture into the future.

Reduction of consumption in industrial societies, however, can have severe repercussions. Since about two-thirds of gross national product or its equivalent in developed countries consists of consumer purchases, it seems obvious that any severe reduction of consumer expenditures would have serious implications for employment, income, investment, and everything else tied into economic growth. Lowering consumption could be self-destructive to advanced industrial societies. Yet if such measures aren't taken, Durning warns, ecological forces may eventually dismantle advanced societies anyhow, in ways that we can't control, and that would be even more destructive.[35]

Is there any way out of this dilemma? Several things suggest themselves. Corporations could be more responsible in their advertising and promotion activities and consumers in their consumption activities by promoting and buying products that have less adverse impacts on the environment. This was supposed to be the goal of *green marketing,* which is discussed at some length in another chapter, but because corporations were more concerned with exploiting a trend to increase market share than they were with promoting more responsible consumption, the effort has not been able to realize its potential. The goal of green marketing could be to change consumption patterns, not necessarily to limit consumption. If this kind of consciousness were to be expanded throughout society, much could be done to mitigate environmental impacts by promoting more ecologically sound products and packaging.

But if consumption does need to be limited, the adverse impacts on employment and other aspects of a growth-oriented economy could be mitigated by promoting more employment and investment in companies that produce goods and services that directly enhance the environment. In other words, more people would be employed and more investment made in an environmental sector, where technologies are developed to deal with environmental problems related to pollution and waste disposal, and services are provided related to recycling and restoration of the environment. Growth could still increase under this scenario, but people would be employed and profits made in a different manner by producing things and providing services that directly enhance the environment rather than devoting so much of our economic resources to producing and providing consumer goods and services that destroy it in the interests of more and more consumption.

Finally, perhaps there needs to be a new concept of growth promoted in the society, a reeducation of the American consumer to realize that growth can mean more than mere

Protestant Ethic	Consumption Orientation	Environmental Ethic
Limited consumption	Limited saving	Limit consumption
Promoted investment in productive capacity	Promoted consumption	Promote investment in environment
		Alternative meanings of growth

FIGURE 11-1 Changing Ethical Concerns

accumulation of things and that wealth can mean more than just material wealth. Perhaps Druning is right in suggesting that consumers in industrial societies can curtail the use of those things that are ecologically destructive and cultivate the deeper nonmaterial sources of fulfillment that he claims are the main psychological determinants of happiness—things like family, social relationships, meaningful work, and leisure.[36]

There is thus a need for a new understanding of the relationship of business to the natural environment and for the development of a new ethical consciousness consistent with current realities (Figure 11-1). While the Protestant ethic served an important function in limiting consumption to build up a productive base, once that base was established, people needed to consume more in order to keep the system going. Such increased consumption, however, has precipitated environmental problems related to pollution and resource usage, so that there is a need for a new ethic that again provides moral limits to consumption and supports increased investment in environmental technologies and services and provides as well an alternative meaning of growth.

If this is so, then American pragmatic philosophy can make a contribution on both counts. Its understanding of growth emphasizes that growth means neither mere accumulation nor mere economic development, but rather involves the integrative expansion of both the individual and the community through ongoing dynamic interaction. Growth involves constructive reintegration of problematic situations in ways that lead to widening horizons of self and community. Growth can best be understood as an increase in the moral-esthetic richness of experience, an increased infusion of experience with meaningfulness and expansion of value. Moreover, as seen in the last chapter, pragmatism offers a unifying moral framework for understanding and supporting the latest shift in the moral milieu of business activity.

Questions for Discussion

1. What is the Protestant ethic? How did the discovery of this ethic come about? What evidence supports its existence? What was the nature of the Protestant ethic? How was it related to the development of capitalism? What kind of a person did such an ethic produce?

2. What changes took place in American society during the 1950s in particular? What kind of society was created? What were some of the social forces behind these changes? What environmental impacts did these changes produce? What issues began to be discussed in society brought about by environmental problems?

3. How does the concern about limits to growth differ from the concern about sustainable growth? Do advanced industrial nations need to cut back on their consumption activities? How much is enough? Is there a need for a new environmental ethic? What would it look like? How would lifestyles be changed?

4. What are the implications of the issues discussed in this chapter for business organizations? What role could business adopt in society that would be more consistent with changes in the ability of the natural environment to support an ever increasing standard of living? What are the ethical issues involved in this kind of change?

Endnotes

[1] Max Weber, *The Protestant Ethic and the Spirit of Capitalism* (New York: Charles Scribner's Sons, 1958).

[2] Richard LaPiere, *The Freudian Ethic* (New York: Duell Sloan, and Pearce, 1959), p. 16.

[3] Weber, *The Protestant Ethic,* pp. 90–92.

[4] Ibid., pp. 35–40.

[5] Ibid., pp. 39–40.

[6] The Marxist analysis of history holds that religion is a part of the superstructure built upon the organization of the productive forces of society. Thus, religion is a product of the material conditions and the economic organization of society and is in no way an active agent in giving shape to these factors. This kind of causality is also supported by other scholars who have argued that religion had to shape itself to the capitalistic organization of production. For example, Tawney says that: "As a result of the Reformation the relations previously existing between the Church and State had been almost exactly reversed. In the Middle Ages the Church had been, at least in theory, the ultimate authority on questions of public and private morality, while the latter was the police officer which enforced its decrees. In the sixteenth century, the Church became the ecclesiastical department of the State, and religion was used to lend a moral sanction to secular social policy. . . . Religion has been converted from the keystone which holds the edifice together into one department within it, and the idea of a rule of right is replaced by economic expediency as the arbiter of policy and the criterion of conduct." Richard H. Tawney, *Religion and the Rise of Capitalism: A Historical study* (New York: Harcourt Brace & Co., 1926*), pp. 141, 228–229. Another example comes from C. E. Ayres who says: ". . . as industry and thrift came to be recognized as Christian virtues, inevitably the Christian conscience adjusted itself to the rewards of industry and thrift—to the accumulation of capital." C. E. Ayres, *Toward A Reasonable Society* (Austin: The University of Texas Press, 1961), p. 280.

[7] David C. McClelland, *The Achieving Society* (New York: The Free Press, 1961), p. 48.

[8] Gerhard W. Ditz, "The Protestant Ethic and the Market Economy," *Kyklos,* Vol. 33, no. 4 (1980), pp. 626–627.

[9] Christopher Lasch, *The Culture of Narcissim: American Life in an Age of Diminishing Expectations* (New York: Norton, 1978), pp. 52–53.

[10] The University of Michigan Survey Research Center asked 1,533 working people to rank various aspects of work in order of importance. Good pay came in a distant fifth, behind interesting work, enough help and equipment to get the job done, enough information to do the job, and enough authority to do the job. "Work Ethic," *Time,* October 30, 1972, p. 97. Also see *Editorial Research Reports on the American Work Ethic* (Washington: Congressional Quarterly, 1973); Harold L. Sheppard and Neal Q. Herrick, *Where Have All the Robots Gone?* (New York: The Free Press, 1972); Special Task Force to the Secretary of Health, Education, and Welfare, *Work in America* (Cambridge: M.I.T. Press, 1973); and Judson Gooding, *The Job Revolution* (New York: Walker & Co., 1972).

[11] Clyde Kluckhohn, "Have There Been Discernible Shifts in American Values During the Past Generation," *The American Style: Essays in Value and Performance,* Elting E. Morrison, ed. (New York: Harper & Bros., 1958), p. 207.

[12] Ibid., p. 184.

[13] Ibid., p. 207.

[14] Ibid., p. 192.

[15] Daniel Bell, *The Cultural Contradictions of Capitalism* (New York: Basic Books, 1976), p. 70.

[16] Ibid., p. 21.

[17] Ibid., pp. 64–65.

[18] Ibid., pp. 71–72.

[19] Ibid., p. 75.

[20] Daniel Yankelovich, *New Rules: The Search for Self-Fulfillment in a World Turned Upside Down* (New York: Random House, 1981).

[21] Ibid., p. 3.

[22] Ibid., p. 9.

[23] Ibid., p. 39.

[24] Ibid., p. 10.

[25] Lasch, *The Culture of Narcissim,* p. 53.

[26] Ibid., pp. 68–69.

[27] See John Kenneth Galbraith, *The New Industrial State* (Boston: Houghton Mifflin, 1967).

[28] See Donella H. Meadows, Dennis L. Meadows, Jorgen Randers, and William W. Behrens, III, *The Limits to Growth: A Report for the Club of Rome's Project on the Predicament of Mankind* (New York: Universe Books, 1972); Mihajlo D. Mesarovic, *Mankind at the Turning Point: The Second Report to the Club of Rome* (New York: Dutton, 1974).

[29] William C. Clark, "Managing Planet Earth," *Scientific American,* Vol. 261, no. 3 (September 1989), p. 48.

[30] Ibid., p. 49.

[31] Ibid., p. 53.

[32] Alan Durning, *How Much Is Enough?* (New York: W.W. Norton, 1992), p. 13.

[33] Ibid., p. 25.

[34] Ibid., p. 38.

[35] Ibid., p. 107.

[36] Ibid., p. 137.

Suggested Readings

Bell, Daniel. *The Cultural Contradictions of Capitalism.* New York: Basic Books, 1976.

Clark, John W. S. J. *Religion and the Moral Standards of American Businessmen.* Cincinnati: South-Western Publishing Co., 1966.

Durning, Alan. *How Much Is Enough?* New York: W.W. Norton, 1992.

Gilchrist, John. *The Church and Economic Activity in the Middle Ages.* London: Macmillan Co., 1969.

Halberstam, David. *The Fifties.* New York: Villard Books, 1993.

Kluckhohn, Clyde. "Have There Been Discernible Shifts in American Values During the Past Generation," *The American Style: Essays in Value and Performance.* Elting E. Morrison, ed. New York: Harper & Bros., 1958.

LaPiere, Richard. *The Freudian Ethic.* New York: Duell Sloan, and Pearce, 1959.

Lasch, Christopher. *The Culture of Narcissim: American Life in an Age of Diminishing Expectations.* New York: Norton, 1978.

McClelland, David C. *The Achieving Society.* New York: The Free Press, 1961.

Pahlke, Robert C. *Environmentalism and the Future of Progressive Politics.* New Haven: Yale University Press, 1989.

Weber, Max. *The Protestant Ethic and the Spirit of Capitalism.* New York: Charles Scribner's Sons, 1958.

Whyte, William H., Jr. *The Organization Man.* New York: Simon & Schuster, Inc., 1956.

Yankelovich, Daniel. *New Rules: The Search for Self-Fulfillment in a World Turned Upside Down.* New York: Random House, 1981.

SHORT CASES

The Body Shop

The Body Shop opened in Brighton, England, on March 27, 1976, selling all-natural personal care products. By 1991, the company then called The Body Shop International PLC was conducting business in 39 countries, with nearly 600 stores and 6,000 employees worldwide. From 1988 to 1990, its revenues, profits, and earnings per share grew at more than 30 percent per year. The company insists on selling only environmentally safe and natural products, which gave it a unique position in the cosmetics industry. Its level of commitment to environmental policies and programs has been compared to the zeal of a missionary. The company is an agent of positive social change while also being financially prosperous.[1]

Since it has been in operation, the company has run 19 major campaigns having to do with the environment, and completed 475 community projects including protection of rain forests, the elimination of hunger in the Third World, initiating a petition against animal testing that was signed by 2.6 million people, and recycling of its own waste material. The values of the founders of the company are ecocentric in nature and part of the mission and vision of the company includes environmental protection and sustainability. These values pervade all aspects of company operations including product development, production, waste and energy management, consumer protection, and social and environmental policies. Employees are also selected and choose to work for the company, in large part, because of mutual agreement on environmental values.

The company goes against every basic tenet of the cosmetics industry because its products are all natural in an industry that is dominated by chemical concoctions. All the ingredients for the company's products come from renewable sources such as plants, herbs, fruits, flowers, seeds, nuts, oils, soils, water, and juices. There are certain natural products the company does not use such as musk because it is extracted in a rather cruel manner from the glands of male musk deer. The Body Shop actively opposes and campaigns against animal testing as it believes that animals should not suffer for the vanity of humans. The company believes that it is neither right nor scientifically accurate to test skin- and hair-care products on animals, and requires suppliers to provide confirmation that no animal testing has been performed on their behalf within the previous five years.

The company also tries to eliminate all unnecessary packaging, as it believes the main products of the cosmetics industry are packaging and waste. The three criteria of product compatibility, strength over useful life, and safety are used in the design of packaging. Customers are encouraged to refill existing containers through a 25 percent discount on each refill offered by the company, but customers who do not want refill packages can return them to the Body Shop for recycling. All plastic bottles that the company uses have recycling identification, and recycled paper is used for all office needs and advertising. All wastepaper is shredded and used as padding for mail-order packages, and employees are encouraged to bring their wastepaper to the office for shredding.

The Body Shop has been advocated as a model for businesses of the future; however, not all companies may be able to follow the approach of the company. The company is able to invest so much money and effort in social and environmental programs because of its prosperity. Basic financial viability is a necessary condition for effective greening. There is also a need for charismatic leadership provided by the founders, Anita and Gordon Roddick, as much of the zeal and energy for the company's efforts come from these people. When they depart, this missionary zeal may not continue. However, there are several elements of success that can be learned from their efforts and applied to other companies.

1. Clear values and vision of environmental responsiveness, shared widely among employees, and charismatic leaders who strongly support these values.

2. Employees with personal commitment to environmental and social causes.

3. A management culture that encourages innovation, tolerance, and experimentation. A work culture that allows the whole individual to function.

4. Financial prosperity that allows resources to be diverted into environmental and social programs.

5. Use of simple, low-technology solutions and renewable resources that are inherently less burdensome on the natural environment.

The benefits of missionary greening are said to be apparent in the financial success and rapid growth of the company. The Body Shop has distinguished itself competitively in an industry with maturing demand, as its emphasis on environmentalism created a viable and profitable market niche. This niche gave the company entry into the mainstream cosmetics industry where it was able to firmly establish itself as an industry leader. The competitive advantage it was able to gain because of its greening effort was effective in many different countries, making the company a global success.

1. Is The Body Shop truly a model for the future? Has it responded to many of the issues related to the environment mentioned in the chapter? Is it implementing a new ethic in its operations and in its product that is consistent with environmental preservation?

2. Can many companies duplicate or even come close to duplicating The Body Shop's commitment to environmental values? What are the critical ingredients for its success? Can these ingredients be inserted into other companies to make them more environmentally responsive?

Source: Information from this case was taken from "Missionary Greening: The Body Shop," Paul Shrivastava, *Greening Business: Profiting the Corporation and the Environment* (Cincinnati: Thomson Executive Press, 1966), pp. 74–85.

Ben & Jerry's

Ben & Jerry's is an unusual company in many respects, but its most distinctive feature is its commitment and approach to environmental concerns. Perhaps the word *organic* best captures this commitment, as environmental efforts seem to occur naturally and effortlessly within the company. Environmental goals are separated from operating functions within the company, as they are an integral part of everyday activities rather than something tacked on as an afterthought. Everyone in the company participates in environmental activities through something called the Green Team, which is a vehicle for widespread participation.

The company was founded in 1978 by two young men, Ben Cohen and Jerry Greenfield, who started making ice cream in their home kitchen. From these humble beginnings, the ice cream they produced became a national brand, as in 1984 the company went public. By 1992, the company had $131 million in revenues, about 350 employees, and 100 franchised scoop shops. It had managed to capture a 36 percent market share of the superpremium ice-cream segment where Häagen-Dazs was its major competitor. This rapid growth was impressive in a mature industry, where ice-cream consumption remained constant or was even declining.

The founders of the company were idealists and social activists, growing up in the 1960s when social activism and environmentalism were popular. They started the company with a goal of not only making profits, but also wishing to promote social change. Their original vision for the company was to use business as a vehicle for social change, and this vision is part of the company's mission. This mission is achieved through product development that is linked to social causes, organic environmentalism, and green stakeholder programs. The company's green vision includes a product mission, a social mission, and an economic mission.

> The product mission is simply to make, distribute and sell the finest quality all-natural ice cream and related products in a wide variety of innovative flavors made from Vermont dairy products. Its social mission is to operate the company in a way that actively recognizes the central role that business plays in the structure of society by initiating innovative ways to improve the quality of life of a broad community: local, national, and international. The economic mission is to operate the company on a sound financial basis of profitable growth, increasing value for shareholders and creating career opportunities and financial rewards for employees.

An ice cream made by the company called Wild Maine Blueberry used wild blueberries picked by the Passamaquoddy Indians of Maine from their reservation. This effort gives them a steady source of income and enables them to support themselves. The company also buys Brazil nuts and cashew nuts grown and harvested by natives living the the Amazonian rain forest, and in this manner helps them maintain their traditional lifestyles and helps protect the rain forest. The company is also committed to supporting family-owned farms, by buying all the cream it needs from a dairy cooperative of such farms. It also uses peaches from a family farm in Georgia for its Fresh Georgia Peach Light Ice Cream. It buys brownies from Greystone Bakery, which provides training and employment for homeless people. All of these efforts give the company a competitive advantage in certain segments of the market.

The production system of the company integrates energy conservation, resource management, production, packaging, and waste treatment into a single comprehensive system. The company's environmental programs try to compensate for all the adverse environmental effects of company operations. These programs include management of waste streams, conserving energy and resources, exploring sources of sustainable alternative energy, establishing linkages between products and environmental causes, and setting up community environmental awareness programs.

Ben & Jerry's encourages employees to develop environmental and social projects and provides them with the supplies and other resources to actually implement these projects. Thus, much of the initiative for environmental activities comes from employees themselves who become members of the Green Team, which meets every month to brainstorm environmental issues. The team plans new actions and assesses progress on ones already being implemented. The more complicated and technical environmental problems are given to other professional groups who have the expertise to deal with them.

While the company has had a great deal of success in implementing its environmental and social mission, it is not without problems. One problem concerns its product, which while of high quality, contains large amounts of fat and sugar, which can be harmful to human health when consumed in excess of bodily needs. The company suggests moderation in consuming ice cream, which will be further encouraged as the company provides more complete nutritional information on its packages. The long-range challenge will be to maintain the integrity of its social, product, and economic missions as it experiences more pressure to behave like a large, established, traditional company.

1. What do you think of Ben & Jerry's priorities? Can it keep focused on its social and environmental missions, or as it becomes an even more established company, will profits become more and more important? Will it eventually come to behave like a more traditional company?

2. What do you think of the company's efforts to integrate environmental concerns into all aspects of the company's operations? Is this a better approach than to focus on just a few aspects such as waste management? Is this approach one that more companies can realistically adopt?

Source: Information from this case was taken from "Organic Greening: Ben & Jerry's Homemade Ice Creams, Inc.," Paul Shrivastava, *Greening Business: Profiting the Corporation and the Environment* (Cincinnati: Thomson Executive Press, 1966), pp. 119–132.

Green Marketing

Your company is going through a strategic planning process, attempting to identify new areas where the company might make an impact in the future and help secure its market position. It is a furniture company that makes a variety of high-quality items for the home. You have been reading a good deal lately about the environmental problems that countries all over the world are having to deal with, and wonder how your company could contribute to solving some of these problems.

There are several obvious things your company could do, such as trying to reduce its waste and starting an office recycling program, but you wonder if a green marketing program makes sense and would be a good thing for your company to consider. You are aware that several companies have gotten into trouble by making misleading claims about their products' biodegradability, for example, and you know your company would have to be careful not to mislead consumers. But you still think that it would be a good idea for the future and might give your company a competitive advantage.

Your company could advertise, for example, that its foam padding contains no CFCs, that some of its cheaper line of furniture is made from recycled wood, that some of its coverings are synthetic, and other features that might have an environmental appeal. Before you bring this idea up with your manager, however, you want to think through the implications of such a program. Can the company really make an impact in this area such that it can obtain a competitive advantage? Will it be making a contribution to society while at the same time promoting environmental consciousness? These are questions that you think your manager will ask and you want to be able to answer.

1. Is green marketing something that can change consumers' consumption patterns and promote environmental consciousness? What pitfalls exist in implementing such a program? What questions should management ask before it goes ahead with this idea?

2. How can such a program be implemented? What is the best way for a company to advertise and promote the environmental characteristics of its products? Should it use the services of one of the environmental rating groups such as Green Seal or Green Cross and tout this in its advertising?

Environmental Services

As an MBA student about to graduate, you are naturally contemplating what kind of a job to get after graduation. You have entrepreneurial instincts and think you would like to go into business for yourself rather than work for a large corporation. You have some money left to you by a rich aunt and, thus, are not totally dependent on raising all your capital needs for starting a new business. But you are not at all sure of what kind of business you would like to start.

You took a course dealing with environmental issues for business and remember that the instructor made a big pitch for people starting environmental service companies that would provide needed services for larger corporations or some other entity in society. These services could range all the way from waste cleanup to providing recycling services for companies or cities. There were many things that came to your mind as you took the course that might make good business opportunities.

But now is the time to get serious about these ideas, and decide if this is really what you want to do with your immediate future. There are many risks involved in starting a new business, as you well know, but the risks of working for a large company are also increasing. These jobs are not as secure as they once were, and so there is more appeal to going into business for yourself. You also wonder if starting an environmental services company has a future, and whether or not you could make a real contribution to society in this area as well as some money for yourself.

1. What questions do you need to ask before trying to start such a company? Will there be a future for environmental service companies? Are more companies outsourcing their environmental departments so that there are increasing opportunities to provide these kinds of services to large corporations?

2. You also wonder about the potential for expansion once you do get such a company started. Are there markets in other countries for such services? What will the competition be like? Are these kinds of companies the wave of the future? Are environmental problems going to demand more attention all over the world?

Business in Its International Environment

As business becomes increasingly internationalized and a global economy has developed, ethical issues that affect business in the international arena have also become of increasing importance. When countries trade with each other and when they are open for foreign investment and technology, they are also more open to outside influences. The increased magnitude of international trade and investment that has taken place over the past several decades has led to greater interdependence among individual national economies. These economies have become linked together to form a truly global economy, and companies competing in this arena are open to influences from all over the world.[1]

Multinational Companies

This internationalization of domestic economies around the world is most directly the result of decisions private firms make to engage in international trade and investment. Some attention thus needs to be given to the role of the multinational corporation (MNC) in the international economy. Because of its role in promoting trade and investment between countries, the MNC has become a major force in internationalizing national economies and creating a global economy. The MNC is the major institutional means through which international trade and investment are accomplished.

> The multinational corporation is probably the most visible vehicle for the internationalization of the world economic system. As the economies of different nations have become increasingly linked and functionally integrated, the multinational corporation seems to have been the institution most able to adapt to a transnational style of operation. Indeed, multinational corporations are a major result of and a prime stimulus for furthering the number and complexity of transnational interactions.[2]

The term *multinational corporation* has been defined as any enterprise that undertakes foreign direct investment, owns or controls income-gathering assets in more than one country, produces goods or services outside its country of origin, or engages in international production.[3] Multinational corporations are generally headquartered in industrialized countries and pursue business activities in one or more foreign countries. They exercise influence over the various entities (branches, subsidiaries, joint ventures) in those countries. This allows them to adopt a common globally oriented corporate policy with respect to sharing of information, use of resources, and division of responsibilities. Thus, the term *multinational* can refer to many different kinds of business enterprises and is not limited to a single type of business.[4]

Growth in trade between nations and international investment means that MNCs have significant economic and social impacts on national economies and political systems.[5] Their activities have become very visible, making them subject to criticism from many quarters. They have something of a love-hate relationship with many developing countries. On the one hand, they welcome MNCs because they have the potential to assist these countries in pursuing their own economic growth and development. Yet these same countries view MNCs as a threat to their national sovereignty and autonomy; they do not want to become economically and technologically dependent on institutions outside of their control. They often find MNCs hard to live with, and yet impossible to live without.[6]

THE STATELESS CORPORATION

The world corporations that we see developing today are a dramatic evolution from the U.S. multinationals that developed in the 1960s and 1970s. The multinationals that we became familiar with during those years treated foreign operations more or less as distant appendages for producing and marketing products that were designed and engineered in U.S. facilities. These foreign operations were controlled by management in the United States, and the chain of command and nationality of these U.S.-based companies were fairly clear and straightforward.

Today, new technologies, capital, and talents flow in many directions, not just one way as in the past. The chain of command and nationality of many of these world corporations are not at all clear. The wave of mergers, acquisitions, and strategic alliances that has taken place during the past decade has further clouded the question of national control. Many so-called U.S. companies sell more of their products outside the United States than they do at home. Nearly 70 percent of General Motors's 1989 profits, for example, came from non-U.S. operations. Over the past several years, Coca-Cola has made more money in the Pacific and Western Europe than it did in the United States. For all intents and purposes, IBM has lost its American identity with major operations in Europe and the Far East. At the same time all this is going on, foreign-based multinationals are arriving on American shores in greater strength than ever before. Such companies spent $200 billion over the past four years on acquisitions and new plants in the United States.[7]

Although world companies appear totally localized wherever they operate, they are actually more global in scale than ever before. The old multinationals tried to maintain stand-alone entities that operated more or less by themselves in different nations and paid dividends to the home office. World companies, on the other hand, try to orchestrate the efforts of all their subsidiaries on a regional or global level. They try to maintain a balance between functioning as a global organism while customizing products to local tastes. They have abandoned identification with a single nation as they try to become what are in effect local companies in many different nations of the world.[8]

In reality, there may be no such thing as an American corporation. Companies that stake their futures abroad may not deserve preferential tax treatment from this country, or subsidized financing, loan guarantees, and research grants. At the same time, foreign rivals with a growing U.S. presence in the sense of actual investments in this country, such as Philips and Sony, for example, maintain they can be as loyal to U.S. interests as so-called American companies, and deserve government support and military contracts. These developments raise some interesting issues that have many ethical dimensions to them such as fairness and equitable treatment.[9]

World corporations are changing social, economic, and political landscapes around the world. They are in the process of creating a worldwide culture that is homogeneous in terms of basic values and lifestyles. This development creates a whole new set of ethical problems that are not related to reconciling different sets of values, but are more in the nature of finding ways of controlling the activities of world corporations so they contribute to the social or common good. These world corporations can hold nation-states hostage in the same way companies in the United States often play states off against each other to get the best deal for themselves. The market system by itself does not guarantee that the environment, consumers, and workers will be adequately protected. Who is going to look after the rights of these constituencies? What mechanisms of social control exist to shape the behavior of world corporations and make them more socially responsible?

MULTINATIONALS AND NATIONAL GOVERNMENTS

Expansion beyond national boundaries is much more than a step across the geographical line of a country. It is also a step toward new and different social, educational, political, and economic environments where different values and cultures mean that there are different ways of conducting business in various countries. As conflicts arise between MNCs and host and home countries, these differences cause problems for managers of multinational corporations. These conflicts are often resolved through regulatory measures shaping the conduct of multinational enterprises. Regulations are often adopted to deal with these differences and managers of MNCs have to pay as much attention to these measures as they do to regulation in their own countries. But this additional regulation increases the chances that the regulations of different countries will clash, with multinationals caught in the middle.[10]

Many countries find it difficult to control the activities of MNCs within their territories. The flexibility of MNCs enables them to move capital, goods, personnel, and technology across national boundaries. This flexibility enables them to play one country off against another to get the best deal for themselves. Since the activities of MNCs affect the level of social and economic development in many countries, particularly developing countries, there has been an increasing interest in developing some form of international regulation to control the activities of MNCs and give host governments some control over their activities. Third World nations in particular believe that in the absence of international regulation, MNCs would only show interest in profit maximization without any regard to the development needs of host nations.[11]

MNCs are accused of creating numerous negative externalities for host countries including the following: (1) The benefits of foreign investments are poorly or unfairly distributed between the MNC and the host country; (2) MNCs preempt the development of an indigenous economic base by squeezing out local entrepreneurs; (3) they employ inappropriate capital-intensive technology adding to host-country unemployment; (4) MNCs worsen the distribution of income in the host country; (5) they alter consumer tastes in the host-country, thus undermining the culture; and (6) foreign investors subvert host-country political processes by co-opting the local elites, using their influence to keep host governments in line, and structuring the international system to respond to their needs to the detriment of host authorities.[12]

Most conflicts arise from the fact that MNCs have some degree of economic power because of the decisions they make concerning product lines, location of plants, technology employed, trade flows, and other business considerations. These decisions are made with regard to corporate objectives related to profits and market share, and are not necessarily made in the interests of the host country or even the home country. Investment decisions and operational practices are geared to the need of MNCs to survive and grow by maintaining or increasing world market shares, gaining a competitive edge over rivals, shifting operations to take advantage of access to natural resources or cheap labor markets, and other such factors where policies and strategies are developed that are global in nature, scope, and character. MNCs do not and cannot take into account the interest of each and every country in the decisions they make because the interests of the various countries affected by these decisions very rarely coincide. MNCs must maintain that they are looking after their own interests within a worldwide strategy they have developed for themselves.

Yet governments are not likely to let important decisions be made by a foreign private institution without exercising some kind of influence.[13] Host governments influence multinationals in a variety of ways. The underlying motive is to set the rules of the game. Government regulation is theoretically nondiscriminatory, since all the parties are nominally subject to the same rules of the game. But governments in reality are political creations and are often motivated by purely political considerations. Another major problem facing multinationals is that the regulatory environment varies considerably from country to country. Many regulations governing multinationals are difficult to interpret and are not consistently enforced. Moreover, in large parts of the Third World there is a distinct absence of regulations or mechanisms for enforcing those regulations that do exist. They often lack the necessary legal and administrative institutions and the technical proficiency to implement and enforce national policies.

The development of world corporations makes sorting out national economic interests difficult at best. Do foreign companies pay adequate U.S. taxes? Should we require foreign multinationals to provide information on their investments? Do antitrust laws apply to foreign companies operating here and to U.S.-based companies operating overseas? Does it really make any difference what a company's nationality is as long as it provides jobs and enables people to earn a decent income? What nation controls the technology developed by world companies? What obligations do they have to adhere to rules imposed by Washington, Paris, or Tokyo on their foreign operations?[14] The sovereignty of national governments has been circumscribed, and stateless corporations have increasingly learned to shape national policies by offering technology, jobs, and capital. They can play one country off against another until they get what they want, and have a privileged position with respect to political participation.

Multinationals and the Issue of Cultural Relativism

Some of the more interesting problems that arise in the case of multinational operations in foreign countries are ethical in nature. Every country has its own standards with regard to the conduct of business, and these standards are often in direct conflict with the standards of acceptable conduct in the United States as expressed in custom or in formal legislation. What is a company to do when faced with this kind of conflict and which set of standards should it adhere to in the conduct of its business? These conflicts can arise in almost every area of activity including anticompetitive conduct, marketing practices, environmental policies, and hiring practices. The multinational can be caught between different standards and expectations regarding ethical behavior.

From an ethical point of view, the issue is one of cultural relativism. Is ethics relative to each culture such that different cultures have different standards of ethical behavior that are valid and legitimate for that culture? According to cultural relativism, moral beliefs and principles that prescribe acceptable forms of human behavior are closely connected in culture to other cultural characteristics, such as language and political institutions. Anthropological studies show that moral beliefs differ greatly from culture to culture. Thus, moral standards are held to be simply a historical product sanctioned by customs that have developed over a long period of time in response to conditions in which the society functions. Moral beliefs and standards are relative to groups and individuals who make up a culture, and consequently, there are no universal norms that apply to all people and cultures.[15]

If cultural relativism is valid, then what is a multinational to do with regard to its conduct when confronted with conflicts between the host country in which it is doing business and the home country in which it is headquartered? Shall it adopt a "when in Rome do as the Romans do" policy and adapt its behavior to conform with the standards of each country in which it does business? Or should it adopt a uniform standard for its worldwide operations that it follows in every country with regard to issues such as hiring practices or environmental policies? Should it attempt to do business throughout the world the way business is conducted in the United States, or should it view this approach as cultural imperialism and adopt a more relativistic approach to its conduct in foreign countries?

Some scholars think such universal standards do exist with respect to many business practices, and that such guidelines may be found embedded in several multilateral compacts adopted by governments in recent years. Taken as a whole, these normative guidelines are believed to comprise a framework for identifying the essential moral behavior expected of multinationals regardless of where they are conducting operations. This set of normative prescriptions embodies a moral authority that transcends national boundaries and cultural differences, thereby invoking or manifesting a universal or transcultural standard of corporate ethical behavior that should be adhered to in every country in which a multinational does business.[16] Taken as a whole, these compacts cover the areas of employment practices and policies, consumer protection, environmental protection, political payments and involvement, and basic human rights and fundamental freedoms. The specific guidelines that can be derived from these compacts expressed in these categories are shown in Exhibit 12-1.

These guidelines are said to have direct implications for a wide range of specific corporate policies and practices. These policies and practices include pollution-control efforts, advertising and marketing activities, child care, minimum wages, hours of work,

Multinational Guidelines

EMPLOYMENT PRACTICES AND POLICIES

MNCs should not contravene the manpower policies of host nations.

MNCs should respect the right of employees to join trade unions and to bargain collectively.

MNCs should develop nondiscriminatory employment policies and promote equal job opportunities.

MNCs should provide equal pay for equal work.

MNCs should give advance notice of changes in operations, especially plant closings, and mitigate the adverse effects of these changes.

MNCs should provide favorable work conditions, limited working hours, holidays with pay, and protection against unemployment.

MNCs should promote job stability and job security, avoiding arbitrary dismissals and providing severance pay for those unemployed.

MNCs should respect local host-country job standards and upgrade the local labor force through training.

MNCs should adopt adequate health and safety standards for employees and grant them the right to know about job-related health hazards.

MNCs should, minimally, pay basic living wages to employees.

MNCs' operations should benefit lower-income groups in the host nations.

MNCs should balance job opportunities, work conditions, job training, and living conditions among migrant workers and host-country nationals.

CONSUMER PROTECTION

MNCs should respect host-country laws and policies regarding the protection of consumers.

MNCs should safeguard the health and safety of consumers by various disclosures, safe packaging, proper labeling, and accurate advertising.

ENVIRONMENTAL PROTECTION

MNCs should respect host-country laws, goals, and priorities concerning protection of the environment.

MNCs should preserve ecological balance, protect the environment, adopt preventive measures to avoid environmental harm, and rehabilitate environments damaged by operations.

MNCs should disclose likely environmental harms and minimize risks of accidents that could cause environmental damage.

MNCs should promote the development of international environmental standards.

MNCs should control specific operations that contribute to pollution of air, water, and soils.

ENVIRONMENTAL PROTECTION (con't)

MNCs should develop and use technology that can monitor, protect, and enhance the environment.

POLITICAL PAYMENTS AND INVOLVEMENT

MNCs should not pay bribes nor make improper payments to public officials.

MNCs should avoid improper or illegal involvement or interference in the internal politics of host countries.

MNCs should not interfere in intergovernmental relations.

BASIC HUMAN RIGHTS AND FUNDAMENTAL FREEDOMS

MNCs should respect the rights of all persons to life, liberty, security of person, and privacy.

MNCs should respect the rights of all persons to equal protection of the law, work, choice of job, just and favorable work conditions, and protection against unemployment and discrimination.

MNCs should respect all persons' freedom of thought, conscience, religion, opinion and expression, communication, peaceful assembly and association, and movement and residence within each state.

MNCs should promote a standard of living to support the health and well-being of workers and their families.

MNCs should promote special care and assistance to motherhood and childhood.

Source: William C. Frederick, "The Moral Authority of MNC Codes," paper presented at the Conference on Socio-Economics, Harvard Business School, March 31–April 2, 1989, pp. 6–8. See also William C. Frederick, "The Moral Authority of Transnational Corporate Codes," *Journal of Business Ethics,* Vol. 10, no. 2 (1991), pp. 165–177.

employee training and education, adequate housing and health care, severance pay, privacy of employees and consumers, safety and health programs, and other policies and practices. It has been argued that these guidelines are believed to have direct applicability to many of the central operations and policies of multinational enterprises, and comprise a set of universal standards that crosses national boundaries and transcends cultural differences.[17]

Other scholars have different standards that they believe are universal in nature. Richard DeGeorge, for example, believes there are several general ethical norms that apply to any business operating anywhere. These norms are universally applicable, he argues, because they are necessary either for a society to function at all, or for business transactions to take place. These norms include (1) the injunction against arbitrarily killing other members of the community to which one belongs, (2) the positive injunction to tell the truth and its negative corollary not to lie, (3) respect for property, (4) the injunction to honor contracts, and (5) exercising fairness in business contracts.[18]

From these basic norms, DeGeorge develops seven moral guidelines that multinationals should follow when operating in Third World countries. These include (1) MNCs should do no harm, (2) MNCs should produce more good than bad for the host country, (3) MNCs should contribute by their activities to the host country's development, (4) MNCs should respect the rights of their employees, (5) MNCs should pay their fair share of taxes, (6) to the extent that local culture does not violate moral norms, MNCs should respect the local culture and not work against it, and (7) MNCs should cooperate with the local government in the development and enforcement of just background institutions.[19]

Tom Donaldson, another expert in international ethics as it applies to multinationals, has a similar list utilizing the concept of rights as a moral vehicle (see box). These rights establish minimum levels of morally acceptable behavior and are the rock bottom of modern moral deliberation regarding the responsibilities of multinationals operating abroad. While the list may be incomplete, Donaldson argues that the human claims it honors and the interests those claims represent are globally relevant.[20]

The United Nations Centre on Transnational Corporations (UNCTC) provides numerous services for member nations with respect to the operation of what it calls *transnational corporations* (TNCs) within their borders. The UNCTC has been in the process of developing an international code of conduct to regulate the activities of TNCs with regard to the internal affairs of host countries and to encourage TNCs to facilitate the achievement of the development activities of Third World countries. This code represents the first time a comprehensive international instrument is being developed for regulating a wide range of issues arising from relations between TNCs and host governments.[21]

The code is meant to provide a stable, predictable, and transparent framework that can facilitate the flow of resources across national boundaries, enhancing the role of foreign investment in economic and industrial growth. The code is also meant to minimize the negative effects of TNCs by setting out, in a balanced manner, the rights and responsibilities of TNCs and host governments. As a result of this twin focus, it is hoped the code

---

BOX 12-1

Ten International Rights That Serve to Establish a Moral Minimum for the Behavior of All International Economic Agents

- The Right to Freedom of Physical Movement
- The Right to Ownership of Property
- The Right to Freedom from Torture
- The Right to a Fair Trial
- The Right to Nondiscriminatory Treatment
- The Right to Physical Security
- The Right to Freedom of Speech and Association
- The Right to Minimal Education
- The Right to Political Participation
- The Right to Subsistence

Source: Thomas Donaldson, *The Ethics of International Business* (Oxford: Oxford University Press, 1989), p. 81.

will help to reduce friction between TNCs and host countries and enable the flow of direct foreign investment to realize its full potential.[22]

The problem with all such international codes is to make them general enough to secure ratification by a number of nations with diverse interests and yet specific enough to have some real meaning in concrete situations. This difficulty has undoubtedly been responsible for the delay in issuance of the code. Another problem is implementation. Third World countries generally want such codes to be binding and are in favor of setting up some institutional machinery for enforcement purposes, while industrialized countries generally want such codes to be voluntary in nature without any binding authority. This problem of international enforcement authority has undermined other efforts of this nature and is likely to produce the same result with respect to the UNCTC code.

For the managers of multinational companies, moral guidelines such as these could be taken to represent a growing consensus among the world's peoples about what is thought to be morally desirable action by private enterprises. While these guidelines do not cover all possible issues that are of concern to people nor are they universally adhered to by all countries, they could be taken to represent the general outlines of a globally oriented system of normative principles governing corporate behavior.[23] Corporate leaders of multinational institutions would be well advised to take them into account when developing policies and strategies for their companies as the internationalization of the world proceeds and grows more complicated.

Issues Affecting Multinational Corporations

The United States has numerous laws and regulations that apply to the operations of MNCs and raise important issues relative to the operation of MNCs in foreign countries. Some of these laws pertain to bribery in foreign countries, and impose the standards we adhere to in this country regarding bribery on the operations of U.S. companies in overseas transactions. There are concerns related to economic sanctions and their effect on the target nation(s) as well as on the country or countries imposing the sanctions. There are concerns related to marketing that are international in scope. And finally, environmental concerns are becoming more and more important all over the world, particularly with respect to global problems that require international agreements. These concerns are also becoming a significant part of trade agreements.

THE FOREIGN PAYMENTS CONTROVERSY

The dilemma cultural relativism poses for MNCs is nicely illustrated by the foreign payments controversy that erupted in the early 1970s, when it was discovered that many large corporations made contributions to political campaigns in foreign countries on a rather extensive scale. These payments were most often contributions to politicians for political campaigns or favors and payments made to agents of government officials to win contracts. The term most often used in the media to refer to these contributions was *questionable payments* because there was some question about the ethics of these payments.

Revelation of the extent to which these questionable payments were made abroad to further the interests of American businesses stirred great concern among government officials and other public and private figures in the 1970s and resulted in broad condemnation of these practices. Such revelations shook foreign government officials, rocked American corporate management, and tarnished the image of American private enterprise at home and abroad. For example, the revelations of questionable payments abroad by American corporations shook the governments of Belgium, Holland, Honduras, Italy, and Japan and contributed to the decline of confidence in American business leadership. One commentator stated that: ". . . the leadership of American big business has never been held in such low regard since perhaps the days of the Great Depression . . . big business is now close to the bottom rung in measures of public trust and confidence."[24]

Foreign payments were defined as "any transfer of money or anything of value made with the aim of influencing the behavior of politicians, political candidates, political parties, or government officials and employees in their legislative, administrative and judicial actions."[25] Lawful payments included contributions to political parties or candidates in countries where this behavior is not illegal as it is in the United States. Many countries allow corporations to make such contributions. It is also true that in some cases the initiative for many payments came from foreign officials who demanded payments and may even have threatened sanctions. But in many other instances, payments were made on the initiative of American corporate officials.

Business tried to defend these practices by explaining that these payments were a necessary cost of doing business—that payments of this kind were an accepted practice in other countries. Business was transacted in many of these countries through agents who collected high fees for their services and passed some of this money on to government officials. In other cases, government officials were paid directly to award favors to companies. Customs officials were paid low salaries or wages with the expectation that their income would be supplemented by payments from foreign corporations. Some argued that when in Rome, one had to do as the Romans, and we should not impose our ethical standards on other countries. In addition, if companies in this country did adhere to "higher" standards, the business would simply go to a non-U.S. corporation that was not so virtuous and we would be shut out of many foreign markets.

The public's concern about these payments was based, on the one hand, on the belief that such payments corrupted the free enterprise system under which the most efficient producers with the best products are supposed to prevail. As put by one treasury official: "When the major criterion in a buyer's choice of a product is the size of a bribe rather than its price and quality and reputation of its producers, the fundamental principles on which a market economy is based are put in jeopardy."[26] Such payments were believed to subvert the laws of supply and demand and result in free markets being replaced by contrived markets.

On the other hand, the public's concern for these payments stemmed from our beliefs about the proper relationships between the economic and political systems, and the behavior of public officials and private managers. The idea that official power vested by the state in government officials can be bought and sold on the marketplace is repugnant to the American mind. We make a clear separation between business and government, between the commercial and the political, and draw a boundary line between marketable goods and services and nonmarketable political rights, duties, and authority.[27]

Theoretically, the best way to deal with foreign bribery would be for some international body to pass measures regulating this practice. And in fact, resolutions on foreign payments were prepared by the secretariats of both the United Nations and the Organization of American States. But these resolutions were never formulated into an international code of some kind that could be implemented in countries all over the world. Despite pressure from the United States for such a code, the issue faded away on the international level. Many countries believed their national laws were already adequate to deal with the situation. Some countries did not consider such payments to be unethical and were not motivated to eradicate them from the system. If the United States wanted to do something to stop foreign payments, at least for corporations headquartered in this country, it appeared that unilateral action was the only course available.[28]

Eventually, a new public policy measure was passed by Congress and signed into law by the president. The Foreign Corrupt Practices Act (FCPA) of 1977 has been characterized as the most extensive application of federal law to corruption since the passage of the 1933 and 1934 securities acts.[29] The law contains both antibribery provisions and accounting provisions. Passage of this act raises many questions related to public policy that have ethical and moral dimensions. The negative effects of bribery were generally considered to be (1) the warping of economic and social objectives in the country as a result of altered decisions, (2) the upsetting of political processes resulting in undesirable decisions, (3) a potential reduction in national security, and (4) the destabilization of international relations.[30] But who is responsible for dealing with these negative effects? In which country should ethical criteria originate to deal with this issue? And if international action proves impossible to attain, should one country act unilaterally to deal with what is an international issue? Are there universal standards with respect to this issue that should be adhered to regardless of cultural differences?

INTERNATIONAL MARKETING

An important dimension of the ethical performance of multinational corporations relates to international marketing practices and the operations of multinational corporations in overseas markets. When multinational corporations of industrialized nations turn to markets in developing countries, for example, the problems that they face are not only different in degree but also often in kind from those they face in their home countries. The environment is often radically different from that of developed countries so that in many cases multinational corporations are unable to forecast the consequences of some of their actions and policies. There is often a lack of reliable information. The regulatory processes of most of these host countries are either inconsistent or unpredictable, at least from the standpoint of the multinational corporation. Poverty and illiteracy are frequently present on a scale unknown or unfamiliar to the industrialized nations.

The rules of the game, which involve pricing and distribution, advertising and promotion, and product quality and safety in foreign countries, are often ambiguous, contradictory, and rapidly changing, and sometimes absent altogether, and an ethical sensitivity is required of companies that intend to do business in these countries.[31] David J. Fritzsche lists issues in Exhibit 12-2 as important to address when decisions are made about a firm's marketing operations in foreign countries.

Other important issues of this kind include the following: (1) Should a product banned in the United States be sold by American multinational corporations abroad? (2) Should the same marketing strategies, policies, and tactics that have proved successful in Western Europe, Japan, or North America be employed in developing countries regardless of differences in consumers' needs, values, and abilities, and the suitability of the product to their needs? (3) Are multinationals responsible for uncontrolled sales of prescription drugs in host countries? (4) What is the appropriate price of high-technology

---

EXHIBIT 12-2

Important Issues in Overseas Marketing

PRODUCT ISSUES

Is the product damaging to the people or the environment of the target market country?

Will the product enhance the lives of people in the target market country?

PROMOTION ISSUES

Will the promotion be viewed as a bribe or a payoff by the home country or by the foreign market?

Will the promotion mislead or confuse the people in the target foreign market?

DISTRIBUTION ISSUES

Is a bribe or payoff required to enter the foreign market?

What is the likelihood that an agent within the foreign market could force extortion payments for access to the market?

PRICE ISSUES

Will the price charged in the foreign market be viewed as dumping by foreign competitors or governments?

Is the price charged in the foreign market competitively fair given current operating costs?

Source: David J. Fritzsche, "Ethical Issues in Multinational Marketing," in Gene R. Laczniak and Patrick E. Murphy, eds., *Marketing Ethics: Guidelines for Managers* (Lexington, MA: Lexington Books, 1985), p. 95.

---

products in host countries when the manufacturing cost may only be a small fraction of that price? (5) Does it make sense to ask multinational corporations to transfer their high-technology products to the developing countries with little return on their investments? (6) How far do manufacturers' liability and accountability extend for the safety and effectiveness of their products, often used and misused under widely differing circumstances?

These are typical of the questions that constitute ethical issues in international marketing facing marketers in the international arena. Marketers have to answer these questions when the company they work for is considering marketing pesticides or drugs banned in the United States in overseas countries, or when the company is considering stepping up marketing of a product such as cigarettes in developing countries when cigarettes are under question in the United States and sales are declining because of health problems.

In spite of differences between countries, multinational corporations often revert to traditional marketing approaches by simply taking products that have been designed to meet consumer needs and desires back home and marketing them as if they had been intended for developing-country markets all along. Rarely does one find a situation in which a multinational corporation adapts its entire marketing strategy to less developed countries. The tendency to treat these countries as an extension of the industrialized marketplace creates a very significant potential for conflict.[32]

In effect, both traditional marketing theories and marketing practices are confronted with challenges that have not as yet been mastered. These challenges are essentially due to the fact that as corporations extend the sphere of their activities beyond their national boundaries, they are confronted with changes in the expectations of society, different degrees of government intervention in the private sector, changes in the legal environment, changes in the marketing environment, and different desires, needs, and values of people. The consequences of these differences are not fully understood in many cases, at least not in the short run. Thus, multinational corporations are confronted with the task of selling abroad under a highly uncertain external environment without many benchmarks to guide them.

> If an organization is to address fundamental issues instead of symptoms, it must identify and analyze them. Such a task is formidable. First, the basic issues are inherently difficult to understand. There is little established theory to guide the decision makers. Relevant empirical questions are usually unanswered. Issues tend to be dynamic and interrelated. The real problems are frequently not visible to the public. . . . The information systems of involved organizations are not oriented toward, or effective in, obtaining information that will enable such organizations to detect underlying social issues.[33]

In effect, the problems marketers face in the domestic environment are greatly magnified as their reach extends into the international marketplace. V. Terpstra has identified three types of marketing practices in the international environment: (1) international marketing that deals with the marketing across national boundaries, (2) foreign marketing that deals with marketing within foreign countries, and (3) multinational marketing that deals with coordinating marketing in multiple markets.[34] Each one of these types will force the marketer to be concerned not only with traditional marketing functions, but also with designing international marketing operations to meet the needs and the values of various stakeholders in countries that have diverse sociocultural, economic, and political environments. Therefore, the marketer must adapt to an international environment in which "marketing is both a cause and effect of conditions within . . . the environment and culture."[35]

INTERNATIONAL ENVIRONMENTAL ISSUES

The physical environment is beginning to have more impact on the conduct of multinational business and is becoming a major factor in the globalization of the economy. There are several facets to this developing environmental concern that deserve some consideration. One facet concerns the so-called global environmental problems, which are a new class of problems with unique characteristics that did not exist previously. The second set of concerns revolves around the disposal of hazardous waste on the international level. And the third facet involves the impact the environment is making on trade agreements, both at the international and regional levels.

Global Problems

In the 1980s, environmental problems appeared that were truly global in nature in that they affected people all over the world and required international cooperation to deal with them effectively. Two problems of this nature that have received most of the attention are global warming and ozone depletion. Global warming is a phenomenon involving a warming of the earth's atmosphere because of the buildup of infrared absorbing trace gases such as carbon dioxide, methane, CFCs, and nitrous oxide, all of which have increased dramatically in past decades. Scientists have documented a 25 percent increase in carbon dioxide in the past 100 years, and some scientists expect the present level to double by the year 2050. Atmospheric methane has doubled during this same time period. The buildup of these gases traps heat that would normally escape into the atmosphere, and is believed to lead to an increase in the temperature of the earth's atmosphere producing the so-called greenhouse effect.

The major culprit in global warming is believed to be the burning of fossil fuels, particularly coal, which releases carbon dioxide into the atmosphere. Deforestation also adds carbon dioxide to the atmosphere, as trees and other vegetation absorb CO_2 as they grow, and release an equal amount when they are burned or decay naturally. It has been estimated that a doubling of CO_2 or an equivalent increase in other trace gases would warm the earth's average surface temperature by between 3.0 and 5.5 degrees Centigrade, a change that would be unprecedented in human history. Such a change would mean hot, dry summers for many parts of the world, and a melting of polar ice caps and glaciers that would cause sea levels to rise several feet by mid-century. Many cities near low-lying coastal areas would be flooded, and people would have to either erect sea walls or move to another location. Temperate zones would move further north leaving areas that were primary agricultural zones, such as the midsection of the United States, useless as far as growing crops is concerned.

Everyone in the scientific community agrees that atmospheric concentration of carbon dioxide and other trace gases is on the rise. And most believe that this increase cannot help but have some effect on the climate.[36] But whether or not the greenhouse effect is already apparent and thus needs to be dealt with now is a matter of some debate. Some scientists say that the the buildup of carbon dioxide and the warming of the globe are circumstantial. The warming that has been experienced could be due to natural causes and attributable to atmospheric cycles or other naturally occurring factors. The greenhouse theory has not been proven conclusively, and to take action at this time to reduce emissions of carbon dioxide or other trace gases may be spending a good deal of money unnecessarily.[37] Others question the accuracy of the models used to predict future temperature increases related to the continued buildup of carbon dioxide.[38]

To deal with this problem would require international cooperation, as one nation could not solve the problem by itself. All nations of the world would have to agree to take steps to limit the release of carbon dioxide and other trace gases to have a major effect on global warming. Such an agreement was adopted at the Earth Summit in Rio de Janeiro in 1992, but the United States, which up to that point had largely taken a wait and see attitude, was able to keep goals and timetables out of the pact. After the summit, however, the Clinton administration committed the country to roll back emissions of greenhouse gases by the year 2000 to 1990 levels, a commitment that involved a debate over which sectors of the economy should bear the cost of the reductions.[39]

Another global environmental problem of this nature is the depletion of the ozone layer in the stratosphere. This layer absorbs most of the ultraviolet radiation that comes from the sun, and depletion of this layer would allow higher levels of ultraviolet radiation to reach the surface of the planet. Too much ultraviolet radiation can damage plant and animal cells, cause skin cancer and eye damage to humans, and kill many smaller and more sensitive organisms. Each 1 percent drop in ozone is projected to result in 4 to 6 percent more cases of skin cancer. Increased exposure to radiation also depresses the human immune system, lowering the body's resistance to attacking organisms.[40]

The culprit was identified in 1974 by two scientists at the University of California at Irvine, who theorized that chlorofluorocarbons (CFCs) eventually drifted up to the stratosphere to react chemically with ozone molecules in a destructive fashion. While many chemicals that are released into the atmosphere decay in weeks or months, CFCs are so chemically inert that they often can stay intact for a century. This gave them ample time to rise through the atmosphere to reach higher altitudes and do their damage to the ozone layer. Because of the nature of the chemical reactions, a single molecule of chlorine can destroy thousands of ozone molecules. Later it was discovered that other compounds such as methyl chloroform and carbon tetrachloride assist the CFCs in ozone destruction. And another family of compounds called halons, which contain bromines, were discovered to be a hundred times more efficient than the chlorine compounds at ozone destruction.[41]

When first discovered, CFCs proved to be remarkable compounds. Since they were inert, they did not react with other chemicals with which they were mixed. They were also neither toxic nor flammable at ground level. The number of CFC compounds grew quickly into the dozens, and were used as a universal coolant, refrigerating 75 percent of the food consumed in the United States; as a blowing agent in rigid insulation forms; as an aerosol propellant; as a solvent to remove glue, grease, and soldering residues from microchips and other electronic products; and as a component of foam packaging containers. Between 1958 and 1983, the average production of some forms of CFC compounds grew 13 percent a year, and could continue to grow more or less indefinitely.[42]

When the theory was first developed, the United States banned the use of CFCs as an aerosol propellant, but most of the rest of the world continued to use them for this purpose. No international action was taken until the discovery of the ozone hole over Antarctica. By the spring of 1987, the average ozone concentration over the South Pole was discovered to be down 50 percent, and in isolated spots it had actually disappeared. The report on this discovery also indicated that the ozone layer around the entire globe was eroding much faster than any model had predicted. Ozone depletion was said to be occurring far more rapidly and in a different pattern than had been forecast. While the role of CFCs in ozone depletion had been hotly contested after the theory was formulated in 1974, within a matter of weeks the report's conclusions were widely accepted and the need for immediate policy decisions became apparent to many of the world's leaders.[43]

On September 16, 1987, after years of debate and heated negotiation, the Montreal Protocol on Substances that Deplete the Ozone Layer was signed by 24 countries. By mid-November 1988, that total had increased to 35 countries. The agreement included a freeze on CFC production at 1986 levels to be reached by 1989, a 20 percent decrease in production by 1993, and another 30 percent cut by 1998. Halon production was also subject to a freeze based on 1986 levels starting in 1992. In order to obtain this many signatures, the treaty included extended deadlines for some countries, allowances to accommodate industry restructuring, and loose definitions of products that can legitimately be traded internationally. Developing countries were given a ten-year grace period past the industrial-country deadline during which CFC production could be increased to meet "basic domestic needs."[44]

In June 1990, representatives from 75 countries met in London to sign another accord that strengthened provisions of the original treaty. Projections showed that if industrialized countries phased out CFCs as scheduled, but the less developed countries did not go along, these countries' use of CFCs would soar from 15 to 50 percent of world usage by the end of the century. This increase would leave chlorine levels slightly above the current level even with reduction by developed countries. Thus, the new pact called for eliminating CFC usage worldwide in a decade, and set up an international fund of $200 billion to help less developed countries join the campaign. This aid will help subsidize purchase of CFC substitutes by less developed countries and build new plants to produce refrigerators and other products that use CFC substitutes.[45]

This treaty and its subsequent revision were an unprecedented effort to deal with a global problem and may provide a model for agreements to deal with other global problems such as the greenhouse effect. The impact on industry is expected to be severe, as the estimated annual world production of these chemicals is worth about $2.2 billion, and the industries that use CFCs had annual sales of many additional billions of dollars.[46] Du Pont, the world's largest manufacturer of CFCs, estimated that banning them would render useless or require altering capital equipment valued at $135 billion in the United States alone. Substitutes are going to be difficult to develop and require the investment of additional billions of dollars in new plant construction.[47]

Hazardous Waste Disposal

The development of global trading in hazardous waste is another environmental problem that has international dimensions. In order to save money and avoid regulatory hurdles, cities and waste disposal companies in the United States and other industrialized countries ship large amounts of hazardous waste to other countries. Most of these legal exports from the United States go to Canada and Mexico. To ship waste to these and other countries, all U.S. companies have to do is to notify the EPA of their intent to ship this material, get written permission from the recipient country, and file an annual report with the agency.[48] Such lax provisions encourage countries such as the United States to transport their hazardous wastes problems to other countries.

These legal shipments of hazardous wastes, however, may be only the tip of the "sludgeberg," as it is called, as there is increasing evidence of a growing trade in illegal shipments of hazardous wastes between countries. Waste disposal firms can charge high prices for picking up hazardous wastes from companies that generate them, and if they can dispose of them legally or illegally in other countries at low cost, they can make large profits. Most of the recipient countries, however, are beginning to realize that importation of hazardous waste can threaten the health and environment of their country and weaken long-term economic growth. Many are adopting a "not in our country" (NIOC) attitude similar to the "not in my back yard" (NIMBY) phenomenon in this country.[49]

In late 1990, it was reported that millions of tons of toxic waste were being dumped in Latin America each year, leaving poisonous residues that will endanger lives for decades. Everything from household trash to radioactive sludge was said to be sent to the region because lax antipollution laws there made disposal of such waste easier and cheaper. Scientists in Brazil called the dumping of hazardous waste in their country an illicit trade that is shrouded in secrecy and often done by small and unregistered companies. This dumping was devastating the environment and said to cause cancer, birth defects, nerve damage, and blood disorders. According to Greenpeace, Latin America made a perfect dumping ground as there were lots of space, loads of corrupt inspectors, and widespread ignorance of the problem.[50]

Leaders from 116 countries drafted an international treaty in 1989 that was designed to help control the export of hazardous waste material. The treaty would ban such exports unless the government of the receiving country gave prior written permission to receive the waste material. Many environmentalists want Congress to ban all exports of hazardous waste to other countries, believing that the United States has an ethical obligation of take care of its own waste material and not export the problem where it will affect the health and environment of other countries.[51]

The Environment and Trade Agreements

Finally, environmental issues are becoming more and more important with respect to trade agreements between nations. This phenomenon is most evident in the discussions that took place over passage of the North American Free Trade Agreement (NAFTA), which has probably done more to promote international environmental concerns than any other trade agreement. Opponents of NAFTA argued that American firms would engage in a mass exodus to Mexico where they can freely pollute and ruin a global environment. In response to these criticisms, the Bush administration conducted a nine-month study of the environmental impact of the agreement with public hearings in six cities. The agreement itself expressly forbids the United States, Canada, and Mexico to lower environmental standards to attract investment, and also supports the harmonization of increased environmental standards and allows the three nations to adopt more rigorous standards should they desire. The so-called side agreements appended to NAFTA will create a Commission on Environmental Cooperation that will give citizens and interest groups unprecedented ease of access to international dispute resolutions regarding the environment.[52]

NAFTA was almost dealt a fatal blow when a federal judge ruled in 1993 that an environmental impact statement had to be prepared in connection with the agreement. He argued that the National Environmental Policy Act (NEPA) passed in 1970 required such a report on the environmental effects of the agreement. The preparation of this report would have taken months and perhaps even years to prepare, and given opponents more time to mount their opposition. While NEPA was designed to prevent the commitment of federal resources to programs whose environmental impact has not been considered, many doubted whether congressional leaders intended that the law also be applied to international trade agreements.[53] An appeals court eventually agreed and ruled that the agreement was exempt from formal environmental review, and could thus go before Congress without the preparation of an environmental impact statement.[54]

However, NAFTA is not the only trade agreement that has been impacted by environmental considerations. The United States imposed an embargo on tuna exported from Mexico in 1990, saying that the use of nets without dolphin-protection measures to catch tuna was a violation of the Marine Mammal Protection Act. This action was appealed by Mexico with support from several other nations, and even though the General Agreement on Tariffs and Trade (GATT) ruled in Mexico's favor by arguing that, while the United States could restrain trade to protect the environment and natural resources within its own borders, it could not seek to extend these actions extraterritorially, compromises still had to be reached with the United States because GATT decisions have no enforcement provisions. This controversy made many realize that GATT is not presently equipped to handle environmental disputes among its members, and needs to at least acknowledge that environmental matters can be used as nontariff barriers to trade among nations.[55]

The World Community

From the preceding discussion it should be clear that what is emerging through international trade and the international economic and environmental issues and problems that result is not merely increasing contact between diverse communities, but rather a growing global or world community. In this situation, the diverse inputs of individual nations are in an ongoing process of mutual adjustment with a common other of global dimensions. The means of adjudication, which would constitute such a global community and enable the resolution of conflicts between countries, have not yet been adequately developed as countries are exploring new and better ways of resolving issues that arise in the world community.

What is implied in this chapter regarding the actual unfolding of this process is neither an absolutism of universal rules imposed on others from "on high" nor a relativism of self-enclosed cultural "choices," but rather an open perspectivalism on ongoing dialogue. An emerging consensus regarding international business conduct is coming from a deepening attunement to the concrete sense of shared human existence and the common values contained therein that underlie the welter of cultural differences. This consensus must be "coaxed out of hiding" through ongoing dialogue and an accompanying growth process that allows one to more adequately take the perspective of the other.

As the world moves toward the development of a true international community, there are few benchmarks to use as guides and, hence, the combination of attunement to deeply embedded human value experience and the creative grasp of possibilities for ongoing reconstruction of the organs of adjudication is greatly needed. In this ongoing, experimental process, emerging rules will need to be continually tested for their adequacy in providing guidance in concrete situations, and new problems within concrete contexts will in turn alter the developing rules. Though this process may be slow and difficult, only a world community with its organs for adjudicating the ongoing adjustments between the unique input of individual nations and MNCs and a general other of global proportions can hope to grapple with the kinds of issues that are emerging in the context of the international business scene.

Questions for Discussion

1. What is a multinational corporation? What role do multinationals play in the international economy? What social and political impacts do they have? What public issues arise with respect to multinational corporations?

2. Are there universal ethical principles that apply to the conduct of business in all countries? Or do you want to develop an argument to defend cultural relativism? What does the process approach to ethics have to say about this issue?

3. What do you think of the principles listed in the chapter that came from several international agreements? What would you add to or delete from this list of principles? Do DeGeorge's or Donaldson's suggestions add anything to these considerations?

4. What were foreign payments and for what purposes were they made? Were they really necessary to do business in foreign countries? How did business attempt to defend these payments? Was this defense justified? Why didn't the public accept the "necessity" of such payments? What was the basis for public concern?

5. What form can economic sanctions take? For what purposes are they imposed? Under what conditions are economic sanctions most likely to be effective? What limitations do economic sanctions have as far as achieving political objectives are concerned? What ethical considerations apply?

6. What are global environmental problems and how do they differ from the more traditional environmental problems of air and water pollution? What needs to be done about them in your opinion? What are the ethical dimensions of these problems? Can business solve these problems on its own without international agreements? Why or why not?

Endnotes

[1] H. Hal Mason and Robert S. Spich, *Management: An International Perspective* (Homewood, IL: Irwin, 1987), p. 9.

[2] David H. Blake and Robert S. Walters, *The Politics of Global Economic Relations* (Englewood Cliffs, NJ: Prentice-Hall, 1983), p. 83. See also William J. Holstein, "The Stateless Corporation," *Business Week,* May 14, 1990, pp. 98–105.

[3] Thomas J. Biersteker, *Distortion or Development? Contending Perspectives on the Multinational Corporations* (Cambridge, MA: M.I.T. Press, 1981), p. xii.

[4] The term *transnational corporation* (TNC) is often used to refer to this same entity. See Kwamena Acquaah, *International Regulation of Transnational Corporations: The New Reality* (New York: Praeger, 1986), p. 48.

[5] See William J. Holstein, "Japan's Clout in the U.S.," *Business Week,* July 11, 1988, pp. 64–66.

[6] Acquaah, *International Regulation,* p. 44. As an indication of the power of MNCs, it is useful to note that in 1984, only 25 nations had GNPs greater than the total sales of Exxon, the world's largest MNC, and the total sales of Exxon surpassed the sum of the gross national products of 44 African countries. Donald A. Ball and Wendell H. McColloch, Jr., *International Business: Essentials,* 2nd ed. (Plano, TX: Business Publications, 1985), p. 5.

[7] Holstein, "The Stateless Corporation," p. 99.

[8] Ibid., p. 101.

[9] Ibid., p. 104.

[10] Douglas E. Rosenthal and William M. Knighton, *National Laws and International Commerce: The Problem of Extraterritoriality* (Boston: Routledge & Kegan Paul Ltd., 1982), p. 1.

[11] Acquaah, *International Regulation,* p. xii.

[12] Jack N. Behrman, *Essays on Ethics in Business and the Professions* (Englewood Cliffs, NJ: Prentice-Hall, 1988), pp. 59–60.

[13] Ibid., p. 240.

[14] Holstein, "The Stateless Corporation," p. 99.

[15] Tom L. Beauchamp, *Philosophical Ethics: An Introduction to Moral Philosophy* (New York: McGraw-Hill Book Co., 1982), pp. 34–35.

[16] William C. Frederick, "The Moral Authority of MNC Codes," paper presented at the Conference on Socio-Economics, Harvard Business School, March 31–April 2, 1989, p. 2. See also William C. Frederick, "The Moral Authority of Transnational Corporate Codes," *Journal of Business Ethics,* Vol. 10, no. 2 (1991), pp. 165–177.

[17] Ibid., p. 8.

[18] Richard T. DeGeorge, *Competing with Integrity in International Business* (New York: Oxford, 1993), pp. 19–21.

[19] Ibid., pp. 45–56.

[20] Thomas Donaldson, *The Ethics of International Business* (New York: Oxford University Press, 1989), pp. 80–82.

[21] Behrman, *Essays on Ethics,* p. 111.

[22] Ibid., p. 114.

[23] DeGeorge, *Competing with Integrity,* p. 24. In 1995, the Clinton administration unveiled a voluntary code of principles for U.S. companies operating abroad. Under the code, companies doing business overseas would be expected to recognize the rights of workers to organize, and to not use either forced labor or child labor in the production process. The code also asked companies to report on their activities abroad. The code is strictly voluntary and doesn't contain any enforcement provisions. See Robert S. Greenberger, "Clinton, Retreating From Tough Pledge, To Unveil Code for Businesses Abroad," *The Wall Street Journal,* March 24, 1995, p. A2.

[24] Nicholas Wolfson, U.S. Senate, Committee on Banking, Housing and Urban Affairs, Foreign Corrupt Practices and Domestic and Foreign Investment Disclosure: Hearing on S. 305, 95th Congress, 1st Session, March 16, 1977, p. 215.

[25] Neil H. Jacoby, Peter Nehemkis, and Richard Eells, *Bribery and Extortion in World Business* (New York: Macmillan, 1977), p. 86.

[26] Gordon Adams and Sherri Zann Rosenthal, *The Invisible Hand: Questionable Corporate Payments Overseas* (New York: The Council on Economic Priorities, 1976), p. 3.

[27] Jacoby, Nehemkis, and Eells, *Bribery and Extortion,* p. 127.

[28] Behrman, *Essays on Ethics,* p. 289.

[29] American Bar Association, Committee on Corporate Law and Accounting, "A Guide to the New Section 13(b)(2) Accounting Requirements of the Securities Exchange Act of 1934 (Section 102 of the Foreign Corrupt Practices Act of 1977)," *The Business Lawyer,* Vol. 34, no. 1 (November 1978), p. 308.

[30] Behrman, *Essays on Ethics,* p. 290.

[31] Thomas M. Gladwin and Ingo Walter, *Multinationals Under Fire: Lessons in Management of Conflict* (New York: Wiley, 1980), p. 330.

[32] Ibid., p. 334.

[33] Burton Marcus, *Modern Marketing* (New York: Random House, 1975), p. 55. Quoted with permission.

[34] Vern Terpstra, *International Marketing,* 2nd ed. (Hinsdale, IL: Dryden, 1978), p. 5.

[35] Sidney J. Levy and Gerald Zaltman, *Marketing, Society and Conflict* (Englewood Cliffs, NJ: Prentice-Hall, 1975), p. 113.

[36] Bill McKibben, *The End of Nature* (New York: Random House, 1989), p. 29.

[37] See Carolyn Lochhead, "The Alarming Price Tag on Greenhouse Legislation," *Insight,* April 16, 1990, pp. 10–13.

[38] Carolyn Lochhead, "Global Warming Forecasts May Be Built on Hot Air," *Insight,* April 16, 1990, pp. 14–18.

[39] Mary Beth Regan, "Hot Air on Global Warming," *Business Week,* August 16, 1993, pp. 86–88; "Clinton Postpones Plan to Curb Greenhouse Gas," *Times-Picayune,* August 16, 1993, p. A-3.

[40] Cynthia Pollock Shea, "Protecting the Ozone Layer," *State of the World 1989* (New York: Norton, 1989), p. 82.

[41] McKibben, *The End of Nature,* pp. 39–40.

[42] Ibid., p. 39.

[43] Shea, "Protecting the Ozone Layer," p. 81.

[44] Ibid., pp. 93–94.

[45] Vicky Cahan, "Fixing the Hole Where the Rays Come In," *Business Week,* July 2, 1990, p. 58.

[46] Laurie Hays, "CFC Curb to Save Ozone Will Be Costly," *The Wall Street Journal,* March 28, 1988, p. 5.

[47] Amal Kumar Naj, "As CFC Phase-Out Looms, Doubts on Substitutes Arise," *The Wall Street Journal,* March 6, 1989, p. B4.

[48] G. Tyler Miller, *Living in the Environment,* 6th ed. (Belmont, CA: Wadsworth, 1990), p. 478.

[49] Ibid.

[50] Todd Lewan, "Officials: Waste Producers Dump on Latin America," *Times-Picayune,* December 11, 1990, p. A-17.

[51] Miller, *Living in the Environment,* p. 478.

[52] William H. Lash, III, *NAFTA and the Greening of International Trade Policy* (St. Louis, MO: Washington University Center for the Study of American Business, 1993), pp. 4–13.

[53] Ibid., pp. 6–9.

[54] Bob Davis, "NAFTA Clears Hurdle in Appellate Court, But Faces Tough Battle in Congress," *The Wall Street Journal,* September 27, 1993, p. A3.

[55] Lash, *NAFTA,* pp. 1–4.

Suggested Readings

Acquaah, Kwamena. *International Regulation of Transnational Corporations: The New Reality.* New York: Praeger, 1986.

Anderson, Kim, and Richard Blackhurst, eds. *The Greening of World Trade Issues.* Ann Arbor: University of Michigan Press, 1992.

Anderson, Kim, and Richard Blackhurst, eds. *Regional Integration and the Global Trading System.* New York: St. Martin, 1993.

Anderson, Thomas. *Managing Trade Relations in the New World Economy.* New York: Routledge, 1993.

Berry, Brian J., et al. *The Global Economy: Resource Use, Locational Choice and International Trade.* Englewood Cliffs, NJ: Prentice Hall, 1992.

Bolotin, Fredric N., ed. *International Public Policy Sourcebook.* New York: Greenwood, 1989.

Brewer, Thomas L., ed. *Political Risks in International Business: New Directions for Research, Management, and Public Policy.* New York: Praeger, 1985.

Brittan, Leon. *EC Competition Policy.* New York: Macmillan, 1992.

Corporate Counsel's Guide to International Antitrust Laws. Washington, DC: Business Laws Inc., 1991.

Daoudi, M. S. *Economic Sanctions: Ideals and Experience.* Boston: Routledge & Kegan Paul, 1983.

DeGeorge, Richard T. *Competing with Integrity in International Business.* New York: Oxford, 1993.

Deresky, Helen. *International Management: Managing Across Borders and Cultures.* New York: Harper Collins, 1994.

Dixon, C. J., et al., eds. *Multinational Corporations and the Third World.* New York: Westview, 1986.

Donaldson, Thomas. *The Ethics of International Business.* New York: Oxford University Press, 1989.

Doxey, Margaret P. *International Sanctions in Contemporary Perspective.* Basingstoke, England: Macmillan, 1987.

Doz, Yves L. *Multinational Strategic Management.* New York: Pergamon, 1986.

Doz, Yves L., and C. K. Prahalad. *The Multinational Mission.* New York: Free Press, 1987.

Epstein, Gerald, et al., eds. *Creating a New World Economy.* Philadelphia: Temple University Press, 1993.

Frazer, Tim. *Monopoly Competition and the Law: The Regulation of Business Activity in Britain, Europe and America.* New York: St. Martin, 1988.

Fugate, Wilbur L. *Foreign Commerce and the Antitrust Laws,* 4th ed. Boston: Little Brown, 1990.

Garland, John, and Richard N. Farmer. *International Dimensions of Business Policy and Strategy.* Boston: Kent, 1986.

Gentry, Bradford S. *Global Environmental Issues and International Business.* Washington, DC: BNA, 1990.

Giersch, Herbert. *The World Economy in Perspective.* London: Ashgate Publishers, 1991.

Greanias, George C., and Duane Windsor. *The Foreign Corrupt Practices Act.* Lexington, MA: Lexington Books, 1982.

Grossman, Gene M. *Imperfect Competition and International Trade.* Cambridge, MA: M.I.T. Press, 1992.

Hanson, Gote. *Harmonization and International Trade.* New York: Routledge, 1993.

Hoffman, W. M., et al., eds. *Ethics and the Multinational Enterprise.* Washington, DC: University Press of America, 1985.

Howell, Thomas R., et al., eds. *Conflict Among Nations: Trade Policies in the 1990s.* New York: Westview, 1992.

Hufbauer, Bary Clyde. *Economic Sanctions Reconsidered,* 2nd ed. Washington, DC: Institute for International Economics, 1990.

Hurrell, Andrew, and Benedict Kingsbury, eds. *The International Politics of the Environment.* New York: Oxford University Press, 1992.

Jacoby, Neil H., et al. *Bribery and Extortion in World Business: A Study of Corporate Political Payments Abroad.* New York: Macmillan, 1977.

Kaempfer, William H. *International Economic Sanctions: A Public Choice Perspective.* Boulder, CO: Westview, 1992.

Kennedy, Tom, and Charles E. Simon. *An Examination of Questionable Payments and Practices.* New York: Praeger, 1978.

Kimball, Lee A. *Forging International Agreements: The Role of Institutions in Environment and Development.* Washington, DC: World Resources Institute, 1992.

Kiwaunka, J. L. *Environmental Protection: International Legal Aspects.* New York: Vantage, 1990.

Kline, John M. *International Codes and Multinational Business: Setting Guidelines for International Business Operations.* New York: Quorum, 1985.

Koekkoek, K. A., and L. B. Memmes, eds. *International Trade and Global Development.* New York: Routledge, 1991.

Krugman, Paul. *Rethinking International Trade.* Cambridge, MA: M.I.T. Press, 1990.

Marcus, Alfred A. *Business and Society: Ethics, Government and the World Economy.* Homewood, IL: Irwin, 1992.

Martin, Lisa L. *Coercive Cooperation: Explaining Multilateral Economic Sanction.* Princeton, NJ: Princeton University Press, 1992.

Mason, Hal R., and Robert S. Spich. *Management: An International Perspective.* Homewood, IL: Irwin, 1987.

Mathews, Jessica T., ed. *Preserving the Global Environment: The Challenge of Shared Leadership.* New York: Norton, 1990.

Miller, Morris. *Debt and Environment: Converging Crises.* New York: United Nations, 1991.

Noonan, John Thomas. *Bribes.* New York: Macmillan, 1984.

Oxley, Alan. *The Challenge of Free Trade.* New York: St. Martin, 1990.

Porter, Gareth, and Janet W. Brown. *Global Environmental Politics.* New York: Westview, 1991.

Poynter, Thomas A. *Multinational Enterprises and Government Intervention.* New York: St. Martin, 1985.

Salscuse, Jeswald W. *Making Global Deals: What Every Executive Should Know About Negotiating Abroad.* New York: Random House, 1992.

Scovazzi, Tullio, and Francesco Francioni, eds. *International Responsibility for Environmental Harm.* Netherlands: Kluwer Academic, 1991.

Twomey, Michael J. *Multinational Corporations in the North American Free Trade Association.* New York: Praeger, 1993.

United Nations Centre on Transnational Corporations. *Transnational Corporations in World Development: Third Survey.* New York: United Nations, 1983.

Whalley, John. *The Future of the World Trading System.* Washington, DC: Institute for International Economics, 1993.

SHORT CASES

Nestlé Corporation

Nestlé, a large international conglomerate, was attacked by Ralph Nader, Dr. Benjamin Spock, Cesar Chavez, Gloria Steinem, and by such groups as the United Auto Workers, The National Council of Churches, the World Health Organization, the Infant Formula Action Coalition (INFACT), the Interfaith Center for Corporate Responsibility (ICCR), and a host of other church, health, and international agencies. These individuals and groups claimed that a rising infant mortality rate in Third World nations was due to the aggressive sales promotions of the infant formula companies, which influenced women to switch from traditional breast-feeding methods to the more "modern" idea of bottle-feeding. Their primary target was the Nestlé Company of Switzerland, which accounted for 50 percent of Third World sales of infant formula. The decade-long debate was labeled by the press as "The Infant Formula Controversy" and "The Bottle-Baby Battle." The issues, however, were not merely as simple as "misguided propaganda" over infant formula, but rather a complex interplay of social, political, economic, and cultural factors.

Infant formula is a specially prepared food based on cow's milk for infants under six months old. It is scientifically formulated to approximate the most nearly perfect of foods, human breast milk.[1] A recent decline in breast-feeding throughout the developing world is associated with the increased availability of infant formula and modern baby bottles. The international manufacturers of infant foods and formulas mounted vigorous marketing campaigns in many of these countries making their products available in ever-expanding areas. Because of this effort, many of them were accused of unfair marketing practices by consumer groups and health professionals.

The declining birth rate in industrialized countries, which began in the 1960s, caused all of the infant formula companies concern. They had seen the popularity of formula feeding greatly expand their sales during and after World War II, but in the 1960s their sales began to diminish as the market became saturated. They viewed developing and underdeveloped countries as potential sources of new markets to restore declining sales. Many of these countries had a large portion of their populations suffering from malnutrition, and this, too, encouraged the manufacturers to look to the Third World to revive sales of infant formula.

As reports began to appear that indicated that women in the Third World were beginning to abandon breast-feeding, many health professionals became alarmed because of the widespread lack of basic nutritional knowledge and adequate sanitation in the Third World, two conditions that were necessary to use infant formula safely. It was estimated that only 29 percent of the rural areas and 72 percent of the urban areas in the Third World had potable water for mixing formula or for sanitizing feeding equipment.[2] The lack of sanitation facilities and the absence of clean water would only be remedied with further development.

The lack of education in underdeveloped countries often means that a mother did not properly mix a formula or did not follow correct sanitary procedures. Sometimes a poor family would also stretch the formula by adding additional water. While these practices were not the manufacturer's fault, when consumers do not have even a basic understanding of sanitation and nutrition, and the company is aware of this, it would seem to bear some responsibility to correct these conditions so its product could be used safely and would provide adequate nutrition for children.

Third World countries presented other problems for the infant formula companies. These problems included the relatively high cost of infant formula compared to the average earnings, the frequent lack of refrigeration, inadequate sanitation and impure water, and an uneducated consumer. When questioned about the high cost of their product to Third World consumers, some major manufacturers argued that substitute breast milk was a relatively free good. Although the money required to purchase equipment and formula to feed an infant for six months approximately equaled the per capita income of a person in one of these countries, the companies reasoned that if bottle-feeding allowed the mother to work, the added cost was offset by additional income.[3]

Despite these problems, the infant formula companies mounted aggressive marketing and promotional campaigns in Third World countries. These marketing and promotional practices included extensive mass media advertising; large quantities of free promotional samples to doctors and maternity wards; gifts of equipment, trips, and conferences for medical personnel; and the use of company representatives called "milk nurses" whose jobs entailed promoting and explaining formula feeding to new mothers. Billboards and posters prominently displayed pictures of fat, rosy-cheeked babies, subtly suggesting that the healthiest babies were those fed formula.

As controversy over the marketing of infant formula in Third World countries mounted, manufacturers responded to these concerns in various ways. In 1972 Abbott Laboratories adopted a policy that limited promotion of its product to health professionals and stated that where no health care counseling is available, their product was inappropriate. Other firms suspended marketing of formula in areas where safe potable water or sanitation facilities did not exist. This policy resulted in a careful and costly segmentation of the Third World market as well as the necessity of forgoing many growth opportunities.[4]

By 1977 an organization called the Infant Formula Action Coalition (INFACT) had been formed in Minneapolis to address the problem. This organization attempted to create public awareness and economic pressure through a nationwide boycott of all Nestlé products. Nestlé was chosen because it had the largest share of the world market and also because it was based in Switzerland and could not be pressured through shareholder resolutions in the United States. The boycott, which had the support of the National Council of Churches, had little effect on Nestlé's business, but the antiformula movement did get the attention of some very powerful groups.

To combat the negative image that was developing around the world and to ascertain exactly what its responsibility was, Nestlé initiated the formation of the International Council of Infant Food Industries (ICIFI), a coalition of formula makers, to develop self-regulatory controls for the industry. Abbott Laboratories set up an office to investigate bottle-feeding practices, Borden curtailed all promotional activity of its Klim formula in Third World countries, Abbott Laboratories took its "milk nurses" out of white uniforms, and Bristol Meyers met with church groups to disclaim responsibility for misuse of its products and issued a report of its promotional activities.

In 1977 Nestlé also initiated a public relations campaign to describe to church and community leaders its response to the issue. The company followed this with an announcement in 1978 that it had terminated its advertising and promotion practices in the sale of infant formula to the Third World. Despite Nestlé's initial reluctance to go along with an International Code of Breast Feeding and Infant Formula Marketing adopted by the World Health Organization in 1981, in March 1982 the company announced that it would observe the code. In a further step, Nestlé set up the Infant Formula Audit Commission, composed of doctors, scientists, and church people under the direction of former secretary of state, Edmund Muskie, to monitor its own conduct.

In general, the industry through ICIFI recommendations and the World Health Organization started to "demarket" its products. *Demarketing* means that efforts to sell a product are reduced or stopped completely because of risks to health or safety and is usually initiated because of management decisions, public pressure, or government regulation. Demarketing is ordinarily carried out in declining markets or markets in which a company can no longer compete successfully, but in the developing countries, demarketing decisions were made for growing markets and were contrary to usual business practice.[5]

In January 1984, the groups that had criticized Nestlé's marketing of infant formula in Third World countries finally called off their boycott of Nestlé's products that had been instituted earlier. In negotiations with the Nestlé International Boycott Committee, the company agreed to observe the World Health Organization's marketing code for infant formula.[6] Thus ended a long and bitter controversy that involved numerous stakeholder groups and that received comprehensive coverage in the press. Perhaps Nestlé learned that public opinion and pressure are not to be ignored in setting its policies.

1. What are the ethical issues in this incident? How do these issues affect the economic aspects of the case? What issues were most important in Nestlé's initial policies regarding infant formula?

2. Are the actions of INFACT, the National Council of Churches, and others opposing the actions of Nestlé warranted? What role did these organizations play in resolving issues of this nature?

3. Can a sophisticated consumer product like baby formula be ethically marketed in the social, political, and cultural environment that exists in developing nations? What factors need to be considered in marketing a product of this nature?

4. What can companies like Nestlé learn from this incident? How can they improve their capability to respond to issues of this nature? Would a code of ethics have been helpful in this situation?

[1] James E. Post and Edward Baer, "Demarketing Infant Formula Consumer Products in the Developing World," *Journal of Contemporary Business,* Vol. 7, no. 4, 1978, p. 18.

[2] Ibid., p. 29.

[3] Ibid., p. 19.

[4] David O. Cox, "The Infant Formula Issue: A Case Study," in *Business Environment/Public Policy: The Field and Its Future,* 1981 Conference Papers, ed. by Edwin M. Epstein and Lee E. Preston (St. Louis, MO: American Assembly of Collegiate Schools of Business, 1982), pp. 126–131.

[5] Post and Baer, "Demarketing Infant Formula," p. 23.

[6] "Nestlé Alters Policy on Infant Formula: Boycott Called Off," *Dallas Times Herald,* January 26, 1984, p. A-8.

Source: Rogene A. Buchholz, *Public Policy Issues for Management,* 2nd ed. (Englewood Cliffs, NJ: Prentice Hall, 1992), pp. 323–325.

Dresser Industries

Dresser Industries, Inc., of Dallas, Texas, had agreed in June 1978 to provide to Russia $144 million in technology and equipment related to the construction of a drill-bit plant on the Volga River, 500 miles east of Moscow. This agreement received a validated export license under the Export Administration Act of 1969 as amended in 1977, which provides the president with broad powers to prohibit exports where necessary to further U.S. foreign policy. The act gives the president the power to prohibit the export of goods or technologies that are subject to U.S. jurisdiction or exported by any person subject to

U.S. jurisdiction. The act also allows the president to impose criminal penalties as serious as the extradition and jailing of offending company officials.

To obtain the export license for the drill-bit plant, Dresser had received the approval of all interested governmental departments including the Departments of State, Commerce, Defense, and Energy. But later that same summer, the Carter administration, seeking to express its disapproval of the treatment of Soviet dissidents, considered the cancellation of the Volga River contract as a show of force to promote human rights. Charges were also made by the government that certain equipment in the plant would help the Soviets militarily.

Dresser's reaction was swift and forceful. The chief executive officer of Dresser, John V. James, expressed grave concern over the advisability of using exports as a lever in foreign policy. He pointed out that four federal departments had approved the transaction and that the technology involved was readily available to the Soviets from suppliers outside the United States. James also added that it might be better to assist the Soviet Union to develop its own oil resources rather than face the possibility of a showdown with that nation over the resources of the Middle East.[1] By the end of the summer, the White House announced that upon President Carter's personal review, the sale was approved.

But Dresser's troubles were far from over. Just before leaving office in January 1980, the Carter administration did revoke the license held by Dresser to export oilfield technology to the Soviet Union. All of the equipment had been shipped before the trade embargo was imposed, and all that remained to complete the contract were some training in assembly and operations and some minor revisions to technical data that had already been supplied. A senior vice president for Dresser noted that "As far as the contract was concerned, the effect was insignificant; but the export license cancellation put Dresser in the light of an unethical supplier, and it may serve to threaten foreign trade and undermine our energy and foreign policy interests."[2]

The Carter administration took a hard line toward the Soviet Union because of its invasion of Afghanistan. The administration had earlier prevented the American Olympic team from competing in Moscow in the summer of 1980 because of the Afghanistan incident. The Dresser decision was just the reverse of a decision made by the administration in November that same year. That decision cleared the way for Caterpillar Tractor Corporation to pursue the sale and export of about $79 million in pipeline-laying equipment to the Soviet Union. The administration had apparently approved the Caterpillar deal because it did not involve new technology and because similar equipment was available from U. S. competitors, particularly the Japanese.[3]

In late 1981, a deal was signed by Western European countries and the Soviet Union to build a pipeline to supply Western Europe with gas at stable prices. Many Western European, Japanese, and American companies (with divisions in Europe) hoped to get contracts for the pipe and other necessary hardware. The Western Europeans were anxious to gain access to the 1.4 trillion cubic feet of Russian gas that was expected to flow by the mid-1980s and the expected $11 billion worth of equipment sales that the project would require.[4] The Soviets were expected to take about 85 percent of the gas volume for their own use. The Western European countries supported the project even though they could fill their own energy needs by tapping North Sea gas reserves. However, the new pipeline provided an opportunity for thousands of jobs and contracts, and a source for new energy.

But in June 1982, the Reagan administration placed an embargo on the sale of all equipment destined for use in the construction of the European pipeline because of the martial law imposed by Poland with the support of the Soviet Union. Reagan sided with Defense Secretary Weinberger, and against Secretary of State Haig on the pipeline issue. The president wanted to penalize Russia for its actions in Poland by toughening trade sanctions aimed at blocking construction of the European pipeline.[5] The president later extended the sanctions to apply to European subsidiaries of U. S. firms, which ensured that the Russians would not have access to U. S. technology.

The Reagan administration placed the ban on American and foreign sales for the following reasons: (1) the military rule imposed on Poland, (2) the possibility that our NATO allies could be blackmailed with the threat of a gas cutoff, and (3) the embargo was to curtail the flow of technology to the Soviet Union. President Reagan had earlier warned that stringent action would be taken if the Soviet repression wasn't eased in Poland and if U.S. manufacturers of oil and gas equipment and technology continued to supply Russia. The Western European countries, Great Britain, France, and West Germany opposed the U.S. embargo along with Italy, calling the application of U.S. law outside the United States unacceptable, charging that it amounted to an infringement of national sovereignty.[6]

The Western European countries were very resentful of U.S. interference in their internal affairs. They were acting in the best interests of their economy. The pipeline would create jobs and provide them with a new source of energy. The countries concerned decided to comply with the contracts that they had with the Russians despite Reagan's urging to cancel. The Soviet Union announced that the U.S. embargo instilled a deeper conviction in the Soviet Union to finish the pipeline on time without U.S. technology or equipment. The U.S.-built pipe-laying machines by Caterpillar Tractor Company and gas-pumping turbines built by General Electric would be replaced by equipment built by European, Japanese, or Soviet manufacturers. Great Britain, France, West Germany, and Italy exempted their industrial concerns from having to comply with the U.S. order, and France even went so far as to order its companies to comply with the signed contracts with the Soviets.

The ban on doing business with the Soviets put the European subsidiaries of American firms in somewhat of a dilemma. If they did not complete the Soviet contracts, they could be fined by the European host governments, but at the same time, if they completed the contracts, they would be ignoring the clause in the U.S. contracts that required them to comply with all U.S. export terms, thereby opening themselves to fines in the United States. At the time of the ban, "the restrictions affected Caterpillar Tractor, which had a $90 million contract to provide pipe layers, and General Electric Co., which had contracts to provide $175 million worth of turbine rotors" to their European-affiliated companies.[7] Dresser Industries, Inc., of Dallas was affected because it was to supply compressors through its French subsidiary.

These compressors, valued at $1 million each, were designed to provide pressure to carry natural gas through the Soviet pipeline. Dresser-France was scheduled to deliver three of 21 compressors in July 1982. However, in June the parent company informed the subsidiary not to ship the compressors because of the U.S. sanctions. Dresser obviously intended to fully comply with the U.S. order. Dresser had a management policy that it would abide by the "spirit and letter" of the laws of all countries in which it operates.

On August 24, 1982, Dresser-France was ordered to defy the American embargo and supply the compressors to the Soviet Union by the French Ministry of Research and

Industry. Edward R. Luter, acting as the parent company's spokesperson said, "As an American company we fully intend to obey U.S. law. But it is our position that our French subsidiary is a French company that must obey the laws of that country."[8] Dresser thus found itself caught in the middle of a power play between two nations with dual obligations to abide by conflicting French and American orders. The situation was not resolved until the sanctions were lifted.

1. Should the government have the right to use U.S. trade policy to bring about desired results in foreign policy? Does this usage take foreign trade seriously enough? Should the government have the right to require export trade licenses from American corporations to sell products abroad? If so, on what basis should they be issued?

2. Should the U.S. government be concerned about the sanctity of a contract in international trade? How should this concern be weighed against foreign policy interests? Should the government be responsible for the loss of profits and jobs that may be the result of voiding a contract?

3. Should business lobby for the right to have unrestricted trade policies? How can this be done effectively? How can business take the national interest into account? Should business be concerned about the foreign policy implications of its activities?

4. Are sanctions of this sort ever effective in terms of attaining political objectives? Under what conditions should they be imposed? Where they have not been effective and only hurt American interests, what justification has been offered for their imposition? Is this justification valid?

[1] Darwin Payne, *Initiative in Energy Dresser Industries, Inc.* (New York: Simon & Schuster, 1979), p. 369.

[2] "Dresser Industries Loses License to Export Oil Field Technology to the Soviet Union," *The Wall Street Journal,* December 4, 1980, p. 12.

[3] Ibid.

[4] "A Big Gas Deal Strains U.S. Embargo," *Business Week,* December 15, 1980, p. 40.

[5] "Pipeline Ban: Reagan Digs in His Heels," *U.S. News & World Report,* June 28, 1982, p. 8.

[6] "A Deal in the Pipeline," *Time,* November 22, 1982, p. 77.

[7] "An Anti-U.S.-Backlash Over Russia's Pipeline," *Business Week,* July 5, 1982, p. 21.

[8] Thomas J. Lueck, "Dresser-France, S.A. Ordered to Comply," *The New York Times,* August 24, 1982, p. D1.

Source: Adapted from Rogene A. Buchholz, et al., *Management Response to Public Issues,* 2nd ed. (Englewood Cliffs, NJ: Prentice Hall, 1989), pp. 179–192.

Economic Sanctions

You are the CEO of a company headquartered in the United States that has a rather large investment in the country of Iran. You have a plant there employing several thousand people that has consistently been one of your best profit makers. Your company has seriously considered expanding operations in Iran to take advantage of other profitable opportunities there.

Pressures have been building in the United States, however, to force American companies to disinvest rather than invest in Iran because of its terrorist activities. Your company has always adhered to antiterrorist principles in its hiring of employees and has a good record in this regard. Nonetheless, critics argue that disinvestment and other economic sanctions are the only strategies that will work to change Iran's behavior.

You have mixed feelings about this strategy. Historically, economic sanctions have not worked very well, and it is not at all clear to you that this situation is any different than many others so that there is some hope that sanctions may work and accomplish something constructive. And the moral implications of sanctions bother you as well. Does one sovereign nation have the right to impose its will on another? Should a company be guided in its investment decisions by moral criteria rather than economic criteria?

1. Would disinvestment make a constructive contribution to the resolution of the situation in Iran? Should the company act unilaterally, work through the industry trade group, or promote the development of government policy regarding sanctions that would affect all American firms considering operations in Iran?

2. What are the pros and cons of disinvestment? Assuming the company chooses to stay, what more could it do to promote constructive social change in Iran so that antiterrorist activities are curtailed in a way that does not tear the country apart in the process?

Foreign Payments

You're in an exotic city somewhere in the Middle East, trying hard to sell military equipment to a local government. You've spent months of hard work checking out specifications, figuring costs on various kinds of configurations, and explaining the advantages of your product to the local generals. Now the deal, which will mean millions of dollars in sales for your company and an almost certain promotion for you, is almost closed.

Before closing the deal, however, you are called to the office of the minister of war for the government. Because of a legal technicality, he says he can't award the contract to your company. You walk out of his office not knowing what has happened. An hour later, a general whom you have come to know quite well calls and states that if you donate $500,000 to a local charity, which just happens to have a Swiss bank account, the legal problems can be resolved and you can close the deal tomorrow.

Perhaps in earlier days, a payment to the Swiss bank may have taken care of the situation and no one would have been the wiser. Now, however, the United States has a law making bribery to obtain business illegal, with stiff fines for the executives and individuals involved and up to five years in jail for the executives who carried out such actions. Several companies in your industry have been hauled to Washington recently and confronted by Securities and Exchange Commission lawyers investigating improper payments abroad. Your own company has set up a committee of outside directors who aim to crack down on such payments.

1. What would you do in this situation? How would you feel about being up against foreign competitors for this contract who are not subject to the same public policy restrictions? Is this an unfair situation for American companies?

2. Why do some foreign countries do business in this manner? Is it necessary to adapt to their rules to do business in these countries? What about your own personal integrity and the integrity of American business?

Source: Rogene A. Buchholz, *Business Environment and Public Policy: Implications for Management,* 5th ed. (Englewood Cliffs, NJ: Prentice Hall, 1995), pp. 522–523.

CHAPTER **13**

Business and Consumers

The marketplace where consumer products are sold is a very complex institution. There are, in most instances, many different competing products to choose from and the consumer is confronted by a bewildering array of products promising to do various things. Accurate information about these products is often hard to come by, as advertising does not necessarily provide the kind of information the consumer needs to make an intelligent choice and is more often than not geared to the emotional side of human beings. Consumers are inundated by all sorts of advertising everywhere they look that is trying to persuade them to buy this or that product. Safety is also a major concern in such a complex situation as the average consumer has no way of judging whether or not adequate testing has been done on a product so that it can be purchased with confidence.

In this kind of complex situation, trust forms the basis of successful marketplace transactions and is the most important ethical issue with respect to the marketplace. Consumers must have some basic level of trust that the products they buy are safe to use as directed and will give them the value they expect. They need to have trust in the companies that produce products for the marketplace and in the brands that companies promote. In some sense, the trust that consumers place in products they buy in the marketplace is basic to the continued operation of a free enterprise system and ensures that companies earn a profit on the goods and services they produce. Without that trust, the marketplace would not work very efficiently and consumers would be reluctant to buy the products that are available.

Yet it is obvious that maintenance of this trust is not inherent in the marketplace itself as it is not automatically maintained by the forces of competition. The marketplace has been subjected to all sorts of outside influences over the years that have been geared to establish trust so the marketplace can function effectively. This trust has apparently been violated by business organizations over the years functioning solely in a market context so that the need for these outside influences to protect consumer interests has increased as the marketplace has become more complex. These outside influences, including government and consumer groups or advocates, have generally expressed themselves through a movement called consumerism, which has developed to protect the rights

293

of consumers and provide something of a balance of power between the interests of consumers and business organizations.

> Consumerism is a movement designed to improve the rights and powers of consumers in relation to the sellers of products and services. It is a protest movement of consumers against what they or their advocates see as unfair, discriminatory, and arbitrary treatment. Consumerism is as old as business but has taken on new dimensions and thrusts in recent years. . . . Consumerism does not mean that caveat emptor—let the buyer beware—is replaced by caveat venditor—let the seller beware. It does mean, however, that protecting the consumer is politically acceptable and that the government will survey consumer demands for better treatment and respond to them with new guidelines for and regulations over business.[1]

Government has been concerned about various aspects of the products consumers buy ever since the marketplace has existed. The need for the federal government to protect consumers has deep roots in this country, and the seeds of consumer protection were planted at the turn of the century. Since 1906, with the passage of the original Pure Food and Drug Act, Congress has seen fit to pass consumer protection legislation and establish regulatory agencies and procedures to deal with product-related problems. During the 1960s and 1970s, however, Congress passed more consumer protection legislation than at any time in its history dealing with various aspects of the marketplace. This legislation led to the creation of new regulatory agencies and the addition of new responsibilities to existing agencies. These public policy activities have arisen in areas where there are concerns of consumers that business organizations have not addressed effectively.

There are also many private groups and individuals, generally called consumer advocates, who are concerned about consumer protection and play various roles in the area of consumer protection activities. These groups and individuals raise issues in society with respect to products and services provided by business and work within government to press for more legislation and regulation to address specific issues that affect consumer interests. Some groups are developed to provide consumers with more accurate and unbiased information about the products they are buying. Still others are concerned with educating consumers about the marketplace and helping them make more intelligent purchasing decisions.

Given all this activity by the federal government and consumer advocates, it seems obvious that the idea of consumers' rights being automatically protected by an unregulated marketplace has not worked in our society. If the amount of outside activity in this area of consumer protection is any kind of indication, it would seem that business in a competitive context has not been able to fulfill its moral responsibility for consumer welfare. There have been too many unsafe products sold on the market, too much misleading and deceptive if not fraudulent advertising, and not enough opportunities for consumers to obtain redress and compensation for legitimate grievances and injuries related to products.

The argument for consumer protection measures is based on the view that because sellers in today's marketplace are much more powerful than consumers, some balance of power between consumers and business must be restored by the activities of government and consumer advocates. The marketplace must be augmented by different kinds of consumer protection measures to protect the rights of consumers. From an ethical point of view, a rights-based approach has been taken by government and consumer groups based on the belief that extending rights to consumers and building protection of these rights into the regulatory and legal process will establish trust in the marketplace and enable it to function more effectively than would a completely unregulated market subject to only the forces of competition. This approach both embodies and creates ethical dilemmas as will be seen in an examination of specific issues in the marketplace.

Setting the Moral Context

Because government has become so involved with the moral issues related to protecting consumer and worker rights, the following discussion of specific issues will largely focus on regulatory actions. However, it must be pointed out that the primary interest is not in regulatory actions per se, but in the moral perceptions that guide their development. The goal of the ensuing discussions about specific issues in the marketplace as well as in the following chapters about workplace issues is not to provide answers to the moral dilemmas involved in these issues, but to clarify these issues as much as possible and bring into focus the moral dimensions operative throughout.

In dealing with specific issues in the marketplace and the workplace, it must be remembered that, here as elsewhere, moral development involves an enrichment of the capacity to perceive moral dimensions of situations rather than a way of simplifying how to deal with what one does perceive and put the problem to bed, so to speak. The goal of such a process is not to make the most unequivocal decision, but rather to promote the richest existence for all those involved. Furthermore, the key role legislation plays in these specific issues must not obscure the fact that merely following the laws and regulations that protect consumers and workers does not absolve the corporation of moral responsibility. Legal statutes when at their best embody morality but legality is not the same as morality and it is the moral issues that are the ultimate concern in the following discussion of consumer and workplace issues.

The legal system may seem to provide "cut and dried" answers to some dilemmas; the enacting of a law may seem to stop the process. But laws are continually changing and the process of rethinking laws is an ongoing moral challenge. Laws never exhaust morality, and there is a need for morally responsible decision making not only in determining the direction laws take and revising them as necessary, but there is the need for morally responsible behavior that goes beyond what the law requires.

A moral issue that keeps recurring throughout much of what follows is the issue of rights—individual rights and group rights. The pragmatic perspective on rights developed in Chapter 3 needs to be kept in mind here. As was seen in that chapter, individual rights are not something absolute, such that group rights are an automatic infringement upon one's "natural" freedom. Rights so understood lead to factionalism and relations that are by their very nature adversarial. Rather, rights emerge in the ongoing process of community adjustments, and in the very having of rights one has obligations. Conflicts of rights are themselves founded on shared communication and shared values, no matter how elusive, as the basis for the meaningfulness of the conflicts that emerge.

Furthermore, individual freedom does not lie in opposition to the restrictions of norms and authority, but in a self-direction that requires the proper dynamic interaction of these two poles operative within the self. Finally, it should be remembered that in looking at the tensions between individuals and groups, one is not looking at individuals versus the whole. For the whole is community, and community is a process of ongoing adjustment between the individual and common other or group. The whole must embody the proper relation between the rights of individuals and the rights of the group or common other to function as it should, and thus the good of the whole must be a community that maintains this proper balance. The ongoing tension between individual rights and group rights must be placed in the context of ongoing community adjustments in which the common goal of both the individual and the group is the good of the whole, of the community, of the proper balance between these two poles. It is always from the backdrop of this pragmatic perspective that the discussion of individual and groups rights is intended to proceed.

The Modern Consumer Movement

The modern consumer movement began in 1965 with the publication of Ralph Nader's *Unsafe at Any Speed*, which eventually became a well-known book if not a best-seller. The book was critical about the safety of the Corvair automobile and indicted its producer, General Motors, for a lack of concern about automobile safety. The issue received national attention when it became public knowledge that General Motors had hired private investigators to follow Nader and investigate him while he was a witness for a Senate subcommittee. The president of General Motors, James Roche, apologized to Nader for these actions at a public hearing of the subcommittee. This apology, of course, received national television coverage and was very embarrassing to the company.

Not only did Nader receive instant publicity and notoriety because of this event, he also filed suit against General Motors and eventually settled out of court for $425,000, most of which was used to start his organization. Thus, General Motors ironically helped Nader rise out of obscurity and financed his start in the public interest arena. This is not to suggest that without the General Motors incident a new consumer movement would never have begun. If it had not been Nader and automobile safety, it probably would have been someone else on some other issue.

The time was ripe for a new consumer movement to be concerned with a range of issues that grew out of a highly affluent population, a technologically sophisticated marketplace, and a society that in general had high expectations and aspirations for the fulfillment of higher needs. The complexity of many modern products made it difficult for the average consumer to make a rational choice among products and impossible to repair them when broken. This modern consumer movement had no particular focus, as did the previous movements, but was concerned about a variety of issues related to the marketplace, including product safety, quality of products, reliability and product obsolescence, truth in advertising and packaging, uses of credit, completeness of information, product warranties, product liability, and other issues. This range of issues is exemplified in the consumer legislation that came pouring out of Congress in the latter half of the 1960s and early 1970s to protect consumers in the marketplace.

Not only was Congress active in responding to consumer issues, the executive branch was active as well. President Kennedy delivered a special message to Congress calling for a broad range of legislative and administrative action to assist consumers. Kennedy directed that the Council of Economic Advisers create a Consumer's Advisory Council and that heads of federal agencies concerned with consumer welfare appoint spe-

---

BOX 13-1

The Consumer Bill of Rights

President Kennedy first listed four rights of consumers that he believed needed protection: the right to safety, the right to a choice, the right to know, and the right to be heard. These rights were later supported by Presidents Johnson and Nixon. To these might be added several others of later vintage. Thus, a complete consumer bill of rights contains the following:

1. The Right to Safety: The consumer has a right to be protected from dangerous products that might cause injury or illness and from the thoughtless actions of other consumers.

2. The Right to a Choice: The consumer has the right to be able to select products from a range of alternatives offered by competing firms.

3. The Right to Know: The consumer must have access to readily available, relevant, and accurate information to use in making purchase decisions.

4. The Right to Be Heard: The consumer must be able to find someone who will respond to legitimate complaints about abuses taking place in the market and products that do not meet expectations.

5. The Right to Recourse and Redress: The consumer has a right to expect full compensation for injuries or damages suffered as a result of unsafe products or abuses in the marketplace.

6. The Right to Full Value: The consumer has a right to expect a product to perform as advertised and meet expectations that were created so that full value is received for the money spent.

7. The Right to Education: Consumers must have access to educational programs that help them understand and use the information available in the marketplace to make rational purchase decisions.

8. The Right to Representation and Participation: Consumer interests must be represented on policy-making bodies that deal with issues related to the marketplace.

---

cial assistants to advise them on consumer issues. In addition, Kennedy enunciated what has since come to be called the consumer bill of rights (see box).

While the marketplace is not quite the same as it was in the 1960s when Ralph Nader's book, *Unsafe at Any Speed,* began a new consumer movement, these rights are still the important ones that government and consumer advocates believe need continual protection. There have been several recent concerns that have continued to make the public aware that its interests are at risk and that additional consumer protection measures are necessary to protect these rights. In the late 1980s, consumers were inundated with health claims about various types of foods, which resulted from a change in the rules regulating health claims about products. Thus, consumers were subjected to all sorts of conflicting claims about the health benefits of various foods and had no way of sorting out which claims were true and could be relied upon in making purchase decisions consistent with a healthier diet. All of this hype made government intervention necessary in the form of new food labeling guidelines to provide consumers with accurate and consistent information about fat content and other ingredients so that valid comparisons between foods could be made.

Concern about the environment was another area where companies saw an opportunity to exploit a trend in order to increase market share. Companies advertised their products as photodegradable, ozone friendly, recyclable, and perhaps worst of all, as biodegradable. Anyone who knows anything about landfills knows that such claims were patently false. Most biodegradable products need sunlight to biodegrade, something they never get when buried under tons and tons of other rubbish. Hubert H. Humphrey III, the attorney general of Minnesota, stated that "the selling of the environment could make the oat-bran craze look like a Sunday school picnic."[2] Again, marketers were quick to exploit a trend for purposes of increasing market share rather than to educate the public about the environment. And again, under external pressure, marketers have had to back off from some of these claims and be more honest about their product and its beneficial effects on the environment.

Another concern that has been on the agenda for several decades but that continues to be of concern to consumers and business alike is the area of product liability, where thinking has changed to open up the legal process for more lawsuits to be filed by consumers to obtain compensation for damages they have suffered. Companies are also hit with punitive damages to punish them for alleged transgressions in the marketplace. These damages can sometimes run into the millions of dollars, making product liability a serious concern for business organizations. There have been efforts for several years to pass some kind of federal uniform product liability bill to give business some relief from some of the uncertainties they have to deal with in this situation, but none of these bills have been able to pass Congress because of strong opposition.

The primary source of frustration for many consumers and their advocates in today's marketplace is that there are so many problems they are not able to give them the attention they deserve.[3] As the service economy continues to expand, new problems will appear with respect to the quality of services consumers are receiving and the prices they are paying for these services.[4] And as the environment gets more attention, there will undoubtedly be more efforts to emphasize the sale of ecologically sound products, and consumers will have to sort out legitimate claims from those that are unsound and make unsupported ecological claims.[5] There will thus be a continual need for government, consumer advocates, and business to be concerned about protecting consumer interests to maintain trust in the marketplace and respond to the ethical concerns of consumers in an ever-changing marketplace.

Safety Concerns

There are various strategies that can be pursued to protect the rights of consumers and promote trust in the marketplace. One set of consumer protection strategies is concerned about the safety of products the consumer buys and assumes that business organizations will not address the safety issue adequately if left to their own devices. Advocates of strategies to promote safety believe that today's marketplace is so complex that the individual consumer finds it impossible to collect, evaluate, and understand all the information necessary to make good choices. Many consumers are either ignorant of what is good for them, or too uninformed to make choices consistent with their best interests. They are not capable of protecting themselves. Thus, the consumer is basically helpless when it comes to safety concerns, either subject to corporate power or overwhelmed by the complexities of the marketplace. Help is needed in the form of legislation designed to protect the consumer from unsafe products or fraudulent business practices. Also needed are standards that set at least minimum levels related to the quality or performance of products. Consumer advocates focus their efforts on identifying unsafe products and deceptive practices and initiate appropriate political action through informational and lobbying campaigns directed at various levels of government.

Policy measures based on this philosophy have the advantage of providing protection for all consumers regardless of their access to information about particular products, their ability or willingness to use that information, their financial condition, or other relevant factors. If dangerous products are kept off the market, society does not need to worry about the thoroughness or rationality of particular consumers. These policies have the disadvantage, however, of requiring an intrusion into the free market by placing restrictions on freedom of choice of both business and consumers. The people who draft legislation and set the standards for acceptable products and practices may use different criteria than consumers would use in deciding whether or not to buy a product, and thus the protectors may force values and criteria upon the protected that are not consistent with the latter's actual preferences.

With respect to business and its moral responsibilities for the safety of its products, it must be stressed that merely following the rules is not enough. Regulations may and often do have unrecognized loopholes that allow for endangering activities or products. Corporations specializing in particular areas may also recognize profitable ways to exploit regulations to their own advantage. Companies that are morally sensitive must refrain from taking advantage of these situations and instead see them as something that must be further resolved to protect consumers rather than as something to be exploited for profit. Moral responsibilities, for individuals and corporations alike, extend beyond legal and regulatory demands; they are not determined by these demands.

The corporation is also more than just a passive follower of the rules handed down by the various regulatory agencies involved in consumer protection. The emergence of regulations is the result of a community process of ongoing adjustment among three major participants: the regulatory agencies, consumer advocates, and corporations. If this process is to embody community rather than sheer interest-group factionalism, the corporation's goal cannot be one of minimizing the impact of regulations on its bottom line, but rather its goal must be a moral one of interacting with the other participants to achieve the common goal of consumer protection.

This means, first of all, that the test results a corporation provides about its products must not be skewed toward its own desire to enhance profits. Remembering the intertwining of fact and value, test results need interpretation, and it is all too easy to overinterpret the data to fit values operative either explicitly or implicitly in individuals or corporations. Such overinterpretation, which evolves ever so subtly into falsification, may be done deliberately. But such a process may be operative even when decision makers in corporations think they are impartially collecting and reporting their results. Unless decision makers attempt to bring forth and openly confront the biases operative in their stance, these biases can color and distort what they think is a pure collection of the facts.

These comments also apply, of course, to government agencies as well as consumer advocates, who have their own personal and institutional biases. As will be shown in the following discussion of specific areas of consumer safety, regulatory decisions involve and generate moral dilemmas of their own that must be resolved. There will be disagreement among the participants in the process concerning the direction in which to go when moral dilemmas arise, and there will be disagreement as well on the interpretation and import of some of the data presented to support various positions. It must be remembered, however, that diversity does not negate but rather furthers community as long as such diversity does not dissolve into sheer interest-group factionalism but instead operates within the framework of a common goal, in this case the self-directed evolution of increasing consumer safety protection.

FOOD SAFETY

Consumers are obviously concerned about the safety of the food they eat, and have not been able to rely on business or the marketplace to ensure adequate protection in this area, as a brief review of the history regarding the development of food safety protections will show. In 1906, the first federal food safety law was enacted by Congress. Prior to this time, food manufacturers were permitted to sell adulterated and mislabeled food to consumers. The law was passed because some food packers were putting foreign substances into food in order to make it last longer or increase its bulk so it weighed more.[6] Scandals regarding contaminated and spoiled food contributed to the public outcry, which led to the passage of the Pure Food and Drug Act on June 30, 1906, by the 59th Congress. Its purpose was "to prevent the manufacture, sale, or transport of adulterated, misbranded, poisonous, or deleterious foods, drugs, medicines, and liquors."[7]

The law was renamed the Federal Food, Drug, and Cosmetic Act in the 1938 amendments. This amended law was designed to prohibit the sale of adulterated and mislabeled food, drugs, and cosmetics in interstate commerce. Food was considered to be adulterated if it contained ingredients that made it harmful to the consumer's health, or if a vital ingredient had been left out, or some other ingredient had been substituted.[8] The penalties for violating the law are a fine and imprisonment, and the contaminated articles are liable to be seized. The crime of adulterating food is considered to be a misdemeanor.

In 1958, the act was amended again to deal with food additives, which were being increasingly used in the marketplace. Food additives can be classified into functional groups such as intentional food additives and incidental food additives. Intentional or direct additives are purposely added to food for a specific function such as stabilizers, colors, antioxidants, flavoring compounds, and special sweeteners. Unintentional additives have no purposeful function in food and include those materials added during production, processing, or storage of food, materials from nature, materials in water used for preparing food, and residues of both plant and animal origin.[9]

Prior to the 1958 amendments, producers could sell food that may have been harmful to consumers until an FDA scientist could prove that substances in the food were injurious to public health. To provide stronger protection for consumers, the 1958 food additives amendment contains the Delaney Clause (named after Congressman James Delaney of New York), which specifies that "no additive shall be deemed to be safe if it is found to induce cancer when ingested by man or animals, or if it is found, after tests which are appropriate for the evaluation of the safety of food additives to induce cancer in man or animals."[10] It should be noted that the clause does not apply to carcinogens that occur naturally in foods; it applies only to food additives. Food additives also can include packaging materials that can get into the food.

The Delaney Clause is always interpreted as meaning "zero tolerance" for additives that are discovered to induce cancer in humans or animals; that is, there is no threshold level below which carcinogens are safe. Theoretically, even one molecule could be hazardous. Given that laboratory techniques can now detect the presence of food additives in proportions as tiny as one part per billion, some people believe that almost everything one eats can be shown to contain a confirmed or suspected carcinogen. The Delaney Clause is thus believed to be unnecessarily restrictive because it does not allow for controlled use of a substance or a gradual phasing out of its use, which many believe would be a better way to deal with weak carcinogens.

> Unlike most other regulatory actions, actions initiated by implementation of the Delaney Clause allow for almost no discretion by the FDA. Instead, once a test has shown that an additive causes cancer in any animal (or if a cancer test is simply judged "appropriate"), the FDA must ban the substance. The FDA has no power to determine how great the risk of cancer is, or to compare it to benefits that would be lost if the substance were banned. The ability of the FDA to measure risk is the central issue in the controversy surrounding the Delaney Clause.[11]

Amendments have been proposed to the Delaney Clause that introduce concepts of "significant risk" into the decision-making process. This would change the way the FDA evaluates risk and give the agency some leeway in making decisions about banning food additives. The Hatch-Wampler bill, for example, suggested that suspected carcinogens be assessed for risk to see if they are significant hazards. It also proposed that safety decisions be based on such assessment of risks to humans when the additive is used under normal conditions. The bill proposed the use of an independent group of scientists to help with these decisions.[12] But no matter what changes may eventually be made in the way risk is determined, scientists will continue to raise hard questions about both old and new additives.

The problem of pesticide residues on food and the risks they pose to children has surfaced in recent years. Some studies estimate that by the end of their first year, average children have been exposed to more risk of cancer from pesticides than the EPA states they should get over their entire life span. One particular problem that contributes to this exposure is that legal residues, which are the amounts of pesticides that are allowed to remain in food, are calculated with adults in mind, so that if a child is exposed to this allowable limit, the risk of cancer would be hundreds of times greater than what the EPA considered to be acceptable. Since children's bodies are also smaller, the effect of pesticides on them is likely to be greater. Because of this risk, pressure was brought against the EPA to lower allowable pesticide residues.[13]

A whole new area of concern arose in the early 1990s as bioengineered foods began to appear on the market. Products such as sweeter tomatoes, longer-lasting peppers, leaner pork, and healthier cooking oils, all bioengineered with these characteristics, posed problems for regulators. The biotech industry asked for clarification as to the manner in which food additive regulations would be applied to bioengineered products. The government issued guidelines for these products in May 1992, by stating its concerns extend only to food from plants, and does not affect biotechnology research involving meat, poultry, fish, or dairy products. With regard to plants, the FDA intended to invoke its power to regulate food additives only if a totally new substance was added to the food or if the composition of the food had been altered enough to raise safety concerns. In other words, if a new substance is introduced such as a sweetening agent that did not exist before, or if an existing substance were significantly increased, then marketers must obtain FDA approval. Otherwise, they would be spared from having to obtain approval for each and every genetically engineered product.[14]

Perhaps the most important moral question that underlies all of these regulations is the question of which standards of safety should apply and which risk levels are acceptable. These are ultimately neither legal nor scientific questions but involve the moral dilemma of balancing the desire of individuals and corporations in a free market context for free choice and the collective need for protection when the choices are complex. This situation is further complicated by the fact that free choice in the use of unsafe products can lead to burdens on society such as increases in health care costs. Some states, for example, are currently suing the tobacco companies to recover the increased medical expenses they have incurred that they claim resulted from smoking.

There is no hard-and-fast line to be found that will answer these questions once and for all time. Even though the line has to be drawn some place at any one time, any place it is drawn will generate new dilemmas with new moral dimensions needing resolution. Both regulatory activities and the use of scientific data must be guided by moral perceptions and both are pulled in different directions by these perceptions. Sincere individuals with no hidden agendas may well disagree on where the line should be drawn. Here, as elsewhere, debates involving the moral dimension will not be resolved by abstract principles of individualism and the right of free choice versus abstract principles of the common good and the right to protection. These debates will be resolved by envisioning and evaluating consequences and by remaining attuned to concrete dilemmas as these are worked through in specific problematic contexts. Any resolutions, however, are experimental in nature and must be judged by their workability in terms of promoting food safety and establishing trust in the marketplace.

DRUG REGULATION

In addition to the moral dimensions highlighted thus far in this chapter, the area of drug regulation introduces a unique and pressing moral issue. While it is important for drugs to be safe, it is becoming more and more true that new drugs, though not yet having had the time to pass the various stages in the drug approval process, may have the ability to save the lives of individuals who have no other hope of survival, such as victims of AIDS or cancer. Should it be argued that in these situations individuals have the absolute right to make the decision as to whether or not to take the drug? It will not be available for the public at large; therefore, these drugs can do no harm to others and do not violate any collective rights. Allowing the use of drugs in these cases will not impose an added burden on society, as the burden will in all probability either lessen or remain the same. On the other hand, does society have a moral obligation to prevent the taking of any drug under any circumstances until it has been officially approved?

Again, a line must be drawn somewhere, but the moral issues involved in drawing this line are not the same as those involved in food safety. And again, these decisions cannot be made and continually reevaluated on the basis of absolutely held abstract principles, but must be developed and be continually available for evaluation and revision on the basis of the way the decision works out in concrete cases and the way moral perceptions become more attuned to the various dimensions of the issue as embedded in concrete situations. The following description of drug regulation can be seen as an illustration of the attempt to work various and diverse moral perceptions into the regulatory process.

The FDA's responsibility for drug regulation is carried out by the Bureau of Drugs, which administers rigid premarket testing procedures. No new drug in the country can be marketed until teams of physicians, pharmacists, chemists, and statisticians from the Bureau of Drugs have completed a thorough assessment. Firms wanting to place a new drug on the market must develop data to show that it is safe and effective and must also prove to the bureau's satisfaction that adequate controls are provided to ensure proper identification, quality, purity, and strength of the new drug. The FDA now also requires pharmaceutical companies to monitor usage and side effects of drugs after they have been placed on the market. This procedure will strengthen the FDA's "postmarketing surveillance" system to discover defective products and have them removed from commercial channels and to detect previously unsuspected adverse side effects of drugs.[15]

Critics of drug regulation argue that this process denies Americans the benefit of new drugs that are available in foreign countries with a shorter approval process. Thus, the health of American people is being adversely affected rather than enhanced. The FDA is held to a "substantial evidence" standard in demonstrating that a drug will work before it is allowed on the market. The law defines substantial evidence as "adequate and well-controlled investigations, including clinical investigations, by experts . . . on the basis of which it could fairly and responsibly be concluded by such experts that the drug will have the effect" it claims. This definition leaves the FDA little room to approve drugs that are probably effective and does not allow the agency to consider the needs of patients who have no adequate alternative drugs available.[16]

Proposals are continually being made to speed up the process. Some proposals would give the government power to approve breakthrough drugs before testing on them was completed. This approval could be granted in cases where lack of the drug could result in severe, life-threatening illness. Another proposal would allow approval of certain drugs for limited distribution, say, only from a hospital or from people with special training and experience. Such limits could be used on a drug that otherwise would have been denied approval. Other proposals would permit approval of new drugs based solely on foreign data, if the tests are well conducted and done by recognized researchers. Recent proposals recommended expanding the review process by using private medical staff under contract with the FDA and blending the agency's review standards with those of other developed nations.[17] In 1992, Congress was also considering user fees, by requiring drug makers to pay millions of dollars in fees so the FDA could hire new staff members to cut product review times.[18]

In late 1988, the FDA announced a major revision of the rules for approving drugs developed to treat diseases that are life-threatening or severely debilitating. The early release of experimental drugs to patients in life-threatening situations was also speeded up by the policy change. Approval of the drug AZT used in treating AIDS was completed much more quickly than normal because the agency worked with company researchers on the project and released it for use before it was officially approved for marketing.[19] Other beneficiaries of the policy change were said to be victims of cancer, stroke and heart attacks, Alzheimer's, Parkinson's, blindness, osteoporosis, and rheumatoid arthritis, who would be able to obtain new drugs faster than before.[20]

The need for drug regulation is based on a persistent lack of moral responsibility on the part of some corporations regarding the safety and effectiveness of their product. The consequences of such morally irresponsible behavior are wide ranging as is illustrated in the following story. In 1989, the FDA was hit by a scandal involving generic drugs. Generics are designed to work as effectively as their brand-name counterparts and cost much less; thus, Congress in 1985 made generics more readily available by speeding up the approval process. After the patent on a brand-name product has expired, usually a 17-year period, a pharmaceutical company can replicate the original drug's components, making a generic much less expensive to develop. In order to speed up the approval process, companies need only show the FDA that their generic product is "bioequivalent" to its brand-name counterpart. The FDA is also allowed to rely on the manufacturer's in-house lab tests to establish a product's effectiveness. The temptation to cut corners is strong, since the first companies to gain approval of a new generic drug are likely to capture the largest market share.[21]

After a year-long investigation by the Justice Department and the FDA itself, evidence was uncovered showing that some makers of generic drugs had falsified laboratory test results and then had paid off FDA chemists to gain faster approval for their products. The scandal began to unravel after Mylan Laboratories began to suspect the FDA of favoritism. The company hired its own detectives to spy on the agency, and they uncovered enough evidence to justify an investigation by federal officials.[22]

In response to the scandal, the FDA investigated the nation's 12 leading generic companies for manufacturing and record-keeping irregularities, later expanded to 20 companies, and tested the potency and stability of the 30 top-selling generic products on the market.[23] Problems were found at ten of the 12 firms initially investigated, which raised additional questions about whether the industry can be trusted to supply accurate information to the agency. While five generic companies were accused of submitting false data or substituting brand-name drugs in premarket testing, the investigation turned up no evidence that the drugs were not safe to use as directed.[24]

Some may try to argue that since the drugs were found to be safe, no harmful consequences resulted from falsifying test results. The means justifies the end, and since the end product was safe and inexpensive, it should be on the market. Falsifying the data made the product available to the public much more quickly than would have otherwise been the case, and the public was anxious to have the product. This argument represents a confusion of short-range narrow expediency with long-range, broadly conceived workability as well as an absolute separation of means and ends—problems that were discussed in section one. And the inadequacy of such an argument can be illustrated by a more in-depth look at the consequences involved.

In response to the scandal, the FDA's generic testing division was reorganized and changes were made to the approval process that would undoubtedly raise the cost of generic drugs and lengthen the approval process. Generic drug makers must now show that their versions are equivalent to the brand-name drugs, and regulations of the data used in these studies are much more rigorous. One of the most onerous requirements is specific product manufacturing inspections every time a company seeks approval. These changes have impacted the number of approvals for generic drugs. Before the scandal, the FDA was approving about 40 to 60 applications a month. At the height of the scandal, approvals practically halted. After the scandal passed, approvals averaged 20 to 25 a month. The tightening of regulations also made it difficult for small companies to enter the market, leading to a market dominated by fewer firms where competition was less with smaller cost savings to consumers.[25]

These, then, are the harmful consequences to innocent companies as well as to the public at large. These consequences are the result of stricter drug regulations, but the drug regulations are, in turn, a response to a breakdown of trust in an ongoing community endeavor to provide consumers with safe drugs that are becoming more and more complex with possible harmful side effects. Instances such as these only provide more evidence that companies cannot be trusted, and since consumers cannot evaluate the safety of drugs on their own, more regulation is the only answer. Community endeavor is an ongoing process of communication and adjustment, and in this instance the process was violated.

But the negative consequences of such actions are even more morally insidious. A quote from Dewey introduced in an earlier chapter is relevant here with some adjustment for the context involved. "[This] act is only one of a multitude of acts. If we confine ourselves to the consequences of this one act we shall come out with a poor reckoning. Dispositon is habitual, persistent. It shows itself, therefore, in many acts and in many consequences." An act of falsification "may be judged, for example, by its immediate overt effects," more stringent regulations, fines, and so on; "it may also be judged by its consequences upon character," setting up an enduring disregard for the truth, a persistent and pervasive deceitful way of life, an inability to trust others, and perhaps even a contempt for others. "To take the latter effects into account is equivalent to taking a broad view of future consequences, for these dispositions affect future companionships, vocations and avocations, the whole tenor of domestic and public life."[26] The more deeply one can perceive moral dimensions and moral consequences and the more intimately intertwined one understands the means-end continuum, the more morally developed one becomes.

PRODUCT SAFETY

Product safety represents an area where corporations have more of a direct input into the process of regulation. The standard-setting process in this area is complicated and time-consuming, and hasn't worked out very well in practice. Only a few standards have actually been set and enforced over the many years regulation has been in existence with respect to product safety. The rule-making process is slow and cumbersome, and often results in standards that are very costly to consumers as well as operationally difficult to implement, and thus voluntary standards have been emphasized. This poses both a moral challenge and a moral opportunity for business organizations.

Are companies going to act with moral sensitivity to the possible harm products can cause and develop creative programs that deal with safety concerns and open testing procedures that do not hide adverse results? Are they going to discuss in open dialogue with other interested parties the question of how safe is safe, as risk in this and any other area cannot be reduced to zero, or are they going to exploit this opportunity for their own interests? Consumers must not be exposed to unreasonable risk and companies have a moral responsibility to reduce such risks to protect the consumer.

The Consumer Product Safety Commission (CPSC) was created by the Consumer Product Safety Act of 1972 to protect the public against unreasonable risks of injury associated with a wide range of consumer products. The background of this act was a National Commission study on product safety, which found that 20 million Americans were injured severely enough each year because of product-related accidents to require medical treatment. Some 110,000 of these people were permanently disabled and 30,000 were killed, at a cost to the economy of more than $5.5 billion annually.[27] Thus, a crisis situation was believed to exist that demanded government attention in the form of direct regulation. Business organizations were not paying enough attention to the safety of their products and the marketplace was not providing adequate protection for consumers.

The jurisdiction of the commission covers a broad range of consumer products, including ladders, swings, blenders, televisions, stoves, as well as stairs, ramps, windowsills, doors, and electrical wiring. The only consumer products not covered by the act are foods, drugs, cosmetics, automobiles, firearms, tobacco, boats, pesticides, and aircraft, all of which are regulated by other agencies. The agency was also given responsibility for enforcing specific consumer legislation, including the Flammable Fabrics Act, the Refrigerator Safety Act, the Hazardous Substances Act, and the Poison Prevention Packaging Act.

The CPSC has the authority and responsibility to (1) develop and enforce uniform safety standards governing the design, construction, contents, performance, and labeling of all the consumer products under its jurisdiction; (2) ban consumer products deemed to be hazardous; (3) initiate and monitor recall of hazardous products; (4) help industry develop voluntary safety standards; (5) help consumers evaluate the comparative safety of products; (6) conduct applied research and develop test methods for unsafe products; (7) collect, analyze, and publish injury and hazard data; and (8) help to harmonize federal, state, and local product safety laws and enforcement.

Regarding its enforcement powers, the commission can order a manufacturer, wholesaler, distributor, or retailer to recall, repair, or replace any product that it determines in the course of its research to be unreasonably risky. Where the action is deemed to be justified because of the hazard involved, the commission can simply ban the product from being sold on the market. In addition, the act also requires manufacturers, wholesalers, distributors, or retailers to report within 24 hours the existence of any substantial product hazard that is known. The agency can then demand corrective action including refunds, recalls, dissemination of public hearings, and reimbursement to buyers for expenses they incur in the process. In 1984, the Toy Safety Act was passed, which gave the commission the power to recall dangerous toys from the marketplace much more quickly than before.

The Consumer Product Safety Act constrains the ability of the CPSC to develop its own standards with a requirement that it look for other parties to develop safety standards that deal with the problems the CPSC has identified. The commission can maintain a scrutiny over this process, but its ability to do so is limited by financial and personnel resources. In many cases, it lacks the analytical resources to determine whether a proposed standard will actually solve the problem it has identified. The CPSC is also under a time limit to act within 30 days on a standard proposed by an offeror.[28]

The Consumer Product Safety Amendments of 1981 changed the rule-making procedure of the commission by placing more emphasis on voluntary standards. An advance notice of proposed rule making has to invite the development of a voluntary standard. The commission must then assist industry in developing a voluntary standard, and if it appears likely that this standard will eliminate or adequately reduce the risk of injury and it is likely that there will be substantial compliance with the standard, the CPSC must terminate its mandatory rule-making effort and defer to the voluntary standard. This provision along with other provisions in the amendments severely restricted the agency's rule-making authority, but also provided for more direct input from business organizations.[29]

AUTO SAFETY

Concerns about auto safety have increased over the years as the number of cars on the highway has increased and cars have become ever more powerful and sophisticated. Statistics show that people are much more likely to be injured in an automobile accident than in flying or other forms of transportation. These concerns will only increase as the federal government has recently given states the responsibility for setting their own speed limits. Since this action, at least one state has abolished speed limits entirely and others have raised the limit above what it was previously under federal mandates. Studies show a correlation between speed and number and severity of accidents, so while people may be able to get places faster because of higher speed limits, the risks they face on the highway will also increase.

The National Highway Traffic Safety Administration (NHTSA) was created by the National Highway Traffic and Motor Vehicle Safety Act of 1966 to set safety standards for motor vehicles and motor vehicle equipment. The purpose of the commission is to protect the public from unreasonable risk of injury resulting from the usage of motor vehicles. The Energy Policy and Conservation Act and Clean Air Amendments of 1970 also gave it authority to set standards for fuel economy and emissions. The responsibilities of the agency include setting and enforcing mandatory average fuel economy standards for new motor vehicles, regulating the safety performance of new and used motor vehicles and their equipment, such as tires, and investigating auto safety defects and requiring manufacturers to remedy them.

Regarding safety standards, the agency has focused on problems that statistics show pose the greatest hazards to motorists and pedestrians. In proposing a standard, NHTSA must take into account the number of accidents and injuries that the standard will hopefully reduce, and the practicality and reasonableness of applying the standard under normal conditions. The determination of reasonableness must include consideration of the cost of compliance with the standard. The standard must also either reduce the likelihood of accidents or reduce injuries or death from accidents that do occur.[30]

Manufacturers are required to report defects connected with motor vehicle safety and noncompliance with standards to NHTSA within five days after their discovery. The agency can also conduct independent investigations to discover safety defects and noncompliance with safety standards. If the situation is serious enough, NHTSA can order the manufacturer to engage in a notification and remedy campaign, commonly known as a recall, even for defects not covered by standards. Such recalls have become rather commonplace in the automobile industry. These recalls cover a variety of defects from engine mounts, gas tanks, seat backs, faulty carburetors, transmissions, brakes, and similar problems.[31]

While automakers do extensive testing on the safety of new automobiles, there have been many instances of bumpers that did not give adequate protection to the rest of the automobile, of fuel tanks that were not well enough protected, of automatic transmissions that did not work properly, of tires that did not perform safely, and many other such problems. Business executives who make decisions about safety must keep in mind the concrete consumer who can be seriously if not fatally harmed by an automobile. Abstractions such as benefit-cost analysis or other such quantitative techniques must not get in the way of concern for humans and their well-being.

Advertising and Product Promotion

Those who are opposed to government's making direct decisions related to whether or not products are allowed to be sold on the market often advocate another approach based on the assumption that consumers have the native intelligence and willingness to make sound purchase decisions in their own best interests. However, the nature of today's marketplace with the rapid proliferation of products, the increasingly technical nature of the products, and the confusing way much information about these products is presented by business organizations means that the consumer has to make decisions about products with much less than perfect knowledge.

According to this view, government programs should be aimed at providing consumers with better product information that is consistent and understandable. Consumer advocates should put their efforts into testing products and collecting and disseminating accurate product information to consumers. Business itself should provide more accurate, relevant, and understandable product and product-related information.

Such policies are more consistent with a free market philosophy since they are aimed at making the market work better by providing more perfect information to consumers. Business firms should be more willing to voluntarily undertake programs consistent with this philosophy, thus reducing the need for government intervention. Consumer information programs are usually less costly to implement than other forms of consumer protection measures. Such policies also avoid the problem of restricting consumers' freedom of choice, as instead of taking products off the market or banning them from being sold, these policies ensure that consumers are more fully informed of the potential risks of a particular product, and allow them to make their own choices.

One disadvantage of this approach is that it is often difficult to determine what is accurate and relevant information and in what form it would be most useful to consumers. There are many questions about how sophisticated consumers are in their ability to process information. Another disadvantage of this approach is that it ignores the fact that many consumers seem unwilling or unable to make effective use of the information that is available about products. Environmental factors such as age, education, income level, and occupation affect the ability and willingness to use information. Many products are purchased habitually or routinely on the basis of past learning and brand loyalty. There are costs involved such as time in gathering and using information; it is not a free good to consumers. Many consumers make choices based on more emotional factors, such as convenience, friendliness of personnel, or social status, rather than on more rational factors such as technical product information.

The development of legislation and regulation in the various areas of this section is concerned with providing consumers with accurate and relevant information so they can make informed decisions concerning the products they buy on the marketplace. A company has, of course, a need to present its product in the best light possible, and advertise and promote it in such a way as to convince consumers that it is the product they want rather a competing brand. But at what point does this effort turn into misleading advertising or even outright deception? At what point do certain techniques or strategies, such as using sex to promote products, undermine important values in the society at large?

Companies under pressure to market their products and make a profit are not likely to ask the difficult questions of moral responsibility to consumers, but will tend to slant their advertising and promotion to be more appealing. This effort may be due to an explicit "fudging" of the product's appealing properties, or it may be the result of the values that color the way the facts about the product are perceived. While the latter may seem more morally innocent, the refusal to face up to the hard truth about one's operative values itself involves a moral culpability. One cannot begin to draw the line if there is no awareness that one may be overemphasizing a product's appealing properties.

Moreover, does the company have a responsibility not just to refrain from outright deceptive claims, but also for the way it states the truth? What sense did it make, for example, to consider a can of soda as consisting of two servings? Obviously, it allowed companies to claim less calories per serving, thus appealing to consumers who were becoming more weight conscious. Most consumers drank the whole can and considered this a serving, as this is the way the product is normally used. Thus, they thought they were consuming half the calories that were actually present. Those who paid attention to the calorie content of their food and could thus be misled were precisely those who were concerned about their caloric intake and would probably not buy the product at double the calorie count.

During the health advertising craze, other companies cut the size of their package in half, and then claimed that their new and improved product had half the fat of their previous product. Consumers who were not aware of this fact, and many undoubtedly were not aware, were quite obviously misled even though the company was stating the literal truth. At the time, these practices were not in violation of any laws, but were they morally responsible? The intent of these practices was clearly not to inform the consumer but to sell more product. Such practices are now illegal with the advent of food labeling regulations.

Further questions can be raised as to whether corporations should take some responsibility not just to be truthful and to state the truth in easily understood terms, but also to make and advertise products in a way that will lead consumers toward healthier, more enriching lifestyles that preserve the environment. Developing and advertising products that are good for individuals and good for the environment can create a market for these goods where none existed previously. It may be argued that such concerns are outside the domain of corporate responsibility, but much advertising is directed not merely at maintaining or increasing market share, but in creating a demand for a product. Such extended ethical concerns need not be in conflict with the need to make a profit.

TRUTH IN ADVERTISING

This section as well as the next two sections involve types of moral issues already noted in this chapter, namely, issues of truthfulness and trust in the marketplace. The purpose of advertising is to promote a company's products over those of its competitors in order to gain or maintain market share and create a demand for a product. Advertisements often do not include much information that is useful for making a decision because their primary function is not that of providing unbiased information to consumers. Consumers cannot trust companies to have consumers' interests in mind when devising advertising strategies, and thus a healthy skepticism is called for when trying to judge truth value in advertising. Some advertising where puffery is obvious probably does little or no damage in terms of misleading consumers, but much advertising can be questioned as to its misleading and deceptive character. Advertisements should, of course, not try to mislead or deceive consumers in the process of inducing them to buy the product.

Deception usually involves some form of lying about the product, making claims that have no basis in fact and that cannot be substantiated, while misleading advertising does not necessarily involve outright lying but does involve conveying false impressions about a product.[32] But what constitutes deception and what is misleading are partly in the eye of the beholder, making it difficult to come up with a firm definition of these terms. And society changes with respect to what it will tolerate in advertising as new products and concerns surface.

Concern with advertising is part of the ongoing responsibility of the Federal Trade Commission (FTC) to deal with deceptive acts or practices in commerce. Several strategies have been adopted by the FTC over the years to deal with advertising that was judged to be less than adequate in terms of disclosing information that consumers could trust in making product decisions. Actions were taken to protect the consumers' rights to accurate and relevant information about the products they were buying.

One such strategy was affirmative disclosure, which required companies to tell the whole truth about their product. Nutrient labeling of food products fell under this strategy. The idea was to provide consumers with more information on the theory that more is better. Another strategy adopted by the FTC several years ago was called ad substantiation, which required companies to back up their advertising claims with specific research data filed with the FTC before the ad was made public. The FTC, for example, wanted proof from Ford Motor Company that its LTD model was actually quieter than other cars that were more expensive. Bristol-Myers Co. was ordered to stop claiming its pain relievers were proved superior to similar ones unless it had adequate scientific proof of these claims.[33]

In 1983, the FTC adopted a new rule regarding deceptive advertising that was based on deciding whether or not a "reasonable" consumer would be hurt by the advertisement. The old standard held an ad to be deceptive if it had the capacity or tendency to deceive a substantial number of consumers regardless of their level of sophistication. Further refinements were added in 1984, when the agency announced it would no longer routinely survey entire industries to collect evidence backing advertising claims, and that under some narrow circumstances, it would consider supporting evidence that is gathered after ads have been run.[34]

Another strategy used by the FTC was that of corrective advertising, which was based on certain behavioral assumptions about the effects of advertising on consumers. Merely stopping a deceptive advertisement from being continued may not result in any decrease in the positive attitude that has been built up over time toward the product. Corrective advertising is needed, the FTC argued, to undo some of the positive effects of the ads and restore the market to the condition it was in before the deception took place. Some research on the effects of advertising tended to support these assumptions.[35]

The FTC asked for corrective advertising in such cases as Hi-C Fruit Drink, Profile Bread, Wonder Bread, Domino Sugar, Chevron F-310, and Listerine. In a case involving Hawaiian Punch, the R.J. Reynolds Foods Company was asked to cease and desist alleged misrepresentations and also to disclose the true facts ("guaranteed to contain not less than 10 percent fruit juice") until such time as a substantial proportion of consumers were no longer misled into thinking that Hawaiian Punch contains major amounts of "seven natural fruit juices," that is, until a true process of unlearning, decay, or extinction and relearning successfully occurred. The commission apparently felt that consumers must be carefully exposed to the fact that what they learned earlier was in error, lest they continue to suffer from the misleading effects of that earlier "learning."[36]

FOOD LABELING

In the late 1980s, consumers were inundated with all the hype about oat bran, all-bran cereals, lite foods, and other foods that had certain characteristics that were supposedly going to promote health. Reputable companies such as General Mills and Kellogg's jumped on the bandwagon and made exaggerated claims about what their product would do to promote lower cholesterol levels and reduce the risk of heart attacks, a clear example of ethics sinking to the lowest common denominator. Consumers were legitimately confused about all the health claims and had no way to determine the truth of these advertisements.[37]

This "anything goes" era regarding health advertising began in 1987 when the Food and Drug Administration, under pressure from industry and the Reagan administration, abandoned a 90-year-old rule barring all health assertions about food. Manufacturers were then free to start making claims about what their products would do to prevent disease. Prior to this change, the FDA had said that any product that claimed it could prevent or treat disease had to be considered a drug and be subjected to the high levels of scientific proof needed to declare a drug safe and effective. As a result of this change, 40 percent of new products and a third of the $3.6 billion worth of food advertising in 1989 trumpeted such messages, with manufacturers proclaiming the disease-preventing qualities of items as diverse as fruit juice, breakfast cereal, and margarine.[38]

Undoubtedly, many of these products did have some positive health benefits, but the exaggerated claims and the battle for more market share that took place over oat bran and other health aspects of food products gave marketing a bad image and was misleading to consumers. Finally, under external pressure from consumer groups and government agencies such as the FDA, which began to consider issuing new food labeling guidelines, marketers backed off from some of the exaggerated claims.[39] The controversy over oat bran died down, particularly after an article appeared in the *New England Journal of Medicine*, reporting the results of a study that showed that oat bran has no special power to reduce cholesterol levels.[40]

Controversy erupted again, however, when the FDA pressured Procter & Gamble to stop using the word *fresh* on its orange juice made from concentrate. Federal prosecutors seized 12,000 gallons of the company's Citrus Hill Fresh Choice Label orange juice from a Minneapolis warehouse on the basis that it was mislabeled. The company agreed to stop using the words *fresh choice* in its label and to stop using any phrases that imply or suggest that nothing is added.[41] The FDA also went after companies that were making what were regarded as misleading claims about the benefits of no cholesterol in their products. Such claims would no longer be tolerated in foods that had high fat content because excess fat increases the likelihood of cancer and other diseases. Food manufacturers that only told consumers about cholesterol levels were telling them only half the story.[42]

Finally, the government issued new food labeling rules in late 1992 that would carry out the 1990 Nutrition Labeling and Education Act and apply to all packaged foods the FDA regulates. The rules took effect in 1994 and required all processed foods to show calories, total fat, saturated fat, cholesterol, sodium, carbohydrates, and protein in the context of a daily diet of 2,000 calories and 65 grams of fat. Serving sizes are also uniform and such designations as "low fat," "high fiber" and "light" are based on federally imposed definitions.[43] The intent of the rules is to force food manufacturers to disclose what is in their products in a uniform manner so that shoppers can make valid comparisons. The FDA estimated that it would cost between $1.4 billion and $2.3 billion for the industry to change 250,000 food labels in the U.S. marketplace.[44]

GREEN MARKETING

Similar concerns about truth in advertising appeared in the area of green marketing, which is a response companies have made to an increasing demand for environmentally sensitive products. The products in this so-called green market include biodegradable products, recycled products, more fuel-efficient cars and appliances, products that contain no CFCs, and other products advertised as being environmentally friendly. Consumers are increasingly becoming concerned about the environment, and this concern began showing up in the marketplace as consumers increased their demand for environmentally friendly products.

The biodegradability issue surfaced as many companies began to advertise these features of their products in order to appeal to the emerging green consumer market. Most of these claims were false, as they failed to inform the consumer that biodegradable products need sunlight to decompose, and when buried under tons of other trash and dirt, do not receive sunlight under normal conditions. Thus, the consumer was being misled. Eventually, the public did a 180-degree turn on its thinking about degradability and environmental groups, like the Environmental Defense Fund, called for a consumer boycott of many products that carried such claims. People began to realize that most garbage is sent to covered landfills where the degradation process is limited at best.

Green marketing, while initially appearing to be a new area for marketers to rush into in a competitive race, quickly became more complicated. Consumers wanted to express their concerns about the environment through marketplace behavior, but in the absence of knowledge about the environment, they were easily exploitable and were left without any means to evaluate environmental claims being made by companies. The federal government and the states became increasingly concerned about these claims and began to investigate the advertising and promotional campaigns of several companies in order to prevent the process from getting out of hand.

Eventually, the environmental theme hit a sour note, as consumers began to become more wary about environmental claims and companies began to discard their environmental messages.[45] In late 1990, two reports were issued that indicated environmental claims made by manufacturers were confusing rather than helpful to consumers, and called for the development of national standards. One report urged business to adopt specific and substantive environmental claims backed up by reliable evidence. The report suggested that companies avoid vague phrases such as "environmentally friendly" and clarify whether environmental claims are being made for the package or the product. The term *recycling* also needed to be clarified, as any claims about recyclability were meaningless unless people have access to recycling facilities.[46]

State legislation began to appear, as several states enacted legislation that governed the use of environmental terms. And state attorneys general circulated final recommendations for "responsible environmental advertising" in a separate effort that was geared at least in part to prod the federal government into action, as they wanted to see the FTC or the EPA develop national green marketing standards. These standards are necessary, it was claimed, so that consumers would have the information they need to make purchasing decisions based on environmental considerations.[47] Eventually such standards were developed.

Two private services also developed to evaluate environmental claims and help consumers sort through all the hype by offering environmental seals of approval for products. The Green Cross Certification Company was founded in April 1990 to address the growing confusion over environmental advertising claims in the marketplace. Green Cross certification means that specific environmental claims made about products have been thoroughly checked out, and that these claims meet high standards of performance.[48]

The Green Seal program is led by Earth Day organizer Dennis Hayes, and sought comment from advertisers, consumers, and environmentalists to establish criteria for guidelines for the first five product categories it will approve. These categories included facial tissues, toilet paper, light bulbs, house paint, and laundry detergent. The program intends to use a "modified" life cycle assessment process that measures a product's environmental acceptability from manufacture through disposal.[49]

The debate on national green marketing standards has thus been enjoined. Until definitions and other aspects of the situation are settled, marketers face the challenge of making truthful environmental claims for their own products while wondering if other companies will do the same or engage in questionable advertising practices to gain market share. This is an age-old problem for marketing that appears in all markets, but especially in newly developing ones like environmental marketing. Marketing offers great potential to deal with environmental problems through the market mechanism without a resort to further government regulation. But the consumer needs to develop a trust in what companies claim about their products and companies need to develop a moral sensitivity to the contribution they can make to the environment through responsible green marketing. Regulations and guidelines, no matter how sound, set minimum standards for moral behavior but do not exhaust moral responsibility.

Products Liability

Regardless of how many standards are developed and enforced to ensure that products are safe, and regardless of how much information is made available to consumers, some consumers will continue to be harmed by products and, depending on the circumstances, deserve compensation for the damages they have incurred. Because of the increased technical sophistication of today's products, there is an increased probability that something will go wrong after a purchase is made and use of a product may result in injuries of one sort or another.

Policies that make it easier for consumers to obtain compensation or redress for losses suffered in the marketplace are thus important to consumers. Consumer advocates argue that government should pass legislation or initiate programs designed to make it easier and less costly for consumers to take action and obtain satisfaction for losses and grievances against business organizations. The products liability system should be opened up to be more consumer friendly. Consumer groups can offer the services of people with expertise in dealing with the market and the legal system to advise consumers and advocate the causes in attempting to gain compensation for legitimate harms and losses. Business can set up better systems to handle consumer complaints and inquiries and establish honest and fair methods to settle grievances.

These approaches have the advantage of being realistic about the marketplace and human nature in assuming that risk and fraud will never be completely eliminated from the marketplace. They simply make it easier for consumers to be heard and obtain appropriate compensation and redress for damages and complaints. An obvious disadvantage, of course, is that it is difficult to obtain compensation of any sort if one has been killed by a defective or unsafe product. And if one is injured seriously, compensation will not restore a lost arm, eyesight, or other serious deformity that may have been caused by dangerous or faulty products. Additionally, many people such as the poor, aged, or minorities may not have access to, be aware of, or be capable of taking advantage of such programs to obtain redress for their grievances. Broad exposure and help must be provided to these groups for these approaches to work fairly.

Ethical issues relative to products liability center around the concepts of compensatory and retributive justice. What is an appropriate level of compensation for particular kinds of harm and what kinds of factors should be taken into account? What is a just compensation for the loss of a loved one or the loss of one's health? Should consumers who are harmed through their own negligent use of a product be compensated for that negligence? Should companies be required to pay punitive damages and under what circumstances? How can such damage awards be made consistent and proportional to the wrong committed so that retributive justice is served? Does the area of products liability need reform to give business more defenses? The area of products liability is fraught with ethical issues of this sort even though it is by and large a legal problem. Different perceptions of these issues can be seen as operative in the ongoing evolution of products liability laws.

THE EXTENT OF THE PROBLEM

In 1985, insurance costs more than doubled for 40 percent of U.S. Chamber of Commerce members. About a fourth of these companies experienced price hikes of more than 500 percent. Nearly three companies in 20 could not get any coverage at all, and seven in 20 were considering going without coverage. Only the most bare-bones coverage was available for catastrophic losses such as might occur from a disaster at a chemical plant.[50] While insurance costs have recently stabilized, they have done so at a very high level and many risks are now excluded from coverage. In addition to high insurance premiums, manufacturers and their customers face billions of dollars in additional costs from attorneys' fees, nuisance suits, and unwanted damage awards. Some estimates put the ultimate costs of product liability suits concerning asbestos alone at potentially $40 billion.[51]

While the first million-dollar verdict did not occur until 1962, the average verdict in product liability cases now tops $1 million. There were 474 awards of over $1 million in 1988, an increase from 398 the previous year. Ten juries handed out awards of $25 million or more in 1989, the awards ranging from $25 million to $76 million and totaling $475 million. The largest jury award of 1989 was for a total of $76 million going to two workers who had become ill from exposure to asbestos.[52] In 1993, a $105.2 million award in compensatory and punitive damages went against GM from the death of a teenager whose pickup truck, where the fuel tanks were mounted outside the frame rails thus making it vulnerable to rupture in a collision, burst into flames after a crash. A state court judge refused to reduce the $101 million punitive damage part of this award, but GM believed it had a good chance to reduce the verdict on appeal.[53]

These kinds of awards still give evidence that the liability crisis has not abated. Such giant awards provide a target for plaintiffs and their attorneys to try to attain, and motivate defendants to make high offers to settle out of court rather than take a chance on what a jury might do with the case. Juries are prone to award compensation for nonquantifiable things such as pain and suffering that can amount to a good deal of money, and hand out punitive damage awards that can go far beyond the actual damages incurred.[54] These developments gave rise to a liability crisis in the United States, a crisis that sparked a national campaign against huge damage awards, which was led by insurers, doctors, defense lawyers, and part of the business community. Changes in the liability area have caused manufacturers to abandon products and markets they have spent years in developing, have increased prices because of higher insurance costs, and have hindered product innovation.[55]

CHANGES IN PRODUCTS LIABILITY THINKING

The liability crisis started with a change in legal thinking regarding product liability. This change can be described as a shift from the old rule that manufacturers or sellers are liable for damages only when they have been negligent or unreasonably careless in relation to products or breached an express or implied warranty, to a theory of strict liability, which holds a manufacturer or seller responsible for damages if a consumer is injured as a result of a product defect regardless of the degree of care exercised. This change resulted in more products liability cases being filed because it was easier for consumers to file such suits and gave lawyers new incentives to seek such cases with a higher probability of winning.

Under product liability theory based on negligence, manufacturers would be held liable only if they failed to take reasonable steps to make the product safe for consumers who are likely to use the product. Manufacturers who failed to conform to the reasonable person standard risked liability to plaintiffs who were injured. Under warranty laws, manufacturers were liable for breach of contract. Products were expected to live up to express representations, and an implied warranty existed that the goods were fit for ordinary purposes for which such goods are used.

Under a theory of strict liability, manufacturers can take every precaution in producing and distributing the product, but if it proves defective and injures consumers, they are strictly liable for damages. Thus, the plaintiff's burden in proving a case has been considerably eased and more suits are being filed. Consumers seeking damages need not prove that the manufacturer was negligent or violated an express or implied warranty. All they need prove is that the product caused the injury, and that a defect in design or production made the product unreasonably dangerous. Even negligent use of the product by consumers is not always an effective defense for the manufacturer. Consumers who have improperly used products have nevertheless received sizable awards.

Thus, the courts have expanded liability for insurers by reinterpreting and redefining policy language in insurance contracts, and forcing them to cover risks they never intended to cover and for which they never collected premiums. Once-solid legal principles such as fault, causation, negligence, assumption of risk, and others have been undermined by judges and juries expanding liability for manufacturers. Insurance and manufacturing companies were considered to have "deep pockets" and thus be able to share a greater part of the risk in using products than consumers who are often unable to accurately assess the risk they are taking. The concept of strict liability shifts the cost burden of defective products to manufacturers that are able to recoup losses in the form of higher prices. Ultimately, then, the burden of these added costs is borne by the consumer. Here, as elsewhere, the individual's right to sue has far-reaching consequences for the rights of the group or common other, and a proper balance must be struck.

Punitive damages have received increasing attention in recent years as they have steadily grown in size and frequency along with the litigation explosion. Punitive damages are awarded in civil cases as punishment in the hopes they will deter misconduct. Such damages are awarded in addition to compensatory awards to plaintiffs for loss or injury, and may be awarded in a variety of cases. Over the past several years, many states have set monetary caps on such damages or toughened evidentiary standards for their award. One state even abolished them entirely.[56] The states thus took some action to relieve business from the burden of facing unlimited punitive damage awards from juries prone to believe business needs to be punished for its transgressions and to be sympathetic to plaintiffs.

Almost all the nation's business organizations, the insurance industry, the medical profession, and assorted groups of educators and public officials favor some kind of limitations on damage awards in personal injury suits. On the other side backing the consumer's right to sue is an alliance of personal injury lawyers, labor unions, and consumer and environmental groups.[57] Because of the strength of the opposition, Congress has been unable to pass product liability legislation in over a decade. With the election of the Clinton administration, chances for reform of product liability to make things more favorable to business seemed to fade even further. Measures to restrict punitive damages and awards for pain and suffering were not likely to be high priorities, and plaintiff and consumer groups were gearing up to press for changes that would aid rather than deter the pursuit of personal injury lawsuits.[58]

Modern product liability thinking seems to have made the system into some kind of insurance scheme and has spread the risks associated with products across the entire society. Insurance costs for any injury involving a product are built into its price, and consumers have to buy the insurance without having any choice in the matter. The insurance is said to be very inefficient, however, and comes with high litigation costs. And as some economists point out, the system is very regressive. Everyone pays the same premium in a sense, making higher prices more onerous for low-income consumers, and high-income consumers collect more from jury awards because compensation awards are calculated according to the plaintiff's income.[59] The higher cost of insurance premiums resulting from litigation thus involves moral issues over and above those involved in the higher cost for consumer products and introduces more complexity into the rights of individuals and groups.

Responses to Consumer Rights

Responses to issues involving consumer rights reflect certain assumptions about consumers and the marketplace. Agencies that have the responsibility to approve products before they can be introduced into the marketplace or to develop safety standards for products, or that have the power to ban them from being sold are operating on the basis that consumers are helpless to make these decisions for themselves and these decisions must be made by experts to protect consumers from unsafe products. Efforts to provide more accurate and consistent information to consumers assume that consumers can make intelligent decisions if they are given accurate information in a form that can be understood. And changes in product liability thinking have opened up the legal process so that consumers can obtain compensation more easily for injuries and deaths caused by products whether or not the companies were negligent in their operations.

It seems obvious given all these outside influences that consumers do not trust companies to give adequate consideration to their concerns. How can this trust be established? The rights-based approach as reflected in most of the consumer legislation that has been passed and regulations issued creates problems of its own as can be seen throughout this chapter. Regulators are punished for making the wrong decision about a product that has the potential to harm people; thus, they tend to be conservative in their decision making and err on the side of caution. But business and consumers pay the price if this caution keeps useful and beneficial products off the market. This same caution leads to an overconcern with safety in some instances, forcing design changes in products that are sometimes unreasonable and overly costly to consumers.

To reestablish trust in themselves and in the marketplace, companies must put the consumer first in their considerations when it comes to the products they manufacture, not profits or maximization of shareholder wealth or some other economic consideration. Producing a safe product should be of top priority in the design and manufacturing of a product. And marketing, rather than exploiting an emerging trend to gain more market share, should be concerned to educate consumers and encourage them to develop more healthy eating habits and redirect their consumption into more environmentally friendly products that will truly make a difference with respect to environmental impacts. Companies must take their eyes off the bottom line and be concerned about consumer needs as a first priority. If they are able to do this, the bottom line will most likely take care of itself quite nicely.

The competitive system places limits on the ability of any single company to go very far in this direction. If one company begins to gain a larger market share because of advertising the health benefits of its products in a misleading fashion, other companies will have to engage in the same kind of hype in order to survive in the market. Ethical behavior again has the problem of sinking to the lowest common denominator. Thus, there will always be a need for public policy measures to adjudicate some of the conflicts that arise between the company's need to make a profit and the public's right to be protected from unsafe products and false and misleading advertising.

This is an area where the market process and public policy process interact and complement each other, as both are needed to allow the market to function effectively. Ultimately, however, the public policy process and the market process can only be as good as the moral perceptions that guide them. The ongoing interaction of the market system and public policy must be guided by responsible moral reflection, and the conflicting evaluations of the outcomes of this process in specific instances must be open to dialogue. Moreover, it must be recognized that no matter how well the interactive process is working, the regulations established can never be exhaustive of what constitutes morally responsible behavior.

Questions for Discussion

1. Are you in favor of further government regulation to protect consumers' rights? Why or why not? How would you improve the present regulatory process? Can regulation be avoided by adopting other approaches to consumer protection?

2. What are consumer advocates? What functions do they perform? Whose rights are they protecting? Should they be limited to specific kinds of activities? What strategies do they pursue in order to promote their interests?

3. What are the main ethical issues when it comes to the safety of products? What are the basic issues with respect to food safety that are unresolved? What have been the effects of drug regulation? Why are product safety standards difficult to design and implement? What are the major ethical concerns with regard to automobile safety?

4. What is the purpose of advertising and product promotion? Are changes needed in these activities to make them more ethically acceptable? If so, what changes would you recommend? What implications do your suggestions have for the kind of marketing education you are receiving in a business school?

5. Describe the changes in product liability. What impacts have these changes had on business? What are the reasons for this change in thinking? What responses can management make that are likely to be effective? What reforms do you believe are necessary to make the system more fair to business and consumers?

6. What are the limitations to a rights-based approach to consumer protection? What other approaches could be taken to establish trust in the marketplace? What does the process approach to ethics advocated in this book have to say about consumer issues? What new issues are likely to arise in the consumer area that should be of concern to business? Are we seeing the end of the current consumer movement?

Endnotes

[1] George A. Steiner and John F. Steiner, *Business, Government, and Society: A Managerial Perspective* (New York: Random House, 1980), pp. 273–274. Quoted with permission.

[2] Randolph B. Smith, "Environmentalists, State Officers See Red as Firms Rush to Market Green Products," *The Wall Street Journal,* March 13, 1990, p. B1.

[3] Ibid., pp. 8–9.

[4] See "Pul-eeze! Will Somebody Help Me?", *Time,* February 2, 1987, pp. 48–55. See also William E. Blundell, "When the Patient Takes Charge: The Consumer Movement Comes to Medical Care," *The Wall Street Journal,* April 24, 1987, p. 1-D; Joan Berger, "In the Service Sector, Nothing Is 'Free' Anymore," *Business Week,* June 8, 1987, p. 144.

[5] Francine Schwadel, "Retailers Latch on to the Environment," *The Wall Street Journal,* November 13, 1989, p. B-1.

[6] American Council of Science and Health, *The U.S. Safety Laws: Time for a Change?,* March 1985, p. 5.

[7] *U.S. Statutes at Large,* 1906, 59th Congress, 34:1, p. 768.

[8] *U.S. Statutes at Large,* 1938, 75th Congress, 52:1, p. 1046.

[9] Thomas E. Furia, *Handbook of Food Additives,* The Chemical Rubber Company, 1968, p. 9.

[10] Thomas H. Jukes, "Current Concepts in Nutrition," *Medical Intelligence,* Vol. 297, no. 8 (August 1977), p. 428.

[11] American Council on Science and Health, *The U.S. Food Safety Laws: Time for a Change?,* 1982, p. 7.

[12] Ibid., p. 10.

[13] Sharon Begley, "Better Watch Those Fresh Fruits," *Newsweek,* July 5, 1993, p. 53.

[14] Bruce Ingersoll, "New Policy Eases Market Path for Bioengineered Foods," *The Wall Street Journal,* May 26, 1992, p. B1; Diane Duston, "Food Tests Not Required for Gene-Altered Crops," *Times-Picayune,* May 27, 1992, p. A-4.

[15] "FDA Is Requiring Pharmaceutical Firms to Conduct Postmarketing Drug Survey," *The Wall Street Journal,* January 23, 1980, p. 12.

[16] "Dying for Drugs," *Regulation,* no. 3, 1988, pp. 9–10.

[17] "FDA to Speed Drug Approvals," *Times-Picayune,* November 14, 1991, p. A-10.

[18] Bruce Ingersoll, "Plan to Speed Drug Approvals Clears Congress," *The Wall Street Journal,* October 8, 1992, p. B1.

[19] "FDA to Shorten Testing Stage for Some Drugs," *The Wall Street Journal,* October 20, 1988, p. B-4.

[20] "Finally, the Patients Benefit," *The Wall Street Journal,* October 20, 1988, p. A-16.

[21] Christine Gorman, "A Prescription for Scandal," *Time,* August 28, 1989, p. 56.

[22] Ibid.

[23] Bruce Ingersoll, "FDA Finds Problems at 10 of 12 Firms Being Probed in Generic-Drug Scandal," *The Wall Street Journal,* September 12, 1989, p. A-4.

[24] Bruce Ingersoll, "FDA Says Tests of Generic Drugs Find Only 1.1% Deficient in Safety, Quality," *The Wall Street Journal,* November 20, 1989, p. B-4.

[25] Jyoti Thottam, "Generic-Drug Makers Prepare for Their Next Battle," *The Wall Street Journal,* August 9, 1993, p. B4.

[26] John Dewey, "Human Nature and Conduct," *The Middle Works,* Vol. 14, Jo Ann Boydston, ed. (Carbondale and Edwardsville, IL: University of Southern Illinois Press, 1983), pp. 45, 47.

[27] R. David Pittle, "The Consumer Product Safety Commission," *California Management Review,* Vol. XVIII, no. 4 (Summer 1976), p. 105.

[28] Nina Cornell, Roger Noll, and Barry Weingast, "Safety Regulation," in *Business and Its Environment,* George A. Steiner, ed. (Los Angeles: UCLA Graduate School of Management, 1977), p. 222.

[29] Consumer Product Safety Commission, *1982 Annual Report* (Washington, DC: U.S. Government Printing Office, 1982), p. 4.

[30] John D. Blackburn, Elliot I. Kayman, and Martin H. Malin, *The Legal Environment of Business: Public Law and Regulation* (Homewood, IL: Richard D. Irwin, Inc., 1982), p. 293.

[31] One of the latest incidents involves GM trucks that had fuel tanks mounted outside the underbody framework. In October 1994, the secretary of transportation ruled that the trucks were essentially deathtraps, a ruling that could result in a recall of as many as 6 million vehicles at a cost of some $1.2 billion. Later in the year, however, the secretary agreed to drop the recall in exchange for a contribution of $51.3 million from GM to support safety programs of the agency. See Rich Thomas, "Forget About the Experts," *Newsweek,* October 31, 1994, p. 42; James Bennet, "GM Dodges Recall of Pickups," *Times-Picayune,* December 3, 1994, p. A-1.

[32] Deception is usually believed to involve three conditions: (1) the author of a communication must intend to have the audience believe something false, (2) the author must know it is false, and (3) the author must knowingly do something that will lead the audience to believe the falsehood. See Manuel G. Velasquez, *Business Ethics: Concepts and Cases,* 3rd ed. (Englewood Cliffs, NJ: Prentice Hall, 1992), p. 300. Another definition of deception holds that "deception occurs when a false belief, which an advertisement either creates or takes advantage of, substantially interferes with the ability of people to make rational choices." See John R. Boatright, *Ethics and the Conduct of Business* (Englewood Cliffs, NJ: Prentice Hall, 1993), p. 309.

[33] "FTC Curbs Bristol-Meyers, Sterling Drug on Certain Claims in Pain-Reliever Ads," *The Wall Street Journal,* July 14, 1983, p. 10.

[34] Jeanne Saddler, "FTC Alters Its Policy on Deceptive Ads by 3–2 Vote, Sparks Congressional Outcry," *The Wall Street Journal,* October 24, 1983, p. 47.

[35] See Harold Kassarjian, "Federal Regulation of Advertising," *Business and Its Environment,* George A. Steiner, ed. (Los Angeles: UCLA Graduate School of Management, 1977), pp. 233–255.

[36] "High Court Rejects Warner-Lambert Bid to Review Order to Correct Listerine Ads," *The Wall Street Journal,* April 4, 1978, p. 2.

[37] Zachary Schiller, "The Great American Health Pitch," *Business Week,* October 9, 1989, pp. 115–122.

[38] "Taking a Bite Out of Food Hype," *U.S. News & World Report,* February 19, 1990, p. 12.

[39] Joanne Lipman, "Some Food Marketers May Shelve Outlandish Health Claims," *The Wall Street Journal,* January 29, 1990, p. B1; Richard Gibson, "General Mills Quietly Withdraws Cereal That Sparked Flap Over Health Claims," *The Wall Street Journal,* January 4, 1990, p. A8.

[40] "Hold the Oat Bran," *Time,* January 29, 1990, p. 80; David Stipp, "Oat Bran's Cholesterol Benefits Are Challenged by Study," *The Wall Street Journal,* January 18, 1990, p. B1. Later studies offered some support for the ability of oat bran to lower cholesterol levels. See Jerry E. Bishop, "Quaker Gets Boost for Oat-Bran Line As Study Shows Declines in Cholesterol," *The Wall Street Journal,* April 10, 1991, p. B4; Carole Sugarman, "Oat Bran Has Merit, Study Finds," *Times-Picayune,* June 24, 1992, p. A-2.

[41] "FDA Puts the Squeeze on P&G Over 'Fresh' Labels on Juice," *Times-Picayune,* April 27, 1991, p. C-7. See also Bruce Ingersoll and Alecia Swasy, "FDA Puts Squeeze on P&G Over Citrus Hill Labeling," *The Wall Street Journal,* April 25, 1991, p. B1.

[42] Bruce Ingersoll, "FDA Takes on 'No Cholesterol' Claims," *The Wall Street Journal,* May 15, 1991, p. B1.

[43] Diane Duston, "Food Labels Must Tell All, Stricter U.S. Standards Say," *Times-Picayune,* December 3, 1992, p. A-1.

[44] Richard Gibson, "Label Law Stirs Up Food Companies," *The Wall Street Journal,* June 2, 1993, p. B1.

[45] Randolph B. Smith, "Plastic Bag Makers Discarding Environmental Claims," *The Wall Street Journal,* March 30, 1990, p. B1.

[46] Joann S. Lubin, "Environment Claims Are Sowing More Confusion, 2 Reports Say," *The Wall Street Journal,* November 8, 1990, p. B8.

[47] Jennifer Lawrence and Steven W. Colford, "Green Guidelines Are the Next Step," *Advertising Age,* January 29, 1991, p. 28.

[48] Letter to the author from Mitchell Friedman, Public Relations Manager, Green Cross Certification Company, September 30, 1991.

[49] Laurie Freeman, "Ecology Seals Vie for Approval," *Advertising Age,* January 29, 1991, p. 30.

[50] "The Insurance Crisis: Now Everyone Is in a Risky Business," *Business Week,* March 10, 1986, p. 88.

[51] Milton R. Copulos, "An Rx for the Product Liability Epidemic," *Backgrounder,* The Heritage Foundation, May 15, 1985, p. 1.

[52] Amy Dockser Marcus, "Juries Rule Against 'Tort Reform' with Huge Awards," *The Wall Street Journal,* February 9, 1990, p. B-1.

[53] Milo Geyelin and Neal Templin, "Court Refuses to Lower Punitive Award of $101 Million in GM Truck Fire Case," *The Wall Street Journal,* April 16, 1993, p. A3. Many such appeals are successful. A 1987 study by Rand Corporation found that jury verdicts of $1 million or more were reduced on average by 30 percent, and verdicts of $10 million or more by 40 percent. And 60 percent of the cases examined resulted in reduced awards through settlements. See Amy Dockser Marcus, "Few Large Jury Awards Survive Appeal," *The Wall Street Journal,* January 28, 1991, p. B6.

[54] "Sorry, Your Policy Is Canceled," *Time,* March 24, 1986, p. 20.

[55] A survey of more than 500 chief executives conducted by the Conference Board in 1988 found that four out of ten believed product liability concerns have had a "major impact" on the businesses.

One-third of the firms surveyed had canceled new products because of liability worries, and more than half discontinued existing product lines. Many reported that they had to close plants and lay off workers. And more than one-fifth believed they had lost market share to foreign competition because of increased product liability expenditures. Carolyn Lochhead, "Liability's Creative Clamp Holds Firms to the Status Quo," *Insight,* August 29, 1988, p. 38.

[56] Charlotte Low Allen, "When Awards Become Too Punitive," *Insight,* April 17, 1989, pp. 46–47. Some studies show that punitive awards are not as bad as many believe. In the majority of cases, punitive damage awards are thrown out or reduced by the presiding judge or by an appeals court. Since 1965, the median punitive damage award for all product liability cases actually paid was $625,000, only slightly above the $500,100 median award for compensatory damages. Punitive damages were significantly higher than compensatory damages in only about 25 percent of the cases studied. See Milo Geyelin, "Product Suits Yield Few Punitive Awards," *The Wall Street Journal,* January 6, 1992, p. B1.

[57] Brooks Jackson, "Proposals to Curb Damage Awards in Lawsuits Lead to Flood of Lobbying Efforts on Both Sides," *The Wall Street Journal,* April 9, 1986, p. 56. See also Stephen Wermiel, "Lawyers Reject Damage Award Limits, But Urge Control on Punitive Amounts," *The Wall Street Journal,* February 18, 1987, p. 5.

[58] Milo Geyelin, "Product-Liability Groups Take Up Arms," *The Wall Street Journal,* January 29, 1993, p. B1.

[59] Carolyn Lochhead, "All Are Liable in Product Liability," *Insight,* February 15, 1988, p. 47.

Suggested Readings

Asch, Peter. *Consumer Safety Regulation.* New York: Oxford, 1988.

Bloom, Paul N., and Ruth B. Smith. *The Future of Consumerism.* New York: Lexington Books, 1986.

Brobeck, Stephen. *The Modern Consumer Movement: A Guide to the Sources.* New York: Macmillan, 1990.

Burditt, Michael F., ed. *Product Safety Management and Engineering,* 2nd ed. New York: ASSE, 1993.

Campbell, Colin. *The Romantic Ethic and the Spirit of Modern Consumerism.* New York: Blackwell, 1987.

Epstein, David G., and Steve H. Nickles. *Consumer Law in a Nutshell,* 2nd ed. St. Paul, MN: West, 1991.

Henderson, James A., Jr., and Aaron D. Twerski. *Products Liability: Problems and Process.* Boston: Little-Brown, 1987.

Hunter, Thomas A. *Engineering Design for Safety.* New York: McGraw-Hill, 1992.

Magat, Wesley A., and Kip W. Viscusi. *Informational Approaches to Regulation.* Cambridge: M.I.T. Press, 1991.

Magnuson, Warren G., and Jean Carper. *The Dark Side of the Marketplace.* Englewood Cliffs, NJ: Prentice-Hall, 1968.

Mayer, Robern N. *The Consumer Movement: Guardians of the Marketplace.* New York: Macmillan, 1989.

McGuire, E. Patrick. *The Impact of Product Liability.* New York: Conference Board, 1988.

Nadel, Mark V. *The Politics of Consumer Protection.* Indianapolis, IN: Bobbs-Merrill, 1971.

Nader, Ralph. *Unsafe at Any Speed: The Designed-in Dangers of the American Automobile.* New York: Grossman Publishers, 1972.

Pertschuk, Michael. *Revolt Against Regulation: The Rise and Pause of the Consumer Movement.* Berkeley, CA: University of California Press, 1982.

Ramsay, Iain, ed. *Consumer Law*. New York: New York University Press, 1992.

Shapo, Marshall S. *Law of Products Liability*. New York: Warren Gorham & Lamont, 1987.

Sheldon, Jonathan. *Unfair and Deceptive Acts and Practices,* 3rd ed. Washington, DC: National Consumer Law, 1991.

Silber, Norman I. *Test and Protest: The Influence of Consumers Union*. New York: Holmes & Meier, 1983.

Uusitalo, Lisa. *Environmental Impact of Consumption Patterns*. New York: St. Martin, 1986.

Viscusi, W. Kip. *Product-Risk Labeling: A Federal Responsibility*. Washington, DC: American Enterprise Institute, 1993.

Walz, Michael K., and Barbara M. Killen. *The Law and Economics: Your Rights as a Consumer*. New York: Lerner Publications, 1990.

Weber, Nathan. *Product Liability: The Corporate Response*. New York: Conference Board, 1987.

Weston, Glen E., et al. *Unfair Trade Practices and Consumer Protection,* 5th ed. St. Paul, MN: West, 1992.

S H O R T   C A S E S

The Rely Tampon

Procter & Gamble (P&G) began developing a tampon in 1974 called the Rely tampon. This tampon contained new superabsorbent fibers that were supposedly able to absorb 17 times their own weight in fluid.[1] After test marketing, Rely was introduced nationally in 1979. In less than six months, it had captured an astonishing 20 percent share of the market.[2]

By 1980, Rely had captured a substantial chunk of its two major competitors' market shares. Tampax, the industry leader, went from 52 to 38 percent of the market; and Playtex, owned by Esmark, went from 28 to 24 percent.[3] Industry analysts believed that Rely had the momentum to overtake Tampax. Procter & Gamble was also planning to place the product into foreign distribution.[4]

The $700 million/year tampon industry came under attack, however, when the Centers for Disease Control (CDC) in Atlanta reported in early spring of 1980 that the use of tampons increases the risk of developing a rare disease called toxic shock syndrome. The term *toxic shock syndrome* (TSS) was introduced in 1978 to describe an acute illness whose signs and symptoms include fever, rash, hypertension, involvement of various organ systems, and subsequent peeling of skin, especially on the palms and soles. A strong association had been shown between the occurrence of TSS and the presence of staphylococcus aureus, a bacterial species known to cause various human illnesses.[5] The CDC contended that tampons may act as a breeding ground or as a carrier of bacteria into the vagina. The bacteria causes high fever, vomiting, diarrhea, and skin disorders followed by shock.

Before 1977, all tampon products were made of cotton, rayon, or a blend of the two, according to manufacturers. Beginning in about 1977, tampon manufacturers began to make more absorbent products and to vary the composition of tampons. These new products garnered a substantial share of the market. The finding of an increased association between more highly absorbent tampons and TSS in one study focused interest on the chemical composition of tampons, but the data relating composition to TSS were preliminary.[6]

Procter & Gamble first became aware of toxic shock syndrome in May 1980, when the CDC in Atlanta published its first indication that many new cases of TSS affecting menstruating women were being reported. On June 13, CDC contacted P&G and other major tampon manufacturers requesting data concerning tampon usage. At this time there was no specific information linking TSS to tampon use. Then on June 19, the CDC invited tampon manufacturers to a June 25–26 meeting and asked them to provide market information for further study. After analysis, CDC confirmed that there was a statistical correlation between TSS and tampon use, but the incidence was too low to warn women to stop using tampons. CDC also found no significant link between TSS and any specific brand of tampon.

At this point, P&G started its own study on TSS. Because P&G was prevented by the Federal Privacy Act from getting the names of the women whose cases had been analyzed by the CDC or their doctors, the company had to find its own doctors and case histories and obtain piecemeal information and statistics from state boards of health. Procter & Gamble's study confirmed what the CDC had reported in June. There was no significant link between TSS and any particular brand of tampon, although studies released in June by the state health departments of Wisconsin and Minnesota had shown a statistical link to the Rely tampon.[7]

Meanwhile, the CDC continued studying toxic shock and found that cases reported in July and August did link the Rely tampon to TSS. The findings were announced September 15, 1980. In a sample of 42 women with TSS, 71 percent had used the Rely tampon.[8] A few days later, the Utah Health Department released findings that supported the CDC, and Rely tampon was in trouble.[9]

The September 15 announcement by the CDC brought about a meeting between Procter & Gamble, the Food and Drug Administration (FDA), and CDC officials. (The FDA is the regulatory agency charged with acting on the CDC's findings.) When the meetings first started between Procter & Gamble and the FDA on September 18, P&G had worked up a warning statement that it was willing to put on the Rely package. After the first meeting, however, P&G realized that the FDA wanted much more; it wanted complete withdrawal of the product.

On Sunday, September 21, the Scientific Advisory Group at Procter & Gamble met to review all the available data. The group could not determine that the P&G product, Rely, was more associated with TSS than any other brand, but at the same time, there was not enough evidence for the group to say that the statistical information provided by the government could safely be ignored. Thus, the company decided to pull the product off the shelves.

On September 22, 1980, Procter & Gamble announced to the public that it was withdrawing Rely from the market. The next day, the FDA and P&G drafted a consent agreement under a previously unused provision of the 1976 Medical-Devices Amendment to the Food, Drug, and Cosmetics Act. In it P&G denied that Rely was defective or that the company violated any federal laws. In return, the FDA got P&G to undertake a big advertising campaign warning women not to use Rely and educating people about toxic shock.

The agreement also required P&G to buy back any Rely tampons that consumers still had, including those received as free samples in P&G's $10 million introductory promotion. By September 26, the consent agreement was finalized, and P&G began pulling Rely out of stores.[10]

Procter & Gamble's decision to withdraw Rely was certainly both painful and expensive. The 1982 Annual Report states that a reserve of $75 million after taxes or $0.91 per share was established to cover the one-time loss. The company believed this reserve will cover all costs that may arise from the controversy.[11]

As of March 1982, over 400 lawsuits had been filed against P&G.[12] It may take years before all of these cases come to trial, and it was impossible to predict whether or not Procter & Gamble will be held liable for damages in any of these cases. However, the company thought it likely that its product liability coverage and its $75 million reserve would prevent any seriously adverse effects on the company's operations or on its financial condition.[13]

Edward Harness, P&G's chairman and chief executive at the time, said, "We did the right thing in suspending the brand. I don't think we could have moved any sooner than we did because we couldn't get any data. And we couldn't have moved any slower or else we would have gotten into a blood bath of wholly negative publicity." Owen Butler, P&G's vice chairman, has added, "I think we did what we could with the information we had at the time."[14]

1. Was P&G's reaction to this problem a responsible form of management decision making? Was it a responsible action as far as consumers were concerned? Stockholders? Other stakeholders? Did management act ethically in this situation?

2. What role did the press play in this incident? How can the truth about these situations be discovered and publicized? What problems does business face in getting its story across as far as credibility is concerned?

3. Should products that are suspect be banned or removed from the marketplace? Or should warning labels be required and consumers choose whether or not to use the product based on this information? Should cigarettes be banned? Diet soda? What makes these products different from tampons?

4. What is the appropriate level of risk regarding the use of products? Who should make the decision as to the level of risk to which people should be exposed? What role should government agencies play in this decision? Corporations?

[1] N. Friedman, "A Major Report on Tampon Safety," *Working Woman,* January 1981, p. 58.

[2] "Rely Tampons Recalled by Maker: Linked to Toxic Shock Syndrome," *The New York Times,* September 23, 1980, p. 1.

[3] "Not Relied On," *The Economist,* September 27, 1980, p. 100.

[4] Dean Rotbart and John A. Prestbo, "Killing a Product: Taking Rely Off Market Cost Procter and Gamble a Week of Agonizing," *The Wall Street Journal,* November 3, 1980, p. 1.

[5] Procter & Gamble Company, *1982 Annual Report,* p. 4.

[6] Dean Rotbart and John A. Prestbo, "Procter and Gamble Isn't Ready to Give Up on Tampon Market Despite Rely's Recall," *The Wall Street Journal,* November 5, 1980, p. 4.

[7] Institute of Medicine, *Toxic Shock Syndrome: Assessment of Current Information and Future Research Needs* (Washington, DC: National Academy Press, 1982), p. 51.

[8] Richard Severo, "Rely Tampon Recalled by Maker: Linked to Toxic Shock Syndrome," *The New York Times,* September 23, 1980, p. 1.

[9] "Rely Tampon Could Cost P&G Over $75 Million," *Chemical Week,* October 1, 1980, p. 22.

[10] Rotbart and Prestbo, "Killing a Product," p. 1.

[11] P&G, *1982 Annual Report,* p. 31.

[12] "A Verdict on Tampons," *Time,* March 29, 1982, p. 73.

[13] P&G, *Annual 10K Report,* p. 6.

[14] Rotbart and Prestbo, "Killing A Product," p. 1.

Source: Rogene A. Buchholz, *Public Policy Issues for Management,* 2nd ed. (Englewood Cliffs, NJ: Prentice Hall, 1992), pp. 247–250.

McDonald's Coffee

On the morning of February 27, 1992, Stella Liebeck pulled into a McDonald's in Albuquerque, New Mexico, to order some breakfast and coffee. She had just driven from Santa Fe to drop off her son at the Albuquerque airport, and did not have time to have breakfast at her daughter's house. Stella ordered a Mcbreakfast, and took it and a cup of coffee back to her car that her grandson had parked.

She looked for a place in the car to set the coffee cup down so she could get the top off, but the dash would not hold the cup because it was slanted at too steep an angle and there was no cup holder in her car. Since both hands were busy with the breakfast, she put the cup between her knees and tried to work the top off so she could drink the coffee. After tugging at the top to get it off, it finally came loose, but in the process scalding, 170-degree coffee spilled into her lap. She screamed and tried to get her sweat suit off, but before she could do so, the coffee had burned her skin. Her grandson drove her to the emergency room of the nearest hospital where she was found to have second- and third-degree burns across her buttocks, thighs, and labia.

Stella spent about seven days in the hospital, and about three weeks recuperating at home with her daughter. She was then hospitalized again for skin grafts, which were as painful as the original burns. She lost 20 pounds, which reduced her total weight to 83 pounds, and was practically immobilized. She wrote McDonald's in August suggesting that the company reduce the temperature of the coffee it sells and asking that her out-of-pocket expenses be covered. This amounted to about $2,000 plus the lost wages of her daughter who had to stay at home to attend her mother. She initially wasn't thinking of suing, but when McDonald's offered her only $800, her daughter began to look for an attorney.

She eventually settled for Reed Morgan of Houston, who filed a complaint charging McDonald's with "gross negligence" for selling coffee that was "unreasonably dangerous" and "defectively manufactured." The suit asked for $100,000 in compensatory damages, which included payment for pain and suffering, and triple punitive damages. McDonald's defended the temperature of its coffee, blaming Liebeck for the accident by alleging she was the "proximate cause" of the injury. McDonald's refused a proposed settlement for $300,000 forcing the case to go to trial.

Many of the jurors were annoyed at having to listen to testimony about this case, as they initially thought the whole case was frivolous. After listening to testimony, however, they changed their minds about the case. Witnesses mentioned that despite receiving 700 burn complaints over a ten-year period, the company had not lowered the temperature of its coffee. Experts testified that 170-degree coffee would cause second-degree burns within 3.5 seconds of spilling on a person's skin. McDonald's defense was that its customers wanted it hot, and that Liebeck had only herself to blame because of her unwise action in placing the coffee cup between her knees.

It took the jury only four hours to find in favor of Liebeck, and awarded her $200,000 in compensatory damages, knocking off 20 percent because of her contribution to the accident. Then they awarded $2.7 million in punitive damages in order to get McDonald's attention and motivating it to do something about lowering the temperature of its coffee. The trial judge later reduced the award to $640,000, which was three times the compensatory damages. After further skirmishing after the trial, the case was settled out of court, with both sides keeping the final amount of the settlement secret.

The case became a *cause célèbre* for those politicians concerned with reforming the tort system. It made several television shows and became the subject of jokes by Jay Leno. Reformers had an example they could point to as evidence that the courts had gone crazy and that the system was at fault. The American Tort Reform Association used the case as its key example of an "outrageous" lawsuit. The association was able to make its case by citing the headlines but giving none of the details. In response, Liebeck and her family of self-described conservative Republicans delivered a statement at a Public Citizens press conference defending the award.

1. Is this case really so outrageous once the details are known? Was the award fair as far as the plaintiff was concerned? Did she deserve compensatory damages, especially for pain and suffering? Who was at fault in this situation?

2. What do you think of punitive damages? Are they a reasonable and fair manner to punish corporations for wrongdoings and force them to change their behavior? Do you think limits ought to be put on these kinds of damage awards?

Source: Information for this case came from Aric Press, "Are Lawyers Burning America?" *Newsweek,* March 20, 1995, pp. 32–35.

Product Liability

Acme International, a large toy manufacturer, has developed a new toy for children ages 4–10 that promises to be an excellent seller. Already the company has received a number of large orders from toy stores and shipment of a considerable consignment is planned for September 1 in anticipation of the Christmas shopping season. On August 25, management learned that one of the machines used to produce the toy had developed a problem with the result that several days' production worth about $100,000 was left with a slight burr on the side of each toy. The burr could be dangerous to a child who handled the toy roughly. The loss from abandoning the marred toys would include not only the $100,000 but also buyer ill-will from not being able to deliver the toys on time. Repairing the toys was impossible. Acme International was proud of its reputation for manufacturing safe toys. It also was dependent on good Christmas sales to close out the year on a profitable note for shareholders.

1. What are the responsibilities of the company to its various stakeholders? In view of these responsibilities, what should the company do in this situation?

2. What are the ethical issues in this kind of situation? How shall management analyze these issues in making a decision? What kind of decision would be in the best interests of the company? Of society?

Source: Rogene A. Buchholz, *Business Environment and Public Policy: Implications for Management,* 5th ed. (Englewood Cliffs, NJ: Prentice Hall, 1995), pp. 411–412.

Food Safety

The Eat-Well Food Company has a reputation for producing safe food for consumption. It has never in its history used a food additive that, when used in one of its food products, caused a safety problem. Even before the FDA regulations on food safety went into effect, the company had a reputation for safety and demonstrated a concern for consumer health.

While just plain good luck may be a factor, the main reason for such a record seems to be the company's extensive testing program. The company has always had an elaborate testing program, utilizing animals for testing food additives whose health effects are unknown. The company used various means to introduce these substances into animals and various dosage levels to show what effects might develop. It always erred on the side of caution, preferring not to introduce a new additive if there were any doubts about its safety as shown in the animal tests.

While animal testing is expensive and time-consuming, the company nonetheless thought the time and expense were worth the effort. Thus, the company has used many animals in its testing laboratories over the years. Recently, the demand for more animals has increased along with the increase in food additives that need to be tested.

However, animal rights activists have begun to raise questions about the use of animals for testing purposes. These groups have begun to criticize companies like Eat-Well for using animals so extensively and for mistreating them during the testing process. They have taken their case to the press and have begun to raise the issue at the annual meetings of some corporations. Some of these groups are also beginning to pressure their state and national politicians for legislative action on this issue.

1. What can companies such as Eat-Well do to deal with this issue? What political strategies should Eat-Well adopt that may contribute to the successful resolution of this issue?

2. What rights do animals have in our society? How should these rights be balanced against the rights of consumers for safe products? Are there any alternatives to animal testing that are likely to work as effectively?

Source: Rogene A. Buchholz, *Business Environment and Public Policy: Implications for Management,* 5th ed. (Englewood Cliffs, NJ: Prentice Hall, 1995), p. 412.

CHAPTER **14**

The Changing Workplace

Many changes have occurred in the workplace over the years as employees and employers have developed new relationships that reflect changing interests and concerns. Changes have taken place relative to the place of work in people's lives and the way in which they understand this activity. These changes are basic to people's attitudes toward work and the workplace and are reflected in the policies of private and public institutions. New institutions have been developed to deal with these changing interests and new forms of public policy have appeared to address particular concerns of employees and society. One of these changes involved the rise of labor unions to look after the interests of employees, an institution that is currently in decline and being replaced by the notion of employee rights contained in public policies of one sort or another. Related to these changes is the way in which the contract between employers and employees is changing with respect to a changing workplace.

The Changing Nature of Work

The notion of what work means and how work is defined has undergone major changes throughout history. To the ancient Greeks, work was a curse to be avoided if at all possible. It was seen as a burdensome task that brutalized the mind and made people unfit for the thinking of truth or the practicing of virtue.[1] The elite of Greek society, in their search for a changeless vision, avoided such effort. By the time the Greek city-states were established, the free citizen had managed to escape all need to labor, as all work in the city-states was performed by slaves, serfs, or outlander noncitizens. Thus, it was easy to see how Greek thought developed the conception that work was inherently servile and degrading.[2]

The ancient Hebrews saw work as a punishment for sin—an activity that resulted from the fall of Adam in the Garden of Eden, which was a universal symbol for the fall of mankind. The world was a workhouse where man might atone for the sin of his ancestors and cooperate with God in working to save the world. Primitive Christianity followed the same line of thought but added one positive note—work was necessary to share the things produced with one's needy brothers.[3]

During the Renaissance, work began to be viewed more positively and became the means whereby man could glorify himself and discover his own powers. People began to revolt against the idea that it was sinful to obtain satisfaction from human achievements. Human accomplishment began to be viewed as worthwhile when it gave pleasure—as essential to human well-being as the need for salvation. Craftmanship and technical processes became more gratifying and intrinsically meaningful. The sense of achievement was awakened as an important need during this period.[4]

The industrial revolution built on this notion of achievement as it was expressed in the work ethic tradition, which largely came from the Protestant Reformation and the doctrines contained in particular denominations such as Lutheranism and Calvinism. Work became the most important activity in a person's life and was seen as something good in itself that bestows dignity on a person; it is a vocation that demands one's best efforts and dedication. Individual members of the society were credited or blamed for their own circumstances according to the degree of their prosperity. By working hard, a person was supposed to be able to overcome every obstacle that life presents and make his or her own way in the world. Success was thus directly linked to one's own efforts and the material wealth a person accumulated was a measure of how much effort he or she expended. Thrift was an important value in this tradition along with a capacity for deferring immediate gratification, a kind of worldly asceticism. Wealth should be wisely invested to earn still greater returns and not foolishly spent on personal consumption.

The work ethic was particularly relevant to the early stages of industrialization when jobs were largely mundane and sometimes difficult to perform and when there was a need to build up a capital base of factories and technology utilizing the savings of the society. As industrial societies advance, technology eliminates some of the hardest and most physically demanding kinds of work, and many people are able to find greater personal fulfillment in the jobs they perform. Consumption is also encouraged so that the system can be maintained. The increasing affluence of society means that people have more leisure time to spend doing something other than working. Thus, there have been changes in the way work is understood in our society just as there have been changes in the notion of deferred gratification related to consumption activities.

With the growth of large corporate organizations, something called an organizational ethic began to evolve. This understanding of work was particularly relevant during the 1950s when there was a good deal of literature dealing with the organization man syndrome.[5] The pressures of society began to build against those of the individual, and this was true of the workplace along with life in general as conformity and regimentation became important values. Some of the major propositions of the organizational ethic included a belief in the group as the source of creativity and a belief in belongingness as the ultimate need of the individual. There were books written about the other-directed individual where conformity to group norms became of paramount importance.[6] It became more important, according to some commentators, for the individual to integrate well with his or her peers in the organization than to stand out for personal excellence or superiority. Dependence became a major virtue to be extolled and the independent person became the social isolate who failed to integrate successfully with the group. The dependent person found fulfillment in a sense of belongingness and togetherness with other members of the group.

Thus, work takes on meaning only as it affects the group or the organization, and group or organizational effort is what is valued rather than individual effort. Work is not so much an end in itself as it was in the work ethic, but is more of a means valued largely for the way in which it serves group interests and contributes to one's success in the organization. Success is not directly connected with one's own individual effort, but is much more dependent on the group or organization and how one is able to "fit in" and conform to the existing values and standards of the group or organization. One thus finds identity and meaning by being an IBM man, for example, and identifies with that culture rather than being concerned about individuality and uniqueness.

As society became more affluent and people came to have more leisure time, another view of work emerged to challenge traditional understandings of work and legitimate leisure activities. Thus, a so-called leisure ethic developed, which holds that work has no meaning in itself. Work cannot be made meaningful or fulfilling but is a necessary evil to produce needed goods and services and enable one to earn the money to buy them. Human fulfillment is found in leisure activities where one has a choice regarding the use of one's time and can find pleasure in pursuing activities of interest to one personally. These leisure activities allow a person to be creative and involved. Thus, the fewer hours one can spend working and the more leisure time available, the better. Consistent with this thinking is the development of a large leisure industry in our society to exploit this trend toward more leisure.

Perhaps the most serious challenge to the traditional understanding of work was presented by the humanistic understanding of work, a development that began with the human potentials movement. A humanistic understanding of work centers on the possibility of making work meaningful and fulfilling for individuals. The workplace can be organized, according to this ethic, to allow for human growth and development. This is a more important concern than anything else having to do with the workplace. The focus of humanistic concern is on the self rather than on the work itself, the group or organization in which one functions, or on the leisure activities one pursues. Work is not only an inescapable necessity for most people but also involves a liberation from nature and the creation of a social and independent being. Through work, people come to know themselves and their powers.[7]

The humanistic school is troubled by development and growth of the self in an industrial environment that emphasizes output and productivity rather than human growth and development. These priorities can and must be changed, say the humanists, to allow people to become self-actualized in work and reach higher stages of development than fulfillment of mere material or lower-order needs.[8] Work is to be taken seriously as the way in which people discover themselves and fulfill themselves as human beings. Technology and the workplace must be redesigned to serve people's needs for growth and development. The organization is necessary to provide the setting in which people work, but it is not an end in itself. Hard work is not valued for its own sake but valued in terms of what it contributes to personal development. Leisure is acceptable, but not as a replacement for the fulfillment that work can provide.

All these understandings of work and its place in life are being challenged by current changes in the workplace. Rapid change has become the order of the day because of global competition and rapidly developing technology. Lifetime employment is becoming a thing of the past and job security is a major concern for workers. Terms like *mobility, empowerment, teams, virtual offices, telecommuting, reengineering, restructuring, delayering, outsourcing,* and *contingency* are new buzzwords.[9] Companies have downsized by laying off many workers and eliminating layers of middle management. Firms have restructured by forming teams and empowering these teams with authority to get the work done. They have outsourced many departments in order to escape paying benefits to full-time employees. Many offices are virtually empty, and employees spend their time mainly in the field.

The last decade, some commentators believe, has produced a profound redefinition of the way we work, perhaps more than at any other time since the advent of mass production.[10] Instead of lifelong employment, the emphasis is on lifelong employability. While employers have an obligation to provide opportunity for self-improvement, employees have to take charge of their own careers and can no longer rely on a secure place in the organization. They must continually acquire new skills to keep up with the development of new technologies. Employees are expected to share responsibility for their employment and in many places are gaining greater control over what they do in the workplace.

The divide between those with more skills and those with fewer has dramatically widened. Forecasts indicate that the future holds more of the same, as the demand for professional, managerial, and technical skills that pay high wages is expected to increase, while the demand for crafts jobs and those of operators and laborers is expected to decrease.[11] Those who know how to process information and make decisions will be in demand, as changes in information technology make more information available to those close to the customer. Organizations need fewer people and those who get jobs must be better trained and equipped for the twenty-first century.

Fully a quarter of all those employed work on a part-time or contract basis. The number of part-time workers grew by 2.2 million from 1973 to 1994, and this is believed to be almost entirely because of necessity, not because people choose to work part time.[12] Such a contingent work force is much more flexible as far as the corporation is concerned. When business falls off, the temporary workers go first, being much easier to cut than a full-time work force. The virtual corporation is composed of transitory teams of people who deal with other transitory teams.

These changes are weakening and even breaking the traditional bonds between employers and employees, and among employees themselves. The nonmaterial rewards that come from collegeality and commonality of interest are diminishing. The intangible values that come from work—a sense of community, the shared goals of employees and employers, the exchange of ideas in the workplace, and a sense of achievement—are said to be disappearing.[13] What will take their place is anybody's guess, but it is clear that many of the traditional understandings of work mentioned earlier may no longer be relevant in this kind of world. These changes raise many ethical questions that will be mentioned in the following sections.

Collective Bargaining and Employee Rights

All of these changes have had implications for unions and the protection of employee rights in the workplace. As industrialization took hold in this country, workers found that the market system was unable to address many of the problems they were experiencing in the workplace, including long hours, poor working conditions, low wages, and arbitrary hiring and firing practices. To deal with these problems, they began to form unions to counter the power of management with an organized labor movement. Before the depression of 1929, however, management held an overwhelming advantage over the formation of unions. Companies could fire workers for joining unions, force them to sign a pledge not to join a union as a condition of employment, require them to belong to company unions, and spy on them to stop unionization before it started. The courts upheld the right of employers to do almost anything to prevent unionism from developing. Thus, the attempt to form unions without government help was not very successful, and before the depression, workers' interest in unionism was declining.

The National Industrial Recovery Act (NIRA) rekindled interest in unionism. The NIRA authorized businesses to form trade associations to regulate production, and a few union leaders insisted that the bill also give employees the right to organize and bargain collectively. With the support of government policy and with job security at the forefront of workers' concerns because of the depression, labor leaders found it easier to organize segments of the labor force. When the NIRA was found unconstitutional in 1935, a more comprehensive labor relations law called the Wagner Act was passed. This act not only extended the right to organize and bargain collectively to workers, it also proscribed employer actions that interfered with that right, and established the National Labor Relations Board as the enforcement mechanism. After World War II, two additional laws were passed to amend certain provisions of the Wagner Act, namely the Taft-Hartley Act of 1947 and the Landrum-Griffin Act of 1959. These laws created the framework of rules that governs labor-management relations today.

Labor unions grew in size and influence in society for several decades, and several significant strikes were held by major unions that had the effect of crippling the American economy. Unions were a force to be reckoned with and won major benefits for their members in confrontations with management. During a 40-year period (1935–1975) unions grew in numbers and bargaining power with employers. A key factor that stimulated union growth at the beginning of this period was, of course, the Wagner Act, which established the right of labor to organize unions and bargain collectively as a matter of public policy. For much of this period, the U.S. economy was relatively closed as far as the rest of the world was concerned because its traditional competitors were rebuilding and the developing nations were not yet ready to compete effectively. Thus, union demands were strong and employer resistance weak for several years, which favored the growth of unions.[14]

Total union membership grew from 4 million in 1935 to 23 million in 1976. As a proportion of nonagricultural employment, union membership rose from 13 percent in 1935 to a peak of 35 percent in 1954, followed by a slow decline to 29 percent in 1975. Unions won most of their organizing elections and won most of their big strikes. They elected more and more of their chosen candidates to federal, state, and local political offices and became the dominant community organization in many localities.[15]

The consequence of this union strength was high wage and benefit costs relative to the rest of the world, especially developing nations. Industry also found itself saddled with many uneconomic work rules, overmanning, slow work paces, and limitations on overtime. These increasing production costs went into rising domestic prices as productivity gains slowed, making U.S. industry vulnerable to new forms of competition from abroad. A union mentality became deep-rooted, contributing to an ongoing adversarial relationship with management.

There are many ethical issues connected with union activity. One of the major issues concerns the nature of unionism. It is a collective activity, and as such can interfere with the operation of a corporation. In some sense, it constitutes a restraint on trade, as collective bargaining agreements interfere with the ability of individual employers to establish wages and other working conditions. Thus, unions had to seek and eventually win an exemption from the antitrust laws. They cannot be taken to court under these laws as posing a violation because they restrain trade and commerce. Is such an exemption ethical? What is the proper balance between employee rights as expressed through union activity and the rights of employers to run their organization?

Strikes, particularly in key industries such as transportation, have an effect on consumers. They are not able to get the products they need or travel as they wish if strikes have shut down an industry or particular companies. Is it ethical for unions to hold consumers or the public at large hostage in order to obtain their goals of higher wages and better working conditions? Is the adversarial relation that usually exists between unions and employers healthy and of long-run benefit to the society? In some industries, this adversarial relationship disappeared as companies adopted an "enlightened" attitude toward unions and tried to avoid strikes by largely adhering to union demands, knowing that the added costs could be passed on to consumers. Is this fair to consumers and were they in some sense victims of the system of collective bargaining?

Should employees in the public sector have the right to strike? Is it ethical for firefighters and police to go on strike and deprive the public of the essential protections these employees provide? Does the right to strike in this case give public employees an unfair advantage that can be exploited to the detriment of the public at large? If they don't have the right to strike, what kind of bargaining power do they have? Are they then at the mercy of public administrators and the public who may not want to vote for increases in taxes or fund bond proposals to provide money for increased wages and better working conditions?

Other ethical issues have to do with breaking picket lines and the hiring of nonunion employees to keep the company going during a strike. There is also the issue of the rights of individual employees who don't want to join unions. For many years, nonunion employees benefited from union activity in receiving higher wages than they would have gotten in the absence of unions without having to pay union dues and otherwise support union activities from which they benefited. Is this fair? Is it right that employees working on public projects receive union wages, or should the Davis-Bacon Act, which makes this a legal requirement, be repealed?

Throughout the whole history of unionism, rights have been at the center of controversy and have often involved intense factionalism: the rights of union workers versus the rights of management, the rights of unions versus the rights of society, the rights of union workers versus the rights of nonunion workers. The intensity of this factionalism has manifested itself in violent situations that have occurred from time to time as rights of labor and management have been asserted. In many, if not most, cases the process has moved these interrelationships away from any sense of community.

Perhaps at least in part because of this factionalism, labor unions have declined as a dominant force in American society. Since about 1975, the balance of power in collective bargaining has been shifting back to management. Unions have been declining in numbers and bargaining power over this period of time. Labor lawyer Steven Early states that the labor movement is in its worst slump since the 1920s, as the forces of foreign competition, capital flight, nonunion competition, and deregulation have weakened traditional union strongholds.[16]

Between 1975 and 1980, it began to become apparent that labor-management relations were undergoing significant changes. These changes were accelerated with the election of the Reagan administration, which took a strong antiunion stance. Labor unions and management found themselves subject to new forms of competition. One form of this competition was domestic, involving the penetration of domestic markets by nonunion companies. Within certain industries, this penetration was spectacular. The second form of new competition was the increasing penetration of U.S. markets by foreign producers.

These new forms of competition forced management of highly unionized industries to search for new options to reduce the high costs of unionism. New strategies were called for if unionized companies were going to be able to survive in competition with nonunionized companies in this country and with lower-priced goods from abroad. These new options that management adopted included (1) importing parts or assemblies from lower-cost facilities abroad, (2) building new plants in nonunion communities, (3) developing a nonunion division to compete with union divisions within the same company, (4) ceasing union operations at the end of a contract period and opening up nonunion operations, (5) holding the line on existing wages in present collective bargaining contracts but establishing a two-tier wage and salary structure to pay new workers lower wages than present employees, (6) automating and robotizing existing facilities as rapidly as possible so as to change production from labor-intensive to capital-intensive technology, (7) starting up new facilities with personnel policies designed to keep unions out, such as greater worker participation, employee stock ownership, and similar measures, and (8) selling the plant to workers under an employee stock ownership plan (ESOP) if the union refused to make concessions.[17]

One of the more morally controversial options used by management to cope with the high costs of unionism was to declare bankruptcy and then reorganize as a nonunion company. This option was used by several airline companies as the usual pattern of collective bargaining caused severe problems in the newly deregulated areas of transportation, such as airline and bus transportation. Airline pilots earning six-figure salaries contributed to the financial problems experienced by some airlines. In the past, high wages and costly restrictive work rules negotiated as part of the labor contract with the airline company could simply be passed on to the consumer because of the regulated nature of the airline industry. With the advent of deregulation, this option was no longer available. Some remedy was thus needed, but was the unilateral action taken by these corporations a morally responsible action? Perhaps a better reconstruction of the problem situation could have been developed.

The combination of a changing economic environment, the use of new management options to reduce the high costs of unionism, and an administration that was anything but supportive of union growth combined in the 1980s to create a difficult time for unions. Annual wage gains achieved by unions in negotiations in 1983 and 1984 were reduced to around 3.5 percent compared with an expected rise of 4.8 percent in the cost of living for 1985 and a 4.4 percent gain in wages and salaries for the nonunion sector of the work force.[18]

Many of labor's automatic cost-of-living clauses were dropped or modified. Industrywide bargaining and pattern bargaining were broken. Overall union membership declined from a peak of 23 million in 1976 to around 18–19 million. Union membership as a segment of nonagricultural employment declined from a peak of 35 percent in 1954 to about 19 percent in 1984, the lowest in nearly half a century. Public approval of unions also declined as many citizens blamed union demands for the failure of many U.S. companies to survive foreign competition.[19]

These trends continued, as in 1991, only 16.1 percent of the work force was organized, and that number was continuing to fall. In 1993, fewer than 4 million workdays were lost to strikes and lockouts, the lowest figure in the 47 years that the government has been keeping such statistics.[20] While there was some increase of union activity in 1994, the resurgence of management strength in collective bargaining is likely to continue, at least in the immediate future. There will most likely be no more big wage and benefit increases that can automatically be passed on to consumers, and throughout most of the 1980s, blue-collar wages trailed inflation partly because unions represented fewer workers.[21]

Do the decline of unions and the demise of collective bargaining as a means of gaining concessions from employers mean that workers' rights are not being respected? Not necessarily, as the courts and state legislators in particular are becoming the most effective champions of employee rights in today's nonunion climate. Many states have laws protecting whistle-blowers, right-to-know laws that require employers to identify hazardous substances used on the job, and laws restricting the ability of companies to close plants for economic reasons. Other states have made it illegal for companies to force retirement at any age, and some have taken steps to modify the employment-at-will doctrine.[22]

Couple these new directions with federal laws related to employee rights that have been in existence for several years and it seems clear the collective bargaining system that has dominated employee relations for several decades is being replaced by a web of public policy measures that involves governments at many levels imposing substantive terms on the conditions of employment. Thus, companies will not be able to return to employee practices of the 1940s and 1950s as the threat of collective bargaining and union organizing diminishes.

The notion of employee rights is firmly embedded in American society and has found its way into numerous public policy measures that restrict management's ability to deal with employees in any manner they desire.[23] These rights include the right to a safe workplace, the right to deal with family interests, the right of equal opportunity in the workplace, and several other rights of interest from an ethical point of view. Questions can be asked as to whether or not this change is in the long-run interests of society. Collective bargaining at least involved labor and management in face-to-face relations. Is the use of government as an adjudicating mechanism and the passage of more laws and regulations a good substitute? Does this development mark a turn away from factionalism?

The Family-Friendly Corporation

One kind of newly emerging right in the workplace involves the relation of the corporation to the family. This issue is broader than the relation of the corporation to its workers, for it involves the very fabric of our society and the recognition that the family represents the most critical unit of society. Without time for and recognition of parenting as the key nurturing force in society, we are faced with the potential disintegration of our social fabric.[24] But the key question is how far can companies go in terms of this recognition and still remain viable economic entities? How much responsibility do they have from a moral point of view to change their practices and policies to be more family friendly, and how much from a more practical point of view can they actually do to mitigate their impact on family life?

The traditional approach that the corporation has taken to the family is largely to ignore it, expecting the family to make the adjustments necessary for corporate careers. The family had to move whenever the employee was asked to move, to adapt to changing work schedules, and to cope with increased demands for travel. This arrangement was more or less satisfactory when the male was the sole wage earner and the wife was by and large in charge of the household and raising the children. But such a relationship is no longer satisfactory when both parents may be working or where single parents are involved.

In 1940, only 8.6 percent of women with children worked outside the home, and many of these jobs did not involve corporations. By 1988, 55 percent of American women were already in the work force, holding 44 percent of all available jobs. Some 80 percent of these women were of childbearing age, and 41 percent of married working women had husbands who earned less than $15,000 per year. By the year 2000, it is expected that 85 percent of new work force entrants will be women, minorities, and immigrants.[25] These figures give some idea of the changes in the workplace taking place with regard to composition of the work force. These changes have implications for a change in the way corporations relate to the family.

A family-friendly corporation can be defined as an organization that acts on its responsibilities to provide employees with the means to manage the conflicting demands between work and family. Creating a family-friendly workplace involves recognition of a responsibility to help employees meet the needs of their families, commitment from the highest levels of management, development and implementation of strategies to help employees meet these conflicting demands, and continuing support from the company for these efforts. The commitment to be more family friendly must be more than just a one-time program or fanfare event.

There are many types of programs that companies have adopted in some form to help employees take care of family needs. One type of program is flextime where employees can work the same number of hours but determine their starting and stopping times with a range of parameters. A typical program allows a two-hour differential, where employees can have a two-hour leeway regarding starting and stopping times, meaning all employees will be on duty for at least six hours, making a core time when they can interrelate as needed. Given this flexibility, one parent can then come to work late if he or she needs to take children to school before coming to work, and another parent can take off work early to get the children from school. There are many other examples where this arrangement allows parents more flexibility to meet family needs.

Part-time work or job sharing is another program or strategy that can help parents meet family needs. Part-time work may give parents some days off during the week to take care of family responsibilities and is consistent with the needs of corporations mentioned earlier. The problem with this approach is that benefits and vacation do not usually go with part-time jobs. Job sharing involves two people doing essentially the same job so that each one gets some time off during the week. The critical element in this strategy is that the job itself must be of such a nature that two people can switch into and out of the job without a great deal of disruption for the organization.

The provision of on-site or near-site day care centers is of obvious benefit to single parents but can also be of use to two-parent families when both are working. If these child care centers are of high quality, their provision will obviously give parents a great deal of security that their children are getting good care, and save them the trouble of arranging for their own care at home. Having the children in close proximity also gives them the opportunity to see them at lunchtime and quickly respond to emergencies. Some studies suggested that the availability or nonavailability of quality child care was a paramount factor for women in the choice of jobs and careers.[26]

Providing time off when employees need it is another strategy that can work effectively. If employees can take time off when a child is sick or when an aged parent needs some special attention, this can be of great help and comfort to employees who have these responsibilities. This privilege must not be abused, however, and without an extensive system of checking up on employees, it is subject to being abused. Such abuse on the part of irresponsible employees will only hurt all employees, particularly those who are responsible and only ask for such time off for legitimate reasons.

Using compressed work schedules is another strategy that involves giving workers a choice over the length of their workweek. Instead of working the traditional five 8-hour days, employees can choose to work four 10-hour days instead, and even in some cases, three 12-hour days. Such a compressed workweek leaves more time to spend with children or care for aged parents. Some companies allow employees to bid on these compressed schedules based on seniority in order to allocate these schedules on some kind of a fair basis.[27]

Finally, family leave policies are another strategy that has much to benefit employees. Most such policies initially took the form of parental leave referring to the time a parent takes away from work to be with a child after birth, adoption, or serious illness. Before family leave was mandated by the government, such policies varied a great deal from company to company, with some organizations providing no form of paternal leave, while others provided only maternity leave based on the disability portion of childbearing. Still others expanded parental leave to family leave, which included taking time off to care for family members other than a child. Some companies granted such leave to men as well as women, and eventually an appeals court ruling stated that any employer with 15 or more workers must provide a man with unpaid child-rearing leave if that benefit is offered to female workers.[28] Thus, company policies varied with regard to salary continuation, coverage, duration, and job protection measures.[29]

With the passage of the Family Leave Act of 1993, companies with 50 or more employees are required to grant full-time employees the right to take up to 12 weeks of unpaid leave a year for specific family and medical reasons. During that time, the employer must continue to pay for the employee's health, dental, and optical insurance, and at the end of the leave, the employer is required to reinstate the employee to the same job or an equivalent one.[30] There are several conditions that apply to the implementation of this law; for example, a person qualifies for a leave if he or she requires hospital care or continuing medical treatment for such illnesses as morning sickness, prenatal care, and recovery from childbirth. If a person is ill or needs to care for a seriously ill family member, all 12 weeks do not have to be taken at once. If a husband and wife work at the same company, they are each granted 12 weeks off to take care of a sick child, but in the case of birth, adoption, or care of an elderly family member, a total of 12 weeks is granted between the two spouses.[31]

Family-friendly policies can help employees resolve the conflict between work and family, but they also can cause other problems. Among small businesses in particular, they can breed resentment in workers who have to pick up the slack. Are such policies fair to employees who do not have families? Many companies can ill afford such policies and are cutting core benefits such as health insurance and pensions in an era of global competition. But many companies have found that helping employees resolve work and family conflict boosts morale and increases productivity. Thus, there can be a positive bottom-line impact when companies have programs that are well conceived and implemented and are geared to employee needs rather than organizational rigidities. There is a need for experimentation in this area to find other ways of meeting the needs of employees and society.

The Changing Social Contract

Changes in the nature of work and in the role of labor unions have resulted in changes in the contract between employees and the corporation. By and large the old contract held that employees had obligations related to satisfactory attendance at work, acceptable levels of effort and performance, and loyalty to the corporation and management. In return for these commitments, employers provided fair pay and fringe benefits that were competitive, the chance for advancement based on seniority and merit, and some degree of job security. While job security was never really explicitly guaranteed in labor contracts, it was implied.[32]

As job security has evaporated because of restructuring, downsizing, and other changes in the workplace, so too have prospects for advancement and predictable wage and benefit increases. Management demands for individual commitment and responsibility have largely taken their place. They want the survivors to buy into long-term visions of the company and be committed to corporate goals while at the same time expecting them to cope with an ever present threat of termination. Such changes seem to be one-sided and certainly have implications for employee loyalty and other obligations employees had to employers. The old contract has collapsed and a new one has not yet emerged.

These changes have obviously affected worker morale and attitudes toward jobs and the company. Pollster Daniel Yankelovich has identified five patterns of employee response to the changing workplace. These include (1) employees no longer believe that their job is for life, (2) they no longer believe in employer loyalty and concern, (3) they are losing confidence that they will be rewarded for learning and expanding their skills, (4) they are beginning to equate the corporate emphasis on quality with downsizing, and (5) work has become a less reliable source of satisfaction and of rewards other than money.[33]

Yankelovich goes on to say that the current wave of restructuring, reengineering, and the use of total quality management (TQM) as a way to cut jobs has violated, or threatens to violate, the unwritten contract between employees and the corporation. Once the unwritten contract is violated, the whole relationship is put at risk with unpredictable results. Furthermore, the effects of downsizing are distributed bimodally. Top executives are well rewarded and are given generous job security provisions when companies merge or jobs are eliminated, while middle managers and clerical and production workers face much greater uncertainty.[34]

The forces driving these changes in the workplace, such as global competition and rapid technological change, will continue for the foreseeable future, making further restructurings and downsizings necessary. The foundations of the old social contract will continue to erode, making it increasingly clear that the old social contract cannot be preserved or reestablished. The question then becomes what kind of a new contract will emerge that will be satisfactory to both parties and yet deal with these new realities of the workplace. What moral issues do these changes raise with respect to the relationship between employees and employers? Do companies have a moral responsibility to provide at least some degree of job security for their employees? Can the system function effectively if employee trust and loyalty disappear and responsibility for the employee's well-being is no longer a corporate concern?

The Clinton administration has taken the position that training is a large part of the answer, and has redefined job security as employment security. It has indicated that workers will not accept changes that come from trade agreements, productivity gains, or technological advances unless they are confident they can get new jobs and thus benefit from the changes. Employment security has been defined as having skills and benefits that are portable. The administration has been largely unsuccessful in getting any new government-run training programs through Congress, and thus has indicated that it is the responsibility of employers to provide the training necessary to keep workers employable. But it also has passed new benefit mandates such as the Family and Medical Leave Act and proposed compulsory employer-provided universal health care coverage, adding to an already long list of employee rights protected by federal laws and regulations.

There are some benefits to this emphasis on employment security rather than job security. What employees need in this kind of society is opportunity rather than security, but they must have the skills to take advantage of the opportunities that come along. This calls for continual growth on the part of employees, a willingness to learn new skills, an emphasis on continual learning and creativity, and an openness to change. Security in a given job or company can lead to stultification and boredom and create a work force that is resistant to change. On the other hand, an opportunity society can degenerate into a free-for-all where it's every man for himself and the devil take the hindmost. No matter what kind of a new contract eventually evolves between employees and employers, there is a need for trust and responsibility.

Unions, particularly the AFL-CIO, have taken a position on this issue of a new contract between employees and the corporation. A report issued by its Committee on the Evolution of Work criticized management by stating the current efforts related to work reform have amounted to little more than attempts to make workers feel good and work harder. The report acknowledges that distrust between labor and management is endemic to the old system, and that any new contract can function effectively only if these deep suspicions are replaced by mutual respect. In order to present something specific and positive, the report presents five principles for a new system of work organization.[35]

- Rejection of the traditional dichotomy between thinking and doing, conception and execution. This process requires a fundamental redistribution of decision-making authority from management to teams of workers. Workers must also be given the opportunity to develop and refine analytic and problem-solving skills.
- Jobs that are redesigned to include a greater variety of skills and tasks and greater responsibility for the ultimate output of the organization. Workers should be free to do the right thing, rather than being compelled to do the prescribed thing.

- Substitution of a flatter management structure for the traditional, multi-layered hierarchy. The aim is to enable workers to be self-managers who are responsible for their own performance.
- A decision-making role at all levels of the enterprise for workers, through their unions. Strategic decisions are to be jointly made by workers—acting through their unions—and the other stakeholders.
- Rewards realized from transforming the work organization to be distributed on equitable terms agreed upon through negotiations between labor and management. This means a negotiated agreement to protect income and employment security to the maximum extent possible. It means a negotiated agreement to compensate workers fairly for their enhanced contribution to the success of the organization through increases in base wages or agreements providing for some form of supplementary contingent compensation (such as gain-sharing, profit sharing, stock ownership or the like).[36]

Top management of many companies have made suggestions related to a new social contract for their organizations. Some CEOs have emphasized the need for employers and employees to share in both the risks and rewards as an alternative to the disappearance of long-term job security, which is similar to a provision in the AFL-CIO statement. Others, such as IBM, which recently had to abandon its long tradition of no layoffs, are seeking to reshape their corporate culture and redefine the social contract (Figure 14-1). They have begun a change from the notion of a "caring management" to one of "principled leadership" as an employee expectation. Thus, the paternalistic tone of caring management is being replaced with the idea that management will conduct itself with integrity and will provide a sense of direction for the company, while leaving a good deal of initiative to the employee.[37]

Kenneth Chilton and Murray Weidenbaum of the Center for the Study of American Business have suggested a new social contract that is comprehensive in nature and emphasizes partnership (Figure 14-2). This contract attempts to reconcile a variety of paradoxes including (1) enhancing productivity while reducing the work force, (2) increasing competitiveness while meeting new employee mandates, (3) decentralizing decision making in the face of increasing workplace regulation, (4) dealing with worker insecurity and golden parachutes for top management, (5) motivating American workers while expanding globally, and (6) emphasizing the need for honest communication consistent with a change from command and control management to a coaching or teamwork style of management.[38]

The key elements in this contract are the joint expectations of employers and employees. Both groups must come to understand that the highly competitive environment in which they function and the uncertainty that results bind them together in a mutual enterprise. Both employer and employees must see each member of the company as a source of the firm's competitive advantage. Such a partnership involves a level of trust and commitment that is new in the workplace, and a willingness to bury antagonisms and abandon stereotypes that have shaped workplace relations for decades. This presents challenges for both employers and employees that have not been met before.[39] Employees and unions must realistically acknowledge that the old social contract does not work in the modern economy, involving a basic reorientation of thinking on the part of workers. Business managers must initiate the development of a new social contract suitable to their company. Employees at all levels need to be involved in the development of this contract, and this is a key element in restoring trust and credibility.[40]

FIGURE 14-1 IBM Efforts to Redefine Its Workplace Compact

	Old Social Compact		Evolving Social Compact	
	Employer	**Employees**	**Employer**	**Employees**
Expect to Receive	Ethics and Honesty Satisfactory Performance Retraining as Required Compliance/Support Loyalty to Company	Respect/Fair Treatment Caring Management Good Pay Broad-Based Benefits Opportunity to Advance Assistance to Succeed Safe and Healthy Workplace Job Security	Ethics and Honesty Superior Performance Continuous Improvement Ideas/Participation Commitment to Business Success Personal Investment	Respect/Participation Principled Leadership Success-Based Pay Cafeteria Benefits Opportunity for Growth-Résumé Learning Climate Safe and Healthy Workplace Work/Life Flexibility Secure Transitions Trust. . .
Willing to Give	Defined Expectations Assistive Management Merit/Good Pay Promotion from Within Leading Company Paid Benefits Training/Retraining Job-Related Information Job Security Family Relationship	Diligence Flexibility/Move, Retrain Satisfactory Performance Plus/Overtime Lifetime Employment Loyalty/Trust	Trust/Empowerment Facilitative Management Variable-Pay Earning Opportunity Opportunity for Growth Leading Contributory/Cafeteria Benefits Learning Support Information Access Transition Assistance Diversity/Work Life Programs	Participation/Involvement Willingness to Challenge Superior Performance/Sacrifice Lifelong Learning Commitment to Vision . . . Business Success

Source: Ross J. Williams, Director of Leadership and Human Resource Development, Presentation to the 21st Issues Management Conference, Human Resources Institute, St. Petersburg, FL, February 18, 1993.

342

Employer Expectations of Employees	Employee Expectations of Employers	Joint Expectations
• Performance to the best of one's ability • Commitment to the objectives of the firm • Participation (suggestions) • Willingness to take training to improve productivity • Ethical and honest behavior	• "Fair" pay and benefits proportionate to contribution to company success • Security tied to fortunes of the company and ability to perform • Respect, recognition, and participation • Opportunities for growth • Access to timely information and openness by candid leaders • Safe and healthy workplace	• Partnering replaces paternalism • Employees are value-adding resources, not merely costs to be cut • Employee and employer must focus on customer needs and desires

Source: Kenneth Chilton and Murray Weidenbaum, *A New Social Contract for the American Workplace: From Paternalism to Partnering* (St. Louis, MO: Washington University Center for the Study of American Business, 1994), p. 43.

FIGURE 14-2 Outline for a New Social Contract

It is obvious that much change is going on in the American workplace, calling for new understandings and new relationships between employees and employers, and new roles for government and labor unions. Some of the key elements in dealing with this change are ethical in nature—the need for trust and respect for each employee and employer, the need for open and honest communication, the need for participation at all levels of the organization, the need to treat people as human beings rather than simply factors of production, and the need for commitment to cope with change in a manner that is not destructive for the employee or the organization. These ethical challenges are perhaps the most difficult of all in regard to the changing workplace.

The present situation is one in which past organs of adjudication between employers and employees are breaking down, and new ones must be established. And the past does not necessarily contain guidelines for the emerging future. What this calls for is creative imagination in envisioning possibilities for the reconstruction of the means of adjudication, based on an attunement to the conflicting concrete demands that need to be reorganized into workable interrelationships. Employers and employees must each strive to take the perspective or viewpoint of the other in coming to grips with the diversity of interests to be satisfied. The working out of new organs of adjudication cannot be mandated from on high either by employee representatives or employer decrees but will be an ongoing experimental process over time. Such a fundamental reconstruction houses an opportunity for a real growth process on the part of all parties.

Furthermore, from the characterization of some of the features that are being put forward for the new contract to emerge, it can be seen that what is being called for are new relationships between employers and employees, which can better allow the corporation to function as a true community. These features explicitly require community dialogue by recognizing all the participants as autonomous, morally responsible individuals whose creative inputs and diverse interests are vital to the interactive process of adjustments and accommodations in the ongoing growth of the corporation. These features also explicitly call for the rejection of the traditional dichotomies between thinking and doing, conception and execution, thus recognizing that these elements are inseparably intertwined. Taking all these features together, it can be seen that what is needed is the recognition of concrete human beings who cannot be dismembered to become a diversity of cogs in a corporate machine, but who can, in their concrete unities, function as diverse centers of creativity in a unified corporate community.

Questions for Discussion

1. What is happening to work in the modern world? What changes are taking place that are offering challenges to the way people have come to view work and its place in their lives? What are the implications of these changes for the corporation and society?

2. What functions have unions served over the years of their existence? What gave unions the impetus to develop and grow and become a major force in society? How have unions changed in recent years? What are some of the forces behind these changes?

3. What implications does the decline of unions have for the protection of workers' rights? What has replaced the functions unions played in this regard? Is this a good trend in your opinion? Are workers' rights adequately protected in modern society?

4. What is a family-friendly corporation? What kinds of programs have corporations adopted to make them more responsive to family needs? Describe the Family Leave Act of 1993. Is this a good law in your opinion? What impact will it have on corporations?

5. How is the social contract between employers and employees changing? What implications does this have for the rights and obligations of employers and employees? Are these changes likely to be beneficial to society in the future?

6. What is a new contract between employers and employees likely to look like? Are any of the suggestions mentioned in the chapter helpful in this regard? Are they realistic? What kind of thinking needs to be done to develop a new contract that is workable?

Endnotes

[1] Stanley Parker, *The Future of Work and Leisure* (London: MacGibbon and Kee, 1971), p. 34.

[2] Clifton D. Bryant, *The Social Dimensions of Work* (Englewood Cliffs, NJ: Prentice-Hall, 1972), p. 46.

[3] Parker, *The Future of Work and Leisure,* p. 34.

[4] Frederick Herzberg, *Work and the Nature of Man* (New York: The World Publishing Company, 1966), p. 22.

[5] William H. Whyte, *The Organization Man* (New York: Simon & Schuster, 1956).

[6] David Riesman, *The Lonely Crowd* (New Haven: Yale University Press, 1950).

[7] Erich Fromm, *The Sane Society* (Greenwich: Fawcett Publications, Inc., 1955), p. 159.

[8] See Abraham Maslow, *Motivation and Personality* (New York: Harper & Row, Inc., 1954).

[9] Keith H. Hammonds, "The New World of Work," *Business Week,* October 17, 1994, p. 76.

[10] Ibid.

[11] Ibid., p. 80.

[12] Ibid., p. 85.

[13] Jack Patterson, "Welcome to the Company That Isn't There," *Business Week,* October 17, 1994, p. 87.

[14] John B. Parrish, "U.S. Labor Relations in Revolution," *The Journal/The Institute for Socio-economic Studies,* Vol. IX, no. 4 (Winter 1985), p. 24.

[15] Ibid., pp. 24–25.

[16] Ibid., p. 23.

[17] Ibid., pp. 28–30.

[18] Ibid., p. 31.

[19] Ibid.

[20] Bernard Baumohl, et al., "Unions Arise—With New Tricks," *Time,* June 13, 1994, p. 56.

[21] Aaron Bernstein, "Why America Needs Unions," *Business Week,* May 23, 1994, p. 70.

[22] "Beyond Unions: A Revolution in Employee Rights Is in the Making," *Business Week,* July 8, 1985, pp. 72–77.

[23] Ibid.

[24] Edward F. Zigler and Meryl Frank, eds., *The Parental Leave Crisis: Toward a National Agenda* (New Haven: Yale University Press, 1988), p. 149.

[25] Ibid., pp. 24–25.

[26] Carol Kleiman, "Child Care Key Reason Women Leave Jobs," *Times-Picayune,* January 20, 1991, p. G-1.

[27] Sharon Allred Decker, "We Had to Recognize That People Have Lives," *Business Week,* June 28, 1993, p. 88.

[28] See Robert Barker, "Taking Baby Steps Toward a Daddy Track," *Business Week,* April 15, 1991, pp. 90–92; Clare Ansberry, "Parental-Leave Provisions by Employers Must Be Granted to Men, Court Rules," *The Wall Street Journal,* May 23, 1990, p. A3.

[29] Many states passed family leave bills as well. See John F. Dolan, "States Take the Lead on Family Leave Laws," *AARP Bulletin,* Vol. 31, no. 9 (October 1990), p. 7.

[30] *Family and Medical Leave Act of 1993.* Public Law 103-3, February 5, 1993.

[31] Office of the Secretary, Women's Bureau, *Family and Medical Leave—Know Your Rights* (Washington, DC: U.S. Department of Labor, 1993).

[32] Kenneth Chilton and Murray Weidenbaum, *A New Social Contract for the American Workplace: From Paternalism to Partnering* (St. Louis: Washington University Center for the Study of American Business, 1994), p. 2.

[33] Daniel Yankelovich, "Corporate Logic in the 1990s," Address to the 1994 Arthur W. Page Society Spring Seminar.

[34] Ibid.

[35] *The New American Workplace: A Labor Perspective* (Washington, DC, AFL-CIO Committee on the Evolution of Work, February 1994), p. 8.

[36] Ibid.

[37] Chilton and Weidenbaum, *A New Social Contract,* pp. 26–27.

[38] Ibid., pp. 30–38.

[39] Ibid., p. 42.

[40] Ibid., p. 41.

Suggested Readings

Bryant, Clifton D. *The Social Dimensions of Work.* Englewood Cliffs, NJ: Prentice-Hall, 1972.

Chilton, Kenneth, and Murray Weidenbaum. *A New Social Contract for the American Workplace: From Paternalism to Partnering.* St. Louis: Washington University Center for the Study of American Business, 1994.

Fromm, Erich. *The Sane Society.* Greenwich: Fawcett Publications, Inc., 1955.

Herzberg, Frederick. *Work and the Nature of Man.* New York: The World Publishing Company, 1966.

Maslow, Abraham. *Motivation and Personality.* New York: Harper & Row, Inc., 1954.

The New American Workplace: A Labor Perspective. Washington, DC, AFL-CIO Committee on the Evolution of Work, February 1994.

Parker, Stanley. *The Future of Work and Leisure.* London: MacGibbon and Kee, 1971.

Riesman, David. *The Lonely Crowd.* New Haven: Yale University Press, 1950.

Whyte, William H. *The Organization Man.* New York: Simon & Schuster, 1956.

Zigler, Edward F., and Meryl Frank, eds. *The Parental Leave Crisis: Toward a National Agenda.* New Haven: Yale University Press, 1988.

SHORT CASES

A New Work Ethic?

You would think that employees would do something if they discovered that a customer had died on the premises. But that's not necessarily so, according to the Associated Press, which reported that police discovered the body of a trucker in a tractor trailer rig that had sat—with its engine running—in the parking lot of a fast-food restaurant for nine days. Employees swept the parking lot around the truck but ignored the situation for over a week until the stench got so bad that someone finally called the police.

That lack of response doesn't surprise James Sheehy, a human resources manager in Houston, who spent his summer vacation working "undercover" at a fast-food restaurant owned by a relative.[1] Introduced to co-workers as a management trainee from another franchise location who was being brought in to learn the ropes, Sheehy was initially viewed with some suspicion, but by the third day the group had accepted him as just another employee. Sheehy started out as a maintenance person and gradually rotated through various cooking and cleaning assignments before ending up as a cashier behind the front counter.

Most of Sheehy's fellow employees were teenagers and college students who were home for the summer and earning additional spending money. Almost half came from upper-income families and the rest from middle-income neighborhoods. More than half were women, and a third were minorities. What Sheehy reports is a whole generation of workers with a frightening new work ethic: contempt for customers, indifference to quality and service, unrealistic expectations about the world of work, and a get-away-with-what-you-can attitude.

A recent survey shows that employee theft accounts for seven times more revenue loss for retailers than shoplifting.[2] Sheehy's experience was in line with this. He writes that the basic work ethic at his place of employment was a type of gamesmanship that focused on milking the place dry. Theft was rampant, and younger employees were subject to peer pressure to steal as a way of becoming part of the group. "It don't mean nothing," he says, was the basic rationale for dishonesty. "Getting on with getting mine" was another common phrase, as co-workers carefully avoided hard work or dragged out tasks like sweeping to avoid additional assignments.

All that customer service meant, on the other hand, was getting rid of people as fast as possible and with the least possible effort. Sometimes, however, service was deliberately slowed or drive-through orders intentionally switched in order to cause customers to demand to see a manager. This was called "baiting the man," or purposely trying to provoke a response from management. In fact, the general attitude toward managers was one of disdain and contempt. In the eyes of the employees, supervisors were only paper-pushing functionaries who got in the way.

Sheehy's co-workers rejected the very idea of hard work and long hours. "Scamming" was their ideal. Treated as a kind of art form and as an accepted way of doing business, scamming meant taking shortcuts or getting something done without much effort, usually by having someone else do it. "You only put in the time and effort for the big score" is how one fellow worker characterized the work ethic he shared with his peers. "You got to just cruise through the job stuff and wait to make the big score," said another. "Then you can hustle. The office stuff is for buying time or paying for the groceries."

By contrast, they looked forward to working "at a real job where you don't have to put up with hassles." "Get out of school and you can leave this to the real dummies." "Get an office and a computer and a secretary and you can scam your way through anything." On the other hand, these young employees believed that most jobs were like the fast-food industry: automated, boring, undemanding and unsatisfying, and dominated by difficult people. But they dreamed of an action-packed business world, an image shaped by a culture of video games and action movies. The college students in particular, reports Sheehy, identified with the Michael Douglas character in the movie *Wall Street* and believed that a no-holes-barred, trample-over-anybody, get-what-you-want approach is the necessary and glamorous road to success.

1. How typical are the attitudes that Sheehy reports? Does his description of a new work ethic tally with your own experiences? What are the implications of the work ethic that Sheehy describes for the future of American business?

2. Is it reasonable to expect workers, especially in a capitalist society, to be more devoted to their jobs and more concerned with quality and customer service than Sheehy's co-workers were? In what ways does the culture of our capitalist society encourage attitudes like those Sheehy describes?

[1] James W. Sheehy, "New Work Ethic Is Frightening," *Personnel Journal,* June 1990.

[2] "Workers Out-Stealing Shoplifters," *San Francisco Chronicle,* November 24, 1990, p. B3.

Source: William H. Shaw and Vincent Barry, *Moral Issues in Business,* 6th ed. (Belmont, CA: Wadsworth Publishing Company, 1995), pp. 175–176.

Levi Strauss

The top management of Levi Strauss has tried to implement an ethical vision in its organization that has to do with making a profit in the traditional sense but also making the world a better place in which to live. What this vision seems to reflect is that the making of profits is not enough to justify the company's activities, but that it must do something more to be, as top management put it, a "responsible commercial success." Such a vision is consistent with the notion of social responsibility that the company has been concerned to implement for several years.

With regard to employees, *empowerment* and *diversity* are the key words the company would like to promote in its employment policies. Management says it is out to make all workers no matter what their position feel as if they are an integral part of the company. Different views on all issues, no matter how controversial some of these views may be, are heard and respected. By letting people express their views on company issues, employees will feel they are a valued part of the company and not just workers to be exploited for purposes of making a profit.

With respect to diversity, creating tangible opportunities for minority employees is a large part of implementing this concept. The company does not want a homogeneous work force but wants to promote a more diverse work force made up of different groups of people. Such diversity is to be valued and honestly rewarded rather than suppressed. The company has created a Diversity Council composed of blacks, Asians, Hispanics, gays, and women that has a direct link to senior management.

These two goals of empowerment and diversity are interconnected. A more diverse work force means there should be more points of view to be expressed. The company claims that it is not implementing these concepts to make top management feel good or because it is the politically correct thing to do. The company believes that there is a connection between business success and liberating the talents of its work force. Conformity and lack of creativity go together, so it is believed. Companies that involve their employees in decision making should do better in the marketplace.

In 1994, however, sales of the company slowed and profits declined. The company proved to be slow to develop new products and slow to get goods into its retail outlets. Some critics of the company's values-based approach suggested that all this emphasis on values distracted top management from the nuts and bolts of running the company on a daily basis. The CEO disagreed, but the company did plan to spend $500 million to restructure its marketing and distribution systems. In the long run, the CEO insisted that a culture devoted to empowerment and diversity will make the company all the more responsive in the marketplace.

An example of where these values paid off is provided by the company's experience in advertising in the Hispanic community. Television ads of the Levi's jeans stressed grit and independence, and these themes drew in young customers. But they didn't resonate with the company's Hispanic employees and customers. They gave some feedback to company executives, which suggested that independence would not work in the Hispanic community, and that ads stressing friends and family could work better in their culture. In response to this information, Levi's developed a new series of ads that downplayed individualism and emphasized camaraderie, and sales of jeans in the Hispanic community boomed.

Diversity remains something of a problem, however, in the top ranks of management. The executive committee consists of seven middle-aged white men and one middle-aged white woman. The CEO openly recognizes this disparity at the upper echelon of the company and explains that building talent for top management takes time. He is quick to point out that Levi's has doubled the percentage of minority managers to 36 percent since 1984 when he took over the company, and over the same time period, women have climbed from 32 percent of management to 54 percent currently. In both cases, Levi's outperforms the average corporation in the United States, according to federal statistics.

1. Are the goals of empowerment and diversity part of a new social contract the company is trying to establish with its employees? In your opinion, are these goals that are worth pursuing? Will they help to promote employee loyalty and dedication to the company?

2. How well has the company been able to implement these concepts? Where does it still fall short? Has management paid too much attention to its values and ignored the business aspects of its activities? Or will the pursuit of such values pay off eventually?

Source: Information for this case is taken from Russell Mitchell, "Managing by Values," *Business Week,* August 1, 1994, pp. 46–52.

Issues Management

Stay-Alert, Inc., is feeling the pressure from its women employees. The company hires many women for a variety of jobs; in fact, more than half its work force is female. However, the great majority of these women end up in lower-paying jobs and very few of them make it into supervisory and management ranks. Thus, the average salary for men is much greater than that of women throughout the company, reflecting the national pattern.

The women are becoming angry over this disparity. They are beginning to talk about organizing and going out on strike or something equally disruptive. The women are well aware of the comparable worth issue, as is the management of the company. Management knows that several states and cities have adopted a point system to rank jobs on the basis of what they are worth to the organization rather than on the basis of what the market dictates. Thus far, however, no private corporation has embraced the concept, arguing that the market should continue to set wage and salary levels.

The management of Stay-Alert wonders what it can do to stay on top of this issue. It doesn't want to change its way of determining wages and salaries, believing that to do so would open up a can of worms, so to speak. Yet it doesn't want a nasty incident either, which would give the company negative press coverage. The company is also worried about government regulation, as some state legislators have begun to make noises about requiring comparable worth of large corporations.

1. What can forecasting contribute to helping management develop a strategy for this issue? What specific factors should the company look at in order to predict what will happen to this issue on both a local and national level? How can it monitor the development of this issue?

2. What strategy should the company adopt? Should it become one of the first private corporations to embrace the concept of comparable worth? Is a more vigorous affirmative action program the answer? What other alternatives does the company have?

Source: Rogene A. Buchholz, *Business Environment and Public Policy: Implications for Management,* 5th ed. (Englewood Cliffs, NJ: Prentice Hall, 1995), p. 596.

Outsourcing

Because of the nature of its production process, your company has significant impacts on the environment. For several years it has had a rather large environmental department that is responsible for identifying environmental problems for the company and ensuring that it is in compliance with government regulations. The department is headed by a vice president who reports directly to the chief executive officer, giving an indication of the importance the company attaches to environmental issues. The department has employees within it who do a variety of jobs connected with the environment, and some of them have been with the company for many years.

Recently, however, the company began downsizing because of intense competition in the industry. To cut costs, the company has laid off many employees and closed plants around the country. It has begun to look for other ways to save money. One of the ideas floating around top management is outsourcing some of the staff functions it has developed over the years. By outsourcing these functions, the company would save the costs of benefits, which would be a significant savings given the way benefit costs have risen in recent years.

One of the staff functions being considered for outsourcing is the environmental department. The people in this department would essentially be cut loose from the company and would become part of another company headed by the vice president of the environmental department. This company would have the parent company as its sole customer for starters, but it could take on other customers as it became established. The parent company would not pay any benefits to the employees of the environmental department, as these would have to come from the new company itself. The new company would operate on a contract basis with the parent company, selling its services for a reasonable price agreed upon by both parties.

1. Is outsourcing a fair way to treat employees who have been with the company a long time? Are they as likely to get as good a benefit package as they have had with the parent company? Is this a reasonable way for the parent company to cut costs to be more competitive?

2. What implications does outsourcing have for employee loyalty? What would outsourcing environmental functions say about the company's commitment to be environmentally responsible? Are there other ways the company could deal with this problem?

Discrimination in Employment

The concept of equal opportunity is consistent with free enterprise philosophy because the most efficient combination of resources should result if those with the best abilities and talents get the best economic opportunities—the best jobs, the best chances to start a new business, the best investment opportunities. Society is better off because people will end up in positions where their abilities can best be utilized, and those who are unfit for that position will have to find jobs elsewhere. The principle of equal opportunity helps to ensure that the best performers in society, no matter where they were born, what they believe, or what race or sex they are, have a chance to rise to the top based on their proven ability to use society's resources efficiently and wisely, or, in other words, to do something society wants done and is willing to reward commensurately.

This concept of equal opportunity never held that people would be of equal ability or that such free and open competition for existing opportunities would bring about equal results in terms of economic condition. Equal opportunity, strictly speaking, does not raise questions about the results of the competitive process; it is not concerned with distributive justice in the sense of equal results, since it assumes that unequal results are morally right and just. People with superior ability will obviously get ahead and are morally justified in receiving a greater share of the rewards society has to offer if they use their abilities to the fullest and contribute to society's well-being. The important thing about equal opportunity is that people should be free to compete equally on the basis of merit for the rewards society offers and be free to go as far as their abilities, interests, ambition, and whatever else is relevant to performance will take them.

Merit is at the heart of this concept of equal opportunity. Merit dictates that an opportunity should go to those who deserve it on the basis of their ability to take advantage of the opportunity to its fullest. Equality of opportunity means that everyone in our society should be able to compete fairly and honestly for the rewards society has to offer on the basis of merit, where merit refers to the ability of an individual to perform in some capacity. Irrelevant considerations such as race, sex, religion, creed, or national origin are not supposed to be a factor in the distributive outcomes of our society. The rewards are supposed to go to those who perform the best and thus are able to compete most effectively.

For much of our history, equal opportunity along with equality before the law have been important ideals and a part of free enterprise ideology and folklore.

In the 1960s, however, many recognized that equal opportunity never existed in this country for some groups, since they recognized what the institution of slavery had done to opportunities for blacks, understood the effects of poverty on the opportunities individuals had to develop their abilities, and may even have recognized the phenomenon of role stereotyping in regard to women. Such beliefs became rather widespread and it was recognized that because of prejudice and stereotyping, something called systemic discrimination was built into our major institutions, preventing members of some groups, most notably minorities and women, from being free to compete on an equal basis with white males for available opportunities and to utilize or develop their abilities to go as far as they might. Barriers were built into the employment practices of businesses and other institutions. There were barriers to starting a new business and barriers to an equal education that prevented members of these groups from gaining experience and training to become qualified and thus having a true equal opportunity to compete with the predominant white male culture.

Thus, it came to be recognized that the market was not by itself effectively implementing the concept of equal opportunity and making it a reality for all members of society. The people making the key decisions about who got what opportunities (employment decisions, loan decisions, purchasing decisions) were by and large white males, and not surprisingly, most of these decisions were made in favor of other white males who were in advantageous positions. Women and minorities were simply not "qualified" for better positions in society. The problem was one of prejudice and discrimination that prevented some groups from being treated equally with respect to employment opportunities.

Prejudice and Discrimination

Prejudice and discrimination enter into decisions very subtly and unknowingly. The nature of prejudice is such that it produces a tendency to evaluate individuals on the basis of their membership in a group rather than their individual characteristics. Group membership becomes a primary and ruling consideration when making judgments about people. All the characteristics that are believed to be true about that group are automatically assigned to individuals who are members of that group, whether or not they actually possess those characteristics. The individual is seen through the veil of the group stereotype, since prejudice does not allow the assumptions made about individuals to be tested against reality.

People thus become stereotyped. Every black person is believed to be inferior to every white person on many dimensions related to job performance because this is what is believed about the black population as a whole. When it comes to making decisions about job opportunities, whites are assumed to have naturally superior ability to perform. Every woman is believed to be too emotional to make rational decisions required of a manager because this is believed about women as a whole. When decisions are made about management opportunities, men have the inside track because it is believed they have superior ability to perform this function.

This kind of stereotyping builds barriers around members of a group that are very difficult to break through. Not only are these characteristics about individuals in a group believed true by people outside the group, they often come to be believed by members of the group itself. Thus, prejudice and stereotyping have a transactional aspect. Whites use blacks to build a superior identity. Blacks internalize this identity and reinforce the pattern. The behaviors of these two groups become a function of each other and the identities of individuals in the groups become a social product.

The way characteristics originally become assigned to certain groups is not clearly understood. Prejudice enters in when these characteristics are assumed to be true of an entire group—that a whole race of people is believed to be by nature inferior and that another group has been destined to be superior for all times and places because of native endowment; or that an entire sex has been assigned to stay at home to be good wives and mothers, and if they want to enter the business world, they have to be content with lower-paying, nonprofessional, nonmanagerial jobs because they are not inherently equipped for the better-paying, more rewarding opportunities that are available.

The roots of racism and sexism are deep and the dynamics complex. There are economic, social, psychological, cultural, and other reasons for prejudice and stereotyping. Factors such as jealousy, frustration, guilt, fear, and power enter into the development and maintenance of prejudice and stereotypes. They are passed from generation to generation by complex and subtle mechanisms that are often very difficult to unveil. Sometimes it almost seems as if prejudice is in the air and is assimilated by the process of osmosis.

Nonetheless, the effects of prejudice and stereotyping are quite visible in discriminatory behavior against certain groups in our society. The relationship between prejudice and discrimination is shown in the following list, which depicts the different kinds of relationships that can take place between groups on a continuum from friendly to hostile. As attitudes toward a group change from friendly to hostile, behavior changes from cooperation and respect to discrimination and perhaps even scapegoating.

A cooperative relationship implies that both groups accept each other and interact in a color-blind and sex-blind manner in most job-related endeavors. They work and play together in a mutually fulfilling manner with little or no exploitation of each other. Respect does not necessarily mean that the groups will interact much; in fact, they may stick very much to themselves. But they at least do recognize each other's rights to share equally in the opportunities and rewards of society.

Continuum of Social Relations Among Human Groups

Friendly	Cooperation
	Respect
	Tolerance
	Predilection
	Prejudice
	Discrimination
Hostile	Scapegoating

The word *tolerance,* as used in this schema, implies that there may be some kind of hostility already present, but the groups at least allow each other a certain degree of coexistence and do not engage in open warfare or overt discrimination. Predilection is defined as the simple preference of an individual for members of one culture, color, sex, or language as opposed to another. While this kind of preference may be seen as inevitable and natural, it opens the door to prejudice, since group interaction is minimal and knowledge of what individuals in other groups are really like is not readily available.

Prejudice arises when a predilection becomes rigid, inflexible, and exaggerated, and myths arise because of the strangeness of the groups to each other. Each group in isolation may overrate its own virtues and exaggerate the vices of the other. These beliefs become very strongly held and form part of an individual's identity. An act of discrimination is an act of exclusion based on these prejudices. Those who make decisions about individuals in the group do so on the basis of characteristics assumed to be true of the group rather than on an individual's intrinsic characteristics. Scapegoating is the ultimate form of hostility, involving full-fledged aggression in word or deed where the victim of discrimination is abused verbally or physically.

Equal Opportunity and the Workplace

The implementation of equal opportunity is aimed at eliminating those factors such as race and sex that should have no bearing on an employment decision if it is truly based on merit and merit alone. The implementation of equal opportunity became a matter of public policy rather than being left solely to market forces. Many public policy measures were adopted in the 1960s and 1970s that were directed at rooting out systemic discrimination and overcoming the disadvantages of race and sex to give members of disadvantaged groups a fair and equal chance at the opportunities and rewards society has to offer. Fair and equal in this context means that they should be able to compete on the basis of merit, and irrelevant factors such as race, sex, religion, national origin, and creed should not hamper their ability to compete.

The Civil Rights Act is, of course, the cornerstone of equal employment opportunity and was passed at the height of concern about civil rights in the 1960s. The amendments to the act in 1972 are important to note as they considerably broadened the act and allowed for enforcement action to be brought in the courts. The act was further amended in 1978 to deal with the problem of pregnancy for women, and again in 1991 to offset the effect of court decisions in the 1980s that had weakened some provisions. The Civil Rights Act is administered by the Equal Employment Opportunity Commission (EEOC) and remains the major piece of civil rights legislation in the country.

Another avenue through which equal opportunity is pursued is through the issuance of executive orders that affect government contractors. These orders are an example of the usage of government's power as a buyer to pursue social values. These executive orders require affirmative action programs to be filed in an attempt to force contractors to take equal opportunity seriously. The Office of Federal Contract Compliance Programs (OFCCP) is responsible for the administration of these executive orders. Other public policy measures deal with equal pay for women, age discrimination, and handicapped and disabled persons.

This approach to equal opportunity focuses on the workplace and is aimed at rooting out the kind of discrimination that prevents members of certain groups, most notably minorities and women, from having an equal chance at the job opportunities that are available. The basic issue here is not necessarily one of poverty or disadvantages that make it difficult to compete in the workplace because of the lack of fundamental skills or work habits. The issue is one of prejudice and discrimination that prevent certain groups from utilizing to the fullest the skills and abilities they already possess, or from gaining the experience and training that are necessary to become qualified for the better opportunities society has to offer.

To discriminate in employment is to make an adverse decision (or set of decisions) against employees (or prospective employees) based on their membership in a certain class. Discrimination of this sort involves three basic elements: (1) It is a decision against one or more employees based solely on the fact that they are members of a certain group and not on their ability to perform a given job, (2) the decision is based on the assumption that the group is inferior to other groups and therefore less worthy of equal treatment, and (3) the decision has a harmful or negative effect on the interests of the employees, perhaps costing them jobs, higher positions, or better pay.[1]

AFFIRMATIVE ACTION

The implementation of equal opportunity has been fraught with problems. The Civil Rights Act of 1964, taken literally, ruled out any form of preferential treatment, thus forbidding such devices as quotas, and seemed to treat discrimination as an intentional, deliberate act of exclusion. It ignored both the moral question of whether or not groups that had been discriminated against in the past were owed something more than simply an equal chance to compete with those who had benefited from past discrimination, and the more practical question of how discriminated groups were supposed to get the education and experience necessary to qualify for jobs—particularly those professional and managerial jobs that commanded the most money and status—without some kind of preferential treatment that would make up for deficiencies in education and experience that were the result of past discrimination.

It was recognized early in the federal contracting procedure that a passive approach to implementing the concept of equal opportunity would not work. What was needed was some kind of an affirmative action program where positive steps would be taken to hire more minorities and women and promote them into better-paying positions. Federal contractors were required to analyze their work force to determine where deficiencies existed, and then file an affirmative action plan with goals and timetables to show how these deficiencies were going to be corrected. These written affirmative action plans were to contain the following information.

- An analysis of all major job classifications, with an explanation of any underutilization of minorities in any of the job classes.
- Goals and targets and affirmative action commitments designed to relieve any deficiencies. But a contractor's compliance will not be judged solely by whether or not it reaches its goals and meets its timetables. Instead, a contractor's compliance will be judged by reviewing the contents of the program, the extent of the contractor's adherence to it, and the contractor's good faith efforts to make its program work toward realization of the goals within timetables set for completion.

The guidelines for affirmative action programs also outlined suggested procedures for use in establishing, implementing, and judging an acceptable affirmative action program. These guidelines offered more concrete information as to how an affirmative action program should be constructed. The contractor had to consider such factors as the following in developing an acceptable affirmative action program that would meet with approval.

- Minority population of the labor area surrounding the facility and the size of the minority unemployment force.

- General availability of promotable minority employees within the contractor's organization.

- Availability of promotable minority employees within the contractor's organization.

- Anticipated expansion, contraction, and turnover in the labor force.

- Existence of institutions capable of training minorities in the requisite skills.

- Degree of training that the contractor is reasonably able to undertake as a means of making all job classes available to minorities.

- The written programs "must relate to all major job categories at the facility with explanations if minorities or women are currently being underutilized." Where there are deficiencies, goals and timetables are required to utilize minorities and women at all levels and in all segments of the work force.[2]

There are various approaches to affirmative action (see box), but the use of quotas and goals became fairly widespread as the most useful device to ensure compliance with the executive order as applied to federal contracting. Eventually, the courts came to regard the Civil Rights Act as requiring similar procedures to implement the intent of Congress. The use of quota systems and implementation goals became a preferred means of correcting deficiencies where they were known to exist and to demonstrate to the government that a company was making a good faith effort to comply with equal opportunity legislation.

The difficulty of proving intent to discriminate is obvious. One would have to find some internal memoranda that clearly indicated race or sex was a factor in the employ-

---

BOX 15-1

Types of Affirmative Action Programs

1. Passive nondiscrimination. This involves a willingness, in all decisions about hiring, promotion, and pay, to treat the races and sexes alike. However, this posture may involve a failure to recognize that past discrimination leaves many prospective employees unaware of present opportunities.

2. Pure affirmative action. A concerted effort is made to expand the pool of applicants so that no one is excluded because of past or present discrimination. At the point of decision, however, the company hires (or promotes) whoever seems most qualified, without regard to race or sex.

3. Affirmative action with preferential hiring. In this posture, the company not only ensures that it has a larger labor pool to draw from but systematically favors women and minority groups in the actual decisions about hiring. This might be thought of as a "soft" quota system, i.e., instead of establishing targets that absolutely must be met, the top officers of the company beef up employment of women and minority-group members to some unspecified extent by indicating that they want those groups given a break.

4. Hard quotas. No two ways about it—specific numbers or proportions of minority-group members must be hired.

From Daniel Seligman, "How Equal Opportunity Turned into Employment Quotas," *Fortune,* March 1973, p. 162. Copyright © 1973 Time, Inc. All rights reserved.

ment decision or find someone who was in on the decision who would testify in court to that effect. It is much easier to infer that discrimination exists from the composition of the work force, by comparing the percentage of minorities and women employed overall with some relevant population parameter such as the percentage of minorities or women in the labor force from which the company could be expected to draw its employees and by comparing the percentage of minorities and women in various occupational categories within the company itself.

Where these statistics showed there was an obvious lack of women or minorities in the total work force, or where they were obviously concentrated in lower-paying occupations, discrimination was inferred to exist. The best way to correct these deficiencies was through the use of quotas and goals, which in effect gave preferential treatment to women and minorities to bring them up to some kind of statistical parity. The assumption behind this approach, of course, is that skills and abilities are randomly distributed throughout the population, so that minorities and women could be assumed to be on a par with white males.

Thus, the concepts of equal opportunity and affirmative action are not the same. Equal employment opportunity means that everyone gets an equal chance at a job or promotion. Affirmative action implies a set of specific, result-oriented procedures designed to achieve equal employment opportunity at a pace beyond that which would occur normally. The objective of an affirmative action program is to achieve within a reasonable period of time an employee work force that in all major occupational categories reflects the makeup of the relevant external labor market. Affirmative action programs establish specific goals and timetables designed to accomplish this objective.

REVERSE DISCRIMINATION

The widespread use of goals or quotas to implement affirmative action meant that inevitably reverse discrimination would be a factor. This phenomenon occurs when a minority-group member or a woman is equally qualified when compared with a white male and is given preference over the latter for a job or promotion, or where quotas resulted in hiring minorities or women who are actually less qualified than white male applicants for the same position. While the phenomenon was tolerated for a while, cases of reverse discrimination began to receive attention, and eventually the courts began to rule that civil rights laws applied to whites as well as blacks and preferential treatment was a violation of these laws. The EEOC itself was found guilty of discrimination against white male professionals in its hiring and promotion practices.[3] Several key court cases illustrate how the society tried to cope with achieving some kind of balance between supporting affirmative action programs and dealing with the problem of reverse discrimination that they sometimes caused.

The most publicized case involving reverse discrimination was the so-called *Bakke* case. The California Supreme Court, in a 6–1 ruling, banned minority quotas in the graduate schools of California's state university system.[4] The case was brought by Allan Bakke, who contended that he was denied admission to the medical school at the University of California's Davis campus in 1973 and 1974 because of reverse discrimination. Of the 100 openings for entering classes in those two years, 84 places went to those selected by normal admissions standards, which emphasized college grades and entrance examination scores. The other 16 openings were filled under an admissions program giving preference to nonwhite applicants.

The university acknowledged that it admitted minority applicants it rated substantially below Bakke. The court said the medical school's reserved places for minority students who did not necessarily score as high as white students violated the Constitution's Fourteenth Amendment guarantees of equal protection to all persons regardless of race. Universities could consider factors other than grades and test scores in admitting students—such as the needs of society—but without regard to race. The University of California appealed this ruling to the U.S. Supreme Court, which agreed to hear the case. Many people thought the country would finally have a definitive ruling on preferential treatment and reverse discrimination.

Such a definitive ruling, however, was not the result. The Court split 5–4 on the decision, which essentially had two parts.[5] On the one hand, the Court affirmed by a 5–4 margin the lower court order admitting Bakke to medical school at the University of California at Davis because its special admissions program for minorities did violate Title VI of the Civil Rights Act of 1964, which forbade racial discrimination in any program or activity receiving federal financial assistance. Quotas based entirely on race where no previous discrimination had been found were held to be illegal. This provision left open the use of quotas to correct deficiencies as part of a settlement where previous discrimination had been found.

On the other hand, a majority of the Court, again by a 5–4 margin, with Justice Lewis Powell being the swing vote in both cases, ruled that a university could continue to take race into consideration in admissions. Exactly how this was to be done was unstated, but Justice Powell referred to the admissions policies at Harvard as a possible model. Race is a factor that was considered at Harvard along with geographical location or athletic or artistic ability. Other factors Justice Powell mentioned that could be considered along with race included unique work or service experience, leadership potential, maturity, demonstrated compassion, or a history of overcoming disadvantage.[6]

The justices of the Supreme Court wrote six different opinions, reflecting their own diversity as well as that of the nation as a whole (see box). This case attracted more briefs than any other case that had ever been considered by the Court. Yet the decision was hardly the landmark decision many had hoped for—the Court ruled narrowly and delicately, trying to find a middle ground. The decision was not definitive and left room for

---

BOX 15-2

Preferential programs may only reinforce common stereotypes holding that certain groups are unable to achieve success without special protection. . . . There is (also) a measure of inequity in forcing innocent persons in (Bakke's) position to bear the burdens of redressing grievances not of their making (Supreme Court Justice Lewis Powell writing for the majority in the *Bakke* decision).

I suspect that it would be impossible to arrange an affirmative action program in a racially neutral way and have it successful. To ask that this be so is to demand the impossible. In order to get beyond racism, we must first take account of race. There is no other way. And in order to treat some persons equally, we must treat them differently (Supreme Court Justice Harry Blackmun in a dissenting opinion on the *Bakke* decision).

Regents of the University of California v. Bakke, 98 S.Ct. 2752, 2807 (1978).

further development, which on the whole may have been a positive approach to such a complex situation.

Another case that dealt with this issue that had more relevance to business organizations was the so-called *Weber* case, in which an employee of Kaiser Aluminum and Chemical Corporation sued his employer and the Steelworkers Union, claiming that he had been illegally excluded from a training program for higher-paying skilled jobs in which half the places had been reserved for minorities. The Fifth Circuit Court of Appeals agreed with Weber, observing that the quota system used by the company improperly favored blacks who had not been the subject of prior unlawful discrimination.[7] The Supreme Court disagreed, however, and by a 5–2 vote ruled that employers can give blacks special preference for jobs that had traditionally been all white.[8]

Whether or not it has had discriminatory job practices in the past, the Court said, a company can use affirmative action programs of this type to remedy "manifest racial imbalance" without fear of being challenged in these efforts by the courts. The Court emphasized the temporary nature of the program and the fact that it was not intended to maintain racial balance, but simply to eliminate a manifest racial imbalance. The program would end when the percentage of black skilled craft workers in the plant approximated the percentage of blacks in the local labor force. Thus, the Supreme Court backed job preference programs for minorities that had been voluntarily established to eliminate conspicuous racial imbalance in traditionally segregated job categories.[9]

The key elements in this decision were that the program was designed to correct a manifest racial imbalance, it was voluntary in nature, and it was only temporary until such time as the manifest imbalance was corrected. These principles seemed to be upheld in further decisions by the Supreme Court and became the major guidelines for business organizations that were concerned about developing affirmative action programs that could not be challenged by employees adversely affected by the programs. There are many moral issues in these principles such as whether or not they are fair to white employees who deserve a job or promotion, but they constituted a reasonable compromise between the different positions on this issue for quite some time.

An even more significant decision was handed down in 1987, when the Court upheld an affirmative action plan voluntarily adopted in 1978 by the Santa Clara County, California, transportation agency. The primary goal of the plan was to correct a conspicuous imbalance of women in skilled and managerial positions. Among skilled craft workers, none of the 238 jobs had ever been held by a woman. It was a temporary plan designed to fill 36 percent of skilled jobs with women to mirror the percentage of women in the area labor market. Thus, when the job of road dispatcher opened up in 1979, the agency interviewed nine people and found seven qualified. Among those qualified was Diane Joyce, a road maintenance worker, who was eventually given the promotion even though she had an interview score that was two points lower than a white male who wanted the same job and eventually sued the county.[10]

The Court argued that the Santa Clara plan merely set up flexible goals that didn't put male workers at a disadvantage. The plan established realistic guidance for employment decisions that visited minimal intrusion on the legitimate expectations of other employees. This decision was said to provide the clearest declaration yet on the role of affirmative action as a remedy for inequality in the workplace, giving employers greater freedom to engage in broad affirmative programs without having to prove or admit prior discrimination against individuals. All that is necessary to support an affirmative action program, the Court indicated, is evidence of a manifest imbalance in the number of women or minorities holding the positions in question. The case also established the rights of women as well as blacks and other minorities to receive preferential treatment in certain situations.[11]

PREFERENTIAL TREATMENT

The key moral issue in affirmative action (AA) programs and reverse discrimination is, of course, whether or not blacks and women deserve some kind of preferential treatment to compensate them for past wrongs or to promote certain social goals such as reducing social injustice. Regarding the issue of compensation, supporters of preferential treatment argue that since we think veterans are owed preferential treatment because of their service and sacrifice to the country, we may similarly think blacks and women are owed preferential treatment because of their economic sacrifices, systematic incapacitation, and consequent personal and group losses. Under preferential treatment, no one is asked to give up a job that is already his. Rather the job opportunity for which the white male competes belongs to the community. Thus, the community takes the job opportunity away from him in the competitive process in order that it may make amends for past wrongs. White males as a whole have profited from the wrongs of the community and many have been direct beneficiaries of policies that excluded or downgraded blacks and women.[12]

Opponents argue that preferential treatment violates the moral requirements of compensatory justice by requiring that compensation should come from all the members of a group that contains some wrong doers, and requiring that compensation should go to all the members of a group that contains some injured parties. Only the specific individuals who discriminated against minorities and women in the past should be forced to make reparation of some sort, and they should make reparation only to those specific individuals against whom they discriminated. AA programs are morally wrong because the beneficiaries are not the same individuals who were injured by past discrimination and the people who must pay for their injuries are usually not the ones who inflicted these injuries.[13]

Preferential treatment has also been justified as necessary to attain equal justice and strive for a society with greater equality of opportunity. Preferential treatment neutralizes the competitive disadvantage with which women and minorities are currently burdened and helps bring them up to the same starting point. The goal of such programs is the reduction of a great social injustice, not proportional representation of the races in all institutions or professions.[14] Equality for all can only be achieved through temporary preferences given to groups that have historically suffered discrimination. It is perverse to use civil rights laws to block the very goals these laws were intended to further.

Opponents argue that AA programs discriminate against white males and thus violate the principle of equality itself in allowing a nonrelevant characteristic to determine employment decisions. They harm women and minorities because such programs imply that women and minorities are so inferior to white males that they need special help to compete. Thus, programs based on preferential treatment to attain social justice create social injustices of their own that perpetuate the very problem they were meant to correct.[15]

Civil rights legislation has been in effect for over 30 years and affirmative action programs have been in place for several decades. While AA may only have been intended as a temporary measure, should corporations now assume that they will be required to indefinitely maintain AA plans based on goals and timetables monitored by the federal government? Or will we look back on AA as a program that peaked in the 1970s and then was phased out over the next few decades as burdensome and associated with reverse discrimination?[16] When will the debt owed to minorities and women because of past discrimination be paid and the books balanced?

> The broad public policy problem is how to recognize and pay the general debt in ways that do not damage investment incentives and that impose no unfair penalties on anyone. A heavy handed approach by government, unions, or corporations risks inflicting a new injustice. Affirmative action is not a punitive concept. It is intended to help produce a fairer distribution of income and opportunity, such as the distribution that presumably would exist today had there been an open and fairly competitive society all along.[17]

In the late 1980s, the Supreme Court began to take the lead in changing the interpretation of affirmative action by a series of 5–4 decisions, reflecting the new conservative majority that was put in place during the Reagan administration.[18] The effect of these rulings was to make it more difficult to prove discrimination and harassment and opened up more avenues for white males to pursue reverse discrimination suits. Lawyers were said to be turning away clients because many job-discrimination claims were viewed as impossible to win under the new rules and too costly to litigate. The ranks of civil rights lawyers were expected to be thinned.[19] To reverse the effects of these decisions by the Supreme Court, a coalition of Democrats and liberal and moderate Republicans introduced comprehensive legislation in Congress that would amend civil rights legislation. After a lengthy and contentious debate, a new civil rights bill was passed in 1991 that reestablished some of the old principles and extended new rights regarding punitive damages to women and the disabled. Despite this new law, however, opposition to affirmative action programs and preferential treatment continues to mount in government and in society at large.

No doubt a large part of the reason for this increasing opposition to affirmation action programs is because concrete situations are arising, such as those cases cited earlier, that bring into clear focus the complexities of the moral issues involved in the whole debate. Should discrimination be treated on an individual basis and compensation be awarded accordingly, or is it a group phenomenon that requires group remedies? Given that intent to discriminate is so difficult to prove in practice, is it fair to use statistics to infer discrimination, which perpetuates treating discrimination on a group basis? Do affirmative action programs build community or are they inherently divisive in nature? Are these programs violating the rights of the white male? Is it true that in order to get beyond racism and sexism, race and sex must be taken into account for some period of time in the programs that are developed to promote equal opportunity? Are there better ways to get beyond racism and sexism, or any other ism for that matter?

Women and Equal Opportunity

There are several issues that apply to women in this area of equal opportunity that deserve discussion. These issues have a moral dimension that must be highlighted at the outset. Sexual harassment involves treatment of women as sex objects rather than treating them as concrete human beings who are full partners in the corporate enterprise. They deserve to be respected by men as colleagues and not as sexual playthings that can be exploited. Women should also have the opportunity to go as far in the corporate organization as their ambition and talents will take them, and not have to run up against a glass ceiling when it comes to the top positions. Women can make significant contributions to corporations and must be judged accordingly.

SEXUAL HARASSMENT

The issue of sexual harassment received increased attention during the late 1970s and came into its own, so to speak, during the 1980s, as it increasingly became a legal matter. During the early 1990s, Clarence Thomas, a Supreme Court nominee at the time, was accused by Anita Hill, a former government employee who had worked for him at the Equal Employment Opportunity Commission when he was head of the agency, of sexual harassment. Because the hearings were televised, the issue became front-page news for several weeks, and could be called the issue of the decade in the area of equal employment opportunity. More attention began to be paid to sexual harassment, and more women were encouraged to bring forth charges of sexual harassment against their employers.

With respect to business organizations, when the federal government and the courts began to insist that sexual harassment constituted illegal discrimination in employment, it was no longer a laughing matter. After some major employers lost lawsuits charging them with failure to act against harassment, hundreds of corporations, colleges, hospitals, and other institutions took steps to deal with the problem and protect themselves against lawsuits. Many issued formal policies and some attempted to make employees more sensitive to the problem through training and strengthening internal grievance procedures. The continuing surge of women into the work force, many of them single parents who are particularly vulnerable because of their financial situation, increased the potential for sexual harassment.

The number of sexual harassment lawsuits increased in the early 1980s, and were as likely to be filed against a small company as a large corporation. Harassment was charged in 6,342 job-discrimination cases filed in 1984, which was an increase from the 5,110 claims filed the previous year. In 1985, the number of complaints rose again to 7,273 cases. During the previous six years, federal courts had heard only about 300 sexual harassment cases.[20] After the Anita Hill–Clarence Thomas hearings, the EEOC logged a record 9,920 cases, which was an increase of 50 percent over the previous year.[21] The number of complaints increased again to 10,532 in 1992, which was nearly double the number filed five years earlier. Some research showed that 90 percent of *Fortune* 500 firms had to deal with sexual harassment complaints, and that employers spent an average of $200,000 on each complaint. More than a third of these companies were sued at least once and about 25 percent were sued several times.[22]

These suits can be divided between so-called quid pro quo cases where an employee has been promised promotion for sexual favors or hasn't been promoted because of refusing such sexual advances, and work-environment cases where sexual harassment creates an environment that is abusive, hostile toward women, and intimidating. Sexual harassment cases must be based on a persistent and calculated pattern of antisocial behavior that constitutes a hostile working environment, or on a single quid pro quo type of situation. In 1992, third-party harassment began to be considered a serious offense that was said to be rampant in the workplace. Such harassment takes place when a client, customer, or supplier is the harasser. Women professionals and sales representatives whose jobs require them to meet with clients and vendors outside the work setting were said to be particularly vulnerable to such forms of harassment.[23]

Defining sexual harassment is difficult, let alone proving that it has taken place. In November 1980, the EEOC issued guidelines to deal with sexual harassment. The EEOC defined sexual harassment as sexual advances of a verbal or physical nature that are unwelcomed. To constitute sexual harassment, these types of behavior must meet the following conditions: (1) submission to such conduct is made explicitly or implicitly a term or condition of employment, (2) submission to or rejection of such conduct is used as a basis for employment decisions affecting the individual, or (3) such conduct has the purpose or effect of unreasonably interfering with an individual's work performance or creating an intimidating, hostile, or offensive working environment.[24]

The employer has strict liability for sexual harassment perpetuated by its agents and supervisors. When the employer knows or should have known of sexual harassment in the workplace and does not take immediate and appropriate action, it will also be held responsible for the actions of nonsupervisory employees and nonemployees. The guidelines also state sex discrimination will be charged against an employer if individuals can prove they were qualified but were refused advancement, while a person who submitted to a request for sexual favors received preferential treatment. This provision was upheld by a 1984 decision, which was first to be brought under this section of the guidelines. Employers were urged to crack down on such affairs between supervisors and subordinates.[25]

A series of court decisions since 1977 has generally upheld the EEOC's guidelines. Courts have ruled that sexual harassment encompasses not only requested sexual favors, but also off-color jokes, sexual leers, pats on the rear, and requirements for sexually revealing uniforms. In 1986, the Supreme Court ruled that workers may sue their employers for sex discrimination on the grounds that sexual harassment by supervisors created a hostile job environment even if loss of a job or promotion wasn't involved.[26] After this decision, more cases were filed in which the whole environment was alleged to be a source of sexual harassment rather than the actions of a single individual. In such an environment women are viewed as men's sexual playthings rather than as their equal co-workers.[27]

Further clarification came in a court ruling where the civil rights laws were said to cover any remark or behavior that a "reasonable woman" would find to be offensive. The court acknowledged that a woman's perception of such behavior might be different from a man's, that conduct that men might consider unobjectionable might offend many women. Companies aiming to comply with the law must regard reports of sexual harassment from the standpoint of a "reasonable woman."[28] The courts also ruled in another case that pictures of naked and scantily clad women displayed in the workplace qualified as harassment. Pornography in the workplace was believed to result in reduced job satisfaction and emotional trauma for women workers.[29] In May 1993, a federal court in Minnesota allowed the first class-action suit in a sexual harassment case to be brought, which if extended throughout the country, could have significant implications for employers.[30] Over the past several years there has thus been some clarification as to the meaning of sexual harassment.

In order to deal with this problem of sexual harassment, it has been suggested that companies develop formal sexual harassment policies that clearly specify the types of behaviors perceived as sexual harassment. These policies should be communicated, along with the potential penalties for engaging in sexual harassment. In addition, companies should also establish in-house grievance and complaint procedures to be followed in the event of sexual harassment. Established systems of this nature should allow for the resolution of sexual harassment problems before they reach the litigation stage.[31] Companies that have well-defined policies against sexual harassment stand a much better chance of escaping liability for hostile-environment cases, but to prevail in court they must have clear procedures for handling complaints that arise in their companies.

Research has shown that (1) both supervisors and co-workers can sexually harass; (2) sexual harassment can occur when people have just started working together or after they have been working together a long time; (3) sexual harassment can occur in a private or a public place; (4) offensive behavior can be personal comments, asking for a date, or sexual advances; and (5) a harasser need not have harassed repeatedly nor a victim have been victimized repeatedly for a given incident between them to be a case of sexual harassment.[32]

One point to remember is that sexual harassment guidelines cover both men and women. In 1982, a male employee of the Wisconsin Department of Health and Social Services won $196,500 in damages for sexual harassment. The plaintiff contended that his female superior demoted him from his job as a disability-insurance supervisor because he refused her sexual advances. The jury believed his contention and also held a higher-level administrator of the agency liable for not remedying the plaintiff's harassment complaints.[33] Sexual harassment charges filed by men are expected to increase in the future as women assume more positions of power in corporations and other institutions.[34]

WOMEN IN MANAGEMENT

Women presently constitute about 41 percent of corporate managers, compared with about 27 percent a decade earlier. The economic shift from manufacturing to services gives women better opportunities at landing top managerial jobs because this sector accepted women managers earlier. And as the number of women expanded in business schools, men became accustomed to them as peers and are less threatened by women managers when they move into corporate positions. Thus, women are starting to achieve equal representation in middle- and lower-management positions. In 1992, half the entry-level management crop was female, which represented an increase from 15 percent 15 years previously.[35]

In spite of these gains, however, less than 3 percent of top executives of *Fortune* 500 companies are women. In the early 1970s, 99 percent of senior management was male; after 20 years of progress some 97 percent of senior management was still male. The wage gap also increases as women move up the corporate ladder. A report issued by the U.S. Chamber of Commerce found that corporate women at the vice presidential level earned 42 percent less than their male counterparts.[36] In 1986, women from the vice president's level on up earned only about half as much as their male counterparts, $124,623 for women executives compared with $213,000 for men executives.[37] Because of these trends, a study published by the Women's Research and Education Institute claimed that at the current pace, it will take 75 to 100 years for women to achieve equal representation and pay at all management levels.[38]

The situation doesn't seem to be any better in the federal government. A survey by the U.S. Merit Protection Board completed in 1992 found that while nearly half the white-collar jobs in government were held by women, relatively few had gained access to executive and supervisory positions. Only about one in four federal supervisors were women, and only one in ten senior federal executives were women. Women remain clustered in lower-paying jobs that offer little chance for advancement into higher-paying positions. The report concluded that the progress women have made in obtaining top jobs in the federal government has been so slow that they are likely to be underrepresented in these jobs for more than the next 25 years.[39]

Black women face a particularly difficult situation. They made up just 2 percent of managers in companies with 100 or more employees in 1988, and none were represented among the top 25 black managers in corporate America. While they accounted for 10 percent of the work force in 1988, they seem to be largely bypassed for promotions and are relegated to staff positions that are vulnerable to corporate layoffs. They suffer from isolation, a lack of mentors that is more serious than for white women, and stereotyping. Since they fulfill two equal opportunity obligations, they are often called "twofers," a label that undercuts their credibility and legitimacy.[40]

Based on a study by the Labor Department, which dealt with glass ceilings for both minorities and women, the OFCCP announced in the summer of 1991 that it would step up enforcement of its antidiscrimination provisions regarding women, levying the same penalties as for other forms of discrimination including disqualification of companies that refuse to correct discriminatory practices. The new enforcement guidelines were also to focus on more subtle forms of discrimination such as differences in perks including club memberships and expense accounts.[41]

In early 1989, a firestorm was set off by a *Harvard Business Review* article written by Felice Schwartz in which she proposed formalizing a two-track system for the promotion of women into higher management positions. The plan would relegate working mothers to a slower career path called the "mommy track" while only women who were willing to set aside family considerations would be placed on the fast track to higher executive positions. Schwartz argued that corporations must find a way to segregate "career-primary" women from "career and family" women in order to cope with high turnover rates of women who quit high-pressure jobs when they cannot reconcile the conflicting needs of work and family. Working mothers would gladly trade advancement and high pay, she argued, for the chance to spend more time with their families, and corporations would benefit from retaining them in less demanding middle-management positions.[42]

While Schwartz seemed to think her proposal would give women the best of both worlds, many women did not agree and were morally offended. Critics feared that corporations might accept the notion that it was a bad investment to groom working women for higher-level positions, thus reducing the opportunities for women to move into the top ranks of management. Others argued that the idea of a mommy track recalled the old-fashioned notion of singling out women rather than men to make all the sacrifices to raise children. If such a thing as a mommy track makes sense for companies, why not also a daddy track? Another problem is that such a system would put a woman on a slow track for her whole career, even though the years spent in raising a child constitute only one phase of a woman's life span.[43]

Nonetheless, the glass ceiling still seems to exist in corporate America that prevents many women from moving beyond middle management. Many women feel stuck on the lower rungs of the executive ladder, which is why they leave to become self-employed. These women are more vulnerable to layoffs during downturns in the economy or restructuring of companies that eliminates middle-management positions. During recessions, white-collar cutbacks fall more heavily on women than men because they lack seniority or hold managerial positions in such vulnerable support functions as personnel, marketing, finance, and public relations.[44] Many women believe that the playing field for the higher-paying positions in corporate America is anything but level.

WOMEN IN SOCIETY

By 1990, women constituted 45.4 percent of the labor force, compared with 12 percent in 1900 and 29 percent in 1950. They provided services that ranged from teaching, air traffic control, medicine, and legal advice to administrative and technical support. Some 57 percent of women were in the work force. Over the next decade, only 15 percent of new entrants to the work force will be native white males, compared to 47 percent in that category in the late eighties. Nonwhites, women, and immigrants together are expected to make up more than five-sixths of the net additions to the work force between 1990 and the year 2000, although they make up only about half of the work force presently. Almost two-thirds of the new entrants will be women. Some 60 percent of all women of working age are expected to have jobs by the year 2000 and about 47 percent of the work force will be women. This increase means that demands for day care and for more time off from work for pregnancy leave and child-rearing duties will increase.[45]

In 1988, at least 3.7 million of the more than 13 million sole proprietorships in the country were owned by women, which was nearly double the 1.9 million such enterprises they owned ten years before. These firms generated revenues estimated to be more than $100 billion a year and paid $37 billion in federal taxes and another $13 billion in state and local taxes. The majority of these enterprises were service companies as women owned nearly half of all retail businesses in the country. But female entrepreneurs were also making headway in manufacturing, construction, mining, and other industries. The Small Business Administration expected that one-half of all self-employed people would be women by the end of the century.[46]

A study released in 1993 by Ralph Nader's Center for Responsive Law found that women in the United States pay more than men for the same goods and services, ranging from cars to health care and dry cleaning. Women buy about half the new cars sold each year, but they pay about $150 more for the same car as their male counterparts. The same discrepancy is found in other areas, indicating that women are discriminated against in the marketplace as well as the workplace.[47] Another study conducted by the General Accounting Office found that even though women were included in studies of new drugs, their numbers were not representative of women in the general population who suffered from the disease in question.[48]

Although tens of thousands of women lose their jobs each year because of pregnancy, some gains have been made against this type of discrimination. More such cases have been filed in recent years, as the EEOC has indicated that the 3,000 pregnancy-discrimination cases it handles each year are less than 5 percent of the cases filed in courts around the country. Still, the Pregnancy Discrimination Act of 1978, which covers such discrimination, has some major loopholes. It exempts federal employees and companies with 14 or fewer workers, which translates into 16 million female employees who can be fired legally when they become pregnant. The law also fails to provide protection for employees who work for companies that do not have a sick leave policy.[49]

While women increasingly chose to enroll in M.B.A. programs during the 1980s, the bloom seemed to be coming off the rose in the early years of the next decade. Many of the leading management schools in the country reported significant decreases in women's enrollment. This may simply reflect demographics, but it may also reflect women's disappointment with a business career. In addition to the problems in breaking the glass ceiling, the earnings disparity mentioned earlier may be having an effect. Studies show that women project their annual postdegree earnings at $5,000–$10,000 less than men, and may be concluding that the M.B.A. degree is not worth the cost of tuition and the risk of leaving a job they may already have.[50]

Despite these setbacks, the enrollment of women in professional education as a whole increased dramatically over the past decade. These graduates are making major inroads into management and the professions. The participation rate for women was expected to average about 60.3 percent by 1995 compared with 53.7 percent in 1985, a jump of almost 7 percent. An increase of one percentage point in the participation rate increases the number of women in the job market by nearly 1 million. Thus, no matter what wage differential now exists, the forces set in motion by the changing employment patterns of women are expected to prevail during this decade and beyond. Women's income has become essential to maintaining the income levels of most families, as only 19.6 percent of families now fit the traditional pattern of the male breadwinner and female homemaker that was dominant just a few decades ago. Thus, the dynamics of the labor market and prevailing social and economic trends are geared to providing increasing opportunities for women, strengthening the pressures against sex-based wage and salary discrimination.[51]

Other Issues Involving Discrimination

Handicapped rights became an issue in 1987, when the Supreme Court ruled that the Vocational Rehabilitation Act of 1973 protects those with contagious diseases as well as those with physical handicaps. The case involved a third-grade teacher who suffered a flare-up of tuberculosis symptoms and was dismissed by the school board who feared she could spread the disease. The Court ruled that the teacher's rights had been violated and that the 1973 law had been passed to ensure that handicapped individuals are not denied jobs or other benefits because of the prejudiced attitudes or the ignorance of others.[52]

Employers could still dismiss someone who is incapable of performing the job or who poses a significant risk of spreading disease. But each case must be judged in the light of medical evidence that such a risk exists and a showing that safe alternative work cannot be found. This ruling was expected to have implications for people suffering from other diseases that often prompt discrimination, most particularly AIDS victims who have been discriminated against. The broad language of the Court in this case involving tuberculosis suggests that people suffering from AIDS would also be able to use the 1973 law as a protection against job discrimination.[53]

Finally, President Bush signed into law sweeping provisions to protect the disabled from discrimination in employment, public services, public transportation, public accommodations, and telecommunications services. The Americans with Disabilities Act (ADA) required that by 1994, all private employers of 15 or more workers will have to abide by antidiscrimination provisions. The law bans employers from discriminating against qualified disabled people in various areas, including job applications, hiring, promotion, and compensation. The law also requires employers to make "reasonable accommodations" for "qualified individuals with disabilities." This could include modifying job sites or work schedules and providing disabled employees and prospective employees with auxiliary aids and services they need to perform their work.[54]

Suits dealing with age discrimination increased dramatically in the early 1980s. In 1980 alone, the EEOC received 8,779 such complaints as against only 3,097 filed in 1979, when the Labor Department was still handling such cases. Another 8,000 such complaints were probably received by state and local agencies.[55] Since 1971, there has been a 100 percent increase in the number of age-discrimination charges brought against employers, including a 12 percent increase from 1984 to 1985 alone. Thirteen states have outlawed mandatory retirement altogether, and as of January 1, 1987, all U.S. companies are required to do the same because of federal laws passed at the end of the previous year.[56] In 1991, age-discrimination cases jumped 20 percent to 17,449 because of layoffs. Requests for information on age discrimination increased 155 percent over the year before, indicating that lawsuits were likely to increase in the future.[57]

Diversity in the Workplace

In the nineties, a new phrase began to appear with respect to equal opportunity, as companies began to emphasize "management of diversity." As the country itself became more culturally and ethnically diverse, this diversity began to be reflected in the workplace. While debates in society took place over multiculturalism, companies were faced with the reality of managing a work force that is going to become more diverse in the future. Companies responding to these changes target institutional racism and sexism that may be built into their organizations and challenge the dominant assumptions of a white-male corporate culture. Training programs emphasize value differences and managers are urged to let minorities and women "be themselves" in order to increase productivity.[58]

While some are suspicious of this emphasis on diversity as avoiding the issue of discrimination, for others the concept and its approaches offer the possibility of getting beyond racism and sexism per se and dealing with these problems in a larger context. There are limitations to a rights-based approach to eliminating discrimination in the workplace. Where does one draw the line with respect to which groups deserve special treatment because of discrimination? There have been cases involving obese people who won discrimination suits.[59] What about left-handed people who have to put up with phones designed for right-handed people? And what about people who are tall who are terribly uncomfortable in airplane seats? What about people who are not very good-looking?[60] As more and more groups are extended rights, everyone eventually comes to have some rights because of discrimination, and we are back where we started. Perhaps an emphasis on diversity offers a way out of this dilemma.

The process perspective lends support to this diversity approach, as can be seen by picking up on some of the themes discussed in Chapter 3. It was seen there that the common goal that characterizes a community of any sort, including a corporate community, can best be understood not in terms of some specific content, but rather in terms of ongoing and enriching growth and development. And this, in turn, indicates that differences should not be melted down, for these differences provide the materials by which a community can continue to grow.

Minorities and women can indeed "be themselves" rather than being compelled to "melt" into the majority group; however, "being themselves" does not mean being isolated from the majority group but should involve an ongoing interplay of all individuals. The healthy pluralism of perspectives, which provides the vitality for growth, is not a pluralism in which varying groups are enclosed within self-contained, myopic, limiting frameworks or points of view, cutting off the possibility of real communication. Rather, the common perspective enters into the development of the individuals in their diversity, and this diversity, in turn, feeds back into the common perspective and its tradition, leading, ideally, to growth for all.

This approach allows both for the evaluation of individuals qua individuals rather than as members of a group demanding rights, and also for the recognition that as members of particular groups having a shared history, they bring with them the diversity of various group perspectives. This diversity, far from needing either to be "melted down" to a common denominator or seen in isolationist terms, can add vitality to the ongoing growth of shared values within the corporate community.

It must be cautioned, however, that diversity is another abstraction that can get in the way of treating people as concrete human beings. Diversity can result in focusing on people as members of groups rather than as individuals in their own right. Ultimately, perhaps the only way to get beyond racism, sexism, or any other kind of ism is to develop the ability to look at people as human beings and evaluate what kind of contribution they can make to the organization and what needs they have that the organization can fulfill. Somehow, we need to get to the point where we can evaluate people as individual human beings who may happen to be male or female, white or black, handicapped or not handicapped, gay or heterosexual, obese or thin, good-looking or ugly, or whatever. These external characteristics say nothing about who the individual person is or what that person has to contribute to an individual corporation.

Prejudices about any of these characteristics have to be set aside in the interests of promoting and maintaining community. But these prejudices do not seem to be disappearing because of affirmative action programs, which may only be promoting further divisiveness in society. An emphasis on diversity has its own problems in this regard. The fundamental moral issue is one of getting beyond prejudices to one's own humanness, and treating others accordingly, thereby promoting growth of the entire human community rather than only for those groups who because of historical reasons have attained favored positions.

Accomplishment of this goal requires attunement to concrete situations and concrete human beings. It requires the ability to get beneath abstractions and take the perspective of the other. It requires growth of oneself, for growth of the self incorporates an ever more encompassing sympathetic understanding of varied and diverse interests, thus leading to tolerance not as a sacrifice but as an enlargement of the self. Treating people as individual human beings will not be achieved by impositions from "on high" but by a deepening to a more fundamental level of human rapport.

Questions for Discussion

1. Define prejudice. How does prejudice differ from stereotyping? Enumerate different places where prejudice can enter into employment decisions. What are the roots of racism and sexism? Are prejudice and stereotyping a figment of the imagination? What do you believe about theories of inherent inferiority, say, with respect to intelligence?

2. What is the difference between equal opportunity and affirmative action? What types of affirmative action programs or approaches are there? Why did quotas come into widespread use? Is there a difference between goals and quotas? What is the objective of affirmative action programs?

3. Is preferential treatment of minorities and women morally justified? How can preferential treatment be awarded without reverse discrimination? Does reverse discrimination violate the civil rights laws? Is it morally reprehensible, or must race and sex be taken into account in rectifying moral wrongs?

4. Describe the *Bakke* case. Was it a definitive case in its implications for business organizations? Did the *Weber* case provide more guidance for employers? What were the key provisions of this decision that gave employers some indication of the kind of affirmative action programs that were acceptable? Are these provisions morally acceptable?

5. Define sexual harassment and think of some examples from your own experience where this definition might have applied. Is sexual harassment a serious problem in the workplace? What can be done to make it less of a factor in employee relationships? What are the moral issues involved in sexual harassment?

6. Does a glass ceiling exist with respect to women advancing into management positions? How can this glass ceiling be broken? Why did the "mommy track" proposed by Felice Schwartz receive such negative criticism? Would you be in favor of such an arrangement? What are its moral implications?

7. What other issues are there with respect to discrimination in the workplace that have received some attention? Describe the new Americans with Disabilities Act and outline its impact on corporations. What other areas of discrimination exist that are likely to receive attention in future years?

8. Is affirmative action a concept that has run its course? Should preferential treatment for any groups be abolished? Has the society overcome its most discriminatory attitudes so that diversity can be implemented in our institutions? Has the debt to past groups that have suffered from discrimination been paid?

Endnotes

[1] Manuel G. Velasquez, *Business Ethics: Concepts and Cases* (Englewood Cliffs, NJ: Prentice-Hall, 1982), p. 266.

[2] Reprinted by permission from Michael D. Levin-Epstein, *Primer of Equal Employment Opportunity,* 3rd ed. (Washington DC: The Bureau of National Affairs, Inc., 1984), pp. 130–131. Copyright © by The Bureau of National Affairs, Inc., Washington, DC.

[3] "When Antibias Efforts Seem to Discriminate," *Business Week,* October 11, 1982, p. 40.

[4] *Allan Bakke* v. *the Regents of the University of California,* 553 P.2d 1152 (1976).

[5] *Regents of the University of California* v. *Bakke,* 98 S.Ct. 2733 (1978).

[6] "Bakke Wins, Quotas Lose," *Time,* July 10, 1978, p. 11.

[7] *Weber* v. *Kaiser Aluminum Corp.,* 563 F.2d 216 (5th Cir. 1977).

[8] *United Steelworkers of America* v. *Weber,* 99 S.Ct. 2721 (1979).

[9] "What the Weber Ruling Does," *Time,* July 9, 1979, p. 48.

[10] Stephen Wermiel, "Supreme Court, in 6–3 Vote, Backs Hiring Goals to Correct Sex Bias," *The Wall Street Journal,* March 26, 1987, p. 3.

[11] "Balancing Act: In a Sweeping Decision, The High Court Expands Affirmative Action," *Time,* April 6, 1987, pp. 18–20.

[12] Judith Jarvis Thomson, "Preferential Hiring," in Tom L. Beauchamp and Norman E. Bowie, eds., *Ethical Theory and Business,* 2nd ed. (Englewood Cliffs, NJ: Prentice-Hall, 1983), pp. 487–492.

[13] Velasquez, *Business Ethics,* pp. 281–282.

[14] Thomas Nagel, "A Defense of Affirmative Action," in Tom L. Beauchamp and Norman E. Bowie, eds., *Ethical Theory and Business,* 2nd ed. (Englewood Cliffs, NJ: Prentice-Hall, 1983), pp. 483–487.

[15] See Sonia L. Nazario, "Policy Predicament: Many Minorities Feel Torn by Experience of Affirmative Action," *The Wall Street Journal,* June 27, 1989, p. A-1.

[16] Daniel Seligman, "Affirmative Action Is Here to Stay," *Fortune,* April 19, 1982, p. 144.

[17] Richard F. America, "Affirmative Action and Redistributive Ethics," *Journal of Business Ethics,* Vol. 5, no. 1 (February 1986), p. 77.

[18] In *Wards Cove* v. *Atonio,* the Court ruled that those bringing race bias charges must prove that an employer has no business reason for imposing the job requirement they are contesting. This ruling reversed a 1971 precedent established in *Griggs* v. *Duke Power* where the Court ruled that employers must show their hiring and promotion practices were related to job performance even if the practices were not intended to discriminate. The burden was placed on the company to show that a requirement of employment had a manifest relationship to the employment in question. In another case involving firefighters in Birmingham, Alabama, the Court allowed white firefighters to challenge an eight-year-old Court-approved affirmative action plan if they could show reverse discrimination. Finally, in *Patterson v. McLean Credit Union,* the Court ruled that an 1866 civil rights law does not apply to cases of racial harassment or other discrimination by an employer after a person is hired. This law was passed to allow newly freed slaves to negotiate and enforce contracts. The Court ruled that the law prohibits discrimination in hiring but does not allow lawsuits involving harassment on the job or other conditions of employment. See Paula Dwyer, "The Blow to Affirmative Action May Not Hurt That Much," *Business Week,* July 3, 1989, pp. 61–62.

[19] Arthur S. Hayes, "Job-Bias Litigations Wilts Under High Court Rulings," *The Wall Street Journal,* August 22, 1989, p. B-1.

[20] "Sexual Harassment: Companies Could Be Liable," *Business Week,* March 31, 1986, p. 35.

[21] Julie R. Grace, Julie Johnson, and Andrea Sachs, "Anita Hill's Legacy," *Time,* October 19, 1992, pp. 56–57.

[22] Anne B. Fisher, "Sexual Harassment: What to Do," *Fortune,* August 23, 1993, pp. 84–88.

[23] L. A. Winokur, "Harassment of Workers by 'Third Parties' Can Lead into Maze of Legal, Moral Issues," *The Wall Street Journal,* October 26, 1992, p. B1.

[24] 29 CFR, Sec. 1604.11.

[25] "An Office Romance Unfairly Discriminated Against a Worker, a Court Says," *The Wall Street Journal,* March 20, 1984, p. 1.

[26] Stephen Wermiel and Cathy Trost, "Justices Say Hostile Job Environment Due to Sex Harassment Violates Rights," *The Wall Street Journal,* June 20, 1986, p. 2.

[27] Joseph Pereira, "Women Allege Sexist Atmosphere in Offices Constitutes Harassment," *The Wall Street Journal,* February 10, 1988, p. 19.

[28] Priscilla Painton and Andrea Sachs, "Office Crimes," *Time,* October 21, 1991, pp. 52–64.

[29] Susan Tifft, "A Setback for Pinups at Work," *Time,* February 4, 1991, p. 61; Amy Dockser Marcus and Ellen Joan Pollock, "Judge Rules Against Pinups in Workplace," *The Wall Street Journal,* January 23, 1991, p. B2.

[30] "Lawyers Keep a Close Eye on a Class-Action Sexual-Harassment Suit," *The Wall Street Journal,* July 20, 1993, p. A1.

[31] David E. Terpstra and Douglas D. Baker, "Outcomes of Sexual Harassment Charges," *Academy of Management Journal,* Vol. 31, no. 1 (1988), p. 193.

[32] Kenneth M. York, "Defining Sexual Harassment in Workplaces: A Policy-Capturing Approach," *Academy of Management Journal,* Vol. 32, no. 4 (1989), p. 847.

[33] "Role Reversal: Man Wins Office Sex Suit," *Business Week,* August 2, 1982, p. 19.

[34] Neal Templin, "As Women Assume More Power, Charges Filed by Men May Rise," *The Wall Street Journal,* October 18, 1991, p. B3.

[35] Amanda Troy Segal, "Corporate Women," *Business Week,* June 8, 1992, pp. 74–78.

[36] Claudia Sallis, "Onward, Women!" *Time,* December 4, 1989, p. 85.

[37] Timothy D. Schellhardt, "Despite Surge in Women Workers' Ranks, Pay Slid to 59.7% of Men's, Agency Finds," *The Wall Street Journal,* October 11, 1983, p. 41; Michael J. McCarthy, "Women's Salaries Reflect Disparities in Executive Suites," *The Wall Street Journal,* December 1, 1986, p. 29.

[38] "Crashing the Ceiling," *The Wall Street Journal,* March 16, 1993, p. A1.

[39] Bill McAllister, "Glass Ceiling: Women Held Back in Government, Too," *Times-Picayune,* October 29, 1992, p. A-9.

[40] Keith L. Alexander, "Both Racism and Sexism Block the Path to Management for Minority Women," *The Wall Street Journal,* July 25, 1990, p. B1.

[41] Susan B. Garland, "Can the Feds Bust Through the 'Glass Ceiling'?" *Business Week,* April 29, 1991, p. 33; Susan B. Garland, "Throwing Stones at the 'Glass Ceiling'," *Business Week,* August 19, 1991, p. 29.

[42] Janice Castro, "Rolling Along the Mommy Track," *Time,* March 27, 1989, p. 72.

[43] Ibid. See also Elizabeth Ehrlich, "The Mommy Track," *Business Week,* March 20, 1989, pp. 126–134; Robert J. Samuelson, "The Daddy Track," *Newsweek,* April 3, 1989, p. 47.

[44] Joann S. Lubin, "White-Collar Cutbacks Are Falling More Heavily on Women Than Men," *The Wall Street Journal,* November 9, 1982, p. 29. See also Carol Hymowitz, "Layoffs Force Blue-Collar Women Back into Low-Paying Job Ghetto," *The Wall Street Journal,* March 6, 1985, p. 33; Julie Amparano Lopez, "Study Says Women Face Glass Wall as Well as Ceilings," *The Wall Street Journal,* April 3, 1992, p. B1.

[45] Task Force on Economic Growth, *Louisiana Department of Labor, Louisiana 2000,* December 1988, pp. 10–11.

[46] Janice Castro, "She Calls All the Shots," *Time,* July 4, 1988, pp. 54–57.

[47] Diane Duston, "Women Paying More for Goods, Services," *Times-Picayune,* May 18, 1993, p. C-1.

[48] Marlene Cimons, "GAO: Drug Tests Short of Women," *Times-Picayune,* October 29, 1992, p. A-15. See also Joan Hamilton, "When Medical Research Is for Men Only," *Business Week,* July 16, 1990, p. 33.

[49] Aaron Bernstein, "The Mommy Backlash," *Business Week,* August 10, 1992, pp. 42–43.

[50] Gilbert Fuchsberg, "Female Enrollment Falls in Many Top M.B.A. Programs," *The Wall Street Journal,* September 25, 1992, p. B1; Barbara Kantrowitz, "Giving Women the Business," *Newsweek,* November 16, 1992, p. 98. See also Monica Roman, "Women, Beware: An MBA Doesn't Mean Equal Pay," *Business Week,* October 29, 1990, p. 57.

[51] "The Lasting Changes Brought by Women Workers," *Business Week,* March 15, 1982, p. 64. See also Peter Dubno, "Attitudes Toward Women Executives: A Longitudinal Approach," *Academy of Management Journal,* Vol. 28, no. 1 (March 1985), pp. 235–239.

[52] "Handicap Rights: Even AIDS Seems Covered," *Time,* March 16, 1987, p. 66.

[53] Ibid. See also "AIDS Goes to Court: Victims of the Disease Sue to Stop Discrimination," *Time,* December 8, 1986, p. 73.

[54] Nancy Traver, "Opening Doors for the Disabled," *Time,* June 4, 1990, p. 54; Albert R. Karr, "Disabled-Rights Bill Inspires Hope, Fear," *The Wall Street Journal,* May 23, 1990, p. B1.

[55] Robert S. Greenberger, "Fired Employees in 40s Filing More Bias Suits," *The Wall Street Journal,* October 8, 1981, p. 25.

[56] "Mandatory Retirement Gets Put Out to Pasture," *Business Week,* November 3, 1986, pp. 31-32.

[57] Linda Grant, "Out With the Old . . . In with the Young?" *Times-Picayune,* September 30, 1992, p. C-1.

[58] Frederick R. Lynch, "Multiculturalism Comes to the Workplace," *The Wall Street Journal,* October 26, 1992, p. A14.

[59] See Margaret Carlson, "And Now, Obesity Rights," *Time,* December 6, 1993, for the story about the extension of rights to obese people. In 1993, a federal appeals court upheld an order that required the state of Rhode Island to pay $100,000 for not hiring a 320-pound woman.

[60] See Jerry Adler, "Beyond the Bell Curve: Forget Intelligence—What Matters in Our Society Is Looks," *Newsweek,* November 7, 1994, p. 56.

Suggested Readings

Acker, Joan. *Doing Comparable Worth: Gender, Class and Pay Equity.* Philadelphia: Temple University Press, 1991.

Allen, Shelia, and Carole Truman, eds. *Women in Business: Perspectives on Women Entrepreneurs.* New York: Routledge, 1993.

Allport, Gordon. *The Nature of Prejudice.* Cambridge, MA: Addison-Wesley, 1954.

Blanchard, F. A., and F. J. Crosby, eds. *Affirmative Action in Perspective.* Holland: Springer-Verlag, 1989.

Blum, Linda M. *Between Feminism and Labor: The Significance of the Comparable Worth Movement.* Berkeley: University of California Press, 1991.

Bowie, Norman E., ed. *Equal Opportunity.* New York: Westview, 1988.

Chan, Anja A. *Women and Sexual Harassment.* New York: Harworth Press, 1993.

Clayton, Susan D., and Faye J. Crosby. *Justice, Gender, and Affirmative Action.* Ann Arbor: University of Michigan Press, 1992.

Coyle, Angela, and Jane Skinner, eds. *Women and Work.* New York: New York University Press, 1988.

Davidson, Marilyn J., and Cary L. Cooper. *Shattering the Glass Ceiling: The Woman Manager.* London: Taylor & Francis, 1992.

Erierson, James G. *Employer's Guide to the Americans with Disabilities Act.* Washington, DC: BNA, 1992.

Evans, Sara M., and Barbara N. Nelson. *Wage Justice: Comparable Worth and the Paradox of Technocratic Reform.* Chicago: University of Chicago Press, 1991.

Ezorsky, Gertrude. *Racism and Justice: The Case for Affirmative Action.* Ithaca, NY: Cornell University Press, 1991.

Fagenson, Ellen A. *Women in Management: Trends, Issues, and Challenges in Managerial Diversity.* New York: Sage, 1993.

Graham, Hugh D. *The Civil Rights Era.* New York: Oxford University Press, 1992.

Gutek, Barbara A. *Sex and the Workplace.* San Francisco: Jossey-Bass, 1985.

Gutman, Arthur. *EEO Law and Personnel Practices.* New York: Sage, 1993.

Jackson, Susan E., et al. *Diversity in the Workplace: Human Resource Initiatives.* New York: Builford Press, 1992.

Jones, Augustus J., Jr. *Affirmative Talk, Affirmative Action: A Comparative Study of the Politics of Affirmative Action.* New York: Praeger, 1991.

Karston, Margaret F. *Management and Gender: Issues and Attitudes.* New York: Praeger, 1994.

Kellough, J. Edward. *Federal Equal Employment Opportunity Policy and Numerical Goals and Timetables: An Impact Assessment.* New York: Praeger, 1989.

Killingsworth, Mark R. *The Economics of Comparable Worth.* New York: W. E. Upjohn, 1990.

Larkin, Geraldine A. *Woman to Woman: Street Smarts for Women Entrepreneurs.* Englewood Cliffs, NJ: Prentice Hall, 1993.

Levin, Martin L. *Age Discrimination and the Mandatory Retirement Controversy.* Baltimore: Johns Hopkins, 1989.

Lynch, Frederick R. *Invisible Victims: White Males and the Crisis of Affirmative Action.* New York: Praeger, 1991.

Mason, Philip. *Race Relations.* London: Oxford University Press, 1970.

McBroom, Patricia A. *The Third Sex: The New Professional Woman.* New York: Paragon House, 1992.

Morrison, Ann M., et al. *Breaking the Glass Ceiling: Can Women Reach the Top of America's Largest Corporations?* Boston: Addison-Wesley, 1992.

Powell, Gary N. *Women and Men in Management,* 2nd ed. New York: Sage, 1993.

Rapoport, John D., and Brian L. Zevnik. *The Employee Strikes Back.* New York: Macmillan, 1989.

Rhoads, Steven. *Incomparable Worth: Pay Equity Meets the Market.* Cambridge: Cambridge University Press, 1993.

Rosenfeld, Michel. *Affirmative Action and Justice: A Philosophical and Constitutional Inquiry.* New Haven: Yale University Press, 1991.

Schneid, Thomas D. *The Americans with Disabilities Act: A Practical Guide for Managers.* New York: Van Nostrand Reinhold, 1992.

Schwartz, Rosalind M., ed. *Managing the Multicultural Workforce.* Los Angeles: University of California Press, 1992.

Sedmak, Nancy, and Michael D. Levin-Epstein. *Primer on Equal Employment Opportunity,* 5th ed. Washington, DC: BNA, 1991.

Turner, Margery A., et al. *Opportunities Denied, Opportunities Diminished: Racial Discrimination in Hiring.* New York: Urban Institute, 1991.

Utofsky, Melvin. *A Conflict of Rights: The Supreme Court and Affirmative Action.* New York: Macmillan, 1991.

White, Jane. *A Few Good Women: Breaking the Barriers to Top Management.* Englewood Cliffs, NJ: Prentice Hall, 1992.

SHORT CASES

Price Waterhouse

Ann Hopkins was a successful manager at Price Waterhouse's Washington office. In 1982, she sought to become a partner in the firm. At that time, Price Waterhouse had 668 partners, of whom only seven were women. Ms. Hopkins was the only woman among the 88 partnership candidates being considered for promotion that year. According to some reports, there was little doubt that Ms. Hopkins was qualified for the position, as she had won at least $34 million of major consulting contracts for the company, the best record of all the candidates, and had billed more hours than any of the other candidates in the fiscal year prior to the partnership nominations.[1]

Of the 32 partners who submitted written reviews, eight abstained from making a recommendation because they didn't know her well enough, 13 wanted her to be made a partner, eight did not want to make her a partner, and three wanted her candidacy held over for the next go-around. After a lengthy evaluation process, the firm put her candidacy on hold for at least another year, and then later decided not to propose her for partnership again. The firm deemed her unsuitable for promotion because she was an overbearing, arrogant, and abrasive manager. In their reviews, some of the partners wrote that Ms. Hopkins had "an abrasive personality and poor interpersonal skills." They noted her "impatience, insensitivity, and use of profanity in dealing with the staff."[2] Others described her as being too "macho" and in need of a "charm school."[3]

After being denied partnership, while 47 of the male candidates were selected, she met with the chief partner in the Washington office who was one of her big supporters. He offered her a few tips to enhance her chances in the future. In court testimony, Ms. Hopkins said that the chief partner suggested that she "walk more femininely, talk more femininely, dress more femininely," and that she wear makeup, have her hair styled, and wear jewelry. Disgusted by this advice, Hopkins resigned and filed a lawsuit under Title VII of the Civil Rights Act, which says that an employer may not discriminate against an employee because of an individual's race, color, religion, sex, or national origin. She claimed that her stridency and occasional cursing would have been overlooked if she had been a man because of her exceptional record.[4]

The district judge in the court where she filed ruled in her favor, a decision that was upheld by an appeals court. The district court found that Price Waterhouse had discriminated against Ms. Hopkins by "filtering her partnership candidacy through a system that gave great weight to negative comments and recommendations, despite evidence that those comments reflected unconscious sexual stereotyping by male evaluators based on outmoded attitudes toward women." The court stated that an inability to get along with staff and peers was a legitimate reason to deny partnership, but the "evident sexism" in the firm's evaluation system raised concerns that stereotyping had caused the denial. While Ms. Hopkins had not proved discrimination to be the direct cause of the denial, the firm's decision was tainted because it had failed to root out such evident sexism from its evaluation system.[5]

In upholding the decision, the appeals court was convinced that Price Waterhouse had discriminated against Ms. Hopkins in "subtle and insidious" ways and that it "took no steps to discourage sexism, to heighten the sensitivity of partners to sexist attitudes or to investigate negative comments to ascertain whether they were the product of such attitudes." The appeals court also ruled that it was up to the firm to prove that sex discrimination was not a decisive factor in the decision, and it would have to do this by presenting "clear and convincing" evidence rather than by the less rigorous requirement of a "preponderance" of evidence.[6]

The case was appealed to the Supreme Court, which in a 6–3 ruling upheld the decisions of the lower courts. Justice William Brennan, who wrote the lead opinion, stated, "An employer who objects to aggressiveness in women but whose positions require this trait places women in an intolerable and impermissible Catch-22: out of a job if they behave aggressively and out of a job if they don't." The burden of proof was shifted to Price Waterhouse in that it would have to establish that it would have rejected Hopkins's partnership application based on purely nondiscriminatory factors. However, the firm would not have to present "clear and convincing" evidence to establish its position, but only meet the less rigorous standard of a "preponderance" of evidence. The firm had been held to too high a standard in earlier rulings, and thus when the case was reheard in a lower federal court, its task would be less onerous.[7]

Women hailed this decision as a victory believing that this decision would put pressure on firms to root out bias from their evaluation systems. Personnel making promotion decisions would have to be properly trained to ensure that race and sex were not part of the decision. Hopkins, who had become a senior budget officer at the World Bank, declared herself delighted by the decision. The prolonged litigation was an embarrassment for the firm, but even after the litigation had ended, only 28 of the firm's 900 partners were women.[8]

1. What is sex stereotyping? What is discrimination? How can stereotyping affect personnel decisions so as to produce discrimination? What can be done to eliminate this problem in organizations?

2. Was stereotyping a factor in the decision about Hopkins's partnership? How did it become a factor? What happened with regard to her candidacy for partner? Was she treated fairly and in a nondiscriminatory fashion?

3. How did the lower court rule on the case? What was the critical factor in its decision? How did the Supreme Court see the situation? What were the different parts of the ruling from the Supreme Court? What was the final outcome of the decision?

4. What does the future look like with respect to women in the workplace? What impact will your projection have on sex discrimination? What future issues are likely to be on the agenda with respect to sex discrimination?

[1] Michael J. McCarthy, "Supreme Court to Rule on Sex-Bias Case," *The Wall Street Journal,* June 14, 1988, p. 33.

[2] Ibid.

[3] Andrew Sachs, "A Slap at Sex Stereotypes," *Time,* May 15, 1989, p. 66.

[4] McCarthy, "Supreme Court," p. 33.

[5] Ibid.

[6] Ibid.

[7] Sachs, "Sex Stereotypes," p. 66.

[8] Ibid.

Source: Rogene A. Buchholz, *Public Policy Issues for Management,* 2nd ed. (Englewood Cliffs, NJ: Prentice Hall, 1992), pp. 180–182.

Rights Up in Smoke

The last thing Darlene Lambert felt like the first thing Monday morning was breathing in the smoke from Frank's and Alice's cigarettes. Darlene wasn't really crazy about breathing other people's smoke under the best of circumstances, especially after reading that nonsmokers like herself can get lung cancer and heart disease from doing so, but today she was suffering from a mild cold and the prospect of those cigarette fumes made her feel slightly nauseated.

Darlene worked with one other person, a nonsmoker, in a small office of the personnel depertment at Redwood Associates, but her job required her to spend extended periods on and off throughout the day in the main files room where Frank and Alice worked and smoked. Darlene had told them that she didn't like breathing cigarette smoke. They were nice people and sympathetic to her feelings; they tried not to smoke too much when she was there. But, of course, the smell of cigarettes permeated the room whether they had a cigarette going or not. And as nice and friendly as they were, Frank and Alice nevertheless figured that since their desks were located in that room, they had a right to smoke there. Alice had as much as told Darlene that she thought Darlene was oversensitive to smoke, and Frank sometimes joked about smokers being persecuted these days for their habit.

At 9:05 A.M., Darlene marched into the office of her supervisor, Charles Renford, and told him that she couldn't work in the files room today because of the smoke. Renford was caught off guard and more than a little put out by Darlene's announcement because top management was suddenly requesting a report—"due yesterday"—and he needed Darlene to begin assembling the data in the files room. He reminded her that Redwood Associates made an effort to accommodate nonsmokers by guaranteeing that certain areas of the building be smoke free, but it wasn't prepared to ban smoking altogether. Not only do smokers have rights, Renford said, it would hurt productivity and morale to make employees leave the building to smoke. "They should quit smoking," Darlene rejoined. "It would be for their own good."

"Maybe, it would," said Charles, "but the company shouldn't force them to quit. Besides, it is easy for you, who's never smoked, to talk about quitting. I know, I used to smoke myself."

Renford brought the conversation back around to the required report and its importance. Darlene simply said, "I'm sorry, Charles, but if it means going in that room—and it does—then I'm simply not going to do it." And then she got up and returned to her office, leaving Charles Renford trying to figure out what he was going to do.

1. Would Renford be within his rights to fire Darlene Lambert for insubordination? Can he order Frank and Alice not to smoke so that Darlene can work in the room? How would you deal with this situation?

2. Do employees like Frank and Alice have a right to smoke? Does Darlene have a right to a smoke-free workplace? How should these rights be balanced?

3. What policy on smoking would you recommend to Redwood Associates? Is it possible for employers to find some compromise between smokers and nonsmokers? Is it appropriate for companies to ban smoking altogether inside their facilities?

4. In 1914, Thomas Edison had a policy of employing "no person who smoked cigarettes." Is such a policy discriminatory? Is it reasonable?

Source: William H. Shaw and Vincent Barry, *Moral Issues in Business,* 6th ed. (Belmont, CA: Wadsworth Publishing Company, 1995), pp. 288–289.

Interest Groups

The Rights-for-Left-Handers Association (RLHA) has been in existence for less than a year, but already it has gained a great deal of visibility nationwide. The group primarily is pushing for companies to take the needs of left-handed people into account when designing products. One of its most recent targets has been the garden-variety pay telephones that have been designed for right-handed people and installed in phone booths around the country.

Pleasant Valley is a medium-sized city in the Midwest with an all-American image. One of the major employers in the city is the Black & White Company, which manufactures pay telephones. The RLHA has targeted this company for a major campaign to persuade it to redesign its phones to accommodate left-handed people. The group has hit upon an effective tactic to gain attention for its cause. It has organized an around-the-clock sit-in of all the public telephone booths throughout the city.

Complaints have been pouring into the mayor's office from irate citizens and out-of-towners who want to use the public phones. The mayor is reluctant to adopt a hard-line posture and use tough police tactics to forceably remove the sitters for fear of damaging the city's image. Several other major companies are considering locating there because of the attractive business climate and good living conditions. The attention of the nation has been focused on the city because of extensive media coverage and the whole world is watching what happens.

In desperation, the mayor has called a meeting for local government officials, representatives of the RLHA, and company management to try and resolve the situation.

Mr. Gray, CEO of Black & White, is wondering what position he should take, and has called a meeting of senior management to discuss the company's options. He believes that most executives will advocate the company take a hard-line position and not give in to the demands of the group or to the pressures they may get from the mayor's office.

1. What options does the company have in this situation? What can Mr. Gray do to help his senior management thoroughly evaluate these options? What should be the company's objectives in this situation? Is a hard-line position likely to accomplish these objectives?

2. What interests do the various stakeholder groups have in the outcome of this controversy? Is a balancing of these interests feasible? How would one go about trying to reach some kind of compromise where a balancing of interests takes place?

Source: Rogene A. Buchholz, *Business Environment and Public Policy: Implications for Management,* 5th ed. (Englewood Cliffs, NJ: Prentice Hall, 1995), pp. 125–126.

Comparable Worth

To deal with the comparable worth issue, Benson Rosen, Sara Reynes, and Thomas A. Mahoney, in an article entitled "Compensation, Jobs, and Gender" (*Harvard Business Review,* Vol. 61, no. 4, July–August 1983, pp. 186–190), mention three strategic options that are available to management. The first option is a choice not to take any steps to reduce or eliminate the earnings gap between men and women. The law does not currently require the comparable worth concept to be implemented by employers, and the political environment, at the time the article was written, made passage of something like a "Comparable Worth Act" highly unlikely. Employers who adopt this option, however, must keep abreast of changes in the social and political environments so that such a conservative position does not become outmoded.

The second option is to attempt to reduce the earnings gap between men and women by taking affirmative action to speed up the selection, training, and promotion of women to higher-paying positions. This approach raises women's earnings without disrupting established methods of salary determination. Advocates of this option argue that once women become employed in positions now held exclusively by men in proportionate numbers, salary differences between the sexes will disappear.

The third option is to attack comparable worth head on and reexamine the entire compensation system of the organization. Companies that adopt this option must decide which of their compensation practices require revision and must assess the economic feasibility of moving toward a comparable worth philosophy on which to base job evaluation. Such bold action, however, may avoid strong government regulation and gain a progressive image for the company.

1. What is the current status of the comparable worth issue? As more and more cities and states decide to change their job evaluation practices to something like a comparable worth approach, does this put additional pressure on the private sector to do likewise?

2. Which of the foregoing options would you recommend for management at this point? What advantages and disadvantages are there to each approach? What kind of a forecast would you make regarding the comparable worth issue and what are the implications of this forecast for business organizations?

Source: Rogene A. Buchholz, *Business Environment and Public Policy: Implications for Management,* 5th ed. (Englewood Cliffs, NJ: Prentice Hall, 1995), pp. 341–342.

CHAPTER 16 Rights and Obligations of Employers and Employees

In addition to the issue of discrimination, which was covered in the previous chapter, there are several other issues having do with specific aspects of employer-employee relationships where ethics is a most relevant consideration. These issues can be analyzed from an ethical point of view and questions asked about the ethical dimensions involved in the relationship between employer and employee. The issues covered in this chapter include termination and job ownership, plant closings, safety and health, insider trading, confidentiality and trade secrets, conflicts of interest, whistle-blowing, and privacy.

Termination and Job Ownership

Studies have shown that two out of every 1,000 employees who are dismissed by companies are fired for unjust causes, which means that some 50,000 to 60,000 workers are fired every year for causes that are believed to be unjust. Some of these discharge cases go to arbitration, and of those that do, more than 50 percent are decided against the employer. The most common reason for these victories by employees is that management failed to abide by union contracts that protect workers against unjust dismissal. Another reason is that employees were fired because they refused to perform an action that was in violation of a law that prohibited the action.[1] The problem of unjust dismissals has resulted in a trend toward curtailment of management's freedom to fire for any reason whatsoever and has extended the notion of rights to the job itself in the form of job ownership.

David Ewing, who wrote *Do It My Way or You're Fired,* argues that the steady buildup in the rights of workers has been natural, inevitable, and desirable. Ewing believes that "an employee has a kind of property right in his or her job."[2] This means that the job must be

381

treated as a species of property rather than as a contractual claim, and as such cannot be bought or sold or taken away from a natural owner without due process. Peter Drucker writes that the evolution of the job into a species of property can be seen as the correct, if not the only, answer to the problem of alienation, which Karl Marx identified over a century ago as resulting from the divorce of the worker from the means of production.[3]

Historically, employers viewed employment as something that could be terminated "at will" without due process of any kind. This has been called the employment-at-will doctrine. Most workers in the United States have no protection against dismissal without good reason or for bad or improper reasons. Only about 35 to 40 percent of the work force is protected against unjust dismissal because of union contracts or federal laws dealing with discrimination.[4] The rest are subject to being fired at any time for any reason or no reason.

This employment-at-will doctrine was expressed in a court decision of nearly a century ago that read: Employers "may dismiss their employees at will . . . for good cause, for no cause, or even for cause morally wrong, without thereby being guilty of legal wrong."[5] Several years later, another court stated that the "arbitrary right of the employer to employ or discharge labor, with or without regard to actuating motives, is a proposition settled beyond peradventure."[6] This employment-at-will doctrine had an economic rationale, namely, that the factors of production, in this case employees, should be free to seek their most productive uses without any restrictions placed on either the employer to fire employees at will or on employees to quit and seek other employment.

With regard to firing based on this economic rationale, employees were not supposed to be fired unless they were not performing adequately and the company would be more productive without them. The doctrine never meant that productive employees should be fired for other reasons having nothing to do with performance. This doctrine was abused by employers, however, as otherwise productive employees were often fired for quite arbitrary reasons and for unjust reasons, and employees had no legal defense. Because of this abuse, this at-will doctrine has been eroded during the past few years by court decisions that have placed restrictions on the ability of management to fire employees without cause.

As society has become accustomed to banning firings based on race, sex, or union activities, it seems the next logical step is to extend the ban to unfair firings. This extension would give workers something like a property right in their jobs, something that could not be taken away except through due process. But what constitutes an unfair firing is not clear. Under this doctrine, some believe that almost any type of firing could be challenged in one way or another.[7] At the present time, courts have opened up three new areas under which fired employees may make claims against employers.

Promises. Claims have been made that a firing violates an employment contract in that it does not conform with promises made in the employee handbook or hiring interview. In recent years, several state courts have ruled that expressed or implied corporate policies are considered to be employment contracts. Fired employees have convinced courts in these states that personnel policies contained in such corporate documents as job applications, handbooks, and stock-option plans should be considered employment contracts. Thus, fired employees have claimed that they were fired without just cause in violation of the company's employee manual.[8]

Public Policy. The public policy action theory holds that a discharge is wrong when an employee is discharged for refusing to do something that public policy condemns or if an employee is discharged for some action that public policy encourages. Between 1962 and

1982, at least 20 state courts invalidated employee dismissals on the public policy theory. These firings conflicted with public policy because they were spurred by something like jury duty or refusal to lie to a grand jury.[9]

Good Faith. This is a claim that the firing did not live up to the employer's obligations to treat its workers fairly and in good faith. This approach was used by Massachusetts judges in a case involving a salesman for NCR Corporation. The employee contended that he was fired just before the company was about to sign a major contract on which he had worked for months in order to avoid paying him a big commission that was due him for making the deal.[10]

These new rules and court decisions are only the leading edge of the issue, and court actions continue to put pressure on legislatures to codify judicial law in formal statutes. By 1992, 45 states had legislation embracing at least one of these areas, and eight have bills covering all three of the new doctrines.[11] These bills subject corporations to "unjust dismissal" claims, but in some cases these claims are settled in arbitration, freeing companies from the time and expense involved in formal litigation. Furthermore, some of these bills would prevent employees from winning punitive damages. Problems encountered in relation to plant closings, downsizing, technological replacement, dislocated workers, employment of the disadvantaged, and other changes in the workplace have brought increased pressure on granting concessions in what may be called the right to a job, lifelong employment, or job ownership.

The trend toward job ownership is partly the result of the decline of unionism in the United States, which traditionally has been the means by which many employees have had their rights respected in the workplace. As unions decline and fewer workers come under union contracts that protect them from unjust dismissals, state courts may be more willing to put employee rights above the private property interests of employers. Another reason the courts have listened to dismissed employees is because the employees who file suit are in many cases educated, professional men and women who know their rights and have the resources to fight for them. Alan F. Westin of Columbia University states: "Today the ordinary American feels that fair treatment means that he can be fired for lack of business but not for lack of cause by abusive managers."[12]

How can business operate in an environment in which its right to remove nonproductive, noncooperative, and nonloyal workers is restricted? Unjust discharge is not fair to the person who was fired because of the stigma it leaves on the discharged employee. Unjust continued employment, however, is a problem for employers because of the stigma it leaves on the productive employees and its negative impact on the bottom line and our competitive system. Peter Drucker offers the following advice to businesses that are trying to cope with this problem.

> How can modern economies cope with the emergence of job property rights and still maintain the flexibility and social mobility necessary for adapting quickly to changes? At the very least, employing organizations will have to recognize that jobs have some of the characteristics of property rights and cannot therefore be diminished or taken away without due process. Hiring, firing, promotion and demotion must be subject to pre-established, objective, public criteria. And there has to be a review, a pre-established right to appeal to a higher judge in all actions affecting rights in and to the job.
>
> Standards and review will, paradoxically, be forced on employers in the United States by the abandonment of fixed-age retirement. For companies to be able to dismiss even the most senile and decrepit oldster, they will have to develop impersonal standards of performance and systematic personnel procedures for employees of all ages.

> The evolution of jobs into a kind of property also demands that there be no expropriation without compensation, and that employers take responsibility to anticipate redundancies, retraining employees about to be laid off and finding and placing them in new jobs. It requires redundancy planning rather than unemployment compensation.[13]

The increasing rights of fired employees are causing some businesses to implement or, in some cases, strengthen existing internal grievance procedures for nonunion employees. Hundreds of companies now have some type of voluntary system to review dismissals. The publicity surrounding the proemployee court decisions on this issue has increased interest in voluntary programs. Some companies even allow the use of outside arbitration procedures or have turned over firing authority to independent panels.[14] The phrase "corporate due process" has emerged to refer to procedures that have been set up to handle employee complaints promptly and equitably. Some believe that most termination problems could be eliminated through a better counseling and complaint system.[15] Other companies are eliminating any promise of job security from their employee handbooks and taking steps to better document their dismissals.

A conflict of rights is clearly at issue in this debate about job ownership. If the job is considered the property of the employee, then there is a conflict of property rights between employees and managers who represent the owners. How are clashes between these different property rights to be resolved? If a job is not considered in this manner, there remains the conflict between the rights of employees to be treated in a fair and just manner when it comes to dismissal versus the right of managers to fire employees when they deem appropriate.

Plant Closings

Restrictions on the ability of company management to close a plant are an issue that appears when companies move to another location or close a plant because it is outdated or for other reasons. Such closings are particularly acute during periods of recession when jobs are not readily available elsewhere in a particular community. Closing of a plant means loss of jobs for those who worked there, but the impact that the closing of a plant can have on a community can also be quite severe, depending on the size of the community and diversification of industry in the community. Thus, plant closings are a concern of both the communities affected and the employees who are thrown out of work.

States and municipalities face fiscal difficulties because of plant closings, as their tax base erodes and public spending is increased to pay for the social costs of dislocation. These costs can include increased unemployment benefits the state may provide, increased welfare payments for the unemployed families, increased juvenile delinquency, crime, divorce, and mental illness. These social costs of plant closings are very real and can be quite significant. Communities have been known to suffer a severe decline in economic activity and an erosion of economic wealth because the major employer in town decided to move elsewhere or close down altogether.

The major victims of a plant closing are, of course, the laid-off workers and their families, who suffer all the hardships that loss of a job entails in our society. The massive layoffs that result from the closing of a major plant often flood the labor market and overwhelm local employment opportunities. Thus, workers and their families may have to move out of the community to find another job, and in many cases, may even have to move to a new region of the country where the economic opportunities are better. These dislocations cause severe problems for those who have lived in a given community for many years and have extensive ties to family and friends. Workers may also need retraining to equip themselves for new jobs if their skills and knowledge are outdated.

The issue of plant closings became a political issue when communities and employees, through their unions or other organizations, began to bring pressure to bear to place restrictions on the freedom of management in closing plants and to make companies bear some of the social costs involved when a plant is closed. Politicians at the state and local levels responded to these concerns by holding hearings on the issue and in some cases passing legislation that imposed certain responsibilities on management when a plant is closed.

These restrictions generally have taken the form of requiring the firm to (1) give long-term notice of its intention to close, thereby giving employees ample time to find a new job and communities time to adjust, (2) pay substantial severance benefits to laid-off workers so they and their families will not have to suffer a severe loss of income before a new job is found, and (3) make restitution payments to the affected community and help bear some of the social costs involved in a plant closing.[16]

Proponents of plant closing legislation argue that firms have a social responsibility to their workers and to the communities in which they do business, a responsibility that extends beyond the labor contract and the economic condition of the enterprise. Businesses have a moral obligation, it is argued, to reinvest profits in the company to keep plants open by modernizing them and to reinvest in the community in which profits are earned.[17] Advocates fear that without government regulation of this sort, employees and communities will be left without protection from the effects of a plant closing. Restrictions on closing a plant will protect employee rights and keep companies from seeking higher profits by locating to areas of cheaper labor. Thus, proponents claim that they support the "little person," the low-income worker as well as the higher-paid skilled worker who may otherwise be exploited by the system.[18] Proponents also argue that reinvestment of a company's profits in the community will have a multiplier effect—that the employment growth in the community will be several times the number of jobs directly associated with the investment projects.[19]

Opponents of plant closing legislation point out that regulations of this sort will restrict the mobility of capital and labor to seek the most profitable economic opportunities available in the country, and thus society will suffer from an inefficient use of its resources. Costs will be higher because of having to keep an inefficient plant open or pay for the social costs of dislocation. Opponents argue that any law that requires firms to reinvest profits in their community would also restrict companies in other areas from investing in the community. Such restrictions would discourage people from assuming the risks of operating a business and would, in the aggregate, deter saving and investment, making the country less able to compete with foreign firms. Economic growth as a whole would be curtailed, which would inevitably have effects on the communities involved in plant closings. Opponents also point to the beneficial effects of the free flow of domestic resources and argue that restrictive laws related to plant closings mean that domestic plants and equipment will become economic hostages of the state.[20] Long-term experimentation and evaluation of specific contextual results will be needed to test the validity of these hypotheses concerning the dire moral consequences of restrictive legislation.

In 1987 the federal government passed the Worker Adjustment and Retraining Notification Act (WARN), which requires employers of more than 100 workers to provide 60-day advance notification of a closing or a massive layoff. While business believed such legislation would result in lost productivity after such notice was given, other evidence suggested that providing workers with advance notice of layoffs generates substantial benefits to displaced workers, their families, local communities, and the economy in general. Advance notice stems the loss of worker incomes and saves the economy unemployment benefits and other social costs by shortening the duration of unemployment.[21]

Advance notice gives workers time to make plans and take steps to find a new job before a layoff is imminent. Some of the advantages that the early warning provision provides workers are said to be (1) it is easier to enroll workers in adjustment programs before they are laid off; (2) it is easier to enlist managers and workers as active participants in displaced workers' projects before the closing or layoff; (3) with time to plan ahead, services to workers can be ready at the time of layoff; and (4) with enough lead time, it is sometimes possible to avoid layoffs altogether.[22]

Should federal, state, or local governments pass legislation to restrict the closing of a manufacturing facility and/or the movement of that manufacturing facility to another location? Should management be required to negotiate such closings with the workers and give advance notice to the workers and the community of a plant closing? Plant closings are a concern of the workers and communities that are affected as they can lead to mass layoffs, high unemployment for the community affected, and the deterioration of public services such as schools, police, and fire protection as the tax base for the community erodes. Whose rights take priority in this situation, the rights of managers to run their enterprises as they see fit or the rights of employees and the communities involved to their livelihood?

The reality is that there will continue to be plant closings and there will be new plant openings. There may be such things as negotiated closings, advance notice, severance pay, plant buyouts by the workers, or other arrangements where labor and management work together to deal with the situation or where legislation requires these arrangements. There will always be a need to close a factory just as there will always be a need to build new factories. Plant closings will remain an issue. The question is how to deal with them—government legislation, cooperative agreements, employee stock-ownership plans, or some other means as yet untried.

There does not seem to be a way to develop a general ethical rule that will hold for all plant closings. Every plant closing is enmeshed in concrete circumstances that set it apart from others. The solutions to these closings will have to be worked out on a case-by-case basis. From the ongoing resolution of concrete closings, rough guides of action will no doubt begin to emerge, but their contours will continually be shaped and reshaped as new plant closings give rise to unforeseen types of problems.

Safety and Health

During the early years of industrialization in this country, not much thought was given to improving working conditions related to occupational safety and health. The dramatic oversupply of labor in the late 1800s and early 1900s made workers so cheap that labor was thought of as a commodity to be secured at the lowest possible price rather than a human resource to be carefully husbanded for humanitarian or economic reasons. Because much of the work done was of an unskilled nature, investment in training and experience was low, making replacement of injured workers much cheaper than efforts to protect them from hazards in the workplace.

Safety efforts were seen as directly conflicting with the maximization of profits, and many owners and managers tended to take an extremely cavalier attitude toward them.[23] Interestingly enough, employees' attitudes were often similar. Accidents were accepted as simply part of working for a living and it was believed they could not be eliminated. This attitude may have been fostered by the Protestant ethic approach toward work, which contained a certain sense of fatalism and created the expectation of a life full of adversity. Workers did not expect safety to receive much attention from employers and learned to accept the unsafe conditions that existed in many of the nation's workplaces.

The attitude of the courts and common law doctrine toward workplace injuries reflected this social climate. Suits against employers were uncommon and awards to employees rare. Employees were understandably reluctant to risk their jobs to sue an employer, and fellow employees were similarly reluctant to risk their jobs to testify on the injured party's behalf. Even if an injured employee should be brave enough to sue and fortunate enough to win, legal fees usually ate up a good portion of any award. Thus, the liability law of these early years failed to protect employees, proved wasteful of time and money (for legal action), and failed to stimulate any action toward accident prevention.

As technology became more sophisticated, the risks to workers increased, particularly in the area of health risks related to chemicals and other substances workers might be exposed to in the course of their employment. This increased risk brought with it an increased interest in promoting safety and health concerns in the workplace. The first substantial effort to promote safety and health in the workplace came from the states in the form of workers' compensation laws. These laws required the employer to either carry insurance to cover damages or to pay out-of-pocket damages to employees injured on the job regardless of who was at fault. Workers' compensation laws brought insurance companies into the accident prevention field. They were able to interest business in substantial accident prevention programs because lower accident frequency and severity rates meant lower insurance premiums. Even with these economic incentives, however, the worker compensation system proved to be inadequate in protecting workers across the country.[24]

State regulation was also attempted, but state laws varied widely in their stringency and coverage, and many were enforced only weakly. Pressures mounted for a federal program that would set and enforce uniform standards to protect workers and extend such rights into the workplace. As one person stated: "More than 90 million Americans spend their days on the job. They are our most available national resource. Yet, until 1970, no uniform and comprehensive provisions existed for their protection against workplace safety and health hazards. . . . In terms of lost production and wages, medical expenses and disability compensation, the burden on the nation's commerce was staggering. Human cost was beyond calculation."[25]

The federal government finally came to the workplace to deal with the safety and health problem in the form of the Occupational Safety and Health Act of 1970 (Williams-Steiger Act). The act was passed by a bipartisan Congress "to assure so far as possible every working man and woman in the Nation safe and healthful working conditions and to preserve our human resources."[26] Under the act, the Occupational Safety and Health

Administration (OSHA), which has legislative and executive functions with respect to safety and health programs, was created.

The safety problem in workplaces relates to injuries that result from hazardous conditions that go undetected or uncorrected. Occupational injuries are generally noninfectious and nonchronic and are usually traumatic types of incidents that happen to workers under certain situations. The causes of injuries are not difficult to recognize and define as being work related. There is usually some hazardous condition such as an unguarded machine or unsafe ladder that is directly related to the injury. Thus, a program aimed at reducing injuries in the workplace must reduce these hazardous conditions in the workplace.

Illnesses, on the other hand, are more often than not difficult to define operationally, and it is not always clear that an illness can be attributed to a specific workplace hazard. Illnesses such as cancer have long latency periods and multiple causes, and employees with varying levels of susceptibility are exposed to many substances both on and off the job that may or may not act in a synergistic fashion to cause the illness. Thus, the health problem in workplaces is much more complex than the safety problem, and a program directed at dealing with illnesses in the workplace must deal with reducing exposure to hazardous substances in the work environment that could cause serious problems.[27]

OSHA does its work through the setting of standards related to safety and health conditions. A safety or health standard has been defined as "a legally enforceable regulation governing conditions, practices, or operations to assure safe and healthful workplaces."[28] There are two types of standards on safety: horizontal regulations that apply to all industries and relate to such items as fire extinguishers, electrical groundings, railings, machine guards, and the like; and vertical provisions that apply to particular industry groups, such as the maritime industry and construction. OSHA safety standards fall into four major categories: general industry, maritime, construction, and agriculture.

Health standards relate to particular substances such as benzene, lead, or cotton dust that workers may come into contact with in one way or another. The agency must proceed on a substance-by-substance basis in regard to health standards. This process is subject to many delays and frustrations, as there are many unresolved issues in the standard-setting process with regard to health that make it tremendously complex and lengthy. Many of these issues may have to be decided by the Supreme Court, as it agrees to hear cases dealing with health standards. There seems to be no conclusive scientific evidence to resolve some of these issues, given the current state of knowledge and medical technology.[29] Health standards are thus subject to political pressures from interested parties with ideological biases.

The process of setting safety and health standards is thus filled with controversy. The establishment of health standards in particular is an area where facts and values are particularly intermingled. These standards, even at their best, must be supplemented by individuals within business organizations who understand the particular dangers to workers and have a sense of moral responsibility to self-mandated initiatives to protect workers. Safety and health concerns cannot be left to government alone.

In the 1980s, more attention began to be paid to toxic or hazardous substances and the worker's "right to know" about the dangers associated with the substances they were handling. Pressures were put on managers to disclose to their employees and the public the names and potential health hazards of any toxic substances workers are exposed to in the workplace. Proponents of these laws argued that if the right to know in the workplace is to be adequately protected, there must be an affirmative duty to disclose information about health hazards to workers in addition to a duty to honor worker-initiated requests for access to records. Employees should be aware of hazards that they may encounter so that they can make an informed decision as to whether or not they wish to work in that environment, and know the precautions that they should take to avoid or minimize the possibility of suffering any adverse effects from the hazards.

An important issue for business relative to safety and health is whether or not executives can be prosecuted for criminal charges by state and local officials. The Justice Department prosecuted only four of the 30 cases referred to it for criminal investigation since 1980 because prosecutors complain that penalties are so weak that they are reluctant to go to court. Criminal negligence is also difficult to prove under the 1970 act because prosecutors must prove that employers intentionally disregarded safety regulations, not just that they were negligent.[30] State and local prosecutors tried to fill this void and open the door to criminal prosecution by arguing that OSHA does not bar states from prosecuting corporate officials for work-related injuries and deaths.[31] Whether prosecuted or not, however, they are morally culpable if the charges are correct.

In September 1991, fire swept through an Imperial Food Products, Inc., plant in Hamlet, North Carolina, killing 25 workers. The plant was in the business of cooking, weighing, and packing fried chicken parts for fast-food restaurants. The workers were killed because the owners of the plant routinely kept the doors locked to keep workers from stealing chicken parts. This practice was in clear violation of OSHA regulations, which require employers to keep exit doors clear of obstructions so they can serve as escape hatches in case of fire. Three officials of the plant were indicted on involuntary manslaughter charges, and the owner was eventually sentenced to 19 years and 11 months in jail as part of a plea bargain that let his son, the operations manager of the plant, get off without being sentenced. This was the stiffest sentence ever awarded for a worker-safety criminal charge.[32]

What seems to be the moral culpability that led to this disaster? The persons responsible for locking the doors to prevent theft certainly did not deliberately decide to sacrifice the lives of workers for a few chicken parts. Rather, most likely they did not take the time, make the effort, or assume the responsibility for envisioning the concrete consequences that could result from their actions. They were seemingly not willing to accept the possibly dire consequences of their actions as real possibilities. They reacted to an immediate situation that was costing them money and ignored any possible adverse consequences.

An area of responsibility for workers' health that grew in the 1980s was the area of emotional stress on the job, as the number of stress claims grew, expanding the liability of the workers' compensation system in many states. In 1985, all but nine states paid compensation for job-related emotional problems. Workers' compensation premiums covering this problem hit $35 billion in 1988, which was double the 1980 level. Many of these states had no legislation limiting the nature of these claims, creating an open-ended possibility for filing claims. The National Institute of Occupational Safety and Health also put psychological disorders on its list of leading work-related illnesses, and cited reducing stress in high-tech offices as a primary objective.[33]

In the late 1980s, more attention began to be paid to hazards in the workplace that may affect workers' ability to reproduce. Some evidence suggested that a variety of chemicals and even video display terminals may pose such health risks, although a study conducted by NIOSH in 1991 found that working long hours before a video display terminal did not increase the risk of a miscarriage for pregnant women.[34] Regarding other reproductive hazards, however, there was little consensus on what action to take, and only 15 of the 500 largest U.S. companies in 1987 had comprehensive policies covering reproductive hazards. This issue was called one of the most sensitive hazards in the workplace because attempts to deal with the problem, usually by banning pregnant or fertile women from certain types of work, often caused controversy and even lawsuits alleging discrimination.[35] Are these attempts a disguised form of discrimination? Do they unfairly limit an individual's freedom of choice? This situation poses both a moral and a legal dilemma as the right to hold a particular job for which one is competent comes in direct conflict with protection from health hazards.

Repetitive-motion injuries also received increasing attention in the late 1980s, as it was estimated that more than 5 million people or about 4 percent of the work force in the United States suffered from motion injuries in 1986, and the cost to employers through lost earnings and expenses for medical costs and treatment amounted to more than $27 billion annually. These injuries stem from thousands of repetitive movements in jobs like typing and meat cutting, and result in painful nerve conditions such as carpal tunnel syndrome that debilitate the hands and arms. The number of reported cases almost doubled in 1987, making repetitive-motion injuries the fastest-growing occupational injury in the 1980s.[36] As seen earlier, technology and the way it is structured are the source of this problem.

By 1990, an estimated 185,000 workers were affected, and repetitive-motion injuries accounted for more than half the country's occupational illnesses, costing employers as much as $20 billion a year from workers' compensation claims and other expenses.[37] Some scholars expected this area to become the next tort law fiasco after asbestos, as claims began to mount into the hundreds of thousands and possibly millions.[38] OSHA began to pay increasing attention to this issue as well, beginning rule-making proceedings aimed at upgrading the regulations on repetitive-motion injuries in a wide range of industries. More emphasis was put on ergonomics, which involves adapting the workplace to the needs of workers by taking engineering or other steps to eliminate such hazards rather than making workers adjust to the workplace.[39]

In the early 1990s, OSHA had to deal with the AIDS problem, by issuing new regulations to protect health care workers from AIDS and other diseases. The roughly 80 new regulations, which took effect in 1992, require protective clothing such as full-length gowns, gloves, and masks when touching patients; storing of needles in puncture-proof containers; better disposal of medical waste; and new record-keeping requirements for health care employers. Violations of these guidelines could result in fines of as much as $70,000 per incident. The rules were expected to affect about 5 million workers in hospitals, nursing homes, and doctors' and dentists' offices, and cost in the neighborhood of $812 million annually.[40]

Finally, something called the "sick building syndrome" began to emerge as a health hazard. Complaints about headache, nausea, sore throat, or fatigue were commonplace among workers at the office, which usually cleared up when leaving the building. Many buildings were found to have inadequate ventilation, which allowed indoor contaminants from smoking and vapors from photocopying machines, cleaning liquids, and solvents to accumulate. The Environmental Protection Agency estimated that the economic cost of indoor air pollution totaled tens of billions of dollars annually in lost productivity, direct medical care, lost earnings, and employee sick days.[41]

There seems to be no end of problems in the safety and health area relative to workplaces. While government data indicated that worker safety was still a problem in many workplaces, other studies suggested that the situation may be even far worse than the government implies.[42] Other studies showed that we were losing the job safety war to Japan, which had far fewer private sector injuries and illnesses.[43] In the early 1990s, the administration stressed more input by workers to deal with the safety and health problem through worker-safety committees and other measures. States were also passing laws to mandate such committees as the federal government debated whether or not to create a similar national mandate.[44] Thus, there is a continual need for managers to pay attention to safety and health issues and be concerned about the rights of workers in this regard.

What is needed is, again, the willingness to view the worker as a concrete human being rather than as something factored into profit and loss statements, and to envision the problems that could arise from the position in which workers are placed. Technology and the way it is employed can create some real hazards for workers that need to be taken into account. Managers must think of the corporation as a community rather than just as an economic entity, and treat workers as valued members of this community who deserve protection from hazards in the workplace.

Insider Trading

Insider trading has been of concern in the financial world since the beginning of the century, but it made the headlines for several years during the 1980s, when so-called financial geniuses such as Michael Milken, Ivan Boseky, Martin Siegel, and Dennis Levine were caught in an insider trading scandal that rocked Wall Street. Since that time, insider trading hasn't received quite so much attention, but it still continues. Over the years, Congress has passed and amended many acts dealing with this problem and has offered many alternatives to prosecute those found guilty of insider trading.

Although there is no precise definition of insider trading, it can be broadly defined as buying or selling securities while in possession of nonpublic information about a corporation or about the market for a corporation's securities. One example of insider trading activity would be if an individual within a company, who knew about the earnings of the company before they were announced to the public, traded in the company's stock because of this nonpublic information and made a profit in the market. Most of the profits insiders made during the 1980s were based on nonpublic information they had regarding mergers and acquisitions because of their position in brokerage houses and investment banks that put these deals together. With this information they could buy stock in the acquired company before everyone else, and make a great deal of money, since the acquired company's stock usually went up when a merger was announced.

Insider trading is difficult to detect in many cases because the insiders go to great pains to cover their actions, but an even bigger problem is how to punish the offenders. Since 1934, when the U.S. Congress decided that insider trading was not good for the financial markets, the Securities and Exchange Commission (SEC) has regulated this activity. The foundation for U.S. insider trading law is the 1934 Securities and Exchange Act, which contains a section relating to trading by certain insiders and has a general antifraud provision. This section was not cited in insider prosecutions for many years, however, because insider trading was not explicitly defined within the act, and subsequent amendments did not add a definition. The relevant sections of the 1934 act focused on penalties and sanctions rather than on demarcating the border between acceptable and unacceptable behaviors.[45]

The lack of a definition of insider trading poses something of a problem in deciding when insider trading has actually occurred, but keeping the definition vague does help prosecutors and regulators by not creating loopholes.[46] If insider trading were strictly defined, insiders would look for ways around the law that were not in the definition. The lack of a definition also enables prosecutors and the SEC to expand their concerns into areas not anticipated by the securities laws, which were written over 50 years ago. These laws were initially written to curb abuses in stock trading, but in today's financial world, many other areas permit abuses if not carefully checked.[47]

Insiders at the upper levels of a corporation are the most visible to regulators, but anyone outside the corporation who obtains nonpublic information about a company that is material in nature is considered to be an insider as far as trading is concerned. The SEC stated in 1961 that corporate insiders in possession of material, nonpublic information were required to disclose that information or to refrain from trading.[48] Since that time, this rule has been extended to persons who are not corporate insiders. People who get information from insiders, called tippees, and those who in some sense become insiders because of some work they perform for the company have been held accountable in some cases.[49] Financial printers and newspaper columnists have also been found guilty of insider trading. Thus, the term *insider* has more and more come to refer to the kind of information a person possesses rather than to the status of the person who trades on inside information.[50]

Under rule 10b-5 of the SEC, an individual must be linked with the company whose security is traded or with the nonpublic information in such a way that the use of this information in trading is deemed to breach some fiduciary duty. This fiduciary duty may derive from (1) working inside the firm as an officer or director of the company whose securities are traded, and as such these agents may not misrepresent inside information in a manner that is detrimental to the firm or may not earn insider trading profits at the expense of the firm's shareholders; (2) working outside the firm in a capacity that leads to an obligation to shareholders such as investment bankers, lawyers, or public accountants for the company whose securities are traded; and (3) receiving information from another individual whose conveyance of the information itself constitutes a breach of duty.[51]

Insider trading is defended on grounds that have to do with efficiency, as it is held that if insiders are permitted to trade freely on their private information, this information then becomes more rapidly reflected in securities prices. Insider trading is thus held to contribute to efficient markets and to allocational efficiency, as proper capital asset pricing leads to optimal allocation of capital resources.[52] Profits from insider trading are also said to constitute the only effective compensation scheme for entrepreneurial services in large corporations. Individuals do little innovation, according to this view, except when they are given the opportunity to share in the value they create, and insider trading is basically the only mechanism for employees to obtain compensation for their innovations.[53] Furthermore, insider trading is essentially a victimless crime, as the insiders' gain is not made at anyone's expense.[54]

Ethical arguments against insider trading include the fairness argument, which focuses on the disparity of information between the two parties to the transaction. Trading in securities should take place on a "level playing field" and disparities in information tilt the field toward one player and away from the other. Insider trading is unfair because the two parties do not have equal information, and the party that lacks information is put at a disadvantage. It is also argued that insider trading is unfair because the insider has access to information that is not accessible to the ordinary investor, and this advantage cannot be overcome by the hard work and ingenuity of the ordinary investor.[55]

Insider information can also be seen as a form of property, much like trade secrets and inventions, and thus trading on this property is wrong because it involves a violation of property rights. While usage is not exactly like theft, because the person who uses inside information does not deprive the company of the use of the same information, it does deprive the company of the sole use of the information. Insider traders are thus believed to "misappropriate" such information that belongs to the company and use it in a way that was not intended. This misappropriation theory has taken hold in the courts and played a major role in the prosecution of R. Foster Winans, a *Wall Street Journal* reporter who leaked the contents of his "Heard in the Street" column to friends who subsequently traded on this information.[56]

There is also the argument that the practice is harmful to ordinary investors who engage in trades with insiders. Ordinary investors may sell their shares too early because they did not know a merger was in the works and that the stock would rise in subsequent market activity. A second version of the harm thesis holds that insider trading erodes investors' confidence in the market, causing them to pull out of the market and harming the market as a whole. If people get the impression that the market is stacked against them, they are not going to be willing to invest. The market will be harmed accordingly and will not be able to perform its role of allocating capital resources in our economy.[57]

Other scholars present different ethical arguments against the practice of insider trading. Jennifer Mills Moore holds that insider trading threatens the fiduciary relationship that is central to business management, a view that is consistent with SEC rules mentioned earlier. The fiduciary relationship is one of moral and legal obligation; fiduciaries are bound to act in the interests of those who depend on them even if these interests do not coincide with their own. According to Moore, permitting insider trading does not increase the likelihood that insiders will act in the interest of the firm and its shareholders, and in some cases, may actually cause conflicts of interest, undermining the fiduciary relationship that is essential to managing the corporation.[58]

Patricia Werhane argues that insider trading both in its present illegal form and as a legalized market mechanism undermines the efficient and proper functioning of a free market. Insider trading thwarts the very basis of market competition because the same information is not available to everyone, so competition, which depends on the availability of equal advantage of all parties, is precluded. Insider trading allows the insider to indulge in greed, and works against the very kind of market in which insider trading might be allowed to function. Thus, insider trading is economically inefficient for the very reason it is immoral.[59]

While insider trading seemed to have reached a peak in the 1980s, it still continues. As mergers picked up again in the mid-1990s, so did evidence of insider trading. There were unexplained run-ups in stock prices and/or trading volume accompanying many of the largest mergers. But the activity seems to have shifted from Wall Street to Main Street, as corporate executives, their friends and relatives, lawyers and consultants were said to be taking up the slack from brokerages and investment banks.[60] It seems clear that the temptations to make quick and easy money from insider trading will always be with us and will have to be policed by regulatory activity. Furthermore, it is clear that the arguments pro and con regarding insider trading are not merely economic in nature but have moral implications affecting not only the limited community of investors but the larger community in which they function.

Confidentiality and Trade Secrets

Confidential information includes advanced product plans; unpublished financial data; unannounced plant construction, expansion, or improvement; the amount of capital investment for new, expanded, or renovated facilities; proposed product prices and warranties; projected earnings; possible dividend action; major forthcoming changes in management or policy; personally identifiable data relating to composition of the work force; unpublished drawings, specifications, or operating characteristics; test reports and data; manufacturing methods and other proprietary business systems and methods; information on suppliers' prices, quantities, and relations; and documents marked "confidential."

The sources of confidentiality are contractual agreements that are entered into by the company with outside parties, the custom or experience of the company and the industry, unilateral promises made by the company, and those areas where trade secrets are involved. Each employee has an individual responsibility to safeguard corporate information that has been learned in connection with his or her employment. Approved access to corporate information does not confer any authority to act as spokesperson for the corporation concerning the information.

Access to personal employee information is generally limited to those persons having a legitimate need for such information in the performance of their job responsibilities. It is important that the employees in no way compromise the position of the company by improper or premature disclosure or leaking of confidential information to outsiders or to other employees who do not require the information for the performance of their duties. Employees are generally restricted in the use of "material" inside information, which is confidential, corporate information not known to the public and to which a reasonable person would attach importance in deciding whether to buy, sell, or hold the corporation's stock.

The principle of confidentiality also extends to information from parties outside the company. It is generally expected that no improper means will be used to acquire confidential or proprietary information from any competitor, supplier, or customer. Improper means could include any form of industrial espionage, the payment of money or giving of any favor or consideration, or the hiring of a competitor's employees to obtain confidential information. Information that may not be sought could include data on a competitor's unannounced new products or confidential data relating to costs, prices, or profits.

The confidentiality principle extends to all business transactions including dealings with suppliers and contractors, potential and current employees, and in particular, the use of proprietary information. Employers must be able to expect that their employees will respect this principle so that information can be used within the company without extensive and expensive safeguards that can hamper productivity and create inefficiencies. Information has to be able to flow freely to the appropriate people in the company, and the company has to have confidence that this information will not be improperly disclosed.

Many, if not most, disputes over trade secrets arise between corporations and their former employees. These cases involve usage of information acquired during employment of a former employee who is currently employed by another company or who has formed his or her own company. There are usually three circumstances under which this situation can occur: (1) The departing employee passively receives and uses proprietary information that he or she had no hand in developing; (2) both the employer and employee contributed substantially in developing a technological innovation; and (3) the proprietary information is mainly the product of the employee's own initiative, creativity, and diligence, with the employer as the passive recipient.[61]

The ethical issue involved in these kinds of cases is one of deciding what rights employers and employees have respectively in trade secrets and what impacts a decision to favor one or the other will have on innovation. The first case seems relatively straightforward, as common sense notions of fairness would seem to dictate that the employee has no right to use trade secrets that were conferred upon them in confidence. Without legal protection against such conduct, companies would regard expenditures on research and development as futile and would cut back on such expenditures. Even in the second situation, a good argument can be made against an employee's use of proprietary information. If a company has spent millions of dollars developing a new technology, it has a claim that would seem to be superior to that of any individual contributor.[62]

The third type of case is more complicated, especially if an employer refuses to market the employee's discovery because the company believes it will not be technologically feasible or make money for the company, or because the innovation may threaten the company's investment in its existing product line. Should employees be prevented from using their own work, even if that would result in the suppression of the technology and hence of its potential benefit to society? Further complications arise when employees have signed all rights to ideas, inventions, and discoveries they may make during the course of their employment over to the employer. Should these agreements be binding and prevent employees from all opportunities to pursue these ideas on their own?[63]

In all of these situations, however, clarity is needed as to exactly what is a trade secret. Companies need to know with some degree of certainty whether or not they have a proprietary technology before they spend millions in development. Employees who leave the company need to know with some assurance what information in their possession can or cannot be used in a new venture or new company. And firms that hire a key employee from a competitor need to know what information they can use that is in the possession of the former employee and what their prospects are for being sued.

Some think the most vexing problem in trade secret law is distinguishing between proprietary information, which former employees may not utilize after terminating their employment, and an employee's general knowledge and experience, which they should be able to use for their own purposes. A company that spends money developing information naturally tends to regard that information as its own and regards its unauthorized use by others, including former employees, as theft and a breach of confidentiality. Employees who appropriate that same information in the normal course of their employment, and may even enhance the nature and quality of the information, regard the content of their thoughts as their own, and any restrictions on the use of this information is seen as compromising the employee's ability to earn a living and as an infringement of personal freedom and autonomy.[64]

Some examples may help to put the problem into perspective. If an employee acquires the capability to perform some task because of training and on-the-job experience, and this ability is not widely available in the industry, does this knowledge belong to the employer or to the employee? If an employee is hired by a company because he or she possesses a special expertise, and the application of this expertise results in certain innovations, may the information embodied in these innovations be freely used by the employee, or is it proprietary information? With regard to knowledge of research objectives and experimental results, or just plain know-how acquired on the job, can these be company trade secrets?[65]

The problem of distinguishing between general employee knowledge and skill on the one hand and company proprietary information on the other is complicated and by no means definitively settled. Some criteria related to deciding whether or not information is proprietary were set forth in a treatise entitled the "Restatement of Torts" that may provide some help in this regard. These criteria include (1) the extent to which the information is known outside of the business; (2) the extent to which the information is known by those involved in the business; (3) the nature and extent of measures taken to protect the secrecy of the information; (4) the value of the information; (5) the amount of time, effort, and money expended in the development of the information; and (6) the degree of difficulty with which the information could be properly acquired or duplicated by others.[66]

These issues surface whenever employees leave companies and there are indications that they are using information obtained while working for their former employer. It is impossible for companies to prevent departing employees from walking off with trade secrets, especially information contained in their minds. Courts usually do not consider anything that an employee remembers or reconstructs, as opposed to a document that an employee steals or copies, as a trade secret. To be considered a trade secret, information must be generally unknown and unlikely to be discovered by lawful means. In addition, the information must have economic value to outsiders, and the company must have made an effort to keep it confidential.

Companies have been encouraged to develop policies with respect to trade secrets. These policies involve deciding what information is to be protected, deciding who will have access to the information, providing adequate security for the information, and establishing procedures for dealing with confidential information with respect to departing employees. During exit interviews, for example, employees should be warned that the company will enforce its rights if the employee discloses trade secrets in subsequent employment. Trade secret protection programs can go a long way toward clarifying some of the difficult issues in this area and help to reduce trade secret theft. A program that is well developed and implemented will also be an asset for a company should there eventually be a lawsuit.[67]

Conflicts of Interest

There is a whole set of situations faced by employees that falls under the heading of a conflict of interest. A conflict of interest arises when a duty owed to another is compromised by either a personal interest or by a mutually exclusive duty owed to a third party. Personal interests could include stock held in another company, family relationships, friendships, and other matters where personal interests are operative. In any organization, a conflict of interest arises when employees at any level have an interest in or are parties to an interest in a transaction that is substantial enough in value that it either does or can reasonably be expected to affect their independent judgment in acts involving the organization.

There are two categories related to conflicts of interest. An actual conflict of interest exists when employees violate their contract of employment by using their position for self-interested purposes that are at odds with the best interests of the firm. A retail purchasing agent who pays a higher price to a distributor from whom he has accepted a bribe is an instance of an actual conflict of interest. A potential conflict of interest arises when employees might reasonably be expected to sacrifice independent judgment because of the situation. An employee who does advertising with his or her brother's advertising agency, even though no favors have been involved and the brother is the low-cost bidder, is in a potential conflict of interest situation.[68]

Duties to act on behalf of others, including organizations, are created through employment relationships, contracts and noncontractual promises, role obligations, and legal requirements. The underlying principle is that employees should avoid any activity, investment, or interest that might reflect unfavorably upon the integrity or good name of themselves or of the organization. Employees should not engage in any activity that is detrimental to the company for which they work and should not use their positions to benefit themselves, relatives, friends, or other businesses (Exhibit 16-1).

Conflicts of interest reduce economic efficiency by distorting market outcomes and interfere with the right of individuals to rely on reasonable expectations in business relationships. The ethical employee takes steps to mitigate even the appearance of an unresolved conflict of interest. Even though there may not be an actual conflict involved, it is important to stay out of situations where it might appear to a reasonable person that a conflict of interest is involved.

There are many areas where a potential conflict of interest may appear. In the procurement and contracting function, where employees are interacting with people from other organizations, employees must act in the best interests of the organization for which they work in all transactions, even though there will be many opportunities for personal benefits in the form of gifts and other favors that may be offered, as well as outright bribery that may rear its ugly head from time to time.

In hiring, promotions, and terminations, there may be family or other kinds of personal ties that are involved with respect to the individuals under consideration that pose conflicts of interest. With regard to proprietary information, there may be opportunities for personal benefit that arise from time to time with regard to the use of this information. The same is true for use of company resources. There are many situations where potential

---

EXHIBIT 16-1

Types of Conflicts

- Accepting gifts or expenses from suppliers
- Offering gifts or expenses to customers
- Consulting of other business relationships outside the firm
- Trading in equities in which the employer has positions
- Trading in the firm's stock
- Attending entertainment or sports functions at a supplier's expense
- Purchasing personal items from vendors at special discounts

or actual conflicts of interest may be present, and employees must keep themselves aware of where these conflicts are present and take steps to mitigate them before they become serious problems.

There are several methods that can be utilized to mitigate conflicts of interest. One method is disclosure of information to each interested party of all information relevant to an evaluation of the fairness and propriety of the arrangement. This gives everyone an equal chance to use the information in the making of decisions and levels the playing field so that one supplier or contractor does not have an unfair advantage. Any nondisclosure that is based on an assumption that the client already knows should be supported by empirical evidence to that effect.

Another method is to obtain an expert who is disinterested in and yet knowledgeable about the situation and have the expert objectively assess the transaction and determine whether or not it is fair to all relevant parties. This expert can be someone from inside the company or someone from outside who knows enough to be able to understand the situation. The critical issue in this method is assessing whether or not the party is genuinely independent. When financial transactions are involved, it is often difficult to find someone who is simultaneously disinterested and yet sufficiently knowledgeable to render a useful opinion.

One can also abstain from making a decision with respect to a given transaction and simply withdraw, claiming that it is impossible to be objective given the circumstances. This method will often be useful to avoid even the appearance of a conflict of interest, and is often the only way to prevent oneself from being accused of acting in one's own interest to the detriment of the company. Use of this method assumes that there is someone prepared to step in with enough knowledge of the transaction to make a good decision that is in the best interests of the company.

Opt-out provisions can also be utilized to give a chance for parties to a transaction to rescind the agreement if they later determine the outcome is not satisfactory because a conflict of interest may have been involved. These provisions must be agreed to by all parties to the transaction before it is consummated, and proper methods of notification and documentation must be established. This method gives time for all parties to examine the agreement after it is accomplished and reflect on the implications for themselves and the situation that existed at the time the agreement was made.

Companies usually deal with conflicts of interest in a code of ethics, indicating where conflicts can arise and how to deal with them. Employees are also encouraged to be aware of actual and potential conflicts and ask the appropriate questions related to the situation. For example, with respect to accepting gifts if one is a purchasing agent, the following questions are pertinent: (1) What is the value of the gift, (2) what is the purpose of the gift, (3) what are the circumstances under which the gift was given, (4) what is the position and sensitivity of influence of the person receiving the gift, (5) what is the accepted business practice in the area, (6) what is the company's policy with respect to gifts, and (7) what is the law?[69]

Whistle-Blowing

Whistle-blowing has been defined as the attempt by an employee or former employee of an organization to disclose what he or she believes to be wrongdoing in or by the organization. In other words, whistle-blowing is an effort to make others aware of practices one considers illegal, unjust, or harmful. Whistle-blowing becomes an issue when an employee is ordered to perform some act or has obtained knowledge that the institution is engaged in activities that (1) are believed to cause unnecessary harm to third parties, (2) are in violation of human rights, or (3) run counter to the defined purpose of the institution.

Some specific situations that may warrant whistle-blowing include the production of defective vehicles; waste of government funds; illegal dumping of hazardous wastes; illegal campaign contributions; discrimination because of race, sex, or age; misuse of pension funds; sale of unsafe food; deceptive advertising; corruption in the company; fraudulent practices; and suppression of data about a serious occupational disease. In regard to acts of this nature, it is important for the whistle-blower to see the difference between dissent on grounds of policy and revelations of actual abuse or neglect that alone give adequate cause for whistle-blowing.

There are different kinds of whistle-blowing. When an employee informs his or her supervisor or higher management of the wrongdoing, meaning the employee makes an effort to deal with the situation within the organization, whistle-blowing is considered to be internal in nature. When disclosure of the practice is made to outside individuals or groups, such as reporters, public interest groups, or regulatory agencies, whistle-blowing is external in nature. When an employee resigns his or her present position and obtains another before blowing the whistle, this is considered to be alumni whistle-blowing. Such action protects an employee from being fired, receiving damaging letters of recommendation, or being blacklisted from the profession.

Whistle-blowing can be done openly and honestly, with no effort made to hide the identity of the person blowing the whistle. Such an open effort puts the employee's career on the line, so to speak, and opens up the possibility of retaliation from those in the company who are engaged in the practice in question. Open whistle-blowing has the advantage, however, of enabling one to use whatever force one's position or integrity within the company can add to the effort. Anonymous whistle-blowing protects the employee from retaliation but may not be as effective as open whistle-blowing in certain situations.

The ethical issue in whistle-blowing can be framed as one of the obligation of loyalty to the organization versus the right to moral autonomy. Employees have a stake in the firm for which they work and have to consider such obligations and the damage to the firm and fellow workers they could cause by their actions. Those who claim whistle-blowing is always wrong consider loyalty to be the employee's highest obligation. But there is also an obligation to do something about wrongful practices in the organization, which could also harm the firm and fellow employees, as well as society.

The decision to blow the whistle or remain silent is not an easy one for employees. There are potentially severe costs that the whistle-blower may have to bear, such as loss of job, health, or family, to say nothing of legal costs if a lawsuit is involved. Whistle-blowing also creates a climate of suspicion in the organization and has implications for employee loyalty. But there are also significant benefits to be gained from a successful effort, including the prevention of serious harm being done to some individuals, preserving the reputation of the company, saving the company money in legal fees from lawsuits, and the protection of society from harm. Certain things ought to be considered before the whistle is blown.

1. *How Big Is Your Whistle?* Questions must be asked about the seriousness of the offense. Will the action or practice under consideration do serious and considerable harm to the public or other persons? The whistle-blower is advised to have accessible, documented

evidence that would convince an impartial observer that the situation is serious. Examination of motives is important in deciding whether or not to blow the whistle. An employee should also consider his or her position in the organization. Is the employee known for integrity and honesty so that he or she will be taken seriously?

2. *When Should You Blow the Whistle?* The whistle preferably should be blown before the action or practice is committed to prevent harm from being done. But after the action or practice has been committed, there may be a need to punish the wrongdoers and prevent the same thing from recurring. The question of whether or not an employee should resign first and then blow the whistle is relevant at this stage. Protection may be available in the industry, at the state or even federal level. If these protections are available, the appropriate guidelines should be followed and any deadlines met without delay.

3. *How Loud Should You Blow the Whistle?* Usually, it is appropriate to exhaust all internal channels for dissent before going public. There is a duty of loyalty to the firm that obligates workers to seek an internal remedy before informing the public of a misdeed. But this obligation may be mitigated by certain conditions within the organization. An employee's supervisor may be the one who is responsible for the wrongdoing, and it is often dangerous to go around one's immediate supervisor to higher management. Organizations differ considerably in both their mechanisms for reporting wrongdoing and how they respond to wrongdoing, and these characteristics must be taken into consideration. There may also be unjustified delays in correcting the problem, and blowing the whistle internally may give time for people to destroy evidence the employee needs to substantiate his or her allegations.

If external whistle-blowing seems to be the best course of action, then an employee must determine the type of wrongdoing that is under consideration and to whom it should be reported. If the wrongdoing amounts to a violation of certain kinds of laws and regulations that the company is supposed to follow, then perhaps the disclosure of the wrongdoing should be made to the government agency administering those laws and regulations. If the wrongdoing consists of actions that are legal but contrary to the public interest, then perhaps a public interest group should be contacted. If none of these seems appropriate, then disclosing the wrongdoing to the press may be a reasonable course of action.

4. *How Long Should You Blow the Whistle?* If there is no immediate response on the part of the company to rectify the situation, an employee has to determine whether or not continued whistle-blowing has some chance of success. Perhaps the consequences should be considered and the whistle-blowing stopped before too much damage has been done to one's career. On the other hand, the employee may feel morally compelled to pursue whistle-blowing to its bitter end regardless of the consequences. Here it must be remembered that the consequences of one's act are not just economic consequences or other "practical" consequences but also involve consequences related to the character of one's self as an autonomous and developing moral agent.

In any event, it is wise for the employee to anticipate and document retaliation on the part of the company. Such retaliation can take the form of harassment from superiors, removal of job responsibilities, change in type of position, monitoring of office telephone, psychiatric or medical referral, forced retirement, or similar measures. Every step the employee takes and every response of the company should be documented with letters, memos, records, tape recordings, and a diary of daily actions and events. These will be useful in court, if nothing else, should the whistle-blowing go to that length. Consulting a lawyer at every stage of whistle-blowing is also advisable.

Several states have passed laws to protect whistle-blowers by curbing the ability of companies to fire or otherwise discipline workers who expose illegal activities. Others have extended protection to whistle-blowing related to practices that may not be specifically illegal but nonetheless endanger public health and safety. In spite of these laws, whistle-blowers still face many obstacles within the company. If an employee can't be fired, he or she can still be transferred to a remote plant in an undesirable part of the country or other things can be done to make the life of the employee miserable. There are many subtle things that employers can do that the law may not be able to reach.

Some companies have taken steps to encourage internal whistle-blowing by establishing a hot line where employees can disclose practices they think are illegal or wrong in an anonymous fashion or in a manner that will protect their identity. Many of these hot lines have been established in response to the sentencing guidelines, which encourage companies to utilize monitoring and auditing systems to detect criminal conduct. Other companies have set up a corporate ombudsman or ethics officer to whom employees can complain without fear of retaliation. The key to the success of these efforts is the perception that the company will actually do something in response to complaints. Still other companies provide financial rewards for legitimate disclosure of wrongdoing.[70] The success of these efforts to encourage whistle-blowing and protect those employees who disclose corporate wrongdoing has been mixed.[71]

Privacy

Privacy has been defined as the state of being free from intrusion or disturbance in one's private life or affairs. One's private life is considered to be that which is not of an official or public character, that solitary or secluded part of life that does not include the presence of others. The private part of life is the most intimate and personal part of life that is not exposed to the public or available to outsiders for whatever reason. Privacy refers to that sphere of life where one's behavior, thoughts, feelings, and so on are unknown to others and are not available for their scrutiny.[72]

The self requires a space of its own to be what it is, and this space is the private world. While people play many social roles in the context of a society, the underlying self, the so-called real person, is seen as the ultimate moral unit, deserving of protection and respect in its own right, and not just because of the functional role it occupies. Neither its creativity nor dignity is reducible to the specific social fields it occupies, and implicitly imposes a limit on what can be done to beings to achieve any particular social objective. It is capable of standing in opposition to society or taking a critical attitude toward things going on in society, even if this critical attitude is unwelcome.

Yet the self is not an atomic unit independent of other selves but is formed through interaction with others. Our dependence on others accounts for most of our moral qualities and accounts for most of what we are and can hope to become. This susceptibility to others is a prime and salutary feature of being human, but it also threatens us in ways that need to be limited. In different historical settings, and in different contexts, different levels of susceptibility to others are appropriate. The concept of privacy limits the amount and effectiveness of social control over an individual. In various settings, different levels of self-direction are appropriate. Privacy protects the individual by limiting scrutiny by others and the control some of them have over our lives.[73]

On the narrow end of the spectrum, privacy relates exclusively to personal information and describes the extent to which others have access to this information. A broader conception extends beyond the informational domain and encompasses anonymity and restricted physical access. The most embracing characterizations of privacy include aspects of autonomy, particularly those associated with control over the intimacies of personal identity. For advocates of this interpretation, privacy is the measure of the extent an individual is afforded the social and legal space to develop the emotional, cognitive, spiritual, and moral powers of an autonomous agent.[74]

As social beings, we may be more vulnerable to social than to legal coercion, and the strategies that we construct to combat social coercion will be different from those that insulate us from legal coercion. The strategies that protect individuals from the overreaching power of government are mostly dependent on legal remedies. In the social realm, the defenses will have to be of a more nuanced and informal character as represented in social norms. Given the awareness of the dangers of social control, it is curious that so little mainstream philosophical attention is placed on rights and wrongs of social control mechanisms.[75]

With respect to privacy, it is interesting to note that the U.S. Constitution does not explicitly mention a right to privacy, although the Bill of Rights does protect what could be called zones of privacy, including the free exercise of religion and security from unreasonable searches and seizures. Not until 1966, however, did the Supreme Court affirm that a right to privacy exists in a case involving a Connecticut law restricting contraception. While this case pertained to marriage and the family, it wasn't long before this right to privacy was transformed into an individual right that has had many permutations. In *Roe v. Wade,* Justice Blackmun had the following to say about the constitutional right to privacy.

> The Constitution does not explicitly mention any right of privacy. In a line of decisions, however . . . the Court has recognized that a right of personal privacy, or a guarantee of certain areas of zones of privacy, does exist under the Constitution. In varying contexts, the Court of individual Justices have, indeed, found at least the roots of that right in the First Amendment . . . in the Fourth and Fifth Amendments . . . in the penumbras of the Bill of Rights . . . in the Ninth Amendment . . . or in the concept of liberty guaranteed by the first section of the Fourteenth Amendment. . . . These decisions make it clear that only personal rights that be deemed "fundamental" or "implicit in the concept of ordered liberty" . . . are included in this guarantee of personal privacy.[76]

The Fourth Amendment to the Constitution guarantees the right to be secure in one's person, houses, papers, and effects against unreasonable search or seizure. The First Amendment affords people free exercise of religion and freedom of speech, the press, and assembly—freedoms we associate with freedom of conscience. The Fifth Amendment ensures that people cannot be required to testify against themselves, and the Fourteenth Amendment provides that they cannot be deprived of life, liberty, or property without due process of law. In tort law there are four categories of individual protection: (1) intrusion upon a person's seclusion, solitude, or private affairs; (2) disclosure of private, embarrassing facts; (3) public disclosure of a person in a false light; and (4) appropriation of another's name, image, or other aspect of identity, for one's advantage or profit, without that person's consent.[77]

Privacy has been held to be the most comprehensive of all rights and is the right that is most cherished by civilized individuals. It has also been described as the kernel of freedom and as the most basic right from which all other freedoms stem.[78] Whether or not privacy is this basic is subject to debate, but there seems to be no doubt that privacy serves some basic human need, that there is some kernel to the self that needs to be protected from intrusion and from scrutiny by other people. There apparently are some things that must be kept inviolate and unknown in order for humans to have some space that is entirely their own and is unavailable to others.

The question in an advanced society, with all kinds of interconnections between people and in which people are dependent on one another for the performance of certain jobs, is where the sphere of privacy ends and the public's need to know begins. Many of the issues that involve privacy in our society can be stated in terms of the individual's right to privacy versus the society's need to know. Other issues, particularly with regard to private property, can be stated in terms of the right to use things in one own interests versus the public's right to regulate that usage in the public interest. These questions are complex and have no easy answers.

With regard to business organizations, privacy is an issue relating to drug testing, testing for AIDS, computer privacy, and other issues. Drug abuse constitutes a significant problem in the workplace, contributing to impaired productivity and job performance, increased accidents and injuries, violations of security, theft of company property, and diminished employee morale. Highly focused programs such as drug testing can be a valuable deterrent in discouraging nonusers from beginning to use drugs, deterring experimental users from graduating to more serious abuse, motivating nonaddicted users to discontinue using drugs for fear of getting caught, and challenging addicted users to seek medical help.

Drug testing is especially appropriate in safety-related work, particularly where public safety is involved. In 1994, new federal regulations doubled the number of workers who needed to be tested for drug and alcohol use at work. Government required both random alcohol and drug testing each year for 25 percent of transportation workers in such safety-sensitive areas as trucking, aviation, railroads, and pipelines. Only random drug testing was required before this law went into effect. The rules also covered mass-transit workers, and expanded drug testing to intrastate truckers and bus drivers.[79]

These new rules were expected to cover 7.5 million workers as compared with 3.5 million previously. In addition to the expanded coverage required by these rules, testing for drugs was on the rise generally as more companies were testing job applicants and employees. An American Management Association survey reported that in 1993, 85 percent of the 630 companies surveyed had drug-testing programs, including 73 percent of manufacturers and 66 percent of financial service companies. Since 1987, the number of companies with drug-testing programs had tripled.[80]

Drug tests can be applied to many different kinds of samples and materials, but most often urine is tested because of the ease of getting a sample, the speed of conducting the analysis, and the low cost involved. But urine tests can be considered an invasion of privacy because the tests can disclose numerous other details about one's private life, such as whether or not an employee or applicant is pregnant or being treated for various medical conditions in addition to evidence of illegal drug usage. Drug testing is less intrusive if the actual giving of the sample is not observed, since most people using the toilet or urinal usually have an expectation of privacy. However, the absence of supervision means that an employee who does use drugs is able to substitute someone else's "clean" urine or otherwise tamper with the sample.

In addition to the moral issues involved, there are many practical problems with drug testing that make it a less than accurate method of detecting drug usage. For one thing, the tests do not measure the degree of impairment at the time of the test but show only a positive or negative result as to the presence of drug traces in the urine. Cocaine may show up in a urine test as much as three days after consumption and marijuana may register for as much as three weeks after its consumption. While employers claim to be testing for drugs such as cocaine or heroin, these drugs vanish from the bloodstream in 48 to 72 hours; thus, employees can test drug free by staying off the drug in question until after the scheduled examination. Tests may also give false-positive readings because the employee is using prescription drugs or over-the-counter drugs such as Advil or Nuprin.[81]

Testing for AIDS has many of the same problems with regard to privacy but is different in many important respects. For one thing, there is as yet no cure for AIDS, so identifying people who have the disease will not help them to get on some rehabilitation program to get over the disease. AIDS sufferers also run a greater risk of discrimination than do people on drugs, where the same elements of fear are not present. Once identified as a carrier of the AIDS virus, an individual runs the risk of losing friends, employment, housing, and insurance, despite laws protecting them from discrimination. Another problem is that the results of testing can be misleading as well as inaccurate and result in unjust treatment of individuals. In spite of these problems, however, many people in the general public believe mandatory testing is necessary, particularly in those instances where there is a risk of exposure where they are willing to set the right to privacy aside in the interests of protecting public health.

The Americans with Disabilities Act was passed in 1990 to eliminate discrimination against disabled citizens in the workplace. After the law was passed, HIV positive and AIDS victims came to be classified as disabled and therefore protected under its mandate. The stated purposes of the act are (1) to provide a clear and comprehensive national mandate for the elimination of discrimination against those individuals with disabilities; (2) to provide clear, strong, consistent, enforceable standards addressing discrimination against people with disabilities; (3) to ensure that the federal government plays a central role in enforcing the standards established in this act on behalf of individuals with disabilities; and (4) to involve the sweep of Congressional authority, including the power to enforce the Fourteenth Amendment and to regulate commerce, in order to address the major areas of discrimination faced daily by people with disabilities.

Problems in the computer field traditionally had to do with security breaks into the computer network, the accuracy of credit information, and other such problems. Technological changes have brought other issues on the agenda of concern such as monitoring of electronic mail (e-mail) and employee performance. Do employers have the right to read employees' electronic mail correspondence, or do employees who work on the equipment own the data even though the employer owns the infrastructure or pays for the service? Is it an invasion of privacy to monitor employees' performance using computer technology without their knowledge? Companies have been encouraged to develop policies on these issues and legislation has been introduced into Congress to require companies to alert workers in advance if they regularly monitor e-mail messages and place limits on how many times a worker could be monitored for performance.[82]

Rapid advances in computer and telecommunications technology have taken individual records and individual papers from the home and private safes out of the control of the individual. The record-keeping explosion of the computer age has prompted both government and the private sector to keep previously unimagined records and papers relating to the individual.[83] Technology has again created these possibilities, but the moral issues arise in the way technology is used or employed and to what purposes it is directed.

The right to privacy is not absolute in an organized society, for privacy must always be balanced against other needs of society. The public's need to know must be balanced against the individual's right to privacy in most democratic societies. People who fly in airplanes are at risk under normal circumstances, and they want to know if they are faced with an additional risk involving pilots who may be on drugs and not able to function properly. Individual managers may want to know what kind of conversations are taking place between employees over electronic mail or voice mail, but employees want to keep these conversations private as they do with other conversations with fellow employees.

The examples offered in this section are only a few of the many areas in the workplace where privacy is a concern. In all of these cases, decisions have to be made about where the zone of privacy ends and where other members of the public have a legitimate right to know in order to protect their own interests. What protections are needed to preserve that core of the individual and protect that space that is necessary for human beings to function, and what intrusions on this space are valid to promote other people's legitimate interests in knowing something about that individual and what he or she is doing? These are difficult questions that any society and its institutions have to continually grapple with as changes in technology and society bring up new issues that were not previously of concern. The moral issues intertwined with the rapid development of the computer age, for example, cannot be dealt with in terms of a past that did not include this technology and its inherent moral problems.

The novel ethical dilemmas being continuously engendered by the rapid rise of the computer age and information technology make very obvious some previously made points about process theory. First, these moral issues are contextually emergent properties of situations in which technology is embedded. Second, the solutions to these emerging issues cannot be imposed from on high by eliciting the standards of a past that does not contain the means of resolution. A more fundamental and creative level of activity is required, which can reconstruct problem situations through attunement to conflicting interests and envisionment of emerging possibilities. While we can draw from lessons of the past, this looking backward is not some passive recovery of what once was, but rather is a construction taking place in the present and directive for a novel future. The process of coming to grips with the issues posed by technology will obviously be experimental and subject to ongoing reconstruction in the light of consequences. These consequences cannot be understood in merely economic terms, for what is at issue is the enrichment of human life and the respect for individuals whose enrichment is at stake.

Questions for Discussion

1. What is the employment-at-will doctrine? What is the rationale behind this doctrine? Does this rationale make sense? What areas have recently been opened up by the courts regarding claims employees may make against employers regarding wrongful termination? Are any of these areas more important than others? What are some of the factors behind these restrictions on the termination-at-will doctrine?

2. What impacts do plant closings have on employees and communities? Do workers have a right to know about such closings in advance? Do employers have a moral obligation in this regard? What laws have been passed or advocated with respect to plant closings? What are the advantages and disadvantages of such legislation?

3. What new issues are appearing in the safety and health area? Are these important enough to warrant the attention of safety and health officials? What new regulations, if any, are likely to be the result? What can business organizations do to deal with these issues? What moral responsibilities do they have with respect to these problems?

4. What is insider trading? Give some examples of insider trading. What advantages does the lack of a legal definition give the enforcement agencies? Should this lack be corrected? How is insider trading defended from an economic perspective? What are the ethical arguments against the practice? Which arguments do you agree or disagree with? Why?

5. Where do most issues of confidentiality and trade secrets arise? What are the ethical issues in these cases? What harms may result to the parties involved from restrictions or the lack of restrictions on the use of information? What criteria can be used to judge whether or not information is indeed proprietory? Are these rules relevant to the issue in your opinion?

6. What is a conflict of interest? Give some examples, if possible, from your own experience. What impacts can conflicts of interest have on an organization? On an individual involved in a conflict? What is the moral issue regarding conflicts of interest? What can be done to mitigate the problem?

7. What specific practices are most likely to warrant whistle-blowing? What are the ethical issues involved in whistle-blowing? What harmful effects can it have on the employee and the organization? Who benefits from whistle-blowing? What questions should be asked before blowing the whistle?

8. How would you define privacy? Why is privacy important? Is there a constitutional right to privacy in this country? If not, from where does concern about privacy stem? Where do privacy issues arise in corporate organizations? How would you frame the ethical issues in these areas where conflicts exist?

Endnotes

[1] "Limiting the Right to Fire," *Dallas Times Herald,* July 17, 1985, p. C-1.

[2] David Ewing, *Do It My Way or You're Fired* (New York: Wiley Publishing Co., 1983), pp. 1–25.

[3] Peter F. Drucker, "The Job as Property Right," *The Wall Street Journal,* March 4, 1980, p. 18.

[4] M. J. Fox, Jr., and Robin Robinson, "Employment At Will: A Time for Change," *Industrial Management,* July–August 1985, p. 17.

[5] *Payne* v. *Western & A.R.R.,* 81 Tenn. 507, 519-520 (1884).

[6] *Union Labor Hospital Association* v. *Vance Redwood Lumber Co.,* 158 Cal. 551, 555 (1910).

[7] "It's Getting Harder to Make a Firing Stick," *Business Week,* June 27, 1983, pp. 104–105.

[8] In 1994, an employee of Johnson & Johnson filed a $3.2 wrongful termination suit claiming the company did not live up to statements about a "sense of security" and "feel free to make suggestions and complaints" contained in its credo. See Joseph Weber, "J&J: Tripped by Its Own Credo?" *Business Week,* November 21, 1994, p. 6.

[9] "It's Getting Harder to Make a Firing Stick," pp. 104–105.

[10] Ibid.

[11] Milo Geyelin and Jonathan M. Moses, "Rulings on Wrongful Firing Curb Hiring," *The Wall Street Journal,* April 7, 1992, p. B3.

[12] John Hoerr, "Beyond Unions: A Revolution in Employee Rights Is in the Making," *Business Week,* July 8, 1985, p. 76.

[13] Drucker, "The Job as Property Right," p. 18.

[14] "Who Fires?" *The Wall Street Journal,* May 12, 1992, p. A1.

[15] "Legal Challenges Force Firms to Revamp Ways They Dismiss Workers," *The Wall Street Journal,* September 13, 1983, p. 1.

[16] Richard B. McKenzie, *Plant Closings: Public or Private Choices?* (Washington, DC: Cato Institute, 1982), preface.

[17] McKenzie, *Plant Closings,* 1982, p. 4.

[18] Ibid., p. 142.

[19] Ibid., p. 2.

[20] Ibid., p. 3.

[21] Lawrence R. Mishel, "Advance Notice of Plant Closings: Benefits Outweigh the Costs," *Challenge,* July–August 1988, p. 58.

[22] Ibid., p. 59.

[23] Frank E. Bird, *Management Guide to Loss Control* (Atlanta, GA: Institute Press, 1974), pp. 2–3.

[24] Albert L. Nichols and Richard Zeckhauser, "Government Comes to the Workplace: An Assessment of OSHA," *The Public Interest,* No. 49 (Fall 1977), pp. 40–41. Workers' compensation systems are still in trouble as runaway costs and bulging caseloads threaten the systems in many states. See Eric Schine, "Worker's Comp Goes Under the Knife," *Business Week,* October 19, 1992, pp. 90–91.

[25] U.S. Department of Labor, *All About OSHA,* OSHA 2056, 1991 (revised), p. 1.

[26] *Occupational Safety and Health Act,* Public Law 91-596.

[27] See *General Industry Digest,* U.S. Department of Labor, OSHA 2201, 1988 (revised), pp. 1–4.

[28] U.S. Department of Labor, *All About OSHA,* OSHA 2056, 1982 (revised), p. 8.

[29] See Andrew Purvis, "The Double Take on Dioxin," *Time,* August 26, 1991, p. 52.

[30] Milo Geyelin, "Study Faults Federal Effort to Enforce Worker Safety," *The Wall Street Journal,* April 28, 1989, p. B-1.

[31] Susan B. Garland, "This Safety Ruling Could Be Hazardous to Employers' Health," *Business Week,* February 20, 1989, p. 34.

[32] Susan B. Garland, "What a Way to Watch Out for Workers," *Business Week,* September 23, 1991, p. 42. See also Richard Lacayo, "Death on the Shop Floor," *Time,* September 16, 1991, pp. 28–29; "Price of Neglect," *Time,* September 28, 1992, p. 24.

[33] "Stress Claims Are Making Business Jumpy," *Business Week,* October 14, 1985, p. 152. See also Joann S. Lubin, "On-the-Job Stress Leads Many Workers To File—and Win—Compensation Awards," *The Wall Street Journal,* September 17, 1986, p. 31; Sana Siwolop, "Stress: The Test Americans Are Failing," *Business Week,* April 18, 1988, pp. 74–78.

[34] Michael Waldholz, "VDTs Are Said Not to Increase Miscarriage Risk," *The Wall Street Journal,* March 14, 1991, p. B1.

[35] Barry Meier, "Companies Wrestle with Threats to Workers' Reproductive Health," *The Wall Street Journal,* February 5, 1987, p. 21. See also "Bias or Safety?" *Time,* October 16, 1989, p. 61.

[36] Maria Mallory, "An Invisible Workplace Hazard Gets Harder to Ignore," *Business Week,* January 30, 1989, pp. 92–93.

[37] Janice M. Horowitz, "Crippled by Computers," *Time,* October 12, 1992, pp. 70–72.

[38] Lester Brickman, "After Asbestos, the Next Tort-Law Fiasco," *The Wall Street Journal,* October 21, 1992, p. A17.

[39] Albert R. Karr, "Repetitive Motion Injuries Are Target of OSHA Program," *The Wall Street Journal,* August 31, 1990, p. A3.

[40] Jonathan Weil, "Federal Regulations to Prevent Infection of Health-Care Workers Will Be Costly," *The Wall Street Journal,* July 2, 1991, p. B1.

[41] Amy Dockser Marcus, "In Some Workplaces, Ill Winds Blow," *The Wall Street Journal,* October 9, 1989, p. B-1. See also David Holzman, "Elusive Culprits in Workplace Ills," *Insight,* June 26, 1989, pp. 44–45.

[42] "Workplace Injuries May Be Far Worse Than Government Data Suggest," *The Wall Street Journal,* February 2, 1993, p. A1.

[43] "Falling Behind: The U.S. Is Losing the Job-Safety War to Japan, Too," *The Wall Street Journal,* May 26, 1992, p. A1.

[44] Jyoti Thottam and Kevin G. Salwen, "As U.S. Mulls Worker-Safety Mandate, Some States Require Company Action," *The Wall Street Journal,* June 22, 1993, p. A2.

[45] There is still no legal definition of insider trading. See Stan Crock, "Insider Trading: There Oughta Be a Law," *Business Week,* December 12, 1994, p. 82.

[46] Gordon L. Cravitz, "The SEC Overstepped When It Made Insider Trading a Crime," *The Wall Street Journal,* December 19, 1990, p. A17.

[47] Michele Galen, "The Insider Trading Cops Widen Their Dragnet," *Business Week,* July 8, 1991, p. 74.

[48] Jennifer Moore, "What Is Really Unethical About Insider Trading?" *Journal of Business Ethics,* No. 9 (1990), p. 172.

[49] Ibid.

[50] Ibid.

[51] Lawrence M. Ausubel, "Insider Trading in a Rational Expectations Economy," *American Economic Review,* Vol. 80, no. 5 (December 1990), p. 1024.

[52] Ibid., p. 1025.

[53] Henry Manne, *Insider Trading and the Stock Market* (New York: Free Press, 1966), p. 116.

[54] Ibid., p. 61.

[55] Moore, "What Is Really Unethical About Insider Trading?" pp. 172–173.

[56] Ibid., p. 175.

[57] Ibid., pp. 176–177.

[58] Ibid., pp. 178–179.

[59] Particia H. Werhane, "The Ethics of Insider Trading," *Journal of Business Ethics,* No. 8 (1989), pp. 841–845.

[60] Amy Barrett, "Insider Trading," *Business Week,* December 12, 1994, pp. 70–80.

[61] Robert A. Spanner, "Trade Secrets versus Technological Innovation," *Technology Review,* February–March 1984, p. 12.

[62] Ibid.

[63] Ibid., p. 13.

[64] Robert A. Spanner, *Who Owns Innovation?* (Homewood, IL: Dow Jones-Irwin, 1986), p. 47.

[65] Ibid., p. 5.

[66] Ibid., p. 10.

[67] Paul B. Hunt, "Preventing Trade Secret Theft," *Machine Design,* July 9, 1992, p. 102.

[68] Vincent Barry, *Moral Issues in Business* (Belmont, CA: Wadsworth Publishing Co., 1979), p. 194.

[69] Michael Brommer, et al., "A Behavioral Model of Ethical and Unethical Decision Making," *Journal of Business Ethics,* No. 4 (1987), p. 275.

[70] Marcia P. Micele and Janet P. Near, "Whistleblowing: Reaping the Benefits," *Academy of Management Executive,* Vol. 8, no. 3 (August 1994), pp. 65–72.

[71] March Mason, "The Curse of Whistle-Blowing," *The Wall Street Journal,* March 14, 1994, p. A14.

[72] Stuart Berg Flexner, *The Random House Dictionary of the English Language,* 2nd ed. (New York: Random House, 1987), p. 1540.

[73] Ferdinand David Schoeman, *Privacy and Social Freedom* (New York: Cambridge, 1992).

[74] Ibid.

[75] Ibid.

[76] *Roe* v. *Wade,* 410 US 113, 1973.

[77] Schoeman, *Privacy and Social Freedom,* p. 12.

[78] Marc Rotenberg, "Communications Privacy: Implications for Network Design," *Communications of the ACM,* August 1993, p. 61.

[79] Anne Newman, "Drug Testing Firms Face Pluses, Minuses in New Rules," *The Wall Street Journal,* March 15, 1994, p. B4.

[80] Ibid.

[81] Dan Davidson, "Employee Testing: An Ethical Perspective," *Journal of Business Ethics,* No. 7 (1994), p. 215.

[82] Michael Allen, "Legislation Could Restrict Bosses from Snooping on Their Workers," *The Wall Street Journal,* September 24, 1991, p. B1.

[83] Warren Freeman, *The Right of Privacy in the Computer Age* (New York: Quorum, 1987).

Suggested Readings

Ashton, Inidira. *Monitoring for Health Hazards at Work,* 2nd ed. New York: Blackwell, 1992.

Bakalay, Charles G., and Joel M. Grossman. *Modern Law of Employment Contracts.* New York: Law and Business, Inc., 1983.

Baldwin, Dawn A. *Safety and Environmental Training: Using Compliance to Improve Your Company.* New York: Van Nostrand Reinhold, 1992.

Berns, Bruce D. *The Rise and Pitfalls of the Employment-At-Will Doctrine: The Implied-In-Fact Contract Exception.* Washington, DC: Washington Legal Foundation, 1989.

Brown, Marianne, and John Fronies, eds. *Technological Change in the Workplace: Health Impacts for Workers.* Los Angeles: UCLA Industrial Relations, 1993.

Coombs, Robert H., and Louis J. West. *Drug Testing: Issues & Options.* New York: Oxford, 1991.

Cranor, Carl F. *Regulating Toxic Substances: A Philosophy of Science and the Law.* New York: Oxford University Press, 1992.

DeCew, Judith W. *Drug Testing: Balancing Privacy and Public Safety.* New York: Hastings Center Report, 1994.

Ewing, David. *Do It My Way or You're Fired.* New York: Wiley, 1983.

Falco, Mathea, and Warren I. Cikins. *Toward a National Policy on Drug and AIDS Testing.* Washington, DC: Brookings Institution, 1989.

Fay, John. *Drug Testing.* Boston: Butterworth-Heinemann, 1991.

Freeman, Warren. *The Right of Privacy in the Computer Age.* New York: Quorum, 1987.

Goetsch, David L. *Industrial Safety and Health in the Age of High Technology.* New York: Macmillan, 1993.

Gunderson, Martin, David J. Mayo, and Frank S. Rhame. *AIDS: Testing and Privacy.* Salt Lake City: University of Utah Press, 1989.

Kenen, Regina. *Reproductive Hazards in the Workplace: Mending Jobs, Managing Pregnancies.* New York: Haworth Press, 1992.

Langevoort, Donald C. *Insider Trading Regulation.* New York: Clark Boardman Co., 1988.

Lewis, P. *Health Protection from Chemicals in the Workplace.* Englewood Cliffs, NJ: Prentice Hall, 1993.

McGarity, Thomas O., and Sidney A. Shapiro. *Workers at Risk: The Failed Promise of the Occupational Safety and Health Administration.* New York: Praeger, 1993.

McVea, Harry. *Financial Conglomerates and the Chinese Wall: Regulating Conflicts of Interest.* New York: Clarendon Press, 1993.

Mount, Ellis. *Top Secret/Trade Secret: Accessing and Safeguarding Restricted Information.* New York: Neal-Schuman Publishers, 1985.

Schoeman, Ferdinand David. *Privacy and Social Freedom.* New York: Cambridge, 1992.

Spanner, Robert A. *Who Owns Innovation?* Homewood, IL: Dow Jones-Irwin, 1986.

Stellman, Jeanne M. *Work Is Dangerous to Your Health: A Handbook for Workers in Every Field.* New York: New Press, 1993.

Stevenson, Russell B., Jr. *Corporations and Information: Secrecy, Access, and Disclosure.* Baltimore: Johns Hopkins University Press, 1980.

Stewart, James B. *Den of Thieves.* New York: Simon & Schuster, 1991.

Werhane, Patricia. *Persons, Rights, and Corporations.* Englewood Cliffs, NJ: Prentice-Hall, 1985.

Wokutch, Richard E. *Cooperation and Conflict in Occupational Safety and Health.* New York: Praeger, 1990.

SHORT CASES

Pickering v. Board of Education

In 1964, a public school teacher in Illinois was fired from her position for writing a letter to a local newspaper criticizing the school board for placing too much emphasis on athletics at the expense of the educational program. She argued for the importance of basic academic subjects and urged voters to turn down an upcoming bond referendum for new athletic facilities. After her dismissal, she filed suit for wrongful discharge, claiming that what she did on her own time was not relevant to an employment decision.

An Illinois court upheld her dismissal, accepting the contention that employees have an obligation to accept the policy choices of their employer and that her public solicitation for support was disruptive and in conflict with support of the school system's objectives. However, the U.S. Supreme Court reversed this decision of the state court and ruled in favor of the woman who was dismissed. Its reasoning was quite different from that of the state court.

The Supreme Court stated that it is essential to maintain a balance between the rights of public employees as citizens and the interests of public employers in providing services to the community. In order to set aside individual rights, the Court argued that it is necessary for public employees to show that their ability to function properly and provide effective services to the employer is seriously threatened. In this case, the Supreme Court was not convinced that such a situation existed and ordered that the dismissed employee be reinstated.

1. Which court decision do you agree with? Why? Do employers have any rights with respect to what employees do with their own time? Should employees be able to do anything they want even if it conflicts with the objectives of the employer?

2. How far should loyalty of employees to the organization for which they work extend? What expectations are reasonable for employers in incidents like the preceding case? Are there any kinds of employee obligations that come with the job?

Benzene

Benzene is a colorless, sweet-smelling gas that has a high vapor pressure that causes rapid evaporation under ordinary atmospheric conditions. The gas has long been recognized as a potentially dangerous substance capable of causing toxic effects and diseases. Over 70 percent of the benzene manufactured in the United States is eventually released into the atmosphere. It is used in the processing and manufacturing of tires, detergents, paints, pesticides, and petroleum products. Ninety-eight percent of all benzene produced is used in the petrochemical and petroleum-refining industries. Over 270,000 employees are exposed to benzene in product-related industries.[1]

In May 1977, OSHA issued an emergency temporary standard (ETS) ordering that worker exposure to benzene be reduced from the regulated level of 10 parts per million (ppm) to 1 ppm, and proposed to make this standard permanent in all industries except gasoline distribution and sales pending a public hearing as required in its enabling legislation. At the time the ETS was issued, little medical evidence existed showing a relationship between benzene and cancer at any level found in the industry. Nonetheless, OSHA decided to drop the exposure level because (1) adverse health effects were evident at certain exposure levels and thus a reduced exposure was necessary to maintain a customary factor of safety, and (2) there is no safe level of exposure to carcinogens suggesting that exposure should be reduced to the lowest level that can be easily monitored.

Industry pressed for the use of benefit-cost analysis in setting such standards, arguing that the law defines a standard as a regulation "reasonably necessary or appropriate" to protect workers' health and safety. A standard that flunks a benefit-cost test is not reasonably necessary or appropriate, industry maintained. Based on this argument, a federal appeals court in New Orleans set aside the ordered reduction, ruling that OSHA cannot legally regulate occupational health hazards without using a benefit-cost analysis to "determine whether the benefits expected from the standard bear a reasonable relationship to the costs imposed." The Supreme Court, in a 5–4 decision, upheld the lower court ruling, but for mostly different reasons.[2]

The court held that OSHA must make a "threshold determination" of significant risk at the standard's present level before moving to a lower level. To the Court a safe work environment is not necessarily a risk-free work environment, and OSHA must adequately prove that there will be significant health benefits at the lower level. The ruling stated that OSHA had established a risk at levels above 10 ppm, but that the agency failed to prove that any substantial benefit would result from dropping the level. While the Court refused to uphold the 1 ppm standard, it in no way rejected the agency's right to regulate industry on a less strict standard.

Under pressure from labor unions and public advocacy groups, OSHA proposed a new rule for occupational exposure to benzene in December 1985, which again dropped exposure to 1 ppm. In proposing this rule, OSHA adhered to the standards set by the Supreme Court ruling. Quantitative risk studies were done to assess whether or not benzene exposure posed a threat to workers. OSHA then assessed whether or not the new standard would provide significant benefits to exposed workers. Finally, the agency looked at available data to set an exposure limit that was technologically and economically feasible.

1. Is the use of benefit-cost analysis appropriate when dealing with regulation of substances like benzene? What ethical theory is benefit-cost analysis based on? What are the problems in applying this theory to making decisions about appropriate regulations?

2. Is it possible to create a risk-free work environment? If not, what level of risk is appropriate and ethical to ask workers to accept? Should they be in on the decision about the risks they face in the workplace? What is a fair way to handle these kinds of issues?

[1] Unless otherwise noted, material for this case comes from Tom L. Beauchamp, *Case Studies in Business, Society, and Ethics,* 2nd ed. (Englewood Cliffs, NJ: Prentice-Hall, 1989), pp. 203–211.

[2] *Marshall* v. *American Petroleum Institute,* 581 F.2d 493 (5th Cir. 1978). See also "Court Battle over Benzene Safety Raises Issues of Weighing Agency Rules, Cost Against Benefit," *The Wall Street Journal,* January 9, 1980, p. 44; and "Regulations Limiting Worker Exposure to Benzene Are Voided by High Court," *The Wall Street Journal,* July 3, 1980, p. 6.

Source: Rogene A. Buchholz, *Business Environment and Public Policy: Implications for Management,* 5th ed. (Englewood Cliffs, NJ: Prentice Hall, 1995), pp. 347–348.

Trade Secrets

Speed took a job with a computer software company shortly after graduating from college. He learned a great deal about the computer software industry while with the company and had access to the company's client list and was a member of the new software development team. After several years with the company, Speed became disgruntled because the software he helped to create was doing well in the market and many of his clients were purchasing the package.

Believing that he could be making more money and finding more opportunity for advancement elsewhere, Speed took a job with a rival software company. In the following months, the new company came out with a software package similar to the one developed at Speed's former company but priced slightly lower. Many of Speed's former clients switched over to the new package and were lured away to his new company.

Speed's former employer filed suit claiming theft of property and improper use of trade secrets. The suit, however, got tied up in a lengthy court battle. Since Speed's former company is a small company, the loss of many of its clients put it in serious financial difficulty. Meanwhile, Speed feels bitter and betrayed after being accused of theft by his former employer and believes all he was doing was using what he had learned about the computer industry to get ahead in a new position.

1. What is a trade secret? Was the knowledge that Speed had about the new software package a trade secret that belonged to his former employer? Was the client list that Speed took with him a trade secret? What are the ethical issues in this incident?

2. How should situations like that portrayed in this case be handled? Would clearly stated policies with respect to trade secrets be helpful to make employees aware of where to draw the line on what information they can legitimately use with a new employer?

Insider Trading

Professor Prolific is employed by Easy University in a large midwestern city. In addition to his teaching duties, he is also area coordinator responsible for scheduling and staffing classes for his area of interest. Since the school is short of full-time faculty, he has to hire several part-time instructors each semester to offer students a full range of classes in his area. Finding qualified people to teach classes on a part-time basis is usually not a problem, since there are several large employers in the city that have people trained in the subject matter.

Professor Prolific is interviewing one of these people in his office to determine if the person is qualified for teaching a class at the university. In the course of the interview, the potential part-timer happens to mention that he has recently visited one of the warehouses that the company he works for has built around the country to hold inventory of its products. He states that this particular warehouse was full of the company's new home computer, which to him was evidence that the computer was not selling.

He then went on to state that he believed that one of the best investments anyone could make in the near future was to sell short the stock of the company he worked for, thinking that the company was due to experience a big loss for the coming quarter because of the unsold inventory of home computers. You know that his particular company has a history of developing new technologies but is terribly inept at marketing them successfully. Thus, it doesn't surprise you that its new computer isn't selling well. Therefore, you are tempted to take the advice of this employee and sell some of its stock short to make a quick killing on the stock market.

1. If Professor Prolific acts on this information given to him by the employee of the company, would this be considered inside information? Would he be subject to being found guilty of insider trading should he go ahead and invest in the company and make a lot of money should the predictions of the employee prove true?

2. What would you do in this situation? What ethical issues should you consider in making your decision? Would anyone be hurt by your making a lot of money in taking the advice of the employee? Would such an act be unethical in any respect?

CHAPTER 17

Leadership in Business

Previous sections of this book have dealt with theoretical aspects of business ethics in presenting a new theory called a process approach that is different from traditional approaches, discussed the nature of the corporation and its relationship to society, and covered a number of ethical issues that confront business organizations. This chapter will discuss the implications of the process approach for current issues in the debate about the nature and function of leadership in general and in particular for the leadership of business organizations.

The Nature of Leadership

One of the most fundamental issues in the current literature on leadership revolves around a discussion of the very nature of leadership itself. After a careful study of existing empirical studies related to leadership, for example, David D. Van Fleet and Andrew Yukl conclude that as the result of decades of research on leadership, what we are left with is a bewildering mass of findings related to leadership that do not allow any firm generalizations to be drawn about the nature of leadership. This same conclusion has been reached by other scholars in their writings.[1] Thus, there is a confusion in the literature regarding the nature of leadership and how leadership is to be understood in modern organizations.

James MacGregor Burns sees the problem as a lack of theoretical foundations for the study of leadership. This view of the problem is seen in his claim that: "Without a powerful modern philosophical tradition, without theoretical and empirical cumulation, without guiding concepts, and without considered practical experiences, we lack the very foundations" for understanding leadership.[2] His work incorporates empirical and theoretical dimensions, which contribute to a better understanding of leadership, but he does not develop the "powerful modern philosophical tradition" that he argues is needed for the emergence of what he calls a "school of leadership."[3]

What is found in the history of discussions regarding the nature of leadership are some of the same assumptions that have plagued business ethics and have led to an unstated moral pluralism. One of these assumptions is again the atomistic view of individuals that is found in so many ethical theories, a view that is rooted in the presuppositions of a passive "spectator" theory of knowledge in which reality is viewed as atomic, separable, isolatable units that can be considered individually. In keeping with this assumption, the individual is considered to be the basic building block of a society or a community, and a society is no more than the sum of the individuals of whom it is comprised.

This long-standing view of atomic individualism provides a common basis for positions as diverse as traditional individualistic or interest-group liberalism and traditional conservative laissez-faire economics.[4] Yet, while peripheral ties may be established when antecedent individuals enter into contract with one another or come together through other means of collection in order to more readily secure their own individualistic goals, these bonds cannot root them in any ongoing endeavor that is more than the sum of their separate selves, separate wills, separate egoistic desires. Thus, at the deepest level, humans are separate from each other and from the communities in which they live and find their identities.

Directly flowing from this is the view that any one individual stands over against the community as a whole in an external relationship. The leader is an atomic individual, standing over against other atomic individuals who constitute, collectively, a group of followers. In this way, there is a leader and there are followers. Burns has expressed the implications of this view by stating that "one of the most serious failures in the study of leadership has been the bifurcation between the literature on leadership and the literature on followership."[5]

This bifurcation between leaders and followers, and the atomistic individualism upon which it is based, is evidenced in many of the well-known empirical studies on leadership that have been undertaken over the past several years. Indeed, what one finds in empirical research is in large measure a result of the way one structures the set of issues or questions to be investigated. The way these issues and questions are structured is directed by philosophical assumptions, which are by and large only vaguely and implicitly held by the researcher, but which are nonetheless powerful directive forces in the structuring of the research.

This phenomenon can be seen in the way in which Lewin and Lippitt, in their early examination of leadership, attempted to understand leadership activity in terms of the democratic versus autocratic leader.[6] The autocratic leader engages in a top-down process, making all decisions and directing all activity. The democratic leader acts as coordinator and utilizes majority-rule decision making when dealing with significant issues. Here, the leader still stands in an external relation to the members of the group, collecting the sum totals of their individual wills and desires.

Fiedler and Chemers, in their 1974 study, stress the importance of interaction, but such interaction is in fact an external link among disparate, inherently bifurcated qualities of leaders and followers that remain essentially unchanged in the interaction.[7] The view of atomic individuals pursuing their own separate goals is clearly manifest in the claim by House that performance is so tied to personal, individual goals that if these goals are obtainable in other ways, the individual will not be a high producer.[8] Hence, the major role of the leader is to effect such a unique link between personal goals and organizational performance.[9] The study by Braen and Schiemann makes a sharp distinction between the relation of the leader to the group and the leader to the individual in such a way as to clearly indicate that the group is the collection of atomic individuals, which in turn absorbs the individual into the collection, thus again pitting the atomic individual over against the group as the collective whole.[10]

The work on leadership over the last decade has shown an increasing distancing from these types of views, which gain their direction from the unexamined assumption of atomic individualism. But, while the work has been highly instructive for understanding the dynamics of leadership, there has been no explicit formulation of a philosophical basis that replaces the long tradition of the atomic individual and, concomitantly, the group as merely a collection of such individuals. For example, a study by Jones in 1983 distances itself from explicit personal reward and punishment or output control by turning to the function of role formalization as the important work of leadership.[11] Such role taking, as will be discussed later, can itself best be understood as an inherently internal dynamic relationship between the individual and the group. In short, it can best be viewed from the perspective of a new understanding of self and community, which cannot be adequately handled in terms of the atomism of a long philosophical tradition.

Toward New Philosophical Foundations for Leadership

Warren Bennis has well summarized the problem of leadership in its relation to an understanding of the self: "American cultural traditions define personality, achievement, and the purpose of human life in ways that shower the individual with glory . . ." There is "a celebration of 'the self' in terms of excessive individualism." As he continues, "We are in danger of losing individualism's opposite, a sense of community, of collective aspirations, of public service."[12] An adequate contemporary philosophy of the self must undercut the opposition between self and community, and herein lies the strength of the pragmatic process approach.

In the discussion that follows, the term *participatory leadership* will be used to indicate the type of leadership that emerges from this approach. While this term is not intended to capture an understanding of leadership that is not already available in some of the contemporary work in the area, it will prove useful in capturing the various features of leadership available in the literature and relating these features to the new philosophical understanding of the dynamics of self and community contained in the pragmatic process approach. Participatory leadership incorporates, at an "enlarged" level, the human dimensions that need to be cultivated, to some degree, in humanity in general. This way of proceeding will also provide an opportunity to summarize and review some of the major tenets of the pragmatic process approach that were developed in the first section of the book and utilized throughout.

To briefly recap this approach, all knowledge and experience are infused with interpretive aspects stemming from a perspective or point of view. Knowledge is not a copy of anything pregiven but involves a creative organization of experience that guides the way we focus on experience and that is tested by its workability in directing the ongoing course of future activities. In this way, experience and knowledge, in being perspectival, are at once experimental, providing a workable organization of problematical or potentially problematical situations. Furthermore, this situation incorporates a perspectival pluralism, for diverse groups or diverse individuals bring diverse perspectives in the organization of experience.

In communicative interaction, individuals take the perspective of the other in the development of their conduct, and in this way there develops the common content that provides community of meaning. To have a self is to have a particular type of ability, the ability to be aware of one's behavior as part of the social process of adjustment, to be aware of oneself as an acting agent within the context of other acting agents. Not only can selves exist only in relationship to other selves, but no absolute line can be drawn between our own selves and the selves of others, since our own selves are there for and in our experience only insofar as others exist and enter into our experience. The origins and foundation of the self are social or intersubjective.

In incorporating the perspective of the other, the developing self comes to take the perspective of others in the group as an interrelated whole.[13] In this way the self comes to incorporate the standards and authority of the group; there is a passive dimension to the self. Yet, in responding to the perspective of the other, the individual is a unique center of activity that responds; there is a creative dimension to the self. Any self thus incorporates, by its very nature, both the conformity of the group perspective and the creativity of its unique individual perspective. Thus, the tension between conservative and liberating forces lies in the very nature of the self.[14] And thus, also, freedom does not lie in opposition to the restrictions of norms and authority but in a self-direction that requires the proper dynamic interaction of these two poles within the self.

The concept of role formalization, which was mentioned previously as marking an early, implicit move away from atomic individualism, can find conceptual underpinnings from this dynamic of creativity and conformity.[15] Using a variation on Mead's example of a baseball team as an instance of a social group, a participant must assume the attitudes of the other players as an organized unity, and this organization controls the response of the individual participant.

Each one of the participant's own acts is set by "his being everyone else on the team," insofar as the organization of the various attitudes controls his own response. Yet, each concrete situation is unique, and individual players feed into the group dynamics in terms of their own unique responses, which in turn shape the ongoing dynamics of the group.

Because of the very nature of the self, the individual is neither an isolatable discrete element in, nor an atomic building block of, a community. Rather, the individual represents the creative pole within community. The unique individual both reflects and reacts to the common perspective in its own peculiar manner. And, when the individual selects a novel perspective, this novelty in turn enters into the common perspective that is now "there" as incorporating this novelty. In this continual interplay of adjustment of attitudes, aspirations, and factual perceptions between the common perspective as the condition for the novel emergent perspective and the novel emergent as it conditions the common perspective, the dynamic of community is to be found.[16]

The adjustment between the self and the other is neither assimilation of perspectives, one to the other, nor the fusion of perspectives into an indistinguishable oneness, but can best be understood as an "accommodating participation" in which each creatively affects and is affected by the other through accepted means of adjudication. Thus, a community is constituted by, and develops in terms of, the ongoing communicative adjustment between the activity constitutive of the novel individual perspective and the common or group perspective. Moreover, each of these two interacting poles constitutive of community gains its meaning, significance, and enrichment through this process of participatory accommodation or adjustment.[17] Because of these dynamics, the leader does not "stand apart" from a following group, nor is the leader an organizer of group ideas, but rather leadership is by its very nature in dynamic interaction with the group, and both are in a process of ongoing transformation because of this interaction.

Novelty within an organization is initiated by individuals, but such initiation can occur only because individuals are continuous with others and with the historically situated social institutions of which they are a part.[18] The novel perspective is an emergent because of its relation to institutions, traditions, and patterns of life that conditioned its novel emergence, and gains its significance in light of the new common perspectives to which it gives rise. As stressed by Bennis and Nanus, the constructive creativity of leadership arises out of awareness of a present as it has been informed by a general heritage from the past.[19] Such an interdependence is concisely stated in their claim that leadership at once creates, alters, or reconstructs the shape of understanding, and does so in such a way as to secure ongoing tradition.[20] It is the interrelation of novelty and continuity at the core of the pragmatic process approach that provides the conceptual tools for understanding how the uniqueness of the individual and the norms and standards of the group are two interrelated factors in an ongoing exchange, neither of which can exist apart from the other. Because of the inseparable interaction of these two poles, goals for the whole cannot be pursued by ignoring consequences for individuals affected, nor can individual goals be adequately pursued apart from the vision of the functioning of the whole.

The development of the ability both to create and to respond constructively to the creation of novel perspectives, as well as to incorporate the perspective of the other, not as something totally alien, but as something sympathetically understood, is at once growth of the self and the organization. Thus, to deepen and expand the horizons of the organization is at once to deepen and expand the horizons of those involved in the ongoing dynamics of adjustment. Any problematic situation can be viewed through the use of social intelligence in a way that enlarges and reintegrates the situation and the selves involved, providing at once a greater degree of authentic self-expression and a greater degree of social participation. In this way, an organization controls its own evolution. Any authentic organization involves a shared value or goal, and the overreaching goal of an organization that is not to die of stagnation is, in Mead's words, precisely "this control of its own evolution."[21] Thus, the ultimate goal involving the working character of universalizing ideals is growth or development, not final completion. This ongoing evolution, as Bennis and Nanus stress in their discussion of leadership, involves the ongoing creativity of problem finding[22] and revision or reconstruction in terms of experimental method.[23]

To unite around a common goal such as that indicated previously does not promote an ideal in which diversity has disappeared. Rather, diversity provides the materials for ongoing reconstructive growth. As Dewey emphasizes, growth by its very nature involves the ongoing resolution of conflict.[24] That leadership, as opposed to sheer power, invites, indeed, requires this type of situation is brought home by Burns in his statement that "Leaders, whatever their professions of harmony, do not shun conflict: they confront it, exploit it, and ultimately embody it."[25]

Moreover, what must be stressed in light of the preceding development is that the creativity of participatory leadership is two-directional by its very nature. The leader not only changes but is changed. James captures this interactional process in his observation that "the influence of a great person modifies a community in an entirely original and peculiar way, while the community in turn remodels him. This is because both at any given moment offer ambiguous potentialities of development.[26] As Burns emphasizes, in the highest level of leadership, what he calls "transforming leadership," the leader and the led are both transformed.[27] He gives as the best modern example the life of Gandhi, "who aroused and elevated the hopes and demands of millions of Indians and whose life and personality were enhanced in the process."[28]

Leaders Versus Managers

One of the most important issues in leadership is the distinction often made between being a leader of an organization as opposed to being a manager. In coming to grips with the nature of a leader as opposed to a manager, the features of innovation and creativity are often considered under various labels as crucial to the distinction. Thus, it has been stressed that leaders, as opposed to managers, are seen as "active instead of reactive, shaping ideas instead of responding to them," changing "the way people think about what is desirable, possible, and necessary."[29] Managers are said to be concerned with the operational side of an enterprise and are considered to be the custodial caretakers of an organization. They are concerned that things get done and their purpose and focus are transactional in nature. Leaders, on the other hand, are concerned with what and why things get done. Their focus is conceptual and directional, and leadership is understood as transformational and visionary in nature.[30]

As has been aptly noted, "All leaders have the capacity to create a compelling vision, one that takes people to a new place, and the ability to translate that vision into reality."[31] These statements lead to the moral dimension of leadership, and to the pragmatic process understanding of the value dimension that pervades human existence and that reflects the bipolar dynamics of adjustment. It has been seen that this approach undergirds a new understanding of the ethical dimension of human activity in general and, hence, it will as well undergird a new understanding of what it means to speak of ethical leadership.

The experience of value emerges as both shared and unique, as all experience is both shared and unique. The adjustment between these two aspects, the shared and the unique, gives rise to the novel and creative aspects within moral community. Though the social context itself affects the vital drives, the energies operative within a situation, and though neither the emergence of moral norms and practices nor the emergence of brute valuings occurs apart from the social interaction of concrete human beings, yet the creative advancement of the individual in its uniqueness brings unique tendencies and potentialities into the shaping processes of social change; brings creative perspectives to the resolution of the conflicting and changing value claims; and restructures the very moral behavior or moral practices and the institutionalized ways of behaving that helped shape its own developing potentialities.

Reconstruction of the moral situation, as involving authentic growth, requires not imposition of abstract principles from on high, but a deepening attunement to the pulse of human existence. Through such attunement, the leader can not only lead individuals to think differently about what is desirable, what ought to be, but can change the actual concrete desires of the individuals involved. While the organization of concrete valuings provides the material for envisioning the valuable, new recognitions of the valuable in turn can change the immediate qualitative "felt" dimension of concrete experience, changing the immediate "tastes" of the individuals involved.

Thus, Zaleznik emphasizes the role a leader exerts not just in establishing different objectives and expectations, but also in altering moods and desires.[32] Similarly, it is the ability to shape and alter not just ideals but the concrete motives, desires, or valuings that are reintegrated by ideals, which Burns characterizes as transforming leadership as opposed to transactional leadership, the latter being a bargaining to aid the separate interests of individuals or groups, who then proceed along their separate ways.[33] Indeed, unless leadership results in the transformation of both the desirable and the desirings, the valuable and the valuings, the reintegration of the individuals involved cannot take place, and the ideals and the vision cannot exert a compelling force or exhibit any vitality. And, again, this transformation involves both the leader and those led in an ongoing participatory dynamic. This move to the highest level of leadership, which Burns characterizes as inherently moral, requires the move from the atomic individualism implicit in his foregoing characterization of transactional leadership to a new dynamic understanding of community interaction.

The reconstructive growth in participatory leadership in turn aids in the further development of the creativity of the individuals involved, expanding, often changing its ongoing path. And, without the development of this active creative dimension, there is no real moral freedom. Thus, Lisa Newton, in distinguishing what she calls the stages of "control leadership" and "inspirational leadership" from the highest level of "empowering leadership," stresses that empowering leadership encourages the "full moral agency" of the individual. While control leadership leads to "a batch of obedient people," inspirational leadership, through reward, precept, and most importantly by example, "by openly and visibly living" what one wants others to become, leads "not only to doers but believers."[34] Yet this is not enough, for belief in what a leader believes in will not cover all cases. Hence, empowering leadership must lead the doers and believers to think independently, to be able to make reasoned, responsible evaluations and choices on their own—to be, in short, free moral agents. Leadership involves a process of engagement in which the leader is the major player in the communicative, transforming engagement process. Far from imposing ideology from on high, leadership and the sense of vision it conveys come from and encourage in others a deepening attunement to conflicting concrete demands operative within a specific context as the matrix for ongoing reconstructive growth. In this way leadership encourages the development of free moral agents who can affect the direction of such constructive change.

Bennis and Nanus, in delineating the difference between leaders and managers, stress that "one of the clearest distinctions" between managers and leaders is that while managers operate on the physical resources of the organization, leaders operate on the emotional and spiritual resources of the organization, on its values, commitments, and aspirations.[35] The transforming leadership explicated by Burns is the highest form of leadership precisely because it draws upon and raises to higher levels the spiritual, value-laden dimension of all in a process of ongoing participatory growth.

Perhaps too much is made of this distinction between leadership and management, and even though leadership and management may not be the same thing, these two dimensions are not so neatly separable. As many have pointed out, leadership is not merely good management, but good management would seem to be at least part of the overall job description of every leader. And leadership would also seem to be part of good management. Thus, at times leaders must manage, and managers must lead. There is an interaction between these two dimensions that must not be forgotten, and any one person can and should incorporate both these dimensions in their activities with respect to the corporate organization.[36] An organization should bring out the leadership qualities in all its employees, especially its managers who run the organization on a day-to-day basis.

In any event, the understanding of leadership has undergone a gradual shift away from early work in the field, which clearly reflected the atomism of a long-standing philosophical tradition and a view of the business organization as an amoral institution. This shift houses an implicit rejection of the philosophical foundations offered by past philosophy and requires the explicit acceptance of an alternative philosophical framework as providing examined assumptions to be used as directive forces for the way one structures the issues and questions to be investigated in ongoing empirical research. An alternative framework will focus attention on different issues and will enable new views of leadership to emerge as further investigation proceeds. This alternative framework also has implications for management to the extent that management incorporates a leadership dimension.

The alternative framework utilized in this book provides an understanding of the nature of the self as inherently social or relational; of community as constituted by the dynamics of participatory and mutually transforming adjustment involving a common goal of ongoing self-directed growth; of growth itself as involving not mere accumulation or mere economic development, but development of the esthetic-moral richness of humans and their experience; of the moral dimension of experience as involving not the following of rules but the ongoing development of rules that integrate the diverse and often conflicting valuings of concrete human beings embedded in concrete situations; and of the need for the functioning of the whole person in these ongoing, inextricably interrelated participatory and transforming processes. These various features were shown to be manifest in the current literature on leadership, thus making the pragmatic process approach to ethics well suited to provide a new philosophical position, which Burns sees as necessary for developing what he calls a "school of leadership."

Moral Management

It should be clear from the foregoing discussion that the corporation is considered to be a community and not just a collection of individuals who voluntarily decide to be associated with each other to accomplish some agreed-upon purpose. Ethics is also considered to be of critical importance to the management of corporate organizations as communities. Moreover, ethics is considered to be at the heart of leadership, as managing ethically is what leadership with respect to the corporate organization is all about, and good management incorporates such leadership. In fact, the manager as leader is a "moral manager."

One important implication of this philosophy is that corporations can be viewed as basically ethical in nature. They are organizations that create values that are important to people and to the society in which corporations function. If ethics is understood as having something to do with actions that are directed to improving the welfare of people, then one primary mission of business is to enhance the economic welfare of society by producing goods and services that make people's lives better and more enriched. In this sense, business creates economic value by taking resources and combining them in such a way as to produce something that has utility and will sell in the marketplace.

Business, however, is not just an economic institution that has to do only with economic value; its activities have other dimensions. Business is also a social institution that can create social value. If business pollutes the environment in the process of creating economic value, it is destroying a social value of great significance for human life and survival. If, on the other hand, business spends money to dispose of its toxic wastes properly and protects the drinking water of a community, it is creating or at least protecting a social value of great significance to the community.

Moreover, if business undermines the trust and confidence of the public through fraudulent and deceptive practices, it is destroying community value by violating ethical principles that form the basis of marketplace transactions. If it is honest and straightforward in all its transactions and fulfills its contractual obligations, however, the organization is creating or at least upholding community values by respecting the norms and standards inherent in a free enterprise economy and a civilized society.

Business is also a human institution that can enhance human value for its employees. If business treats its employees with respect and as autonomous individuals with rights that should not be violated, it is creating and enhancing human value, not just treating people as a means to profits and production. If, on the other hand, business treats its employees as simply another factor of production and ignores important human needs that may not be directly related to the production of goods and services, it is destroying human value and treating people as mere things to be manipulated in the interests of higher production levels and profits.

Thinking of corporations as ethical systems that can enhance or destroy various kinds of value relating to the welfare of society and its constituents means that a corporation must be guided by a moral vision. This view means that the management task is primarily ethical in nature, and the primary task of management becomes the management of values rather than the management of people, machines, money, or other more traditional elements of productive activity. Its responsibility is to create values that enhance the well-being of society and of the people in that society, not merely to manage resources efficiently to create as much economic value as possible. Managers as leaders can also create social, community, and human value that enhances the welfare of people just as does the creation of economic value.

The obvious question to ask about this view is what rewards or incentives exist for one to be concerned about creating social and other kinds of values. Why should one be socially responsible and concerned about pollution? Why should one be concerned about enhancing the quality of the workplace so employees' lives can be enriched in more than monetary terms? Why should one be concerned about adhering to ethical standards if more money can be made by engaging in bribery or other fraudulent practices? Profits are a reward for creating economic value. What rewards exist for creating other kinds of value? Are the only incentives negative in the sense that government regulations are the likely result if business isn't responsive to social concerns or that the corporation may be fined and receive a great deal of negative publicity if fraudulent practices are discovered and disclosed?

Here is where the dimension of leadership comes into play. The pursuit of profit or the creation of economic value is simply not important enough to absorb all of a manager's time and effort and all of the energies and devotion a manager brings to the organization. Managers should be encouraged to think more highly of their own task and recognize that they can contribute much more to society than the creation of economic value. This is not to suggest that economic value isn't important, only to say that it is not enough. Managers should be encouraged to accept the challenge that a broader view of the corporation entails, to think of corporate performance in broader terms than mere economic performance, and to develop an awareness of the manifold impacts they can have on an economy and a society through their decisions and actions. The managerial task is an incredibly significant role in our society and in the world, but its significance cannot begin to be captured by focusing only on the notion of economizing and marketplace transactions.

Are these ideas suggesting that virtue is its own reward? In some sense, this is probably true. Managers cannot expect to receive economic rewards that are directly tied to good performance along social and other value dimensions. It could be argued that if we expect to receive economic rewards for everything we do, this denigrates these other values and reduces them solely to economic values. Managers must find intrinsic rewards in creating other kinds of value, rewards that come from the satisfaction of having made something useful out of one's life and from having made the maximum contribution to society that is possible. Human beings want to feel good about themselves and feel their lives have counted for something important. Managers are in a unique position to develop this sense of significance by utilizing resources under their command that society has entrusted to them because of their expertise. They must be leaders in the true sense of the word, and not just managers who are solely concerned about the organization and their own position in the organization.

Is there then no connection between being ethical in the sense just described and good business? Some of the literature on leadership reviewed in this chapter would suggest otherwise. If management has taken great pains to produce a good product that is safe to use and will enhance people's lives, there should be a confidence that it can be sold at a profit in the marketplace without bribery or dishonest advertising. If a company treats its employees well and gains a reputation as a good place to work, it should have no trouble finding good employees who are willing to devote their energies to the production of goods and services in that company. If the company becomes known throughout the investment community as a well-run company, it should have no trouble attracting investors who are willing to put their money into its stock in good and bad times.

The final implication of this view is that good ethics is not only good business, but that the fundamental business of business is ethical, the creation of values that enhance the welfare of humans and the communities in which they live, as well as the world community at large. Thus, ethics is central to the managerial task; in fact, it is *the* task of management. It was seen in Chapter 5 that according to the traditional market system approaches, good ethics and good business were also understood as part of the same package, but there is a world of difference. For according to that traditional approach, the ethical notion of business was subsumed under, and in fact ultimately conflated with, economic considerations. Now the economic performance of business is subsumed under the ethical notion of business as an organization that creates or destroys different kinds of values that are of great moral significance. A managerial philosophy that takes this view seriously cannot, then, be built on principles solely related to efficiency or expediency, but must be built on ethical considerations related to a host of relationships and activities of management that have moral significance. The notion of business performance must be broadened to include the social and human aspects of business activities, for the corporate community always opens onto a broader community with all the moral implications this involves.

Questions for Discussion

1. What are the most important problems with respect to the current literature on leadership? What assumptions about the individual and community are embedded in much of this literature? Has some recent work deviated from these assumptions? If so, in what ways?

2. How does the process approach based on pragmatic philosophy provide a foundation for new directions in leadership? What does the term *participatory leadership* mean in this context? How are the individual and community related in this approach and what implications does this have for leadership?

3. What is the difference between leaders and managers as seen by many authors on leadership? Is too much made of this distinction in your opinion? What is the difference between transactional and transformational leadership? Is this an important distinction?

4. What is moral management as described in the chapter? How does this concept of management relate to leadership? What kinds of values does business create or enhance? Can any kind of priority be placed on these values?

5. Is virtue its own reward? What is the connection, if any, between being ethical and running a good business? What does it mean to say that the fundamental business of business is ethical? How does this differ from the traditional view of business?

6. From a moral point of view, what should a managerial philosophy incorporate? How can this philosophy be put into practice? What kind of changes in the capitalistic system or in corporate organizations would be necessary to implement the philosophy of leadership and management portrayed in this chapter?

Endnotes

[1] David D. Van Fleet and Andrew Yukl, "A Century of Leadership Research," *Papers Dedicated to the Development of Modern Management* (1986), reprinted in *Contemporary Issues in Leadership,* 2nd ed., William E. Rosenbach and Robert L. Taylor, eds. (Boulder, CO: Westview Press, 1989), pp. 65–90. See also Bernard M. Bass, *Leadership and Performance Beyond Expectations* (New York: Free Press, 1985).

[2] James MacGregor Burns, *Leadership* (New York, Hagerstown, San Francisco, London: Harper Colophon Books, Harper & Row Publishers, 1978), p. 2.

[3] There can be a confusion of terminology here unless clarified. By *modern* Burns obviously means the same thing as *contemporary*. Yet, in the history of philosophy, a distinction is made between modern and contemporary, a distinction to which this essay adheres.

[4] This point is developed in some detail in our paper, "Communitarianism vs Individuality: A Pragmatic Perspective," delivered at the annual meeting of The Society for the Advancement of Socio-Economics, Paris, 1994.

[5] Burns, *Leadership,* p. 3.

[6] K. Lewin and R. Lippitt, "An Experimental Approach to the Study of Autocracy and Democracy: A Preliminary Note," *Sociometry,* Vol. 1 (1938), pp. 292–300.

[7] F. E. Fiedler and M. M. Chemers, *Leadership and Effective Management* (Glenview, IL: Scott, Foresman, 1974).

[8] R. J. House, "A Path-Goal Theory of Leader Effectiveness," *Administrative Science Quarterly,* Vol. 16 (1971), pp. 321–338.

[9] See also two studies by M. G. Evans, "The Effects of Supervisory Behavior on the Path-Goal Relationship," *Organizational Behavior and Human Performance,* Vol. 5 (1970), pp. 277–298, and "Leadership and Motivation: A Core Concept," *Academy of Management Journal,* Vol. 13 (1970), pp. 91–102.

[10] G. Braen and W. Schiemann, "Leader-Member Agreement: A Vertical Dyad Linkage Approach," *Journal of Applied Psychology,* Vol. 63 (1978), pp. 206–212.

[11] G. R. Jones, "Forms of Control of Leader Behavior," *Journal of Management,* Vol. 9 (1983), pp. 159–172.

[12] Warren Bennis, *Why Leaders Can't Lead* (San Francisco and Oxford: Jossey-Bass Publishers, 1990), pp. 71–72.

[13] G. H. Mead refers to this as the "generalized other." See *Mind, Self, and Society,* Charles Morris, ed. (Chicago: University of Chicago Press, 1934).

[14] John Dewey, "Authority and Social Change," *The Later Works,* Vol. 11, Jo Ann Boydston, ed. (Carbondale and Edwardsville, IL: University of Southern Illinois Press, 1987), p. 133.

[15] G. H. Mead, *Mind, Self, and Society,* p. 4.

[16] A person may be a member of more than one community, for there are diverse levels and types of communities. Any community consists of many subgroups, and though individuals may feel alienated from a particular society, they cannot really be alienated from society in general, for this very alienation will only throw them into some other society. *Mind, Self, and Society,* pp. 353–354.

[17] Thus, in Dewey's terms, "No amount of aggregated collective action of itself constitutes a community. . . . To learn to be human is to develop through the give-and-take of communication an effective sense of being an individually distinctive member of a community; one who understands and appreciates its beliefs, desires, and methods, and who contributes to a further conversion of organic powers into human resources and values. But this transition is never finished." Dewey, "The Public and Its Problems," *The Later Works,* Vol. 2, Jo Ann Boydston, ed. (Carbondale and Edwardsville, IL: University of Southern Illinois Press, 1984), p. 330; p. 332.

[18] Thus, Dewey stresses that a part of the life process itself is the need to adjust the old and the new, the stability of conformity and the novelty of creativity. "Authority and Social Change," p. 249.

[19] Warren Bennis and Burt Nanus, *Leaders: The Strategies for Taking Charge* (New York: Harper & Row, 1985), pp. 97–99.

[20] Ibid., p. 42.

[21] G. H. *Mead, Mind, Self, and Society,* p. 251.

[22] Bennis and Nanus, *Leaders,* p. 41.

[23] Ibid., p. 206.

[24] John Dewey, "Ethics," *The Middle Works,* Vol. 5, Jo Ann Boydston, ed. (Carbondale and Edwardsville, IL: University of Southern Illinois Press, 1978), p. 327.

[25] Burns, *Leadership,* p. 28.

[26] William James, "Great Men and Their Environment," *The Will to Believe and Other Essays* (1979), *The Works of William James,* ed. Frederick Burkhardt (Cambridge: Harvard University Press, 1975), pp. 170–171.

[27] Burns, *Leadership,* p. 20.

[28] Ibid.

[29] See Abraham Zaleznik, "Managers and Leaders: Are They Different?" *Harvard Business Review,* May–June 1977, p. 71.

[30] Al Gini, "Too Much to Say About Something," *Business Ethics Quarterly,* Vol. 5, no. 1 (January 1995), p. 150.

[31] Warren Bennis, "Managing the Dream," *Training,* May 1990, p. 44.

[32] Zaleznik, "Managers and Leaders: Are They Different?" p. 71.

[33] Burns, *Leadership,* p. 425.

[34] Lisa Newton, "Moral Leadership in Business: The Role of Structure," *Business and Professional Ethics Journal,* Vol. 5, pp. 74–90.

[35] Bennis, *Leaders,* p. 92.

[36] Gini, "Too Much to Say About Something," p. 150.

Suggested Readings

Bass, Bernard M. *Leadership and Performance Beyond Expectations.* New York: The Free Press, 1985.

Bennis, Warren. *Why Leaders Can't Lead.* San Francisco and Oxford: Jossey-Bass, 1990.

Bennis, Warren, and Burt Nanus. *Leaders: The Strategies for Taking Charge.* New York: Harper & Row, 1985.

Burns, James MacGregor. *Leadership.* New York, Hagerstown, San Francisco, London: Harper Colophon Books, Harper & Row Publishers, 1978.

Fairholm, Gilbert W. *Values Leadership: Towards a New Philosophy of Leadership.* New York: Praeger, 1991.

Gardner, John W. *On Leadership.* New York: The Free Press, 1990.

Heifitz, Ronald A. *A Leadership Without Easy Answers.* Cambridge, MA: Belknap/Harvard University Press, 1994.

Kellerman, Barbara, ed. *Leadership: Multidisciplinary Perspectives.* Pittsburgh: University of Pittsburgh Press, 1986.

McCollough, Thomas E. *The Moral Imagination and Public Life.* New Jersey: Chatham House Publishers, 1991.

Rosenbach, William E., and Robert L. Taylor, eds. *Contemporary Issues in Leadership,* 2nd ed. Boulder, CO: Westview Press, 1989.

Rost, Joseph. *Leadership for the Twenty-First Century.* New York: Praeger, 1991.

Selznic, Philip. *Leadership in Administration: A Sociological Interpretation.* New York: Harper & Row, 1957.

Sergiovanni, Thomas J. *Moral Leadership: Getting to the Heart of School Improvement.* San Francisco: Jossey-Bass, 1992.

Terry, Robert W. *Authentic Leadership: Courage in Action.* San Francisco: Jossey-Bass, 1993.

S H O R T   C A S E S

Influence Peddling

Senator Robert Dole, who became Senate majority leader when the Republicans took over Congress in the 1994 elections, has flown 187 times since 1983 on small private jet airplanes owned by private corporations. Accepting such rides is not uncommon among politicians, and offering such rides is completely legal. The problem is that many of the corporations that offered these rides had business before Congress that Senator Dole could influence.

For example, the senator traveled most frequently on a jet owned by Archer-Daniels-Midland (ADM), the agribusiness giant. Dole's political committee reimbursed ADM the equivalent of first-class airfare as required by campaign-finance law. However, this amounted to less than 25 percent of the cost of operating a private jet. For years, Senator Dole has strongly supported ADM's pet product, which is ethanol, sponsoring tax breaks worth hundreds of millions of dollars.

The senator also flew a good deal on jets owned by UST Inc., the nation's largest producer of smokeless tobacco. Since 1987, the company contributed $40,000 to Dole's political committees, and its senior vice president is a board member and fund-raiser for a charity for the disabled called the Dole Foundation. With respect to company interests, Dole has worked to hold down taxes on smokeless tobacco. In 1985, an amendment sponsored by the senator set the tax on smokeless tobacco at only a fifth of the levy on cigarettes. In response to criticism, a Dole spokesperson said: "It's ludicrous to suggest that Senator Dole's position on any of these issues has been influenced by campaign contributions or entirely legal and fully disclosed rides on corporate planes."

Dole also flew on a plane provided by the American Financial Corporation, whose chairman is Carl Lindner. In 1994, Lindner and his family gave $20,000 to the senator's political committee, and the company contributed $200,000 to the Republican National Committee. Contributions of $375,000 were also made to the Democratic National Committee and $55,000 to Newt Gingrich's GOPAC. In late 1994, Dole and several other lawmakers were successful in their efforts to persuade the administration to attack European quotas on banana imports. The prime beneficiary of this effort was a Lindner company, Chiquita Banana.

1. Is there a conflict of interest involved in accepting flights on corporate jets and political contributions by corporations? Do you believe the denial of such a conflict by Dole's spokesperson? How would you evaluate these practices from a moral point of view?

2. Is this a moral way for business to influence public policy? Are corporate executives demonstrating moral leadership by offering such favors to politicians? What could they do to influence the public policy process that would be morally acceptable in your view?

Source: Michael Istkoff and Mark Hosenball, "Dole's Frequent-Flier Miles," *Newsweek,* April 24, 1995, p. 32.

The Tylenol Crisis

Johnson & Johnson, with its subsidiaries, is one of the world's largest and most diversified manufacturers and distributors of health care products, which include prescription and nonprescription drug products. During the 1960s, Tylenol, an acetaminophen-based analgesic, was introduced in the market as an over-the-counter product. It was produced by McNeil Consumer Products Company, which had been owned since 1959 by Johnson & Johnson, and rapidly became the best-selling product within the company. The Tylenol line came to represent 8 percent of Johnson & Johnson's total revenue and 17 percent of corporate income. In only nine years, Tylenol captured 35 percent of the $1.3 billion analgesic market.

Of the total Tylenol sales, $125 million was sales of extra-strength capsules, which were the fastest-growing segment in the Tylenol line. However, within a three-day period during the fall of 1982, seven people were found dead in the Chicago area. The apparent cause of death was eventually linked to cyanide in extra-strength Tylenol capsules. Although Tylenol was not initially suspected, the link among the deaths was made after two firefighters in different districts of Chicago compared information about the deaths and noticed that each victim had taken extra-strength capsules shortly before they died. Tests by the Cook County Medical Examiner's Office found as much as 65 milligrams of cyanide in some capsules. Fifty milligrams is considered lethal.

At first, the possibility of a disgruntled employee tampering with the product during the manufacturing process was considered, but local authorities quickly discounted that assumption when it was determined that the bottles, which bore different lot numbers, were not from the same plant.[1] Investigators theorized that the capsules had been tampered with at distribution points, most likely after they reached retail shelves.[2] Officials at McNeil and Johnson & Johnson, who were alerted by Chicago authorities early Thursday morning, September 30, announced an immediate recall of all 93,400 bottles of Tylenol that had been produced in McNeil's Ft. Washington, PA, plant and shipped to 31 eastern and midwestern states in August. The company also sent nearly half a million mailgrams to physicians, hospitals, and wholesalers informing them of the danger.

The victims could have been anyone. Death was random, as the poisoner had no way of knowing who the victims might be. Six bottles containing poisoned capsules were found in five drugstores and another in a grocery store. One of the stores was located in North Chicago, and the others were located in communities in the western suburbs, scattered roughly along a north-south line near Illinois State Route 53. Investigators theorized that the killer drove along Route 53, turning off at randomly selected points, to lace a poisoned bottle of capsules in each store.

Soon after the Tylenol poisonings occurred, the Food and Drug Administration met to draft federal requirements for tamper-resistant packaging. Federal action was necessary to avoid a jumble of conflicting regulations among different states and municipalities, which could adversely affect and limit the distribution of over-the-counter products. The regulations that were eventually established required a statement on the label of over-the-counter drugs to make consumers aware of the specific tamper-resistant features of the package. These requirements went into effect on February 7, 1983. Legislation was also introduced on the Senate floor, which would provide federal penalties for anyone who adulterates or tampers with an over-the-counter product.[3]

The damage sustained by Johnson & Johnson because of the Tylenol tragedy was substantial. While public opinion was not negative toward Johnson & Johnson, once it was established that the product tampering was done in the store and not in the plant, consumer confidence was severely shaken. The chairman of Johnson & Johnson decided to spend whatever millions it would cost to voluntarily withdraw 31 million bottles of Tylenol capsules from store shelves across the nation. This action was taken against the advice of government agents. Food and Drug Administration officials feared that the recall would increase the panic touched off by the deaths of the Chicago area residents. The FBI argued that such an expensive action would demonstrate to potential terrorists that they could bring a $5.9 billion corporation to its knees. The recall cost $50 million after taxes.[4]

Despite the setbacks Tylenol experienced, the company never lost faith in the product and retained confidence in its ability to rebuild the business. Within ten weeks of the recall, the company began putting capsules back on the shelves in the new tamper-resistant packages. These efforts paid off and consumer confidence was reestablished as Tylenol eventually regained more than 95 percent of the market share it held before the still unsolved poisonings. The company was given a great deal of credit for doing the right things to enhance its public image in what could have been a disastrous situation.[5] Throughout the crisis, the company managed to maintain consumer and investor confidence by adopting an open approach in dealing with the situation and a willingness to consider the long-term benefits of its actions rather than short-term expediency.

1. In a complex society based on mass production and distribution, is there no way to guarantee absolute protection against someone who is bent on planting poison somewhere in the system? How can trust in the marketplace be maintained given this situation? Who is responsible for maintaining this trust?

2. Did Johnson & Johnson act responsibly in this incident? Did the management of the company demonstrate moral leadership? Did the company consider itself to be a moral agent in responding to the crisis? What lessons are there to be learned by other companies in responding to similar situations where consumer confidence is shaken?

[1] "The Tylenol Scare," *Newsweek,* October 11, 1983, pp. 32–36.

[2] Ibid.

[3] Lawrence G. Foster, "The Johnson & Johnson Credo and the Tylenol Crisis," *New Jersey Bell Journal,* Vol. 6, no. 1 (Spring 1983), p. 2.

[4] "Tylenol's Miracle Comeback," *Time,* October 17, 1983, p. 67.

[5] Ibid.

Source: Rogene A. Buchholz, *Business Environment and Public Policy: Implications for Management,* 5th ed. (Englewood Cliffs, NJ: Prentice Hall, 1995), pp. 381–383.

The PAC Dilemma

John was a respected manager of a division of the Long-Shot Company. His division manufactured components for the MX missile, and due to the recent action of Congress in approving the building of 50 missiles, his division was working at full capacity. Profits of the division looked good, and the division was meeting its production goals. Rumors were floating around that John was targeted for bigger things with the company because of his recent successes.

The company had a political action committee (PAC), which John suspected gave money to congressmen who supported projects that might benefit the company. One day he received a memo that asked for management to give "voluntary" contributions to the PAC, much like they were asked to give to the United Way. While the memo emphasized that the contributions were voluntary, and John knew the law prevented employees from being coerced into giving money, John also suspected that top management knew who contributed and who didn't, and might take this into account in making promotion decisions.

Besides being concerned about the blatant self-interest that John suspected was behind the formation of the PAC, John was also a Democrat, and he suspected the bulk of the contributions was going to Republican candidates given the political affiliations of the majority of top management and the PAC administrator. The pressure he felt to contribute to an opposing party and the ethical implications of the PAC made John angry, yet he did not want to jeopardize his promotion. He liked the company and enjoyed his work and the community.

1. What can an employee do about subtle pressures of the kind in this case? Are most employees at the mercy of top management? Is John free to speak out against the PAC or against its contribution strategies? What can employees do who are concerned about the political involvement of their corporation?

2. Are PACs a legitimate way for business to exercise moral leadership in our society? Should business attempt to influence public policy in this manner? Are PACs solely an instrument for business to look after its own interests?

Source: Rogene A. Buchholz, *Business Environment and Public Policy: Implications for Management,* 5th ed. (Englewood Cliffs, NJ: Prentice Hall, 1995), pp. 639–640.

Strategic Planning

Mr. Flight, the CEO of Mountain Airlines, has been contemplating forming a strategic planning group within his company. Back in the days of regulation, there wasn't much need for airlines to do strategic planning, since their options were limited. Prices and routes and other aspects of their business were regulated by the federal government. Now that deregulation had taken effect, the airlines were in vigorous competition with each other and adopting competitive pricing strategies that obviously benefited consumers but left most of the major airlines with lower earning than before, forcing some into bankruptcy.

Thus, on the surface, a strategic planning group made sense, as Mr. Flight saw the need for the company to think of its long-term profitability and survivability, and not just react to the short-term actions of its competitors. Yet Mr. Flight had also been reading a good deal of literature that described strategic planners as falling out of favor at many companies. Some large corporations were actually disbanding their groups and going back to their usual way of doing business.

The problem seemed to be that planners had no trouble formulating grandiose strategies for their companies, but they did have trouble implementing these strategies given the resources and culture of the organizations in which they were employed. Thus, Mr. Flight wondered how a strategic planning group would fit into his company and whether or not their recommendations would be accepted by line management.

1. What kind of changes have taken place in the airline industry in recent years? Do these changes lend themselves to strategic planning efforts? What could a strategic planning group provide that would benefit the company?

2. What criteria should Mr. Flight consider before he goes ahead with the idea to form a strategic planning group? What moral considerations are relevant? How can management exercise moral leadership through a strategic planning process?

Source: Rogene A. Buchholz, *Business Environment and Public Policy: Implications for Management,* 5th ed. (Englewood Cliffs, NJ: Prentice Hall, 1995), p. 557.

CHAPTER 18

Ethics and Education

There has been an increasing interest in business ethics over the past several years as more schools of business and management have developed business ethics courses, as more chairs in the subject have been established, and as more centers promoting research in the area of business ethics have been started. Companies have been increasingly concerned to have some kind of ethical considerations built into their management training programs and have developed codes of ethics related to employee behavior throughout the company or to specific functions such as purchasing or accounting. Is all this activity just a passing fad that started because of certain scandals in the corporate world, or is it indicative of something more significant taking place in the way business is conducted and in the values held by society?

Many changes in American society provide evidence that something fundamental has happened over the past several decades and that ethical considerations have become more important to corporations and schools of business and management because of these changes. There is something going on regarding conceptions of human welfare and how best to attain the kind of society where human fulfillment can be attained. Old myths and ideologies are no longer accepted and functional, but there is no consensus that has yet developed to replace the old ones that served us in the past. We are groping our way toward some new understanding of society and its goals and objectives, and the outcome of this search will have significant implications for business organizations. These changes in society and the dilemmas they pose for corporations were stated several years ago in the following manner.

> Executives today are living "between the times"—that is, they are caught between the time when there was a strong social consensus that the market mechanism was the best way to control business activity, and some possible future time when society has a clear consensus about just how business institutions ought to advance human welfare. We are now searching for a new consensus: economic language, which has in the past often provided the sole rationale for corporate decisions, no longer, in itself, strikes a note of legitimacy for the American public. While corporate critics speak in ethical

language employing terms such as fairness, justice, rights, and so on, corporate leadership often responds solely in economic language of profit and loss. Such discussion generates much heat but little light, and the disputing parties pass like ships in the night.[1]

In recent years, it has become more and more recognized, not only by the public at large but also by business itself, that corporations must speak not merely in economic language, but in ethical language. Managers are constantly making ethical decisions whether these are conscious or whether they are made unknowingly. They are creating the future, not only for their organizations, but for the people who work for them, for consumers who use their products, for stockholders who may have invested their life savings in the company, and for the society as a whole that is dependent on corporate activity. Managerial decisions affect human well-being and social welfare and have ethical impacts that are significant for those affected by the decisions. Managers are constantly helping to direct people toward or away from human fulfillment by offering persons better working opportunities or assigning them to uselessness, by making products that enhance people's lives or give them serious illnesses, and by contributing to community life or exploiting physical and human resources that devastate the community.

As we expand our knowledge of the world and develop technology to control the world, we have more and more choices to make concerning the kind of world in which we want to live. These choices must be made but are too often based on some kind of ethical notions that are not consciously examined and debated. The future is thus created by default, and is not the result of an explicit dialogue between those who make decisions and those who have to live with the results. The application of technology is most often under the control of managers of business organizations. This is an awesome responsibility, and one that calls for ethical reflection of the highest nature. The decisions managers make create or destroy important values and affect the lives of hundreds and thousands of people, sometimes scattered around the entire planet.

The vision managers have about the kind of world in which they want to live is all-important, and such a vision must be realistic and consistent with human welfare. There is no perfect man or woman and no perfect society that can ever be reached. Reality is dynamic and always changing. Human beings have neither an end nor a nature in the sense of some fixed, invariable, uniform condition in which they reach a static state. The nature of society and humankind is open and is created by the kind of decisions we make in the present. The future is not the result of some deterministic process whether guided by an all-knowing diety or by a mechanistic universe. The future is largely under our control and depends on the vision we have and the will to implement that vision and move toward it in decision and action. While we cannot create a perfect world, we can create a better world than the one we now have by a responsible appropriation of the possibilities for the future that a dynamic past has embedded in the present.

Ultimately, managers have to become their own moral philosophers and apply moral thinking to the decisions that they make and the actions that they take in their daily lives as managers, and this responsibility cannot be avoided. Managers cannot rely on the market or the invisible hand to take care of moral and ethical concerns. The idea that human welfare is best served when each agent or corporation pursues its competitive advantage should be assigned to the scrap heap of human ideas. It has outlived its usefulness. The working of a free and competitive marketplace will not ensure moral behavior on the part of the organizations and managers in the system. Moral responsibility resides in the hands of the managers of business organizations, not in the invisible hand of the free market system.

Nor should the laws and regulations of government be relied upon to promote moral behavior of corporations and management. If managers think of themselves as no more than rational economic actors with only economic responsibilities, then moral direction will be provided by political managers who will be seen as custodians of the public purpose. Corporations are not, however, amoral entities, and an emphasis on government regulation as the key to business ethics underestimates the capacities for moral responsibility in the private sector and overestimates the capacities of government for moral guidance. Neither the market system nor the public policy process can be relied upon to carry the moral freight of society. Managers themselves must make an explicit effort to introduce ethics into their day-to-day decision making.[2] In so doing, they cannot abrogate responsibility by falling back on so-called absolute rules or norms as a substitute for the use of creative intelligence.

This does not mean that the marketplace or government is going to be replaced by managerial discretion. The competitive marketplace is always going to be the major factor in guiding managerial behavior with respect to economizing in the use of resources and directing managerial efforts toward producing something people are willing to buy at prices they can afford. And government will always be a major factor in guiding managerial behavior where substantial matters affecting the public interest are concerned. But management cannot abandon its ethical responsibilities to these two systems and claim that all of its moral concerns are exhausted either by marketplace performance or by adherence to government regulations.

In both of these areas, management has considerable discretion and the ethical dimension of its task has relevance. Managers have considerable discretion in the marketplace, in gaining competitive advantages through marketing and distribution of products and through planning for sources of supply. They are not managing machines that automatically respond to consumer demand in a mechanical fashion. By the same token, managers are not passive when it comes to government regulation. They have become increasingly sophisticated over the last several years in influencing government and having an impact on designing the rules by which they are going to have to live. Through political involvement, managers have been able to influence public policy and have in some cases prevented legislation from being passed that would adversely affect their interests.

Managers might even be able to increase their discretion if they could win the trust of the public and adhere to ethical standards in all their activities. As long as the public does not trust management to take public interests into account, regulation will be continued to be relied upon to promote values of concern to the public. Managers must self-consciously pursue human fulfillment and the social good in all their activities. To restate what was said at the end of the last chapter, economic self-interest must be subsumed under a broader and more comprehensive notion of the common good or social welfare. The pursuit of self-interest is simply not enough.

This broader notion is a possibility if managers take ethics seriously. The institutionalization of business ethics should not be seen as just another control mechanism for management to extend its power over employees or various aspects of society. Business ethics must be seen as a management responsibility. The questions raised in this book must be dealt with in order to develop a philosophy of management that is ethically sound.

Every manager has a philosophy, but most likely it has not been very well articulated. Management and business school students must be encouraged to develop a philosophy that can serve them well throughout the rest of their careers.

The development of such a philosophy that incorporates ethical concerns requires commitment. External justifications can only go so far, and eventually one will reach a level beyond which such attempts no longer make sense. At that point, a choice is involved, a choice as to whether or not to live a moral life. Individual managers must accept responsibility for whatever choice they make and abandon the hope for some higher level of justification. Their own fulfillment as human beings is at stake in the choice they make, because human beings in the final analysis are moral beings, living in a web of moral relationships, institutional and personal, and one's response to these relationships determines the quality of a person's life.

It is hoped that managers will recognize the web of moral relationships in which they and the organizations they direct function. This recognition is the first step toward realizing that a choice is involved, a choice to promote human fulfillment and welfare in the decisions they make, or to pursue some more narrow goal such as the pursuit of profit or market share and ignore the moral implications of the decisions that they make. In this case, these moral dimensions will be pursued by others who will take action to shape managerial and business behavior to match their conceptions of the good life and the life they believe is worth living. To abandon this moral debate to others, however, would seem to be an irresponsible act of management and an abdication of its responsibilities to shareholders, let alone all the other stakeholders who have an interest in corporate activities.

Managers want freedom to make decisions and business organizations want to be free to pursue their own interests. External control mechanisms of whatever kind are always seen as burdensome and an undue interference with management perogatives. Freedom, however, is a moral concept and is granted only to moral agents. Thus, if business wants freedom to conduct its affairs with a minimum of outside interference, it must see itself as a moral agent accountable to the society as to how this freedom is used to the benefit of society. It only makes sense to ascribe moral freedom to corporations under conditions of moral accountability. Only when corporations acknowledge moral responsibility will they be able to carry out their obligations with relative independence from external control mechanisms.[3]

> The point is that corporate moral responsibility, like its analogue in the individual, requires management; management of people and resources, but most importantly what we might call self-management. The modern challenge for the professional manager lies not with the growing number of tasks associated with the growing complexity of the role. Though formidable, the quantitative dimensions of the challenge can be met by more sophisticated approaches to control, production, and organizational structure. The most dramatic challenge lies in the qualitative domain—the domain in which management must exercise judgment and self-understanding. The competitive and strategic rationality that has for so long been the hallmark of managerial competence must be joined to a more "disinterested," community-centered rationality. Gamesmanship must be supplemented with moral leadership.[4]

Such moral leadership means recognizing the corporation as basically an ethical system that affects various kinds of values that are important to human welfare. The challenge to management is to incorporate these other kinds of values into routine decision making and develop methods of analysis that are appropriate to determining trade-offs between objectives. The holistic perspective is captured in the notion of human welfare, and the decisions of management affect human welfare by affecting economic, social, and human values. All of these dimensions are important to consider in making a decision. Economic values must not always be assumed to be dominant, but in most instances must be considered along with other values in determining the best actions to take that will contribute most to human welfare and enrichment.

Freedom, Responsibility, and Education

What educational process is needed to cultivate moral managers able to provide moral leadership in society? The plight of education is well summarized by Warren Bennis in his claim that the educational process "is far removed from the creative and deeply human process required of leadership."[5] It is this type of education that Lisa Newton sees as allowing one to get beyond the level of committed disciple to the level of empowered autonomous agent.[6] Furthermore, participatory leadership requires the education of the society at large, for, as seen in the last chapter, the ongoing dynamics of community that are reflected in participatory leadership require collective intelligence at work. Thus, Philip Selznic views leadership primarily in terms of education because it "involves transforming men and groups from neutral, technical units into participants who have a particular stamp, sensitivity, and commitment."[7] Participatory leadership transforms individuals by heightening the traits that make leaders, and these traits do not lead to disciples but to the enhanced dynamics of community.

Any community incorporating a dynamic participatory process is far from immune to hazardous pitfalls and wrenching clashes. When there is lacking the reorganizing and ordering capabilities of intelligence, the imaginative grasp of authentic possibilities, the vitality of motivation, or sensitivity to the "felt" dimensions of human existence, all of which are needed for ongoing constructive growth, then conflicting demands lead to irreconcilable factionalism. But ideally, these conflicts can be utilized to provide the material for further growth.

What will resolve present problems and provide the means for ongoing growth of the self and the community is human intelligence with its creativity, sensitivity, imagination, and moral awareness geared to the human condition in all of its qualitative richness and the possibilities contained therein for betterment. Utilization of the total concrete human being, in all its dimensions, is necessary for ongoing constructive dynamics. And this in turn requires the education of the entire person. As Gardner has noted, "neither intellect nor talent alone" is enough.[8]

A true community, then, to maintain itself as a community, requires universal education and requires as well an understanding of the educational process as concerned with the education of the whole person. This in turn indicates that education is not fundamentally the transmission of information but rather the development of the skills of experimental inquiry. Education must provide the skills of experimental inquiry needed not just for the adequate exploration of specific subject matter but for the possibility of the interrelated ongoing reconstruction and expansion of the self, values, and the institutions and practices of the community. In this way, education of the entire person leads to growth of self and growth of community, for it develops in the community an openness to engage rather than passively follow the leader.

The proper method of education is in fact the road to freedom. To the extent that we intelligently participate and independently think rather than passively respond we are free, for we, not external factors, determine the nature of our responses. We are free when our activity is guided by the outcome of intelligent reflection, when we do not let ourselves be passively pushed this way and that by external factors bombarding us, but can take what comes to us, reconstruct it through intelligent inquiry, and direct our activity in terms of the unique synthesis of the data brought about by our unique creativity.

In learning to think, we are learning at the same time to be free moral beings. Freedom involves moral responsibility, but moral responsibility, as has been stressed, does not involve the learning and following of rigid sets of rules, regulations, or principles passed down from on high. Rather, it involves the ability to recognize moral problems and to utilize experimental method to reconstruct the moral situation in order to bring about a reintegration of value experiences. To be free moral beings in an authentic sense, however, we must also cultivate a deepening attunement to the "felt" dimensions of experience, to a sense of the vitality of human existence that ultimately roots diverse values, for it is the goal of expanding and developing this dimension that should shape our moral claims.

This requires a sensitivity to the esthetic dimension that pervades human existence, to experiencing what Dewey calls the qualitative character of an experience as a unified whole.[9] In learning to integrate experience through purposive, experimental activity, one at once enhances its esthetic dimension. And the enhancement of the esthetic dimension enhances other dimensions, for the esthetic involves the emotional, and the emotional enters into the unity of attitudes and outlooks.

The sense of history is also crucial. But again, an adequate historical awareness involves not a passive recovery but a creative, imaginative reconstruction of a present oriented toward a future in light of the possibilities provided by the past. The creative play of imagination and intelligence can extend and reintegrate experience in productive ways only if it is not capricious but rather seizes upon real possibilities that a dynamic past has embedded in the changing present. Students thus must learn to live in the present through the appropriation of a living tradition, which they creatively orient in the light of a projected future.

This focus on experimental method does not ignore content, but rather provides a unifying thread for dealing with the vastly varied and huge amounts of content to which one is exposed. Learning to think is not learning to memorize facts or concepts of the great thoughts of the past. Rather, it is learning to resolve problems through the gathering, evaluation, and interpretation of evidence, through understanding relationships between the causes or actions which instigate and the consequences that follow. In this process, theory is not sacrificed for practice, but rather theory embodies practice, and the operation of reason cannot be isolated from the concrete human being in its entirety.

Creativity, in all its varied dimensions, functions within the context of community, and in turn changes and enriches the community within which it functions. The context within which creativity emerges, and which should in turn gain enrichment from such creativity, is ultimately the community at large. In this way, the proper educational process can be a means for guiding social change, and social change can in turn provide an enriched context for the educational process. Ultimately, the educational process cannot be limited to any one context, for the educational process in a broad sense pervades the life of an individual.

The foregoing understanding of the education of the whole person provides education for life in a true community, for it provides the tools for ongoing adjustment between the new and the old, the precarious and the stable, the novel and the continuous, creativity and conformity, self and other. Furthermore, it nourishes the common "end" that must characterize any community, including a highly pluralistic one, for it helps bring to fruition the universalizing ideal of ongoing self-directed growth. These dynamics of community require throughout that one "rise above" the divisiveness of illusory closures by a "delving beneath" to the concreteness of human existence, which roots the very possibility of reconstructive growth of self, community, and values.

The ultimate goal of the educational process is precisely the development of the ability for ongoing self-directed growth. As stressed throughout this book, growth cannot be understood as mere accumulation. In this sense increases in morally detrimental activity or unfounded beliefs could be considered instances of growth. Nor can growth be reduced to material growth. Rather, the process understanding of growth involves reintegration of problematic situations in ways that lead to widening horizons of self, of community, and of the relation between them. In this way growth and, hence, proper education itself have an inherently moral and esthetic quality. Growth can best be understood as an increase in the moral-esthetic richness of experience, an increased infusion of experience with meaningfulness and the expansion of value.

In a commencement address to business school graduates, a highly successful and highly respected business executive and community leader insightfully pointed out that, "It is not the job that gives your life meaning; it is your spirit, your essence that puts meaning into whatever job you have."[10] If the educational process does not nurture the holistic dimensions of this spirit in its full capacity for ongoing growth through the infusion of experience with meaningfulness and the expansion of value, then it has failed miserably in its task.

Education, properly understood, then, is itself moral in nature, for it nurtures the ability to participate in this growth process. And participatory leadership, as both embodying and nurturing the dynamic interaction of the individual and the community that gives rise to ongoing growth, is by its very nature moral in quality. Participatory leadership can be understood as an ongoing educational process geared to promoting the leadership qualities that are inherent, in various degrees, in the very life process of concrete human beings.

The preceding discussion has focused on the liberal education of the whole person, which must underlie any learning of professional skills. How, then, is this to be implemented in professional schools of management and business administration? Separate courses in business ethics are important in order to understand basic issues and frameworks related to ethical concerns. But this is not enough. There is a need for a thorough integration of moral and ethical concerns into the so-called "mainstream" courses such as marketing, accounting, finance, and so forth.[11]

Furthermore, ethics can serve to integrate these various functional fields of management which, as they have developed over the years, have become more and more specialized with their own bodies of knowledge that are not very well integrated with each other. Thus, finance, for example, has developed its own theories and principles, and people who teach and research in the finance area have difficulty in communicating with people in the other areas of management. Each functional area has dug its own tunnel of specialization deeper and deeper, and in the process, become more and more isolated from the other areas.

Supposedly, all of these functional areas have something to do with business as a whole, but the integration of all these specialized areas into a meaningful whole is a problem for students and faculty alike. At one time, most schools of business and management had a capstone policy course that was to serve as an integrating course in providing an opportunity for students to use their specialized functional knowledge to solve case problems. In the last few years, however, policy has been linked more closely with strategic management or strategic planning that has developed its own literature and body of knowledge. Thus, strategy, which has replaced policy in many schools, has become a field in its own right and has further fragmented knowledge in schools of business and management. This leaves no integrating device in the curriculum that can fit all of the functional areas into some holistic framework in which the student's knowledge and experience can be related to a meaningful whole.

It would seem that ethics is well suited to serve this integrating function. If the management task is fundamentally ethical in nature, as has been argued throughout the previous chapters, then ethics can be the glue that holds all the functional areas together. These functional specialties all have to do with the creation of values, values that will hopefully enhance human welfare and lead to the development of a better life for humanity. Most of the functional areas have to do with the creation of economic value and contribute to economizing in the use of resources. Courses in business and society or public policy could be said to deal primarily with the creation of social value, while courses in human and organizational behavior might have as their primary concern the creation of human value.

However, as stressed throughout this book, isolating these different kinds of values from each other is itself artificial and distortive. Thus, business courses that focus primarily on the production of economic value must themselves be infused with a concern for social and human value. Moreover, while some courses may focus primarily on "social value" while others focus on "human value," such a distinction is an abstraction from a dynamically interwoven process such that neither of these can begin to be adequately discussed without incorporating the other. In brief, not only should all courses contain a value orientation of some sort, but no one type of value orientation can become the sole focus of any course.

All of these courses are meant to contribute to the development of individuals who can help to guide the future course of modern complex business organizations. And each individual brings to a position some kind of a philosophy of business, either explicit or implicit, that is in large measure a result of these courses and experience in organizations. One would hope that this philosophy is based on some broader notions about human welfare and contributions to society than are apparent in the notion of self-interest and profit making. Ethics has a primary contribution to make in the development of a vision that recognizes that business is more than just some loose integration of the functional areas and is more than just making money or gaining an ever larger market share—a vision that recognizes that business itself fundamentally concerns the creation of values that enhance human welfare and contribute to the development of civilization. There is no task that can be more important than this, or more challenging and meaningful to those who choose business as a career.

Questions for Discussion

1. Discuss the significance of the holistic approach to education in general, and for understanding the field of business in particular.
2. Are the ethical resposibilities of management exhausted by marketplace performance and adherence to government regulations? Why or why not? What discretion does management have in this regard?
3. Discuss the role of a value orientation as the tool for offering a unified vision of the nature and function of business.
4. If you disagree with the holistic approach to education in general and/or the holistic approach to understanding business and/or value orientation as the key for a holistic approach, explain why and indicate what you consider to be a better alternative.

Endnotes

[1] Oliver F. Williams and John W. Houck, eds., *The Judeo-Christian Vision and the Modern Corporation* (Notre Dame, IN: University of Notre Dame Press, 1982), pp. 2–3.

[2] Kenneth E. Goodpaster, "The Concept of Corporate Responsibility," *Just Business: New Introductory Essays in Business Ethics,* Tom Regan, ed. (New York: Random House, 1984), p. 316.

[3] Patricia H. Werhane, *Persons, Rights, & Corporations* (Englewood Cliffs, NJ: Prentice-Hall, 1985), p. 76.

[4] Goodpaster, "The Concept of Corporate Responsibility," p. 319.

[5] Warren Bennis, *Why Leaders Can't Lead* (San Francisco: Jossey-Bass Publishers, 1990), pp. 219–220.

[6] Lisa Newton, "Moral Leadership in Business: The Role of Structure," *Business and Professional Ethics Journal,* Vol. 5, pp. 77–78.

[7] Philip Selznic, *Leadership in Administration: A Sociological Interpretation* (New York: Harper & Row, 1957), p. 17.

[8] John Gardner, *Excellence: Can We Be Equal and Excellent Too?* (New York: Harper & Row, 1961), p. 120.

[9] John Dewey, "Affective Thought," Vol. 2, *The Later Works,* Jo Ann Boydston, ed. (Carbondale and Edwardsville, IL: University of Southern Illinois Press, 1984), pp. 106–107.

[10] Sidney W. Lassen, "Commencement Address," Tulane University, 1991.

[11] See Thomas W. Dunfee, et al., *Ethics and the MBA Curriculum: A Proposal for Integration of Ethics into the MBA Core Curriculum* (Philadelphia: The Wharton School, 1986).

Suggested Readings

Altvater, Elmar A. *The Future of the Market.* New York: Verso, 1993.

Bluestone, Barry, and Irving Bluestone. *Negotiating the Future: A Labor Perpsective on American Business.* New York: Basic Books, 1992.

Chamberlain, Neil W. *Social Strategy and Corporate Structure.* New York: Macmillan, 1982.

Daniels, John L., and N. Caroline Daniels. *Global Vision: Building New Models for the Corporation of the Future.* New York: McGraw-Hill, 1993.

Globerson, Arye, and Edgar Krau. *Organizations and Management: Toward the Future.* Brookfield, VT: Avebury, 1993.

Hamel, Gary A., and C. K. Prahalad. *Competing for the Future.* Cambridge, MA: Harvard Business School Press, 1994.

Henderson, Hazel. *Paradigms in Progress: Life Beyond Economics.* Indianapolis, IN: Knowledge Systems, Inc., 1991.

Lipset, Seymour Martin, and William Schneider. *The Confidence Gap: Business, Labor, and Government in the Public Mind.* New York: The Free Press, 1983.

Management in the XXI Century. Washington, DC: AACSB/EFMD, 1979.

National Legislative Conference on Small Business Issues. *Focus on the Future: Small Business in the 1990s.* Washington, DC: U.S. Small Business Administration, 1989.

Theobald, Robert. *Turning the Century.* Indianapolis, IN: Knowledge Systems, Inc., 1992.

SHORT CASES

Hucksters in the Classroom

Increased student loads, myriad professional obligations, and shrinking school budgets have sent many public school teachers scurrying for teaching materials to facilitate their teaching.

They don't have to look far. Into the breach has stepped business, which is ready, willing, and able to provide current print and audiovisual materials for classroom use. These industry-supplied teaching aids are advertised in educational journals, distributed to school boards, and showcased at educational conventions. The Dr Pepper Company, for example, displays at such conventions a recipe booklet titled *Cooking with Dr Pepper.* Each recipe includes sugar-filled Dr Pepper soda. Students can also learn about nutrition with worksheets provided by Chef Boyardee or about how to keep food fresh with information from Reynolds Wrap.[1]

One collective tack taken by the business community has been the ABC Education Program of American Industry, whose annual publication, *Resourcebook,* consists of product-specific "sponsored pages" or ads with accompanying teacher guide sheets. Food and toiletry products are featured, as in the following:

A is for AGREE: the Cream Rinse and Conditioner that helps the greasies.
C is for COCONUT: a tantalizing tropical treat from Peter Paul candies.
E is for EFFECTIVE double deodorant system in Irish Spring (soap).[2]

An integral part of the ABC program is an annual essay-writing contest. Essays must deal with some aspect of a product in *Resourcebook*—its production and marketing, the history or importance of an industry to a community or nation, and so on. To be eligible, entries must be signed by a teacher and include a product label or reasonable facsimile. Student writers can earn up to $50 for entering.

The people at ABC say they want to reflect the positive aspects of the world outside the classroom. And they're convinced that the way to do it is through depicting the wonders and genius of industry. "Thus," says researcher Sheila Harty, "history is taught in terms of 'innovative industrial genius,' as students write their essays on the value of soft drinks (C is for Canada Dry) or the production of tires (G is for Goodyear)."[3]

Some people think corporate-sponsored teaching materials do more than fill curriculum needs. They are also public relations gambits. Thus, in his book *Corporate Response to Urban Crisis,* professor of sociology Ken Neubeck writes:

> Corporations must continually respond to problems which they had a hand in creating in the first place. From this perspective, corporate social responsibility becomes a defensive strategy to be employed whenever the social and political climate become hostile to the active pursuit of corporate economic goals. It is a strategy of "enlightened self-interest."[4]

There is nothing defensive, however, about the strategy of Lifetime Learning Systems, a marketing firm that specializes in pitching to students the products of its corporate customers. "[Students] are ready to spend and we reach them," the company brags, touting its "custom-made learning materials created with your [company's] specific marketing objectives in mind." Many corporations now see education marketing as a cost-effective way to build brand loyalty.[5]

Both Gillette and Schick provide in-school programs to introduce young people to their razors, while other companies sponsor school contests that offer prizes for buying their products. For example, in exchange for 5,125 soup labels, Campbell Soup Company furnishes schools with a filmstrip, the "Boyhood of Abraham Lincoln." Orville Redenbacher Popcorn offers schools ten cents for every label they collect, and Hershey's a nickel for every wrapper. General Mills supplies educational pamphlets on the planet's "great geothermic 'gushers,' " along with General Mills's "Gushers" snack (a candy filled with liquid). The pamphlet recommends that teachers pass the "Gushers" around and then ask the students, as they bite the candy, "How does this process differ from that which produces erupting geothermic phenomena?"[6]

Corporate America's most dramatic venture in the classroom, however, began in 1990 when Whittle Communications started beaming into classrooms around the country its controversial Channel One, a television newscast for high school students. The broadcasts are twelve minutes long—ten minutes of news digest with slick graphics and two minutes of commercials for Levi jeans, Gillette razor blades, Head & Shoulders shampoo, Snickers candy bars, and other familiar products. Although a handful of states have banned Channel One, more than 10,000 schools now receive it.

Whittle provides cash-hungry schools that agree to broadcast Channel One with thousands of dollars worth of electronic gadgetry, including television monitors, satellite dishes, and video recorders. In return, the schools are contractually obliged to broadcast the program in its entirety to all students at a single time on 90 to 95 percent of the days that school is in session. The show cannot be interrupted, and teachers do not have the right to turn it off.[7]

For their part, students seem to like Channel One's fast-paced MTV-like newscasts. "It was very interesting and it appeals to our age group," says student Angelique Williams. "One thing I really like was the reporters were our own age. They kept our attention." But educators wonder how much students really learn. A University of Michigan study found that students who watched Channel One scored only 3.3 percent better on a 30-question test of current events than did students in schools without Channel One. Although researchers called this gain so small as to be educationally unimportant, they noted that all the Channel One students remembered the commercials. That, of course, is good news for Whittle, which charges advertisers $157,000 for a 30-second spot. That price sounds high, but companies are willing to pay it because Whittle delivers a captive, narrowly targeted audience.

That captive audience is just what worries the critics. Peggy Charren of Action for Children's Television calls the project a "great big, gorgeous Trojan horse. . . . You're selling the children to the advertisers. You might as well auction off the rest of the school day to the highest bidders." On the other hand, Principal Rex Stooksbury of Central High School in Knoxville, which receives Channel One, takes a different view. "This is something we see as very, very positive for the school," he says. And as student Danny Diaz adds, "we're always watching commercials" anyway.

1. What explains industry's thrust into education? Is it consistent with the basic features of a free market economy? What moral issues, if any, are involved in the affiliation between education and commercial interests?

2. Do you think students have a moral right to an education free of commercial indoctrination? Should companies be prevented from engaging in these kinds of activities?

3. If you were a member of a school board contemplating the use of either industry-sponsored material or Channel One, what would you recommend?

4. Do you think industry in general and Channel One in particular are intentionally using teachers and students as a means to profit? Or do they have a genuine concern for the educational process? On the other hand, if teachers and students benefit from using these materials, is there any ground for concern?

[1] Sheila Harty, *Hucksters in the Classroom* (Washington, DC: Center for the Study of Responsive Law, 1979); Alex Molnar, "Learning to Ad," *New Republic,* March 22, 1993.

[2] Harty, *Hucksters in the Classroom,* p. 5.

[3] Ibid., p. 11.

[4] Ken Neubeck, *Corporate Response to Urban Crisis* (New York: D.C. Heath, 1974), p. 117, quoted in Harty, *Hucksters in the Classroom,* pp. 11–12.

[5] Molnar, "Learning to Ad," p. 15.

[6] Ibid., p. 16.

[7] See Susan Chira, "Little Help from a School TV Show," *The New York Times,* April 23, 1992, p. A8; Henry Giroux, "School for Scandal," *Transition,* 59 (1993), pp. 92–94; Jonathan Kozol, "Kids as Commodities: The Folly of For-Profit Schools," *Business and Society Review,* 84 (Winter 1993), p. 16; "Mixed Reviews on Classroom Commercials," *San Francisco Chronicle,* March 8, 1989, p. A1, is the source of the quotations in the following paragraph.

Source: William H. Shaw and Vincent Barry, *Moral Issues in Business,* 6th ed. (Belmont, CA: Wadsworth Publishing Company, 1995), pp. 170–172.

General Sherman Goes After Higher Education

Twelve of the Northeast's most prestigious colleges and universities received civil investigative demands (CIDs) from the Antitrust Division of the Justice Department in late summer of 1989. These CIDs are rather like a subpoena from a grand jury to recipients as they are written requests intended to gather information. Receiving a CID can be a frightening experience, as it was for these colleges and universities. The CIDs focused on price fixing that is prohibited by Section 1 of the Sherman Antitrust Act, legislation that in the past had nearly always been applied to for-profit businesses.[1]

The Justice Department's purpose in sending out the CIDs was to gather budgeting and other financial information related to a practice of two dozen or more schools that had been going on for decades. Officers from these schools met each year to agree on the amounts of financial aid they would offer star-quality students. At this meeting, the schools arrange for their aid packages to be nearly identical. In 1989, some 10,000 students were said to have been affected by this practice. Many of the schools freely admitted that they got together to fix aid awards to avoid bidding wars, and defended the practice by suggesting that the conferences were held for the good of education since the agreements helped the schools to keep their costs down.[2]

Defenders of the inquiry argued that fixing aid was an anticompetitive practice, that in a competitive environment student aid would vary, thus making the amount a student ends up paying vary proportionately. Students receiving aid would pay less were the schools to compete on granting aid packages. The schools are no different from other institutions if they conspire to agree on what they are going to charge. Critics contended that the inquiry is novel and not an appropriate area for the antitrust law to be applied. They pointed out that the money was not going to line the college president's pocket. What the schools were talking about was a subsidy rather than a price, and thus questioned whether antitrust should cover how much money to give away.[3]

There are three possible outcomes to the inquiry: (1) Since one out of every five investigations ever goes anywhere after inquiries are completed, the government could simply walk away and do nothing; (2) the schools would be required to abide by some sort of injunction; and (3) the government would accept the promises of the schools to forgo price fixing. The schools could also possibly be hit by a series of class-action suits by former students who could claim they had been hurt by the financial aid agreements and deserve damages.[4]

Such a suit was, in fact, filed by a Wesleyan University student who filed suit against his school and the 11 other private colleges seeking damages on behalf of thousands of other students. The defendants were said to have "engaged in a conspiracy to fix or artificially inflate the price of tuition and financial aid." The suit sought treble damages on behalf of a class of all students who were allegedly harmed by the scheme. The Justice Department, meanwhile, widened its investigation to about 20 schools and was seeking information about not only financial aid, but the way in which the schools set tuition and salaries as well.[5]

1. Were the schools involved in this incident in violation of antitrust laws? Why or why not? Who benefited and who was hurt by their so-called anticompetitive practices? Should the antitrust laws apply to not-for-profit organizations such as universities?

2. What are the ethical issues in this incident? Whose rights, if any, were being violated by the universities? Was what they were doing in any way a conspiracy against society? Were they conspiring against any particular group of people?

[1] Christopher Elias, "Northeastern Fix on Financial Aid," *Insight,* September 18, 1989, p. 48.

[2] Ibid., pp. 48–49.

[3] Ibid., p. 48.

[4] Ibid., p. 49.

[5] Gary Putka, "Twelve Colleges Named in Lawsuit on Price-Fixing," *The Wall Street Journal,* September 18, 1989, p. C-17.

Source: Rogene A. Buchholz, *Public Policy Issues for Management,* 2nd ed. (Englewood Cliffs, NJ: Prentice Hall, 1992), pp. 77–78.

Economic Education

The Public Affairs Office of Drexler Corporation had a new idea that it was very excited about. Based on recent surveys that again indicated the general public was relatively ignorant about economic matters, the Public Affairs Office thought that the company should develop some kind of economic education program that would be available to high schools and colleges. It was well aware that such programs developed by other corporations were accused of being nothing more than attempts to indoctrinate students into the virtues of a free enterprise system and had little or nothing to do with education.

Thus, the Public Affairs Office wanted to develop a balanced program. It consciously tried to tone down the free enterprise rhetoric in the materials it was developing, and give a hearing to critics of the system. A debate was taped, for example, between Michael Novak of the American Enterprise Institute and Michael Harrington who had socialistic leanings. The group tried to focus on economic principles rather than on institutional systems, and it employed some of the best intellectual talent in the country to help develop the materials.

The Public Affairs Office envisioned a series of videotapes and books that would be made available to educational institutions either free of charge or for a very nominal sum of money. While the Public Affairs people were very excited about this project, they wondered if it would sell with top management. They knew top management was 100 percent behind the free enterprise system, and wondered if management would buy the balanced approach they were taking. Thus, they were marshalling their arguments in favor of the approach in preparation for a meeting with top management tomorrow morning.

1. What arguments would you use to defend this balanced approach? In what ways would it be superior to a heavy emphasis on the virtues of the free enterprise system? What argu-

ments are they likely to encounter against the use of a balanced approach? Which approach would be more ethically responsible?

2. Even if the Public Affairs Office is successful in getting approval for this program, is this effort a legitimate exercise for private corporations to be undertaking? Is there economic illiteracy in this country and are corporations the proper ones to do something about this problem? Is an effort of this sort, even if extremely well done, likely to be effective?

Source: Rogene A. Buchholz, *Business Environment and Public Policy: Implications for Management,* 5th ed. (Englewood Cliffs, NJ: Prentice Hall, 1995), p. 640.

The Social Audit

Monolith, a large conglomerate, has recently come under fire from a variety of federal agencies and/or offices because of alleged problems in some of its operations. The Occupational Safety and Health Administration has charged it with certain violations in its steel plants, the Office of Federal Contract Compliance Programs is threatening to cancel some of the government contracts the company enjoys because of its failure to meet affirmative action guidelines, and the Federal Trade Commission is taking a close look at certain aspects of the corporation's advertising strategies. A management consultant called in to study the situation has advised that the company would not be in this predicament if it had periodically conducted a social audit. The consultant recommends that such an audit be taken systematically in the future.

The company is thus considering doing something along these lines, but it is finding that there is no agreement on what a social audit should look like. It has run across various proposals as to what kinds of things should appear on a social audit and what measures are appropriate. There is also the question as to whether such an audit should be used for internal management purposes only or disclosed to the outside public. Nonetheless, the company is committed to developing some kind of means to determine how well it is doing in areas that cannot be measured by the traditional financial statements. It has formed a team to deal with this problem and make proposals to top management as to what exactly ought to be done in this regard.

1. What types of regulations may the conglomerate have violated based on the agencies mentioned in the case? Be as specific as possible. Would an audit of the areas covered by these regulations help the company with its compliance efforts?

2. What do you think of the suggestion to conduct a social audit? As far as the issues raised in this case are concerned, what type of social audit might be most useful to alleviate some of the problems the company is currently facing?

Beech-Nut Corporation

The Beech-Nut Nutrition Corporation, the second largest baby food company in the United States, is a subsidiary of the Swiss food company Nestlé, which bought it in 1979 for $35 million. Beech-Nut was originally founded in 1891 and was incorporated in the state of Pennsylvania as a meat-packing company. The company eventually expanded into other food products and eventually came to focus on baby food and dietetic specialty products. At one time its product line included such diverse products as Life Savers, Table Talk pies, Tetley Tea, Martinson's coffee, chewing gum, and baby food. Over the years, Beech-Nut built a reputation for purity, high-quality products, and natural ingredients.[1]

The Squibb Corporation took over Beech-Nut in 1969, but only four years later, a remnant of the old company was spun off and sold for $16 million to a private group led by Pennsylvania lawyer and entrepreneur Frank C. Nicholas. The company that emerged from the Squibb umbrella concentrated solely on baby food, and while Beech-Nut was still a reliable brand name, its baby food products rarely turned a profit.[2] Baby food was a completely new venture for Beech-Nut's new owners, and to make matters worse, the company was in continuous financial trouble.[3]

During the time he presided over the company, Nicholas promoted the "naturalness and nutrition" of Beech-Nut products.[4] Although Nicholas was a charismatic leader with many good ideas, the company's poor financial position limited its growth and its ability to match the marketing outlays of its competition. The Nicholas group had acquired Beech-Nut almost entirely with borrowed money and ran the company on a shoestring. Its market share in 1977 was only 15 percent compared with a 70 percent share attained by the Gerber Company, its major competitor. By 1978, Beech-Nut, burdened with losses, owed millions to suppliers and was under great financial pressure.[5]

THE PRODUCT

The combination of babies, apple juice, and a well-known name like Beech-Nut made for a potent symbol that could be exploited. For over 50 years, consumers relied on the image that Beech-Nut had created. They had confidence in Beech-Nut's reputation for using high-quality, natural ingredients with no artificial flavorings, no preservatives, and no colorings. Parents were pleased to buy a product that claimed to be 100 percent fruit juice with no sugar added.[6] The fact is that apple juice is not especially nutritious and bottlers often fortify it with extra vitamins, but babies came to love it and found it easily digestible. Parents came to regard apple juice as almost as pure and natural as breast-feeding.[7]

THE PROBLEM

To cope with the threat of insolvency, in 1977 Beech-Nut executives switched to another supplier of the apple juice concentrate. The new supplier, Universal Juice Company and its affiliate Interjuice, offered the concentrate at a price that was 20 percent below the market. The concentrate was actually manufactured by Food Complex Company at a Queens, New York, facility. Since rumors of apple juice adulteration had already spread in the industry, the purchase of concentrate at such a low price raised suspicions among employees in Beech-Nut's research and development department. One Gerber executive later said, "When it comes in at that price, you shouldn't have to test it. You know it's fake."[8]

The uneasy feelings Beech-Nut chemists had were well founded. In 1977, tests by a company-hired laboratory suggested that the cheap apple concentrate Beech-Nut bought from Universal Juice Company might be adulterated. While at the time there was no official adulteration test, there were several procedures that could provide strong evidence of fake ingredients. Later it was discovered that chemists at Food Complex Company, which actually manufactured the concentrate, had learned how to replicate precisely apple juice's numerous components with less expensive substitutes.[9]

Commercially produced apple juice is easily faked because it is manufactured in a bottling facility. The recipes used are designed for mass appeal and low expense. When apple juice finally reaches the consumer, it has been screened, filtered, blended with apples from other orchards, and may even have been dosed with ascorbic acid to help maintain its clarity. Since there was no officially sanctioned test for adulteration at the time Beech-Nut began doing business with Interjuice, a company that was accused of selling an adulterated product could simply claim ignorance.[10]

Because Beech-Nut products containing apple concentrate accounted for 30 percent of its sales, use of the cheap substitute helped the company to keep its head above water.[11] Beech-Nut sold about $60 million worth of the product between 1977 and 1982, while reducing material costs about $250,000 annually. While this savings seems small when compared with a $50 million plus manufacturing budget, the company was under intense financial pressures and even a small savings helped to keep it alive.[12] In 1979, Nestlé bought Beech-Nut and tried to boost sales by investing an additional $60 million. It also increased the marketing budget, but costs were still too high and losses persisted.[13]

Jerome J. LiCari, director of research and development at Beech-Nut's main plant in Canajoharie, New York, suggested to Operations Chief John F. Lavery that they discontinue their association with Interjuice. LiCari noticed how quickly Interjuice could respond to Beech-Nut's suggestions and complaints regarding qualities of the products such as acidity and clarity. He knew that it was not that easy to remedy such problems with natural products. Lavery, worried about the possibility of Beech-Nut's insolvency, disregarded LiCari's suggestion. However, Lavery did ask the supplier to sign a "hold harmless agreement" that would compensate Beech-Nut for any damages that might arise if the concentrate should prove to be adulterated.[14]

LiCari then mounted a major drive to improve adulteration testing. Based on new evidence, he suggested that the apple juice concentrate Beech-Nut was buying to make its juice and other products was a blend of beet sugar, cane syrup, and synthetic ingredients. LiCari made a written report to Niels Hoyvald, then president of Beech-Nut, and Lavery that the concentrate was bogus and suggested getting another concentrate supplier. He believed that continuing to deal with Universal could jeopardize the company's planned product line restructuring that would emphasize nutritional values and the absence of artificial ingredients in its products.[15]

Despite LiCari's efforts, Hoyvald and Lavery took no actions on this matter; they neither confronted Universal Juice Company nor inspected Universal's concentrate source. They called LiCari "Chicken Little," told him he wasn't a team player, and even threatened to fire him. Several months later at a budget meeting with Hoyvald, Lavery did suggest getting a new apple concentrate supplier to avoid the risk that Universal's concentrate was indeed bogus. Hoyvald again refused, arguing that switching to a new supplier would add more costs to an already unaffordable budget. Hoyvald later testified that he had promised Nestlé that Beech-Nut should be profitable in 1982, and using cheap concentrate would save millions of dollars.[16] The company continued to produce and distribute adulterated apple juice under the label "100% fruit juice" for nearly five years before outside investigators first suspected foul play. Licari later resigned when he became convinced that the company was knowingly breaking the law. He became a key prosecuting witness in the investigation and indictment of Beech-Nut and its two executives.[17]

INVESTIGATIONS

An industry trade group called The Processed Apples Institute was aware of long-standing allegations of adulteration of apple juice concentrate. In April 1982, they hired a private investigator to check into rumors about Universal's concentrate. By searching through garbage dumpsters and following delivery trucks, the investigator learned that the concentrate was indeed bogus, and that Beech-Nut was its largest customer.[18] Later it was learned that Universal's Queens plant was only part of a large bogus operation that extended from coast to coast and included wholesalers, brokers, shippers, and ingredient manufacturers. At its peak, the operation was said to have grossed tens of millions of dollars annually.[19]

Beech-Nut was informed about these findings and was asked to join other juice makers in a lawsuit against the Universal operation. Beech-Nut's response to this disclosure was a gross blunder. Had it been honest and cooperative at this point, it could have paid a small fine and gotten out of the situation basically unscathed. Had the company recalled its inventory immediately, it would have shown a good faith effort and been able to portray itself as the innocent victim of unscrupulous suppliers. It would have had to admit only to a civil violation of the Food, Drug and Cosmetic Act, and paid a small fee and minor punitive damages.[20]

Instead it chose to stonewall and refused to cooperate with the investigation or join the lawsuit. Although Beech-Nut did cancel its apple concentrate contracts, it continued to distribute millions of bottles of "fake" apple juice at deep discounts, both in the United States and in other parts of the world. Despite warnings from the Food and Drug Administration and the New York State Agriculture Department, Beech-Nut continued to unload its $3.5 million of inventory of adulterated apple juice, and did not issue a national apple juice recall until late October 1982. This behavior led prosecutors to believe that the company's main concern was making money even if it meant selling a phony product, and that Beech-Nut was not the victim of a crime, but its conscious perpetrator.[21]

Beech-Nut's strategy apparently became one of avoiding publicity and stalling federal and state investigations in order to continue to sell its inventory. The company began special promotions to get rid of the adulterated juice quickly. When the FDA identified specific lots of apple juice as adulterated, Beech-Nut destroyed the lots before the FDA could seize the juice in an apparent attempt to avoid bad publicity.[22] Initially, the FDA had taken no action because the adulterated juice posed no health risk. The agency's first priority was health and safety, not economic fraud. But by 1982, when the fraud amounted to millions of dollars, it was too much for even the FDA to ignore.[23]

The FDA tested four samples of apple juice from the company's warehouse and found the samples contained little or no apple juice. When confronted with these results, Beech-Nut executives lied, saying the company had no knowledge of a reliable method to test the authenticity of its product. At that time, the FDA did not have access to the company's records, and had no way of knowing that Beech-Nut's own chemists had been raising questions about the authenticity of its product for several years. When the agency asked to review the company's juice-testing records, batch production records, and complaint files, Beech-Nut refused access. Thus, the FDA had no knowledge about the quantity of adulterated juice or where it was located.[24]

When Beech-Nut refused to turn over its shipping records, the FDA decided to contact the company's trucking company for shipping information. When Beech-Nut learned of this action, the company backed down and offered to provide the agency with a list of ten locations where adulterated juice could be found. According to later testimony, however, the FDA was misled, as the company put together a list that included companies that would have little or no apple juice left in their warehouses. Beech-Nut's director of distribution later testified that Beech-Nut was trying to delay the FDA's finding of the adulterated product.[25]

On one occasion, the company became alarmed when it believed state officials were about to seize its entire inventory and sent nine trucks to move the entire inventory out of New York to a warehouse in Secaucus, New Jersey. One report described this action as fleeing the law just like a bootlegger. Many cases of this adulterated apple juice were shipped to Puerto Rico, a major Beech-Nut market; the Dominican Republic; and the Virgin Islands. Here the products were sold to innocent consumers at a 50 percent discount in what was called a foreign promotion. American law does not prohibit the selling abroad of products that are banned at home.[26]

In addition to adulterated apple juice, Beech-Nut also had in its inventory a supply of mixed-juice products made with the phony concentrate. Adulteration in this product was said to be difficult or impossible to detect, so the company continued to sell mixed juices made from the bogus concentrate until March 1983—months after its recall of apple juice and after filing its own lawsuit against Universal alleging that the supplier's concentrate was phony.[27] All of these actions allowed the company to get rid of most of its adulterated products. Had Beech-Nut initiated the recall of apple juice in June instead of October, 700,000 cases in inventory might have been affected. Due to the many delays and evasive actions, the company had to destroy only about 20,000 cases of the bogus product.[28]

Beech-Nut executives thought they had gotten away with the fraud and had outsmarted the government. Several months after the recall, LiCari attended a cocktail party at a gathering of the National Food Processors Association, where he overheard the boasting of Beech-Nut executives. When he arrived home, he immediately fired off a letter to the FDA providing details about the fraud that had been going on at the company for several years. At this time, some agency officials were already preparing to recommend that the Justice Department bring criminal charges against Beech-Nut and several of its top executives. The agency had some reason to believe that the company had violated provisions of the Food and Drug Act, but it had no knowledge of the real extent of the conspiracy and cover-up within the company. LiCari's letter suggested that Beech-Nut had knowingly and intentionally broken the law and was more guilty than initially assumed.[29]

CONVICTIONS

While Beech-Nut was initially assumed to be a victim of fraud, it now became clear that Beech-Nut was itself a perpetuator of fraud. The case changed from civil to criminal and became a nightmare for the company and its executives.[30] In June 1985, the Justice Department opened a criminal investigation into the case, using investigative powers that are denied federal agencies (see box). Beech-Nut pleaded guilty to federal charges brought by the FDA on November 13, 1987, that it had intentionally sold adulterated and misbranded juice in 20 states, Puerto Rico, the Virgin Islands, and five foreign countries. The company paid a fine of $2 million, which at that point was the largest fine in FDA history.[31]

Further federal and state investigations disclosed more details of the cover-up, as well as the fact that the company had continued to sell the bogus concentrate in its mixed juices for six months after the recall. New York State fined Beech-Nut $250,000 for selling an adulterated and misbranded product—the largest fine ever imposed by the state for a consumer violation. Indictments were brought against Zeev Kaplansky, former president of Universal, and Raymond Wells of the Food Complex, who had earlier agreed to discontinue production of the fake concentrate in response to the Apple Institute suit.[32]

The FDA then referred the case to the Justice Department for criminal prosecution. Beech-Nut eventually pleaded guilty to 215 felony counts and agreed to pay fines, legal fees, and class-action settlements that were estimated to total $25 million. On February 17, 1988, a jury convicted Hoyvald on 359 counts of violating the Food, Drug, and Cosmetic Act, and Lavery was convicted on 448 counts, which included conspiracy and mail-fraud charges. Each was sentenced to one year and a day in jail and assessed a $100,000 fine.[33] After the sentences, both men were out of jail on appeal on a jurisdictional technicality.

The Nestlé Company defended its subsidiary's acts by spending several millions of dollars in defending the two executives. Hoyvald and Lavery were kept on the payroll at annual salaries of $120,000 and $70,000, respectively, until their appeals were exhausted. When LiCari testified that in 1980 and 1981, he had expressed his concerns to six different Nestlé officials, they had all six officials appear in court to either contradict LiCari's account or state that they had no memory of the alleged conversation. Most of these people were flown in from the company's headquarters in Switzerland to testify. One of these officials was Richard Theuer, who was then a vice president of Nestlé and, in 1986, became the president of Beech-Nut. Theuer hoped to convince the public that the new company would always make decisions on behalf of babies.[34]

Though Beech-Nut and its top executives were eventually fined and sentenced for violating U.S. food and drug laws, it was not before consumers were defrauded of as much as $60 million—the price they paid for sugared water labeled as Beech-Nut apple juice. The U.S. Food and Drug Administration is the agency that is supposed to mind the store for the public. Unfortunately, it doesn't have the key.

As the Beech-Nut saga demonstrates, unscrupulous manufacturers can stay one step ahead of the FDA because the FDA lacks the power necessary to regulate effectively. "Beech-Nut played a cat-and-mouse game with us," said an FDA official in Buffalo. "They thwarted us at every level."

Last year, when Rep. John Dingell, chairman of the House Subcommittee on Oversight and Investigations, asked the FDA to explain why the agency failed to enforce the Food, Drug, and Cosmetic Act effectively in the Beech-Nut case, Hugh Cannon, associate commissioner for legislative affairs at the FDA, responded as follows: "FDA is severely hampered in conducting investigations. . . . The [Federal Food, Drug, and Cosmetic] Act does not provide FDA the authority to subpoena records, compel interviews of employees, or subpoena individuals when the Agency is conducting investigations. The absence of such authority explains why much of the evidence that was disclosed during the trial was not uncovered by FDA's 1982 investigation of Beech-Nut."

The FDA is the only federal regulatory agency that does not have subpoena power. In the 1970s, the FDA repeatedly asked Congress to expand the agency's authority; each time Congress failed to act. In 1981, the FDA again made its appeal, but this time the recommendation was aborted within the administration. "The political climate of the last eight years has been to deregulate, so it's no surprise that it's been a dead issue," said an insider on the Oversight and Investigations Committee.

In order to grant the FDA subpoena power, Congress will have to disregard the wishes of the powerful food, drug, and cosmetic lobbies. We think the Beech-Nut case ought to be the scandal that forces Congress to rethink the FDA's regulatory authority.

Source: "Bad Apples: In the Executive Suite," *Consumer Reports,* May 1989, p. 296.

IMPACTS

The news of the "ersatz apple juice" shocked thousands of parents and created a slump in sales, as the company's share of the $760 million baby food market dropped from a high of 20 percent in 1986 to 17 percent two years later. Its losses in the fruit juice market were even more dramatic.[35] Even though the fake juice was never proven to be dangerous to human health, the mislabeled product was regarded by the FDA as thwarting consumers' intelligent choices and comparison shopping, especially for parents whose babies were on a special diet. By ignoring the well-being of its consumers, Beech-Nut created negative publicity for itself, and its reputation was destroyed—a reputation that would take years to rebuild.[36]

Beech-Nut had several opportunities to get out of the scandal it created. It could have simply labeled the product "apple-flavored drink" instead of selling it under false pretenses. It could have switched suppliers at any time. Finally, it could have cooperated with investigators from the Processed Apples Institute and the FDA. If the company had responded to early warnings of in-house investigators and external regulators and recalled its inventory, it would have shown a good faith effort and would have been able to portray itself as an innocent victim of unethical suppliers. The company would have had to admit only to a civil violation of the Food, Drug, and Cosmetic Act, and paid a small fine and minor punitive damages.

Beech-Nut officials did not respond to any of these opportunities because they believed that they were acting in the best interests of the company and were concerned about its financial health. Apparently, these officials justified their actions on the basis of two premises. First, they assumed that other companies were also participating in such activities, and that they had to do the same in order to compete effectively. Second, they believed that even if the juice was adulterated, no one was being harmed, since the juice was still safe to consume. Both these premises were unfounded.[37]

The Beech-Nut apple juice incident, according to *The New York Times,* is a "case study in the warping effects of blind corporate loyalty."[38] It is particularly disturbing because babies were the consumers of the tainted product. Parents expect only the highest standards of safety when it comes to products that can affect the health of their babies.[39] Thousands of parents were shocked by news of this scandal and switched to other products.[40]

Even the most reputable of companies, through poor judgment, can suffer an ethical breakdown.[41] The financial and competitive pressures that led to Beech-Nut's action exist in many companies. The weakness of the FDA's authority is conducive to such scandals. As a result, consumers cannot be as confident in the quality of their food as they should be under normal circumstances.[42] They must rely on both business and government to learn from this scandal. "Cover-ups usually don't cover a misdeed. They compound it."[43]

Beech-Nut is trying to emerge from the scandal that sent it into a sales slump and brought it such negative publicity. In 1989, the company began a $15 million advertising campaign with Joan Lunden as a sponsor. The co-host of *Good Morning America* was introduced as a Beech-Nut mother, and was scheduled to appear in print ads and two 30-second network and spot commercials to promote Beech-Nut's new baby food line. The company's campaign stressed quality, and was designed to appeal to women who have children toward the end of their childbearing years.[44]

The name of the new product is Stages and it will compete with Gerber's First Foods line. This new baby food comes in different textures according to children's stages of growth. The campaign will have to be a strong one to overcome setbacks from the apple juice scandal, but Beech-Nut is hoping for a second baby boom.[45] By pleading guilty to its actions, the company hopes it has put the past behind it and can get on with the present. It has begun to use new testing procedures to avoid a repetition of the past. Richard Theuer, the new president of Beech-Nut, stresses that feeding babies is a sacred trust.[46] Hopefully, he can carry through on this philosophy.

1. What financial pressures was the company under when the incident first occurred? Were these pressures the cause of the company's ethical transgressions? Or where they simply part of the context in which the incident took place? How could the situation be analyzed to understand why this incident happened?

2. Was Jerome LiCari a loyal employee? Could he be characterized as a whistle-blower? Were his actions ethically justified? What else could he have done? What role did he eventually play in the ongoing investigation?

3. What was the eventual outcome of the incident? Does a cover-up of the kind perpetuated by Beech-Nut ever work? Why or why not? What is there to be learned from the incident? What are the ethical issues in the case that need to be highlighted?

4. What does it take to make an ethical organization? What role does top management play in creating a climate or culture in which ethical behavior is discouraged or encouraged? What could Beech-Nut do in the future to prevent such a scandal from happening again? How can it win back the public's confidence? What role could an ethics code play?

[1] James Traub, "Into the Mouths of Babes," *New York Times Magazine,* July 24, 1988, p. 19.

[2] Chris Welles, "What Led Beech-Nut Down the Road to Disgrace," *Business Week,* February 22, 1988, p. 125.

[3] Traub, "Into the Mouths of Babes," p. 19.

[4] Welles, "Beech-Nut," p. 125.

[5] Ibid.

[6] "Bad Apples: In the Executive Suite," *Consumer Reports,* May 1989, p. 294.

[7] Traub, "Into the Mouths of Babes," p. 18.

[8] Welles, "Beech-Nut," p. 126. Later, a federal prosecutor also contended that the low price of the concentrate should have been enough to tip off most anyone that the concentrate was diluted or adulterated. Another supplier, who had sold Beech-Nut much of its apple juice concentrate until 1977, agreed that there was no question about the fake concentrate in the trade. Traub, "Into the Mouths of Babes," p. 20.

[9] Ibid., p. 125.

[10] "Bad Apples," p. 295.

[11] Welles, "Beech-Nut," p. 125.

[12] Stephen Kindel, "Bad Apple for Baby," *Financial World,* June 27, 1989, p. 48.

[13] Welles, "Beech-Nut," p. 125.

[14] "Bad Apples," p. 295.

[15] Welles, "Beech-Nut," p. 125.

[16] Ibid., p. 124.

[17] Ibid.

[18] "Bad Apples," p. 295.

[19] Welles, "Beech-Nut," p. 125.

[20] Ibid.

[21] Leonard Burder, "Two Former Executives of Beech-Nut Guilty in Phony Juice Case," *The Wall Street Journal,* February 18, 1988, p. D3.

[22] Welles, "Beech-Nut," p. 128.

[23] "Bad Apples," p. 295.

[24] Ibid.

[25] Ibid.

[26] Traub, "Into the Mouths of Babes," p. 52.

[27] Welles, "Beech-Nut," p. 128.

[28] "Bad Apples," p. 296.

[29] Ibid.

[30] Welles, "Beech-Nut," p. 128.

[31] "Bad Apples," p. 296.

[32] Traub, "Into the Mouths of Babes," p. 52.

[33] "Bad Apples," p. 296.

[34] Traub, "Into the Mouths of Babes," p. 53.

[35] Ibid.

[36] Welles, "Beech-Nut," p. 125.

[37] Ibid., p. 126.

[38] Traub, "Into the Mouths of Babes," p. 19.

[39] "Bad Apples," p. 290.

[40] "Beech-Nut: The Case of the Ersatz Apple Juice," *Newsweek,* November 17, 1986, p. 66.

[41] Welles, "Beech-Nut," p. 124.

[42] "Bad Apples," p. 296.

[43] "Stonewalling at Beech-Nut," *Business Week,* February 22, 1988, p. 174.

[44] Judann Dagnoli, "Beech-Nut Ready to Fight Back," *Advertising Age,* November 14, 1988, p. 8.

[45] Ibid.

[46] Welles, "Beech-Nut," p. 125.

Source: Rogene A. Buchholz, et al., *Management Responses to Public Issues* (Englewood Cliffs, NJ: Prentice Hall, 1994), pp. 139–149.

Johnson Controls

Title VII of the Civil Rights Act of 1964 prohibits employers from discriminating on the basis of race, color, sex, religion, or national origin in any term, condition, or privilege of employment. This law forbids discrimination in hiring and firing practices, wages, and fringe benefits; classifying, referring, assigning, or promoting employees; extending or assigning facilities; and training, retraining, apprenticeships, and other employment practices.[1] The Federal Pregnancy Discrimination Act of 1978 expanded the definition of sexual discrimination to include discrimination "on the basis of pregnancy, childbirth, or related conditions."[2] Explicit discrimination against people on the basis of the characteristics mentioned is justified only in circumstances where there is a "bona fide occupational qualification" for making such a distinction. A bona fide occupational qualification refers to cases where these characteristics are believed to interfere with a person's ability to perform a particular job effectively.

In the past, employers frequently limited women's access to traditional male, higher-paying jobs by using many different arguments to support this practice. In one landmark case early in the century, the U. S. Supreme Court upheld an Oregon law that forbade hiring women for jobs that required more than ten hours a day in factories. The Court held this restriction to be reasonable because "healthy mothers are essential to vigorous offspring," and preserving their physical well-being is thus essential to preserving the strength and vigor of the human race. While such blatant sex discrimination in employment is history, for the most part, the Court's decision highlights a contemporary legal question not covered in Title VII or the 1978 act. Can an employer substitute concern for fetal health or concern for women's health as an argument for limiting job opportunities for women?[3]

Some employers have moral concerns about safeguarding potential offspring from being deformed or otherwise adversely affected by exposure to harmful substances in the workplace, and fiscal concerns about avoiding future liability suits on behalf of deformed or stillborn fetuses.[4] Some 15 companies were believed to have fetal protection policies in effect at the time the Johnson Controls case was scheduled to be heard by the U. S. Supreme Court. Monsanto Corporation, for example, barred fertile women from six types of jobs where it was believed chemical exposure would be harmful to an unborn child.[5]

However, the U.S. Supreme Court's decision in *International Union* v. *Johnson Controls* found that fetal protection policies are a violation of the law when they restrict jobs to men and sterile women and are not based on a person's ability to perform the job itself. Women cannot be excluded from job categories on the basis that they are or might become pregnant. The case's ruling applies to all employers that are engaged in interstate commerce.[6]

THE FETAL PROTECTION POLICY OF JOHNSON CONTROLS

Johnson Controls maintained a battery-manufacturing division in Milwaukee, Wisconsin, that employed women. Lead, one of the main components in the manufacturing of batteries, has long been known to be particularly dangerous to children and adults. Occupational lead exposure poses health risks that extend to a fetus carried by a female employee.[7] Lead is one of the oldest known toxic substances. Breathing or ingesting excessive amounts of lead can damage the blood-forming systems; kidneys; and the urinary, central nervous, immune, and reproductive systems of both sexes. In fetuses and young children, lead can affect brain development and cause learning deficits, delays in behavioral development, and even decreased growth.[8]

Lead is commonly found in the environment naturally and as a contaminant. Lead enters the human body through inhalation and through food and beverage consumption. Although lead is a natural component of soil, water, vegetation, and animals, certain human activities tend to increase these levels.[9] Lead generated by industry, for example, can cause an increase in an adult's lead levels to the point where the body cannot adjust to the higher levels. The average lead intake for a normal adult is about 0.14 to 0.45 milligram of lead per day.[10]

Equilibrium in a normal adult can be thrown off by an increase in the level of lead intake.[11] The body's inability to handle an increased level of lead can lead to intoxication. Three forms of lead poisoning exist. The most common form causes problems in the digestive system resulting in loss of appetite, constipation, colic, and general weakness. A more infrequent form of poisoning is a neuromuscular syndrome resulting in atrophy of muscles. The last form of poisoning is lead encephalopathy occurring frequently in children but rarely in adults.[12]

In 1977, Johnson Controls began advising women who planned to have children not to take jobs that would submit them to lead exposure. It alerted women who did take such jobs to the problems related to childbearing and lead exposure. The company did not exclude women capable of bearing children from lead exposure at that time, but it did emphasize that a woman who expected to have children should not choose a job in which she would have such exposure. The company also encouraged women to seek their doctor's advice in making the decision to take such a position.[13] Women who chose to be considered for jobs that would expose them to lead were required to sign a document, which stated that they had been notified of the possible dangers.[14]

Among the risks believed to be associated with lead exposure were a higher potential for spontaneous abortion and other unspecified risks to the fetus.[15] Scientific evidence also suggested that a pregnant woman's exposure to lead could lead to damage of the fetus's nervous system.[16] The Centers for Disease Control (CDC) declared that blood lead levels over 30 µg per deciliter were excessive for children. Between 1979 and 1983, eight employees at Johnson Controls with blood lead levels higher than 30 µg per deciliter became pregnant. None of the children born to these women demonstrated evidence of harm due to lead exposure. However, a medical consultant for the company suggested that the hyperactivity of one of the children could be related to his exposure to lead.[17]

In 1982, Johnson Controls decided it had to be more assertive in protecting pregnant women and their fetuses. The company concluded that its voluntary program, as well as its other safety and health policies, were not effective in protecting pregnant women and their unborn children from excessive exposure to lead. After consulting medical experts on the risks of fetal exposure to lead, the company changed its stance from one of simply warning women of the dangers to one of exclusion from the jobs where exposure to lead was involved. The policy stated:

> women who are pregnant or who are capable of bearing children will not be placed into jobs involving lead exposure or which could expose them to lead through the exercise of job bidding, bumping, transfer, or promotion rights.[18]

Women were considered capable of bearing children unless they could provide medical evidence that proved otherwise. Application of the policy did not consider a woman's family status, age, or intent to bear children. The company stated that its intent was to protect unborn babies, arguing that not all pregnancies are planned or expected.[19] The company thus chose to treat all its female employees as having the potential to become pregnant, unless their inability to bear children could be medically documented.[20]

The policy covered women between the ages of 17 and 70, even though the birth rate for blue-collar women over 30 was less than two percent. Statistically, only one in 5,000 women between the ages of 45 and 49 gave birth each year. None of these facts were considered in developing the policy. One 50-year-old plaintiff, Ginny Green, was divorced and raising a teenager, yet she was transferred to a glorified laundress position.[21]

As a result of this policy, fertile women were transferred to another work area if any employee in the present area had a blood lead level higher than 30 µg per deciliter. Several of these transfers meant pay cuts for women, as the jobs they were transferred to did not require the same level of skill or responsibility and therefore paid less than their previous jobs. The company did not make an effort to adjust pay scales to make up for the difference.[22]

The policy was based on the company's claim that no alternative to lead-acid batteries existed, and that excluding women was the only way to reduce risks to fetuses. However, industry experts claim that a less toxic battery could be produced, although it would be very expensive. It seemed to be cheaper to exclude women from manufacturing batteries than to change the process of production itself.[23]

THE LAWSUIT

In 1984, a class-action suit that claimed the policy violated Title VII of the Civil Rights Act of 1964 was brought against Johnson Controls. Plaintiffs included Mary Craig, who had chosen to be sterilized in order to keep her job; Elsie Nason, a 50-year-old divorcee who was transferred and suffered a loss in compensation; and Donald Penney, who had been denied a request for a leave of absence for the purpose of lowering his lead level because he intended to become a father. The plaintiffs argued that Johnson Controls could not justify its discriminatory treatment because it could not show that an employee's sex was a "bona fide occupational qualification."[24]

The petitioners based their case on two major principles. First, they cited scientific evidence showing that men are subject to as great a risk as women from lead exposure. At levels exceeding 30 µg per deciliter, male fertility decreases and the threat of neurological and cardiovascular damage increases. Animal studies also suggest that lead exposure can cause sperm damage and lead to birth defects. The second principle was based on challenging the validity of animal testing as a whole. Some courts did not believe that animal testing presented the solid scientific data that were necessary to establish that a fetus is equally threatened by a certain lead level in either the mother or the father.[25]

In 1988, the U.S. District Court for the Eastern District of Wisconsin granted summary judgment in favor of Johnson Controls. The court believed that the fetal protection policy was justified as a business necessity. This decision was made primarily on the basis of depositions and affidavits from doctors and environmental toxicologists.[26]

In 1989, the U.S. Court of Appeals for the Seventh Circuit affirmed the district court's decision in a 7–4 opinion. The majority opinion relied on medical evidence of potential risks to the fetus and on their opinion that federal law allows employers to consider potential harm when creating company policies.[27]

The appeals court did not accept the plaintiffs' argument of bona fide occupational qualification (BFOQ), holding the company's policy was justified under a modified and less stringent "business necessity" standard. The business necessity defense applied when a facially neutral employment practice, such as a writing test or a weight requirement, is claimed to have a disparate impact on women. The more limited BFOQ defense applies when the employment practice in question is overt and not neutral in its discrimination against women. The appeals court argued that the business necessity standard applied in this case because precedent had been established by two other courts that had considered this defense to be the appropriate analytical framework for evaluating the propriety of fetal protection policies.[28]

Writing for a majority of the court of appeals, Judge John Coffey articulated a three-part test for determining whether a business necessity justified Johnson Controls's fetal protection policy. First, he sought to determine whether workplace exposure to lead posed a substantial risk of harm to the unborn children of employees. Relative to this point, the judge noted that the parties to the suit agreed that exposure to lead presented a risk to children as yet unborn. Second, he tried to determine whether harm to fetuses occurred only through the women's exposure to lead in the workplace. Relative to this point, the judge cited the expert witnesses of the company who had testified that exposure of men to lead levels meeting federal guidelines did not pose a harm to unborn children.[29]

Finally, the judge considered whether an adequate, less discriminatory alternative to the company's fetal protection policy existed. Since the union representing the women had not suggested any such alternative, he concluded that no such alternative existed. The union's failure to allege facts that met this three-part business necessity standard meant that the company was entitled to summary judgment in its favor.[30]

The decision in favor of the company was upheld by a 7–4 majority, with the dissenting judges strongly disagreeing with the application of the business necessity standard in this case. Judge Frank H. Easterbrook, for example, stated that even if business necessity were the correct standard to apply, the majority's view of what constituted a substantial risk of harm to unborn children was too narrow. The court should have applied a "net" risk analysis, he argued, where the risks to the fetus are balanced against risks posed by other factors such as the mother's loss of income and medical insurance.[31]

THE SUPREME COURT'S DECISION

The U.S. Supreme Court unanimously reversed the decisions of the lower courts. The Court found "obvious" bias in Johnson Controls's policy since the policy was based on gender and childbearing ability rather than fertility alone.[32] The Court stated that the policy did not seek to protect the children of all employees but only those of its female employees. Also, the policy was in direct conflict with the Pregnancy Discrimination Act of 1978 because it was based on the potential for pregnancy. The key factor in determining the outcome of the case was deciding whether the absence of pregnancy or the potential to become pregnant was a bona fide occupational qualification for a battery manufacturing job.[33]

The High Court rejected the appeals court's reasoning that sex-specific fetal protection could be justified as a business necessity. Since Johnson Controls's policy was concerned only with the harms that may befall the offspring of its female employees, the policy was racially discriminatory because it required only female employees to prove that they are not capable of reproducing. The fetal protection policy is thus sex discrimination forbidden under Title VII unless the company can establish that sex is a bona fide occupational qualification.[34]

In this case, the Court concluded that Johnson Controls could not establish a BFOQ because fertile women participate in the manufacture of batteries as efficiently as anyone else. Limitations regarding pregnancy or sex must relate to the ability to perform the duties of the job, and in this case no such evidence could be found. The High Court also said that the fetal protection policy of the company violated the provisions of the Pregnancy Discrimination Act, which states that unless pregnant employees differ from others in the ability or inability to perform the job, they must be treated the same as other employees for all employment-related purposes. Women as capable of doing their jobs as their male counterparts must not be forced to choose between having a child and having a job.[35]

According to the Court, "No one can disregard the possibility of injury to future children; the BFOQ, however, is not so broad that it transforms this deep social concern in an essential aspect of battery making." The Court concluded that Congress had left the welfare of the next generation to parents, not employers. "Decisions about the welfare of future children must be left to the parents who conceive, bear, support and raise them rather than the employers who hire those parents."[36]

The Court also addressed the question of possible tort liability the company could later face from the fetus that was injured due to the mother's job. With respect to this issue, the Court decided that, although the threat of injury was slight, even if injury did occur, the injured child would be required to prove negligence on the part of the company. As long as the company followed standards set by the Occupational Safety and Health Administration (OSHA) and provided employees with full information concerning the risks involved, the Court's opinion was that the likelihood of such a liability would be remote at best.[37] Only one such case had emerged, and it resulted in a verdict on behalf of the company even though it had been in violation of OSHA standards.[38]

Although they agreed with the outcome of the case, several justices disagreed with the BFOQ analysis as it applied to tort liability. They warned that the case could be used to undercut certain privacy rights. They believed that under some circumstances, it would be permissible for employers to exclude women from certain jobs on the grounds that their unborn children could sue the employers at some future date. They reasoned that parents cannot waive the right of their children to sue; that the parents' negligence will not be imputed to the children; and that even in the absence of negligence, the employers could be held strictly liable if their manufacturing process is considered.[39]

The Court reversed and remanded the Johnson Controls case stating that, "It is no more appropriate for the courts than it is for the individual employers to decide whether a woman's reproductive role is more important to herself and her family than her economic role." Congress had left this choice to the woman as hers to make, and the only relevant consideration in this case, was whether pregnancy or the potential to become pregnant was a legitimate reason to exclude women from battery-making jobs because of the ability or inability to perform the job adequately.[40]

CONCLUSION

The Court's opinion in the Johnson Controls case held that recasting sex discrimination in the name of fetal protection is illegal under antidiscrimination laws. Johnson Controls argued that its policy was ethical and socially responsible and that it was meant only to prevent exposing the fetus to avoidable risk.[41] As a result of this case, all employers must be sensitive to policies that restrict or exclude a segment of employees. Policy decisions must be made on the ability or inability of each individual employee to perform the functions of the position. Employers must also review their obligations under federal and state laws dealing with occupational safety and health, to determine their obligations to reduce exposure to toxic substances or to disclose such risks to affected employees.[42]

Concerning risk of fetal harm, lead is not the only or even the most dangerous toxic substance. If fetal protection policies were installed in every occupation in which a fetus could be at risk, the advancement women have made in the workplace could be significantly hindered. According to the Bureau of National Affairs, fetal protection policies such as the one at Johnson Controls could affect over 20 million jobs involving women in industry. Millions of other jobs, such as X-ray technicians, cab drivers, radiologists, and those working on video-display terminals could also be threatened.[43] It is curious that fetal protection policies did not emerge in "women's work" occupations such as laundries and dry cleaners where employees are subject to carbon disulfide and benzene.[44]

The decision in the Johnson Controls case continues the legal and social movement to ensure equal opportunities in the workplace for women and other groups covered by antidiscrimination legislation. Women may choose jobs where exposure to toxic substances is possible because they appreciate that there is no risk-free world. Compared to alternatives, jobs in a battery plant may pay double and triple the hourly wages they could get elsewhere, may deliver better health care benefits, and cause less stress. Most of the women who worked at Johnson Controls would probably not call themselves feminists, but having such jobs gave them a sense of independence and self-confidence that may have otherwise been missing from their lives.[45]

> There is a strong correlation between the health of the infant and prenatal medical care; there is also a powerful link between the parents' income and infants' health, for higher income means better nutrition, among other things. . . . Removing women from well-paying jobs (and the attendant health insurance), or denying women access to these jobs, may reduce the risk from lead while also reducing levels of medical care and quality of nutrition. . . . To insist on zero risk . . . is to exclude women from industrial jobs that have been a male preserve. By all means let society lend its energies to improving the prospects of those who come after us. Demanding zero risk produces not progress but paralysis.[46]

Antidiscrimination laws do not remove the responsibility companies have to provide a workplace that involves minimum exposure to toxic substances. Those specializing in occupational health should continue their work to reduce exposure to toxic substances in the workplace for all workers. This can be done by replacing toxic agents with other, less toxic substances; by reducing the volume of their use; and by encouraging the use of protective gear. Workers should be warned about the health risks that cannot be avoided, and encouraged to be monitored for early signs of damage. Personal physicians could look at the occupational history of their patients and tell them about the risks of exposure to various substances. This is the arena on which company policymakers should concentrate, rather than finding new methods of sex discrimination.[47]

All workers must be made aware of the risks they are exposed to in their workplace. With that knowledge, workers will be able to make informed decisions about their jobs and the risks they are willing to take. Congress and the Supreme Court have made strong statements about the use of fetal protection as a strategy to control or restrict the activities and decisions of women. Neither the courts nor employers should attempt to control women's opportunities and choices on the basis of their reproductive role. The ultimate decision maker must be the workers themselves, whether they are male or female.[48]

1. What are fetal protection policies? Why have some companies adopted them over the years? What effect have they had on women who work for such companies? Do these policies address a legitimate problem?

2. Describe the Johnson Controls policy. Is there any evidence to suggest that the company had a discriminatory intent in adopting this policy? Was the policy discriminatory in its effect? If so, in what manner?

3. What is a bona fide occupational qualification (BFOQ)? How did the Supreme Court rule with regard to this issue? Was this a valid judgment?

4. Do companies have a responsibility to be concerned about the welfare of future children? Or is this concern limited to the parents, as the Court ruled? What potential liability, if any, do employers now face because of the Court's decision?

[1] Howard J. Anderson, *Primer of Equal Employment Opportunity* (Washington, DC: Bureau of National Affairs, 1978), p. 25.

[2] George J. Annas, "Fetal Protection and Employment Discrimination—The Johnson Controls Case," *The New England Journal of Medicine,* 325, no. 10 (September 5, 1991), p. 740.

[3] Ibid.

[4] David L. Krip, "The Pitfalls of Fetal Protection," *Society,* March–April 1991, p. 70.

[5] Cathy Trost, "Businesses and Women Anxiously Watch Suit on Fetal Protection," *The Wall Street Journal,* October 8, 1990, p. A1.

[6] Annas, "Fetal Protection and Employment Discrimination," p. 740.

[7] *International Union, United Automobile, Aerospace and Agricultural Implement Workers of America, UAW, et al., v. Johnson Controls, Inc.,* 111 S. Ct. 1196 (1991).

[8] Trost, "Businesses and Women Anxiously Watch Suit," p. A1.

[9] The Working Group on Lead Contamination, *Survey of Lead in the Atmosphere of Three Urban Communities,* U.S. Department of Health, Education, and Welfare, January 1965, p. 5.

[10] Ibid., p. 12.

[11] Ibid., p. 13.

[12] Ibid., pp. 14–15.

[13] Annas, "Fetal Protection and Employment Discrimination," p. 740.

[14] 111 S. Ct. 1196 (1991).

[15] Annas, "Fetal Protection and Employment Discrimination," p. 740.

[16] "Bias or Safety?" *Time,* October 16, 1989, p. 61.

[17] Annas, "Fetal Protection and Employment Discrimination," p. 740.

[18] 111 S. Ct. 1199 (1991).

[19] Christopher Joyce, ". . . While Supreme Court Debates a Woman's Right to Be Poisoned," *New Scientist,* November 10, 1990, p. 16.

[20] 111 S. Ct. 1203 (1991).

[21] Krip, "Pitfalls," p. 72.

[22] Joyce, "Supreme Court," p. 16.

[23] Krip, "Pitfalls," p. 75.

[24] 111 S. Ct. 1196 (1991).

[25] Joyce, "Supreme Court," p. 16.

[26] Betty Southard Murphy, Wayne E. Barlow, and D. Diane Hatch, "Fetal Protection Policy Invalidated," *Personnel Journal,* May 1991, p. 33.

[27] Annas, "Fetal Protection and Employment Discrimination," p. 741.

[28] "Significant Decisions in Labor Cases," *Monthly Labor Review,* March 1990, p. 59. See *Hayes v. Shelby Memorial Hosp.,* 726 F.2d 1543 (11th Cir. 1984); and *Wright v. Olin Corp.,* 697 F.2d 1172 (4th Cir. 1982).

[29] "Significant Decisions," p. 59.

[30] Ibid.

[31] Ibid., p. 60.

[32] Ibid. See also Murphy, Barlow, and Hatch, "Fetal Protection Policy," p. 33.

[33] Ibid.

[34] Ibid.

[35] Ibid.

[36] Ibid.

[37] Ibid.

[38] Krip, "Pitfalls," p. 74.

[39] Annas, "Fetal Protection and Employment Discrimination," p. 741.

[40] Murphy, Barlow, and Hatch, "Fetal Protection Policy," pp. 33–34.

[41] Annas, "Fetal Protection and Employment Discrimination," p. 742.

[42] Murphy, Barlow, and Hatch, "Fetal Protection Policy," p. 34.

[43] Krip, "Pitfalls," p. 70.

[44] Ibid., p. 75.

[45] Ibid., p. 73.

[46] Annas, "Fetal Protection and Employment Discrimination," p. 742.

[47] Ibid.

[48] Ibid., pp. 742–743.

Source: Rogene A. Buchholz, et al., *Management Responses to Public Issues* (Englewood Cliffs, NJ: Prentice Hall, 1994), pp. 245–254.

LONG CASES

Save the Turtles

The Endangered Species Act was originally passed in 1973 to protect animal species threatened with extinction. It marked the first time a law had been passed in the United States that recognized that animals have a right to exist for their own sake, and that animals must be protected both from human beings and from projects that threaten their existence. The law was based in part on the notion that animals have an intrinsic value apart from their value for human welfare. As such, a law was needed to protect this value as well as give animals a haven from extinction. Since the law's passage, various animals have been placed on the endangered list when their species have become threatened for one reason or another.[1]

Since 1978 all six species of sea turtles found in U.S. waters have been labeled threatened and have been placed on the endangered list to protect them from further decimation. Sea turtles are powerful and imposing creatures that evolved about the time of the dinosaurs. They are fascinating in their own right, and some people are loath to see them disappear. Turtle populations in North America have declined in recent years due to the development of beaches where they breed; butchery of nesting females and theft of eggs from their nests; oil slicks; eating plastic garbage; and nets used to catch fish and shellfish.[2]

The Kemp Ridley sea turtle nests only on one beach—near Rancho Nuevo, Mexico—and is one of the world's most threatened species of sea turtles. The Kemp Ridley's population has declined from 40,000 nesting females a day in the late 1940s to 10,000 in 1960 to little more than 500 in the 1980s. The decline continues at an annual rate of about 3 percent. Their nesting beach is now protected by a detachment of Mexican marines who guard the site against poachers. Shrimp nets are the major suspect in their continuing decline. According to some estimates, approximately 48,000 sea turtles are caught each year on shrimp trawlers in the southeast, and about 11,000 of these turtles die because of drowning, since they must come to the surface every hour or so to breathe. About 10,000 of the turtles that die are Loggerheads, and 750 are Kemp Ridleys.[3]

The Kemp Ridley has a diameter of about 32 inches and may weigh as much as 85 pounds. The breeding season starts in early April and lasts through the first week of September. During this period biologists from the United States and Mexico, together with a contingent of volunteers from both countries, work at the Rancho Nuevo site to improve the turtles' reproduction rate. After a female turtle digs her nest in the sand and lays her 100 or so eggs, she leaves the scene and heads out to sea the moment her clutch has been buried. When left unguarded, the nest may be victimized by predators. To protect the eggs, volunteers transfer them to nests in a nearby corral guarded by the marines.[4]

The shrimping industry disputes government figures showing a close correlation between the number of dead turtles found on beaches and the number of trawlers working in the vicinity. While any one boat may not catch many turtles, the cumulative impact of approximately 7,000 offshore commercial vessels towing 4 to 5 million hours per year can be serious. Shrimpers claim dead turtles are mostly victims of pollution or disease rather than shrimpers' nets. There is evidence supporting both points of view, but there is no doubt that shrimpers are killing a number of turtles along with other nonshrimp organisms. For every pound of shrimp caught, 9 pounds of fish, such as juvenile trout, redfish, whiting, and flounder, are dumped dead over the side of the boat in what is called the by-catch.[5] The by-catch has become more of a problem as shrimping has increased.

Americans eat an average of 2.4 pounds of shrimp a year, making it the most popular seafood in the country. In 1988, 331 million pounds of shrimp, worth $506 million, were caught. The shrimping industry provides jobs for many people in the southeastern part of the United States. More than 30,000 commercial fishermen and their families rely on shrimp for their livelihood, and many more work in shoreside processing plants.[6] Many shrimpers are second and third generation, following in the paths of their fathers and grandfathers. As such, the industry has great social as well as economic value, and any threat to the industry is likely to be met with great resistance.[7]

THE SOLUTION

Such a threat appeared in the form of turtle excluder devices (TEDs), which act as trap-doors in the nets of the shrimpers. The TED is a panel of large-mesh webbing or a metal grid inserted into the funnel-shaped nets of the shrimpers. When these nets are dragged along the bottom of the ocean, shrimp and other small animals pass through the TED and into the narrow bag at the end of the funnel where the catch is collected. Sea turtles, sharks, and other marine species too large to get through the panel are deflected out the trapdoor. The problem is that some of the shrimp escape as well, as much as 20 percent or more of the catch, according to some estimates.[8]

Some fishermen call the TEDs a trawler elimination device. They claim the TEDs, which are about 3 feet in diameter, are dangerous, wasteful, expensive, and unnecessary, often lead to wholesale losses of catch. "Would you all like to go to work with a big hole in the back of your pants?" asked the wife of a Louisiana fisherman. "That's what they're asking us to do. We can't pull a TED." Many shrimpers simply refuse to use TEDs in spite of laws requiring their installation.[9]

Ironically, TEDs were developed to save the shrimp industry. Since the law requires that endangered species in the public domain be protected regardless of the cost, the industry was in danger of being totally shut down if environmental groups were to sue the industry or the federal government. To prevent a total shutdown, the National Marine Fisheries Service (NMFS) sought a technological solution. Between 1978 and 1981 the NMFS spent $3.4 million developing and testing the TED device. By 1981, the agency was promoting voluntary usage of the device and in 1983 began distributing free TEDs to further encourage shrimpers to use them. However, shrimpers rejected the TEDs, claiming they were difficult to use and lost a significant percentage of the shrimp catch.[10]

As more dead turtles washed ashore, environmental groups like Greenpeace and the Center for Marine Conservation demanded an end to the killing. Since the voluntary approach to TEDs had failed, the U.S. Fish and Wildlife Service mandated the use of TEDs, and the Center for Marine Conservation threatened to sue the NMFS and close down the industry completely. Industry representatives agreed to phase in use of TEDs, but rank-and-file fishermen rose up in rebellion. They vowed civil disobedience against what they saw as a threat to their survival, and filed lawsuit after lawsuit, which were all eventually lost in court.[11]

The fight then moved to Congress where the Endangered Species Act was up for renewal. It was hoped that Congress would not require the devices until a study was done to determine (1) whether the turtles to be protected were really endangered; (2) if so, whether the TEDs would protect them; and (3) whether there were better ways, such as increased use of hatcheries, to protect the sea turtle population.[12] After prolonged debate, amendments were passed in early fall 1988 that made the use of TEDs mandatory by May 1, 1989, but only in offshore waters, with the exception that regulations already in effect in the Canaveral, Florida, area remain in effect. Regulations for inshore areas were to go into effect by May 1, 1990, unless the secretary of commerce determined that other conservation measures were proving equally effective in reducing sea turtle mortality by shrimp trawling. Further testing was to be done on TEDs under inshore conditions, but until 1990, inshore turtles had virtually no protection.[13]

FURTHER CONTROVERSY

Disaster struck almost immediately after the amendments were passed. Record numbers of dead turtles began washing up on beaches from Georgia to New Smyrna Beach, Florida. From October to December 1980–1986, 32 Kemp Ridleys had washed ashore, but during these same months in 1988, 70 dead Kemp Ridleys washed ashore along with several other species of sea turtles. Altogether, 201 dead turtles were counted, and since there were 150 to 200 boats working in the area, shrimpers were again blamed.[14] In December 1988 environmentalists pressured the state of Florida into requiring emergency use of TEDs in state waters off Florida's northeast coasts. Florida's mandated use of TEDs was now set for an earlier date than required by the federal government.[15]

As the May 1 federal deadline for implementing TEDs drew closer, fishermen in Louisiana rallied to oppose installation of the device. Officials from across the South pledged to help stop TED legislation from being implemented. Governor Roemer of Louisiana said that state wildlife agents should boycott TED laws until studies showed conclusively that the device worked. Roemer said he would take his concerns to Washington, D.C., and tell George Bush to "read my lips."[16]

Louisiana congressional representatives persuaded the secretary of commerce, who was responsible for implementing TED regulations, to further delay their implementation. This would allow shrimpers additional time to buy and install the devices. Only warnings would be issued through the end of June while a National Academy of Sciences committee studied the issue.[17] However, shrimpers who were caught many times not pulling a TED would be branded flagrant abusers of the new law and could be held liable for civil penalties of up to $12,000 per violation.[18] When the warning period ended, penalties as high as $10,000 would go into effect and the catch confiscated. Criminal violators—those who repeatedly thumbed their noses at the law—could be convicted of a felony and fined $20,000 in addition to losing their catch. Emotions ran high in some Louisiana communities, and many shrimpers vowed to break the law by not pulling TEDs, and dared officials to haul them off to jail. Some vowed to shoot the man who tried to take away their living.[19]

In order to comply with the regulations, many shrimpers installed and tried to use the device. Then nature struck with the largest bloom of seaweed in several years, which clogged the excluder panels and prevented much of a shrimp catch from being taken. Shrimpers who had installed TEDs cut them out of their nets, and the Coast Guard temporarily suspended the regulations for Louisiana coastal waters. Representatives from the state hoped that the secretary of commerce would make the suspension permanent.[20]

Then the secretary of commerce, after initially telling the Coast Guard not to enforce the law, reversed himself. When the shrimpers heard this, they streamed into port to protest, blocking shipping channels in Galveston and Corpus Christi, Texas, as well as several Louisiana locations. The blockade in Galveston halted all ship and ferry traffic, although by midafternoon the shrimpers agreed to let ferries pass through the blockade. The blockade threatened to shut down Houston's oil refineries. There was some violence. An Alabama man was arrested after firing a semiautomatic rifle from his boat in Galveston, and two men were arrested in Corpus Christi for throwing an object through a window of a 41-foot Coast Guard patrol boat. Angry fishermen set fire to a huge pile of TEDs on shore.[21]

The secretary of commerce then announced that he was suspending the use of TEDs until the National Academy of Sciences completed its study. Environmental groups filed suit, claiming that the secretary had caved in to terrorism and had put the Bush administration on a collision course with the Endangered Species Act. Robert E. McManus, president of the Center for Marine Conservation, said the secretary of commerce's decision "is a capitulation to organized violence, assaults against government and private property and individuals, and legitimizes organized efforts by a minority of shrimpers to promote illegal activity."[22]

Meanwhile, researchers for the National Marine Fisheries Service released the results of their research, which showed that nets equipped with TEDs resulted in only a 2 to 5 percent reduction in the shrimp catch. These results were at considerable variance with the 20 to 50 percent loss claimed by shrimpers. The results were based on 1,555 hours of trawling off the coast of Louisiana, which produced 12,185 pounds of shrimp in nets equipped with TEDs and 12,391 pounds of shrimp in nonequipped nets. Shrimpers accused the researchers of fudging their data to keep sea turtle research money flowing into their organization.[23]

Experts on the use of TEDs defended their results and accused the shrimpers of refusing to learn how to use the devices correctly. They argued that if TEDs were installed properly the shrimp catch could even be increased. But shrimpers, as victims of a depressed economy that resulted in an increase in the number of competing boats thus contributing to stagnant prices, believed they were fighting for their lives. TEDs were seen as the deathblow to a dying industry, and research data regarding the use of TEDs were rejected. With such a hardened position, nothing short of a court-ordered settlement seemed likely to resolve the issue.[24]

With respect to the lawsuit filed by environmental groups, a federal judge refused to immediately force offshore shrimpers to use TED, but directed the secretary of commerce to enforce some immediate turtle protection until he ruled on the TEDs issue. The judge stated that the secretary of commerce's decision to suspend the use of TEDs left sea turtles totally unprotected, but it was not the court's responsibility to determine what protection was appropriate. The secretary then published regulations that required shrimpers to limit their tows to 105 minutes so that any sea turtles caught would not drown. Environmental groups were unhappy with these results, and said they would appeal the judge's decision, arguing that restricting tow times is not nearly as effective in protecting the turtles as TEDs. They claimed that turtles could not survive even 90 minutes underwater.[25]

In order to enforce the trawl limits, the secretary of commerce planned to embargo shrimping altogether for 30 minutes after each 105-minute period. The normal trawl times for shrimpers ranged between 2 and 6 hours. Shrimping would be banned for 11 half-hour periods during a 24-hour day. This fixed routine would allow Coast Guard officials to spot violators. Fishermen who pulled TEDs, however, would not have to adhere to this schedule.[26]

After the Coast Guard reported that 88 percent of the shrimp fleet was not complying with the shorter tow times, the secretary withdrew the limited tow times and required TEDs to be installed once again.[27] The new regulations were to go into effect Friday, September 8, 1989, but until September 22 violators would not be fined if they immediately installed a TED upon being caught. Violators caught between September 22 and October 15 would be eligible for reduced fines if they purchased and installed TEDs; otherwise, the fines ranged between $8,000 and $20,000 depending on the circumstances. Agents of the federal government could also confiscate both the boats and their catch.[28]

When President Bush visited New Orleans in September 1989 to address the U.S. Hispanic Chamber of Commerce and the National Baptist Convention, shrimpers and their families lined his motorcade route protesting the use of TEDs, and more than 50 shrimpers blocked nearby waterways. Instead of confronting the shrimpers, the Coast Guard issued citations that could have amounted to $55,000 per vessel. Shrimpers, who sealed off Belle Pass in Lafourche Parish and the Intracoastal Waterway near Intercoastal City, were cited under two little-used maritime laws. Many shrimpers were cited for one count of anchoring in and blocking a narrow channel and two counts of violating a safety zone as designated by a port captain.[29]

Shrimpers then protested an editorial that appeared in the *Times-Picayune* under the headline "Shrimpers as Scofflaws." The protest took place outside the newspaper's main offices in downtown New Orleans. The shrimpers resented being compared to outlaws and wanted the newspaper to listen to their side.[30] The president of Concerned Shrimpers of America then said his group might sue the federal government for cash compensation for losses caused by being forced to use TEDs. Comparisons were made with ranchers who are subsidized by the federal government if endangered animals feed on their cattle. These payments are designed to stop ranchers from killing the endangered species.[31]

To protect shrimpers from an unfair competitive advantage given to countries that did not require the use of TEDs or other actions to protect endangered sea turtles, Congress considered a law barring these cheaper imports. Even though imports constitute 80 percent of shrimp consumption in this country, the law was not expected to have much of an impact. Most of the shrimp imported into the United States are produced by an aquaculture industry that relies on shrimp farming. China and Ecuador, for example, each of which accounts for about 104 million pounds of shrimp imports, run aquaculture industries. The import provision was inserted into a spending bill by U.S. Senators J. Bennett Johnston and John Breaux, both from Louisiana. The measure ordered the state department to negotiate agreements with countries that do not protect sea turtles to institute similar turtle protection measures to those found in the United States.[32]

In February 1990 shrimpers sued the federal government again, saying TED laws placed an unconstitutional burden on their businesses. The suit was filed in federal court in Corpus Christi, Texas, and sought immediate suspension of the regulations requiring the use of TEDs for offshore shrimpers. Attorney Robert Ketchand, who filed the suit on behalf of the Concerned Shrimpers of America, called the TED laws "regulatory taking" of shrimpers' profits.[33]

The controversy had now come full circle, with the shrimpers pursuing the cause through the courts as they did before the amendments to the Endangered Species Act were passed. Nothing yet has been resolved, and a solution to the problem seems nowhere in sight.

1. Is there a technological solution to this problem, or is the nature of the controversy so political at this point that the parties to the controversy have ceased to believe a technological solution exists? If so, what kind of a political solution will work to resolve the controversy?

2. Should the fishermen be paid compensation for the losses they claim because of using TEDs? How should these losses be determined? Who should pay for the protection of endangered species? What is a fair resolution of this issue?

3. Is the on-again, off-again nature of the regulations a serious problem? Was the secretary of commerce right in suspending TED regulations when shrimpers blockaded ports along the Gulf Coast? What else could have been done at this point?

4. What should be done now? Is our system structured in such a way that it can resolve conflicts of this nature? What makes this conflict different from others that seem to get resolved without resort to violence or stonewalling tactics that drag on forever?

[1] Roderick Frazier Nash, *The Rights of Nature: A History of Environmental Ethics* (Madison: University of Wisconsin Press, 1989), pp. 175–179.

[2] Jack and Anne Rudlow, "Shrimpers and Lawmakers Collide over a Move to Save the Sea Turtles," *Smithsonian,* December 1989, p. 47.

[3] Ibid.

[4] "TEDs Couldn't Keep Gilbert from Attacking Turtle's Beach," *Times-Picayune* (New Orleans), September 20, 1988, p. A-4.

[5] Rudlow, "Shrimpers and Lawmakers Collide," p. 49.

[6] Ibid., p. 47.

[7] Ibid., p. 49.

[8] Ibid., p. 45.

[9] Christopher Cooper, "La. Shrimpers Get Break on TEDs," *Times-Picayune* (New Orleans), July 11, 1989, p. B-1.

[10] Rudlow, "Shrimpers and Lawmakers Collide," p. 50.

[11] Ibid.

[12] Susan Finch, "Congress May Delay TEDs Date," *Times-Picayune* (New Orleans), July 16, 1988, p. A-13.

[13] Endangered Species Act Amendments of 1988, Conference Report 100-928 to Accompany H.R. 1467, House of Representatives, 100th Congress, 2d Session, p. 5.

[14] Rudlow, "Shrimpers and Lawmakers Collide," pp. 50–51.

[15] Ibid., pp. 52–53.

[16] Christopher Cooper, "Shrimpers Vow to Defy Law on TEDs," *Times-Picayune* (New Orleans), April 9, 1989, p. B-1.

[17] Rudlow, "Shrimpers and Lawmakers Collide," pp. 52–53.

[18] Christopher Cooper, "TED Honeymoon May Be a Short One," *Times-Picayune* (New Orleans), May 6, 1989, p. B-2.

[19] Christopher Cooper, "Furious Shrimpers Flouting TEDs Law," *Times-Picayune* (New Orleans), July 9, 1989, p. B-1.

[20] Cooper, "La. Shrimpers Get Break on TEDs," p. B-1.

[21] Christopher Cooper, "Shrimpers' TEDs Protest Turns Violent," *Times-Picayune* (New Orleans), July 23, 1989, p. A-1.

[22] Christopher Cooper, "Environmentalists Plan Legal Challenge of TEDs Suspension," *Times-Picayune* (New Orleans), July 26, 1989, p. B-1.

[23] James O'Byrne, "Research Disputes Shrimpers' Claims," *Times-Picayune* (New Orleans), July 27, 1989, p. A-1.

[24] Ibid.

[25] Rick Raber and Christopher Cooper, "Judge Refuses to Force Shrimpers to Use TEDs," *Times-Picayune* (New Orleans), August 4, 1989, p. A-1.

[26] Christopher Cooper, "Trawling Schedules Start for Shrimpers," *Times-Picayune* (New Orleans), August 8, 1989, p. A-1.

[27] Rudlow, "Shrimpers and Lawmakers Collide," p. 55.

[28] Christopher Cooper, "Commerce Department Reinstates TED Regulation," *Times-Picayune* (New Orleans), September 6, 1989, p. A-1.

[29] Christopher Cooper, "$55,000 Fines Are Urged for TEDs Blockage," *Times-Picayune* (New Orleans), September 13, 1989, p. B-1.

[30] Christopher Cooper, "Shrimpers Picket Newspaper to Protest Blockade Editorial," *Times-Picayune* (New Orleans), September 22, 1989, p. B-5.

[31] "Shrimpers May Sue U.S. for Losses," *Times-Picayune* (New Orleans), October 4, 1989, p. B-5.

[32] Rick Raber, "TED Provision OK'd for Shrimp Imports," *Times-Picayune* (New Orleans), October 21, 1989, p. A-4.

[33] Christopher Cooper, "Shrimpers File Federal Suit against TEDs," *Times-Picayune* (New Orleans), February 22, 1990, p. B-1.

Source: Rogene A. Buchholz, et al., *Managing Environmental Issues: A Casebook* (Englewood Cliffs, NJ: Prentice Hall, 1992), pp. 61–70.

The War on Cigarettes

The tobacco industry has been a major employer in the United States since the founding of the country. It has most always been a prosperous industry, but in recent years uncertainty has hit the markets of this once thriving industry. Changing market trends have led to a decline in the sales of tobacco products. From 1965 to 1994, smokers as a percent of the total U.S. population over the age of 18 declined from 42.4 percent to 25.0 percent.[1] The factors behind this declining market have to do with changing consumer tastes, health concerns, and demographics. People are learning about the health hazards of smoking and are becoming more aware of the health problems that smoking can cause. The American public today is more health conscious than in previous years and people are going to greater lengths to improve the general quality of their lives. Increased restrictions on where smokers can practice their habit also contribute to the decline in tobacco sales. The demand for cigarettes might decline still further as the male population ages and employment shifts more toward the service sector.[2]

Perhaps the title to this case best captures what is happening with regard to cigarette smoking in this country and abroad. There is a war being carried on between those who would like to see a smoke-free society and critics of the tobacco companies on the one side, and those who would like to continue smoking and the tobacco industry on the other side of the controversy. This war is taking place on many fronts, which in some sense constitute the major battles in the war on cigarette smoking. These battles include health issues related not only to smokers themselves but also to those inhaling passive smoke and the newer controversy as to whether or not nicotine is addictive, smoking in the workplace, the battle over advertising and marketing practices of tobacco companies, court cases that have taken place as well as those that are still pending, and other battles such as those involving suits by states to recover smoking-related costs and battles with the media.

THE HEALTH ISSUE

The health issue regarding cigarette smoking began to be raised as early as 1953, when findings were presented at the annual meeting of the Dental Society suggesting a connection between repeated cigarette use and lung cancer. In 1954, *Reader's Digest* published an influential article based on medical research which linked smoking with lung disease. In response to these medical reports, which were critical of cigarette smoking and its relationship to diseases like lung cancer, expenditures for cigarette advertising steadily increased, making cigarettes one of the most heavily advertised products in the late 1950s and early 1960s. Public attitudes toward smoking, however, were changing, resulting in a requirement passed by Congress in 1966 that a health warning be placed on all cigarette packages. Since then not only has government become more active, but so have private citizen groups in support of increased legislation and restriction on smoking and the tobacco industry.

The annual mortality rate from cigarette smoking in the United States was estimated at one time to exceed 350,000 lives per year. These deaths are nearly equivalent to the number of American lives lost during World War II, and are in excess of the combined losses experienced during World War I, the Korean War, and the Vietnam War. An estimated 30 percent of all annual deaths from coronary heart disease and cancer are attributable to cigarette smoking. This figure does not take into account the estimated 9,000 deaths due to oral cancer. Chronic obstructive lung diseases account annually for an additional 62,000 smoking-related deaths.[3] Thus, smoking has been universally condemned by many authoritative medical groups and medical officers who work for the government as a leading cause of death and a major public health problem in developed countries around the world.[4] When he was Surgeon General of the United States, Dr. C. Everett Koop, stated:

> We can say again today, with greater certainty than ever, that cigarettes are the most important individual health risk in this country, responsible for more premature death and disability than any other known agent.[5]

Death rates among smokers are uniformly above those of nonsmokers regardless of sex or age at the time of death. For smokers between the ages of 45 to 54, their excess mortality rate is proportionately greater than at younger or older ages. A smoker doubles his or her risk of dying before the age of 65.[6] Low tar and nicotine cigarette smokers have lower mortality rates than smokers of medium or high tar and nicotine cigarettes; however, the death rate for low tar and nicotine cigarette smokers is still 52 percent higher than for nonsmokers.[7] It has been estimated that an average of five and one-half minutes of life is lost for each cigarette smoked. This translates into an average reduction in life expectancy of five to eight years for cigarette smokers.[8] Dr. John Holbrook of the University of Utah Medical Center says: "When you light up, it's like exposing your whole body to a miniature chemical factory." The temperature within the glowing tip of a cigarette soars to 1800 degrees Fahrenheit, which produces an estimated 4,000 chemical reactions between the paper and tobacco.[9]

Cigarette smoking has also been called the greatest threat to the health of American women. Smoking has been changing, it is claimed, from a man's to a woman's preserve,

---

I think historians will marvel at the fact that in the last few decades we have been panicking over the alleged health effects of things like DDT, aldrin, dieldrin, ethylene dibromide, nitrite in cured meat, saccharin, cyclamates, the asbestos in hair dryers, the chemicals in hair dyes. Yet we seem to tolerate a product which kills hundreds of thousands of us every year. No, we just don't tolerate it, we subsidize it and we advertise it and we promote it.

Source: Remarks by Dr. Elizabeth M. Whelan, A Symposium: Doctors and Smoking, "The Cigarette Century," *The New York Times,* April 20, 1986, p. E-8. Copyright © 1986 by The New York Times Company. Reprinted by permission.

as it is estimated that more women than men will be smokers if present trends continue. In 1985, the American Cancer Society estimated that lung cancer killed more women than breast cancer, marking the first wave in what was called a rising tide of formerly "male" diseases among female smokers. The impact of this trend could be so severe, some demographers predict, that the edge in lifespan that women have had, which has been about eight years in women's favor, will disappear because of women's smoking patterns.[10]

In 1994, the American Heart Association released a report, which estimated that 2.2 million American children between the ages of 12 and 17 smoked cigarettes, and that 9 million children younger than 5 years of age lived with a smoker, increasing their risk of asthma and respiratory infections.[11] A report released by the Surgeon General the same year found that 3.1 million adolescents between the ages of 12 and 18 smoked cigarettes, with 3,000 new smokers under the age of 18 beginning every day. The average age at which smokers tried their first cigarette is 14.5 years, and more than 70 percent of those who become daily smokers had acquired their habit by the time they reached 18 years of age.[12] Because of statistics like these, President Clinton made an issue of teen smoking and backed action to curb the habit.[13]

The response of the tobacco industry to these claims of increased mortality rates and incidence of disease is perhaps best represented by Walker Merryman, vice president of the Tobacco Institute, who claims that the health studies relative to smoking aren't conclusive. The institute questions the statistical correlation between cigarettes and diseases, and claims that nobody has clearly shown a cause-and-effect relationship between smoking and lung cancer. If smoking causes cancer, why do nonsmokers get it, he asks, and furthermore why don't all smokers get it if there is a clear cause-and-effect relationship? Merryman claims that studies done by the institute show that 90 percent of the heaviest smokers don't get lung cancer.[14]

Ann Bowder, assistant to the president of the Tobacco Institute, reports that the industry has provided $120 million in grants over the years for research through its Council on Tobacco Research. She also questions whether or not statistical studies show a causal relationship. She calls such studies "helpful, useful, and necessary," but adds that these studies that show a correlation between smoking and disease do not establish a causal connection. "If there were information beyond a shadow of doubt that the industry would have no doubts about—if they were able to induce lung cancer in an animal through the inhalation of tobacco smoke—that would put us out of business overnight."[15]

Robert Stapf, the institute's leading media spokesman, calls the antismoking crusaders a bunch of hypocrites who talk out of both sides of their mouths. They say that they want only to educate people about the risks of smoking, yet they refuse to look at the evidence objectively. Stapf claims that the antismoking advocates are out to scare people and make smoking so socially unacceptable that informed adults won't have a right to make their own choice because of laws and policies that restrict or ban smoking outright. People's right to a choice ought to be respected, whether they are nonsmokers or smokers.[16]

Passive Smoking

Much of the public's attention in recent years has focused on the effects of passive smoking on human beings. Involuntary or passive smoking can be defined as the exposure of nonsmokers to tobacco-combustion products in the indoor environment. James L. Repace, a physicist at the Environmental Protection Agency, and Alfred A. Lowrey, a chemist at the Naval Research Laboratory in Washington, D.C., reviewed 14 epidemiologic studies and reported that all but one study showed evidence of an elevated risk of lung cancer among nonsmokers exposed to cigarette smoke. Repace estimated that depending on the level of smoke one is exposed to "there may be between 500 and 5,000 deaths each year from this disease (lung cancer) among nonsmokers 35 or more years of age, simply because they were exposed to side stream tobacco smoke."[17]

University of Massachusetts researcher, Dr. S. Katherine Hammond, reported that "a filter cigarette will deliver less nicotine to the smoker but not to those present. Filter cigarettes dilute the smoke inhaled by the smoker, but emit the same ash and particles of a traditional cigarette into the surrounding air."[18] Repace concludes that current efforts to eliminate smoking in public places are justified due to the estimated magnitude of the risk from passive smoke. The main targets for antismoking laws are schools, hospitals, theaters, conventions halls, or other public places where people have to stand and wait.

Joseph Califano, former secretary of the Health and Human Services Department, stated that studies show that 5,000 Americans die each year because of secondhand smoke. A Japanese report concluded that nonsmoking wives of heavy smokers had an 80 percent higher risk of lung cancer than women married to nonsmokers. Other studies have associated involuntary smoking with pneumonia, asthma, bronchitis, and heart disease.[19] In 1986, a special committee of the National Research Council of the National Academy of Sciences reviewed the available scientific studies and concluded that nonsmokers incur considerable health risks from passive smoking. The committee did not make any recommendations on whether or not smoking should be limited in public places or workplaces, stating that its charge was only to evaluate the scientific data available on passive smoking.[20]

Because of the concern with passive smoking, most states have passed laws restricting smoking in public places. Many prohibit smoking in subways and 17 states forbid it in offices and other workplaces. There are also many local ordinances against the use of tobacco. These vary widely across the country. For example, in Cambridge, Massachusetts, smoking has been banned in just about all public buildings.[21] In Austin, Texas, every company is required to have a written policy on smoking, and if there is a dispute, the rights of the nonsmoker prevail. Eventually, a report was released indicating that a nationwide ban on smoking in most public buildings could save $39–72 billion and prevent as many as 12,900 premature deaths annually. A bill was introduced into Congress that would require most all nonresidential buildings to establish smoking areas with separate ventilation or force smokers to go outside.[22]

The EPA first got into the act in 1990 by issuing a report that claimed smoking causes 3,800 lung cancer deaths per year among nonsmokers who inhale the smoke from the air with which they are surrounded. The agency also issued a draft guide for employers to help them cope with secondhand smoke in the workplace. It recommended that passive smoking be eliminated wherever possible and mentioned the effectiveness of various methods of reducing worker exposure to secondhand smoke. The proposal treated secondhand smoke as a known human carcinogen and put it in a class with such pollutants as asbestos. While the EPA cannot regulate smoking in the workplace, the Occupational Safety and Health Administration was expected to use the report to raise the issue of workplace exposure to secondhand smoke.[23]

Other evidence continued to mount warning about the dangers of secondhand smoke. In June 1992, the EPA released a draft report claiming that exposure to "environmental tobacco smoke" contributed to as many as 300,000 cases of respiratory illness and about 3,000 cases of lung cancer annually. Based on this report, the EPA's science advisory review board concluded that secondhand smoke should be classified as a known human carcinogen. This action was expected to support further restrictions on public smoking.[24] The same year, the American Heart Association estimated that about 50 million nonsmoking adults over the age of 35 are exposed to secondary smoke. It urged that secondhand smoke be treated as an environmental toxin that should be banned from offices and public places.[25]

The Tobacco Institute takes exception to these findings. It disputes the claim that since 1964 there have been thousands of studies showing that secondary smoke increases the risks of heart and lung disease, by insisting that fewer than 100 studies have been done on the effects of secondary smoke, and claiming that the weight of scientific evidence continues to show no linkage.[26] Philip Morris and RJR Nabisco filed a federal lawsuit against the EPA for ruling that secondhand smoke causes lung cancer and sought to have the report declared "null and void."[27] Meanwhile, another study released in 1994 claimed that secondhand cigarette smoke will cause an estimated 47,000 deaths and about 150,000 heart attacks in nonsmokers, as much as 50 percent higher than previous estimates.[28] Thus, the battle over secondhand smoke continues.

The Nicotine Battle

In May 1988, the Surgeon General released a report which claimed that tobacco, like cocaine or heroin, is addictive, opening up a whole new area of controversy. The Surgeon General stated that "cigarettes and other forms of tobacco are addicting" and urged that they be treated with the same caution as illegal street narcotics. The report was based on two decades of research by 50 scientists, and claimed that in 1986, smoking-related lung ailments accounted for 108,000 deaths and heart disease accounted for 200,000 more deaths. In comparison, cocaine and opiates such as heroin killed only about 6,000 people. Recommendations included warning labels about addiction on packages of tobacco products and a ban on cigarette vending machines in order to curb availability to children.[29]

Eventually, the FDA asserted its legal authority to regulate and virtually ban all cigarettes based on evidence it had accumulated that the nicotine content in cigarettes is being manipulated to stroke a public addiction. The head of the agency, David Kessler, cited research which showed that 77 percent of smokers wanted to quit their habit but could not because of nicotine addiction. The FDA was trying to make a case for considering nicotine a drug that was then subject to the agency's regulations requiring premarket testing. Since such regulatory action could have dramatic effects on society, the FDA asked for a directive from Congress as to what action it should take.[30]

Under pressure from Congress, the largest tobacco companies released a top-secret list of the chemicals in cigarettes. The tobacco companies had long opposed releasing such a list because of fear competitors would steal their trade secrets, but now they wanted to prove that they were not hiding anything sinister. However, tobacco critics said that the list did not let the companies off the hook because some of the chemicals were believed to pose safety problems and the companies did not disclose how much of the chemicals is contained in each puff taken by a smoker. The list contained in all some 599 chemicals that are used to flavor and process cigarettes.[31]

Testifying before a House subcommittee, top executives of the nation's seven largest tobacco companies said that nicotine is not addictive and denied allegations that they manipulated the nicotine content to keep smokers addicted. They also agreed to turn over all studies, research notes, and internal memos about their analysis of nicotine.[32] Philip Morris filed a $10 billion lawsuit against ABC for charging that the industry artificially adds nicotine to cigarettes to keep people smoking and boost profits. The company also took out full-page advertisements in six major newspapers assuring smokers about the safety of its product.[33]

The controversy took a new twist when two former scientists for Philip Morris testified before a House panel that their studies on rats, which were performed more than a decade before, raised serious questions about the potential addictive nature of nicotine. When they wanted to publish the results of their research and present their findings at professional conferences, they were told by the company they could not do so, and eventually their lab was closed.[34] Subsequently documents were discovered which showed that already in 1963, executives at Brown & Williamson had debated whether or not to publicly disclose research which showed that cigarettes caused lung cancer and some heart problems. This information had supposedly been shared with other tobacco companies, although they denied having received any such information.[35]

In 1995, the American Medical Association (AMA) weighed in on the side of the FDA, calling tobacco a "drug-delivery vehicle" that should be regulated the same as other life-threatening drugs. The organization also called for withholding federal funds from cancer research groups that accept money from tobacco companies, the elimination of all tobacco advertising, and severe penalties for those who sell tobacco to young people. These recommendations were made in an editorial in its weekly journal, the first time in modern history, so the AMA stated, that the association's entire board of trustees had joined the editor of the journal in taking an editorial stance.[36]

Later in the year, the FDA proposed rules to curtail the sale, distribution, and advertising of cigarettes to minors. The agency stated that three decades of research suggested that the companies themselves have long believed that cigarettes are addictive and have strong appeal to minors. In its report, the agency noted that almost all the leading experts and public health organizations in the United States as well as in the international community, including the vast majority of scientists funded by the industry itself, recognized the addictive effects of nicotine. If these regulations were to go into effect, they would even outlaw the use of cigarette vending machines. The move met with resistance from the tobacco companies and advertising interests, which went to court to try and halt the initiative.[37]

Finally, a high-level defector from Brown & Williamson (B&W), Jeffrey S. Wigand, former vice president of research for the Louisville-based company, accused his ex-boss of lying under oath to Congress about his views on nicotine addiction. Testifying in a deposition as part of trial preparation for Mississippi's lawsuit seeking compensation from the tobacco companies for smoking-related illnesses, he charged that lawyers for B&W repeatedly hid potentially damaging information about nicotine, including altering minutes of a scientific meeting. The former executive also testified that the company had stopped efforts to develop a safer cigarette because any research on such a cigarette would expose every other product as unsafe and present a liability issue for any type of litigation. The company had tried to prevent Mr. Wigand from testifying by filing a suit in a state court in Louisville, where a judge ordered him to comply with his confidentiality agreement. But another judge in Mississippi had ordered him to appear, agreeing to seal the deposition transcript.[38]

SMOKING IN THE WORKPLACE

Smoking in the workplace is also an issue of recent concern because of the passive smoking issue. Proponents of a smoke-free workplace argue that restrictions on smoking will save lives and money by reducing absenteeism, health insurance costs, property maintenance, and legal liability. The problem for employers is one of balancing the rights of smokers with nonsmokers and the responsibility of the employer to provide a healthy work environment. This is not an easy problem to solve, as many employers are discovering, but more and more companies are dealing with it in some fashion. A poll taken by the Administrative Management Society in 1986 found that 42 percent of the firms surveyed had some kind of smoking policy, up from only 16 percent at the beginning of the decade.[39]

Many companies have designated smoking areas for their employees, which would seem on the surface to be a reasonable solution to the problem. But some companies have found the cost of doing this was too expensive, and so they have banned smoking entirely. The EPA's report linking passive tobacco smoke to lung cancer and other ailments was expected to put added pressure on employers to ban smoking on their premises. New lawsuits were expected including (1) workers' compensation claims by nonsmokers who claim they became ill in a smoke-filled workplace, (2) suits against tobacco companies by nonsmokers who have been exposed to cigarette smoke, and (3) damage suits by customers who experience adverse health reactions at restaurants, bars, and other facilities that permit smoking.[40]

One executive predicted that "we'll get to the point where nonsmoking is a condition of employment."[41] Indeed, USG Acoustical Products Company did just that, by announcing that employees working in its plants must give up their smoking, even at home, or lose their employment. Mineral fibers used in the production of acoustical tiles were believed to be especially hazardous to smokers. The company planned to conduct lung tests to make sure workers were complying with the ban, and those who didn't quit smoking would be fired. This policy affected about 2,000 workers in eight states, and was the first time a company attempted to regulate smoking off the job. Employees were given the opportunity to enroll in a company-sponsored program to help them quit smoking or they could elect to enroll in a program of their own choosing at company expense.[42] Later, under pressure from various groups concerned about this invasion of privacy and lack of respect for workers' rights, the company backed off and announced the employees who didn't quit smoking would not necessarily be fired, but that each situation of this sort would be reviewed on a case-by-case basis.[43]

Smoking is also becoming more hazardous to careers in business. Instead of being a socially acceptable practice, smoking is increasingly seen as a character defect indicating weakness and lack of self-discipline. In some companies smoking is actually becoming an impediment to the climb up the corporate ladder.[44] In other cases, job seekers are finding that smoking can prevent them from getting work. Classified newspaper advertisements sometimes specify that employers are looking for nonsmokers only, while in other situations, one of the first questions asked of job applicants is whether or not they smoke.[45]

Employers justify these actions because they believe tobacco users take too many sick days and raise insurance premiums. Employees who smoke cost too much in health care benefits, lost productivity, and office maintenance. Companies are revising their definition of work performed to include not only how well individuals perform their jobs but whether or not they are good corporate citizens. The opponents of this practice believe that it results in discrimination against smokers and will, no doubt, lead to lawsuits. For some time, however, employers have had wide latitude to regulate company policy with regard to smoking. The federal courts have focused their efforts on employment discrimination based on race and sex and have not had occasion to establish a firm legal framework with regard to the smoking issue.[46]

The tobacco companies turned to state legislatures to protect the right to smoke, and by the middle of 1993, 28 states and the District of Columbia made discrimination against smokers illegal. And at least two states made smoking outside the workplace a civil right for workers. These laws do not affect office smoking bans or smoke-free zones in the workplace, but they prevent companies from refusing to hire workers and from firing employees who fail to stop smoking. In some states, the American Civil Liberties Union supported the tobacco lobby, stating that off-the-job antismoking policies are a corporate intrusion into what is a private matter. Many companies who had tightened their antismoking policies opposed these measures.[47]

In early 1994, the Clinton administration proposed a sweeping ban on smoking in all indoor workplaces, including bars and restaurants. Employers could designate smoking rooms in nonworking areas, but these rooms would have to have outside ventilation and air could not flow from the smoking rooms into the rest of the building. The proposal, which was expected to increase the productivity of the American work force while protecting them from heart disease, lung cancer, and respiratory ailments, would affect some 6 million workplaces. It was expected to cost business $8.1 billion to comply in the first year and $6.6 billion a year thereafter.[48] Later in the year, OSHA clarified regulations by stating that the rules would not apply to private homes or vehicles. This clarification was in response to tobacco industry ads which portrayed the government as dictating what people could do in the privacy of their homes.[49]

ADVERTISING AND MARKETING

The Federal Trade Commission estimated that spending for cigarette advertising in 1980 reached $1.24 billion, making cigarettes one of the most heavily advertised and promoted products in the world.[50] People who are against smoking argue that for over 60 years cigarette firms have used unfounded health claims to encourage people to smoke regardless of the risk or harm involved. Misleading ads were placed as far back as 1929 in some of the leading publications. One Luckies ad, for example, showed a fist labeled "American intelligence: breaking the chain of ignorance," and claimed that Lucky Strike cigarettes caused "No throat irritation—no cough." In later years, smokers were urged to protect the delicate tissues in their throat by using Luckies. Then, as evidence began to mount linking smoking with disease, cigarette makers used medical themes to promote smoking. American brands claimed that 20,679 physicians said Luckies were less irritating to the throat. R.J. Reynolds responded by claiming that "More doctors smoke Camels than any other cigarette!"[51]

One of the most deceptive cigarette advertising campaigns occurred with the introduction of Kent cigarettes in 1952 as having less tar and nicotine than most competing brands. It was claimed that these cigarettes provided "the greatest health protection in cigarette history." The levels of tar and nicotine were so low that addicted smokers complained that smoking Kents was like "smoking through a mattress." By 1955, however, Kent cigarettes had quadrupled in nicotine content and increased sixfold in tar delivery.

The public was not informed about this change, however, and was deceived into believing they were using a "safe" cigarette.[52]

Some believe that the advertising of cigarettes today is still deceptive but in a more subtle manner. Advertising still is believed to communicate to the public that it is reasonably safe to smoke. The industry has conducted major publicity campaigns to create doubt in the public mind about the relationship between smoking and disease. One report accused the industry of adopting a strategy of quoting scientists out of context and selectively citing evidence to make it appear that there is a controversy within the scientific community over the effects of smoking where none really exists.[53]

Since ads may be having a diminishing effect on men, they have been increasingly targeted at young women, projecting smoking as liberating and glamorous. Nonsmokers argue that every freedom, including freedom of speech, entails some responsibility to warn people about the possible dangers of using their product. The industry cannot just think about itself but also needs to consider the health risks and possible deaths associated with smoking.[54]

The American Medical Association called for a ban on the advertising and promotion of cigarettes and smokeless tobacco. Its 371-member, policy-making body voted almost unanimously to back such a sweeping prohibition of cigarette advertising because the health risks were believed to be so great.[55] The AMA also asked for increased educational efforts to attain the goal of a "smoke-free society by the year 2000," and for enlarging that goal to aim for a completely tobacco-free society.[56]

The industry believes that there is no real evidence to support the claim that advertising of tobacco products leads to further consumption. They claim that advertising is not used to entice nonsmokers into smoking, but is used to promote brand loyalty within the existing market and to get people to switch brands, not to start smoking.[57] The industry is not trying to push nonsmokers into a habit, but is trying to promote its product within the market that has already been established. Cigarette makers like to argue that the advertising issue is one of free speech. Any attempt to restrict their efforts to promote smoking is portrayed as a violation of their First Amendment rights. The tobacco industry believes that it has the right like any other manufacturer to advertise its product.[58]

The industry also believes that using the words *addictive* and *death* in proposed warning labels on cigarette packages is lacking in supporting evidence. They have fought against the use of the word *addictive* in particular because of its legal implications. By arguing that smoking is not addictive and that smokers have a free choice to quit at any time, the tobacco industry has managed to win most every lawsuit brought against it thus far in the courts. Industry spokespersons have successfully argued that people smoke voluntarily and are thus responsible for any injury to their health that may result.[59]

Since 1971, there has been a ban on the advertising of cigarettes on radio and television. Antismoking groups want a ban on all forms of cigarette and tobacco advertising. Eventually a bill was passed that made it mandatory to place health warning labels on all tobacco products, not just cigarettes. Plaintiffs involved in lawsuits against the tobacco companies claimed that the cigarette warnings did not adequately warn them concerning the dangers or risks of contracting particular diseases by smoking. They also claimed that industry advertisements directly challenge or criticize health warnings, encouraging smokers to disregard any warnings of health risks.

A three-judge panel of the U.S. Third Circuit Court of Appeals determined that tobacco companies are not obliged to issue health warnings that go beyond those required by the U.S. Cigarette Labeling and Advertising Act. The 1966 federal cigarette labeling law preempts any state law tort claims that "challenge either the adequacy of the warning or the propriety of a party's actions with respect to the advertising and promotion of cigarettes."[60] In October 1985, a new law went into effect requiring four rotating health warnings. Representative Albert Gore, Jr. (D–Tenn.) called this legislation a true compromise between "keeping the essential elements of a comprehensive smoking education program while recognizing the legitimate concerns of the tobacco industry."[61] The new warnings specifically express a relationship between cigarette smoking and lung cancer, heart disease, and emphysema, and warn pregnant women that smoking might result in fetal injury and premature birth.[62]

Legislative proposals have also attacked the current tax provisions that allow for deductibility for advertising and promotion of tobacco products. This legislation was introduced by Senator Bill Bradley (D–N.J.) and Representative Pete Stark (D–Calif.). Senator Bradley contends that the tobacco industry spends about $2 billion annually on advertising and that this legislation would add approximately $2.3 billion over the next three years to federal revenues. Bradley says, "This is not a freedom of speech question. Tobacco companies can advertise all they want. They just aren't going to get my subsidy."[63]

In 1990, RJR had to withdraw plans to test market a cigarette aimed at blacks after public pressure led by Louis W. Sullivan, the secretary of Health and Human Services. Sullivan claimed that the message of the new marketing plan for Uptown, as the new cigarette was called, meant more disease, suffering, and death for a group of Americans already bearing more than their share of smoking-related illness and mortality. Many blacks considered the introduction of the new cigarette an insult because of the company's blatant admission that Uptown was aimed at the black community. This fiasco was expected to make it more difficult for tobacco and liquor companies to target their products to minorities, women, and youth. Because fewer and fewer Americans are smoking, tobacco companies thought that new brands aimed at specific groups would help them gain market share.[64]

Research published in the *Journal of the American Medical Association* (*JAMA*) in 1991 indicated that even though companies deny targeting children in their ads, ads for Camels featuring the Joe Camel mascot are highly effective in reaching children. The cartoon camel was recognized much more often by children than adults in the studies, which suggested to one researcher that such advertising causes children to become addicted to cigarettes. The company running the ads argued that brand recognition does not mean children are buying cigarettes, but the studies also showed that Camels are smoked by a higher percentage of children who smoke than adults, matching closely the brand recognition. As a result of these studies, major health associations asked the Federal Trade Commission to ban advertising featuring the Camel character.[65]

R.J. Reynolds, maker of Camel cigarettes, instead of giving in on this issue, pushed the controversial campaign even harder. It boosted spending on Joe Camel ads and attacked the *JAMA* articles.[66] It even introduced female characters into the ad campaign, which infuriated critics who called this effort a blatant attempt to broaden the traditionally male brand's appeal to women smokers.[67] Indeed, studies released in 1994 showed a sharp increase in smoking by teenage girls in the late 1960s and early 1970s because of widely advertised cigarettes for women.[68]

As the battle over smoking and children became more politically charged, Philip Morris unveiled a plan to discourage minors from smoking cigarettes including discontinuing all giveaways of samples by handouts and mail, pushing for laws requiring all cigarette retailers to be licensed, and placing "underage sale prohibited" labels on all cigarette packs.[69] Eventually, even Joe Camel was quietly demoted by Reynolds, appearing in fewer and fewer places. The company claimed it was not reacting to criticism of the campaign, but that the ads had largely outlived their usefulness.[70]

In late 1995, the FDA proposed restricting the advertising and marketing of tobacco products. The proposal was aimed at reducing cigarette smoking among minors, and would declare cigarettes a drug-delivery device. It would ban sales of cigarettes through vending machines, sponsorship of sporting or entertainment events by tobacco-product brand names, and billboard advertising of tobacco products within 1,000 feet of schools. The proposal sparked a storm of protest from many companies not in the tobacco industry who would be affected.[71] Advertising trade groups as well as the tobacco industry filed lawsuits claiming the FDA had overstepped its legal bounds in regulating advertising.[72]

COURT CASES

In December 1985, a jury ruled in favor of R.J. Reynolds Company in a $1 million product liability suit. The suit was brought by the family of John Galbraith, who had died in 1982 from heart and lung ailments after smoking for 50 years. The jury was not convinced that Galbraith had been addicted to cigarettes or that he had died of tobacco-caused disease.[73] In April 1986, the U.S. Court of Appeals for the Third Circuit in Philadelphia said that the federally mandated health warning printed on cigarette packages protects the industry from claims that it failed to warn smokers adequately that cigarettes are dangerous. The court also denied the claim that advertising had the effect of negating this warning. This decision overturned a lower court ruling in a case filed by the estate of Rose Cipollone, who died at the age of 58 from lung cancer allegedly caused by smoking.[74] The Supreme Court allowed this ruling to stand without comment.[75]

These victories were important for the tobacco industry, as even a single verdict against one of the tobacco companies could trigger thousands of other lawsuits seeking compensation for smoking-related deaths or diseases. Because of this threat, tobacco companies have been strengthening their defenses, hiring the best law firms in the country to represent them, and retaining psychologists, economists, physicians, and medical researchers to testify at trials. The cost of all this effort is unknown, but lawyers' fees for only one trial were $3 million.[76]

In June 1988, something of a landmark victory was handed down by a federal jury in Newark, which represented the first loss handed to the tobacco industry in any of the lawsuits brought against one of the companies. The case again involved Rose Cipollone, who had died of cancer in 1984, supposedly from cigarette smoking. The case dragged on for five years, but finally a six-member jury awarded her husband $400,000 in compensatory damages to be paid by the Liggett Group, maker of the Chesterfield and L&M brands. Out of more than 300 lawsuits filed against the tobacco companies since 1954, this was the first in which a company was found at least partly liable and ordered to pay damages.[77]

The suit was only a partial victory, however, as the jury agreed with only part of the plaintiffs' broad allegations. Two of the companies charged in the case were exonerated from liability because Cipollone smoked these brands later in life after warnings were required. Federal appeals courts have found these warnings, which went into effect in 1966, sufficient to absolve tobacco companies from liability. And the jury did not find the companies guilty of fraud and conspiracy to hide the hazards of smoking from the public, which might have produced much greater damage awards. Even so, antismoking activists expected the case would boost the confidence for the other 110 plaintiffs who at that time were pursuing similar cases against the tobacco companies.[78]

Just a few days later, a federal jury in Philadelphia found that an American Brands unit was not liable for the death of a former shipyard worker, who had smoked for more than 40 years. While the jury did find that cigarettes made before 1966 were "defective" because the company failed to warn consumers about possible injury, the jury was not convinced that the shipyard worker's smoking habits would have been affected by such warnings. The case was complicated by the fact that the plaintiff was exposed to asbestos in his line of work, and it is believed that people exposed to asbestos who also smoke are many times more susceptible to lung disease than those only exposed to asbestos.[79]

The Supreme Court finally agreed to decide whether or not the federal law that requires health warnings on cigarette packages bars smokers from suing for damages from smoking-related illnesses. This was the first time the Supreme Court agreed to venture into this high-stakes controversy that would have serious implications for the tobacco industry. The Court agreed to hear an appeal by Thomas Cipollone, a member of the Cipollone family who had been carrying on a long battle with the companies. The cigarette companies themselves said they welcomed the Court's intervention because there were so many similar lawsuits pending. The issue the Supreme Court had to decide is whether Congress intended to supercede the personal-injury laws of all 50 states when it passed the labeling law in 1965, or whether it meant to leave the state liability systems undisturbed. Tobacco companies have long argued that the 1965 law preempted state laws that allow lawsuits for personal injuries.[80]

The decision, handed down in the summer of 1992, stated that warning labels did exempt tobacco companies from liability in cases where smokers claim that they were not adequately warned of the risks of smoking after 1969, which was four years after warning labels were required. The decision also stated that plaintiffs cannot base their suits on promotions that were put into effect after the same year. But the decision also opened the door for cases that involve allegations that tobacco companies misrepresented or fraudulently withheld information concerning the health effects of smoking. Since some believed that there was ample evidence that tobacco companies had misrepresented the dangers of smoking, this decision was expected to expose the tobacco companies to new and uncertain legal risks that could result in a major financial impact on the industry.[81]

Suits, such as the one filed by seven flight attendants in November 1991, could proceed under this ruling if they could find evidence in company files that secondhand smoke posed a risk to people who were exposed to such a danger. The suit was a $5 billion class-action lawsuit charging tobacco companies with causing cancer and other diseases in flight attendants.[82] However, the first case to go to trial after the Supreme Court's ruling was decided in the tobacco companies' favor. The plaintiff had sought $48 million in damages, but the jury rejected the allegation that the tobacco companies had engaged in a conspiracy to play down the health risks of smoking.[83]

In early 1994, a group of high-profile lawyers filed a $5 billion class-action lawsuit in New Orleans against the major tobacco companies, charging they manipulated the level of nicotine in cigarettes to cause addiction in smokers. Fifty law firms promised an initial investment of $100,000 each to finance the suit. The suit claimed that three New Orleans area residents became addicted to cigarettes as youngsters and could never shake the habit, but damages were sought for all smokers for the effects of nicotine addiction and the costs of attempting to quit smoking. The suit was filed only days after Congressional hearings on allegations that the tobacco industry intentionally maintained nicotine at addictive levels.[84] In February 1995, a federal judge in New Orleans ruled that the suit could move forward.[85]

Finally, also in 1994, a landmark case was filed in which the industry has to defend itself against an alleged death from secondhand smoke. The case involved an individual who never smoked or drank, but who was exposed to smoke from cigarettes in his barbershop. The case is particularly critical for the tobacco companies because it could be the first in which company documents about research into the health risks and addictiveness of nicotine and dangers of secondhand smoke are used as evidence. The companies claim that it is going to be very difficult to prove that secondhand smoke causes lung cancer. Their defense hinges on discovering whether an individual's lifestyle or genetic makeup could have caused the disease.[86]

OTHER DEVELOPMENTS

Despite heavy lobbying by the tobacco industry, in August 1987, the House supported a bill that would ban smoking on all airline flights of two hours or less. This action applied to about 80 percent of all domestic flights and was a serious blow to the industry. This ban also passed the Senate and went into effect on April 24, 1988, affecting about 13,600 flights daily. Northwest Airlines went even further, banning smoking on all domestic flights. Over 60 percent of the airline's domestic revenue passenger miles involved flights of more than two hours. The ban affected flights that carried an estimated 100,000 passengers daily.[87]

In February 1990, smoking was banned on all domestic flights and on trips to Alaska or Hawaii lasting six hours or less. This ban was an extension of the two-hour ban put into effect three years earlier. The Department of Transportation cited a study that found long-term exposure to tobacco smoke in airplanes represented a significant risk of premature death. This was a risk that no one should be expected to take, especially cabin crew members who were exposed to such smoke more frequently than the average passenger. Several airlines decided to even exceed this ban by offering smokeless flights to overseas destinations. The Association of Flight Attendants said the new policy was welcomed by their membership because they believed it was not unreasonable to demand a healthy workplace and a smoke-free travel environment.[88]

The secretary of Health and Human Services in 1990 stated that smoking costs the nation some $52 billion per year and was the only legal product that could cause death when used as directed. State and local officials initiated more antismoking measures, as more than 500 communities restricted smoking in malls, restaurants, and other public places. At the beginning of 1990, Congress was considering 72 bills to restrict tobacco use in various places. Senator Kennedy proposed a $185 million Center for Tobacco Products that would have broad powers to regulate the industry. Even Greensboro, North Carolina, in the middle of tobacco country, had an ordinance that restricted smoking in retail stores and other public places.[89]

In April 1990, the state of California began a $28.6 million cigarette-bashing advertising campaign that was financed by the state's excise tax on tobacco products, which had been increased by 25 cents through a voter-initiated tax increase passed in the 1988 campaign. One of the major themes of the ad campaign was to attack the alleged deception of the advertising about tobacco products. California's health director stated that the state wanted the public to understand that they have been duped by the tobacco companies and that they wanted to portray a more correct image of what smoking is all about. By 1999, the state hoped to achieve a 75 percent reduction in smoking and reduce the $7.1 billion that smoking costs the state each year in health care and lost productivity.[90]

In 1994, states opened up a new front in the war against cigarettes. The state of Florida introduced legislation that would make it easier for the state to hold the tobacco industry liable for the cost of treating smoking-related ailments. The provision strengthened a little used law that allowed the state to sue the parties who are responsible for Medicaid costs by allowing the state to sue on behalf of an entire class of smokers on Medicaid rather than individual by individual.[91] The law was eventually passed and the state sued for $4.4 billion in direct and indirect costs of tobacco-related illnesses.[92]

Before Florida was able to file its lawsuit, however, the state of Mississippi beat it to the punch by suing the tobacco industry to recover the cost of treating tobacco-related illnesses among welfare recipients. Besides seeking compensation for Medicaid and other welfare costs, the state also wants damages from tobacco companies under legal theories related to unjust enrichment and common-law public nuisance. This was the case in which Jeffrey Wigand, a former employee for Brown & Williamson, was asked to testify as mentioned earlier.[93] These state suits opened up a tangle of legal and ethical questions related to the smoking controversy.

Another issue that surfaced in 1993 revolved around children living in homes where the parents smoked. There were a growing number of cases, mainly involving children in divorce custody proceedings, where judges prohibited parents from smoking around children who were sensitive to tobacco. Some critics called the exposure of children to secondhand smoke in the home the most common form of child abuse in America. A legal journal indicated that at least 11 states had dealt with the issue, almost always siding with the nonsmoking parent. Legal experts predicted there would be a continued surge in suits against smoking parents.[94]

Because of the growing number of lawsuits, particularly the class-action suit moving through the New Orleans federal court, companies that supplied the tobacco industry with many of the components of a cigarette, such as paper and filters, began to cut themselves loose from the industry. They began to worry about being drawn into the legal quagmire surrounding cigarette safety and liability. The state of West Virginia included a supplier in its tobacco litigation when it sued Kimberly-Clark, which supplied paper and other materials for cigarettes, along with several tobacco companies. Subsequently, Manville sued R.J. Reynolds to terminate its contract to supply the company with glass fibers believed to be a component of its new smokeless cigarette. In a similar action, Harley-Davidson sued Loews Corporation's Lorillard unit to break an agreement that puts Harley's name on cigarettes. Harley was afraid that the cigarettes might appeal to kids and draw the motorcycle maker into litigation. Other suppliers considered similar actions.[95]

Even sales of tobacco overseas began to be attacked by antismoking activists. In early 1991, a group called the Asian Consultancy on Tobacco Control met in Hong Kong to design a four-year strategy to combat smoking in the region. One of its goals was to persuade Asian countries to adopt uniform tobacco-control regulations. In Hong Kong, where U.S. companies control 80 percent of the cigarette market, the government banned all radio and television ads for cigarettes. Thailand imposed high import duties on cigarettes, a cumbersome customs-clearance procedure, and a stiff ban on cigarette advertising. The activists admit that in countries such as Japan, South Korea, and the Philippines, where more than 60 percent of the males use the product, they have their work cut out for them, but they quickly note that cigarette use in Japan is dropping about 1 percent a year.[96]

ECONOMIC IMPACTS

The core sectors in the tobacco industry employed more than 414,000 persons during 1983 and paid total compensation of $6.72 billion to these employees. Supplier industries employed about 296,000 workers and paid out almost $7.4 billion in compensation. Combined, these industries employed 710,000 workers and accounted for $31.5 billion of gross national product. Another 1.59 million were employed to produce goods and services in all business sectors to meet the consumption demands of workers and their families who received income from the tobacco industry. This employment accounted for another $50.6 billion of gross national product.[97] In 1990, a Price Waterhouse survey for the Tobacco Institute found that there were some 200,000 tobacco-growing and manufacturing jobs with another 468,000 people dependent on the industry as suppliers, wholesalers, and retailers.[98]

In 1979 alone, Americans spent $21.3 billion for tobacco products, which generated a contribution of $57.6 billion to the gross national product (GNP). Directly and indirectly, tobacco accounted for 2.5 percent of all employment in the private sector. Tobacco also generated $22 billion in taxes for state and federal governments.[99] In 1992, total sales amounted to $10.12 billion with the industry contributing $51 billion to GNP and ultimately employing 681,353 people. The payroll was estimated to be about $16 billion a year, and the tax take for federal, state, and local governments amounted to $18.9 billion.[100]

Any major decline in the tobacco industry would obviously affect the financial fortunes of a great number of people. Many of the people now employed in this industry might be left without jobs, and thus the unemployment rate in the country as a whole would increase. They would have to be retrained, as it is doubtful if many of the skills necessary to produce tobacco products would be readily transferrable to other industries. The entire economy would suffer with the decrease in the gross national product that would result from a decline in the industry.

Advertising expenditures are also affected. With sales slipping, cigarette companies are abandoning national magazine advertising and replacing it with discount coupons, sponsorship of sports events, point-of-sale displays, and more sharply focused promotional devices. By the end of 1986, it was estimated that $50 million in advertising revenue or 12 percent of 1985's $434 million advertising budget would be drained from the country's major magazines. This would be on top of a 12 percent decline in 1985 spending.[101] Cigarette advertising on billboards also fell 7 percent in 1986 to $349.4 million and even bigger cutbacks were predicted for 1987.[102] These trends continued into the 1990s, as more questions about advertising were raised as mentioned earlier.

On the other hand, nonsmokers are questioning the economic burden they are being forced to bear to provide medical care for smoking-induced illnesses. Legal restrictions on smoking are following these changes in attitude. Indirect losses from reduced productivity, earnings lost from excess morbidity, and disability and premature deaths were estimated to cost the country $37 billion annually.[103] The U.S. Public Health Service concluded that within a single year cigarette smoking has caused in excess of 81 million person-days lost from work and 145 million person-days spent ill in bed. Twenty-five per-cent of the disability days for men between the ages of 45 and 64 are associated with cigarette smoking. Women who smoke reportedly spend 17 percent more ill days in bed than women who have never smoked.[104]

> Smoking results in a considerably increased morbidity rate, with its conse-quent loss of working days, absenteeism and excessive demands on medical services, both for primary and for hospital care. The cost to the community of premature death, increased illness, and loss of productive capacity resulting from cigarette smoking is very high in countries where the habit has been common for a long time.[105]

Within the United States, the per capita cost for smoking-related disease is estimated at $454 annually. The total costs of smoking represent approximately 11 percent of the comparable aggregate costs of all illnesses in the United States. In 1976, total out-of-pocket health care costs for smoking-related diseases were estimated at $8.2 billion or approximately 8 percent of all U.S. health care costs.[106] In March 1987, the Surgeon General of the United States, Dr. C. Everett Koop, stated that smoking costs the nation $65 billion a year in health care and lost productivity.[107] In February of the same year, the American Lung Association stated that smoking costs the nation $30.4 billion a year in lost work and productivity and another $23.3 billion a year in medical costs.[108] In 1994, the Congressional Office of Technology Assessment estimated that more than 430,000 Americans die each year of tobacco-related causes costing $68 billion in health care expenses and lost productivity, more than the $46.7 billion that the country spent on tobacco products.[109]

COMPANY RESPONSES

In anticipation of a decline in tobacco sales, major tobacco companies started to diversify. Philip Morris, marketer of Marlboro, the country's biggest-selling cigarette, acquired Miller Brewing Company in 1969, R.J. Reynolds acquired Nabisco, and Philip Morris merged with General Foods. These mergers represent diversifications into product areas or lines that have a close fit with the strong consumer marketing required of cigarettes and utilize the same primary distribution channels. These responses by the tobacco industry, however, have not alleviated the pressures of the antismokers, but rather are more in the nature of defensive strategies designed to help the industry survive in case the tobacco market does collapse at some point.[110]

In response to further developments, tobacco companies continued to consolidate their positions in the market by thinning the ranks of farmers, dealers, distributors, and manufacturing facilities. They saw little hope of reversing the slide in sales of cigarettes and other tobacco products and wanted to get as much out of their existing investment as possible. Thus, they continued the strategies of cost cutting, international expansion, and diversification. They even raised prices despite the damage this does to long-run con-sumption. From 1982 to 1987, cigarette prices increased faster than inflation, and coupled with higher taxes, the average price of a pack of cigarettes nearly doubled over that time period. Thus, the cost of maintaining the habit became more and more expensive.[111]

This contraction of the market produced a more concentrated industry. The two largest producers, Philip Morris and R.J. Reynolds, commanded a 70 percent market share in 1986, as sales fell at a compound annual rate of 6.68 percent and 6.73 percent at American Brands and Liggett, respectively. The smaller companies were hit harder while the larger companies found ways to cope and in the process captured a larger share of the market.[112]

Meanwhile, in September 1987, R.J. Reynolds announced a new cigarette that it claimed was nearly smokeless. The cigarette, which was to be test marketed in 1988, used a carbon tip to heat the tobacco rather than burning it, so that it produced no ash, no odor, and virtually no smoke. Most of the compounds produced by burning tobacco were eliminated or greatly reduced, including those most often associated with health problems.[113] This cigarette was obviously aimed at reducing the problem of passive inhalation of smoke. Critics were skeptical about these claims, pointing out that the new cigarette contains about the same levels of carbon monoxide and nicotine as regular cigarettes. They doubted it would substantially reduce health hazards.[114]

On February 28, 1989, the company pulled its smokeless cigarette, Premier, from the market. According to some estimates, the company had spent more than $300 million on development and marketing of the cigarette. One of the major problems with introducing such a cigarette is that a smokeless brand couldn't be marketed as a safe alternative without refuting the industry's claim that regular smoking has not been proven unhealthy. The cigarette also did not taste right when lighted with a match or even with most lighters. Competitors and marketers were surprised that the company had allowed itself to become so attached to the new product that it became convinced that consumers would buy the cigarette despite obvious problems.[115] Meanwhile, later in the year, Philip Morris began to test a nicotine-free cigarette that it claimed would have all the taste and flavor of standard cigarettes. The company hoped that its new product would have the same consumer appeal as decaffeinated coffee or sugar-free soda.[116]

Five years later, R.J. Reynolds started testing a new version of the smokeless cigarette called the Eclipse, which was supposed to reduce secondhand smoke by 85 to 90 percent. The cigarette used a special charcoal tip, which meant the cigarette didn't burn tobacco at all, eliminating secondhand smoke and also reducing the amount of tar and carcinogenic compounds ingested by the smoker.[117] However, the development of the cigarette was threatened when Manville, the supplier of glass fibers for the product, sued to get out of its contract with Reynolds because of fears about being drawn into litigation, as mentioned in an earlier section.[118]

Philip Morris, the nation's largest cigarette manufacturer, began a counterattack against the nonsmokers and other opponents of smoking. It tried to get those who are against tobacco usage to ease the pressure they are placing on smokers, who are being shunted away from more and more nonsmoking areas and accused of harming other people with their habit. The company argued that if smokers want to enjoy a cigarette, they should be able to do so in peace. It appears to some that the antismoking advocates are making smoking into more of a civil rights issue than a health issue, and smokers believe the whole issue is getting blown out of proportion. Thus, the company published a free quarterly magazine that it sent to smokers and put inserts into cigarette packages urging smokers to rebel against tobacco taxes.[119] However, in the early 1990s, the company backed off from this kind of strategy, partly because of a change of leadership.[120]

In a rather bizarre development, as part of their defense against state lawsuits trying to recover the cost of treating illnesses allegedly caused by smoking, lawyers for the tobacco industry began a campaign of arguing that cigarette smoking has an upside for state revenues. In addition to tax revenues from the sale of cigarettes, other supposed benefits come from income taxes levied on doctors and other health care providers who treat smoking-related illnesses, and federal funding of state health care. They even mentioned that the premature deaths of smokers can save the state money because they spare the taxpayers expenses connected with long-term geriatric care. This comment led one critic to comment that the tobacco companies were trying to claim that they are benefiting society by killing off its citizens. The lawyers for the tobacco industry maintained that they were merely trying to find out exactly how much Mississippi has spent in tax dollars treating tobacco-related illnesses among the poor and elderly to find out how much the sale of cigarettes has allegedly cost state taxpayers.[121]

In another interesting series of events, Philip Morris sued ABC for a story carried by ABC's *Day One* program, which claimed that the tobacco industry adds nicotine to cigarettes to make them more addictive. The show gave the impression, according to Philip Morris, that the industry was "spiking" tobacco with nicotine. The company said it merely "re-adds" or "recombines" nicotine that has been removed and, thus, the impression created by the program was misleading. The suit, for $10 billion would have more than wiped out ABC's 1994 revenue of $6.4 billion.[122] After 17 months of aggressively defending the broadcast, ABC agreed to settle the lawsuit with a public apology stating that it was incorrect to imply that tobacco companies add nicotine from outside sources. In addition to the apology, ABC agreed to pay Philip Morris's legal fees and other litigation expenses.[123]

In a related development, CBS decided to withdraw a planned program on *60 Minutes* featuring Jeffrey Wigand, the former executive of B&W mentioned earlier. The executive had signed a confidentiality agreement with the company barring such media contacts, and CBS lawyers worried about being sued for so-called tortious interference, namely, inducing the source to break the agreement. Ordinarily, news organizations are not vulnerable to such lawsuits, but there may have been an exception when the organization paid the source to break an agreement. While CBS didn't pay for the story, it did agree to pay Mr. Wigand's legal fees and any damages in the event he was sued by his former company.[124]

After *The Wall Street Journal* published many of the damaging allegations against B&W made by Mr. Wigand, CBS began broadcasting some of its interviews with the former executive over its regular news program.[125] CBS News's *60 Minutes* finally broadcast its interview on Sunday evening, February 4, 1996, in which Wigand alleged that the former chairman of B&W lied to Congress when he testified that he thought nicotine is not addictive. The broadcast also contained new footage in which Wigand said he began to carry a handgun because of death threats against him and his family. The report devoted almost equal time to what it called B&W's "full-throated campaign" to discredit the former executive.[126]

The aggressive stance taken by the tobacco companies in these incidents shows how important the issue about the addictive properties of nicotine is to the future of their industry. If enough people come to believe that nicotine is indeed addictive, and that the companies knew this and may have used it to their advantage, support will build for regulation of cigarettes by the FDA, which will subject the companies to a lengthy approval process at best, and perhaps an outright ban on cigarettes should the FDA declare them a threat to public health at worst. Furthermore, if nicotine is believed to be addictive, the warning label defense that the companies have used successfully so far in court cases would be discredited. So in some sense, the tobacco industry is fighting for its life over this issue.

Meanwhile, the industry rolls along. While unit sales dropped about 7 percent in the five years after peaking in 1981, at least three of the nation's six cigarette manufacturers reported record profits in 1986 because of price increases and cost-cutting measures. The companies sought acquisitions to lessen their reliance on tobacco, while implementing manufacturing efficiencies to boost margins in their core business. Twenty years ago, cigarette-rolling machines were capable of producing 1,200 cigarettes per minute; today's new machines have the capability to produce 8,000 cigarettes per minute.[127]

After slashing the price of Marlboros by 40 cents a pack in 1993 to staunch the brand's market share deterioration, nine months later its market share rebounded to 25 percent of the U.S. market.[128] Because of these gains and strong international profits, the company reported better than expected results for the 1994 first quarter.[129] Later in the year, however, the company faced pressure from its board and some shareholders to split the company into separate food and tobacco businesses in order to boost its stock price.[130] R.J. Reynolds received similar pressure to spin off its Nabisco unit as a separate business. In spite of these problems, the tobacco companies were expected to report earnings gains for the second quarter of 1995, and Philip Morris's earnings rose 17 percent in the third quarter as its cigarettes racked up gains around the world.[131]

The companies were benefiting from the increasing popularity of American brands in international markets, where unit volume increased at roughly 5 percent a year.[132] Markets in Russia and Eastern Europe opened up because of changes in that part of the world. Potential smokers comprise more than one half the world's population, and much of this potential is in Third World countries where governments are not so quick to spend already scarce funds on antismoking campaigns and are reluctant to give up tax revenues from tobacco sales. Cigarette manufacturers are not required to provide warning labels on products exported outside the United States unless they are going to a U.S. military base.[133]

CONCLUSION

The primary factor that initiated this war over cigarettes and the battle between smokers and nonsmokers was the medical discoveries that smoking did indeed entail certain health risks for everyone exposed to cigarette smoke. This caused a division between those who smoked and those who wanted it eliminated for health reasons. Despite this issue, the tobacco industry continues to maintain a profitable business and promote the use of cigarettes and other tobacco products, acting as if no serious problem exists. Meanwhile, the antismoking campaign persists and continues to cause problems for the tobacco industry on all the fronts mentioned previously.

The industry uses two main arguments in the fight against the antismoking campaign. The first argument is that everyone has had fair warning about the possible negative health effects of smoking and the second is that the link to adverse health effects has not been scientifically established. Mr. John Strauch, an attorney for R.J. Reynolds, says: "We've got to draw the line somewhere on what we're going to require from people in the way of accountability for their own choices." The industry's first line of defense, he says, is this issue of personal responsibility.[134]

Thus, the war continues as legal and medical coalitions form to pool information, strategies, theories, and money. There are many cases pending against the tobacco industry, including the massive class-action suit in New Orleans. A single defeat could lead to an avalanche of costly lawsuits that could swamp the companies in litigation costs even if they win most of them.[135] Yet, tobacco continues to be a profitable product and the companies continue aggressive efforts to defend their product and keep an industry that provides jobs and income for many people viable.

While there are so many ethical issues in this controversy that is impossible to list them all, perhaps a few key issues can be identified. In a society that values freedom so highly, to what extent should steps be taken to prevent the spread of harmful substances throughout the community? To what extent should individuals be allowed to engage in dangerous self-destructive behavior that entails personal, social, and economic consequences for other people? People's rights are affected by the steps that are taken to deal with this issue. Nonsmokers want a healthier environment free from cigarette smoke. They want specific areas designated for them where smoking is prohibited. Smokers, on the other hand, resent their freedom being restricted in this manner, and feel it is unfair and unjust to be allowed to smoke in only designated areas of public places. Smokers' preferences are being shunned and they are now considered, in a manner of speaking, to be second-class citizens. Their rights are no longer considered to be so important.

Another complaint brought by nonsmokers is that the tobacco industry, which markets one of the most dangerous products sold in the United States, is the only industry that has been sheltered from product liability. It has been suggested that the tobacco industry's failure to warn the public of the dangers that smoking entails is an "unparalleled display of corporate indifference" and exposes the tobacco industry to civil liability.[136] Because of this problem, it has been suggested that the tobacco industry be made financially liable to nonsmokers who are injured or killed in cigarette-caused fires in hotels, hospitals, airplanes, and other public places. Health insurance members also insist that smokers pay a fair share of extra tobacco-related health care expenses, and that smokers make up for the extra costs of Medicare, Medicaid, and veterans' benefits inflicted upon nonsmokers.[137]

The future of the tobacco industry depends mainly on what the courts will decide in the many product liability suits filed against major tobacco companies. Many analysts believe that no strong precedent has been set in the cases that have been decided thus far, and believe that pending cases will provide crucial tests for the industry. The industry's future also depends on how the general public will respond to new research findings of the hazards of smoking, and, most importantly, the hazards of inhaling secondary smoke and the alleged addictive properties of nicotine.

Nonetheless, a former Surgeon General of the United States predicted that for all its enormous economic power, the cigarette industry will virtually disappear over the next 20 years. The tobacco industry is currently a formidable adversary and is the biggest obstacle to the antismoking campaign in this country. But as per capita cigarette consumption continues to decline, the former Surgeon General claimed that the industry will become less and less formidable with every tomorrow.[138] Thus, the prospect of a relatively smoke-free society is a real one and the war will continue for the foreseeable future.

1. Can you distinguish between facts and values in this case? What are the facts of the situation regarding the health effects of cigarette smoking? How do you account for the differences between the antismoking movement and the tobacco industry regarding the facts about cigarette smoking? Are these differences simply differences in values rather than facts? Are changing values responsible for the plight of the industry?

2. How would you go about establishing the facts about cigarette smoking and its health effects? Is statistical evidence conclusive in showing the relationship between health

problems and smoking? What kind of cause-and-effect relationship would be conclusive in proving the facts regarding smoking and health problems such as cancer or lung diseases? Would these facts be acceptable to the Tobacco Institute?

3. Are cigarettes an ethical product? If not, are the people who work in this industry unethical people? If so, how does smoking contribute to the welfare of people and promote human fulfillment? Why do people smoke? What does the promotion of smoking say about the values of the industry? What values do the antismoking advocates hold?

4. Would a benefit-cost analysis help in making decisions about the advertising of tobacco products and the banning of smoking in public places? Where would values enter into these calculations? Is benefit-cost analysis a useful decision-making tool in these complex situations? Why or why not?

5. What are the rights of smokers and nonsmokers with regard to the provision of non-smoking areas or the outright banning of smoking in public places? Are companies that ban smoking in their facilities guilty of discrimination? Are they violating any laws with regard to the rights of smokers? What is the future likely to hold with respect to the question of the rights of smokers versus nonsmokers?

6. Do tobacco companies have the right to advertise their product? Was the banning of such ads from television an unethical action? Why or why not? Should advertising of tobacco products be banned entirely? Is this an issue of free speech or is it one of responsibility? What ethical criteria should take precedence in this decision?

[1] Linda Himelstein and Laura Zinn, "Tobacco: Does It Have a Future?" *Business Week,* July 4, 1994, pp. 24–29.

[2] John Merwin, "Tobacco," *Forbes,* January 2, 1984, p. 222. See also "U.S. Market for Smoking Tobacco Declines," *Tabak Journal International,* December 1985, p. 463.

[3] Jonathan E. Fielding, "Smoking: Health Effects and Control," *The New England Journal of Medicine,* Vol. 313, no. 8 (August 1985), p. 491. In 1993, the U.S. Centers for Disease Control linked 434,000 deaths to smoking. See Alix M. Freedman and Laurie P. Cohen, "Smoke and Mirrors: How Cigarette Makers Keep Health Question 'Open' Year After Year," *The Wall Street Journal,* February 11, 1993, p. A1. See also Bob Geiger, "Study: Tobacco Is Leading Killer of Americans," *Times-Picayune,* November 10, 1993, p. A-5.

[4] American Cancer Society, *Dangers of Smoking, Benefits of Quitting & Relative Risks of Reduced Exposure,* Revised Edition (New York: American Cancer Society, Inc., 1980), p. 5. In 1992, a study published in a British medical journal claimed that one in five people in industrialized countries will die from smoking cigarettes, more than the entire population of the United States in that year. See Randi Hutter Epstein, "Half of All Smokers May Die from It, Study Says," *Times-Picayune,* May 22, 1992, p. A-7.

[5] Irvin Molotsky, "Congress Votes Stiffer Warnings of Tobacco Risk," *The New York Times,* September 27, 1984, p. A-1. Copyright 1984 by The New York Times Company. Reprinted by permission.

[6] "Controlling the Smoking Epidemic," *Report of the WHO Expert Committee on Smoking Control,* Technical Report Series 636, World Health Organization, Geneva, 1979, p. 9.

[7] American Cancer Society, *Dangers of Smoking,* p. 11.

[8] Fielding, "Smoking: Health Effects and Control," p. 491.

[9] David Holzman, "Where the Smoke Goes," *The Washington Post,* March 20, 1985, p. 10.

[10] "Smoking Called Biggest Health Threat to Women," *Dallas Times Herald,* November 11, 1985, p. A-1. See also Bill Sloan, "Women and Smoking: Have They Come a Long Way?" *Times-Picayune,* January 10, 1991, p. E-1. In 1992, the World Health Organization predicted that the

number of women killed each year by cigarettes will double to more than 1 million in the next 30 years. See Clare Nullis, "Cigarette Deaths Among Women to Double," *Times-Picayune,* April 2, 1992, p. A-24.

[11] "Kids Lighting Up, Living with Smoke," *Times-Picayune,* January 17, 1994, p. A-2.

[12] Barri Bronston, "Nico-Teens," *Times-Picayune,* March 14, 1994, p. C-1.

[13] Laurie McGinley and Rick Wartzman, "Clinton Backs Action to Curb Teen Smoking," *The Wall Street Journal,* July 14, 1995, p. A3. See also Bob Cohn and Bill Turque, "Firing Up the Politics of Teen Smoking," *Newsweek,* August 21, 1995, pp. 25–26.

[14] Bella Stumbo, "Where There's Smoke: On the Front Line with the Tobacco Lobby," *Los Angeles Times Magazine,* August 24, 1986, p. 14.

[15] "Mass Tort Litigation Predicted: Legal Attack on Tobacco Flares," *American Medical News,* September 20, 1985, p. 30.

[16] Stumbo, "Where There's Smoke," pp. 12–13.

[17] "Effects of 'Passive Smoking' Lead Nonsmokers to Step Up Campaign," *Journal of the American Medical Association,* Vol. 253, no. 20 (May 1985), pp. 29–37.

[18] Gayle Young, "Nicotine a Problem in Passive Smoking," United Press International, April 14, 1986.

[19] "Restrict Smoking in Public Places?" *U.S. News and World Report,* July 21, 1986, p. 65.

[20] Alan L. Otten, "Passive Smoking Heightens Health Risks for Nonsmokers, a Federal Study Says," *The Wall Street Journal,* November 17, 1986, p. 68.

[21] "Where There's Smoke," *Time,* February 23, 1987, p. 22.

[22] John Schwartz, "Smoking Ban Will Save Lives, Money, Study Says," *Times-Picayune,* April 22, 1994, p. A-12.

[23] Rose Gutfeld, "Tougher Rules Urged on Smoking in the Workplace," *The Wall Street Journal,* June 26, 1990, p. B4.

[24] John Cloud, "Second-Hand Smoke from Tobacco Called Carcinogen by Panel," *The Wall Street Journal,* July 23, 1992, p. A3. See also Timothy Noah, "EPA Declares 'Passive' Smoke a Human Carcinogen," *The Wall Street Journal,* January 6, 1993, p. B1.

[25] Richard Keil, "Doctors Target Passive Smoking," *Times-Picayune,* June 11, 1992, p. A-6.

[26] Ibid. See also Robert J. Barro, "Send Regulations Up in Smoke," *The Wall Street Journal,* June 3, 1994, p. A10.

[27] Eben Shapiro, "Passive-Smoke Ruling Sparks Industry Suit," *The Wall Street Journal,* June 23, 1993, p. B1.

[28] Paul Raeburn, "Secondhand Smoke May Kill 47,000 This Year," *Times-Picayune,* August 2, 1994, p. A-3.

[29] "Why It's So Hard to Quit Smoking," *Time,* May 30, 1988, p. 56. See also Ed Bean, "Surgeon General's Stature Is Likely to Add Force to Report on Smoking as Addiction," *The Wall Street Journal,* May 13, 1988, p. 17.

[30] Edwin Chen, "Evidence of Tobacco Addiction Could Lead to Labeling as Drug," *Times-Picayune,* February 26, 1994, p. A-1. See also Angela Shah, "FDA Cites Evidence of Cigarette Makers Keeping Nicotine at Addictive Levels," *The Wall Street Journal,* February 28, 1994, p. B4.

[31] Lauran Neergarrd, "Secret Chemicals in Cigarettes Listed," *Times-Picayune,* April 14, 1994, p. A-1; Eben Shapiro, "Firms Release Cigarette-Ingredients List as Disclosure Raises Fresh Concerns," *The Wall Street Journal,* April 14, 1994, p. B3.

[32] Eben Shapiro, "Tobacco Executives Tell Panel Nicotine Is Not Addictive," *The Wall Street Journal,* April 15, 1994, p. A4.

[33] Massimo Calabresi, et al., "The Butt Stops Here," *Time,* April 18, 1994, pp. 58–64.

[34] "Scientists: Nicotine Study Was Quashed," *Times-Picayune,* April 29, 1994, p. A-12.

[35] Eben Shapiro, "Disclosure of Smoking's Harm Was Known Seen Turning Up Heat on Tobacco Firms," *The Wall Street Journal,* May 9, 1994, p. A4.

[36] Jerry E. Bishop, "AMA Urges FDA Regulation of Tobacco," *The Wall Street Journal,* July 14, 1995, p. B3.

[37] "Nicotine Attack: Cigarette Regulation Is Formally Proposed: Industry Sues to Halt It," *The Wall Street Journal,* August 11, 1995, p. A1.

[38] Alix M. Freeman, "The Deposition: Cigarette Defector Says CEO Lied to Congress About View of Nicotine," *The Wall Street Journal,* January 26, 1996, p. A1.

[39] "Where There's Smoke," p. 23.

[40] Edward Felsenthal, "EPA Report Sparks Antismoking Plans," *The Wall Street Journal,* January 7, 1993, p. B3.

[41] "A Burning Issue on the Job and Off," *Newsweek,* January 13, 1986, p. 9.

[42] Mark Weaver and Nora Zamichow, "Company Tells Smokers: Quit or Be Fired," *Dallas Times Herald,* January 21, 1987, p. A-1.

[43] "Company to Relax Plan That Would Ban Smokers," *Dallas Times Herald,* January 28, 1987, p. A-3.

[44] Alix M. Freedman, "Harmful Habit: Cigarette Smoking Is Growing Hazardous to Careers in Business," *The Wall Street Journal,* April 23, 1987, p. 1.

[45] "Thou Shalt Not Smoke," *Time,* May 18, 1987, p. 59.

[46] Jube Shirver, Jr., "Smoking: A Burning Work Issue." *Los Angeles Times,* November 21, 1985, p. 1.

[47] Junda Woo, "Employers Fume Over New Legislation Barring Discrimination Against Smokers," *The Wall Street Journal,* June 4, 1993, p. B1.

[48] Bob Geiger, "No-Smoke Workplace Sought," *Times-Picayune,* March 26, 1994, p. A-1.

[49] Daniel Pearl, "OSHA Says Workplace Smoking Rules Won't Apply to Private Homes, Vehicles," *The Wall Street Journal,* September 20, 1994, p. A22.

[50] "Skimming Cream from the Crop," *Advertising Age,* January 31, 1983, p. M-11.

[51] Joe B. Tye, "Cigarette Ads Reveal a History of Deceit," *The Wall Street Journal,* August 5, 1986, p. 26.

[52] Ibid.

[53] Joe B. Tye, "Cigarette Marketing: Ethical Conservatism or Corporate Violence?" *New York State Journal of Medicine,* July 1985, p. 324.

[54] Tye, "Cigarette Ads," p. 26.

[55] "Setting Off the Smoke Alarm," *Time,* December 23, 1985, p. 56.

[56] "AMA Calls for Ban on Tobacco Products Ads," *Dallas Times Herald,* December 11, 1985, p. A-1.

[57] "Setting Off the Smoke Alarm," p. 56.

[58] The Supreme Court issued a ruling in 1986 that seems to support the AMA position that a ban on cigarette advertising is constitutional. In a 5–4 ruling, the Court upheld a Puerto Rico ban on gambling advertisements, stating that such a ban does not violate the First Amendment protections for commercial speech. The majority opinion stated that states may ban advertising of products and services that are legal to sell, so long as the legislature also has the power to ban their sale outright. See "Supreme Court: Ad ban does not violate First Amendment speech protections," *American Medical News,* July 18, 1986, pp. 2, 34.

[59] John Riley, "Smoking Suits Dealt a Setback," *The National Law Journal,* April 21, 1986, p. 45. See also Kathleen Clute, "Cigarette Health Warnings Protect Tobacco Companies," United Press International, April 11, 1986.

[60] M. F. Goldsmith, "Tobacco-Addiction Death Link Shown But Labels Don't Tell It," *Journal of the American Medical Association,* February 1986, pp. 997–998.

[61] "4 Cig Warning Backed," *The New York Times,* May 18, 1984, p. A-10.

[62] Molotsky, "Congress Votes Stiffer Warnings," p. A-1.

[63] Robert Doherty, "Attack on Tax Deduction for Tobacco Advertising," United Press International, February 20, 1986.

[64] James R. Schiffman, "Uptown's Fall Bodes Ill for Niche Brands," *The Wall Street Journal,* January 22, 1990, p. B1.

[65] Kathleen Deveny, "Joe Camel Ads Reach Children, Research Finds," *The Wall Street Journal,* December 11, 1991, p. B1; "Cigarette Study: Cartoon Camel Ads Enticing Children," *Times-Picayune,* December 11, 1991, p. C-1.

[66] Maria Mallory, "That's One Angry Camel," *Business Week,* March 7, 1994, pp. 94–95.

[67] Kevin Goldman, "A Stable of Females Has Joined Joe Camel in Controversial Cigarette Ad Campaign," *The Wall Street Journal,* February 18, 1994, p. B1.

[68] Jane E. Brody, "Study: Tobacco Ads Linked to Teen Smoking," *Times-Picayune,* February 23, 1994, p. A-8.

[69] Suein L. Hwang, "Philip Morris Co. Unveils Plan Aimed at Curbing Cigarette Smoking by Minors," *The Wall Street Journal,* June 28, 1995, p. A3.

[70] Suein L. Hwang, "Joe Camel Is Missing, But Who's Walking Miles to Find Him?" *The Wall Street Journal,* July 14, 1995, p. A1.

[71] Timothy Noah, "Tobacco-Marketing Rules Anger Many Non-Tobacco Industries," *The Wall Street Journal,* October 17, 1995, p. B1.

[72] Wade Lambert and Milo Geyelin, "FDA's Planned Tobacco-Ad Rules Spur Suits Over Agency's Powers," *The Wall Street Journal,* August 14, 1995, p. B6.

[73] "A Jury Takes Tobacco Companies Off the Hook—For Now," *Business Week,* January 13, 1986, p. 36.

[74] Ed Bean, "Cigarette-Pack Warnings Protect Firms in Liability Suits, Appeals Court Rules," *The Wall Street Journal,* April 10, 1986, p. 2.

[75] "High Court: Warning Labels Cut Tobacco Firms' Liability," *Dallas Times Herald,* January 13, 1987, p. A-1.

[76] Patricia Bellew Gray, "Legal Warfare: Tobacco Firms Defend Smoker Liability Suits with Heavy Artillery," *The Wall Street Journal,* April 29, 1987, p. 1.

[77] Stephen Koepp, "Tobacco's First Loss," *Time,* June 27, 1988, p. 48.

[78] Ibid., pp. 48–49.

[79] Laurie P. Cohen, "American Brands Unit Wasn't Liable for Smoker's Death, Federal Jury Rules," *The Wall Street Journal,* June 27, 1988, p. 6.

[80] Stephen Wermiel, "Supreme Court Will Consider Tobacco Issue," *The Wall Street Journal,* March 26, 1991, p. A3.

[81] Walecia Konrad, "This Decision May Be Hazardous to Tobacco's Health," *Business Week,* July 6, 1992, p. 33.

[82] Paul Raeburn, "Flight Attendants Seek $5 Billion in Tobacco Suit," *Times-Picayune,* November 1, 1991, p. A-12.

[83] Junda Woo, "Jury Rejects Claim That Tobacco Firms Conspired to Play Down Risks of Smoking," *The Wall Street Journal,* February 1, 1993, p. B5.

[84] Mark Schleifstein, "Suit: Tobacco Companies Push, Cause Addiction," *Times-Picayune,* March 31, 1994, p. B-2; Eben Shapiro, "A Crafty Lawyer Turns Up the Heat on Tobacco," *The Wall Street Journal,* May 19, 1994, p. B1.

[85] Bill Veolker, "Tobacco Class Action OK'd," *Times-Picayune,* February 18, 1995, p. A-1; Suein L. Hwang and Milo Geyelin, "Tobacco Industry, Plaintiffs Square Off as Cigarette Suit Is Ruled Class Action," *The Wall Street Journal,* February 21, 1995, p. A2.

[86] David Greising, "Where There's Secondhand Smoke . . . ," *Business Week,* August 8, 1994, pp. 43–44.

[87] Judith Valente, "Northwest Plans Smoking Ban on U.S. Flights," *The Wall Street Journal,* March 24, 1988, p. 29; David Webb, "Up in Smoke: Airlines Banning Cigarettes Today," *Dallas Times Herald,* April 24, 1988, p. A-1.

[88] "Smoking Light Goes Out for Domestic Flights," *Times-Picayune,* February 25, 1990, p. A-10.

[89] John E. Gallagher, "Under Fire from All Sides," *Time,* March 5, 1990, p. 41.

[90] Sonia L. Nazario, "California Ads Attack Cigarettes," *The Wall Street Journal,* April 11, 1990, p. B1. A study released in early 1992 claimed that the California campaign reduced smoking among California adults by 17 percent over a three-year period. Ron Winslow, "California Push to Cut Smoking Seen as Success," *The Wall Street Journal,* January 15, 1992, p. B1. See also "No-smoking Campaign Effective," *Times-Picayune,* March 24, 1994, p. A-14.

[91] Junda Woo, "Tobacco Firms Face Greater Health Liability," *The Wall Street Journal,* May 3, 1994, p. A3.

[92] Milo Geyelin, "Tobacco Companies Are Set Back by Actions in Florida, Mississippi," *The Wall Street Journal,* February 22, 1995, p. B12.

[93] Junda Woo, "Mississippi Wants Tobacco Firm to Pay Its Cost of Treating Welfare Recipients," *The Wall Street Journal,* May 24, 1994, p. A2.

[94] Andrea Sachs, "Home Smoke-Free Home," *Time,* October 25, 1993, p. 56.

[95] Suein L. Hwang and Yumiko Ono, "Companies Crush Out Ties to Cigarettes," *The Wall Street Journal,* April 3, 1995, p. B1. See also Stephanie Anderson Forest and Maria Mallory, "Nicotine Stains on Kimberly-Clark?" *Business Week,* December 19, 1994, pp. 117–118.

[96] Pete Engardio, "Asia: A New Front in the War on Smoking," *Business Week,* February 25, 1991, p. 66.

[97] "The Economic Impact of the Tobacco Industry in the United States Economy in 1983," *Chase Econometrics Letter: Business Trends Forecaster,* Vol. 1 (Philadelphia: Chase Econometrics, 1983), p. 179.

[98] Yumiko Ono, "If Cigarette Industry Coughs, Remote Areas Expect to Catch Cold," *The Wall Street Journal,* October 26, 1995, p. A1.

[99] "Skimming Cream from the Crop," *Advertising Age,* January 31, 1983, p. M-11.

[100] Charles M. Madigan, "Tobacco: Government Hooked on Tax Revenue," *Times-Picayune,* April 3, 1994, p. A-16.

[101] "Good-bye to the Marlboro Man," *Forbes,* June 2, 1986, pp. 207–208.

[102] Ronald Alsop, "Billboard Firms Lure New Ads as Tobacco, Liquor Sales Slide," *The Wall Street Journal,* May 7, 1987, p. 29.

[103] Fielding, "Smoking: Health Effects and Control," p. 491.

[104] American Cancer Society, *Dangers of Smoking,* p. 14.

[105] "Controlling the Smoking Epidemic," WHO, p. 10.

[106] American Cancer Society, *Dangers of Smoking,* p. 62.

[107] Sharon Eglebor, "Koop: Smoking Costs Too High," *Dallas Times Herald,* March 28, 1987, p. A-1.

[108] "Cigarette Smoking Kills 350,000 in U.S. a Year, Report Says," *Dallas Times Herald,* February 21, 1987, p. A-1.

[109] John Carey, "It's Time for Regulators to Stop Blowing Smoke," *Business Week,* March 14, 1994, p. 34.

[110] "Tobacco Takes a New Road," *Time,* November 18, 1985, pp. 70–71.

[111] "Big Tobacco's Fortunes Are Withering in the Heat," *Business Week,* July 27, 1987, p. 47.

[112] Ibid., p. 48. See also "American Brands Is Breaking Its Cigarette Habit," *Business Week,* September 14, 1987, pp. 86–94.

[113] Carlos Byars, "Near-Smokeless, Odorless Cigarette Is Developed," *The Houston Chronicle,* September 15, 1987, p. 1–1.

[114] Ed Bean, "RJR's New Cigarette May Be 'Clean' But Specialists Say It Still Isn't Safe," *The Wall Street Journal,* September 15, 1987, p. 7. See also John Heylar, "RJR Nabisco Inc. Is Expected to Unveil New 'Smokeless' Cigarette to Market Soon," *The Wall Street Journal,* September 14, 1987, p. 4; Ed Bean, "Anti-Smoking Forces Set Strategy to Fight 'Smokeless' Cigarettes," *The Wall Street Journal,* March 2, 1988, p. 25.

[115] Betsy Morris and Peter Waldman, "The Death of Premier," *The Wall Street Journal,* March 10, 1989, p. B1.

[116] Alix M. Freedman, "Philip Morris Begins Testing Nicotine-Free Cigarette," *The Wall Street Journal,* May 31, 1989, p. B1.

[117] Suein L. Hwang and Alix M. Freedman, "RJR Is Testing a 'Smokeless Cigarette' Five Years After Similar Product Failed," *The Wall Street Journal,* November 28, 1994, p. A5.

[118] Maria Mallory, "For Reynolds, Where There's Smokeless . . ." *Business Week,* March 27, 1995, p. 39.

[119] Trish Hall, "Smoking Guns: Philip Morris, Seeking to Turn Tide, Attacks Cigarettes' Opponents," *The Wall Street Journal,* February 4, 1986, p. 1. See also "Breathing Fire at the Antismoking Campaign," *Business Week,* August 19, 1985, pp. 55–56; Robert Bruce Slater, "One Magazine We Can Do Without," *Business and Society Review,* no. 60 (Winter 1987), pp. 45–47.

[120] Joanne Lipman, "Philip Morris Curtails Defense of Smoking," *The Wall Street Journal,* May 7, 1992, p. B1.

[121] Milo Geyelin, "Tobacco Lawyers Cite Tax Benefits of Smoking, Such as Early Deaths," *The Wall Street Journal,* September 6, 1995, p. B8.

[122] Alix M. Freedman and Amy Stevens, "Philip Morris Is Putting TV Journalism on Trial in Its Suit Against ABC," *The Wall Street Journal,* May 23, 1995, p. A1.

[123] Alix M. Freedman and Elizabeth Jensen, "ABC Agrees to Run On-Air Apology to Settle Philip Morris Libel Lawsuit," *The Wall Street Journal,* August 23, 1995, p. B10.

[124] Alix M. Freedman, Elizabeth Jensen, and Amy Stevens, "CBS Legal Guarantees to '60 Minutes' Source Muddy Tobacco Story," *The Wall Street Journal,* November 16, 1995, p. A1.

[125] Elizabeth Jensen and Suein L. Hwang, "CBS Airs Some of Wigand's Interviews, Accusing Tobacco Firm, Its Ex-Chief," *The Wall Street Journal,* January 29, 1996, p. B5.

[126] Scott Williams, "Tobacco Whistle-Blower Says He Fears for His Life," *Times-Picayune,* February 5, 1996, p. A-3.

[127] "Tobacco Company Profits Just Won't Quit," *Business Week,* December 22, 1986, pp. 66–67.

[128] Laura Zinn, "The Smoke Clears at Marlboro," *Business Week,* January 31, 1994, pp. 76–77.

[129] Eben Shapiro, "Philip Morris's 1st-Quarter Earnings Outperformed Analysts' Expectations," *The Wall Street Journal,* April 20, 1994, p. A8.

[130] Eben Shapiro and Gautam Naik, "Philip Morris Board Considers Splitting Lines," *The Wall Street Journal,* April 15, 1994, p. A4. See also Laura Zinn, "A Rumor of War in the Philip Morris Boardroom," *Business Week,* June 13, 1994, p. 40.

[131] Meera Somasundaram, "Tobacco Companies Expect to Report Earnings Gains for the Second Quarter," *The Wall Street Journal,* July 17, 1995, p. B8; Suein L. Hwang, "Philip Morris's Earnings Rose 17% in 3rd Period on Growth in Cigarettes," *The Wall Street Journal,* October 18, 1995, p. A12.

[132] "Tobacco Company Profits Just Won't Quit," pp. 66–67.

[133] American Cancer Society, *Dangers of Smoking,* p. 63.

[134] Ed Bean, "Tobacco Industry's Court Victories Fail to Slow Product-Liability Suits," *The Wall Street Journal,* January 30, 1986, p. 29.

[135] William P. Barrett, "Smoldering Lawsuits: Smokers Want Tobacco Companies to Pay for Their Illnesses," *Dallas Times Herald,* September 8, 1985, p. A-1.

[136] R. Roemer, "Combating the Smoking Epidemic: Why Legislation," *Proceedings of the Fifth World Conference on Smoking and Health,* Vol. 1, W. F. Forbes, R. C. Frecker, and D. Nostbakken, eds. (Canada: Canadian Council on Smoking and Health, 1983), pp. 593–602.

[137] D. W. Garner, "The Legal Implications of Cigarette Smoking," *Proceedings of the Fifth World Conference on Smoking and Health,* Vol. 1, W. F. Forbes, R. C. Frecker, and D. Nostbakken, eds. (Canada: Canadian Council on Smoking and Health, 1983), pp. 523–532.

[138] Sharon Eglebor, "Koop: Smoking Costs Too High," p. A-1.

The Generic Drug Scandal

Drug regulation has been in effect since 1962 when the Harris-Kefauver amendments to the Food and Drug Act were passed. These amendments required extensive testing of new drugs for safety and efficacy, and had a significant impact on the industry a few years after passage. The average time required for clinical study and agency approval increased from 2.7 years in 1966 to 6.6 years in 1973. The number of applications for clinical study fell to 41 in 1973, down from 85 a decade earlier. The number of new drugs approved averaged 17 per year in the postregulation period, compared with more than three times that amount in the five years before the Harris-Kefauver amendments were passed.[1]

The rate of return and expenditures on research and development in the drug industry plummeted to about one-third the 1960 level. Drug companies have cut back on basic research—the discovery of new and better drugs—and have put more money into product development. During the ten-year period from 1970 to 1980, domestic research and development expenditures grew at an annual rate of only 0.3 percent, adjusted for inflation, while expenditures by U.S. companies abroad rose from 7.5 percent of total research and development expenditures in 1965 to 19 percent in 1980.[2]

Finally, from 1960 to 1977, the cost of discovering and developing a new drug increased eighteenfold. These costs, half of which have been attributed to drug regulation, forced many smaller companies out of the market. Between 1957 and 1961, the four largest drug companies' share of innovational output amounted to 24 percent of total industry output. After the amendments, between 1967 and 1971, the share of the four largest companies increased to 48.7 percent.[3] The number of independent firms introducing new chemical entities declined from 51 (1954 to 1958) to 41 (1963 to 1967), and finally to 36 (1976 to 1980).[4]

> There thus has been a decline in annual new drug introductions accompanied by strong upward trends in the costs, times, and risks associated with discovering and developing new drugs. In economists' terminology, there has been a shift in the "production function" for new drug innovation in the direction of lower R and D productivity–that is to say, fewer drug introductions are emanating from larger resource commitments by the industry.[5]

Responsibility for drug regulation is carried out by the Food and Drug Administration (FDA), more specifically the Bureau of Drugs, which administers rigid premarket testing procedures. No new drug can be marketed in the United States until teams of physicians, pharmacists, chemists, and statisticians from the Bureau of Drugs have completed a thorough assessment. Firms wanting to place a new drug on the market must develop data to show that it is safe and effective and must also prove to the bureau's satisfaction that there are adequate controls to ensure proper identification, quality, purity, and strength of the new drug. The FDA also requires pharmaceutical companies to monitor usage and side effects of drugs after they have been placed on the market. This procedure strengthens the FDA's "postmarketing surveillance" system to discover defective products, to have them removed from commercial channels, and to detect previously unsuspected adverse side effects.[6]

The drug approval process used by the FDA proceeds in three phases. In Phase I, a new drug is tested to assess toxicity and determine how a drug is metabolized in the human body. These studies typically involve 10 to 50 healthy subjects and are generally completed in a few months. In Phase II, a drug is administered for the first time to patients with the condition it is intended to treat. These studies are usually randomized controlled trials involving 50 to 200 subjects and take from several months to two years to complete. In Phase III, studies typically involve 200 to 1,000 patients, although some studies can require as many as several thousand people. Many of the Phase III studies take from three to four years.[7]

Critics of drug regulation argue that this process, because it denies Americans the benefit of new drugs that are available in foreign countries having a shorter approval process, adversely affects rather than enhances the health of the American people. The Food and Drug Act requires a "substantial evidence" standard in demonstrating that a drug will work before it allows that drug on the market. The law defines substantial evidence as "adequate and well-controlled investigations, including clinical investigations, by experts . . . on the basis of which it could fairly and responsibly be concluded by such experts that the drug will have the effect" it claims. This definition leaves the FDA little room to approve drugs that are probably effective and does not allow them to consider the needs of patients who have no adequate alternative drugs available.[8]

Supporters of the FDA argue that approval delays actually protect Americans against possibly hazardous drugs until the FDA is satisfied they are safe. The FDA claims that the decline in drug innovation has been largely confined to marginal drugs and is due more to depletion of research opportunities than to regulation.[9] The drug regulatory apparatus in this country was developed as a response to the Thalidomide tragedy in Europe, which caused a rash of birth defects. Even though the drug had not been approved in the United States, the scandal provided the political impetus for the 1962 amendments which established the current process for drug approval.

Proposals have been made to speed up the process. Some proposals would give the government power to approve breakthrough drugs before testing on them was completed. This approval could be granted in cases where lack of the drug could result in severe, life-threatening illness. Another proposal would allow approval of certain drugs for limited distribution, say only from a hospital or from people with special training and experience. Such limits could be used on a drug that otherwise would have been denied approval. Other proposals would permit approval of new drugs based solely on foreign data, if the tests are well conducted and done by recognized researchers.

GENERIC DRUGS

Generic drugs have proven to be the right prescription for rising health care costs in the United States over the past decade. In 1988, sales of generics totaled $6.8 billion, and represented 29 percent of the total drug market.[10] These drugs are medically comparable imitations of brand-name drugs that sell for much less. The generic drug industry got a boost in 1984 when Congress made the FDA's approval process for generic drugs more efficient. Since then, the generic drug market has grown steadily at the expense of brand-name pharmaceutical companies.[11] The segment of the U.S. prescription market accounted for by generics rose from 2 percent in 1982 to 33 percent in 1989. The use of generics is saving U.S. consumers $7 billion annually.[12]

There are about 200 U.S. companies producing generic drugs for the market. Most are privately held companies with less than $1 million in annual sales. However, there are some large companies with annual sales of over $100 million, including Mylan Laboratories, Bolar Pharmaceutical, and Rugby Laboratories.[13]

Generic drug sales are predicted to rise from the 1986 level of $5 billion to $15 to $17 billion by 1995. There are several reasons for this expected increase. First, according to New York market research firm Frost & Sullivan, about 200 brand-name drugs worth approximately $14 billion in sales, including some of the industry's best sellers, will come off patent protection by 1995. All of these drugs will be susceptible to competition from generic substitutes.[14] For this reason, the generic drug industry is about to enter a tremendous growth period. Industry analyst Leonard S. Yaffe foresees phenomenal growth for the industry from 1991 to 1995.[15]

Second, the generic drug industry also benefits from the expanded use of health maintenance organizations (HMOs) which generally require pharmacies to dispense generic drugs to member patients unless a physician has instructed otherwise. Third, export demand for generics is growing rapidly. Some consultants believed that the world market for generics would nearly double in 1991 from the level reached in 1986, to some $15 billion.[16] And finally, increased cost-consciousness within the health-care community and the pharmacy buying groups has led to a greater market for generic drugs.[17] The impact of all of these factors could cause the generics to capture 50 percent of the market over the next few years.[18]

However, the future of the generic industry is on shaky ground. Although the market share of generics will probably continue to increase, the money-saving power of generics will be reduced due to more rigid testing by the FDA in the future. This tougher testing was a response to a scandal in the generic drug industry, and will lead to an increase in the cost of generic drugs.[19]

THE INCIDENT

The 1984 legislation that made the approval process for generic drugs easier was well intentioned. This legislation, called the Drug Price Competition and Patent Term Restoration Act (PL 98-417), gave brand-name drugs longer patent life to compensate for long periods of testing on the part of government agencies and allowed generic drugs to enter the market quickly and cheaply once the patents had ended. This law abolished the requirement that generic drugs had to be proven safe and effective before they could be marketed. Instead, manufacturers of generic drugs would only have to show that the copy was "bioequivalent" to the brand-name drug. This means that they would only have to demonstrate that the generic would have the same effect as the brand-name drug.[20] The fast pace of this approval process allowed the industry to become extremely profitable.[21]

However, it was that part of the legislation along with the deregulatory policies of the Reagan administration that made scandal more likely. While brand-name drugs had to undergo strict testing to prove that they were safe and effective, generic drugs now only needed to pass limited tests to show that they were comparable to brand-name drugs.

Generics can only be approved when the original brand-name products come off patent protection; therefore, producers of generic drugs race to have their products approved.[22] The first generic drug manufacturer to get approval captures at least 20 percent of the market.[23] And at times, the first generic on the market can snare almost half of the market.[24] Peter B. Hutt, former counsel for the FDA, said that fortunes could be made or lost depending on who got approved first. "Some companies would do almost anything to be first, and several did."[25]

Improprieties in the approval process came to light when Mylan Laboratories, Inc., filed a complaint with Dr. Marvin Seife, then head of the FDA's Generics Division. Mylan claimed that FDA officials were unfairly favoring their competitors in the approval process by speeding up the approval process for certain companies. When Seife refused to investigate, Mylan began its own investigation and eventually uncovered proof of foul play by some FDA employees and some generic drug manufacturers.[26] Mylan then brought the results of its investigation to the attention of Representative John D. Dingell (D-Mich.), head of the House Energy and Commerce Committee, because it didn't trust the FDA itself.[27] Mylan's distrust was well founded, as Seife was later convicted of two counts of perjury; Charles Y. Chang, a supervisory chemist and branch chief pleaded guilty to racketeering charges; and three other FDA drug reviewers pleaded guilty to accepting illegal payoffs from drug companies.[28]

A government investigation of the FDA generic drug approval process ensued. Investigators probed allegations of foul play, such as bribery and fraud. The branch chief of the FDA's generics division, Charles Y. Chang, pleaded guilty to charges that he had received around $13,000 in gifts from American Therapeutics, a generics producer that was not charged. Two of Chang's subordinates as well as Par Pharmaceuticals and its subsidiary, Quad Pharmaceuticals, were also charged with making or receiving illegal gratuities.[29] Quantum Pharmics, Ltd., a subsidiary of American Home Products Corporation, suspended production of its generic drugs after it was discovered that the company had a "cozy relationship" with an ex-FDA official who would accelerate the approval process for some companies while holding back others.[30]

FDA officials could slow down or speed up the approval process for particular companies in several ways. Some chemists were known to be more finicky than others. The branch chief admitted to assigning the testing of a favored company's products to swifter reviewers. FDA employees testified that officials had the power to determine the speed at which an application was processed. Some reviewers were also directed to test products out of order.[31]

The FDA began an investigation of its own, motivated by the Congressional probe that had unearthed embarrassing skeletons in the agency's closet.[32] Their investigation found that some generic drug producers had been faking test results and other data reported to the agency.[33] The investigation began a survey of the quality of the top 30 generic drugs. These drugs made up 75 percent of the industry's $5.1 billion in sales.[34] The number of generic drug manufacturers involved in the scandal was relatively small, as they produced only 18 percent of the 8,000 generics available. However, FDA investigators reported discovering "significant problems" of falsification, poor documentation, and failure to comply with FDA regulations in 11 of the 13 companies that were targeted for its investigation.[35]

Par Pharmaceuticals admitted to providing the FDA with false information regarding one of its drugs. Vitarine Pharmaceuticals conceded that employees had substituted the brand-name blood-pressure drug Dyazide for its own drug for testing purposes.[36] Bolar Pharmaceuticals also lost FDA approval of its generic substitute for Dyazide when suspicions arose.[37] Bolar's reputation suffered again when a 1982 letter from an independent laboratory, which scolded the company for submitting a brand-name drug as its own for testing purposes, was released. Bolar maintains that the incident was caused by a manufacturing mix-up.[38]

REACTION

Most brand-name drug manufacturers responded to the generic scandal in one of two ways. They either questioned the bioequivalence of their generic competition or began producing generics themselves.[39] Eventually, brand-name manufacturers came to account for about 60 percent of generic drugs in the U.S. market. As this trend continued, many companies that produced only generics were forced out of the industry, and the brand-name companies competed against their own generic equivalents.[40] Douglas G. Watson, president of Ciba-Geigy Ltd.'s Pharmaceuticals, pointed out that three companies had the opportunity to become the leading generic maker against their own brand,[41] thus ending the low prices associated with generics and increasing the nation's health bill.[42]

Although many brand-name companies have become involved in producing generics, sales from their generic divisions account for only a small portion of their entire revenue.[43] Brand-name companies support any measures to take generics out of the market because they would prefer not to compete with the lower-priced drugs.[44] Some big companies began campaigns to discredit the safety of generics and to scare lawmakers into limiting the use of generics. Federal regulators have referred to several of these campaigns as "false and misleading."[45]

For example, an FDA investigation discovered that Ciba-Geigy paid a marketing firm to create mailgrams from doctors and pharmacists and send them to state officials. The mailgrams bashed the use of generic drugs. The FDA says that the claims in the mailgrams were unfounded.[46]

AFTERMATH OF THE SCANDAL

Only 5 of the 52 generic drug manufacturers investigated by the House Oversight and Investigations Subcommittee from 1988 to 1991 have remained unblemished. Bolar Pharmaceuticals, for example, finally agreed to pay $10 million in fines in response to charges of obstructing justice, tainting drugs, and falsifying information.[47] The scandal cast a dark shadow over the multibillion-dollar generics industry, which boomed in the late 1980s and made up almost one in three prescriptions sold in the country.[48] A Gallup poll taken after news of the scandal emerged revealed that public faith in generics had declined. Of those aware of the scandal, over 75 percent indicated that their confidence in the quality of generic drugs had been as least somewhat disturbed.[49]

Congressional sources claimed that the scandal raised doubts about the safety and effectiveness of many drugs.[50] The American Academy of Family Physicians warns doctors about prescribing generic drugs to patients who are over 75 years old or who have illnesses like heart disease, asthma, or diabetes. The academy argues that the FDA testing processes do not give us the assurances we need to prove that generic drugs are comparable to the brand-name medications they replace. The FDA only requires generic drugs to match the active ingredients in their brand-name counterparts. They can use different inactive ingredients as long as the absorption rate into the patient's bloodstream does not differ by more than 20 percent.[51]

Other experts have maintained that generic drugs are still viable substitutes for brand-name drugs, and safe for patients that use them.[52] According to Dr. Peter Rheinstein, director of the FDA Office of Drug Standards, "We've had no reason to doubt the safety and efficacy of the vast majority of generics."[53] By April 1990, thousands of tests had been performed on generic drugs and authorities said that the drugs passed with flying colors.[54] Exhibit 1 shows the 30 most commonly used generic drugs.

Health and Human Services Secretary Louis Sullivan and FDA Commissioner Frank Young called on Congress in 1989 to grant the FDA greater enforcement powers, which would allow it to bar companies which had submitted false results from attaining future approvals.[55] Sullivan also began a reorganization to enlarge and improve the generic drug division of the FDA[56] and proposed a broad bill to prevent scandal with the agency. This bill, called the Food, Drug, and Device Fraud and Abuse Prevention Act of 1990, would, according to Sullivan, "provide strong deterrents against the types of improper activity that came to light recently in connection with generic drugs."[57]

In November 1989, FDA Commissioner Frank Young resigned in the middle of the scandal.[58] In order to protect itself from further scandals, the FDA has put internal controls in place. One-on-one meetings between reviewers and officials are not allowed and limits have been set on gifts and travel expenses employees may accept.[59]

In November 1990, David A. Kessler, M.D., became chief of the FDA, and began "an ambitious, no-holds-barred shake-up of the agency that for years seemed to epitomize bureaucratic inaction and ineptitude."[60] He was particularly interested in strengthening the testing process for approving generic drugs and the enforcement of FDA regulations. Each generic drug is now individually inspected, and Kessler insisted that the honor system was thrown out the window. To instill confidence in generics, he also stated that he would prescribe them for his patients.[61]

Representative Dingell backed a bill that would strengthen the FDA generic approval process. This bill would bar any generic drug manufacturer convicted of fraud from the testing process and even from selling previously approved products for at least 18 months. Companies cheating on the tests would also face fines of up to $5 million.[62] Dingell would like the FDA to have greater authority to prevent corruption by dealing with problems quickly and thoroughly.[63]

Dingell compromised on some points and eventually sponsored H.R. 2453, which was expected to get Congressional approval. This bill would give the Department of Health and Human Services (HHS) greater authority to enforce regulations as well as the ability to refuse applications from generic manufacturing companies that had abused the system and to withhold applications of generic producers under investigation. The bill would allow HHS to impose civil fines of up to $1 million, withdraw approvals, and permanently bar abusers from association with the FDA.[64]

The generic drug scandal was the worst scandal the FDA ever faced, but the agency may eventually reap some benefits from the incident. As stated in the *Congressional Quarterly,* "Although public confidence was severely shaken, the scandal focused congressional attention on the FDA for the first time in many years and may lead to a more efficient, more modern and more effective agency."[65]

1. What are generic drugs? Describe the growth of the generic drug market. What are the reasons for this growth? What does the future hold with respect to further growth of this market?

EXHIBIT 1 The Thirty Most Commonly Used Generic Drugs

In the face of growing public concern about the safety of generic drugs, the FDA is testing the 30 top-selling generic drugs and their brand-name counterparts. The 30 drugs are listed here with their brand names in parentheses.

Drug (Brand names)	Description
Amoxicillin (Amoxil, Larotid, Polymox, Trimox)	penicillin antibiotic used to treat a wide variety of bacterial infections including bronchitis and pneumonia
Penicillin VK (V-cillin-K, Ledercillin-VK)	broad-spectrum antibiotic commonly prescribed for numerous infections
Ampicillin (Amcil, Polycillin, Omnipen)	penicillin antibiotic used to treat various infections
Prednisone (Deltasone)	corticosteroid used to treat inflammatory diseases, rheumatoid arthritis
Tetracycline (Panmycin, Robitet, Achromycin V)	widely prescribed antibiotic used to treat a wide variety of bacterial infections including chronic bronchitis
Hydrochlorothiazide (Esidrix, Hydrodiuril)	diuretic often used in treatment of high blood pressure, swelling in certain parts of the body
Doxycycline (Vibramycin, Vivox, Vibratabs)	tetracycline antibiotic used to treat a wide variety of bacterial infections including bronchitis and pneumonia
Ibuprofen (Advil, Motrin, Nuprin)	pain reliever and anti-inflammatory used to tread headaches, cramps, rheumatoidarthritis
Diazepam (Valium, Valrelease)	helps relieve anxiety, insomnia, muscle spasm and seizures
Phenobarbital (Luminal)	to treat insomnia and to relieve anxiety and nervousness
Hydrocortisone cream (Cort-dome, Hytone)	in topical form, used for pain, itching and swelling of rashes and other skin conditions
Sulfamethoxazole with trimethoprim (Bactrim, Septra)	used to treat urinary tract infections, infections of the ear, chest and intestinal tract
Dipyridamole (Persantine)	to treat angina pectoris
Nitroglycerin (Nitrostat, Nitrodisc, Nitrobid)	to treat chest pains and prevent angina attacks
Nystatin (Mycostatin)	used to treat vaginal infections
Triamcinolone (Aristocort, Azmacort, Kenacort)	topical form used to treat skin inflammations, oral form to treat inflammatory diseases—arthritis, rheumatic disorders, lupus
Propoxyphene napsylate with acetaminophen (Darvocet-N)	pain reliever

506

EXHIBIT 1   The Thirty Most Commonly Used Generic Drugs—cont'd

Drug	Description
Erythromycin stearate (Erythomicin Stearate, Wyamycin-S)	antibiotic used to treat a wide variety of infections such as bronchitis and pneumonia
Erythromycin base	see above
Acetaminophen with codeine (Tylenol with codeine)	aspirin substitute used for pain relief
Cephalexin (Keflex)	antibiotic used to treat upper respiratory tract infections such as bronchitis and pneumonia
Amitriptyline (Elavil, Endep)	antidepressant used in treatment of digestive disorders
Furosemide (Lasix)	diuretic used to treat fluid accumulation that may be a byproduct of congestive failure, kidney disease, liver disease; also treats high blood pressure
Lorazepam	used to treat anxiety, insomnia, muscle spasm, and seizures
Imipramine (Tofranil)	antidepressant used to treat digestive illnesses and to relieve the anxiety and nervousness that may accompany them
Thyroid (Armour Thyroid)	used to treat thyroid disorders including goiter
Metronidazole (Flagyl)	antibiotic used to treat systemic infections such as vaginal infections, dysentery and others
Meclizine (Antivert)	antihistamine used to treat motion sickness and inner ear disorders
Allopurinol (Lopurin, Zyloprim)	used to treat kidney stones and gout
Ferrous Sulfate (Feosol)	dietary iron supplement to prevent or correct iron-deficiency anemia

Source: Barbara Coleman, "Drug Safety Charges Draw Challenge," *AARP Bulletin*, 30, no. 9 (October 1989), 18.

2. How long has drug regulation been in effect? What forms has this regulation taken in the United States? What have been some of the positive benefits of drug regulation? What have been some of the more important negative impacts on the industry and on the U.S. drug market?

3. What was done to reform regulation of generic drugs in order to speed up the approval process? What effects did these reforms have on the context in which generic drug makers compete? Did this change create conditions where ethical transgressions were more likely?

4. Describe what happened with regard to ethical improprieties in this case. What kind of control did FDA officials have over the approval process that made them susceptible to bribery and other allegations of ethical misconduct? With regard to test data, what did the companies do that was unethical?

5. What was the outcome with regard to investigations into the situation? Are generic drugs safe to use as directed? What has been done to win back public confidence in generics? Have these efforts been successful?

6. What should be done to prevent future scandals of this nature? Is the answer to abolish government regulation of drugs altogether? What would happen if this was done? Is the answer stricter ethical codes in both government and business? What effect, if any, would these codes have on human behavior?

[1] "The Hidden Cost of Drug Safety," *Business Week,* February 21, 1977, p. 80. See also Henry G. Grabowski and John M. Vernon, *The Regulation of Pharmaceuticals: Balancing the Benefits and Risks* (Washington, DC: American Enterprise Institute, 1983), pp. 29–48.

[2] Grabowski and Vernon, *The Regulation of Pharmaceuticals,* pp. 31–32.

[3] "Hidden Cost," *Business Week,* February 21, 1977, p. 82.

[4] Grabowski and Vernon, *The Regulation of Pharmaceuticals,* p. 33.

[5] Ibid.

[6] "FDA Is Requiring Pharmaceutical Firms to Conduct Postmarketing Drug Survey," *The Wall Street Journal,* January 23, 1980, p. 12.

[7] "Dying for Drugs," *Regulation,* no. 3, 1988, pp. 9–10.

[8] Ibid., pp. 10–11.

[9] Grabowski and Vernon, *The Regulation of Pharmaceuticals,* pp. 33–36.

[10] Reginald Rhein, "Drugs, What's in a Name Brand? Less and Less," *Business Week,* December 5, 1988, p. 172.

[11] Rhein, "What's in a Name Brand?" p. 172.

[12] Joseph Weber, "The Price of No-Name Drugs May Soon Be Hard to Swallow," *Business Week,* October 2, 1989, p. 87.

[13] Rhein, "What's in a Name Brand?" p. 172.

[14] "Updates," *FDA Consumer,* 22, no. 2 (March 1988), 4.

[15] Rhein, "What's in a Name Brand?" p. 172.

[16] Ibid.

[17] "Updates," p. 4.

[18] Holman Jenkins, Jr., "When a Drug Patent Expires, Rivals Vie to Be Next Brand X," *Insight,* September 25, 1989, p. 40.

[19] Weber, "Hard to Swallow," p. 87.

[20] "Generic-Drug Bill Moves Past Panel," *Congressional Quarterly,* August 3, 1991, p. 2174.

[21] Susan Dentzer, "Watchdogs Overdose on Generic Drugs," *U.S. News & World Report,* August 28–September 4, 1989, p. 26.

[22] Ibid.

[23] Bruce Ingersoll, "Congress Widens Probe into FDA's Approval of Drugs," *The Wall Street Journal,* March 16, 1989, p. A10.

[24] "Generic-Drug Bill Moves Past Panel," p. 2174.

[25] Kitty Dumas, "Fallout from Drug Scandal May Be a Stronger FDA," *Congressional Quarterly,* March 3, 1990, p. 666.

[26] Otis Pike, "The FDA's Generic Drug Scandal," *Times-Picayune,* April 29, 1991, p. B-5.

[27] Jenkins, "When a Drug Patent Expires," p. 39.

[28] Pike, "The FDA's Generic Drug Scandal," p. B-5.

[29] Dentzer, "Watchdogs Overdose," p. 26.

[30] Gregory Stricharchuk, "American Home Generic Drug Lines Halted," *The Wall Street Journal,* September 21, 1989, p. A4.

[31] Dumas, "Fallout from Drug Scandal," p. 665.

[32] Jenkins, "When a Drug Patent Expires," p. 38.

[33] Dentzer, "Watchdogs Overdose," p. 26.

[34] Bruce Ingersoll, "FDA Is Gathering Samples of Generic Drugs for Tests," *The Wall Street Journal,* August 17, 1989, p. B1.

[35] Barbara Coleman, "Feds Launch Generic Drug Probe," *AARP Bulletin,* 30, no. 9 (October 1989), pp. 1–2.

[36] Dentzer, "Watchdogs Overdose," p. 26.

[37] Bruce Ingersoll and Gregory Stricharchuk, "Bolar to Lose FDA Approval of Its Dvazide," *The Wall Street Journal,* August 29, 1989, p. A3.

[38] Jenkins, "When a Drug Patent Expires," p. 38.

[39] Ron Winslow, "Generic Drug Scandal Creates Opening," *The Wall Street Journal,* September 6, 1989, p. B1.

[40] Weber, "Hard to Swallow," p. 87.

[41] Rhein, "What's in a Name Brand," p. 176.

[42] Weber, "Hard to Swallow," p. 87.

[43] Michael Waldholz and Gregory Stricharchuk, "Fight Between Generic and Major Drug Firms Heats Up as Stakes Rise," *The Wall Street Journal,* October 4, 1989, p. A1.

[44] John Carey, "Congress Wants a Tougher FDA—But It's Not Sure How Tough," *Business Week,* January 14, 1991, p. 33.

[45] Waldholz and Stricharchuk, "Fight Between Generic and Major Drug Firms," p. A1.

[46] Ibid., p. A12.

[47] Zina Sawaya, "Getting Even," *Forbes,* April 29, 1991, p. 92.

[48] Dentzer, "Watchdogs Overdose," p. 26.

[49] Mitchel L. Zolar, "Generic Scandal Shakes Public," *Medical World News,* January 8, 1990, p. 45.

[50] Dentzer, "Watchdogs Overdose," p. 26.

[51] Barbara Coleman, "Drug Safety Charges Draw Challenge," *AARP Bulletin,* 30, no. 9 (October 1989), 17.

[52] Dentzer, "Watchdogs Overdose," p. 26.

[53] Coleman, "Drug Safety," p. 17.

[54] Don McLeod, "Generics Pass Tough Tests," *AARP Bulletin,* 31, no. 4 (April 1990), 4.

[55] Dentzer, "Watchdogs Overdose," p. 26.

[56] Ingersoll, "FDA Is Gathering Samples," p. B1.

[57] David Strickland, "Scandal Spawns Crackdown Bills," *Medical World News,* June 25, 1990, p. 35.

[58] Dumas, "Fallout from Drug Scandal," p. 667.

[59] Strickland, "Scandal Spawns Crackdown Bills," p. 35.

[60] Don McLeod and Elliot Carlson, " . . . I'm Giving You News Here," *AARP Bulletin,* 32, no. 7 (July–August 1991), 20.

[61] Ibid.

[62] Carey, "Congress Wants a Tougher FDA," p. 33.

[63] Dumas, "Fallout from Drug Scandal," p. 665.

[64] "Generic Drug Bill Moves Past Panel," p. 2174.

[65] Dumas, "Fallout from Drug Scandal," p. 664.

Source: Rogene A. Buchholz, et al., *Management Responses to Public Issues* (Englewood Cliffs, NJ: Prentice Hall, 1994), 168–180.

A. H. Robins

BACKGROUND

On Christmas day in 1967 two longtime friends and their families gathered at the traditional holiday dinner. One of these friends was Dr. Hugh Davis, who was then an assistant professor of medicine at Johns Hopkins University in Baltimore, Maryland, and an expert on birth control. The other friend was a man named Irwin "Win" Lerner, who was an inventor with his own research facility called Lerner Laboratories located in Stamford, Connecticut. Lerner had an electrical engineering degree from Oklahoma A&M University.

Among the topics of conversation at the dinner was the research Davis was conducting into intrauterine devices (IUDs). An IUD was inserted into a woman's uterus to prevent the development of a fertilized egg and thus the conception of children. They were generally made of plastic and were smaller than an inch wide so that they could be inserted easily. Most IUDs had a tail several inches long that served as a signal to an attending physician that the IUD was properly in place. The tail also aided in removal of the IUD from the uterus.

Many experts had hailed the IUD as the cure for the worldwide population explosion because the IUD was relatively easy to use and seemingly very effective. It was unlike birth control pills, which had to be taken every day, and did not have to be monitored very frequently. Because the IUD was largely a mechanical device, many people preferred its use to birth control pills, which contained strong drugs and later were suspected of causing some serious side effects. However, the pregnancy rate—the percentage of women using a birth control method who did become pregnant during the year—was generally much lower for pills than for use of the IUD.

Thus, the IUDs on the market in 1967 were not satisfactory to all doctors. Besides being ineffective in some cases, the IUD ripped the walls of the uterus in some women, causing infection and serious bleeding at irregular intervals. There was also the possibility that the tail of the IUD could act much like a wick drawing bacteria up from the unsterile vagina to the sterile uterus. This could cause extensive infection of the uterus and surrounding areas. It was believed that this wicking effect could be inhibited by the use of a very thin, single-strand tail that would utilize the mucus normally present in the cervix to block any ascending bacteria.

Davis had been working at improving the performance of the IUD for several years. In fact he had applied for a patent on an IUD called the Incon Ring only the year before. But because he was not a manufacturer, he had no way of translating this research into a marketable product. Thus, Davis's relationship with Lerner was a perfect fit for both parties. Although Lerner had never worked on devices for bodily insertion, he was an inventor who had the facilities to turn Davis's ideas into a marketplace reality.

By the time the Christmas dinner ended, the two friends had agreed to develop a better IUD for the market. At the end of the following summer they had already developed a device they called the Dalkon Shield. This name was derived from the last names of Davis, Lerner, and a lawyer of Lerner's by the name of Robert Cohn. The Dalkon Shield looked much like a crab with eight extended legs, thus making it radically different from other IUDs, which were longer and thinner by design. The single-strand tail, which was standard on most IUDs, was replaced by a multifilament tail containing 200 to 400 strands surrounded by a nylon sheath that was open at the lower end.[1]

The device was tested on women who were patients at the family planning clinic that Davis operated at Johns Hopkins Hospital. These tests began in September 1968. While the tests were being conducted, Davis, Lerner, and Cohn were working out the financial arrangements connected with production and marketing of the device. They eventually formed the Dalkon Corporation in January 1969, whose sole asset was the Dalkon Shield device. The stock of the new company was split between the three parties; Lerner got 55 percent, Davis got 35 percent, and Cohn got 10 percent.[2]

The study Davis was conducting of the Dalkon Shield was completed by the summer of 1969 with about 640 women participating. According to Davis the pregnancy rate for the Dalkon Shield was 1.1 percent, which was as low or lower than the rate for birth control pills. The results of this study were written up and submitted to the *American Journal of Obstetrics and Gynecology.* The article was published in the February 1, 1970, issue under the title "The Shield Intrauterine Device: A Superior Modern Contraceptive." The article carried a great deal of prestige because of Davis's affiliation with Johns Hopkins, but nowhere did the article mention that Davis had a financial interest in the device he was evaluating. Thus, to the uninformed reader it appeared that Davis was conducting an objective study with no possible conflicts of interest that might impair that objectivity.

The timing of the article could not have been better as far as its impact was concerned. The nationwide scare about birth control pills had peaked with a committee hearing in the U.S. Senate about the side effects and safety of pills. Davis was called as the lead-off witness at these hearings and proceeded to blast birth control pills as dangerous and to present the IUD as the preferred method of birth control. Davis was asked if he had commercial interest in any IUD, and he replied that he did not. When asked about this several years later, Davis explained that he had answered the question negatively because he had not at the time of the hearing received his stock certificates in the Dalkon Corporation.[3]

The Dalkon Corporation formally started marketing the device in March 1970, but sales were very disappointing. The Dalkon Corporation did not have an established sales organization with salespeople scattered around the country and around the world who could promote the device. The company did not have the money to mount an extensive advertising campaign. Nor did the company have access to medical offices throughout the country. Without these ingredients the Dalkon Shield was headed into oblivion.

THE ENTRANCE OF A. H. ROBINS COMPANY

The New Jersey Practitioner Association held its regular convention in the middle of May 1970 at Host Farms, Pennsylvania. At this convention the medical director of the Dalkon Corporation, who was promoting the Dalkon Shield, drew the attention of a salesman for the A. H. Robins Corporation by the name of John McClure. Robins was a small ($133 million sales) Richmond, Virginia–based manufacturer of pharmaceuticals and other products, best known for Sergeant's Flea and Tick collars, Robitussin cough medicine, and ChapStick lip balm. The salesman contacted his boss, a vice president at Robins, three days later and forwarded information about the device, including the Davis article that reported the 1.1 percent pregnancy rate for the shield.

This information triggered a great deal of activity at Robins including in-house meetings about the Dalkon Shield, consultation with outside experts, and a visit to Ohio to watch the insertion of the device. Apparently, the key visit came on June 8, 1970, when the medical director of Robins, Dr. Fred Clark, Jr., traveled to Baltimore to see Davis and review his files. Upon reviewing this information Clark raised questions about the reported pregnancy rate because data given him for the first 14 months covered 832 insertions with 26 pregnancies that produced a pregnancy rate of 3.1 percent or higher, which was three times that of birth control pills, the IUD's chief competitor.[4]

Clark also noted that Davis and Lerner had made design changes in the Dalkon Shield that made it thinner and more flexible. Thus, the study performed by Davis, which claimed a 1.1 percent pregnancy rate, applied to a different model. Other questions were raised by Jack Freund, vice president of the medical department. Freund apparently stated that the Davis study was "not long enough" and that he had been told by Lerner that the actual pregnancy rate with a follow-up period increased to 2.3 percent. Although Freund lauded the Dalkon Shield for its other characteristics, he did refer to its possible higher pregnancy rate when compared with birth control pills.[5]

W. Roy Smith, the director of product planning for Robins, wrote on June 10 that he was concerned about marketing "a device not identical in composition to that on which the paper was based." Smith noted that copper had also been added to a later model to improve effectiveness in producing an added drug effect for the device. This was later disputed by the company, which argued that copper had been added only to help hold together the plastic material in the shield and not to increase the contraceptive effect. The difference was crucial as at that time the Food and Drug Administration (FDA) required extensive premarket testing of drugs but not devices; thus, if the copper addition was considered a drug to increase contraception, the device could be subjected to three years of testing before it could be sold.[6]

Smith was also concerned about the lack of hard data concerning the Dalkon Shield. "We have relatively limited information on the Dalkon Shield in terms of length of usage, overall cases published, etc.," he wrote in a memo referring to "this relatively limited total case history."[7] Thus, the people at Robins were aware that the Davis study was the only information they had about the effectiveness of the Dalkon Shield and that this study had problems that needed investigation. It was clear that there was some mystery regarding the way in which the study was completed.

Despite these concerns the company went ahead and bought the rights to the Dalkon Shield from the Dalkon Corporation on June 12, 1970, barely three weeks from the time they had first heard about the device. Robins paid $750,000 for these rights and agreed to pay Davis, Lerner, and Cohn a total of 10 percent of future royalties. Davis was to be hired as a consultant to Robins at a salary of $20,000 per year. All profits made from the device after June 15 went to Robins. The company immediately drafted plans to begin marketing the device using its own sales force. Production costs were estimated at 36 cents for each device. The cost to doctors was set at $4.35 less discounts for bulk purchases.[8]

THE BEGINNING OF THE PROBLEMS

Almost immediately after buying the rights, the company started hearing about problems with the device. The marketing department surveyed doctors who had been using the shield produced by the Dalkon Corporation and reported that some of these doctors were quite displeased. Reactions to the device were found to be varied and inconsistent. Two weeks after they purchased the rights, a company official noted that there might be a problem with the tail, which was reported to have a wicking tendency. Thus, the potential for wicking problems was apparently known by the company early in the summer.

Sometime toward the end of July 1970 the company agreed to make further changes in the product in response to Davis's recommendations. The width of the device was reduced slightly, and the legs were fattened and rounded. These changes were not tested before they were marketed and mentioned in the promotional material. Robins had never manufactured a birth control device before and Davis was on staff as a consultant, but the company concluded nevertheless that it did not need to test these changes. Robins later claimed that it had consulted with experts and talked with enough doctors to satisfy itself that the changes would not be adverse.[9]

Robins geared up its nationwide sales network for the debut of the Dalkon Shield, even though several company officials expressed concern about the lack of thorough testing supporting the effectiveness of the model that was about to be sold on the marketplace. The company engaged in an extensive advertising campaign. A patient brochure that was distributed starting on January 1, 1971, when the national marketing campaign began, stated that "you can relax and enjoy the luxury of a truly superior birth control method." Thousands of reprints of the Davis study that found a 1.1 percent pregnancy rate were distributed. These reprints bore the all-important Johns Hopkins reference.[10]

Other pregnancy rate studies, all involving earlier models than the one being sold, were also publicized. One study by Dr. Thad J. Earl reported a startling low 0.5 percent rate, but Earl, like Davis, had an undisclosed financial interest in the Dalkon Shield. Another study that reported a 1.1 percent rate was conducted by Dr. Donald Ostergard, a Los Angeles-area physician. A third study was conducted by Dr. Mary Gabrielson, who computed a 1.9 percent pregnancy rate that she called comparable to the Davis study. As a result of the follow-up studies, however, she revised the rate to 4.3 percent, a figure Robins did not report for several months.[11]

These marketing efforts paid off; the Dalkon Shield captured an impressive 60 percent of the American IUD market in less than a year. Figure 1 shows how sales of the device took off and stayed relatively high for three years despite mounting evidence that the device had serious problems. Because of the questions that were being raised about the safety of birth control pills, the market was ripe for an alternative method of controlling pregnancies. However, events were about to take a significant change.

Up to this point concern had focused on the effectiveness of the Dalkon Shield and whether the limited information that was available about pregnancy rates was accurate and could be believed. After the product was introduced, however, questions began to surface about its safety as well. At least one competing salesman was telling customers that because the tail of the Dalkon Shield was multilayered, the inner core would act as a wick to introduce infection into the uterus. Someone else by the name of Wayne Crowder was also coming to the same conclusion. Crowder was a quality control supervisor at the Chap Stick Company, which was the wholly owned subsidiary manufacturing the shield.

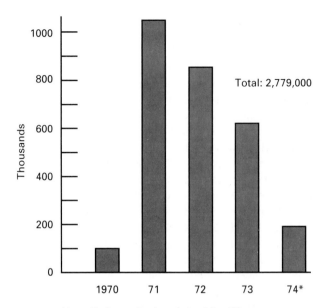

Note: Estimated sales about 2.5 million.
*Shield was voluntarily removed from market in June 1974.

Source: "Testing of Dalkon Shield Questioned by Doctors," *Dallas Times Herald,* February 17, 1985, p. A-22. Reprinted with permission.

FIGURE 1   U.S. Distribution of Dalkon Shield

Crowder conducted a simple experiment by hanging some shields in such a way that their tails ended in a glass of water. The next day Crowder found that he could milk water from the end of the tails. He subsequently informed his superior at ChapStick about the problem. Crowder suggested a way of sealing the ends so they might not cause wicking, but this suggestion was rejected by the president of ChapStick because it would increase the cost of the product. Because of Crowder's efforts, the tail received closer attention from company officials. It began to be viewed as a serious problem, which motivated Robins to actively search for a tail replacement.[12]

It was not long after the Dalkon Shield was first marketed that medical complaints started to arrive at company headquarters. In February 1971, it was reported that two Dalkon Shield wearers developed pelvic inflammatory disease. This disorder occurs when infectious agents enter and spread to the fallopian tubes, ovaries, and surrounding tissues. The disease causes severe pain and tenderness in the lower abdomen and is usually accompanied by a fever. If neglected, an abscess may form in a fallopian tube or ovary, which can cause damage and scarring and may block the fallopian tube, thus preventing conception.

In June of that same year, a physician's wife in Kentucky who was wearing the device developed pelvic inflammatory disease and required a hysterectomy. A Torrington, Connecticut, doctor reported two infections in a Dalkon Shield wearer several months after insertion. A doctor in Utah reported five pelvic infections from wearers of the Dalkon Shield, three of which were severe enough to require hospitalization. Finally, in a study conducted by the Maryland Health Department, one out of every 14 Dalkon Shield patients became infected.[13]

In early 1972 Robins was alleged to have become aware of another safety problem without informing the medical community. Some medical personnel in the company found that the nylon sheath could deteriorate from the effect of bodily fluids, and this deterioration made it more easy for bacteria to ascend the filaments into the uterus. Robins officials were informed that three baboons had died in a recent animal study using the Dalkon Shield, an unacceptably high figure. Kenneth Moore, the project manager for the shield, wrote in reference to this deterioration, "We have a problem. We are desperately searching for a suitable material to replace our currently used nylon string." On March 11, 1971, the Robins research committee recommended that "the string be removed or replaced."[14]

The problems continued. Five doctors who were treating cases of pelvic inflammatory disease suggested that the shield be withdrawn from the market. Meanwhile questions about its effectiveness continued. A doctor in Richmond, Virginia, said that 8.5 percent of his patients who used the shield became pregnant. An army doctor by the name of Russell J. Thompsen blasted the advertised pregnancy rate studies as "pathetically inadequate" because of the short time period involved. The real pregnancy rate, Thompsen suggested, was closer to 10 percent.[15]

The company responded to these allegations by modifying its advertising to say the pregnancy rate was "approximately" 2 percent but that "in a few isolated studies" higher rates had been reported. Robins also changed its labeling by adding infection to the list of possible side effects. In October 1971 Allen Polon, a project coordinator, wrote that an eight-page Robins ad that concluded the 1.1 percent pregnancy rate found by Davis was "outdated and . . . no longer valid" and asked that the company stop using the figure. However, the company continued to use the figure for more than a year after this question was raised.[16]

By the end of 1973 the company was aware of the deaths of six women associated with septic or infected abortions. In early 1974 Robins held a septic abortion conference consisting of experts in the field to reach a decision about continued sale of the shield. The company did not share any of the information it had accumulated about tail wicking with these experts. Five of these doctors said use of the Dalkon Shield increased the risk of septic abortion, five said it did not, and two abstained. One of these doctors, Dr. Howard Tatum of the Population council, further examined the tail of the shield and notified the FDA about the potential wicking problem.

Pressure against the shield was building. Robins sent a "Dear Doctor" letter on May 8, 1974, in which the company warned for the first time of a link between the Dalkon Shield and septic abortion. Robins officials considered taking the shield off the market that same month but were warned by their lawyer that such a move would be a "confession of liability" that would cause Robins to lose many of the lawsuits that at that time were pending against the company. Finally on June 26, 1974, the head of the FDA wrote Robins that "because of its questionable safety" the company should stop selling the device. Two days later the company announced that it was "voluntarily" withdrawing the product from the market. The company did not, however, issue a formal recall of all shields then in use and stated in a press release that "performance has clearly been satisfactory."[17]

THE CONTINUING BATTLE

The failure to issue a recall would cost the company millions of dollars. Many of the women who later filed lawsuits against the company claimed an injury after 1974 when the company withdrew the product from the market. The announcement about the suspension of sales was not as widely publicized as a formal recall would have been, and as a result hundreds of thousands of women continued wearing the Dalkon Shield, apparently unaware that there was a medical problem. The first Dalkon Shield trial took place in Wichita, Kansas, with a settlement of $85,000 against the company. Several months after this trial the company announced that it would not remarket the product but continued to maintain that the shield was safe and effective when properly used.[18]

Lawsuits continued to be filed against the company. A Denver, Colorado, jury in 1979 awarded $6.8 million to the plaintiff, $6.2 million of it in punitive damages. A jury in Los Angeles, California, in 1980 awarded $600,000 to the plaintiff. Three years later a jury in Miami, Florida, awarded $2.75 million (later reduced to $1.45 million), $500,000 of it in punitive damages. In 1983 a Minneapolis, Minnesota, jury awarded $1.75 million in damages, all but $250,000 in punitive damages.[19]

The company was severely criticized for some of its trial tactics, particularly the habit of questioning plaintiffs about their sex lives. The company maintained that its actions were necessary to rule out other possible sources of infection. Roger Tuttle, the chief Dalkon Shield lawyer from 1971 to 1975, later expressed regrets for his role as architect of what he called the company's "hard-nosed, ask-them-lots-of-questions-about-their-sex-life strategy." Tuttle was demoted in 1975 after the company lost its first trial, and he eventually moved to Oral Roberts College in Tulsa, Oklahoma, a religiously fundamentalist school, where he is a law professor. He explained that he had displayed a misplaced zeal for his former employer and that he now saw that a lawyer had a higher obligation to society.[20]

Tuttle also later testified that in 1975 the company had destroyed documents culled from the files of top corporate officials in the spoiled-products incinerator that the company maintained in the basement of its Richmond headquarters. Tuttle maintained that the purpose of the destruction was to help the company deny that Robins's executives knew about the problems with the pregnancy rate or the tail wicking. Such documents would obviously help the plaintiffs in the cases filed against the company. The company later denied these allegations and claimed that management never ordered or permitted the destruction of Dalkon Shield documents.[21]

In January 1985 Robins was involved in allegations of perjury made by a federal appeals court. The court ordered a new trial for a Florida woman who had lost a jury trial in Tampa because of the testimony of an expert witness for Robins by the name of Dr. Louis Keith, of Chicago. Dr Keith testified that wicking studies on the Dalkon Shield were being done under his direction, and implied that he had conducted them. He said they established that the tail did not wick as was believed. However, in a California court eight months later he testified that he had never performed any such studies. Robins's lawyers said the appeals court had misconstrued the testimonies; these lawyers characterized the discrepancies as "minor inconsistencies."[22] Dr. Keith has since been acquitted of perjury charges by a Florida jury.

In September 1980 Robins advised all women to have their Dalkon Shields removed by issuing another "Dear Doctor" letter, citing a possibility of infection from an obscure bacteria. No mention was made of pelvic inflammatory disease. The company again declined to issue a recall of the device and refused several requests by wearers for payment of removal expenses.[23] Then the Centers for Disease Control in Atlanta conducted a study that found that wearers of the Dalkon Shield had a five times greater chance of contracting pelvic inflammatory disease than did nonwearers. This finding came from a large study of contraceptive methods used by women hospitalized with pelvic inflammatory disease.[24]

Despite the growing litigation and negative scientific studies the controversy surrounding the Dalkon Shield dropped from the news for several years, until a judge by the name of Miles Lord decided to speak his mind about the conduct of corporate executives. Lord had presided over a number of Dalkon Shield cases in his Minneapolis courtroom and was becoming exasperated with Robins executives. When asked to approve the settlement of seven Dalkon Shield cases for $4.6 million, Lord demanded that the three top Robins executives appear before him in his courtroom. When they did appear on February 29, 1984, Lord proceeded to denounce the firm's legal tactics and alleged that the interest earned by delaying the settlement of cases covered all the legal fees of the company.

The judge's speech received nationwide publicity (see Appendix One), and even though a federal review court struck the speech from the record in response to a protest by the company, ruling that the judge had been out of line, the episode focused new attention on the A. H. Robins Company and was followed by new action.[25] In October 1984 the company agreed to pay the bills for women who had the shield removed and mounted a $4 million advertising campaign to spread the work across the nation. Also in October, Robins asked the federal court in Richmond to restrict punitive damage awards across the country. The company sought a single nationwide trial on punitive damages to be held in its home town. In November Robins settled 198 cases in Minneapolis for a total of $38 million.[26]

At the beginning of 1985 Robins and its insurer had paid more than $300 million to settle the claims of about 7,700 women. At that time the company still faced more than 3,700 lawsuits and claims across the country. The nationwide total was growing by about 30 each week. Payment of these suits was done for business reasons, according to one of Robins's lawyers, and was not an admission of guilt. The company could not defend against 10,000 suits, it was maintained. Robins has still never formally recalled the device and has maintained its position that the Dalkon Shield was neither defective nor unreasonably dangerous.[27] Some of the specific allegations made by the plaintiffs and the company's response included the following:

> Robins told doctors, regulators, and patients that there were no problems with the Dalkon Shield even though the company's staff had identified the suspected defect and was frantically seeking to correct it. The company said a seemingly damning set of memos was wrongly interpreted.
>
> Robins, which never before had manufactured birth control devices and had no design planning experts on its staff, put the Dalkon Shield on the market with design changes that had not been tested. The company said it took all reasonable steps in light of the information then available and that in any event plaintiffs never claimed these changes caused any injury.
>
> Experts testified on behalf of the women suing and contended that the wider tail with 200 to 400 strands, which was unusual among IUDs, facilitated wicking, particularly because the sheath could keep the bacteria-smothering mucus away from the strands. This was a contention Robins rejected.
>
> Copper was added to the Dalkon Shield to increase its contraceptive effect, but to avoid costly delays for government-mandated testing, Robins

falsely told federal regulators the metal had been added only to increase the IUD's strength. The company said the copper had no contraceptive effect and that no deception was committed.

In promoting the Dalkon Shield Robins published a favorable study conducted by a co-inventor of the product without revealing his financial interest in the device and while the company had its own doubts as to the validity of his data. Plaintiffs contended that Davis falsified the data by selecting women only after they had had favorable experiences. In a statement under oath Davis was unable to say who picked the women for the study, only that many people in his office were involved in the process. Plaintiffs also alleged that Davis improved the results of the study by instructing new patients to use contraceptive foam, a substance that killed sperm, during the first few months of usage. Davis denied this but later conceded that the initial set of instructions published when the Dalkon Corporation first marketed the device recommended that wearers use foam. This recommendation was also made to Robins. The company maintained that Davis conducted an honest study; that such financial disclosures were not customary in those days; and that a Dalkon Shield critic who had invented a rival IUD did the same thing.

In promotional material Robins cited studies that did not exist and made claims for which no research had been done. The company said any such errors were inadvertent. Robins was also alleged to have continued publishing studies showing low pregnancy rates after its officials knew the data were false, misleading, or otherwise invalid. Plaintiffs maintained that the pregnancy rate problems should have made Robins suspicious of the Dalkon Shield in general. The company denied this allegation and argued that the pregnancy rate problems were irrelevant to the infection issue.

Robins officials order the destruction of incriminating company documents in an effort to reduce potential liability. The company said that its former lawyer who so testified, Roger Tuttle, was lying.[28]

Thus far, lawyers for the plaintiffs bringing suit against the company concede that they have uncovered no documents or testimony suggesting that top Robins executives knew their product would cause as much harm as it may have done. Moreover, Robins won 24 out of the first 52 cases that went to trial, usually by showing that the plaintiff's injury in a particular case was not linked to the Dalkon Shield. In only eight cases had juries awarded punitive damages.[29]

FURTHER DEVELOPMENTS

The legacy of the Dalkon Shield continued to haunt the company. On April 2, 1985, the company set aside $615 million to cover expected losses from the thousands of suits that were still pending and would be filed in the future against the company. Robins's chief financial officer called the sum "a reasonable estimate of the minimum cost" of legal fees and compensation in current and anticipated suits filed in the United States. Legal experts stated that the fund was the largest ever established to handle medically related product liability claims. The fund wiped out the company's net worth, thereby creating a deficit of $128 million that required the suspension of dividends until at least 1987 because of a Virginia law prohibiting dividend payments until the deficit was eliminated.

At the time the fund was established, Robins had already paid $314 million to settle some 8,300 suits, with about 3,800 more still pending. Robins estimated that during the next 17 years an additional 8,300 cases could be brought against it in the U.S. courts alone. The average payment in each case through the end of 1984 was about $37,900. The company estimated an average of $53,200 for pending cases and $52,400 for future ones. New lawsuits were being filed at the rate of about 70 a week, the highest rate in the company's history. Company officials attributed this increase to an advertising campaign designed to encourage women still wearing the device to have it removed at the company's expense. Robins claimed that it had paid $1.08 million for 4,437 removals.[30]

The fund was designed to pay compensation only to plaintiffs bringing suit in U.S. courts. The company did not assess how much might be required to cover liabilities to women who used the shield in foreign countries. Of the 4.6 million devices that Robins sold before the product was taken off the market, 1.7 million were sold in overseas markets. The fund also did not cover punitive damages because of the difficulty of measuring potential exposure to this kind of award.[31] Punitive damages were not covered by product liability insurance, and by the end of 1984 Robins had only about $70 million left in compensatory claim insurance.[32]

In addition to establishing the reserve fund, the company also announced that it had settled a stockholder suit that claimed that Robins and three of its officers had made misleading statements about the Dalkon Shield. The company agreed to pay a total of $6.9 million to shareholders who had bought the stocks between March 8, 1971, and June 28, 1974, and who still held their shares at the end of that period.[33]

Five days after the establishment of this fund, the Agency for International Development (AID) released a report that established the agency as the world's largest single buyer of the Dalkon Shield. The agency stated that its large purchases contributed to the product's "illusion of success." The agency had purchased 697,292 Dalkon Shields, or 15.5 percent of the worldwide total of 4.5 million. The devices were distributed in about 40 countries through AID itself, various family planning agencies of foreign governments, and private institutions. Half the stock purchased by AID remained in warehouses and never reached users. The agency claimed that it "moved aggressively" to retrieve unused intrauterine devices once Robins took the product off the U.S. market.[34]

This claim was disputed by Martina Langley, an Austin, Texas, lawyer who said she once worked in a Central American medical clinic. The lawyer was convinced that in the three countries she knew best, El Salvador, Guatemala, and Nicaragua, most of the women who had received a government-funded Dalkon Shield were still wearing them. She claimed that doctors in El Salvador were prescribing the shield as late as 1980, six years after Robins had discontinued sales in the United States and five years after AID said it had retrieved all unused shields. Langley was critical of the decision not to launch Third World publicity programs to have Dalkon Shields removed.[35] In response to this criticism the agency ordered new studies to help determine whether many women in foreign countries were still using the device.[36]

The results of two new studies funded by the National Institute of Health were released in April 1985 and provided additional ammunition to those who were suing the company. The studies were critical of the Dalkon Shield and stated that the device posed a three to eleven times greater risk of infertility than other devices. One of the studies found that 5 percent of the infertile women in the population studied had used the Dalkon Shield, while only 1.4 percent of the fertile women had used the device. The other study found that Dalkon Shield users represented 14.5 percent of all cases of infertility, while they represented only 2.5 percent of fertile women.[37]

Despite these difficulties company officials maintained that the company was financially sound. When asked at a news conference whether the firm would file for bankruptcy, a senior vice president replied, "We are not in danger of that. We are operating today just as we did yesterday. It's business as usual." Some Wall Street analysts agreed. Barbara Ryan of the Bear, Stearns brokerage firm said, "This will cost Robins a lot of money, but the company's survival is not in question."[38]

In spite of these optimistic projections, however, the company did file for bankruptcy in August 1985, citing the mounting cost of the 5,100 claims that were pending against Robins at the time. This action paralleled that of Manville Corporation, which had filed for protection under Chapter 11 in 1982 as a way of dealing with the mounting claims by workers that they were injured as a result of exposure to asbestos. The bankruptcy filing brought a halt to further action regarding the claims already filed and prohibited the filing of any new claims anywhere except in federal bankruptcy court. The president and chief executive officer of Robins, E. Claiborne Robins, Jr., stated that "the continuing burden" of Dalkon Shield litigation forced the company to seek bankruptcy law protection. The filing was made "to ensure that all persons to whom the company has an obligation are treated fairly, to preserve the assets of the company and to maintain its current operations."[39]

As of June 30, 1985, the company and its insurer had paid $378.3 million to dispose of 9,320 cases involving the Dalkon Shield. Legal fees amounted to another $107.3 million. Because new cases were being filed at the rate of about 370 a month, the company expected thousands more in addition to the 5,100 that were pending.[40] Given that the company's request to consolidate thousands of claims for punitive damages into a single proceeding had been denied, the company would have continued to face separate awards for these damages that could have exhausted its finances. This filing was opposed by women's groups, which filed suit asking the bankruptcy court to dismiss the company's request, claiming that by filing for bankruptcy Robins was only trying to delay and diminish compensation to plaintiffs. These groups charged that injured women would receive less compensation under a Chapter 11 settlement than they would if each case went to trial separately.[41]

Subsequently, U.S. district judge Robert Merhige of Richmond set a deadline of April 30, 1986, by which time women who used the Dalkon Shield must have filed damage claims or be barred from suing. A. H. Robins Company agreed to pay about $4 million to mount a three-week advertising campaign across the country to notify women of this deadline and an additional $1 million for publicity in more than 90 other countries. This effort included 30-second announcements that would be shown 41 times on network television and 171 times on major cable superstations. Ads were also to be placed in 225 daily newspapers and 8 national publications.[42]

Even in bankruptcy proceedings, however, Robins's troubles continued. When in bankruptcy a company must obtain court approval before using any company assets to make payments to creditors or company officers for any debt incurred prior to the filing of the petition. Such a requirement is necessary to protect the interests of the remaining creditors who must wait for court approval of a reorganization plan for paying off debts. Yet the company went ahead and made about $1.2 million of deferred compensation payments to executives, about $600,000 to other expenses, and $5 million to settle contract debts for computer services and royalties on drug patents and trademarks, all without court approval.[43]

The company claimed that it did not get adequate advice from its outside law firm, which it subsequently dismissed, and that the officers did not realize immediately that the payments were improper.[44] Judge Merhige ordered Robins to retrieve these payments and considered appointing a trustee to run the company. [45] Such an independent trustee could have been appointed if the court had found evidence of "fraud, dishonesty, incompetency, or gross mismanagement" or if a court had decided that such an appointment would be in the best interests of the creditors.[46] The judge stopped short of appointing a trustee, however, and instead ordered the appointment of an examiner with broad authority to monitor the activities of the company while in bankruptcy proceedings. The examiner's responsibilities were to review Robins's financial data, investigate allegations of any misconduct by company officials, and report to the court on his findings. But management retained control of the company's operations.[47] In September 1986 the examiner asked for and was granted an extension until February 5, 1987, for the company to submit a reorganization plan to the court.[48]

Before this date was reached, American Home Products Company offered to bail out A. H. Robins from bankruptcy proceedings by acquiring the company and assuming its liabilities for the Dalkon Shield product. American Home expected to pay at least $20 for each of Robins's 24,175,000 shares outstanding, or a total of $484 million.[49] American Home intended to establish a huge trust fund for settling the hundreds of thousands of pending claims related to the Dalkon Shield. Just a few days later, however, American Home Products withdrew this bid, thus sending Robins's stock into a sharp decline. Initially the company cited the lack of guarantees that it would be protected against future Dalkon Shield claims and the difficulty of combining the two companies, which would take longer than American Home executives had thought.[50] Eventually it was disclosed that what really may have torpedoed the negotiations were the escalating financial requests of Robins. Apparently Robins wanted five-year employment contracts and severance payments for about 50 top executives and supplemental consulting contracts of about $100,000 a year each for its chairperson, E. Claiborne Robins, Sr., and his son, E. Claiborne Robins, Jr., the company's president.[51]

As a result of this failure, the bankruptcy judge took steps to prevent Robins from sabotaging any future acquisition offers. The judge expanded the powers of the court-appointed examiner and order the company to cooperate in the event of another rescue offer. If Robins failed to comply, it could face the threat of a court-appointed trustee negotiating on its behalf.[52] In April 1987, just before Robins was to face two further motions in court that would threaten its ability to survive as an independent company, Robins submitted its own reorganization plan.[53] The plan would create a $1.75 billion trust for settling claims against the Dalkon Shield and about $100,000 million for paying other creditors. Initial funding for the trust would come from a $75 million cash payment from Robins and a five-year, $1.68 billion letter of credit from a group of banks.[54]

Another development in this continuing saga was a $2.6 billion bid from Rorer Group to merge with Robins. Rorer indicated that it was proposing a true merger rather than a buyout and promised to leave Robins's Richmond operations substantially intact. Rorer offered to issue one share of new convertible preferred stock with a stated value of $30 for each share of outstanding Robins stock. If Rorer's common stock price reached or exceeded $48 in the open market, Rorer would issue 0.625 common shares to Robins holders. The combined company would have sales of about $1.6 billion and would rank sixth among U.S. nonprescription drug makers. The board of Robins signed a letter of intent to accept this proposal, but the proposal also had to be accepted by all parties to the bankruptcy proceedings.[55]

Pressure was being placed on Rorer to sweeten its offer when the French drug maker Sanofi made another takeover proposal. Sanofi proposed to provide full funding for Robin's court-ordered liability trust in exchange for a stake of up to 60 percent of the company. The proposal was attractive to Robins because the Sanofi plan would allow members of the Robins family to retain a large ownership stake in the company and perhaps even retain control. Sanofi proposed to pay Robins $500 million and to guarantee the payment of $2.48 billion to claimants, which would be available much sooner than would payments under the Rorer plan.[56]

This bid was opposed by a committee representing Robins shareholders who believed it was inferior to bids received from other companies. The bidding then escalated as American Home Products increased its bid by offering $700 million in stock for Robins shareholders, $100 million higher than its previous proposal. Eventually, American Home agreed to pay the entire court-ordered $2.48 billion for claimants into a trust fund within one year after Robins emerged form bankruptcy, or provide $2.38 billion to claimants immediately at the end of the proceeding. This plan was endorsed by committees representing Robins shareholders and Dalkon Shield claimants and was eventually accepted by Robins's board of directors.[57]

CONCLUSION

Why was Robins so reluctant to recall the shield, as Proctor & Gamble did with Rely tampons when there was an indication that the product might be linked to toxic shock syndrome, another disease caused by vaginal infection? Perhaps part of the answer lay in the fact that the Dalkon Shield was an extremely profitable product. The shield generated a profit margin of more than 40 percent in the United States and more than 70 percent overseas. Sales of the device were good, perhaps even outstanding. From January 1971 until sales were suspended in the United States at the request of the FDA in June 1974 and overseas in April 1975, Robins sold some 4.6 million shields worldwide, making it the largest selling IUD in the world.[58]

Perhaps the words of Roger Tuttle put the problem into perspective. In an article that appeared in the *Oklahoma Bar Journal* (cited in *Forbes*), Tuttle wrote, "Robins entered a therapeutic area with no prior experience, no trained personnel, and reliance on statistics from an admittedly biased source. Although the device was based on sound scientific principles, Robins over-promoted it without doing sufficient clinical testing in an effort to ride the crest of a marketing wave for financial gain."[59] Morton Mintz, in his book *At Any Cost*, stated, "The Dalkon Shield created a disaster of global proportions because a few men with little on their minds but megabucks made decisions, in the interest of profit, that exposed millions of women to serious infection, sterility, and even death."[60]

1. Where did the A. H. Robins Company go wrong? Why did the company not concern itself more with thoroughly testing the Dalkon Shield before it was marketed, particularly by an unbiased researcher who did not have a financial interest in the product? Was the company solely motivated by profit, or were there other factors involved?

2. Why was the product not recalled after evidence began to mount about its adverse health effects? Was Robins right to defend the product and never admit there might be a problem?

3. What role did the regulatory agencies play in this situation? Should they have taken a more active role early in the controversy? What can government do to protect the public from unsafe products? Is the role government agencies can play in this respect limited? If so, in what ways?

4. Did the judiciary play a key role in this case? What decisions do the courts have to make in product liability cases? Did Judge Lord overstep his authority as district court judge when he lectured Robins's executives? Do you applaud or condemn this action? Why? Are judges accountable for their actions?

5. What is the difference between compensatory and punitive damages? Should punitive damages be assigned to this situation? Why? What purposes do they serve? Do you support Robins's contention that all punitive damages ought to be consolidated in one case? Why do you think the company made this suggestion?

6. What role can consumers play in being diligent about the purchase and use of products? Are consumers at the mercy of producers in the modern marketplace? How can consumers protect themselves from misleading or outright false advertising and unsafe products?

APPENDIX ONE

A Plea for Corporate Conscience

From a speech delivered by Federal District Court Judge Miles W. Lord in his Minneapolis courtroom on February 19, 1984. Lord made his remarks in approving a $4.6 million product-liability suit against the A. H. Robins company, manufacturer of the Dalkon Shield intrauterine contraceptive device, which was found to cause serious and sometimes fatal pelvic infections in many of its users. This settlement satisfied seven of the 9,000 claims that had been brought against Robins. Lord's remarks were addressed to E. Claiborne Robins, Jr., the firm's president; Carl D. Lunsford, senior vice president for research and development; and William A. Forrest, Jr., vice president and general counsel.

Mr. Robins, Mr. Forrest, and Dr. Lunsford: After months of reflection, study, and cogitation—and no small amount of prayer—I have concluded that it is perfectly appropriate to make this statement, which will constitute my plea to you to seek new horizons in corporate consciousness and a new sense of personal responsibility for the activities of those who work under you in the name of the A. H. Robins Company.

It is not enough to say, "I did not know," "It was not me," "Look elsewhere." Time and again, each of you has used this kind of argument in refusing to acknowledge your responsibility and in pretending to the world that the chief officers and directors of your gigantic multinational corporation have no responsibility for its acts and omissions.

Today as you sit here attempting once more to extricate yourselves from the legal consequences of your acts, none of you have faced up to the fact that more than 9,000 women claim they gave up part of their womanhood so that your company might prosper. It has been alleged that others gave their lives so you might prosper. And there stand behind them legions more who have been injured but who have not sought relief in the courts of this land.

I dread to think what would have been the consequences if your victims had been men rather than women—women, who seem, through some quirk of our society's mores, to be expected to suffer pain, shame, and humiliation.

If one poor young man were, without authority or consent, to inflict such damage upon one woman, he would be jailed for a good portion of the rest of his life. Yet your company, without warning to women, invaded their bodies by the millions and caused them injuries by the thousands. And when the time came for these women to make their claims against your company, you attacked their characters. You inquired into their sexual practices and into the identity of their sex partners. You ruined families and reputations and careers in order to intimidate those who would raise their voices against you. You introduced issues that had no relationship to the fact that you had planted in the bodies of these women instruments of death, of mutilation, of disease.

Gentlemen, you state that your company has suffered enough, that the infliction of further punishment in the form of punitive damages would cause harm to your business, would punish innocent shareholders, and could conceivable depress your profits to the point where you could not survive as a competitor in this industry. When the poor and downtrodden commit crimes, they too plead that these are crimes of survival and that they should be excused for illegal acts that helped them escape desperate economic straits. On a few occasions when these excuses are made and remorseful defendants promise to mend their ways, courts will give heed to such pleas. But no court will heed the plea when the individual denies the wrongful nature of his deeds and gives no indication that he will mend his ways. Your company, in the face of overwhelming evidence, denies its guilt and continues its monstrous mischief.

Mr. Forrest, you have told me that you are working with members of the Congress of the United States to find a way of forgiving you from punitive damages that might otherwise be imposed. Yet the profits of your company continue to mount. Your last financial report boasts of new records for sales and earnings, with a profit of more than $58 million in 1983. And, insofar as this court has been able to determine, you three men and your company are still engaged in a course of wrongdoing. Until your company indicates that it is willing to cease and desist this deception and to seek out and advise your victims, your remonstrances to Congress and to the courts are indeed hollow and cynical. The company has not suffered, nor have you men personally. You are collectively being enriched by millions of dollars each year. There is no evidence that your company has suffered any penalty from these litigations. In fact, the evidence is to the contrary.

The case law suggests that the purpose of punitive damages is to make an award that will punish the defendant for his wrongdoing. Punishment had traditionally involved the principles of revenge, rehabilitation, and deterrence. There is no evidence I have been able to find in my review of these cases to indicate that any of these objectives has been accomplished.

Mr. Robins, Mr. Forrest, Dr. Lunsford: You have not been rehabilitated. Under your direction, your company has continued to allow women, tens of thousands of them, to wear this device—a deadly depth charge in their wombs, ready to explode at any time. Your attorney denies that tens of thousand of these devices are still in women's bodies. But I submit to you that he has no more basis for denying the accusation than the plaintiffs have to stating it as truth. We simply do not know how many women are still wearing these devices because your company is not willing to find out. The only conceivable reasons that you have not recalled this product are that it would hurt your balance sheet and alert women who have already been harmed that you may be liable for their injuries. You have taken the bottom line as your guiding beacon and the low road as your route. That is corporate irresponsibility at its meanest. Rehabilitation involves an admission of guilt, a certain contrition, an acknowledgment of wrongdoing, and a resolution to take a new course toward a better life. I find none of this in you or your corporation. Confession is good for the soul, gentlemen. Face up to your misdeeds. Acknowledge the personal responsibility you have for the activities of those who work under you. Rectify this evil situation. Warn the potential victims and recompense those who have already been harmed.

Mr. Robins, Mr. Forrest, Dr. Lunsford: I see little in the history of this case that would deter others. The policy of delay and obfuscation practiced by your lawyers in courts throughout this country has made it possible for you and your insurance company to put off the payment of these claims for such a long period that the interest you earned in the interim covers the cost of these cases. You, in essence, pay nothing out of your own pockets to settle these cases. What corporate officials could learn a lesson from this? The only lesson they might learn is that it pays to delay compensating victims and to intimidate, harass, and shame the injured parties.

Your company seeks to segment and fragment the litigation of these cases nationwide. The courts of this country are burdened with more than 3,000 Dalkon Shield cases. The sheer number of claims and the dilatory tactics used by your company's attorneys clog court calendars and consume vast amounts of judicial and jury time. Your company settles those cases out of court in which it finds itself in an uncomfortable position, a handy device for avoiding any proceeding that would give continuity or cohesiveness to this nationwide problem. The decision as to which cases are brought to trial rests almost solely at the whim and discretion of the A. H. Robins Company. In order to guarantee that no plaintiff or group of plaintiffs mounts a sustained assault upon your system of evasion and avoidance, you have time after time demanded that, as the price of settling a case, able lawyers agree not to bring a Dalkon Shield case again and not to help less experienced lawyers with cases against your company.

Another of your callous legal tactics is to force women of little means to withstand the onslaughts of your well-financed attorneys. You target your worst tactics at the meek and the poor.

If this court had the authority, I would order your company to make an effort to locate each and every woman who still wears this device and recall your product. But this court does not. I must therefore resort to moral persuasion and a personal appeal to each of you. Mr. Robins, Mr. Forrest, Dr. Lunsford: You are the people with the power to recall. You are the corporate conscience.

Please, in the name of humanity, lift your eyes above the bottom line. You, the men in charge, must surely have hearts and souls and consciences.

Please, gentlemen, give consideration to tracing down the victims and sparing them the agony that will surely be theirs.

[1] This account is in major part adapted from William P. Barrett, "Testing of Dalkon Shield Questioned by Doctors," *Dallas Times Herald,* February 17, 1985, p. A-22.

[2] Ibid.

[3] Ibid.

[4] Ibid.

[5] Ibid.

[6] Ibid.

[7] Ibid.

[8] Ibid.

[9] Ibid. In relation to these changes the company made the following statement: "After Robins acquired the patent rights to the Dalkon Shield in June, 1970, the company, at Dr. Hugh Davis' suggestion, made three additional minor changes in the Shield: (1) the tie point for the tailstring at the base of the Shield was strengthened; (2) the standard size Shield was narrowed by two millimeters; and (3) the appendages were rounded or 'tear-dropped.' Each of these improvements was designed to increase tolerance and reduce expulsion. There is no evidence that these changes affected the safety of the Shield or pregnancy or medical removal rates associated with it." See A. H. Robins, "Summary History of the Development and Marketing of the Dalkon Shield." (Richmond, VA: A. H. Robins, undated), 2, p. 9.

[10] "Testing of Dalkon Shield," p. A–22.

[11] Ibid.

[12] Ibid., p. A–23.

[13] Ibid. The company has continued to support the safety of the device by making strong statements about medical evidence and conclusions from this evidence. For example, in a report issued by the company, the following statements appeared: "By 1970, the medical literature was *unanimous* in its conclusion that not only was there no association between IUD use and pelvic inflammatory disease, but that there was no difference between tailed and non-tailed devices in this regard. . . . Because of the *consensus* in the medical literature that there was no association between IUD use and pelvic inflammatory disease, the interviews concentrated more on other events associated with IUD use, including expulsions, medical removals, and pregnancies [italics added]." See Robins, "Summary History," p. 10.

[14] "Testing of Dalkon Shield," p. A–23.

[15] Ibid.

[16] Ibid., p. 24.

[17] Ibid.

[18] Ibid.

[19] Ibid.

[20] William P. Barrett, "I Hang My Head in Shame: Ex-Robins Lawyer Regrets Company's Hard-Nosed Trial Tactics," *Dallas Times Herald,* February 17, 1985, p. A–23.

[21] Ibid. The company also has suggested that Tuttle had made inconsistent statements on the matter.

[22] Francine Schwadel, "Witness for Robins Probed for Perjuary on Dalkon Shield," *The Wall Street Journal,* April 9, 1985, p. 19.

[23] "Testing of Dalkon Shield," p. A-24.

[24] "Dalkon Shield Warning," *FDA Consumer,* July–August 1983, p. 2.

[25] "A. H. Robins Hauls a Judge into Court," *Business Week,* July 16, 1985, pp. 27–28. Robins executives filed a complaint with the U.S. Eighth Circuit Court of Appeals, arguing that the judge had "methodically destroyed their personal and professional reputations" and "grossly abused his office." They charged that Lord's diatribe was an example of judicial irresponsibility at its worst. The complainants asked that he be reprimanded. Five federal judges, including the chief judge of the eighth circuit, heard the case, and three other federal judges gave statements in Lord's defense. "A Panel Tries to Judge a Judge," *Time,* July 23, 1984, p. 88. Disciplinary proceedings against Lord were dismissed. The court ordered Lord's speech to be struck from the record.

[26] "Testing of Dalkon Shield," p. A–24.

[27] Ibid., p. A–22.

[28] Ibid.

[29] Ibid.

[30] William P. Barrett, "Dalkon Shield Maker Concedes Possible User Injuries," *Dallas Times Herald,* April 3, 1985, p. A–8. In May 1985 a jury in Wichita, Kansas, awarded nearly $9 million to a Topeka woman who claimed the use of the Dalkon Shield forced her to undergo a hysterectomy. The jury awarded $1.43 million in actual damages and $7.5 million in punitive damages. See "Woman Awarded $8.9 Million in Damages from Dalkon Maker," *Dallas Times Herald,* May 5, 1985, p. A–11. In a suit filed in Austin, Texas, the plaintiff sought $2 million in damages for pain and suffering and $50 million in punitive damages. Robins asked the judge to rule out such a large damage award. See William P. Barrett, "Dalkon Maker Issues Plea to Judge," *Dallas Times Herald,* May 10, 1985, p. A–22.

[31] "How Robins Will Go on Paying," p. 50.

[32] Frances Schwadel, "Robins Sets $615 Million Pool to Cover Dalkon Shield Claims, Halts Dividend," *The Wall Street Journal,* April 3, 1985, p. 2.

[33] Ibid.

[34] William P. Barrett, "IUD Sales Success Boosted by Agency's Purchases," *Dallas Times Herald,* April 7, 1985, p. A–9.

[35] William P. Barrett, "Foreigners Using Dalkon Shield, Lawyer Claims," *Dallas Times Herald,* April 21, 1985, p. A–6.

[36] William P. Barrett, "U.S. Agency to Study Dalkon Shield Use in 4 Countries," *Dallas Times Herald,* April 25, 1985, p. A–7.

[37] Michael Waldholz and Francine Schwadel, "IUDs Especially Dalkon Shield, Pose Increased Risk of Infertility, Studies Say," *The Wall Street Journal,* April 11, 1985, p. 38.

[38] "The Big Payout," *Time,* April 15, 1985, p. 86.

[39] Frances Schwadel, "Robins Files for Protection of Chapter 11," *The Wall Street Journal,* August 22, 1985, p. 3.

[40] William P. Barrett, "Dalkon Shield Maker Files for Bankruptcy," *Dallas Times Herald,* August 22, 1985, p. A–1.

[41] "Dismissal of Robins's Chapter 11 Petition Sought by Plaintiffs, *The Wall Street Journal,* August 26, 1985, p. 4.

[42] William P. Barrett, "Deadline Given for Claims from Dalkon Shield Users," *Dallas Times Herald,* January 5, 1986, p. 8–A.

[43] Sonja Steptoe, "U.S. Requests that Robins Be Operated by Court Appointee; Spending Is Cited," *The Wall Street Journal,* March 14, 1986, p. 4.

[44] Sonja Steptoe, "Robins Officials Dispute Firm on Payments," *The Wall Street Journal,* June 6, 1986, p. 4.

[45] Sonja Steptoe, "Robins Is Ordered to Seek Retrieval of $6.8 Million," *The Wall Street Journal,* March 31, 1986, p. 34.

[46] Sonja Steptoe, "U. S. Expands Payments Case Against Robins," *The Wall Street Journal,* June 5, 1986, p. 4.

[47] Sonja Steptoe, "Judge Orders Appointment of Examiner to Monitor Activities of A. H. Robins Co.," *The Wall Street Journal,* August 6, 1986, p. 4.

[48] Sonja Steptoe, "Robins Examiner Receives Extension in Chapter 11 Case, *The Wall Street Journal,* September 30, 1986, p. 47.

[49] "American Home Products Is Proposing to Buy Robins in Chapter 11 Bailout," *The Wall Street Journal,* February 5, 1987, p. 2.

[50] Michael Waldholz and Alix M. Freedman, "American Home Withdraws Robins Bid, Citing Risks Involved in Going Forward," *The Wall Street Journal,* February 23, 1987, p. 2.

[51] Sonja Steptoe, "Robins Demand Cited in Failed Takeover," *The Wall Street Journal,* February 17, 1987, p. 6.

[52] Ibid.

[53] Sonja Steptoe, "Robins's Chapter 11 Plan Derailed Sale but May Delay Settling of IUD Claims," *The Wall Street Journal,* April 20, 1987, p. 2.

[54] Sonja Steptoe, "Robins's Reorganization Plan Specifies Added Debt of $1.35 Billion, Asset Sales," *The Wall Street Journal,* April 6, 1987, p. 6.

[55] Sonja Steptoe, "Robins Accepts Rorer's $2.6 Billion Bid; Dalkon Claimants' Lawyer Reacts Coolly," *The Wall Street Journal,* July 6, 1987, p. 3.

[56] Paul M. Barrett, "Sanofi's Bid for Robins Puts Pressure on Rorer, May Trigger Other Proposals," *The Wall Street Journal,* December 21, 1987, p. 6.

[57] Paul M. Barrett, "Robins Accepts American Home's Offer of $3.28 Billion in Major Break in Case," *The Wall Street Journal,* January 20, 1988, p. 3.

[58] Subrata N. Chakravarty, "Tunnel Vision," *Forbes,* May 21, 1984, p. 218.

[59] Ibid.

[60] Morton Mintz, *At Any Cost: Corporate Greed, Women, and the Dalkon Shield* (New York: Pantheon, 1985), p. xiii.

Source: Rogene A. Buchholz, et al., *Management Responses to Public Issues* (Englewood Cliffs, NJ: Prentice Hall, 1994), pp. 276–300.

Index

C